W9-ATX-532

EFFECTIVE RETAIL AND MARKET DISTRIBUTION

A MANAGERIAL ECONOMIC APPROACH

This book is part of
the World series in business administration

Effective
Retail and Market
Distribution

A Managerial
Economic Approach

BY *Robert D. Entenberg,* M.B.A., Ph.D.

Louis D. Beaumont Professor of Marketing and Business Administration,
and Director, Division of Research, College of Business Administration,
University of Denver

THE WORLD PUBLISHING COMPANY

Cleveland and New York

Published by The World Publishing Company
2231 West 110th Street, Cleveland, Ohio 44102

Manufactured in the United States of America

Library of Congress Catalog Card Number: 65-27420

To Ann

Whose love and understanding
make all contributions possible

Foreword

This book has been designed for a broad, interdisciplinary one-semester or one-quarter course in the economics of retail management and effective market distribution. It has been written primarily for upper-division and graduate students of colleges of business, liberal arts, education, or engineering who have completed a basic course in economics.

One of the goals of this book is to prepare students and practitioners in the field to meet and to understand company objectives and the executive decision processes under conditions of uncertainty. The framework in which the text is developed is the changing milieu of competitive innovations and growing complexities found in the total business environment. Another goal of this text is the development of a better understanding of the administrative processes, executive action within the firm, and buyer behavior in the market place.

To meet these and related objectives, the material varies widely from the traditional descriptive approaches. The primary emphasis is upon analysis and decision rather than upon descriptions of commodities and institutions. At the same time, no essential principles or fundamental techniques needed for profitable market planning and store operation have been omitted. These include evaluative analysis of markets and design of marketing strategy needed to meet competitive innovations and new techniques in data-processing and information-retrieval systems. Included in these discussions are analyses of discount-house competition, channel by-passing, changing consumer shopping patterns, evaluation of computer installations, changing trading-area requirements, and new approaches for optimizing branch-store and shopping-center locations.

To provide maximum teaching flexibility, pertinent comparisons based on market actualities are included with the text material. As to treatment of material, the first four chapters are deliberately theoretical and provocative so as to provide the student with a broad conceptual framework in which he can better understand and challenge the nature, scope, and effectiveness of managerial decisions within the firm and in the market. To carry this out, the initial chapters include many divergent and controversial points of view. By this means, particular philosophies of management can be critically examined and at the same time can provide an optimal framework in which the student's own thinking may be projected.

Within the limits of managerial control systems, the decision processes and administrative applications in policy formulation are reviewed analytically. Particular reference is made to the problems arising from choice of channels of distribution, changing locational factors, changing competitive practices and changing organizational needs. These are discussed in Parts II and III, which consist of the fixed factors of enterprise in the external setting and the functions of the organizational structure in the internal setting.

In the four following parts, the basic functional areas of financial planning, merchandising and market management, research and publicity, and the control processes of analysis, evaluation, and reappraisal are presented. In the concluding part, the role of executive leadership and administrative management of the firm operating within the socioeconomic and governmental framework is reviewed and analyzed. Evaluation of the various kinds of retail institutions and technical operational facets will be found in the appendixes.

Throughout the text, pertinent quantitative and qualitative techniques of the behavioral and mathematical sciences are used in conjunction with the managerial economic point of view.

Acknowledgments

This text represents the successful fruition of some six years of effort. During this period of time many friends, colleagues, and individuals of good will have contributed both knowingly and unknowingly to the completion of this work. More specifically, the writer would like to express his appreciation to Professors A. James Boness and Edward Sussna for their reading and review of certain sections of the manuscript; to Dexter E. Robinson for his continuing faith, confidence, and encouragement consistent with the finest traditions of executive leadership; to Professors Theodore N. Beckman and William R. Davidson, and Dean Charles M. Edwards, Jr., for the inspiration they have given me by always exhibiting a high level of scholarship; to William A. Clampett, Jr., Barbara Flannery, Emily Sutter, and Aileen Cooper for their willing cooperation in helping with certain portions of the manuscript; to Professor William M. Morgenroth, Dean T. H. Cutler, Dr. Albert B. Smith, and Mrs. Betty Stiltz for their expressions of confidence and encouragement; and finally, to Shirley Levy and Betty Stenberg, who assisted in typing much of the final portions of the manuscript.

A careful effort has been made to secure permission to reprint copyrighted material and to make full acknowledgment of its use. Any errors or omissions are inadvertent, and will be corrected in subsequent editions.

ROBERT D. ENTENBERG

Contents

Appendix

Part One

The Environmental Setting:
The Field of Distribution

Chapter 1: *The Economic Setting*

Of all the economic changes that have taken place during the last half century, the relative importance and complexity of the marketing processes have assumed most significance. The American economy is no longer faced with the complex problem of producing enough to supply the needs of a large and growing population. Supply has caught up with and far exceeded the demand for consumer and industrial goods.

Total demand has not kept pace with the enormous growth in our productive facilities because of a propensity for consumption to decline in relation to income. Accompanying this decline has been an increasingly inefficient and uneconomic use of resources. This problem of imbalance in our production-consumption function has become especially acute since the end of World War II.

Long-run economic growth, full employment, and the means for competing effectively both at home and abroad depend directly on how well the production-consumption problems can be resolved. Thus, one of the most important problems facing American economic development today is that of maintaining adequate demand to insure full use of resources. The solution to this problem is the task of business management everywhere.[1]

---

[1] Robert D. Entenberg, "Maintaining Adequate Demand to Insure Full Use of Resources," in *Problems of U.S. Economic Development*, Vol. 2, (New York: Committee for Economic Development, 1958), pp. 35–36.

Because of inadequate market demand, a tremendous scramble for market position and survival has been and is taking place in both the manufacturing and consumer-goods sectors of our economy. This struggle has been further accentuated by the fact that consumer purchasing patterns, shopping habits, and wants are in a constant state of flux, thus forcing changes in business operations and methods. One example of these changes is the fact that a majority of the approximately 1,710,000 retail establishments have gone into "scrambled merchandising" operations. "Scrambled merchandising" means the carrying of all kinds of merchandise by all sorts of retail outlets, regardless of classification.

Another example of change is the advent of new forms of competition, such as discount houses, and the development and use of all kinds of promotional devices, such as stamps and tape plans. Such innovations have become part of the everyday retail scene. The competitive stress in the market place has reverberated all the way back through existing channels of distribution—the paths through which goods move from the producer to the consumer. The scramble for market position has forced retailers, wholesalers, distributors, and manufacturers into careful examination of their entire marketing policies and structures.

While most changes in channels of distribution during the last two decades have served to accentuate the shifts in competitive demand, these changes have resulted in little or no substantial increases in either efficiency or profits consistent with the growth and income of an ever-increasing population.[2]

THE MARKETING-RETAILING SYSTEM

The marketing-retailing system embraces all the nonmanufacturing functions involved in moving goods from producer to consumer.[3] This definition includes both wholesale and retail sales. Wholesale sales include sales to businesses, industrial users, and institutions where the commodity is used to further or to facilitate production. The quantity bought or sold is not the criterion for a wholesale sale; the *purpose* for which goods are is! Thus retail sales are those made to ultimate consumers for their personal use and satisfaction in the process of ultimate consumption.

Marketing and retail management operate in a profit-oriented competitive economic system. Profits are the primary objective of the business firm in our society. The owners of a business measure managerial performance by this profit criterion.

---

[2] See *Survey of Current Business*, National Income Number, July 1961, p. 15. (Total expenditures for goods and services in terms of constant 1954 dollars compared with population totals.)
[3] *Marketing*, in the commonly accepted usage of the term, "covers all business activities necessary to effect transfers in the ownership of goods and to provide for their physical distribution. It embraces the entire group of services and functions performed in the distribution of merchandise from producer to consumer, excluding only operations relating to changes in the form of goods normally regarded as processing or manufacturing operations." Theodore N. Beckman, H. H. Maynard, and W. R. Davidson, *Principles of Marketing*, 6th ed. (New York: Ronald Press, 1957), p. 4.

Management performs effectively when it plans, organizes, and controls the destinies of the business organization so as to reap maximum profits.[4]

A business organization is also measured in terms of how well it succeeds in creating public values. To insure its success and continuation, a business firm must deliver wanted goods and services regardless of how these change. To generate such social and economic goals requires organizational creativity and flexibility in the marketing-retailing system.

Historical Role

In the past, the term *trade* embodied what today is the marketing-retailing system. In general, trade was considered nonproductive and parasitic in nature; it is still so considered by many individuals in the economy. This type of thinking is almost as old as civilization itself. For example, both Greek and Roman philosophers felt that agriculture was the only "honorable industry." [5]

Belief in the relative nonproductivity of trade was given varying degrees of emphasis throughout the Middle Ages. And with the advent of the mercantilist philosophy, with its "net product" concepts regarding precious metals, the role of marketing as basic to a country's economic health was not yet perceived.[6]

The advent of French physiocracy in the early eighteenth century contributed no basic changes in recognition of the role of traders or trade. The economic reasoning of the times was guided by basic concepts such as "those who buy and sell are to be accounted as vulgar," with implications that marketing was not part of the *ordre naturel* and did not contribute to a *produit net*. The French economists stated that only from the bounty of agriculture could the other classes of society be nurtured and have a "value added" above the work of applied labor.[7]

During the nineteenth century, manufacturing was recognized as having elements of "value added" above the input costs of land, labor, capital, and the entrepreneur. During this period, however, trade was still considered nonproductive. This idea was embodied by J. B. Say (*Traité d'économie politique*, 1803), who stated that "supply creates its own demand," while blithely ignoring an increasing number of market gluts.

---

[4] The terms *profit*, *costs*, and *distribution* in this text will be used in the accounting or business sense unless it is specifically stated otherwise. *Profit* in this context will refer to the actual amount above cost received from revenues. The term *distribution* will be used interchangeably with *marketing* and may refer to any or all of the functions involved in the movement of goods from producer to consumer—in other words, the nonmanufacturing operations. When the terms are used with their normal meaning in economics, they will be so designated.

[5] Marcus Aurelius, *Meditations* IV, 31.

[6] The implications of the dishonorable status of trade were spelled out early in the seventeenth century. See also Davenant's textbook, *Of the Use of Political Arithmetic*, Vol. I, Works, (London: 1771), p. 139.

[7] *Oeuvres de Quesnay*, ed. A. Oncken, from *Tableau* "Les Ouvriers européens" (Paris: 1855), p. 320; also by Oncken, Ersten Theil—die Zeit vor Adam Smith (*Geschichte der National Ökonomie*, 1902). See also Lewis H. Haney, *History of Economic Thought*, 4th ed. (New York: The Macmillan Co., 1953), pp. 178–203.

Emergence of Distribution as a Productive Economic Function

It was not until the middle of the nineteenth century that the processes of trade—marketing, wholesaling, and retailing—began to be considered as productive and value-creating. During this period, W. Stanley Jevons' writings stressed that value was dependent upon supply and upon utility to the buyer. He pointed out that the interaction of scarcity and utility could be easily translated into the process whereby a buyer is willing to exchange scarce cash freely for particular commodities and services; this exchange process offered comparable utility satisfactions. Jevons also introduced a concept whereby personal utility could be seen in terms of social utility. He implied that social utility could be seen as the prices paid by buyers for having the goods at the right place at the right time.[8]

Maturity of Distribution in the Economy

For the first time in history, at the turn of the twentieth century retail markets had available supply adequate to meet demand, and buyer's markets began to appear in selected areas.[9] The transition from a seller's to a buyer's market created a new market norm at the retail level. This initiated the need for mass marketing techniques to move the fruits of mass production; it became very clear that one could not exist without the other.

Thus, one of the prime functions of retail and market management is to move goods by converting *potential* into *effective* demand; then, having the right goods at the right place, time, and price completes the demand-supply cycle. The effective performance of such marketing functions is always needed to utilize the vast and growing excess production of consumer goods.

Institutional and methodological innovations take place as consumer wants and market competition change. Middlemen, such as wholesalers and retailers, can always be replaced, but never their functions.

The System in Terms of Functions

Effective performance of the marketing-retailing system is basic to our economy. The performance of marketing activities by retail firms includes the functions of exchange—buying and selling; the functions of physical supply—transportation and storage; and the facilitating functions—standardization, grading, financing, and risk bearing.[10] The accomplishment of these functions is the marketing process.

---

[8] W. S. Jevons, *Theory of Political Economy*, (London: 1871), pp. 159ff. It is evident to most consumers that a crate of oranges or cantaloupes has a great deal more value in New England than in Florida or California. Nevertheless, consideration of the total functions involved in the process of getting the goods to the market place is still only partially understood by the average consumer in terms of "value added."

[9] This has continued up to the present except for brief periods of scarcity during and immediately after World War I and World War II. A *buyer's market* is one wherein the purchaser has the opportunity to choose from realistic alternatives.

[10] Theodore N. Beckman and W. R. Davidson, *Marketing*, 7th ed. (New York: Ronald Press, 1962), pp. 40–43. The universality of these functions and their specialized application, in marketing in the American economy are analyzed in this text.

Value is added because buyers are willing to pay an exchange price above operating costs and the actual cost of goods sold. The amount of value added in the exchange depends on available supply and the utility of the goods to the buyer.

PRODUCTIVITY MEASURES IN DISTRIBUTION

In efforts to reinforce the concept of the productivity of marketing, many scholars— among them Harold Barger of Columbia University and Theodore N. Beckman of Ohio State University—have devoted much time to pointing out the productive nature of our distribution system.[11] Dr. Beckman has at last achieved a long- awaited goal in this direction. Through his efforts, the Bureau of the Census of the U. S. Department of Commerce collected data on "Value Added by Whole- saling" for the 1963 census from a sample of about 9,600 firms. This is a mile- stone in the advancement of the science of marketing. It is expected that similar data might at a later date be collected for the retail trade as well.[12]

In compilations of government and business statistics, manufacturing costs plus margins at the point of shipment are generally referred to as the "value added" by manufacture—not "costs" of manufacturing. Differing identifications of this kind leave implications of productivity in manufacturing and nonproductiveness in distribution. For example, in the case of distribution, gross margins are still referred to as the "cost" of distribution—not "value added." [13]

"Value Added" by Marketing

The case for marketing and retailing in adding value above the cost of the com- modities sold is very clear.[14] "Total value" may be defined as the sum total of both the psychological and material satisfactions that consumers derive from their pur- chases. As pointed out, consumers in competitive markets will buy wanted items only when the exchange value in terms of dollars is equal to the psychological and social utilities that they expect to acquire from the purchase. Thus the meas- urement of value can be developed in terms of a dollars-and-cents market-basket system correlated to particular goods classifications.[15]

---

[11] The measurement of "value added" by marketing has also been carried out by D. D. Monie- son, who concluded that the measurement of value added by marketing is essentially equal to gross margin obtained on sales. D. D. Monieson, Value Added as a Measure of Economic Contribution by Marketing Institutions. Unpublished doctoral dissertation, Ohio State Uni- versity (1957).

[12] Dr. Beckman also presented an extensive paper entitled "The Value Added Concept as Applied to Marketing" at the December 1954 meetings of the American Marketing Asso- ciation.

[13] The terms margin and gross margin will be used interchangeably in these initial chapters. These terms will mean the actual amount above the cost of goods received by the seller for merchandise sold.

[14] When the marketing functions are applied to the movement of goods for industrial or busi- ness use, or for further processing, selling, or use, the analyses of these functions lie within the framework of industrial marketing or wholesaling.

[15] See also Irwin D. J. Bross, Design for Decision (New York: The Macmillan Co., 1953), Chapter 5.

"Value Added" by Retailing

The final link in the distributive process is the retailer. As seen in Table 1, it is estimated that in 1964 a total of $63.6 billion was contributed in "value added"

TABLE 1

RETAIL SALES AND ESTIMATED "VALUE ADDED" BY RETAILING

For Selected Years 1939 to 1964

(in billions of dollars)

YEAR	RETAIL SALES	MAJOR COMPONENTS[a]		ESTIMATED "VALUE ADDED" BY RETAILING[b]
		DURABLE GOODS STORES	NONDURABLE GOODS STORES	
1939	$ 42.0	$ 6.7	$ 35.1	$10.5
1948	130.5	22.2	98.7	33.9
1954	170.0	58.2	110.2	39.1
1956	189.7	67.0	123.9	46.0
1958	199.6	67.3	142.0	48.5
1959	215.5	71.7	143.8	52.4
1960	219.6	70.7	148.8	53.4
1961	218.2	67.3	151.5	53.6
1962	235.4	74.9	160.4	57.3
1963	244.2	75.5	168.7	59.6
1964	261.6	85.1	176.5	63.6

[a] Component totals may not equal total retail sales because of rounding.

[b] Estimated on basis of average gross margin attained by various census store-classification groups and applied to total sales of each store group. Total dollar amounts were then combined to arrive at the total "value added." (The total dollars as a percentage of total retail sales, in the aggregate, represent the "per cent" total of value added to the economy by retailing.)

Sources: *Census of Business, Retail Trade* (Washington, D.C., U. S. Department of Commerce, 1939, 1954, 1958, and 1963), and *Surveys of Current Business* for 1956, 1959, 1961, 1962, and 1964 data, (also March 1965).

by retailing. This is based on an average estimated gross margin of 24.3 per cent on $261.6 billion worth of retail sales in 1964. As pointed out, the gross margin is the total amount received above the cost of goods sold for merchandise sales. In effect, the difference represents the "value added" by retailing. This may be illustrated as follows:

$$\frac{\text{Total Net Sales}}{\text{(Price paid by consumers)}} = \underline{\text{Cost of Goods Sold}} + \underline{\text{Gross Margin}}$$

$$\therefore$$

$$\frac{\text{Gross Margin Attained}}{\text{(In competitive markets)}} = \underline{\text{Value Added by Retailing}}$$

$$\frac{\text{1964 Net Retail Sales}}{\text{\$261.6 billion}} = \frac{\text{Cost of Goods Sold}}{\text{\$198.0 billion}} + \frac{\text{Gross Margin}}{\text{\$63.6 billion}}$$

$$\therefore$$

$$\text{Value Added by Retailing} = \text{\$63.6 billion}$$

The estimates of value added, in effect, represent valid measures of productivity by retailing.

IMPORTANCE OF CONSUMER SPENDING

Productivity depends on sales-cost ratios; sales, in turn, depend on consumer spending. Consumer spending is one of the key motivators of economic growth and national welfare. High levels of consumer spending are positive influences in limiting the extent and duration of general depressions or business recessions.

Except for the depression period of the thirties, spending has been increasing both relatively and absolutely. Since 1940, the principal contributing factor to this increase of consumer spending has been a constantly increasing flow of personal income to more and more consuming units. The wider distribution of income tends to offset the disposition to spend decreasing proportions of income as it aggregates to an individual or a family.[16]

Changing Spending-Saving Patterns

Consumer demand also depends on what can be purchased by net money income. The value of net money income depends on its purchasing power in terms of real income. Real income in the aggregate is continuing to increase for broader bands of consumer groups. As pointed out, consumers are spending a decreasing proportion of their total income for goods and services and are saving more. At the same time consumers have been increasing their total spending for services in relation to their spending for goods.[17]

Obviously, then, an understanding of what consumers want and are willing to accept and purchase in the way of goods and services is of major importance—not only to marketing and retail managers, but also to the entire economy. Understanding the changing consumer goals that underlie buying motivations can lead to more efficient distribution.

For example, during the 1930's, most family units were forced to change their consumption patterns in both direction and amount. The average family could barely afford necessities during this period of economic and environmental dislocations.

> ... this pattern continued in alternating fashion until 1940 when the sequential effect of huge national defense expenditures was felt throughout the economy. The ensuing war years brought further dislocations almost before those of the depression were fully digested.

> During World War II, a tremendous growth in population and in the number of households occurred. A constantly expanding "middle-income" group became much more characteristic of the total population. For the first time in more than a decade most household units had the necessary income

---

[16] Louis J. Paradiso and Clement Winston, "Consumer Expenditure-Income Patterns," *Survey of Current Business* (September 1955), p. 23.

[17] Included in this grouping are expenditures for household operation, personal business, medical care, transportation, recreation, personal appearance, religion, education, repairs, installations, and service charges for all kinds of commodities. See *Survey of Current Business*, February 1962.

to transform their increasing wants and desires into actualities. Yet the goods and services necessary to fulfill the latent demands of this new "mass" market were not available. This further increased dislocations in consumer spending-saving patterns. During these years the trend towards increased savings became evident.[18]

During the postwar period, the rapid reconversion to consumer-goods production was quickly effected. As a result, the tremendous backlog of consumer demand built up during the war years was rapidly satisfied. By 1947, however, the existing retail institutions were not able to sell more than two-thirds of the potential output of goods of our consumer-goods manufacturers. As a result, a back-up of manufactured consumer goods built up and cut-price discount houses began to appear in most trading areas. For example, by 1952 the output of the consumer-goods sector of the economy was more than twice that of 1929 and was 25 per cent greater than in 1947 [19]—far more than could be absorbed in the market place at that time.

In effect, the economic setting in the early 1950's was one of an overproduction-underconsumption pattern in the consumer-goods sector of the economy. The net difference between exports and a rising influx of imports merely served to accentuate the problem of inadequate demand to insure a fuller use of resources. The present underconsumption pattern is only partially indicative of the broad economic and social changes that constantly take place in the economy. Spending-saving ratios are not changing as much as consumer tastes with respect to the relative personal importance of goods and services.

The Explosion in Service Expenditures

One of the most significant postwar changes in consumer spending has been the increase in allocations for services. In 1961, consumers spent more than $141.2 billion for service sales of all kinds, an increase of 24.5 per cent since 1958. This amount does not include service charges added to the price of merchandise requiring installations or alterations. Today, almost 42 cents of every dollar spent by consumers represent an expenditure for services! [20]

In the past, most customer-and-merchandise-oriented services were included in the retail price and not "costed" separately. Thus, the costs accompanying full service selling (such as delivery, installations, and alterations) and extremely liberal return policies were all generally included in the merchandise price. This type of inclusive pricing has been rapidly disappearing because of severe price competition and the necessity for quoting the lowest possible price for promotional purposes. Most services offered by retail firms today are quoted as additional extras accompanying a merchandise sale.

---

[18] Entenberg, op. cit., pp. 35–36.

[19] See Survey of Current Business, "National Income Supplement," 1954.

[20] Survey of Current Business (February 1962). By 1965, the amounts spent for service expenditures as a proportion of total consumer expenditures stabilized at approximately 41.5 per cent of all such spending. (Survey, May 1965.)

Other Changes in Spending

Within the "goods" sector of the economy the greatest change in spending has occurred in the automotive group categories (automobiles, parts and gasoline service stations). As can be seen from Table 2, this category increased by 42.7 per cent in the period from 1958 through 1963. Although the amounts spent in food stores increased in dollars, the amounts spent by consumers for food purchases in these establishments were proportionately less.

TABLE 2

UNITED STATES SUMMARY
RETAIL TRADE BY KIND OF BUSINESS GROUPING[a]
Establishments, Sales, and Percentage Change in Sales
1954, 1958, and 1963

KIND OF BUSINESS	ESTABLISHMENTS (IN THOUSANDS)			SALES (IN BILLIONS)			CHANGE IN SALES (PER CENT)	
	1954	1958	1963	1954	1958	1963	1954–58	1958–63
RETAIL TRADE, TOTAL[b]	1,721.7	1,788.3	1,707.9	$170.0	$199.7	$244.2	17.5%	22.3%
Food Stores	384.6	355.5	319.4	39.8	49.0	57.1	23.1	16.4
Eating, Drinking Places	319.7	344.7	334.5	13.1	15.2	18.4	16.0	21.1
General Merchandise Group Stores	76.2	86.6	62.1	17.9	21.9	30.0	22.3	37.0
Department Stores	2.8	3.2	4.3	10.6	13.4	20.5	26.4	53.3
Limited Price Variety Stores	20.9	21.0	22.4	3.1	3.6	4.5	16.1	26.1
Apparel, Accessory Stores	119.7	118.8	116.2	11.1	12.5	14.0	12.6	12.3
Furniture, Home Furnishings, Appliances, Dealers	98.1	103.4	93.7	9.0	10.1	10.9	12.0	8.2
Other Retail Stores	226.9	240.1	244.9	15.6	18.5	21.3	18.6	15.2
Nonstore Retailers[c]	78.5	74.7	79.8	4.5	5.4	6.2[d]	20.0	14.8
Automotive Group	86.0	93.7	98.5	29.9	31.8	45.4	6.3	42.7
Gasoline, Service Stations	181.7	206.3	211.5	10.7	14.2	17.8	32.7	25.1
Drug Stores, Proprietary Stores	56.0	56.2	54.7	5.3	6.8	8.5	28.3	24.9
Lumber, Building Materials, Housewares, Farm Equipment, Dealers	100.5	108.3	92.7	13.1	14.3	14.6	9.2	2.2
Home Furnishing and Appliance Stores			20.3			2.4		

a See Appendix B for selected definitions.

b Contiguous United States, Hawaii, and Alaska.

c Nonstore retailers, part of SIC major group 53, shown separately for 1954 and 1958 (1963 data includes Mail Order Sales, General Merchandise and Dry Goods Store Sales, etc.).

d Within this framework, 2.379 billion dollars of sales of Mail Order Firms and Department Store Lines have been added to Department Store Totals; a similar procedure was followed in 1954 and 1958.

Sources: Census of Business, Retail Trade (Washington, D.C., U. S. Department of Commerce, 1958 and 1963, and Survey of Current Business (Feb. 1962). Only 1963 data include Alaska and Hawaii.

Another significant change in spending occurred in the store classification group known as the "GAF" or "GAFFO" group.[21] In effect, the change indicates an increase in consumer spending for department store merchandise lines. Sales of these store groupings are being used increasingly by retail management as a standard of comparison for measuring their changing competitive market positions. In 1963, GAF group store sales approximated $56.6 billion in sales, an increase of 27.4 per cent since 1958, indicating a lower rate of growth in comparison with the sales growth in the automotive and food group categories.

PROBLEMS OF STUDY IN DISTRIBUTION

The exposition of some of the macro- and micro-facets of the economic setting illustrate the highly complex economic variables that must be considered in any

---

21 This group includes the General Merchandise, Apparel and Accessory, and Furniture and Home Furnishings and Appliances stores (see Table 2). Mail order and catalogue sales relating to this merchandise group are also included in these totals.

study of the retailing-marketing system. Because of the tremendous continuing changes and the interaction of practically all functional fields, more and new kinds of economic and management principles must be applied to problem solving and optimization in the field.

For example, the advent of automation, computer technology and cybernetics—the automatic control of machines and men—has opened up a whole new era of information processing and retrieval. Unquestionably, information availability has grown at a far greater rate than the ability of most organizations to use it. This means that complete rethinking and redirection in the field of administrative management in general business as well as in retail distribution must take place. Rethinking is also needed in present theories of communications, control, and human behavior.

This is the age of the generalist. Policy formulation and administration can no longer be based on the narrow concepts of functional field specializations. Ideas which in the past were considered basic and fundamental are no longer adequately serving as guides for decision making and managerial action.

Most of the developing problems today involve economic reasoning and are primarily managerial in nature. As pointed out, the role of computers is not yet fully understood. Further, the capabilities of computers in many business organizations can never be fully utilized until existing organizational concepts and processes are redesigned. In a sense, information technology (with all its implications) is merely one of the keys to progress. Another is the creative application of the facts, principles, and hypotheses that form the basis of theory. Moreover, theory is needed as the basis for a philosophy of management.

There is no single theory of economics, no single theory of the firm, nor is there a single philosophy of management that can be universally applied in solving business problems. Understanding the dynamic processes of consumption in a complex modern society requires the application of general rather than fixed economic concepts or philosophies of management. Teachers, scholars, practitioners, and students in the field must be prepared to adapt to change. This requires continuing general and critical evaluations of existing structures, organizations, processes, techniques, and goals.

Within this general framework, specialization is still a "must"; and specialization can be most creative and productive when carried out in conjunction with pertinent applications of new knowledge and research from related disciplines. Thus, the role of the social sciences, the humanities and the physical sciences must be reevaluated not only in terms of general completeness in themselves, but also in terms of basic applications to functional field problems. In this context, study and research in the field of the retail-market system can be substantially enriched by interdisciplinary applications of a managerial economic nature.

THE MANAGERIAL-ECONOMIC APPROACH

The improvement of performance in any functional field depends directly on the approaches used to identify, develop, analyze, and utilize pertinent data. Studies in the field of distribution generally and retailing specifically have been carried out from the commodity, the institutional, and the functional standpoints. These have been only moderately successful in improving performances in the field. The commodity and institutional approaches consist of tracing the path of goods from the point of production through various middlemen and institutions to the point of ultimate consumption. Because of continuing changes in consumer spending patterns, institutional strategy and existing channels of distribution change; as a result, the commodity and institutional approaches tend to become obsolete.

The functional approach to the study of retail and market distribution consists of analyses and descriptions of the functions of exchange, facilitation, and product movement; this approach has generally been the least repetitive and most productive. However, this approach no longer meets the need for objective analysis, creative planning, and administrative management, which are necessary today to adapt effectively to change. The managerial-economic approach fulfills this objective.

The Role of Related Disciplines[22]

Retailing, in effect, is a social system in operation. The study of retail distribution as a functional field not only involves conceptual applications from economic theory but also integrates concepts and tools of analyses from related disciplines. While each discipline may have separate areas of application, the over-all objective is to improve managerial performance and market effectiveness.

Sociology. Today, sociology—the study of the individual in the social milieu—is an accepted science in itself. While the history of sociology as a separate discipline can be measured in terms of decades, it includes a wide range of human reflections on society. In effect, sociology is the science of society that deals with the relationship of social structure to human behavior. Inherent in this relationship is the concept of conforming or belonging to a group. The development of any optimum sales promotion program (in retailing or wholesaling) must be based on an understanding of conditions under which the individual either conforms or does not conform to the standards of the group. In this case, the standards of the 65 per cent "middle majority" of the population determine the manner in which advertising appeals or patronage motives are developed.

Sociology also deals explicitly with group behavior patterns found in certain trading areas and geographical locales. An early example of sociological concepts in economics is Engels' "Laws of Consumption," which were concerned with the buying behavior of low-income groups—in this case, German workers. These studies, conducted during the middle of the nineteenth century, represent both sociological and economic research seeking to explain changing consumer buying patterns and outlays in terms of changes in income. Engels' studies are still

---

[22] This brief review of interdisciplinary applications is not intended to be complete. It is rather an initial orientation only.

used as points of reference in seeking better understanding of forces in retail markets.[23]

Psychology.   The area of psychology that deals specifically with the motivation and behavior of the individual in society has always been used in determining demand creation. As in sociology or social psychology, an understanding of the individual in terms of his motivations has always been basic to organizational planning, motivation of sales personnel, and the maximization of promotional efforts in the field of distribution. Freud developed a motivation system which was subsequently enlarged, rephrased, and corrected by Jung, Adler, Fromm, Horney, Sullivan, and others.

Motivation research, for example, and other aspects of psychological motivational systems have always been used to determine specific advertising copy and the choice of media. Although buying appeals and motivation research were not termed "interdisciplinary"—the context used today—these considerations were an integral part of the retail-market process. Essentially, these are sales promotion tools. The contributions of social psychology help sum up and channel consumer drives for personal status within the social system with a total objective of increasing primary and selective demand.

The types of policy formulated, the kind of store image developed, the kind of merchandise carried and the price lines offered by a store are unquestionably based on economic and demographic factors. However, the optimum success of any retail firm depends on the extent to which management uses the new psychological insights in stimulating consumer demand. Contributions from these social sciences are constantly providing new methodologies for improving performance.

Mathematics.   Elements of the exact sciences (more specifically, the quantitative mathematical approaches) are playing an increasingly important role in the solving of business problems and in decision making. At first glance, there seems to be little connection between mathematical applications to problem solving in retailing because, for the most part, nonlinear relationships are involved. However, entirely new decision-making concepts are being developed under the broader ranges of heuristic—nonlinear—relationships.[24] To date, only limited use has been made of these techniques. For example, learning theory and other aids to human thinking were originated and set up without a true understanding of the direction which the theory would take. In a similar manner, new mathematical and behavioral concepts are being applied without any guarantees as to their usefulness. To this end, research is continuing in the simulation of human thinking and behavior processes by programming philosophical points of view into a computer.

---

[23] See Carroll D. Wright, "Supervisory Budget Study of 397 Workmen's Families in Massachusetts" in Wright and Potter, "Sixth Annual Report of the Massachusetts Bureau of Statistical Labor" (Boston: 1875), p. 438. Wright formulated the first complete statement of Engels' "Laws of Consumption." See also Beckman, 7th ed., *op. cit.*, pp. 102–104.

[24] See Herbert A. Simon, *The New Science of Management Decisions* (New York: Harper and Brothers, 1960), pp. 21–30. In this text, Professor Simon discusses new concepts of nontraditional use of computers.

Statistical Decision Theory and Inference. Statistical interpretations and applications of raw data are also basic to many decisions affecting retail markets. Statistics, in reality, is a subdiscipline that permits simulations and mathematical interpretations of data. Such interpretations no longer deal solely with coordinating data and developing functional relationships. Statistical tools furnish retail management with the most precise measures of effectiveness that could result from various alternative decisions.[25]

The concept of statistics itself is also changing. For example, there are two kinds of random procedures in statistics. One is based on *a priori* "probability inferences" (Bayes' Rule) and the other on the "state of nature." In one case, estimates and inferential projections beyond the sample data furnish the basis for decision making; in the other, validated correlations are considered to be the only basis for decision making.

More specifically, inference in statistical decision theory uses existing knowledge or "infinitive insight" in a field to implement the data obtained from a sample. By this means, management infers certain postulates on which to base decisions. "Inference theory" helps bring normal intuition into the decision-making processes and is used extensively at all levels of management.[26]

Philosophy. Philosophy as well as the humanities in general interact in retail-management decisions. More specifically, philosophy gives substance to organized society and organizational structures. Logic gives the proper weight to interpretation of problem solving and goal attainment either within or outside of the organizational framework. It still takes a philosophical interpretation of physical and psychological data to decide on any action. Even Adam Smith was not unmindful of the need for a philosophy of management. In a like manner, retail managers often act without full verification of data or new concepts. Decision making, in this context, involves a philosophy of action which is constantly needed in competitive markets. Thus, retail management is both an art and a science, drawing heavily upon the contributions and logic developed in related disciplines. The managerial-economic approach in effect takes these contributing relationships into consideration in the analysis of effective retail and market distribution.

SUMMARY AND CONCLUSIONS

Distribution deals with people and with the problems accompanying the sale and acquisition of goods and services.

---

[25] Herbert A. Simon and Allen Shewell, "Heuristic Problem Solving: The Next Advance in Operations Research," *Operations Research*, 6 (Jan.–Feb. 1958), pp. 1–10; (May–June 1958) pp. 449–450. Specific applications of both operations research and game theory will be presented in later chapters, as will pertinent applications of other related disciplines.

[26] See Bross, *op. cit.*, pp. 83–84, pp. 212–238. Under the Bayesian system, a series of specific hypotheses are set up, tested and eliminated as disproved. Finally, when one hypothesis remains which cannot be disproved "based on theoretical and computation tests" the resulting hypothesis is "judged" to be sound. See also R. Fisher, *Contributions to Mathematical Statistics* (New York: Wiley and Sons, 1950), Chapters 3–4; and Harvey V. Roberts, "The New Business Statistics," *Journal of Business* (January 1960), pp. 21–30.

Economic analysis helps point out both the issues and solutions involved in the competitive market structure. It is within this framework that retail management's goals of creating public values and long-run profit maximization must be achieved. Improving the efficiency of our marketing-retailing system must be based on improving the techniques of demand creation and of logistic support for its fulfillment.

Manufacturers in a competitive economy tend to overproduce in order to reduce unit costs and to maintain or increase their market shares. As a result, we are faced with an overproduction-underconsumption economic pattern with increasing and constant pressures being put on retail markets to move goods more effectively.

An understanding of the broad economic setting in which retail management must operate and solve its problems must be developed. Within this economic setting, the prediction of change *before* it occurs and how best to recognize, evaluate, and adjust to change represent new frontiers of organizational planning. Some of the tools of analyses from interacting and related disciplines have been reviewed in the framework of the managerial-economic approach. Within this framework, the major determinants of the retail structure are analyzed in the chapter that follows.

Chapter 2: *The Retail Structure and Competition: Determinants and Characteristics*

The functional operation of retail establishments and retailing is so pervasive throughout the economy that many businessmen and most consumers overlook its key role in the economy. Overgeneralizations, both as to its scope and to its importance, are made frequently; for example, "Anyone can open and operate a store."

Total retail sales in 1964 approximated $261.6 billion.[1] This includes over $6 billion in sales by functionaries in the channel classified as "nonstore retailers," a classification that includes sales of direct selling organizations, catalogue stores, mail-order sales, door-to-door distributors, and vending-machine operations. These totals do not include the many "retail" sales made by both wholesalers and manufacturers. On the other hand, these totals do include many "wholesale" sales made by retailers.[2]

Retail establishments are classified by the Bureau of the Census according to sales size, number of employees, legal form of organization, location, and kinds of stores. In the *1963 Census of Business*, there are eleven classes of retail estab-

---

[1] *Survey of Current Business* (May 1965).
[2] See definition of terms, *1963 Census of Business, Retail Trade,* (Bureau of the Census, U. S. Department of Commerce, Washington 25, D.C.) and Appendix A.

17

lishments, and one broad class called "nonstore retailers," which includes firms lacking a definite identity for the purpose of classification.[3]

The largest single class of retail stores is that of the food group, which includes some 319,000 stores; these stores generated over $57 billion in sales in 1963.

As previously noted, there has been a tremendous surge in demand for income-producing services such as travel accommodations; specialized credit-investment counseling; insurance; rentals of all kinds; radio, television, and appliance repairs; reupholstering; and custom-made interior decorating. Retailers offer such services both as an accommodation and as a broader volume base on which to improve profits.

The intensity and pattern of consumer demand is the most important determinant of the retail structure. At the same time, consumer demand is also a dependent variable of the business structure. In circular fashion, the manner and the extent to which consumers allocate their expenditures between durable goods, nondurable goods, and services are of major interest to retail-market managers.[4]

Retail management's major interest is not primarily in such totals, but rather in the much narrower breakdowns of how consumers allocate their incomes for specific merchandise categories. The narrower the sales breakdowns, the easier it is for retail store buyers to forecast merchandise requirements and do a more efficient job. The shifting expenditure patterns between commodities and services, as well as the shifts in the kinds of commodities and services bought in any trading area affect the basic character of the retail structure and its setting.

CONSUMER DEMAND AND MARKET STRUCTURE

Despite periodic variations in total business activity, consumption expenditures in the aggregate have generally been regarded as a comparatively stable function of income. As a result, economic analysts have generally forecast gradual, rather than rapid, changes in the market place. Yet, shifts in consumer spending can and do occur rapidly, and not necessarily with any advance notice.[5] For example, when the Edsel automobile was introduced as a competitive entry in the medium-price field in the late 1950's, the bulk of consumer demand had already shifted to the low-price compacts. The result was market failure. On the other hand, the timing

---

[3] In 1948, sales made through stores classified as nonstore retailers were included with the major store group according to its "kind of business" classification. For example, in the 1954 Census of Business, a leased department in a store was treated as a separate establishment; such a department today is classified on the basis of its particular kind of business or as a nonstore retailer rather than as part of the store within which it operates. In 1948 leased departments' sales were included with the stores in which they were located. In effect, this means that general merchandise store sales are overstated for 1948 and understated for 1954 because of the changes in the classifications of leased departments. (See Appendix B for a summary analysis of principal store types by group.)

[4] For detailed discussion of the circular effects of consumer spending, see Robert D. Entenberg, *The Changing Competitive Position of Department Stores in the United States by Merchandise Lines*, rev. ed. (Univ. of Pittsburgh Press, 1961), pp. 36–45.

[5] Arthur F. Burns, *The Instability of Consumer Spending*, 32nd Annual Report (New York: The National Bureau of Economic Research, 1952), p. 9.

and introduction of the Mustang in 1964 met the market squarely and successfully. In the former case, many Ford retailers disappeared or reorganized; in the latter, many additional Ford dealerships appeared as a result of the Mustang's success.

Because consumer spending patterns can shift rapidly, many innovators have appeared in the market place in the hope of capitalizing on these potential shifts. Since 1946 there also has been a tremendous growth in customer mobility. This, along with population increases and changes in the composition of localized consumer groups, has resulted in further structural changes in retail markets.

Effect of Output and Income

In Table 3, it is seen that since 1948 personal consumption expenditures have been decreasing as a percentage of disposable personal income, thus indicating an increasing predisposition to save more. This may be the result of a sufficiency of goods and/or a lack of fear of inflation in the economy. Personal consumption

TABLE 3

PERSONAL CONSUMPTION EXPENDITURES AS A PERCENTAGE
OF OUTPUT AND INCOME, FOR SELECTED YEARS,
1929–1966

YEAR	PERSONAL CONSUMPTION EXPENDITURES AS A PERCENTAGE OF		
	GROSS NATIONAL PRODUCT	PERSONAL INCOME	DISPOSABLE PERSONAL INCOME
1929	75.9	92.6	95.5
1940	71.1	92.1	95.5
1944	52.2	67.3	75.9
1948	68.7	84.9	94.4
1950	67.8	85.8	95.5
1951	63.1	81.8	92.5
1952	62.7	80.0	92.8
1953	62.6	80.5	92.7
1954	65.6	83.4	92.7
1955	64.6	83.8	94.7
1956	64.4	81.7	92.1
1957	64.4	81.8	93.0
1958	66.1	82.1	92.3
1959	65.1	82.4	93.6
1960	65.2	81.8	93.5
1961	65.0	81.6	92.9
1962	64.2	80.7	92.8
1963	64.2	80.8	93.2
1964	64.1	81.3	92.5
1965 (estimated)	64.2	81.4	92.6

Sources: U. S. Department of Commerce, Office of Business Economics, as found in *Survey of Current Business* (April 1954), p. 7, (April 1956), p. 7; *U. S. Income & Output* (1958), pp. 119, 145; and *Survey of Current Business* (July, August, February, July 1960 and 1961, February 1962, and May 1965).

expenditures have decreased significantly as a percentage of both gross national product and personal income. This means that changes in gross national product and personal income have become less important indicators of both personal consumption expenditures and retail sales. However, the directional shifts in both output and spending patterns by locales form the basic determinants of the retail structure and resulting interfirm competition.

Another aspect of this long-run secular trend shows that because the consumer is saving a greater proportion of his income, he is therefore in a highly receptive position to increase his spending—given the proper stimuli. The proper stimuli to increased spending today can be symbolized by the term "convenience." This means convenience of location (parking, transportation) and of merchandise (competitive prices and complete merchandise assortments in depth). The increasing availability of credit also increases the consumer's short-run expenditure patterns without recourse to depleting savings. In effect, such situations have served to increase entrepreneurial risk-taking with many ventures originating on purely hopeful considerations.

Effects of Consumer Expenditure Shifts

From Table 4, it is clear that consumers are still allocating the greatest proportion of their expenditures for "nondurables" (soft lines), such as clothing, shoes, and food. Yet there has been a decline in the proportion of total spending allocated for these categories. In 1965 consumers allocated some $185 billion or 44.1 per cent of their total spending for nondurables, a decline of 20.7 per cent since 1948, when spending for these categories represented 55.6 per cent of all expenditures. Although total dollar sales for these categories are still increasing, these dollar increases are being generated at a decreasing rate.

During the same period of time, spending for durables increased from 12.5 to 15.7 per cent, or 25.6 per cent increase. In other words, the shift in consumer expenditures has been away from nondurables and in the direction of both durables and service expenditures.

From 1948 through 1961 when a peak in this direction was reached, service expenditures as a percentage of all consumer spending increased from 31.9 per cent to 41.7 per cent, an increase of 30.7 per cent. In other words, consumers are still spending somewhat more than 41 cents of every dollar for services. This major expenditure shift away from nondurable goods to services and durables (primarily automotive) has been forcing basic changes in both the structure and the nature of retail competition. As a result, many retail outlets are faced with shrinking soft-goods markets and increasing service and durable-goods markets. Because the greatest part of service sales are not adaptable for handling by retail stores, many have had to innovate, to carry other commodity lines, or discontinue operations.

Effect of Investment Opportunities

Although shifts in consumer expenditures are a major determinant of the institutional setting, the attractiveness of investment opportunities in the field is another. The availability of investment capital is dependent upon the rate of expected return and the relative security of the investment. With respect to market expansions at the retail level, dominant roles are played by real estate developers, architects, banks, and insurance companies as well as by retail management. The nature of the requirements for the acquisition of investment capital is and has been a

TABLE 4

PERSONAL CONSUMPTION EXPENDITURES BY MAJOR TYPE FOR SELECTED YEARS, 1939–1965

(in billions of dollars)

	1939	1941	1945	1946	1948	1950	1951	1953	1954	1956	1958	1960	1961	1962	1963	1964	1965e
Durable Goods	6.7	9.7	8.1	15.9	22.2	28.6	27.1	29.7	29.4	38.5	37.3	44.3	42.3	48.4	52.1	57.0	66.0
Autos & Parts	2.2	3.4	1.0	3.9	7.3	12.4	10.9	13.1	12.6	15.8	13.9	18.5	16.8	20.6	22.7	24.2	28.1
Furniture & Household Equipment	3.5	4.9	4.6	8.7	11.5	12.9	12.7	12.8	12.9	17.4	17.4	18.8	18.6	20.2	21.4	24.0	24.3
Other Durables	1.0	1.4	2.5	3.3	3.4	3.3	3.5	3.9	3.9	5.3	6.0	6.9	7.0	7.6	8.0	8.8	9.4
Nondurable Goods	35.1	43.2	73.2	84.5	98.7	100.4	111.1	118.9	120.6	131.4	142.0	152.4	155.5	162.0	167.5	177.3	185.0
Clothing & Shoes	7.1	8.8	16.5	10.2	19.6	18.5	19.8	19.8	19.7	24.5	25.7	33.9	28.4	29.9	30.7	33.4	35.0
Food & Beverages	19.2	23.6	41.6	48.8	57.3	58.0	66.5	71.8	73.1	71.2	76.8	80.0	81.8	84.6	87.1	91.7	94.9
Gas & Oil	2.2	2.6	1.8	3.0	4.3	5.0	5.5	6.6	6.9	9.6	10.6	11.6	11.8	12.3	12.8	13.5	14.1
Semidurable Furnishings	.7	.9	1.5	2.0	2.3	2.4	2.5	2.5		2.7	2.7	3.0		—	—	—	—
Tobacco	1.8	2.1	3.0	3.5	4.1	4.4	4.7	5.3	{ 20.8	5.6	6.4	7.5	{ 33.6	—	—	—	—
Other Nondurables	4.2	5.1	8.8	8.9	11.1	11.2	12.0	12.9		17.8	19.8	23.6		—	—	—	—
Services	25.8	29.0	40.4	46.2	56.7	65.0	70.1	81.4	86.8	100.0	114.2	132.2	141.2	146.4	155.3	165.1	173.0
Personal Business	1.4	1.7	2.9	3.4	3.8	3.9	4.1	4.4		15.2	16.8	20.6	21.0	—	—	—	—
Recreation	1.5	1.8	3.0	3.7	3.8	3.9		4.4	{ 37.2	—	—	—	—	—	—	—	—
Other Services[a]	8.0	8.7	11.6	13.7	17.5	20.6	21.9	25.8		—	—	—	—	—	—	—	—
Transportation, Housing, & Household Operation[b]	—	—	—	—	—	—	—	—	—	—	—	—	—	79.4	83.3	88.1	93.2
Totals[b]	57.8	81.9	121.7	146.6	177.6	194.0	208.3	230.1	236.6	269.9	293.5	328.9	339.0	356.8	375.0	399.3	419.5e

a Does not include Transportation, Housing, and Household Operation except for 1962–1965.

b Durable Goods 1929, 1933, 1935—9.2, 3.5, 5.1; Nondurable Goods 1929, 1933, 1935—37.7, 22.3, 29.3; Services 1929, 1933, 1935—32.1, 20.7, 21.9.

c Estimated.

Sources: *National Income Supplement, Survey of Current Business* (1954), Table 50. Figures for later years represent latest adjustments found in *Survey of Current Business* (July 1958, July 1960, July 1961, Feb. 1962, and June 1965).

significant factor in the development, promotion, and composition of shopping centers.

The field of retailing has usually been a relatively attractive outlet for investors. New firms and innovators, because of the comparatively small working capital needed and the relative ease of entry, make almost constant appearances. For example: there are constant streams of new shopping centers and innovative firms of all kinds being integrated into the market—discount houses, cut-rate drugstores, "shopmobiles," leased department expansions, and now the development of "supermarketing" stores (stores that handle any and all kinds of commodities on a mass scale regardless of merchandise relatedness or price lines). These supermarketing outlets closely resemble the "general store" of the past, but on a vastly larger, more competitive scale. Supermarketing stores often take on the guise of discount houses, although they do not seem to operate as such.[6]

Small Store Competition

As a result of the relative ease with which investment money can be secured for ventures in retailing, much overbuilding has occurred and many "overstored" areas have begun to appear. Furthermore, in the scramble for financial and market security, shopping-center promoters and underwriters have adopted leasing policies that often prove highly unfavorable to the smaller independent stores.

Until very recently, most promoters and shopping-center developers were not in any position to lease desirable locations to small independents. This was because the principal underwriters of shopping centers required signed leases with financially top-rated firms before underwriting could be assured. The effect of financial underwriting requirements of this kind meant that the most "economic" locations went to the larger, multi-unit firms. As a result, it was almost impossible for the smaller independent businessman of limited means to secure desirable space at a reasonable rental. In a very large percentage of the more than 10,000 regional, sectional, and local shopping centers built outside central business districts since 1946, this is still true. In Table 2 (page 11), it is seen that for the first time since 1929 there has been a significant decrease in retail establishments, most of these being in the food store categories. A decrease of over 36,000 establishments occurred from 1958 to 1964.

In 1961 the Small Business Administration (SBA), taking formal recognition of this problem, announced that it would, where warranted, underwrite up to $250,000 of shopping-center development costs for each lease signed with a small independent concern. Hopefully, this policy should serve to equalize, to some extent, the tremendous locational and competitive advantages that the larger firms are enjoying in shopping center expansions.

---

[6] John's Bargain Stores can be considered a prototype of these new "general stores," as can the new "Safeway Super S Stores." A discount house may be defined as "any size retail establishment that attempts to continuously sell nationally advertised, easily recognized, branded merchandise at less than a 'list' or manufacturer's suggested retail price." Robert D. Entenberg, "The Discount House—Panic or Panacea," *Georgia Business* (University of Georgia, October 1961).

Despite a major competitive advantage of this kind accruing to the larger multi-unit retail firms, the soundness and vigor of the smaller independent firms remain. Fortunately, the remaining independents and smaller multi-unit firms have been growing and maintaining their share of the market as the larger firms fail to exploit fully their competitive advantages of size, buying power, and preferential locations. In 1961, the smaller firms still absorbed over 78 per cent of total retail sales—approximately the same percentage that they enjoyed in 1946. This fact clearly demonstrates that, despite the growth of retail "giants," the fluidity of retail markets is such that many favorable aspects of interfirm competition at the retail level continue to exist.[7]

THE COMPETITIVE SETTING

Interfirm competition at the retail level has been characterized as monopolistic, imperfect, "naturalistic," and/or "workable." Such competition represents almost a complete range of market settings short of pure competition and pure monopoly.

Unfortunately, many so-called modern analyses of interfirm competition are still set up within a framework of eighteenth-century agrarian societies in which economic scarcities and sellers' markets were the order of the day. More often than not, the standard basis for evaluating competition still is in terms of deviation from a norm of theoretically perfect competition. Moreover, "perfect" competition implies a market with homogeneous products, with full information on the part of consumers, and with price as the automatic regulator of supply and demand. This kind of market simply does not exist. For example, packaging creates product differentiation, and separation of trading areas prevents flow of full information.

The behavior of the firm, especially in market distribution, can be only partially explained in this kind of "perfect model" framework. The actual behavior of retail firms in the market place is competitive and can be characterized as "workable." As pointed out above, the field of retailing has a greater ease of entry and comparatively lower investment requirements.

Basically, then, the essential differences between traditional economic theory and modern management theory of the firm may be found in the differing organizational goals, policy formulation, and market behavior. Retail management generally strives for long-run satisfactory profits rather than short-run profit maximands.[8] Furthermore, organizational goals can be summed up in the manner in which merchandising and operating pricing policies are set up.

Price versus Nonprice Competition

Just as retail structure is determined by consumer expenditures and wants as well as entrepreneurial opportunities, the total market framework is determined by retail structure and the availability of goods. Both the availability and the potential

[7] *Survey of Current Business* (February 1962).
[8] See Julius Margolis, "The Analyses of the Firm: Nationalism, Conventionalism, and Behaviorism," *Journal of Business* (July 1958), pp. 187–199.

amount of goods that can be offered to the public increase daily. The merchandise lines available to the public have developed more similarities than dissimilarities in both variety and depth. Today, "exclusives" on really differentiated merchandise classifications are rare attributes for stores.

Because of buyers' markets and the easy accessibility of competing stores and market areas, product as well as store substitutions are commonplace; they are so commonplace, in fact, that patronage motives in brand and store preferences have to be constantly reinforced in order to maintain competitive market shares. To reinforce institutional and merchandise appeals, many stores have gone all out into nonprice as well as price competition. Nonprice competition can take the form of better service, better selections, more convenient locations, better prestige surroundings, and the projection of a better store image as *the place* to shop.

Thus, the increasing availability and growing similarities of goods and institutional settings in which to shop have increased consumer tendencies to substitute both products and stores in shopping. Diluted customer loyalties and patronage motives of these kinds have served to intensify competition at the retail level. Pricing in such settings is highly competitive. Intense competitive pricing also works, at least in the short run, toward the stimulation of consumer interest because in this setting the consumers often pay a far lower than normal price. Market conditions of this kind also mean that new firms must prove their competitive effectiveness in very short order or be quickly forced out of business.

"Normal" Price and the Firm's Fixed Cost Structure

The "normal" retail price can be considered the cost of the merchandise plus a mark-up that is sufficient to cover operating expenses and still leave a margin for profit.[9] When "price wars" break out, sales are often transacted on a "loss-leader" basis. Loss leaders are sales below cost or below actual costs plus operating expenses. Price competition of this nature soon becomes uneconomic. Where chaotic pricing conditions of this kind continue, marginal stores are often forced out of business, and financially secure firms seek to become more efficient by reducing their fixed cost structure. In striving for greater efficiency, management may often eliminate many previously "free" services, may decrease needed services, and may institute charges for "wanted" services. These form structural changes at the level of the firm. In most cases, despite continuous readjustments in both service expenditures and methods of operation, a firm's fixed-cost structure generally inches upward on a continuum. Fixed costs, when not reviewed and evaluated periodically, tend to become permanent and uneconomic. When this occurs, the firm's flexibility and ability to compete lessens. Uneconomic costs can result from unwarranted executive compensation or uneconomic wage rates operating with outdated procedures, outdated fixtures, improper utilization of selling space, and unrealistic methods of merchandising management.

---

[9] The term *profit* is used in this context in the accounting or financial sense.

In effect, uneconomic costs seem to begin with the basic organic growth cycle of the firm. As the firm moves from the stage of innovation, low cost, and survival, goal objectives change. Often, when store management is motivated to "trade up" and seek status respectability, higher cost ratios accompany the change. Higher cost ratios force a need for higher gross margins and result in an "umbrella" type of pricing structure, less competitive effectiveness, and greater market vulnerability. This is one of the many ways in which the advantages of scale of firm and size of plant are competed away.[10]

Thus, in the long run, it is impossible in a competitive economic order for even the most efficient of firms to undersell continuously and generally all its competitors. While new firms and innovators find constant encouragement to enter the market, these same smaller, newer firms must effectively and almost immediately compete on both a price as well as a nonprice basis. Because the smaller firms have greater flexibility, they can become strong competitors. Again, should they become "entrenched," they too begin to compete increasingly on a nonprice rather than a price basis in attempts to cover their own rising cost structures. Thus the forces that mold retail structure and competition are fluid in nature—and therefore the structure itself is highly fluid.

SUMMARY AND CONCLUSIONS

The most significant demographic and economic changes molding the retail structure during the last three decades have been the continuing increases in disposable personal income and in service expenditures and the decreasing proportion of spending for nondurables. Rural-urban-suburban migrations and, more recently, movements back into urban areas are all illustrative of fluidity in the market place. Despite increasing availability of both choice of goods and accessibility of stores in which to shop, the total allocation of consumers' income spent in retail stores has not increased in relation to expanding disposable personal income.

Yet, total consumption expenditures are still a comparatively stable function of income with changes in spending patterns being in the direction of services and durables—primarily automobiles—and not in the total amount of dollars spent. Accompanying these changing spending patterns, the consumer's propensity to save continues at a high level. To be effective, the stimulation of consumer demand must be set up in light of the constantly changing consumer expenditure patterns and competitive changes in the market place. The increase in savings by more spending units is making the stimulation of primary and selective demand somewhat easier.

The relative ease of entry for new retail firms and innovators of all kinds tends to weaken both store patronage and brand monopolies. More important, the growing similarities of markets, stores, and merchandise offers and prices also dilute cus-

---

[10] See Robert A. Triffin, *Monopolistic Competition and General Equilibrium Theory* (Cambridge: Harvard University Press, 1940), Chapter 5.

tomer patronage motives and the market structure. The over-all result has been an increasing importance of nonprice competition in relation to price competition. Nonprice competition in terms of "convenience" has become a more important value aspect in consumer purchase motivation and interfirm competition. Consumers attempt to maximize their purchase satisfactions provided that such satisfactions can be attained with minimum inconveniences.

Retail managers operate in settings of "workable" or "naturalistic" competition. It has also been pointed out that small differences in the price of shopping and convenience goods do not significantly affect the quantity of goods taken off the market through particular firms. Thus, an important facet of any new market entry is the fact that any initial price differentials offered by new firms tend to disappear over time because of the increasing institutionalization of fixed costs into the operating structure.

Thus the circular interaction of demand in terms of purchasing patterns, wants in terms of conveniences, and the application of investment capital in terms of expected returns determines the characteristics of the retail structure and the degree of existing interfirm competition. These considerations are only part of the new adjustments made in the retail setting. A further evaluation of the final stages of the total distributive structure will be presented in Chapter 3.

Chapter 3: *General Analysis of the Final Stages of the Distributive Process*

Some of the most volatile areas of uncertainty in the distributive process are those of the external setting, such as analyses of potential locations, selection of channels of distribution, evaluation of the effects of mergers, and acquisitions and innovations on the part of competitors. These are merely the more common areas of uncertainty with which retail management must deal.

Any going concern operates and is guided by managerial policy decisions. These decisions, in turn, are strongly influenced and guided by the requirements of the external setting. External settings change in response to changes in the socioeconomic framework known as the market. For example, customers' outlooks change, the size and composition of the population change, consumer purchasing patterns change, as do loyalties to products, brands, and stores. Thus, executive action constantly adjusts to the fluctuating requirements of the external setting. Adjusting to changing organizational requirements internally and new situations externally requires an integrated approach for maximum effectiveness.

DETERMINANTS OF THE CHANNEL OF DISTRIBUTION

The channel of distribution can be defined as the path through which the title of goods passes. The definition itself implies functional activities tied to middlemen operating in a competitive framework of the individual firm in a trading area.

The competitive framework of any store is determined by the total number of retail establishments in the area and the extent, contiguity, and accessibility of competing stores and adjacent shopping center clusters. The size of the trading area as well as the methods of operation, price lines handled, and the kind, variety, and extent of merchandise offerings also make up the competitive framework. The amount of business or drawing power that any store in a group can generate depends upon the size of the cluster and the progressiveness of management in being able to attract customers and correctly analyze and meet any problems created by new forms of competition.[1]

Importance of the Proper Choice of Channel

A channel of distribution may also be defined as the functional manner in which goods move in a distributive path from the producer to the consumer. Several guiding principles govern the choice of the most effective paths through which goods can move effectively. For example, technical products of a high unit value tend to have a short channel of distribution. A relatively short channel of distribution is one in which goods move directly from the manufacturer to the seller without intermediaries. This is illustrated in Figure I.

High fashion and higher-price women's and misses ready-to-wear clothing and accessories, better men's clothing and shoes, better furniture, and major appliances would all fit into the classification of a "technical product." Merchandise in such categories is generally sold directly to the retailer by the manufacturer. Lower-price shopping goods and convenience goods which need wide, nonselective distribution tend to have a relatively long channel of distribution. Goods classified in these categories generally involve many distributors and wholesalers for movement to the ultimate consumer. Other classes of goods, such as specialties in the cosmetic, book, and accessory fields, often move directly from manufacturer to consumer. Avon cosmetics, Book of Knowledge, and Fuller-Brush items move in direct channels.

The retail store (or retailer) represents the final stage or the ultimate middleman in the total distributive process. Basic to "channel" analysis is an understanding of the retail institutions in which customers in particular trading areas prefer to shop. A basic principle illustrating the key importance of functionaries in the channel is that, while it is possible to eliminate the middleman, it is *never* possible to eliminate the functional performance.

However, integration of the functional activities of middlemen in the channel does take place. Nevertheless, integration does not mean elimination, despite severe competitive pressures. For example, the United Parcel Service Company

---

[1] A *cluster group* store is one in any grouping of stores in a local, sectional, regional, secondary, or downtown shopping center that is easily accessible within an unhampered seven-minute walking distance for a shopping customer. Should a store take longer to reach, it should not be considered part of the cluster for maximum promotional effectiveness.

handles merchandise deliveries for stores that consider it more economic or more expedient to "contract out" the function of customer deliveries. Or the management of a retail firm may decide to integrate vertically and conduct warehousing and storing operations normally conducted by wholesalers. In such cases, the retail firm may be seeking added functional discounts, greater efficiency, or both.

The competitive "norm" in the American economy is one of abundance char-

FIGURE I
CHANNELS OF DISTRIBUTION

Most technical products (consumer or industrial goods) of high unit value

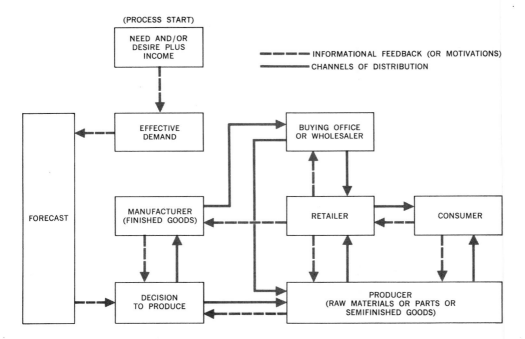

acterized by a continuing buyers' market in which consumers have almost unlimited choice of products as well as institutions in which to shop. In a competitive economy all middlemen must perform wanted services in a reasonably efficient manner in order to justify their existence and to assure their continuity. Otherwise, consumers by-pass the normal channel. Buyers continuously seek to maximize their satisfactions by paying the lowest possible prices for their purchases in the most convenient manner possible. In this type of competitive framework, the buyer is in a highly favorable position to achieve his "maximization" objective.

At the same time, the degree of existing competition and the availability of goods in local markets determine the extent to which purchasers can maximize. The continuous shopping for greater selectivity and lower prices by consumers creates and sustains constant pressure on all the functionaries in the channel to perform at optimum levels. Thus, manufacturers of relatively high-priced "shopping" goods [2] operating in buyers' markets with products such as suits, fabrics, or refrigerators strive to promote their products into a specialty goods category, one on which consumers will insist. Should the producer succeed in developing a high volume of selective demand, such as insistence on a Davidow suit, a Forstmann woolen, or a General Electric refrigerator, he is then in a good position to control both his market and the channel of distribution.

Similarly, at the retail level, the store which carries the greater number of "prestige" specialty brands has, in a great measure, a singularly well-protected market and a reduced likelihood of direct price competition. Thus, the degree to which customers unconsciously classify a brand, a product, or a merchandise line as a shopping or specialty item influences the channel of distribution and the manner in which the item is marketed. In effect, the degree of product acceptance by consumers constitutes an important facet in determining the ultimate choice made by manufacturers and wholesalers in the choice of a channel of distribution. In turn, these choices strongly influence the institutional framework that develops in the market place.

Effect of Product Differentiation on Channels of Distribution

Of course, attempts are constantly being made by manufacturers to change customer acceptance of only particular kinds of stores in which to shop for specific classes of goods. Manufacturers who initiate such changes hope to expand the sales of their products by selling through as many outlets as possible. In some instances they have succeeded, but generally only with lower-price convenience goods.

For instance, in past years such goods as cosmetics, dentifrices, and patent medicines were generally sold primarily in drugstores. Today, customers make volume purchases of these commodities in supermarkets, and department and variety stores, and not solely on an impulse basis. Retail stores today handle widely diverse product lines, regardless of relatedness or previous generic classifications; stores operating under this kind of managerial philosophy are called "scrambled merchandisers." Such offerings of almost limitless ranges of commodities without departmentalization are encountered more frequently as many firms attempt to widen their basic merchandising appeal. To succeed, such stores must be located in high traffic areas.

As a rule, only the retail institutions that stress the most distinctive merchandising features of the products they carry tend to develop strong store image and patronage appeal, which help assure long-run success. Strong consumer patronage motives are the result of the competitive interaction of manufacturers, distributors,

---

[2] *Shopping* goods are normally higher in price than convenience goods, are bought less often, and are subject to price comparisons before purchase. Stoves, washing machines, and small electrical appliances would be in this category. Purchases of goods in this category are also generally postponable.

wholesalers, and retailers in bringing to the consumer the widest possible merchandise choices at the right price and in the most desirable and convenient setting possible. Although consumer buying motivations differ, most consumers tend to set up habit patterns in terms of stores in which they prefer to shop.[3]

COMPETITIVE EFFECT OF NATIONAL AND PRIVATE BRANDS

Manufacturers with strong brands built up over extended periods constantly strive to move their products out of the "shopping goods" category into the "specialty goods" category, where insistence on their brand becomes so strong that the product is almost "pre-sold." [4]

When a manufacturer believes that his brand's market has achieved this position, he often reduces gross margins at the retail level. When the suggested retail price is lower than can be economically justified because of higher wholesale price or a lower list price, the marginal value of the product's contribution to the retailer's profit disappears. When this occurs, the retailer immediately seeks out substitutable products and a "private brand" from which he can derive both better profits and a greater degree of market control.

Manufacturers of nationally advertised merchandise often produce identical products under private labels in order to meet "off-price" competition, widen their market, utilize idle plant time and capacity, and maximize sales and profits. A multiple-brand, multiple-pricing policy of this kind enables the manufacturer to maintain a consistent "list" price policy on national brands. In many cases, independent retail firms have integrated into manufacturing and wholesaling in order to develop and promote a private brand policy for their organization.

Private brands usually enable both the retailer and a sponsoring wholesaler or manufacturer to achieve better margins than are generally available on national brands. Furthermore, a retailer with an acceptable private brand has a product with which no direct price comparisons can be made. With proper quality control and promotion, the acceptance of a private brand can become a strong market factor. Examples of strong private brands are the AMC brands of member stores of the Associated Merchandising Corporation.[5] Other unrepresentative private brands include the Armaid brand of the May Department Stores Company, the Kenmore and Allstate brands of Sears, Roebuck and Company, and the Ann Page and Sultana brands of the A & P Tea Company. Those mentioned are in actuality distributed nationally; however, there are many strong private brands in local and sectional trading areas.

---

[3] Based on Robert D. Entenberg's "Consumer Motivation Studies," Research Report Memoranda, (Graduate School of Retailing, University of Pittsburgh, 1961–1963, unpublished).

[4] Detergent manufacturers of All, Vel, Tide, and small appliance manufacturers of Sunbeam, General Electric, and Westinghouse brands have attempted to place their products in the "specialty goods" category and continue to do so.

[5] The AMC is a store-owned buying office. Stores such as Bloomingdale's (New York City), Filene's (Boston), Carson, Pirie, and Scott (Chicago), and Bullock's (Los Angeles) are representative members of this group. The role of buying offices will be discussed in a later chapter.

GOODS CLASSIFICATION BY PRODUCT AND PURCHASE CHARACTERISTICS

Most products can be classified on the basis of the kind of buying motives that account for the major portion of their sales—the convenience, shopping, or specialty buying motive appeals.

Convenience goods consist of food, soft drinks, tobacco, general cosmetics, and sundries. These frequently bought goods are often selected on an impulse basis, and are generally low in price. Product substitution is common, and purchases are made almost as quickly as the want enters the shopper's mind. Also characteristic of this grouping is the almost complete absence of time-consuming price comparisons. Convenience goods have relatively small seasonal purchase patterns and may often be effectively featured for off-season selling.

Shopping goods consist of apparel, accessories, furniture, home furnishings, appliances, and the like. These goods are higher in price and are bought much more infrequently than convenience goods. Price and value comparisons are usually made before purchase, and quality and service are important purchase considerations. Brands are more important as standards of comparison than they are in convenience goods; however, brand substitution at the point of sale is not uncommon. During slack-season periods, "sales" featuring substantial price concessions are common.

Specialty goods consist of merchandise on which customers will insist. Product or brand substitution is rare. For example, a Christian Dior dress, a Ford "Thunderbird," a *dernier cri* hat by Mr. John, and S. S. Pierce fancy dry groceries may be "specialty goods" items to many consumers. Price in the case of specialty goods is not the basic purchase consideration.

It is evident that most merchandise lines and product categories can be classified into two or even all three of the above categories, because any given type of goods may have completely different types of appeals for various consumers. In such cases, the promotional appeals for effective distribution of the product would have to be broadened.[6]

IMPORTANCE OF GOODS CLASSIFICATION

The classification of goods in accordance with their product and purchase characteristics is important in that the most effective channels of distribution can be more clearly delineated. Delineation of the most effective channel of distribution for a product must also involve selection of the type of store best suited for its sale. Too often, the entire channel of distribution is determined on the basis of value judgments on the part of the producer. The channel chosen must be effective, otherwise both the store and the product will be by-passed.

Many merchandise classifications formerly sold through only one type of store are now sold to any store willing to handle them. For example, toasters, frying

---

[6] See Robert D. Entenberg, "How to Improve Off-Season Sales," *Small Marketers' Aids* (Washington, D.C., Management Division, Small Business Administration, 1961).

pans, and other small appliances can now be bought in practically any kind of retail outlet, including food, drug, and soft-line specialty stores. Regardless of the scrambling of merchandise and outlets, the effective marketing of any product depends on its accurate classification by its most dominant consumer appeal.

SUMMARY OF GOODS CLASSIFICATION AND CHANNELS OF DISTRIBUTION

In a competitive economy the institutional framework evolves as the result of and in response to customer wants. The retail structure is essentially one of imperfect or monopolistic competition. Although many sellers exist in most retail markets, leading sellers can and do exercise a direct influence upon price. However, when the number of buyers is large, the individual seller, regardless of size, is generally unable to affect long-run price.[7] Consumer wants are expressed through various types of preferences, both as to institutions and products. Because consumer spending-saving-consumption patterns are in a constant state of flux, the retail structure will always be highly volatile in nature. Thus, all existing channels of distribution and methods of sales should be periodically reviewed and analyzed.

In this age of increasing competition and decreasing areas of specialization, retail management is on the lookout for merchandise lines and classifications that will fit into the total promotional framework. By properly classifying existing or potential merchandise lines into the correct patterns, management is able to make the best possible merchandising decisions. This procedure is basic to the final stages in the distributive process.

MARKET INTEGRATION AND COMPETITIVE EFFECTIVENESS

Another and more recent trend toward securing competitive effectiveness has been functional integration by many kinds of firms at all stages in the channels of distribution. In general, functional integration can be classified as vertical when more than one stage of functional operation is involved—retailing, wholesaling, and manufacturing. Horizontal integration is that in which expansion takes place within any one stage in the cycle of distribution. The intense competition at the retailing, wholesaling, and manufacturing levels creates pressures to by-pass the normal channels of distribution. Such pressures inevitably lead to the integration of functions—that is, retailers, wholesalers, and manufacturers perform one another's functions.

New product development and product diversification at the manufacturing and wholesale levels represent another type of integration. At the retail level, this type of horizontal expansion may consist of the introduction of new merchandise lines and also of branching out into new store locations. Another motive under-

---

[7] See also John F. Due and Robert W. Clower, *Intermediate Economic Analysis* (Chicago: Richard D. Irwin, 1961), pp. 55–57.

lying a firm's decision to integrate and expand might result from desire on the part of a strong executive manager to expand his own personal power and prestige.

Vertical Integration as a Means of Market Expansion

The term *vertical integration* is used to refer to several processes. First, it may refer to the absorption of the wholesaling and manufacturing functions by retailers. Sears, Roebuck and Company, the J. C. Penney Company, and many other chain-store groups, as well as many of the larger independent stores, expand through this form of combination. Secondly, vertical integration can also refer to the absorption of both the manufacturing and retailing functions by a wholesaler. A third type of vertical integration is the absorption of wholesaling and retailing functions by manufacturers. The Goodyear Tire and Rubber Company sponsors and operates wholesale and retail operations through which it attempts to guarantee a continuing consumer market for its products. When vertical integration takes the form of sponsorship by manufacturers, wholesalers, or retailers, it is referred to as a cooperative voluntary chain. For example, Western Auto Store outlets are classified as wholesale-sponsored, voluntary chain stores in the tire and automobile accessory categories; Butler Brothers, a wholesale distributor, sponsors the Ben Franklin variety store group; cooperatives, such as the I.G.A. stores, are sponsored by a wholesaler, the Independent Grocers Alliance.

These kinds of manufacturers—wholesaler sponsored retail establishments—give an excellent opportunity for enterprising individuals with very little capital to go into business for themselves. The sponsoring firm provides trade credit and operating know-how to the small entrepreneur. At the same time, such sponsorship enables manufacturers and/or wholesalers to maintain and improve their share of the market because sponsorship means purchase of brands and product lines from the sponsoring firm.

An example of vertical integration is the recent organization by Sears, Roebuck and Company of the Kellwood Company. This consists of a combination of some seventeen firms that supply apparel and other merchandise lines to Sears. The Kellwood Company has been established as an "open-end" company to provide a permanent framework for the acqusition of additional suppliers. While it was stated that no further merger "of Sears suppliers was contemplated," it was pointed out that "the 17 firms provide everything from awnings to children's wear and the percentage of Sears soft-goods sales in the market is continually increasing." [8]

Sears' management expects that this new setup of manufacturing subsidiaries will attract top professional management. An additional consideration relating to this new supplier organization is the likelihood that many of the firms making up the new subsidiary might have gone out of existence upon the retirement of their

---

[8] Franchising is another form of expansion and growth at the retail and service levels—for example, Holiday Inns, International Franchise Systems, Inc., of St. Louis, Howard Johnson Restaurants.

owners or managers. It was also reported that Sears will continue to be the largest single stockholder of a companion group consisting of the combination of fifteen manufacturers who supply Sears primarily with hard goods.[9]

Horizontal Integration

Manufacturers, wholesalers, and retailers also integrate horizontally as well as vertically. Horizontal integration refers to any combining of firms that occupy similar levels of activity within a single stage in the channel of distribution. Retailers have been integrating horizontally into all kinds of markets with all types of retail operations through combinations, mergers, and acquisitions—not necessarily with homogeneous retail organizations or merchandise lines. The L. S. Ayres Company of Indianapolis, a prestige department store, is expanding horizontally through "budget" operations that are set up as self-service, check-out stores called Airway. Another example is that of the supermarket chains expanding into nonfood discount stores.

Both vertical and horizontal integration have accounted for the tremendous growth in such organizations as Safeway, J. C. Penney Company, and Montgomery Ward and Company. Each of these organizations generates more than $1 billion in annual volume.

Two completely different types of horizontal integration were evident when the Grayson-Robinson Stores, Inc.—an apparel-stores chain—was purchased outright by the Peerless Camera Stores, Inc. in 1956. In this combination, Peerless was operated essentially as a hard-line, highly promotional discount operation (its *modus operandi* at the time of purchase); but the Grayson-Robinson Stores continued to be operated as a chain of promotional specialty stores. The merger proved unsuccessful.[10]

At the manufacturing level, almost complete horizontal and vertical integration has been successfully achieved by Genesco, Inc. Originally a men's footwear manufacturer, Genesco now manufactures and wholesales shoes, cosmetics, and lingerie, operates men's and women's apparel and accessory retail stores, and also controls prestige specialty stores such as Henri Bendel and Bonwit Teller of New York City. Genesco is now projecting its 1972 volume at $1.8 billion. Its pattern of vertical and horizontal combinations is indicative of the unconfined nature of merger trends involving retail and market distribution.

Influence of Size of Firm

As pointed out above, mergers at the retail level do not necessarily result in greater efficiency and profitability per se; rather, many of these combinations demonstrate a desire for greater economic security through locale dispersions and

---

[9] *Women's Wear Daily*, October 26, 1961, p. 1.
[10] This is an example in which integration and expansion did not provide competitive effectiveness and market security. See Samuel Feinberg, "Diversifying the Risk," *Women's Wear Daily* (June 13, 1958), p. 33.

guaranteed market outlets. Also, larger firms do not necessarily enjoy lower cost structures.[11]

Despite all the mergers and combinations that have taken place at the retail level, in no sense may it be said that on the national scene does any single retail organization or group dominate the field, although this may be so in some local and regional areas. The twenty largest retail organizations in the country—which are listed in Table 5—have grown through various types of combina-

TABLE 5

THE TWENTY LARGEST RETAIL ORGANIZATIONS BY SIZE

ORGANIZATION	PRINCIPAL CLASSIFICATION	SALES VOLUME (IN MILLIONS OF DOLLARS)		
		1960 (POSITION)		1964[a]
Sears, Roebuck	Dept. Stores & Mail Order	4,134	(2)	5,740
Atlantic & Pacific Tea	Supermarkets	5,250	(1)	5,080
Safeway Stores	Supermarket–Discount Stores	2,469	(3)	2,818
Kroger	Supermarkets	1,870	(4)	2,328
J. C. Penney	Departmentized Specialty Stores	1,468	(5)	2,011
Montgomery Ward	Dept. Stores & Mail Order	1,248	(6)	1,697
F. W. Woolworth	Variety & Discount Stores	1,035	(7)	1,338
Food Fair Stores	Supermarket–Discount Stores	771	(11)	1,215
Federated Dept. Stores	Department Stores	785	(10)	1,187
National Tea	Supermarkets	855	(9)	1,123
American Stores	Supermarkets	1,011	(8)	1,119
Allied Stores	Department Stores	680	(14)	893
Winn-Dixie	Supermarkets	739	(12)	872
May Department Stores	Department Stores	684	(13)	782
Jewel Tea	Home Supermarket Service	509	(19)	782
W. T. Grant	Variety & Junior Dept. Stores	512	(18)	770
Grand Union	Supermarket–Discount Stores	604	(15)	740
First National Stores	Supermarkets	537	(16)	723
S. S. Kresge	Variety–Discount Stores	—	—	683
R. H. Macy	Department Stores	517	(17)	638
Colonial Stores	Supermarkets	445	(20)	—
Total Volume (20 largest firms)		26,123		32,539
Total Volume (all retail stores)		219,627		261,630
Per Cent of Total Volume (20 largest firms)		11.90%		12.44%

[a] Department store sales rose 6% in 1964 over 1963 sales, with branch stores up 8% and main stores up 4% (Feb. 1964 to Jan. 1965). Branch store sales accounted for 35.5% of total company sales, compared with 35.6% in 1963. (Net earnings after federal income taxes were 2.3%, compared with 1.8% in 1963. Transactions were 2% higher, and average gross sales rose to $5.59 compared with $5.44 in 1963.)— Controller's Congress, MOR, NRMA Data, 1965.

Sources: *Business Week* (May 6, 1961), *Retail Trade, Annual Report* (Bureau of Census, U. S. Department of Commerce, 1964), and *Moody's Industrial Manual* (1964).

tions, mergers, expansions, and acquisitions. Their growth has resulted from both homogeneous and heterogeneous mergers of almost every conceivable form. The competitive performance of these firms rarely resembles that of either oligopoly or monopoly in the markets where they might enjoy elements of dominance.

At no other level of economic activity can a grouping of the twenty largest firms represent so small a share of the total market as in the field of retailing.

[11] See also Edna Douglas, "Size of Firm and the Structure of Costs in Retailing," *Journal of Business*, No. 2 (April 1962), pp. 158–190: "Retailing appears to be an industry of decreasing costs up to a point. In some lines of trade it appears that the largest operations ... were less profitable than firms which were somewhat smaller."

As shown in Table 5, the twenty largest firms in the field absorbed only 12.44 per cent of total market sales in 1964. At the same time, the market positions of most of these firms shifted during the five-year period.

EFFECT OF COST AND PRICING POLICIES ON RETAIL COMPETITION

Marketing and distribution costs represent approximately 50 to 55 per cent of the final purchase price of goods for ultimate consumption.[12] These figures in themselves do not indicate either efficiency or inefficiency of the marketing processes. Over a period of time, increases in fixed costs tend to be "built into" the total operating structure. As a firm's fixed cost structure increases, downward pressures on profits and internal pressures on upward revision of selling prices result. However, if market competition does not set an upper limit on price, oligopolistic "umbrella" pricing may result. Gasoline prices in divisional areas are set by pricing formulae of this kind. Under such circumstances, prices to the consumer become noncompetitive, and innovators or more efficient operators are encouraged to enter the market. New firms entering a market under favorable conditions of this kind absorb substantial market shares without necessarily expanding total demand.

Thus, the upper range of selling prices is limited by competition, and the low range by a firm's total cost structure. A constant two-way pressure to keep prices in line because of competition externally and requirements for a minimum profit goal internally is always present.

However, values in terms of goods, services, or institutions must be considered from the standpoint of "wanted packages" and of total satisfaction. Values in terms of satisfaction are measured by the consumer in terms of comparative prices. When merchandise offerings and prices in retail markets become noncompetitive, operational efficiency declines, patronage motives shrink, and sales evaporate, causing all levels in the channel of distribution to be adversely affected. In other words, a circular "chain" relationship exists in any marketing economy.

TRADING AREA ANALYSIS

The parameters of retail trade include some 1.708 million diverse, complex, and highly competitive establishments that generated annual sales of some $261 billion in 1964. Compared with other fields of economic endeavor, retailing is relatively easy to enter; most establishments are comparatively small in size. The industry

---

[12] See Table 1 (page 8). "Value added" by retailing and wholesaling can be used interchangeably with "costs" needed to perform effectively the marketing functions in terms of value to the buyer. The gross margins attained by retailing and wholesaling processes together represent the total marketing costs. Estimates on relative marketing costs must be made on the basis of value judgments because the construction of the accounting systems themselves and the way in which accountants may look at a problem determine the measurement of both factory and distribution costs. See also Joel Dean, *Managerial Economics* (Englewood Cliffs, N.J.: Prentice-Hall, 1951).

TABLE 6

Comparison of Selected Retail Establishments and Sales, 1948, 1954, 1958, and 1963
Average Population and Average Annual Business per Store

Kind of Business	Establishments[c] (in thousands)				Sales (in millions of dollars)				Average Population per Store[f]				Average Sales per Store[g] (in thousands of dollars)			
	1948	1954	1958	1963	1948	1954	1958	1963	1948	1954	1958	1963	1948	1954	1958	1963
Retail Trade, Total	1,773.0	1,722.0	1,788.3	1,707.9	$130,521	$169,968	$199,646	$244,202	82	94	97	111	$74	$99	$112	$143
Food Stores, Total[a]	492.7	384.6	355.5	319.4	30,966	39,762e	49,022	57,079	297	419	488	594	63	103	138	179
Groc. Stores (incl. Supermkts. & Dels.)	378.0	279.4	259.8	244.8	24,774	34,421	43,696	52,566	386	577	667	777	126	123	168	215
Meat Markets, Fish (sea food) Markets	29.5	27.4	28.8	20.1	1,776	2,128	2,520	1,705	4,958	5,893	6,018	9,461	60	78	88	85
Fruit Stores, Vegetable Markets	15.8	13.1	12.7	8.9	399	485	505	412	9,268	12,207	13,673	21,367	25	37	40	46
Candy, Nut, Confectionery Stores	32.9	20.5	17.6	15.0	649	568	528	499	4,444	7,860	9,866	12,678	20	28	30	33
Bakery and Produce Stores	20.2	19.0	19.2	18.6	725	862	905	1,080	7,249	8,469	9,044	10,244	36	45	47	58
Eating, Drinking Places, Total[b]	346.6	319.7	344.7	334.5	10,683	13,101	15,202	18,412	422	504	504	569	31	41	44	55
General Merchandise Group	74.1	76.2	86.6	62.1	17,136	17,872	21,879	30,003	1,972	2,115	2,005	3,062	231	235	253	483
Department Stores (incl. Mail Order Sales)	2.6	2.8	3.2	4.4d	10,645	12,163	13,360	22,915	56,125	58,381	55,032	43,220	4,126	4,405	4,232	5,208
Dry Goods, General Merchandise & General Stores, n.e.c.	51.3	51.8	52.5	35.4	3,983	4,233	4,899	4,927	2,847	3,111	3,308	5,372	78	82	93	139
Variety Stores	20.2	20.9	21.0	22.4	2,507	3,067	3,621	4,538	7,229	7,706	8,269	8,490	124	185	172	203
Apparel Group	115.2	119.7	118.8	116.2	9,803	11,078	12,526	14,040	1,268	1,346	1,462	1,637	85	93	105	121
Shoe Stores	19.6	23.9	24.4	24.6	1,467	1,895	2,130	2,390	7,472	6,759	7,116	7,730	75	80	87	97
Women's Clothing, Specialty Stores	46.5	45.2	44.6	44.4	5,424	4,333	4,909	5,592	3,141	3,565	3,893	4,283	117	96	110	126
Furniture, Home Furnishings, Appliance Dealers Total[b]	85.6	91.8	103.4	93.7	6,914	8,994	10,074	10,926	1,707	1,756	1,679	2,030	81	94	97	117
Furniture, Home Furnishings Stores	48.7	50.7	54.5	54.9	4,378	5,374	5,989	6,826	3,003	3,177	3,186	3,464	90	106	110	124
Household Appliances Stores } Radio, Television, Music Stores }	36.9	29.8	48.9	30.7	2,543	3,237	3,811	3,385	3,956	3,976	6,093	6,194	69	80	115	110
Automotive Group, Total[a]	86.2	86.0	93.7	98.5	20,104	29,915	31,808	45,376	1,696	1,875	1,853	1,931	233	348	340	461
Passenger Car Dealers (fran.)	44.0	41.4	38.6	33.3	15,953	25,108	25,326	37,375	3,320	3,893	4,499	5,712	363	606	656	1,122
Passenger Car Dealers (nonfran.)	21.5	20.1	25.3	28.0	2,791	2,424	2,984	3,087	6,784	6,784	6,863	6,792	130	121	118	110
Tire, Battery, Accessories Dealers	20.6	18.8	20.9	20.9	1,360	1,814	2,426	2,548	7,082	8,554	8,308	9,099	66	97	116	122

38

Kind of Business																
Gas, Service Stations	188.3	181.7	206.3	211.5	6,483	10,744	14,178	17,760	776	887	842	899	34	59	69	84
Lumber, Building Materials, Housewares, Farm Equipment Dealers, Total[b]	98.9	100.5	108.3	92.7	11,152	13,124	14,309	14,606	1,477	1,604	1,603	2,051	113	131	132	158
Farm Equipment Dealers	17.6	18.7	19.0	16.4	2,386	2,805	3,186	3,626	8,294	8,625	9,139	11,596	136	150	168	221
Lumber, Building Materials Dealers	26.1	30.2	34.8	29.0	5,127	6,503	7,123	7,023	5,595	5,337	4,976	6,558	196	216	204	242
Plumbing, Paint, Electric, Glass Stores	20.5	16.5	19.7	17.8	1,145	1,115	1,282	1,397	7,113	9,769	8,814	10,684	56	68	65	79
Hardware Stores	34.7	34.9	34.7	29.6	2,494	2,694	2,717	2,560	4,213	4,624	5,004	6,425	72	77	78	87
Drugstores, Proprietary Stores, Total	55.8	56.0	56.2	54.7	4,013	5,252	6,779	8,487	2,618	2,878	3,090	3,477	72	94	121	155
Other Retail Stores, Total[a]	214.5	226.9	240.1	244.9	13,267	15,612	18,468	21,309	681	723	723	777	62	71	77	87
Jewelry Stores	21.3	24.3	23.7	20.9	1,225	1,408	1,495	1,560	6,869	6,643	7,327	9,099	58	58	63	75
Book, Stationery Stores	6.9	8.1	9.4	8.8	549	576	679	719	21,057	19,863	18,473	21,610	79	71	72	82
Sporting Goods, Bicycle Stores	8.5	10.0	11.6	12.8	345	451	624	762	17,113	16,098	14,969	14,857	40	45	54	60
Gift, Novelty, Souvenir Stores	12.5	12.1	14.0	12.6	196	283	389	397	11,672	13,268	12,403	15,093	16	23	28	32
Music Stores	6.1	5.8	—	8.1	337	375	—	715	23,871	27,744	—	23,477	55	65	—	88
Camera, Photography Supplies Stores	3.0	2.9	3.5	3.3	202	278	382	379	48,216	55,660	49,613	57,627	67	96	109	115
Nonstore Retailers, Total	n.d.a.	78.5	74.7	79.8	n.d.a.	4,514	5,401	6,204	n.d.a.	2,053	2,325	2,383	n.d.a.	58	72	78
Mail Order Houses[d]	—	2.0	2.5	4.1	—	(1,605)	(1,986)	(2,379)	n.d.a.	79,838	68,096	46,383	—	—	794	580
Direct Selling (house-to-house) Org.	—	70.8	64.0	66.2	—	2,273	2,574	2,373	n.d.a.	2,278	2,713	2,873	—	—	40	36
Merchandise Vending Machine Operators	—	5.7	8.2	9.4	—	636	842	1,452	n.d.a.	28,204	21,176	20,231	—	—	103	155

[a] Includes data for establishments with no payroll in 1958 and 1954 which have not been classified by detailed kind of business; also includes establishments in kinds of business not separately listed.

[b] Includes data for establishments with no payroll in 1958 and 1954 which have not been classified by detailed kind of business.

[c] There were 1,773,100 retail establishments in 1948 doing a total volume of $130.521 billion. In 1954, there were approximately 1,722,000 doing $169.968 billion. The difference can be accounted for by the fact that retail establishments having a volume of less than $2500 annually were not included in the census of that year.

[d] Establishments include mail order establishments dealing primarily in department store merchandise, in order not to overstate estimated numbers which in many cases may consist of only a desk or leased space in a public warehouse. However, total sales by mail order houses of department store merchandise have been included. These sales total 2.379 billion in 1963.

[e] Sales of $1.887 billion of dairy products stores, milk dealers excluded in 1954.

[f] Census of population figures for those residing in continental U. S. were 146.093 million in 1948; 161.191 million in 1954; 173.646 million (contiguous U. S. less 414,000 in Armed Forces overseas) in 1958; 190.169 million in 1963. Average population per store is the total population divided by the number of stores.

[g] Arrived at by dividing total sales per class by number of stores.

n.d.a.—not directly applicable. n.e.c.—not elsewhere classified.

Source of data: U. S. Census of Business, Retail Trade (Washington, D.C., U. S. Department of Commerce, 1948, 1954, 1958 and 1963).

also recognizes a high failure rate. Retail firms operate in wide varieties of external settings. Because of the broad geographic dispersion of population locales, retailing will remain largely local in character.

Unfortunately, the elements of wide geographic dispersions and the nature of the trading areas are not easily pinpointed by present census classifications. The present Bureau of the Census classifications underemphasize specific trading areas, while far too much emphasis is placed on artificial geographical and political divisions.[13] Yet, in no other segment of the economy are trading areas of such vital importance. A trading area is determined by customer accessibility and by the spending power that can be generated in it. Both considerations—customer accessibility and spending power—are basic prerequisites for the successful operation of any retail institution.

SIGNIFICANT STRUCTURAL CHANGES AT THE RETAIL LEVEL

For the purpose of analyzing structural changes in retailing establishments, the data in Table 6 are presented. It is evident that the retail structure can still be characterized as including a very large number of small stores, a moderate number of medium-size stores, and a very small number of extremely large stores. There has been a decrease of the total number of retail establishments since 1948; at that time there were some 1.8 million stores. Total retail establishments in 1963 still numbered more than 1.7 million units. However, within this relatively constant framework, many significant changes have taken place.

From 1948 to 1963, the average sales per store in the food group increased approximately 184 per cent, from $63,000 to $179,000. During the same period, the total number of food stores declined from 492,700 in 1948 to 319,400 in 1963, a decrease of 35.1 per cent. What has been happening is that the smaller neighborhood grocery stores are fast disappearing and their place is being taken by supermarkets and "superettes"—the smaller independent versions of the supermarket. Because of the smaller total number of stores and expanding food store volume, the annual sales volume of the average food store almost tripled to approximately $179,000 per unit in the period from 1948 to 1964. Another significant change is that it now takes some 594 individuals to support a food store operation, whereas in 1948 only 297 consuming units were needed to assure the possible success of the average food store.

In the third major grouping shown in Table 6—that of general merchandise stores—the greatest percentage increase was in the number of department stores. Department store establishments increased from 2,600 to 4,400—approximately a 69.2 per cent increase. This tremendous increase is the result of suburban branch store expansions of all kinds and of the reclassification of many discount houses

---

[13] See Robert D. Entenberg, "Suggested Changes in Census Classification of Retail Trade," *Journal of Marketing* (January 1960), pp. 39–43. The complete evaluation of Census criteria and suggested changes will be found in Appendix C.

as promotional department stores as they evolved into that census definition.[14]

There has been a significant change in the number of people needed to support a full-line department store. In other words, department store growth (the number of establishments) has corresponded to a greater than average rate of growth in consumer expenditures since 1958. During that year, the average department store generated $4,232,000 annually and needed a market of approximately 55,000 individuals for adequate support in a trading area. In 1963, it took only 43,220 individuals to support a department store, and the average sales per store rose to $5.2 million annually.

As to the other major groups of establishments, in almost every case the average volume per store has increased; the only exceptions were in "nonfranchised" passenger car dealer outlets and in books and stationery stores. The latter are changing in character and are being absorbed into other kinds of classifications.

The significant contribution of Table 6 lies in the fact that the analytical comparisons can be used as *initial* evaluative criteria in determining whether locating a particular type of store in a trading area would tend to create market oversaturation and operating inefficiencies.

For example, an entrepreneur considering opening a women's specialty shop in a metropolitan area with a population of 200,000 would note from Table 6 that the average volume of a women's specialty shop approximates $126,000 (1963) and that some 4,283 individuals are needed to support this type of store. By dividing the population factor of 4,283 into the trading area's population of 200,000 one can see that a community of this size could support almost as many as 47 women's specialty stores.

$$\frac{200,000 \text{ (population of metropolitan area)}}{4,283 \text{ (Number of individuals needed to support the store)}} = \begin{array}{l} 46.7 \text{ or } 47 \text{ (the maximum} \\ \text{number of stores that can} \\ \text{be supported in a trading area} \\ \text{of 200,000 consumers)} \end{array}$$

If the total number of specialty shops in the area is less than 47, one could then proceed. Should there be 47 or more such stores in the area, the decision to enter the market would have to be negative or be very carefully reviewed. Further discussion on goals of store location will be found in Chapter 5.

SUMMARY AND CONCLUSIONS

Analysis of the final stages in the distributive processes involves examination of the underlying manner in which consumers regard and purchase the various kinds of merchandise offerings. The particular category—convenience, shopping, or specialty—determines the selling potential, promotional appeals, and the kinds of stores that should do the selling.

---

[14] See App. A and B for definitions of major store groups and SIC (Standard Industrial Classification) numbers of these stores. Discount stores that meet department store classification criteria are considered "promotional" department stores.

Because of geographic population dispersions and the need for local neighborhood conveniences, the smaller store will continue to represent a significant portion of the retail structure in numbers with approximately half of the total sales volume.

In essence, the retail structure is the product of the socioeconomic setting externally and the philosophies of management internally. The firm itself is the operating result of the goals of the organization and the policies and administration under which it operates. Most innovations that develop in the institutional structure are the result of changing purchase motivations, consumer wants, and market competition. The individual firm has only limited control in this direction.

When horizontal and/or vertical integration occur as a result of competitive pressures, tax considerations—or a desire for market security—create a tendency to merge; increasing the size of the firm and scale of plant does not necessarily guarantee either an efficient or a successful operation.

The management that recognizes and can delineate the social and economic variables with which it must contend has the greatest probability of formulating optimum marketing strategy and of achieving its organizational objectives.

Success in the final stage of the distributive process is the responsibility of retailing management. The extent to which the retail management can maximize its effectiveness depends directly on how well it plans, organizes, and controls the business operation. The goal of retail managers in using the organic functions of management will form the principal subject matter of the chapter that follows.

Chapter 4: *Management of the Retail Enterprise*

The long-run success of any business enterprise is determined by the quality of its executive leadership. The most productive solutions are those based on relevant information and use. When business management bases its decisions on relevant information, resulting policies generally maximize operating effectiveness.

Yet, executive management is never certain that it is making the most of information at its disposal. For example, in the formulation of pricing and/or product strategies, a complete knowledge of the external setting of the market would be the ideal goal; this goal is rarely, if ever, reached. Again, organization factors such as size of firm, scale of plant, operating rigidities, and poor informational flows can lessen the effectiveness of any business decisions.[1]

In recent years, management's inability to maximize effectiveness in many of its decisions has resulted in attacks on the classical theory of the firm. These attacks by both scholars and businessmen, who claimed that businesses are operated by managers believing in this theory, have generally been directed at the lack of predictive value at certain general levels of the firm and the lack of

---

[1] Specific examples of these goals and their achievement are illustrated definitively throughout the text. The larger the firm, the more formal and specialized its organizational functions and the more likely that operating rigidities can develop.

explanatory values at a detailed level. But these lacks are insufficient reasons for discredit of the classical theory of economics. Further, executives still regard their goal as "pursuit of maximum advantage," which is consistent with classical economic doctrines.

Optimal decisions mean effective planning, organizing, directing, and controlling. Effective carrying out of the organic functions of management results in the generation of the greatest possible profits consistent with the maintenance of the strongest possible competitive position in the market place.

Regardless of the theory put forth, optimal decision making remains basically the function of good executive leadership—whether it is influenced by classical economic doctrines or the theories of the firm set forth by Papandreau, March, or Simon.[2] For example, in the expansion goals of retail firms, the decision as to whether or not to open a branch store generally involves three considerations. The first is: if the store is not opened will a competitor go into the proposed location and weaken the firm's total market position? If so, will this affect the firm's expansion policy? A second decision variable is: if the store is opened, how much business will the branch take away from the parent store? Will the new business acquired in the new location offset the sales lost to the parent store? A third consideration is the over-all result of the new branch store: will it strengthen the total store image? Subgoals in opening the branch store are: what lines should be carried? Should they be the same as the parent store? Breadth of lines, decor, display, and pertinent policies are other considerations.

In the goal of optimization, the criteria for evaluating managerial decisions cannot be applied until the decision is made and action carried out. Thus "in time" optimization of decisions can be considered the prime goal of executive management.

POLICY FORMULATION AND ADMINISTRATION

Management is the function of executive leadership; it is today more of an art than a science. Effective top management must be creative and decisive in policy planning, formulation, and administration. This is especially important in certain clearly identified key policy areas. Generally, a policy may be defined as a predetermined course of action set up for application to recurring situations met in daily business operations. Business policies, when properly set up and administered, help to assure and perpetuate a smooth functioning of the total operation. Policies are the vehicles through which most management decisions are carried out.

In formulating business policies, sets of predetermined courses of action are established for various sets of conditions. For example, a store may have a

---

[2] A. Papandreau, "Some Problems in the Theory of the Firm," in B. F. Haley (ed.), *A Survey of Contemporary Economics*, Vol. II (Chicago: R. D. Irwin, Inc., 1952), pp. 183–219; Herbert A. Simon, *The New Science of Management Decision* (New York: Harper and Brothers, 1960), Chap. 1; James G. March and H. A. Simon, *Organization* (New York: Wiley and Sons, 1958), Chaps. 6 and 7.

pricing policy of never being undersold. Once set, a price cut by a competitor on an identical item can then be met immediately by action on the selling floor without waiting for formal markdown authorization.

Policy formulation with respect to problems of a nonrecurring nature is the exception rather than the rule. At the same time, nonrecurring problems generally involve critical time elements, greater uncertainties, and time-consuming attention. Therefore, every effort must be made to utilize, whenever possible, policies that can be administered and controlled at the lowest possible managerial echelon. Only by such means can the over-all effectiveness of management be optimized. This is especially important in multi-unit firms.

As a rule, the less repetitive and routine the condition variables, the higher the management echelon to which the decision is delegated. The more repetitive and routine the conditions, the greater the likelihood that middle or supervisory management is delegated the assignment and the greater the likelihood that the decision choice can be machine-programed and automated. For example, the determination of how many additional personnel would be needed for various sets of sales schedules can be "automated" into fixed policy procedures. If the sales predicted for a department amount to $1,000 for the day and the average or "typical" sales person can generate $125 in sales, eight individuals would be needed for effective sales operations. Again, policies such as spot-checking accounts-receivable statements against sales checks, or determining the number of "open" checkout lanes in a self-service operation, are further examples of areas for "automatic" policy procedures.

Authority and responsibility delegated downward results in the greater decentralization of decisions and the greater autonomy of the lower-echelons. The greater the autonomy, the greater the necessity that policies must be sound and meet the test of universality—that is, they must pervade the organization and apply to basic and vital functions. Policies must also meet the test of "solitariness" —that is, each functional policy, unitarily, should not be combined and controlled with another function.[3] To illustrate this point, adjustment policies in a retail store should be customer-oriented and controlled by an adjustment department. However, when necessary, most department managers and buyers are also permitted to make adjustments on the floor. Store policy dictates satisfying the customer; the department manager may be more interested in maximizing the department's profits. In this kind of situation, the principle of "solitariness" is not met if the customer is not satisfied, although the functions of customer satisfaction and departmental profitability appear momentarily in conflict.

Management policy, once formulated, should clearly show the relationship of all the subordinate operating policies that accompany it. At the same time, management policy should also easily demonstrate how time and expense may be eliminated if a policy is pursued. This helps to assure an effective business plan

[3] R. C. Davis, The Fundamentals of Top Management (New York: Harper and Brothers, 1951), pp. 14–17.

through which it is easy to determine the lines of responsibility and authority. For instance, each individual in the firm should know exactly to whom and what to report.

Policy planning in terms of personnel is as important as planning in terms of techniques; both are key prerequisites for meeting organizational goals. In retailing, management must plan personnel policies with a view toward continuous promotion of all employees to higher echelons at both operative and administrative levels. Policy planning along these lines is especially critical for firms with branches and multi-unit stores, and is essential for the morale of junior management.

THE ORGANIC FUNCTION OF PLANNING

Policy is carried out through a business plan. Policy formulation and administration determine the resulting store organization and store image. The manner in which policies are administered determines how sales, gross margin, inventories, and other specific plans and budgets are forecast and developed.

Business planning and execution must begin with determination of the business objectives. Planning is a process, and along with policies it should demonstrate how procedures may be simplified and expenses saved through carrying out the plan. Once a plan has been determined, the proper delegation of authority and accountability can then be set up with clearly defined objectives. The kind of delegation extended depends on the size of the retail establishment, the types of services to be offered, return policies, and the degree of autonomy necessary for optimal decisions.

Scientific Management and Planning

The proper delegation of authority and responsibility facilitates the use of the scientific method and the proper evolution of administrative management. This means that organizational plans and functions must be set up on a methodical, scientific basis. Such procedures encourage greater use of the scientific method at all other levels of the organization.

The scientific method of decision making begins with a definition of the problem and is followed by preliminary observations and a situation analysis of all the possible variables. At this point it is frequently found that there are so many variables that, often, problems involve a great deal of search activity, imagery, and abstractions. Under such circumstances solutions cannot be handled mathematically. Nevertheless, alternative solutions must be found.[4] The next step is to test the proposed solutions in the form of a plan to find the most practical one available. This is followed by the final testing of an accepted plan for the determination of the best practical solution.

---

[4] D. M. Johnson, *The Psychology of Thought and Judgment* (New York: Harper and Brothers, 1955); A. Newell, J. C. Shaw, and H. A. Simon, "The Elements of a Theory of Human Problem Solving," Vol. 65, *Psychological Review*, (March 1958), pp. 151–166; and Newell and Simon, "Heuristic Problem Solving," Vol. 6, *Operations Research*, (Jan.–Feb. 1958), pp. 1–10.

Testing the plan usually points up uncertain factors that generally enter into preplanning for any type of enterprise; for example, the choice of the best location for a new store, determination of the price lines to be handled on the services to be offered, and effective utilization of the growth factors in the area. This means that suitable provision for adequate alternatives must be made for any possible decision errors.

Scientific evaluation in administrative management should result in a high degree of creative planning. Creative planning can result in relatively smooth transitional processes for decision making in areas of uncertainty and risk. The manner in which nonprogramed decisions are made is determined by the philosophy of management. For example, the choice of assortments, brands, and prices of merchandise to be bought is guided by the type of image that store management wants to project.[5]

Any final plan agreed upon by top management must not be considered a sacred cow. Most policies resulting from business generally will involve areas of conflict both internally and externally. The minimization of such conflicts is another aspect of optimal decision.

OPTIMAL DECISION AND CONFLICT

For maximum effectiveness, decisions must be initiated and carried out with due regard for clearly defined objectives. The creation of public values for the community specifically and organized society generally would encompass the type of service objectives to be formulated. This is of special importance to retail management because of its direct consumer relationships. The social groups primarily concerned are those that reside in a store's trading area.

Meeting service objectives involves the processes of "joint maximization"—that is, maximization from the standpoint of the consumer as well as of the firm. For example, joint maximization involves the consumer as he attempts to maximize in terms of satisfactions and involves the firm as it attempts to maximize in terms of profits. Consumer goals and those of the firm are obviously neither similar nor diametrically opposed. Rather, a balancing of goals is involved. The degree of coincidence of "fit" between maximum consumer satisfaction and entrepreneurial profits is a result of managerial acumen; this is basic for long-run success.

The joint maximization aspect of company goals is not much different from that of classical thinking and is very much a basic part of the retailing-marketing processes.[6] As a result, differing facets of joint consumer-retailer maximization must be included in any model framework simulations of the decision processes of both buyers and retail management.

---

[5] These concepts of scientific management began with Frederick Taylor and were further developed by Henry R. Towns, Henry Metcalf, Henry L. Gantt, and Walter Clark, among others.

[6] See Adam Smith, *The Wealth of Nations* (New York: Random House, Modern Library, 1937), p. 651. The duty of "superintending the Industry" is that of directing employments toward most suitable interests of society.

Conflict enters all areas of decision making wherever the element of choice among alternatives is involved. The choice among alternatives essentially involves conflict, because the goals remain the same while the manner in which they are to be reached differs. Then, too, public and company goals differ. Thus, optimal decision making also means resolving the conflicts of public and company goals, as well as those within the internal organizational structure. This is a prerequisite to achieving any goal of profit maximization. These aspects are reviewed in a later chapter on government and business.

Optimal Decision and Operations Research

Profit is best maximized by improving the operating system as a whole; it is not possible to improve the effectiveness of every segment of a firm's organizational structure. Pursuit of this policy generally means using less than optimal criteria in clearly defined organizational segments, operating areas, and merchandise departments.

In striving for over-all optimal performance, all operating considerations should be brought into a single model framework; then the effects of various combinations of independent variables can be set up into a total input-output system. By this means, the effectiveness of each combination of inputs and corresponding outputs can be measured. The forecast results of various alternative decisions can then be presented to store management as a guide for optimal decision.

The development of these kinds of quantitative data for managerial decision is known as operations research methodology. For example, when decisions involve "waiting lines"—such as deliveries, warehousing allocations—and the scheduling, processing, and marking of incoming merchandise, then the "queuing theory" phase of operations research would be the one used. Where budget forecasts or inventory control problems are involved, a probability sampling or experimental design simulation methodology could be used.[7]

Operations research, although it is one of the newer of the basic management tools for maximizing the effectiveness of the firm, is only one of many possible evaluative criteria that can be utilized. The specific methodology or evaluative criterion used is the one that management feels will best measure the effectiveness of the system as a whole. Regardless of the techniques used, there is no substitute for either executive leadership or perceptive judgment.

Optimal Decision Based on Input Cost Factors

Generally, decisions based on definitive information tend to be better than decisions of the intuitive and stop-gap variety; yet the latter are quite characteristic of retail management. This kind of intuitive decision making is often due to the dynamic nature of the market and the rapidity with which continuing crises seem

---

[7] Operations research will also be referred to as "OR" in the text. Other methods used in managerial decision making will be taken up in functional chapters on research and organization. See C. West Churchman, Russell L. Ackoff, and E. Leonard Arnoff, *Introduction to Operations Research* (New York: Wiley and Sons, 1957).

to arise. Unquestionably, constant market innovations and new competitive pressures of all kinds call for fast and effective decisions, and the time wait needed for reliable data may seem overlong. Carrying out managerial decisions under such circumstances necessitates a higher degree of management coordination at all levels in the organization.

In attempting to improve the effectiveness of the decision-making processes, retail management has initiated the development of all kinds of informational guides. In fact, there has been such a deluge of information that management has been hard put to make use of it. Because of the "cost-profit" squeeze in many retail enterprises, much of the developed information has been in the area of cost estimates. This has raised special problems because of the many areas in which the same cost information is used.

Cost estimates as well as information flows have differing aspects of magnitude and importance depending on the use to which they are to be put. For example, the same data are used for the purposes of satisfying public regulation, financial reporting, decision making, and formulation of management policy.

Thus, informational guides, especially in the area of input cost data, tend to develop "use ambiguity" because of the varying uses to which they are put. "Intuitive" management unfortunately tends to make uneconomic use of cost data set up in a "natural" classification of expense—such as management, operation, and buying—which is discussed in later chapters.

For example, the merchandise manager of the store is generally the chief line officer of the firm.[8] The merchandise manager must be thoroughly familiar with the use of cost data for merchandising and inventory control and for directing and controlling all the merchandise areas. At the same time he must also be familiar with the use of these data for developing a profitable organization; the financial reporting and public regulation aspects of the same cost data are generally the responsibility of the controller.[9]

THE ORGANIZATIONAL STRUCTURE

Another organic management function is organization for carrying out the work of retail management. This function includes the determination of the best organizational structure for achieving company goals. In retailing, as in all business firms, there are two primary forms of organizational structure: the line and the line and staff. All others may be said to be variations of these forms. In Figure II, the line and staff organization depicted was set up to meet the needs of the larger retail firms and to meet certain weaknesses in the pure line organization.

---

[8] The line organization is characteristic of the smaller firm. As the firm gets larger, service and advisory staff groups are added. The line organization is the firm's primary chain of command, and its functioning results directly in the creation and distribution of "salable values." R. C. Davis, *The Fundamentals of Top Management* (New York: Harper and Brothers, 1951), pp. 794–95.

[9] The retail method of inventory is generally used for the control of departmental merchandise performances, and the cost method is used for over-all profit evaluation. Both methods will be detailed in the sections on financial and inventory management.

FIGURE II
FLOW CHART SHOWING PROCESS OF OPERATION OF DEPARTMENT STORE

(Operating steps in time sequence. Read from top to bottom.
Accounting and Control relationships on dotted lines.)

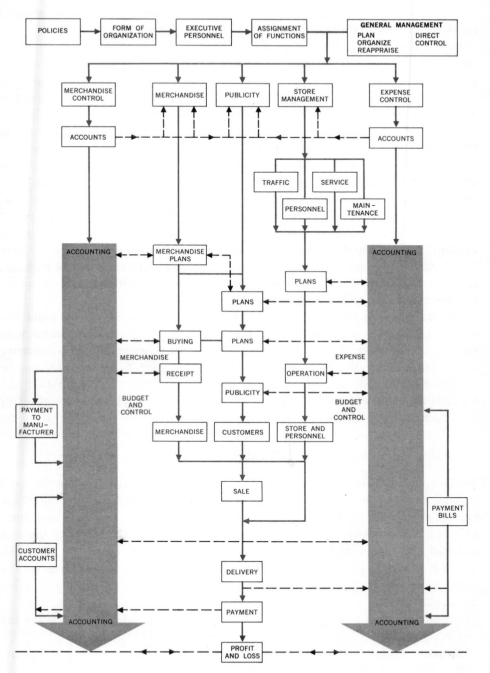

Source: Paul M. Mazur and Myron S. Silbert, *Principles of Organization Applied to Modern Retailing* (1927).

Its essential characteristic is the addition of experts or functional assistants to help the line organization in its management functions. Analysis of the various types of organizations within this framework will be found in Chapters 8 and 9.

One of the important organizational variations being used by retail firms is the functional type of organization, in which specialists have line as well as staff authority in the control of particular functional operations. This has found increasing acceptance by the management of large multi-unit firms because of increasing difficulties in coordinating and integrating widely scattered branch stores.

These problems have altered existing line and staff organizational concepts—especially in management beliefs as to what activities corporate controllers, branch-store managers, buyers, and department managers should supervise in addition to their primary activities. This problem of "scope" along functional lines has not been resolved.

Further, the process flow and time sequences of the various steps needed for store operation have remained substantially the same. Thus, the time sequences and decision flows within the retail organization are not very different today from what they were half a century ago. For example, in the flow chart of Figure II is shown a typical department store operation in the 1920's. It is evident that the line and staff organization had relatively little functional duplications. Today, however, with increasing autonomy and cross-functionalization at the merchandising, buying, and department-manager levels, much duplication of activities and new built-in cost factors have resulted. Uneconomic factors along these lines tend to negate the many advantages that can accrue with greater organizational flexibility. As a result, few increases in store profitability have been evident despite increases in volume.

For example, the buyer is a line executive of the firm as he executes his merchandising activities; when he is on buying trips, a floor or department manager takes over his sales-generating function. As such, the temporary executive replacement becomes a sales-generating rather than a sales-supporting executive. When the buyer returns to the department, he may act in both capacities—sales and sales-supporting; at the same time the floor manager may continue to duplicate the same activities.

The real value of new excursions into changing a firm's organizational structure has been in focusing management's attention on the continuing necessity for organizational adequacy and flexibility. One of the many directions in which organizational changes can proceed is illustrated in Figure III. The lines are broken where sales supervision in the stores is not part of the buyer's responsibility. Organizational decisions along these lines have become very acute in larger and multi-unit firms.

SELLING AND SUPERVISORY PROBLEMS

With growing population dispersions and shopping decentralizations externally and with greater autonomy and flexibility internally, some management prerogatives

FIGURE III

LINE AND STAFF ORGANIZATION, SHOWING FUNCTIONAL INTERRELATIONSHIPS OF DEPARTMENTIZED CHAIN OR INDEPENDENT STORE WITH BRANCHES

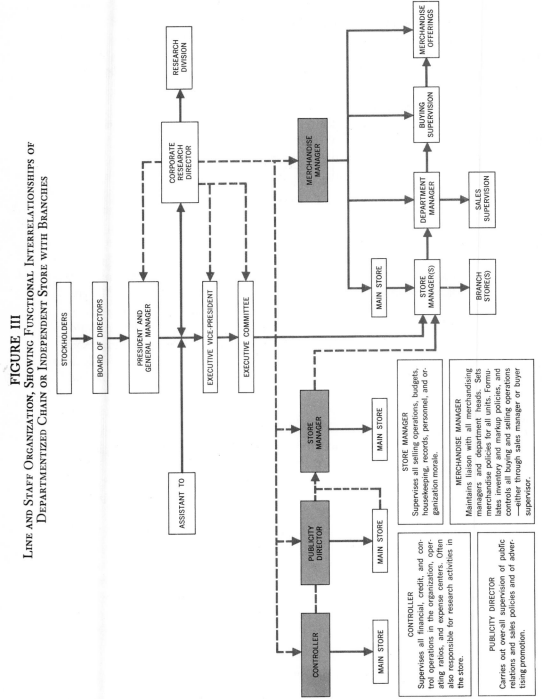

NOTE: Organizational charts do not present reality or give "kinship" patterns—work-flow patterns of relationships or actions. (See Figure II, this chapter, for process-flow relationships.) More significantly, the organization chart does not present the informal organizational structure.

52

are being delegated downward to supervisory and department managers. Automated techniques—such as self-service, check-out, simplified selling, and self-selection procedures—are resulting in fewer but better sales people and operating personnel.

Unfortunately, automation in retailing rarely improves customer services or choices. In addition, store personnel must be much more highly trained and developed, thus offsetting some of the possible savings. Yet, good personnel at the selling and the junior executive levels are problem areas where the functional operations of the retail store are weakest. In a comment on this very point, Peter Drucker states:

> ...The people who are needed are precisely the people most difficult to manage—and also the people in whom management has an investment many times the investment in the skilled worker of today. Add to this, management people will need to have a degree of technical knowledge unknown today, while the technical people need to have a degree of management insight unknown today, and finally that the "production worker" of tomorrow will have to understand practically the entire plant and the entire process in order to be able to maintain the equipment in good running order—and we'll have problems of personnel, or organization, of human relations, which, while perhaps are quite different from those management is familiar with today, are certainly not going to be easier or less important...[10]

FUNCTIONAL CONTROL PROCEDURES

The final organic function of management is that of directing and controlling the retail operation. In this respect the legal framework—whether a partnership, single proprietorship, or a corporation—would be the basic determinant of the most effective type of managerial control needed. For example, in the partnership form of organization, the act of any owner can bind the organization regardless of written contractual agreements as to specific areas of authorization. Thus, a continuing reappraisal of the executive decisions of the partners would be in order because the scope of their activities is not subject to specific limitations. Not so in the corporation: corporate executives may bind the corporation only in designated areas of authority and responsibility. (These aspects are detailed in a later chapter.)

The "One-Man" Organization

Because most retail firms are comparatively small in size, the partnership and sole proprietorship forms of organization are commonplace. As with most smaller businesses, many retail stores are generally operated on an intuitive, "one-man" organizational basis. In the smaller stores also, managerial controls are often

---

[10] From a letter to *Business Week* (March 1953), with reference to an article on "Management in the 1980's" (by T. L. Whisler and H. J. Leavitt).

ineffective because the store's owner-manager attempts to direct too many individuals. In technical terms, this is known as violation of the span of executive control.

The definition of the term "span of executive control" is the control by an executive charged with administrative management of no more than five to seven executives reporting directly to him, for operation at maximum efficiency. At the operating level, the span of control may run from twelve to twenty individuals, depending on the complexity of the function being performed.[11]

Although many of the smaller retail firms are run as one-man organizations, this does not necessarily indicate a lack of efficiency or success. The smaller organizations do have a tremendous advantage in organizational flexibility. Only when a firm has grown to the extent that the spans of executive and/or operating control are violated do the smaller organizations begin to falter. However, violations in the spans of control can and do occur in even the largest organizations.

For example, continuing violations of executive control by merchandise managers result in departmental inefficiencies and the shifting of line authority of many merchandise management functions to controllers. This kind of shifting often leads to better controls but, too often, to losses in merchandising effectiveness—such as letting a controller determine a division's "open to buy."

With each stage in a growth cycle, the entire organizational structure should be reviewed to determine if a new organizational plan is needed. Only by maintaining organizational flexibility can the firm be adequately directed and controlled so as to meet growth objectives in terms of sales and profits. In the long run, profits are the best assurance of a business's continuity as a "going concern."

"GOING-CONCERN" VALUES AND EFFECTIVE CONTROL

The determination of "going concern" values—both as to return on sales and return on investment—is directly dependent on the effectiveness of its administrative management as a coordinating force.

As a basic principle, managerial coordination and control should extend to every phase of the business both within and without the organization. Management secures coordination through the flexible blending of the organizational objectives of the firm and the personal service objectives of its employees. The complexity of size in itself makes it essential that the basic retail organization be flexible, otherwise the problems accompanying the continuing cost-profit squeezes cannot be soundly resolved.

As long as volume increases when new facilities are introduced, underlying managerial weaknesses are sometimes overlooked. This is often the case when organizational complexities and rigidities within the enterprise "mold" the executive,

---

[11] Although there is currently much debate about the spans of control, these concepts are still valid. For elements of the controversy, see J. M. Pfiffner and F. P. Sherwood, *Administrative Organization* (Englewood Cliffs, N.J.: Prentice-Hall, 1960).

rather than the executive molding the enterprise. However, when volume declines or remains stationary, problems accelerate, become acute, and result in a rapid cost-profit squeeze. The pinpointing and correcting of the underlying weakness in a store's management may be too late to re-establish the firm's effectiveness and value as a going concern.

Pinpointing potential weaknesses *in advance* is the function of the managerial control and reappraisal processes. As an organic function of management, the control-reappraisal-feedback function should be planned and set up so that all potential weaknesses as well as growth possibilities can be easily handled.

This over-all control function is one of conservation of assets as well as of furthering and facilitating organizational plans and policies. Effective control also implies an objective evaluation of the various degrees of risk involved with each functional element of a store's operation.

The operating risks that can be economically shifted, such as insurance and the use of specialized leased departments, are relatively simple to evaluate and control. The business risks concomitant to the total operation should always be classified according to profitability, utility, and the degree of control required. This also means checking and implementing the standards of service and performance at every level of the firm and evaluating the soundness of the authority and responsibility delegated for functional performance. Otherwise uneconomic duplication occurs. For example, it should be asked whether the delegation of authority actually facilitates the intended fulfillment of the function.

GENERIC AREAS OF CONTROL

The functional areas of executive management in retailing are generally four in number; these consist of the merchandising, management-operation, publicity-sales promotion, and finance-control divisions.[12] In Figure III the functional interrelationships of some types of retailing organizations are shown.

For example, management division is responsible for operating the physical plant, training, and the supervision of all personnel including salespeople, cashiers, wrappers, and section managers, as well as those concerned with store protection, merchandise deliveries, and all ingoing and outgoing traffic. The management division is directly responsible for selling and customer-service functions, and acts in a staff and facilitating capacity for the buyers and department managers in the merchandising division.

The merchandising division is responsible for carrying out the basic line functions of buying, merchandising, and generating adequate gross margins consistent with the store's public service objectives. The merchandising division is the primary income-producing division of the organization, and its effectiveness is the key to any long-run success that the store might achieve.

The publicity and sales promotion division generally has full line responsibility

---

[12] Each of these divisions will be functionally detailed in subsequent chapters.

for the development of the wanted store image and motivational appeals and all public relations activities; included in its area of responsibility are sales promotion, advertising, and all window and interior displays in the store.

The control division generally acts in both a line and staff capacity. In its staff capacity, the control division facilitates the work of merchandising, publicity, and store management and more recently, research evaluations on all aspects of store operation. In its line capacity, it is responsible for credit extension, flow of fund and ratio analyses.

All these functions must be performed in carrying out the work of retailing. Although they are listed separately, the smaller the firm the greater the likelihood that a single individual performs one or more of these functions in its entirety. Evaluation of these functions from the standpoint of functional integration as well as functional specializations is of paramount importance because most retail establishments are comparatively small in size and, as pointed out, the smaller the size of the firm, the greater the degree of functional integration.

SUMMARY AND CONCLUSIONS

The long-run success of any business is determined by the quality of its executive leadership. Management, being the function of executive leadership, generally has a goal of long-run sales and profit maximization.

Profit maximization is the basic long-run objective of the business enterprise. This objective of the firm coincides with the "pursuit of maximum advantage" as projected in classical economic doctrines.

Profit maximization is achieved through optimal decisions. To make the best possible decisions, the organic functions of planning, organizing, and control of the retail operation must be based on realistic information. This is as true today as it was in the past.

One of the most important aspects of good management lies in the organic function of planning—especially in the area of market and marketing analysis. This involves correctly assessing specific market demand in order to maximize within limited amounts of working capital investment the choices of merchandise lines, assortments, and prices to be offered. This means that available working capital must be used to the firm's best possible advantage. Along with enterprise profitability, market position is one of the key indicators of how successfully managerial decisions have been made and carried out. When a firm shows an increase in the rate of its net profit, it means that the "spread" between total expenses and gross margin has been widened; either expenses have been lowered or gross margins have been raised, or both. The former is a sounder procedure in a competitive framework.

The ability to make optimal decisions also means correctly developing the most effective marketing strategy needed for offsetting both present and possible future competition. Regardless of the size of the firm, it is obvious that the application of sound **economic** and management principles are a must if an enterprise is to achieve success and growth. These, then, are the basic goals of retail and market managers.

Financially, the smaller the retail firm, the greater the degree of functional integration; the larger the firm, the greater the degree of functional specialization. Few changes have been found in the internal managerial processes of the retail firm over time—new techniques and automated processes notwithstanding. However, a greater use of information guides based on market analyses and operations research has become much more commonplace.

SUMMARY OF PART I

In the four chapters that make up Part I, management's over-all functional responsibilities in maximizing the effectiveness of the retail firm were analyzed. In Part II, the analyses and decisions concerned with carrying out the specific functions of retailing as an economic enterprise will be taken up. As the initial consideration, planning for optimum location will be the primary subject matter of Chapter 5.

Part Two

The External Setting: Competitive Factors

Basic and Fixed Factors of Enterprise (Limited Control)

Chapter 5: *Locational Factors: Planning for Optimum Change*

The success of any retail enterprise depends upon its location; in fact, payment for a location represents the largest fixed-cost expenditure of the retail firm. Convenient and rapid access to and egress from a location is the basic determinant of its value.

THE ECONOMICS OF RENT

Land, along with other natural resources, is part of the economy's wealth and capital stock, and the institution of private property implies the necessity of payment for the use of land resources that have been acquired and capitalized in the past. The modern theory of rent may be said to have been initiated by Ricardo and supplemented by Malthus.[1] Both were somewhat pessimistic in their discourses, and discussed rent as the difference in "produce" or net revenues of two similar areas on which the same amounts of labor and capital were expended. This is generally known as the "differentials approach" to rent determination.

The principal shortcoming of the theory in practice is the difficulty in equating the differences in "fertility" (in this case adjacencies) and in the conditions under

---

[1] See David Ricardo, *Principles of Political Economy* (London: J. Murray, 1817).

which any two areas could be "cultivated" or converted. In retailing, the equating process would center on equalizing the differences in the potential of each location by first selecting only complementary types of retail establishments to occupy an area. The conditions of "cultivation" would be determined by the number of of square feet of space available, parking spaces, access, egress, population per trading area and the degree of integrated sales promotion activities.

Economic rent may also be defined as payment to factor unit owners in excess of the amounts necessary to keep the factor units available for use.[2] In the commonly accepted accounting term, rent is the payment for the use of land and durable capital goods. To avoid confusion on the use of the term in this text, rent, unless otherwise designated, will refer to its everyday accounting usage.

OPTIMUM USE AND THE 100-PER-CENT IDEA

The rent paid for any location depends directly on the optimum use to which it can be put. "Optimum use" in this case means choosing the type of establishment that can obtain the maximum possible revenue from a specific location.

For example, a corner location in the heart of a central business district might be the most economic place to locate a large departmentized drugstore handling many impulse and convenience items; however, this location may be a very poor site to locate a women's fashion specialty shop. The drugstore would benefit fully from both the lane[3] and shopping traffic that the location generates. On the other hand, the specialty shop would be paying far too much rent for needless "waste circulation" in the form of lane traffic, which is primarily impulse and nonshopping in nature.

Thus, the amount of rental charged would depend on the maximum expected revenues of the drugstore because it is this type of establishment that can optimize the use and maximize the revenues from this kind of location. If the rental is fixed at the optimum, then any other type of establishment at this location would be paying uneconomic rent. It follows, therefore, that any retail establishment other than the drugstore located at this particular site would have to be charged less rent because it would earn less.

In other words, this site would be classified as a 100-per-cent location for the departmentized drugstore because it would check highest with regard to the kind of traffic desired and would be the only type of establishment that could maximize the revenues from that location.[4] The same location would be classified as only a 70- or 80-per-cent location for the women's specialty shop.

In general, it may be stated that the lower the percentage classification of a

---

[2] Each factor unit of property has attendant costs, such as taxes and handling. Any firm acquiring a site for use must pay the owner of the land (the factor unit) more than enough to make it worth-while for an owner to own the land and to have it used productively so as to furnish him income.

[3] Lane traffic generally consists of individuals who work in the vicinity of a store, or who have entered the trading area in order to attend to personal business other than shopping, such as visiting a doctor, lawyer, bank, etc.

[4] William R. Davidson and Paul L. Brown, *Retailing Management*, 2nd ed. (New York: Ronald Press, 1960) pp. 75–76.

location for a particular type of store, the lower the potential revenue that can be generated in that location, by that type of store and the lower the amount of rent that could be charged by the landlord.

The productivity of any location is subject to constant change. For instance, the amount of income that land and fixed capital assets can be expected to produce tends to decline as per capita income rises in adjacent residential areas. This is because individuals making up the family group whose income is increasing tend to travel shorter distances and for shorter periods of time in purchasing shopping and specialty goods.

THE NEGOTIATION PROCESS AND THE MINIMUM GUARANTEE

The minimum rent guarantee for any location should cover all of the owner's costs—such as taxes, insurance, and imputed return on investment; the owner also seeks a margin for "pure" profits (in the economic sense). At the same time, the minimum rent guarantee must not be uneconomic for the renter. When the rent for the use of land and capital assets is too high in relation to the type of store occupying the premises, then the store must relocate or fail.

As a result, the negotiations for a site center primarily on the rent per square foot of gross space; further negotiations would then involve the length of the lease, number of options, if any, and (where applicable) restrictive clauses as to the kinds of merchandise that the store may handle. The last-named may be applicable only when directly competitive stores are also under leases controlled by the same landlord.

From the standpoint of the entrepreneur, no location should ever be leased unless the minimum rental charge lies within the "typical" expense range criteria shown in Table 7. Also illustrated in this table are some of the other negotiable factors in a lease.

Thus, both owners and renters seek to maximize their returns and minimize the risk of change. Attempts to meet these objectives are reached through a bargaining process within limits set by the terms of leases that have been negotiated in the past for comparable locations and comparable types of stores in similar economic settings. The parameters of the model would be further molded by the relative inelasticity and short-run scarcity of suitable locations within the trading area.

THE DECISION TO RENT

Assuming that a specific location can be deemed favorable in the light of applicable theoretical models, then the decision to rent can be made, if suitable space is available. Favorable interpretation means that the sales projection, on a conservative basis, of a specific volume goal can be reasonably correlated to the asking rental price. A rent is excessive when its ratio to the projected sales volume is higher than the "typical" rental expense for the type of store involved. At the initial renting stage of new firms, the owner of the smaller firm would have

TABLE 7
Shopping-Center Leases
Typical Data—Selected Stores[a]

Type of Firm and Number in Sample	Total Square Feet (gross)	Selling Area (approx.) per cent	Minimum Annual Rental per Sq. Ft. (Actual)	Percentage Against Minimum	Length of Leases (years)	Number of Options	Length of Options (years)
Supermarket (97)	15,000 to 25,000	65 to 75% of Total	.90 to 1.75	1 to 1½%	7 to 20	0 to 5	5 to 10
Variety (62)	13,000 to 30,000	75 to 85	.55 to 1.75	3 to 5%	5 to 25	0 to 5	5 or 10
Drug (67)	5500 to 8000	84 to 90	.92 to 2.00	2½ to 6%	5 to 25	0 to 5	5 or 10
Restaurant (includes cafeterias) (52)	4200 to 6700	80 to 95	1.35 to 2.25	4 to 6%	5 to 21	0 to 4	5 to 10
Women's Apparel (54)	5200 to 7000	80 to 95	1.40 to 2.40	4 to 6%	5 to 21	0 to 2	5 or 10
Men's Wear (28)	2000 to 6000	80 to 93	1.25 to 3.75	3½ to 6%	5 to 20	0 to 4	3 to 10
Jr. Dept. Stores (41)	20,000 to 31,000	80 to 85	.80 to 1.67	2 to 4%	10 to 24	0 to 3	5 to 10
Women's Shoes (24)	4800 to 7800	87 to 96	1.20 to 3.00	4½ to 6%	15 to 30	0 to 2	5 or 10
Men's Shoes (25)	1800 to 8000	88 to 96	1.91 to 2.55	5 to 6%	11 to 20	0 to 2	5 only
Family Shoes (22)	2500 to 36,000 (all)	84 to 95	1.36 to 2.50	4 to 6%	5 to 20	1 to 5	5 to 10
Auto Supply (17)	2000 to 12,000 (all)	80 to 97	1.25 to 2.50	2½ to 5%	5 to 20	0 to 2	5 only
Hardware (21)	2200 to 12,000 (all)	78 to 90	.75 to 2.44	4 to 6%	4 to 5	0 to 2	5 to 10
Bakery (25)	600 to 2000 (all)	60 to 85	2.50 to 4	4½ to 6%	5 to 20	0 to 2	5 only
Candy (11)	600 to 900 (all)	80 to 97	2 to 4.70	5 to 10%	5 to 10	0 to 2	5
Children's Wear (13)	930 to 4000 (all)	80 to 85	1.22 to 5	3½ to 7%	5 to 15	0 to 2	5
Jewelry	800 to 3000 (all)	85 to 90	1.67 to 2.25	5	5 to 15	1	3 to 10

Shopping Center Samples:

Range of Areas———————————→2 to 113 acres
No. of Stores in Centers (range)——→6 to 80 stores
Parking for——————————————→250 to 6,000 cars

Sources: *Chain Store Age*, Adm. Ed. (May 1958), Vol. XXXIV No. 15 pps. 25–45; research data, Retail Research Center, Grad. Sch. of Business, University of Pgh. (1960) (Above data do not include "other" provisions such as contribution for promotions and Asso. dues, etc.) See Appendix B for definition and descriptions of stores.

Range of Areas (in sq. feet)

Supermarket	10,000–72,000
Variety	3,600–50,000
Drug	4,800–22,000
Restaurant	1,500–26,000
Womens Appar.	1,800–30,000
Mens Wear	1,600– 8,000
Jr. Dept. Stores	10,000–60,000
Wos. Shoes	1,800– 9,400
Mens Shoes	1,800– 9,400

little bargaining power and would probably have to pay a maximum rental, while a larger, high-rated firm would generally pay less.

Also influencing the final agreement for the actual rent to be charged for a particular location are, as pointed out, the locale, complementary cluster-group stores in the vicinity, the degree of existing competition, pedestrian and vehicular traffic flows, customer access and egress, availability of parking and adequacy of public transportation facilities, and economic, sociological, and historical trends in the trading area.

The final lease contract is the result, also, of alternative bargaining power and the intensity of the motivational objectives of each of the parties involved in wanting to "close the deal." All these are prime facets of the total location problem. However, the actual research procedure in location determination involves the sequential evaluation of regional, economic, sociological, and marketing data.

The First Approximation

The research procedure used in determining optimum locations for a particular type of store begins with a general evaluation of the region or area in which management wishes to locate. If no regional preference is indicated, then the first choice should be the region with the greatest potential and the minimum amount of competition.

Once the broad area decision has been made, then the region should be subdivided into metropolitan zones and trading areas, for which government and private statistics are readily available. At this point the boundary lines of each market area should be clearly delineated and defined; this should be supplemented by a brief synopsis of the physical, social, and historical characteristics of the trading areas. A typical outline of major locational zones within a standard metropolitan statistical area[5] is shown in Figure IV.

Town, City, and Free-Standing Locations

The Smaller Town as an Integrated Shopping Unit. Smaller towns and cities of around 5,000 to 25,000 in population often take on the growth characteristics of completely integrated regional shopping centers; this takes place when sufficient parking, easy access and egress, and reasonable traffic and police supervision are present and the business community works cooperatively together as an integrated unit in public relations and promotional activities.[6]

---

[5] See Appendix C for definition and concepts of standard metropolitan statistical areas and subdivisions.

[6] See Samuel Feinberg, "Small-Town Stores Take on the Giants," Women's Wear Daily (June 1961). Rutherford, N.J., a town of under 18,000, has a drawing population perhaps five times that number. Yet only minutes away from the fifty-odd stores on the four-block stretch of the main street are the huge Modell and Great Eastern Mills roadside discount stores; some eight miles away (15 to 20 minutes' driving time) are the two regional shopping centers of Bergen Mall and Garden State Plaza; also 20 minutes distant, through the Lincoln Tunnel, is New York City's midtown retail area—all these on top of the usual competition of nearby towns.

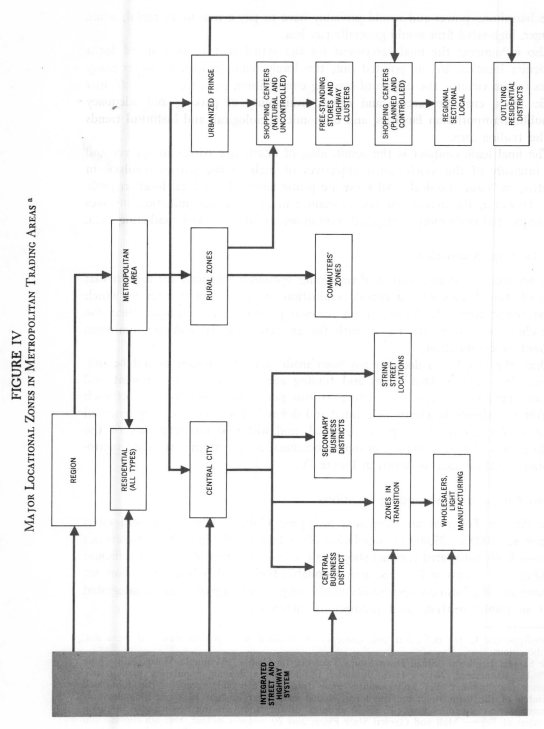

FIGURE IV

MAJOR LOCATIONAL ZONES IN METROPOLITAN TRADING AREAS [a]

[a] See Appendix C for a complete description of the various types of shopping-center locations, and Appendix B for trend factors for different types of trading zones within any metropolitan area.

Trend Characteristics of Urban Locations. The centralization of manufacturing, commercial, and political power has been the chief underlying factor in the growth of cities. In the past, both department stores and wholesalers of all kinds were dominant factors in the growth of the cities as well as their central business districts. Because of population movements to the suburbs, the typical downtown areas today have many vacant stores within and contiguous to the central business districts (CBD). The CBD's are generally surrounded by a mixture of produce and other wholesale businesses, warehouses, extensive slums, and redeveloped areas of varying magnitudes. Despite such questionable characteristics, there are still many locations in downtown areas which are economic because their rentals have fallen drastically.

Free-Standing Locations. Most free-standing locations must derive their volume primarily from motor traffic. Included in this grouping are automobile service stations, drive-in restaurants, auto washing operations, and automobile accessory and service stores. There has also been an increase in furniture, home furnishings, and discount stores operating in free-standing locations. Such locations to be competitively productive need adequate frontage with easily accessible and adequate parking facilities. A corner location is generally the most desirable.

Parking needs, whether in a free-standing store or in a shopping center, must be evaluated from the standpoint of the size of store, type of merchandise handled, amount of possible walk-in business, public transportation schedules, and proximity to the site of possible transit stops.

Population Factors

Once the trading areas are delineated, their population should be examined in relation to the type of store to be opened. This initial analysis should show whether the population per store corresponds roughly to the average in Table 6 (pages 38 and 39). Assuming that a variety store is to be opened, it is seen from this table that in 1963 approximately 8,490 individuals were needed to support the average variety store; further, the average variety store should generate a volume of some $203,000 per store.[7]

If there are more than 8,490 inhabitants per variety store in the trading area being evaluated, then the region is not "overbuilt," and research for a site within the area would appear feasible. This initial step would *not* automatically rule out areas with less than 8,490 people per store, but it would call for a more rigorous examination of any proposed location in the trading zone.

Age, sex, and income have been listed as general population factors to be considered in planning for optimum locations. Other evaluative population criteria are the percentage of white, Negro, and foreign-born, the number of couples at work, the number of dependent children, the percentages of blue- and white-

---

[7] From Table 6, the total volume of variety store sales in 1963 ($4,538 million), divided by the total number of such stores (22,400), gives an average volume of $203,000 per store.

collar workers, and the ratio of retired people to the total employed. The spending characteristics of the community are, of course, dependent on the make-up of the population.

The pay-roll trend in a community is more important as an indicator than the total amount earned at any particular period of time. Unemployment trends by industry should be considered along with population. Because pay rolls are more stable in locations with well-balanced blends of highly diversified industries, it is far preferable, *ceteris paribus*, to choose cities or shopping centers with industries of this type. In some areas the availability of high-caliber full- and part-time employees is an important operating advantage.

Along with the population characteristics, the residential zones within the trading area should be set up in tabular form showing present and possible future land use. This type of tabulation is shown in Table 8, which analyzes the South Hills section of the Pittsburgh Standard Metropolitan Statistical Area. From this table the use and possible growth of an area can be projected.

TABLE 8

LAND USE ANALYSIS

FORT COUCH SHOPPING CENTER AREA OF

PITTSBURGH STANDARD METROPOLITAN STATISTICAL AREA

(South Hills Areas)

TOWNSHIP AREAS	AREA[a]	EXCESSIVE SLOPE AREA[a]	USEABLE LAND AREA[a]	DEVELOPED LAND AREA[a]	1960 POPULA-TION	USEABLE LAND AREA WITH PO-TENTIAL POPU-LATION DEVL.[a]	MAXIMUM POPULATION[b]	
Bethel	11.92	2.14	9.78	4.22	23,606	5.56	56,160	52,676
Upper St. Clair	10.00	2.42	7.58	1.93	8,278	5.65	24,976	30,327
Baldwin	5.44	0.20	5.24	4.55	24.431	0.69	29,543	25,674
Baldwin Twp.	1.00	0.20	0.80	0.65	3,003	0.15	4,142	3,734
Brentwood	1.43	0.48	0.95	0.87	13,678	0.08	15,081	16,220
Bridgeville	1.06	0.19	0.87	0.78	7,094	0.09	11,506	7,339
Carnegie	1.30	0.10	1.20	0.98	11,874	0.22	16,313	14,082
Castle Shannon	1.51	0.39	1.12	0.94	11,809	0.18	18,097	13,569
Collier (part)	6.39	2.03	4.36	0.39	4,075	3.97	40,636	42,392
Crafton	1.14	0.19	0.95	0.61	8,391	0.34	14,085	11,519
Dormont	0.76	0.10	0.66	0.62	13,031	0.04	15,245	13,402
Greentree	2.02	0.84	1.18	0.38	5,229	0.80	14,304	14,523
Heidelberg	0.26	0.01	0.25	0.19	2,118	0.06	3,030	2,862
Mt. Lebanon	5.90	1.04	4.86	3.29	35,308	1.57	45,138	52,579
Pittsburgh (part)	6.99	2.02	4.97	4.62	75,420	0.35	95,839	91,601
Pleasant Hills	2.50	0.96	1.54	0.52	8,495	1.02	14,772	23,094
Rosslyn Farms	0.47	0.18	0.29	0.10	559	0.19	1,724	1,523
Scott	3.75	1.04	2.71	1.48	19,200	1.23	33,918	32,009
Snowden	8.92	2.02	6.90	3.94	7,367	2.96	27,115	12,324
South Fayette	20.95	6.15	14.80	5.03	9,244	9.77	75,104	29,776
Whitehall	3.19	0.59	2.60	1.44	16,547	1.16	18,004	30,631
Canonsburg	1.65	0.11	1.54	1.17	11,768	0.37	c	16,299
Cecil	27.27	9.23	18.04	2.82	8,527	15.22	c	48,673
North Strabane	27.43	9.92	17.51	1.49	7,313	16.02	c	92,173
Peters Twp.	19.77	4.05	15.72	2.04	7,037	13.68	c	51,672
Total	173.02	46.60	126.42	45.05	343,402	81.37	574,732	730,673

[a] In square miles.

[b] Maximum Population: First column based on lot sizes under present zoning; second column based on present land use ratios.

[c] Figures not available.

The use of a table such as this should be supplemented with a population analysis. Other population data that may be considered in location analyses are:

1. Daytime Working Population and Industry:
   a. Total working population; growth and work locales.
   b. Number and percentage employed in commerce, industry, and government, also seasonal factors.
   c. Percentage of residents employed locally; percentage commuting; total available work force.
   d. Number of firms, employee totals, pay roll by standard industrial classifications (SIC).
   e. Retail concentrations relative to site along with possible new developments.
2. Household Income:
   a. Breakdown of households by income group; then per capita income and trends.
3. Current and Historical Land Factors:
   a. Residential housing:
      (1) Number of dwelling units by type; percentage.
      (2) Percentage owner-occupied; percentage renter-occupied.
      (3) Percentage of dwelling units deteriorating; percentage improved (tax assessments).
      (4) Percentage occupancy; average contract rent; average dollar value of owner-occupied homes.
      (5) Changes in land values.
   b. Construction activity:
      (1) Units in proximity to site.
      (2) Number of residential units and dollar values.
      (3) Commercial, industrial, and municipal units and dollar values.

Historical Perspectives and Drawing Power

Generally, only progressive towns and cities should be considered for new locations for expansion. Evaluative data developed by civic groups, chambers of commerce, and bankers should be "shaded" because of possible overoptimism. The population characteristics as to age, sex, income group, and so on are basic indicators of both volume potentials and the kinds of merchandise lines best-suited to an area.

Too often, location decisions are based on only one or two area characteristics. Often sites occupied by national chains are used as a sufficient criterion for site selection. For example, many locate in an area because of "rule of thumb" guides that indicate that most F. W. Woolworth stores in the South are generally located in 100-per-cent locations; the S. H. Kress stores have similarly classified locations in the West; and the W. T. Grant stores have been found to occupy 100-per-cent locations in New England.

TABLE 9

CLASSIFICATIONS

PITTSBURGH MARKET AREA

| AREA | POPULATION[a] | | % CHANGE | DEFINITION |
	1950	1960		
Pittsburgh City	676,806	604,332	−10.7%	The area included within the political boundaries of the corporate city of Pittsburgh.
A B C City Zone	1,157,301	1,198,046	3.5%	A newspaper term defined by the Audit Bureau of Circulations. It includes the city of Pittsburgh and 62 surrounding municipalities. The area is smaller than Allegheny County but accounts for nearly 74% of the county population.
Allegheny County	1,515,237	1,628,587	7.5%	The primary divisions of the state are termed counties. Allegheny County is that in which the city of Pittsburgh is the county seat.
Pittsburgh Standard Metropolitan Area	2,213,236	2,405,435	8.7%	(Standard Metropolitan Statistical Area) A United State Census Bureau and Bureau of the Budget definition. It includes four counties—Allegheny, Beaver, Washington, and Westmoreland.
Retail Trading Zone[b]	2,380,594	2,580,821	8.4%	A newspaper term defined by the Audit Bureau of Circulations. It includes all or parts of nine counties. The counties and percentage of total county population within the RTZ are as listed in footnote b.
The Pittsburgh Market	3,065,624	3,271,453	6.7%	14 counties—10 in Pennsylvania, 2 in Ohio, and 2 in West Virginia—that come within a 50-mile radius of the city of Pittsburgh.

[a] Population figures from 1950 and 1960 Census Reports, final counts.
[b] Allegheny, 100%; Beaver, 100%; Washington, 100%; Westmoreland, 95.3%; Armstrong, 75.3%; Butler, 72.5%; Indiana, 19.5%; Fayette, 13.5%; Lawrence, 10.0%.

A decision based on such factors may be a poor one because a downtown site may be in a desirable 100-per-cent location yet should be discarded because of either insufficient adjacent parking[s] or massive suburban area "build-ups."

Again, the choice of a downtown or suburban location may be determined by the availability of a suburban site at the intersection of two or more main traffic arteries. This is often a deciding consideration for the management of department stores and discount houses. Of course, decisions of this kind may also be influenced by the fact that suburban areas generally have less expensive land costs, greater access to parking areas, and often greater potential for growth. In Table 9 the classifications of a market area by initial location analysis are shown.

In determining total retail sales in an area, it is assumed that approximately

[s] This is based on a general rule that for every estimated million dollars' worth of volume in the vicinity of a site, there should be minimum of a hundred parking spaces adjacent to or within a two-block, a four-minute walking distance of the proposed store.

62 to 65 per cent of personal income is spent in retail stores.[9] The proportion of this spending going into a particular neighborhood would depend on the drawing power of the site itself. There is no metropolitan trading area, community, or town in a modern economy that is entirely self-contained; also, some areas lose business that others gain. Generally, the drawing power of any community or shopping center varies directly with its population and inversely with the square of its distance to the next nearest trading zone.[10]

General Economic and Social Factors

To determine the validity of what is supposed to be true about a zone trading area requires much more analysis than intuition. Other pertinent criteria (in addition to drawing power) that should be analyzed are such economic and social factors as income, transportation, and competition. The ultimate decision to locate in a particular site should be the result of some theoretical as well as pragmatic interpretations of all the data. The number and kinds of business establishments in the area along with gravitational points in relation to the proposed site should be set up in visual form. The particular climate, specific industries, and local customs would furnish specific clues as to what type of merchandise lines should be handled.

Competition. In actuality, the greater the number of shopping and specialty goods stores in any one location, the greater the distance consumers are willing to drive in order to patronize the center. Thus the greater the number of stores of these kinds in a shopping center, the greater its total drawing power. This is not the case with convenience goods because they are widely available, low in price, and have high degrees of product, brand, and institutional substitutability.

It is also important to keep in mind that when a large shopping center is built close to or adjacent to a smaller center, the shopping and specialty goods stores in the smaller center tend to lose volume and become uneconomic, because most purchases of these goods classifications generally accrue to the larger center. On the other hand, the convenience goods stores (such as laundry, dry cleaning, supermarkets, and drugstores) tend to retain adequate measures of previously developed volume and remain relatively profitable.

The amount of existing competition in a city can be estimated by developing a ratio of retail sales to specific pay-roll classification; the number of clerks in competitive stores in a trading area, if ascertainable, is multiplied by an average estimated annual gross sales per clerk.[11] For example, the approximate volume of

---

9 See Robert D. Entenberg, *The Changing Competitive Position of Department Stores in the United States by Merchandise Lines,* rev. ed. (Pittsburgh: University of Pittsburgh Press, 1961), Chapter 4.

10 William J. Reilly, *The Law of Retail Gravitation,* 2nd ed. (New York: Pilsbury, 1953).

11 Pay-roll data of this kind may be obtained from local government sources; clerical and "check-out" lane data may be obtained from pertinent trade associations. The MOR (Merchandising and Operating Results) of the Controllers' Congress of the National Retail Merchants Association (NRMA) develops many pertinent criteria for department and specialty stores.

a service type of variety store with simplified selling procedures can be determined by multiplying the "clerk-average" of $25,000 annually in sales by the number of clerks. Another method is to estimate the number of square feet of selling space and multiply it by the "typical" square-foot sales volume for that type of store.

Another type of competition is for the most desirable sites. Demand for locations in particular areas grows in almost direct proportion to the expansion rate of department and chain stores into the area. Also, when other locations are available in an area, the effect of possible new entries into the field should be evaluated. In most downtown areas, demand for retail locations has decreased, resulting in many commercial vacancies.

The location decision must be made with the view of operating in a setting of monopolistic competition as the condition of normalcy. Only by correctly assessing the competitive settings can the economic processes of the firm within the community be facilitated.[12]

Thus, an optimal location may be found in any setting. In many areas, it may be quite evident that not all the available business in a proposed location is being generated. Similarly, excess capacity and overcompetition manifest themselves quite readily. One of the positive factors in determination of an area's competitive characteristics would be an affirmative reply to the question, "Can new business be introduced on a cumulative compatibility basis without maximizing the competitive hazards?" [13]

The term "cumulative compatibility" implies favorable store affinities. For example, as pointed out, when one specialty shop or department store locates adjacent to or close to another, the total amount of business of both stores in that location is generally greater than either one could have generated individually in nonadjacent locations. Two specialty or shopping-goods stores located competitively will show increases in volume in almost direct proportion to the incidence of the total customer interchange between them. More specifically, a car dealer, an auto-repair shop, a service station, and a used-car dealer would have a high degree of retail affinities. On the other hand, when one supermarket or drugstore moves next to or close to another, the total business of both stores would rarely be doubled or show proportionate over-all increases.

Transportation.   An important facet in site evaluation is transportation. The specific types of transportation facilities that shoppers use or can use to reach the shopping locale must be listed and examined for adequacy. To what extent is public transportation available and used? The other transportation aspects of location analysis to be considered are parking, access, and egress. Finally, point of origin–point of destination shopping surveys should be taken to determine how far and from where consumers have come.

---

[12] See Edward H. Chamberlin, *The Theory of Monopolistic Competition* (Cambridge: Harvard University Press, 1947), pp. 56–63. This concept, as discussed in Chapter 1, places the theory between the earliest theoretical concepts of pure competition and pure monopoly.

[13] See R. L. Nelson, *The Selection of Retail Location* (New York: F. W. Dodge, 1958), Chapter 6.

Real estate agents and land developers almost constantly promote store locations, and many claim to specialize in research data of this kind. When using generalized research, it is always prudent to spot-check the data. For example, it is comparatively easy to spot-check pedestrian and vehicular traffic flows. Whenever possible or feasible, it is best to rely on one's own research.

Imputed versus Explicit Costs

In planning for optimum location a forecast of all costs connected with the location is essential. Imputed as well as out-of-pocket and depreciation costs must be realistically estimated in total operating costs. Total costs must be covered in the long run if the firm is to stay in business; only in the short run can operations be maintained with the coverage of only variable or out-of-pocket costs.

Implicit or imputed costs are those for which no actual cash is paid out. This occurs when the manager-owner of a store is his own landlord. The amount of rent that he would have charged another for the use of his land would be included as an implicit cost of doing business. While implicit cost allocations are not deductible for income tax purposes, they are an essential inclusion for evaluating the true profitability of the business.

Underlying Theoretical Concepts

Another consideration is the tendency for particular specializations to increase as land is used for similar purposes. In many metropolitan areas, irregular and complicated gravitational shopping patterns have developed, with great concentrations of retailers handling similar lines. This often takes place in urban renewal areas.

While such concentrations often result in excess capacity and uneconomic land use, some areas are being enlarged by innovations and other topographical and highway changes; in such cases risk is minimized.[14] Thus, "know-how" in terms of advanced technology, innovations, and readily applicable topographical changes can cushion the increasing scarcity of economic land for commercial purposes. Nevertheless, demand for particular locations is elastic, whereas the availability of suitable sites is inelastic. As a result, there is a general decreasing utilization of natural resources that accompanies economic growth. Maximizing the income from land can still be set up within the principles laid down in the Ricardian model.[15]

OTHER LOCATION THEORIES

Location theories have often been criticized on the basis that too many assumptions, deductions, and chance observations are used in the optimization p

[14] See Richard U. Ratcliff, "The Problem of Site Selection," *Michigan Business Stud* No. 1, (1938), pp. 4–6; see also Eugene J. Kelly, *Shopping Centers* (New Y University Press, 1956), pp. 55–67.

[15] Theodore W. Schultz, "A General View of Natural Resources in Econom delivered to the Conference on Natural Resources and Economic Gro outlined by Edgar M. Hoover in Vol. 14, No. 2, *Items* (June 1960).

and further, that insufficient use is made of indicators developed from carefully determined facts.[16] Yet theoretical location studies do provide much insight into current problems and should be used in conjunction with empirical cost studies.

The principles underlying retail store location have many similarities to those principles used in locating manufacturers' plants and warehouses. In manufacturing, transfer costs—both incoming and outgoing—are often critical in determining location; in retailing, the location is critical in terms of customer conveniences, and transfer costs are secondary. Other facets of locational decisions in agricultural processing, manufacturing, market distribution, and retailing are often quite similar in terms of population density, transportation facilities, adjacencies to the market, and regional growth trends.

For example, an early nineteenth-century economist, J. H. von Thunen, treated the spatial elements and transfer costs accompanying the marketing of agricultural products as a valid area for economic analysis. Only recently have economists been treating spatial as well as time considerations in their analyses.[17] Von Thunen's book on the isolated state, Der Isolierte Staat, describing the managerial operation of an agricultural estate, is one of the best examples in economics of deductive logic. He was one of the first economists to point out that transportation and transfer costs were prime factors in analyzing economic activities. In retailing, this idea is translated as customer conveniences in terms of driving time and distances involved in shopping. Von Thunen's concentric patterns of agricultural land usage are not unlike the various types of trading and industrial zones in present-day urban centers.

Another and much more recent approach to locational analysis was introduced by Alfred Weber. Weber pursued the evolutionary approach of what happens when people occupy an underdeveloped region. His analysis of the varying cost factors accompanying the development and growth of an economic system is quite similar to the economic changes that result when a regional shopping center is located in an "open" area.[18]

The Sales Forecast Method of Site Evaluation

In the sales forecast method of making the final decision to rent a location, the owner of the land attempts to protect himself against the risk of change by getting agreement to the longest possible lease, the highest minimum guarantee, and a fixed percentage return on all additional volume above a stipulated minimum. At the same time, the potential renter seeks to sign for the lowest possible guarantee and minimum rental, and secure a decreasing percentage charge (if this is required) for all sales in excess of the minimum volume guarantee.

---

[16] Coleman Woodbury, ed., The Future of Cities and Urban Development (Chicago: University of Chicago Press, 1953), p. 124.

[17] See Walter Isard, "The General Theory of Location and Space Economy," Vol. 43, Quarterly Journal of Economics (November 1949), pp. 476ff.

[18] William J. Reilly, op. cit., p. 9; A. M. Neilsen, Economic and Industrial Geography (New York: Pitman Publishing Company, 1950), pp. 650–680; and George T. Renner, "Geography of Industrial Locations," Economic Geography, Vol. 25, No. 167 (July 1947), pp. 168–172.

More specifically, the management of a variety store with a projected conservative volume of $150,000 for the first year of operation in a particular location may be asked for a $7,500 minimum rental guarantee. If the volume projection is sound, then $7,500 would represent a 5 per cent rental charge. Again referring to Table 7 (page 64), it is seen that the typical variety store lease ranges from 3 to 5 per cent. On this basis the projected initial conservative volume estimate of $150,000 would be adequate.

If the minimum rental guarantee is $10,000, however, then the store would have to generate at least $200,000 annually to be competitive. Should the entrepreneur feel that he could do only $180,000 the first year, then he must plan his over-all operations with a projected rental expense of 5.56 per cent. Unless research can project a volume of at least $200,000 by the end of the second year, then the store should probably not be leased.

A further example: a supermarket operator in a shopping center may agree to pay $15,000 annual rent for a 20,000-square-foot location with a stipulation for an additional payment of 1 per cent on all sales volume in excess of $1 million annually. Unless store management feels certain that the proposed location can easily generate the $1 million minimum, the site should probably not be leased.

Assuming that the decision is made to lease, then the merchandise lines must be selected with reference to the area's needs and the amount of square feet of selling space available in the store. Further, the equipment and fixtures needs in the store must be set up so that peak-period traffic can be easily handled. In most suburban locations 70 per cent of the traffic generally occurs about 30 per cent of the time. The investment required for necessary alterations in addition to fixtures and equipment should be evaluated to make certain that the "make-ready" costs would not be too great.

Over-all, the two types of expenses critical to a location decision are process costs (the expenses of shaping, sampling, and transforming an area into an attractive retail location) and transfer costs (the expenditures connected with buying, merchandising, and marketing certain classifications of products).

Regardless of the type of store involved, this is the kind of analysis and evaluation that must take place before any final commitments are made. And, in order for any business to be competitive, the store rent must be economic and in line with the projected volume for that location.

SUMMARY AND CONCLUSIONS

An optimum location is not a substitute for good management. Nor is it a substitute for the proper composition and distribution of tenancy and merchandise line offerings in a properly balanced proportion of shopping, specialty, and convenience goods. Locating in an area also requires a sense of social responsibility to the community. When uneconomic use is made of scarce land resources, then delivery, driving time, and competitive costs also tend to become excessive.

Once a location has been chosen, there is no one store and no one design which would be effective for all neighborhoods and situations. Today, new forms of competition, changing hours and manners of shopping, and rapidly changing values of particular locations have a very important bearing on all marketing and distribution costs.

In general, there are two types of site locations: in one—the larger, easily accessible center—the consumer is directly attracted to shop; in the second—the smaller, less accessible location generally found in a "string street"—mostly impulse and convenience-goods shopping takes place. Fortunately, most sizable retail locations combine both types of merchandise attractions.

The underlying social and economic considerations in location development are enormous. For example, the regional shopping center involves some 40 to 100 stores and serves as a "convenience" center for several hundred thousand people. An optimum location in terms of reasonable fixed costs relative to potential sales volume is necessary for efficient management. Marketing and retail distribution create driving-time distance, place and possession utilities. Two of these contributions—those of time and place—are primarily determined by location.

While location and land use theories have undergone radical changes during the last two decades, increasing population mobility and suburban dispersion have accelerated and increased the importance of the spatial facets of location analysis. Improved roads and increasing store and product substitution are still accelerating this trend. As a result, there will be continuing demand for new shopping centers, as well as refurbishing and remodeling of existing centers where warranted.

Location demand will always be fluid, because the three principal generative forces that influence shopping patterns are themselves in a constant state of flux. These forces are the population within a zone, the geographic location of a zone, and the degree of self-sufficiency within a zone.

Because retailers operate in a very highly competitive environment, the lease requirements are prime considerations. Unfortunately, most leases signed in a shopping center today are set at high rates plus a percentage of sales above a minimum level.

The landlord seeks this type of lease to protect himself against economic changes. This kind of lease is also a hedge against inflation, because the value of his property increases with increases in his lessee's sales. However, this kind of lease almost forces a high-mark-up operation on store management. Often managerial efficiency and effectiveness are also lessened because of large constant fixed expense.

Assuming success in securing an optimum location, it must be kept in mind that buying, selling, pricing, and promotion policies determine the value of a business as well as the value of the surrounding land.

In the next chapter, the factors underlying changing competitive practices and marketing strategies will be discussed, along with the effect of new social patterns as they affect buyer behavior.

Chapter 6: *Underlying Facets of Effective Competition and Market Strategy*

Modern retail management came of age during the transition from the boom years of the late 1920's to the great depression of the thirties. During the depression, management, faced with shrinking volume, rising expenses, and declining price levels, had to make effective and almost constant adjustments in order to survive. In many cases, only great organizational and managerial flexibility saved firms from bankruptcy. Those that remained generally proved profitable during World War II.

During the postwar period retail business gradually became "buyer's" rather than "seller's" markets. This period was also characterized by booms in residential construction, movement into the suburbs, and a general superabundance of goods, especially in hard lines; these factors added further to the social and economic dislocations built up during the war years. Despite the rise in consumer income and market demand, less efficient and marginal firms began to disappear quite rapidly because of the growing intensity of retail competition.

NEW SOCIAL AND ECONOMIC PATTERNS

Short-term market demand was increased still further as consumers began to accept credit extensions of all kinds at unprecedented rates; also, a constantly expanding middle-income group became much more characteristic of the population as a whole. This group today represents the new mass market.[1]

The largest single change in the broader macro-economic facets underlying our national economy has been the "stabilizing and directional" factors created by federal government expenditures. In 1961 these expenditures were approximately 19.7 per cent of net national product; in 1965 these constituted over 20 per cent of this total. Government expenditures will in all probability be even greater during the coming years—in contrast to 1929, when these expenditures represented approximately 1 per cent of net national product.[2] The accepted policy of both political parties is the prevention of economic stagnation through active participation with private enterprise in directing the economic course of the nation.

In the midst of these economic changes, all types of retail establishments have expanded into all kinds of areas, merchandise lines, and store operations in order to insure, as fully as possible, their long-run market positions. It has been in the setting of such competitive pressures that the so-called "retail revolution" and accompanying changes in market management and marketing strategy have been taking place.

One of the major changes in the structure of retail competition has been the decline in importance of central city shopping. In attempts to reverse such trends, government and cooperative efforts have been initiated to improve mass transportation facilities, to clear blighted areas adjacent to downtown districts and replace them with modern middle- and high-income apartments, to create more on- and off-street parking facilities, and to enlarge access to and egress from downtown shopping areas.

While many improvements such as these have been carried out, inconveniences (such as a decreasing availability of suitable parking facilities during peak periods) are still proving quite detrimental to downtown sales volume.[3] This kind of shopping impediment has accelerated the trends towards more localized purchasing of shop-

---

[1] Charles F. Schwartz and Robert E. Graham, Jr., "Personal Income by States, 1929–54," *Survey of Current Business* (September 1955), pp. 12–18. The new statistical series recording the income flow of individuals by states has involved the reworking of all statistics back to 1929. This new series developed by the National Income Division, Office of Business Economics, covers personal income flow of all sources. Using 1929 as a base year, the series shows a 233-per-cent increase in personal income from 1929 to 1954, a 263-per-cent change from 1940 to 1954, and a 451-per-cent increase to 1962. (From *Surveys* of August 1959, 1960, 1961, and Tables 4–70 of August 1962.)

[2] See *Survey of Current Business* (February and July 1962); in 1961 federal government expenditures totaled $97 billion, and net national product total was $492 billion. Some of the more specific control and directional efforts of the federal government in the pursuit of a national economic policy furthering a constantly increasing national product and a gradually rising price level are: price supports (on major crops), government loans of all kinds and sizes (home repairs, housing, small business, public works, civic improvements, grants in aid to public health, etc.), and tax privileges (mostly through accelerated depreciation rates, social security benefits, increasing unemployment compensation, and legislation on maximum hours, minimum wages, etc.).

[3] R. D. Entenberg, *The Changing Image of Downtown Department Stores in Pittsburgh— 1959–1964.* Research Studies (Pittsburgh Graduate School of Business, University of Pittsburgh), June 1964.

ping and specialty goods in suburban areas—despite their smaller merchandise assortments and selections.

In addition to the general improvements in central business districts, many of the larger department and specialty stores have found it necessary to enlarge and improve their existing downtown facilities while expanding geographically in order to meet the new competitive challenges in suburban areas.[4]

THE SUBURBAN MOVEMENT

Unquestionably, the most popular of all attempts by central city retailers to regain or improve market position has been geographical and suburban expansion. In most cases, suburban expansion has been necessary in order to gain access to the ever-widening perimeters of residential areas.

The development of shopping centers in response to changing residential and buying patterns has also furthered the trend toward less central and secondary business-district buying of shopping and specialty goods. In addition, the convenience of not needing to "dress up" in order to shop is apparently stabilizing this change in purchasing habits—especially in the case of young marrieds with small children. Most shopping-center promoters try, if it is at all feasible, to develop centers with a well-established department store or a departmentized specialty store as its chief focal point; when this can be done, the center has a proper drawing card for shopping and specialty-goods customers.

The belated movement of department stores into the suburbs has too often been initiated and fostered by real-estate interests and promoters whose research methods, in many cases, leave much to be desired. As a result, many shopping centers are located in marginal and uneconomic areas with inadequate access, inconvenient parking, and growing congestion; and those centers not optimally located are beginning to suffer from much the same types of area obsolescence as those found in downtown areas. For example, in research studies on what they dislike about shopping in these locales, many customers give the same answers regarding shopping centers as they do for the central business district.

TRENDS IN MARKET HOMOGENEITY AND FRAGMENTATION

Another underlying factor molding the nature of market competition has been a growing homogeneity in many sectors of the population. The impact of network television, high-speed communications, increasing impact on consumer tastes of national magazines, and increasing consumer mobility have all had varying effects on the nature of the retail market. On the surface, the increasing homogeneity of the mass market with respect to tastes, purchasing habits, and zones of residence

[4] Examples of such stores are: Rich's, Atlanta, Ga.; The F. & R. Lazarus Co., Columbus, Ohio; Foley Bros. Dry Goods Co., Houston, Texas; Kaufmann's, Pittsburgh, Pa.; and the May D. & F. store and Joslins, Inc. in Denver, Colo.

should make it much easier to predict changes in styles and fashions. Normally, this kind of trend should make longer production runs of mass-produced consumer goods definite possibilities. These possibilities have not materialized because of fragmentations in the mass market.

Sectional and social fragmentations in the mass market are beginning to appear, despite trends to conformity. For example, the older population group has become segmented into those still working and those actually retired; these two groups have different tastes, needs, and wants. There has also been a great increase in the number of working women over the age of forty-five who are, at the same time, consumers. A growing proportion of this group consists of widows and single women who work both full- and part-time—in many cases not out of necessity but to combat boredom.[5]

Another type of market fragmentation is being generated as the rush to the suburbs decelerates; many individuals and family groups are returning to the central city and its adjacent urbanized fringes to live. The heralded increases in leisure time, supposedly for recreational and holiday activities, are taken up more and more with commuting and business travel. To an increasing extent, leisure time is also being taken up with travel to and from work, shopping, and schools by both city dweller and suburbanite. As a result, the "do-it-yourself" market sales have been showing only moderate success.

Another underlying change has occurred in the increasing amount of consumer savings of both the liquid and forced varieties. Forced savings, of course, result from the purchase of high-priced durables on extended-time repayment bases and contribute to a higher standard of living. Liquid savings consist of cash or assets which can be quickly converted to cash.

Economic shifts such as these also have a direct bearing on customer tastes, preferences, and shopping habits. As a result, retail management has to make almost constant adjustments in its operating procedures and merchandising policies in order to remain competitive. In addition, lagging productivity and almost continuous narrowing of gross margins necessitates increasing degrees of organizational flexibility.

Because most of the changing market requirements are primarily the result of changes in consumer behavior, concepts from the behavioral sciences that have a bearing on buyer behavior are, more than ever before, being examined and evaluated for their application to the improvement of managerial effectiveness.

Some of the more pertinent concepts and techniques underlying purchase decisions and buying behavior will now be reviewed.

THE PURCHASING DECISION

By and large, at both the consumer and industrial levels, the decision-making processes as to whether to buy or not to buy flow in relatively the same procedural

---

[5] See Kenneth Schwartz, "Fragmentation of the Mass Market," *Dun's Review and Modern Industry*, Vol. 80, No. 1 (July 1962), pp. 31ff.

channels. The speed and nature of the purchasing process depends on the degree of competition in the market and the strategy used to implement it. For example, in the purchase of industrial goods—goods purchased for resale or to further production—the market strategy of sellers generally stresses the product advantages involved with specification buying and price and quality checks; and, where reciprocity buying may be a factor, this aspect of a potential sale may be discreetly suggested.

The purchasing decisions of the retail-store buyer, the commercial purchaser, or the industrial agent are only a part of several types of decision needed to attain organizational objectives. In addition, different values are stressed by sellers of such commodities. Consumers, too, weigh purchase alternatives in much the same manner as the agents of business firms. What, then, does differ between consumer and industrial buying are the underlying value scales and motivations.

At the consumer level, the decision to buy results in the actual fulfillment of a personal or family objective in terms of direct use, satisfaction, and well-being. At the commercial level, the decision to buy results in another step in furthering production.

BUYING MOTIVES AND MARKET STRATEGY

When groups of consumers can give definite reasons for purchasing specific products or patronizing a particular store, then guideposts for the establishment of store policies can be effectively set up; the store policies most directly affected are advertising appeals, both in mass media and at points of merchandise purchase. In fact, practically every aspect of successful market strategy and merchandising management depends directly on retail-store buyers correctly evaluating the basic motivational appeals underlying the buying decisions of the customers in their trading areas.

For example, many firms have taken high calculated risks in introducing the use of self-selection and simplified selling procedures for high-fashion and better-quality merchandise, when, for the most part, such operating techniques had been employed primarily in the sale of convenience and low-priced shopping goods.[6] Managerial decisions of this kind risk the loss of the service and prestige elements that are generally basic to continuing purchases of high-priced fashion and shopping goods.

The purchase decision of an individual buying something for ultimate consumption is often based on emotional as well as rational motives. The concept of economic man is often used as the standard of comparison in the analysis of buyer behavior; however, the economic-man comparisons assume that the individual has a fairly complete knowledge of the market, free choice, a limited supply of money, and a desire to maximize his satisfactions in terms of individual utilities.

When a consumer cannot give a definite reason for making a purchase, an

---

[6] Ohrbach's, New York City, is an example of this kind of operation.

emotional motive has generally brought him to a decision. In any kind of situation where it is difficult to discriminate as to what to purchase, the decision is likely to be prompted by an emotion. Yet, market strategy directed toward emotional buying appeals is avoided, because the consumer generally rejects direct appeals to his basic emotions. On the other hand, *indirect* appeals of this kind (with pictures, illustrations, and symbols) have proved to be effective market strategy.[7]

In a rationally oriented situation, the purchaser can give a definite reason for buying. For example, market strategy that ties in dependability, economy in use, money gain, convenience in use, or low purchase price to trigger a buying decision would be considered rational in nature. While such concepts are used as examples of the ultimate in rational buying, hidden motivations below levels of awareness often trigger the buying decision. An understanding of the hidden motivations underlying purchasing decisions is of prime importance in maximizing the effectiveness of managerial decisions at the retail level.

Market Strategy Based on Purchase Motivations

Rational motives generally underlie the purchase of most shopping goods; price comparisons are important to consumers of these kinds of goods. Thus, sales maximization of shopping goods would have to be primarily price-oriented with adequate quality and guarantee appeals. Some of the merchandise lines sold with these appeals are automobiles, refrigerators, stoves, washing machines, dishwashers, and television sets.

Brand name emphasis, trade-in allowances, and list and fair-trade pricing comparisons are also important in the sales promotion of these lines. If an item is fair-traded or sold at a fixed price, purchase appeals then revolve around credit arrangements, service, delivery, manner of handling guarantees, installation, and, of course, buying satisfactions. Buying satisfactions quite often result from good salesmanship as well as good products which are fairly priced.

When emotional motives trigger the buying decision, price generally becomes a relatively less important part of the sale. Products in this category may be said to have developed "specialty" characteristics, and consumers will go out of their way to shop for such merchandise.

Stores such as Neiman-Marcus in Dallas and Bergdorf Goodman in New York have developed strong patronage motives and personified "halo" images that encourage consumers to identify themselves with the store. The market strategy of prestige stores of this kind is to base their promotional appeals first around themselves and then around the merchandise they handle. Objectives and competitive strategy of this kind become increasingly difficult as greater numbers of competing stores in adjacent trading areas begin to handle larger amounts of similar and substitutable merchandise. In this process, stores attempt to differentiate themselves

---

[7] See Lincoln H. Clark, ed., *Consumer Behavior* (New York: Harper, 1958). Consumers' emotion is exploited by the linking of stores or products to appeals to prestige, emulation, individuality, conformity, pleasure, creativeness, etc.

and their offerings by placing constant stress on individuality, exclusiveness, service, and prestige.

Motivation Research

To differentiate in the midst of growing similarities of products and stores, management has made increasing use of motivation research techniques of all kinds. The tools of clinical psychologists—such as depth interviews, projective techniques, and focused group interviews—are used constantly in order to pinpoint more specifically the most effective promotional and advertising appeals.

Focused group interviews are attempts to determine group motivations of representative consumers' groups through informal "directed" discussions. The basic objective of these group interviews is to discover and rank the various buying motives according to their importance to the group.

In depth interviews, researchers seek to determine motivations that exist below the levels of awareness. Once discovered, the "hidden" motivations can then be projected into actual buying situations for use in market promotions.

For example: a respondent may state that he is in the market for a refrigerator; he is then asked what make he is thinking of buying, the approximate price, and why. In conversational interviewing, the consumer's opinions and beliefs may not be uncovered. Therefore, motivation research techniques are used. Techniques based on depth interviews, however, do not take into account in attempting to forecast future buying situations and relationships the many unforeseen and uncontrollable variables that enter the actual buyer-seller relationships. Projecting the possible effect of multiple price lines, varying types of credit facilities, new features, special pricing, new competition, and so on, is hazardous at best. Any or all of these variables may enter into the actual buying setting, thus negating the effectiveness of projective forecast techniques.

Consumption and Marketing Strategy

As shown in Part I, any evaluation of modern competitive practices should be carried out in terms of the functional unit of the firm—that is, with regard for all the functionaries involved and with a strong leaning toward consumer interest. Also, the field of retailing has been—and will continue to be—despite its tremendous size, predominantly local in character.

Competitive effectiveness and profit maximization may be said to be circular and almost interlocking in effect. Organizational efficiency is maximized only to the extent that policy decisions are based on the correct evaluation of the social and economic variables. The basic economic variables to be correctly evaluated are those that relate to consumer expenditure patterns.

For example, throughout 1961 consumer purchases of nondurable goods (such as food, beverages, tobacco products, drugs, and toilet articles) continued to show increase over 1960; on the other hand, spending for clothing and shoes did not begin to rise until mid-1961; and for the first time since 1948 service expenditures advanced at a less rapid rate. In 1961 consumer expenditures for automobiles, furniture, appliances, television, and other goods reached or exceeded all previous highs. The increase in household expenditures coincided almost directly with an increase in residential construction.[8] Retail management does not generally act on the basis of such definitive economic information. Unless the items are requested directly and continually by his store customers, his total product offer remains the same, regardless of economic trends. When he is finally faced with higher than average markdowns and an actual decline in volume, he will act positively on market information.

THE ECONOMICS OF CONSUMPTION

Economic studies of consumption-expenditure patterns have been conducted from time to time. One of the first "modern" studies for economic purposes was conducted in 1672 by Sir William Petty, who gathered data on the way in which the average workingman spent his family income. The purpose of his study was to determine the feasibility of trade with Ireland. Another study was undertaken by an English clergyman some one hundred years later to discover the expenditure patterns of agricultural workers in his parish in order to find out why they needed aid from the church.

In the nineteenth century, Frederic Le Play and Ducpétiaux were well known for their case studies of expenditure patterns of selected "typical" families. However, the first statistical study of family expenditure-income patterns was carried out by Ernst Engel in 1857.[9] Briefly, Engel's laws of consumption state that: (1) as family income increases, the smaller is the percentage of outlay for subsistence, and (2) the greater is the percentage of outlay for "sundries"; (3) and (4) whatever the income, the percentage of outlays for household operation (rent, heat, light, etc.) and for clothing remain approximately the same. While these laws may have been true a century ago, only two of these postulates—those relating to subsistence and sundries—hold true today.

Such patterns of expenditures can be confirmed in Table 10, which shows changes in consumer outlays with changes in income. As seen in this table, percentage of allocations for subsistence tends to decrease with increasing income, and the proportion spent for all other categories except that for clothing and accessories tends to remain relatively constant; however, dollar allocations for all commodity groups rise with increases in income.[10]

NATURE OF DEMAND ELASTICITIES

When particular classes of expenditures increase with increases in disposable personal income, these goods are said to have positive coefficients of sensitivity. When

---

[8] "Patterns of Consumer Spending," *Federal Reserve Bulletin*, April 1962, pp. 389–95.
[9] See Beckman and Maynard, *Principles of Marketing* (5th ed. New York, Ronald Press, 1952), pp. 92–99.
[10] *Life Study of Consumer Expenditures*, Vol. 1 (New York, Alfred Politz Research, Inc., 1957).

the demand for goods decreases as concomitant income increases, these goods may be said to have negative coefficients of sensitivity. Other categories of goods may have no income effect.

For example: as income increases, the demand for luxury goods, recreational equipment, and sundries tends to increase. Furniture, new cars, jewelry and watches, drug preparations, furs, and travel have high coefficients of sensitivity.[11] This concept is directly related to the economic concept of product-demand elasticity. Thus, the coefficient of sensitivity is the average per cent by which specific commodity expenditures change in relation to changes in disposable personal income.[12]

TABLE 10

INCOME AND EXPENDITURE BY HOUSEHOLDS IN THE UNITED STATES
(October 1955–December 1956)

	ANNUAL HOUSEHOLD INCOME						
	ALL HOUSE-HOLDS	UNDER $2,000	$2,000–$2,999	$3,000–$3,999	$4,000–$4,999	$5,000–$6,999	$7,000–$9,999	$10,000 OR MORE
Per cent of households	100%	18	14	15	19	20	9	5
Number of households (in thousands)	49,140	8,610	7,080	7,510	9,250	9,680	4,680	2,330
Average persons per household	3.3	2.7	3.2	3.4	3.4	3.6	3.7	3.8
Expenditures (in per cent)								
Food, beverages, & tobacco	29%	36%	33%	30%	29%	28%	26%	24%
Clothing & accessories	12	11	11	13	12	11	13	14
Medical & personal care	5	7	5	6	5	5	5	6
Home operation & improvement	19	17	20	18	19	19	18	18
Home furnishings & equipment	9	7	8	8	8	9	9	10
Recreation & recreation equipment	5	5	5	5	6	5	5	6
Automotive	14	11	13	15	14	16	15	15
Other goods & services	7	6	5	6	7	7	9	7
Total	100%	100%	100%	100%	100%	100%	100%	100%

Source: *Life Study of Consumer Expenditures*, Vol. 1 (New York City, Alfred Politz Research, Inc. 1957), pp. 18–20.

Basically, consumer demand and the intensity of competition at the retail level is determined by supply, distribution, and the manner in which the supply of goods is sold by retailers. In the long run, retail managers as well as all businessmen generally apply the particular pricing formulas best suited to the income and sectional characteristics of their communities. In this way, consumer demand is maintained so as to "clear the market" in terms of satisfactory stock turns.[13]

Consumer demand schedules are affected, then, by the relative extent of price changes in particular categories of goods, such as candy, toys, and canned goods.

[11] See Louis A. Paradiso and Mabel A. Smith, "Consumer Purchasing and Income Patterns," *Survey of Current Business* (March 1959), p. 25.
[12] Ibid.
[13] This is the number of times in the course of the year that merchandise inventories are replaced. This entire economic concept will be discussed in the chapter on inventory management.

Items such as sugar and salt are not in this group, as their demand is relatively inelastic and consumption of these commodities is not significantly affected by price changes. In the case of specialty goods—items for which consumers will go out of their way to shop—the demand is relatively stable except where very large changes in price have occurred.

However, consumer demand for standardized, easily substitutable items is often increased as the result of "price wars." The net effect of intense price competition is to raise the total primary demand for broad categories of products; facial tissues, antifreeze products, detergents, and automobiles are illustrative of goods the demand for which is often increased with almost commonplace price competition.

Demand for particular brands and specialty goods within such groupings, however, can be stimulated when there is a definite degree of product differentiation and a favorable trend in primary demand. Product innovation can also stimulate demand by stressing "hidden qualities" and emotional buying motives. Management must have sufficient money to carry out the planned promotional task, however, if particular product demand is to be sustained. Often, stress on brand names may be an important market factor—for example, "With a name like Smucker's, it has to be good." [14]

Income and Time-Demand Elasticity

In the short run, as real income increases, the level of living tends to remain constant until the recipients of the additional income increments learn to live in accordance with higher income levels. Also, as income increases, the average propensity to consume declines and the average propensity to save increases.

In determining competitive policy in the face of changes in income and propensities to consume, retail management must keep in mind that it is far more likely for income units to draw on savings in order to maintain a previously set level of living than to draw on savings or improved incomes in order to attain higher levels of living. Thus, the amount of savings in a community has a stabilizing effect on either increases or decreases in income. More importantly, the income effect on demand depends directly on the extent of its distribution among consumer spending units; the wider the income distribution, the higher the demand for luxury goods in a trading area.

As pointed out, credit acceptability is widespread throughout the economy. Lengthening the period of repayment for consumer expenditures increases purchasing power and the individual's short-run effective demand. Another factor facilitating the expansion of time-demand elasticity is the fact that many consumers think in terms of amounts of repayment schedules rather than in terms of total costs. When the time period granted for purchase repayment is extended, the average payment becomes smaller and the number of individuals that can afford

---

[14] D. E. Robinson, comments in interview on brand-name effects (August 7, 1965, Cleveland, Ohio). See also E. A. Pessemier, *Analyzing Demand for Branded Consumer Goods* (Pullman, Washington, Bureau of Economic Business Research, Washington State University, 1963).

the commodities becomes greater. Time extensions often have the same effect on sales as lowering prices. In other words, when the time period for repayment can be extended, then upward changes in the price of a commodity generally does not result in a decrease of its sale. This is especially true in the case of high-price durables, such as homes, major appliances, automobiles, and furniture.

Cross Elasticity of Demand

When prices of commodities change, the demand schedules for these commodities as well as for substitutable products also shift. For example, many consumers purchase fresh oranges whenever reasonably available. However, during the course of the year consumers substitute apples, peaches, or plums should their prices be low in relation to the price of oranges. Again, when apples are in short supply and the price goes up, the demand for peaches or plums would increase if their prices decreased or remained relatively constant in relation to the price of apples. The concept and measurement of such changes is known as the cross elasticity of demand. This concept has been well illustrated by Stigler: [15]

Let X = Cross elasticity of demand for peaches (X)
Let Y = The price of apples (Y); then:

$$\frac{\% \text{ change in quantity of } X}{\% \text{ change of price of } Y}$$ results in the cross elasticity of demand for peaches equated in terms of the price of apples.

In retail markets, cross elasticities of demand are encountered in the substitutability of piece-goods materials, in the purchase of used cars, and especially in consumer choices in the purchase of soaps and detergents. In supermarket studies of detergent purchase preferences of consumers, controlled observations show that consumers look for and seek out "trend" because of a real price advantage in the midst of oligopolistically priced items.[16]

The actual rate of change in the cross elasticity of demand depends, of course, on the marginal rate of product substitution. Product substitution is one of the basic parameter frameworks in which consumers make their purchasing decisions. Every retail firm, unless it can boast "exclusive" specialty distribution (in lines such as Steuben glassware or Brooks Brothers suits), must carefully consider and evaluate the marginal rate of product and store substitution in setting up its pricing policies.[17]

During normal times, very few long-run scarcities and seller's markets exist in the American economy. It follows, therefore, that consumer demand and market

---

[15] See George R. Stigler, op. cit., pp. 35–36.
[16] R. D. Entenberg, unpublished research studies on consumer behavior (Memorandum, Graduate School of Business, University of Pittsburgh), June 1964.
[17] See S. C. Hollander, "Entrepreneurs Test the Environment; A Long Run View of Grocery Pricing," American Marketing Association, Proceedings, September 1965. Dr. Hollander points out that the grocery trade is never quite in equilibrium, as he describes the constant change and experimentations constantly taking place in the industry. He gives excellent examples of the way in which—while not stating it as such—cross elasticities of demand influence pricing strategy in this industry.

competition rather than any conditions in the nature of supply are the all-important determinants of pricing and marketing strategies. Although certain products or brands may be temporarily unavailable or too high in price, consumer mobility and product substitutability serve to eliminate supply or locational monopolies. For example, when the amount offered for a trade-in toward the purchase of a new car is considered inadequate, the potential buyer may go to other dealers in the community or to dealers in an adjacent city to seek what he would consider a fair exchange price.

Effective demand for a particular product depends directly on the extent of its differentiation from substitutable products, the existing prices of other products, and expectations about relative changes in the price level. The interaction of supply in terms of substitutable commodities and the competitive effectiveness of the institutions that supply these commodities is, thus, one of the major determinants of price and the nature of consumer demand.

EFFECT OF SCRAMBLED MERCHANDISING

Another increasingly important determinant of price is the effect of impulse demand created by scrambled merchandising. It is again mentioned in this context because of its still growing importance. For example: shoe stores no longer confine themselves to the handling of shoes alone; most variety and drug stores, because of their wide assortments and varied price lines, should be classified as junior department stores; nonfoods in supermarkets are becoming much more important in relation to the total supermarket sales volume.

One of the catalytic factors in this type of merchandise competition stems from commodity scarcities that prevailed during World War II. In that period many specialty stores that handled hard lines such as appliances and housewares had to introduce soft-line merchandise such as underwear and sporting goods in order to have something to sell. When, in the postwar period, merchandise again became available many retailers continued to carry nonrelated, scrambled lines in order to achieve greater market security through broadened merchandise appeals.

The over-all competitive effect of this type of merchandising has proved somewhat chaotic for many retailers and confusing for many consumers. In many cases, stores engaging in such merchandising policies often carry inadequate selections, and the lines must be supplemented and coordinated or merchandising stagnation and chaotic pricing result. As an illustration, the woman who purchases a daytime dress in a supermarket would have a severely limited selection from which to choose. Only low cost and rotation of merchandise, which generally only the more alert chains can manage, prevents excessive markdowns and uneconomic stock turns.

SUMMARY AND CONCLUSIONS

In this chapter some of the more important underlying facets of effective competition and marketing strategy were presented. Some rational concepts of economic man were discussed, along with emotional motivations that affect buying behavior. Also reviewed were applications of both economic analysis and social psychology to the development of selective demand and effective competition.

It was pointed out that the basic appeal of any retail organization is determined by its management policies. The effectiveness of these policies in turn is determined by the manner in which management is able to evaluate and apply the pertinent results of behavioral and market research. Management's well-judged motivation of potential customers should result in greater demand for goods and in increased sales.

Managerial effectiveness depends to a great extent also on the type of image it is able to project for its organization. The store image represents the basic appeal of the retail organization. It is the net result of all public, private, customer, and employee contacts made by any individuals associated with the store and the effect of the total store organization as an entity. The store image is the cornerstone on which the long-run success of the business must rest.

The locale of a store also influences its marketing strategy and competitive effectiveness. This is especially true in the case of the smaller or medium-sized store. A smaller establishment depends to a large extent on the "circular" effect of the stores making up its cluster group for its store image and community acceptability.

The total number of firms in any trading area is another underlying facet of market strategy and competitive effectiveness. The fewer the number of competitors in any specific market, the greater the degree of interaction and interdependence among them. In the field of retail distribution, there is apt to be far less interdependence among firms because of consumer mobility, large number of competitors and relative ease of entry into the field.

Retail management operates in a dynamic, fast-moving setting where the profit criterion can be quickly determined. Managerial behavior in retail markets can be explained in terms of marginal analysis. Marginal analysis, whether labeled as such or not, is always used in connection with the profit criterion. Management alternatives in this respect are employed primarily with controllable variables such as advertising, pricing, personal selling, and merchandise line offerings. The manipulation of these controllable variables determines the store's competitive practices and resulting sales and profits. Demand analyses and action resulting from price, income, and time and product cross elasticities also determine an area's market structure.

Because consumers are numerous, complex, and generally not well informed, the key to maximizing sales and profits is an evaluative understanding of buyer behavior. Consumer attitudes and their change over time, the influences of small groups, and social stratifications of the market are also integral factors underlying competitive practices and market strategy. Retail managers who base their strategy, organizational decisions, and conclusive actions on the evaluation and analyses of these basic considerations are the ones most likely to improve their long-run market positions and profit margins.

The manner in which locational factors and market competition limit the scope of management planning and strategy was reviewed in this chapter and in Chapter 5. In the chapter that follows, adaptation to change and some of the more pertinent aspects of decision making and problem solving in carrying out the work of retailing are analyzed.

Chapter 7: *Adaptation to Change: Problem Solving, Decision Making, and Operational Analysis*

Price competition is not the exclusive province of discount houses. Nor are customer services and extra accommodations the exclusive province of the so-called "traditional" department and specialty stores. Further, discount houses have not taken over, nor will they take over, as the major factor on the American retail scene. The only norm is the certainty of continuing and almost constant change. This, then, is the framework to which management must continually adapt.

Retail management must also be aware of and be able to evaluate correctly all changes in competitive trends. For example, the obvious successes of supermarkets, chain stores, and discount houses have tended to overshadow the continuing development and expansion of independent retail stores into larger units.

THE CHANGING EXTERNAL SETTING

One example of an external change that directly affects retail management is the tremendously improved financial position of the average consumer, despite decreases in the purchasing power of the dollar. In effect, the consuming-spending units in the American economy are growing ever more rapidly into Warner's "middle majority" social class,[1] which comprises about 65 per cent of the total population.

Further, the average wage-earner today has a higher educational level and earns a far higher income in far less time. This has created the necessity for the development of, among other things, more leisure-time wearing apparel. He is far more discriminating, has more paid holidays and more vacations, but he has still not learned how to relax. At the same time he seeks more and more "total" conveniences.[2] The consumer today also has greater amounts of liquid assets and is in a very favorable position to assume the burden of additional installment and charge-account debt. This is an area where demand creation can achieve a most profitable return, an area that responsible retail management cannot ignore.

Consumer surveys at the Retail Research Center and the Division of Research of the Universities of Pittsburgh and Denver (1960–1966) show that style, comfort, and store service can be far more important than price in triggering purchase decisions. It is also recognized that price alone does not account for the success of the discount house. The so-called retail revolution and the success of the cut-price stores are the result of furnishing customer conveniences along with wanted merchandise and services "at a price."

The independent retailer, because of his great flexibility, can offer the customers more variations, better service, and more new items almost as soon as they become available. This is one of the great strengths of the independent. Supermarkets, chains, and discount houses do not attempt to compete on such bases. However, the successful practice of one firm in a competitive market soon finds acceptance and becomes a "competing" practice by firms in the same market.

Successful retail managers constantly seek to apply sound economic principles to meet changing requirements in the market place and to apply deductive reasoning from accepted generalizations. When this reasoning takes place, results directly reflect the persistent attitudes and resourcefulness of supervising executives.

Implications of the External Setting

The point being made is that retail management demands a high degree of ability in order to meet the variegated and constantly changing problems in the field. For example, strategic planning is needed to meet changes such as unparalleled customer mobility, new purchase patterns, changing shopping habits, and completely altered composition and income levels of the population in the midst of suburban and urban mobility. This planning must be formulated in terms of the organizational structure's ability to meet such changes. If the organization cannot do so, then it should be reconstructed.

---

[1] See William L. Warner et al., Social Class in America (Chicago, Science Research Associates, 1949).

[2] From a paper presented by J. Rogers Flannery, Jr., architect and management consultant, to store principals of the Atkins buying group (Hot Springs, Arkansas, April 1962).

The external factors of change can have a serious effect on the competitive market position of any firm whose management does not take into account the underlying social and economic conditions promoting change. For example, the operating policies of many stores have remained essentially unchanged over the years—despite continuing losses in their share of their market. A reappraisal of competitive market position pinpoints many bases for action; this is only one type of continuing analysis that should be undertaken and maintained by any progressive management. In this case, when a firm's merchandise sales show decreases in relation to national or regional sales of the same merchandise lines, remedial managerial action is indicated.

Sociological and Psychological Considerations

Other implications of the external setting are the elements of time, money, and nervous energy expended in getting to many downtown and suburban locations; these are disutilities that must be overcome or minimized if sales are to be improved. The first measures of success in this direction would be determined by how well the elements of convenience have been built into the store image and the extent to which the "convenience" offer has been projected to the shopper. For example, the store layout, by inculcating the customer with a sense of ease, well-being, and relaxation, can help project an image of convenience as well as desirability.

Other convenience factors include the type of dress shoppers are expected to wear in particular locales (i.e., downtown versus suburbs), the number and age of children that can conveniently accompany one or both parents on a shopping trip, and the homogeneity of the consumer groups representing the trading area's social milieu.

Today, shopping centers and downtown modernizations are planned with primary emphasis on convenience; in addition, the retailer is increasingly stressing his social role in the community by offering auditoriums and other modes of convenient meeting places within the store to customer groups. Management's recognition of functional convenience represents a return to the "old-fashioned" concepts of encouraging high degrees of social intercourse in the market place.

FUNCTIONS OF EXCHANGE, SUPPLY, AND FACILITATION

All the sequential and interlocking functions included in the movement of goods from the producer to the consumer for the purpose of ultimate consumption can be delineated as follows:[3]

---

[3] See T. N. Beckman and W. R. Davidson, *Marketing* (7th ed. New York: Ronald Press, 1962), pp. 40–44. Each of these functions will be taken up in detail in later chapters so that the entire process of effective management of each of these major functions can be analyzed fully.

The Functions of Exchange
    1. Buying
    2. Selling

The Functions of Supply
    3. Storage
    4. Transportation

The Facilitating Functions
    5. Standardization
    6. Grading
    7. Marketing and consumer research
    8. Financing

All these activities are found in varying degrees in every business selling a product or a service and are pervasive throughout the marketing-retailing processes. The corner grocer performs these functions, as does the department store or large mercantile corporation—the main difference being the degree of sophistication and risk.

The functions of exchange are carried out by the merchandising division; the primacy of this division is unquestioned because it is generally the only one producing actual income. The merchandising division is generally headed by the top administrative officer, sometimes titled the executive vice-president of the firm. A more common title is general merchandise manager. The type of merchandise to be bought and the price lines to be handled are usually set by the merchandise manager of the firm. Sometimes advice about supplementary acquisitions may also come from the fashion coordinators and trend forecasters.

The facilitating functions of standardization and grading are also part of the merchandise manager's job. Standardization is a general term that refers to the establishment of norms for products; inspection and grading of the product against the norm is also part of this function. Standardization is important because it makes the merchandise easier to sell. If the customer knows it to be of reliable quality or easily serviced, he will continue to buy easily and with confidence.

The gathering of facts about the product (what competitors have and how much, price data, service back-up, etc.) and about the market (consumer purchasing power, where the consumers are located and their number, their motivations and preferences) is essential to many of the major decisions that retail managers must make. The better the research in such areas, the better the decisions about manpower and work-load needs. Other areas of research include evaluations of the effects of capital expansion, promotional expenditures, merchandise pricing, and whether and where a new branch store should be established.

Transportation and storage are obviously necessary. Goods must be moved to and stored in a location where they will be readily accessible for sale. These functions are generally administered by an operating vice-president or superintendent. Also included in the superintendent or store manager's province are personnel management, housekeeping, materials handling, store operation and protection, and traffic flows both within and out of the store.

The merchandising information and market research functions, along with the functional management of advertising, public relations, and sales promotion, are generally handled by a vice-president in charge of publicity. In smaller firms, these activities may often be handled by a sales promotion or advertising manager with very important staff advice emanating from the merchandise manager.

The company treasurer supervises the financial, credit, and control operations within the store and acts in a staff advisory capacity to the store in general. Financing and risk taking are, of course, directly correlated with inventory and other working capital needs.

Effect of Size on Functional Interrelationships

The environment determines the merchandising needs of the retail organization. In turn, the merchandise lines handled determine the over-all policies, marketing strategy, and the kind of functional management that is needed. Where the firm is of sufficient size to warrant separate executives for the needed functions to be performed, functional interaction at all levels in the organization occurs. This is because of the personal nature of most of the economic processes involved in retailing. For instance, the completion of a retail sale involves integration of all functional areas both of sales preparation and sales support. Functional interrelationships in retail firms tend to contain elements of continuing competitive stress at all managerial echelons. For example, if an organization has a strong controller, his activities may take on a "line" control aspect over total store operations rather than that of an over-all supervisory staff function. In effect, the larger the organization, the greater the degree of specialization needed and the more likely that a functional separation of activities will exist. At the same time, the larger the organization, the greater the need for administrative management and coordination for the various divisional segments within the firm.

CROSS-FUNCTIONALIZATION IN THE ORGANIZATION STRUCTURE

In any discussion of the managerial functions necessary to meet changing market requirements, it would be well to set forth again a basic principle of marketing: that it is always possible to eliminate the middleman, but never his function. As business firms grow, they tend initially to integrate and combine operations rather than specialize. As a result, multiple functions are performed by individual executives.

Vertical integration is the ownership of various stages of manufacture or distribution. The automobile firm that processes the steel from mine to assembly line and makes its own spark plugs, glass, tires, and upholstery for its end product would be vertically integrated. By such means, a company has direct control over its source of supply and can dictate what it wants in quality, delivery intervals, and service, with the possibility of general lower over-all costs. The problem in such integration is the high quality and quantity of management talent needed. Such a framework would require a large capital investment and would provide unnecessary independence as a source of supply, with little or no flexibility in times of emergency. Also, it is often the case that outside suppliers specializing in only one product are more efficient and produce a better product because of more specialized research than would be possible in the multiproduct plant.

Vertical integration extended away from production and into marketing means that the company makes the product and sells it through its own stores. An example of this type of vertical integration is Timely Clothes, a Rochester, New York, manufacturer of better men's suits and clothing, that bought a chain of eight retail outlets in the Los Angeles area in order to guarantee themselves a retail outlet for their products. Another example is the direct sale on a house-to-house basis of the Fuller Brush Company or Avon Cosmetics. Very strong control over the total sales effort is the result. Company-owned or leased stores, such as the Firestone Stores of the Firestone Tire and Rubber Company, provide another example.

In any integrated, direct-sale method a high degree of cross-functionalization is found, since representatives or employees of the producer are performing the production as well as marketing functions. Thus, the functions performed by a single individual might be diametrically opposed to each other. Because integration is generally directly related to size of firm, it can be said that the degree of cross-functionalization in an organization varies directly with its size. The greater the number of conflicting functions and goals that an individual has to perform, the lower his effectiveness.

On the other hand, horizontal integration (the combination of plants or operations that handle similar products or operate at the same stages in the distribution process) lessens the possibility of all units having bad business at the same time. Also, horizontal integration means more over-all market security. Many businesses combine both vertical and horizontal integration—as in the case of the large chains that vertically control most of the steps in the manufacture of many of their standard commodities, but at the same time have many different types of sales organizations and outlets that present different appeals and store images in various markets.[4]

It may be concluded, then, that duplication of the same functions may be undertaken by different individuals within the firm, or two sets of functions may be performed by a single individual. This is the essence of the type of cross-functionalization that can occur and that must be avoided whenever possible.

THE INFORMAL ORGANIZATION STRUCTURE

Cross-functionalization within an organization can also be seen in the informal organizational structures existing in most retail firms. In these cases, undirected functional duplications take place. Organization charts and manuals describing the various functional divisions within the firm are commonplace with the larger retail firms, although the content of organization manuals has almost infinite variations from one company to another. The primary purpose of organizational manuals

---

[4] For example, department-store groups such as the Federated Department Stores have multiple budget operations and smaller department store chains appealing to lower-income groups of consumers.

and charts is to describe the company's operating structure so as to facilitate action and guide and coordinate employees' efforts in their daily tasks.

Beneath the surface of every formal organization there is an intricate network of communication and relationships among the people who perform the basic functions of production, distribution and selling, and financing. The formal organization determines the scope of the informal organization, by fixing the structure within which personal associations achieve continuity and remain reasonably consistent. The study of such formal and informal interactions is popularly called "human relations"—in effect, the manner in which people cooperate to produce a product or a sale. This term also refers to the development of a social community within the firm. When a social community evolves, one finds different strata and prestige levels and cliques or groups that are not pictured on the chart. These groups fluctuate in importance and level of activity each time a member leaves or another enters into the group. Thus groups within groups change and adapt to change themselves.

It must be kept in mind that good wages and security do not fully meet the needs of employees that arise as physical and subsistence-level needs are satisfied. Therefore, management must understand the sentiments and attitudes of the employees in order to develop and maintain an effective organization. An awareness of the social ramifications of any group and a realization that the work place is not just a spot where a certain number of people work for a living will result in increased satisfaction for the managers and employees. The need for this awareness is especially true as the formal organization becomes larger; then an employee's contact with his firm is only through others in his immediate working relationship.

The close working relationships so characteristic of the retail processes induce a natural informal cross-functionalization in the performance of daily activities; this cross-functionalization involves almost all managerial divisions and echelons. It is not at all uncommon for middle management to perform supervisory activities actually assigned to other areas of control; for example, department buyers will often guide floor superintendents in making adjustments in nonassigned areas.

In facilitating functional performance the informal organizational structure provides additional communication by simplifying:

(a) the complexity of purpose and technological conditions;

(b) the difficulty of the communication processes;

(c) the extent to which communication is necessary; and

(d) the complexity of the personal relationships involved—that is, the social conditions.

In addition, the informal organization helps maintain cohesiveness in the formal organization by regulating the willingness to serve, stabilizing respect for authority, and helping to maintain the feeling of personal integrity, self-respect, and independent choice of all associated with the firm.[5]

---

[5] See Chester I. Barnard, *The Functions of the Executive* (Cambridge, Mass.: Harvard University Press, 1960), p. 122.

Because of the extreme effectiveness of the flow of information within the informal organization, a concerted effort should be made by each retail organization to insure that the goals of the various informal organizations are guided into general conformance with the goals of the firm. An effective way in which this can be accomplished is for the top executive to periodically view the entire operation with concern for only the communication channels.[6]

While the function of reinforcement of personal attitudes is often deemed destructive of formal organization, it should be regarded as a means of maintaining the personality of the individual against certain effects of formal organizations that tend to disintegrate the personality. The rapid development of an informal organization structure is a fact of life in retailing—more so than in any other business field except in service sales organizations.

Staff Parallelism and Functional Duplication

The development of an informal organization leads to staff parallelism and duplication at most supervisory and middle management echelons. Unfortunately, such developments tend to become institutionalized into a nonproductive aspect of a firm's over-all cost structure. This is one of the key reasons that lowering the cost aspects in the profit squeeze of many retail firms is so difficult a task. Once a functional duplication is institutionalized, it becomes accepted and difficult to correct.

An example of this might be the case of an old-line employee who, over the years, has taken it upon himself to reorder staples needed in his department. Since the buyer is the one formally charged with buying, a functional duplication exists. Unfortunately, staff duplication results in a dual hierarchy, and is a natural follow-up of functional growth; thus, overlapping of management is also often hidden within the organization. As an organization's sales volume increases, business functions tend to become deceptively complex and technical. The nature of most market organizations is such that constant action and interaction occur at all organizational levels. With rapid growth, the administrative coordination of line and staff operations in any firm involves constant reappraisal and control to be sure it remains effective. This is generally easier said than done, because planning for optimum marketing strategy within the pressures of any highly competitive setting is always challenging.

The better the firm is organized, the better are its communications; the higher its morale, then, the less important is its informal organizational structure. On the other hand, the less effective the retail organization, the poorer are its communications; and the lower its morale, the slimmer its growth and profit potentials.

Naturally, it is impossible to provide formally for every potential situation. For example, a section manager may see merchandise improperly displayed or a merchandise manager may see customers unsuitably provided for at a service desk;

---

[6] N. E. McNeill, *A Study of the Decision Making Process and Flow of Information Within the Retail Organization* (being published by Retail Research Institute of the NRMA, New York, 1966).

the section manager may take it upon himself to suggest to the buyer or department manager that it be corrected; likewise, the merchandise manager may step in to see that the customer is satisfied.

Should a buyer or his assistant follow through with a section manager's suggestion, a pattern may be set up for continuation of supervisory efforts of this kind. Should a section manager's suggestion be discarded, then the section manager could report the situation upward to the store superintendent. The store superintendent could then bring the matter to the store manager for action or make the suggestion directly to the merchandise manager involved, provided there was sufficient interdepartmental rapport.

In other words, it is generally far simpler and more efficient and expedient in many instances to listen to and cooperate with direct suggestions, regardless of stipulated authority or responsibility in the formal organization.

THE ECONOMICS OF TRADE

The successful retail store organization is the one that can adapt most easily and quickly to changing requirements resulting from changes in consumer needs and wants. For instance, the consumer is less dependent than formerly on deteriorating inter- and intra-city transportation systems. This means that stores must always be alert to providing new means of access to and egress from their shopping areas in order to remain competitive and improve the long-run market position. Stores located at public transportation system hubs tend over time to lose their locational monopolies; such stores must therefore place greater stress on developing new methods of easy access to the store.

Increasing unionization and widely distributed national brands tend to further "sameness" in retail stores. Local legislation and ordinances help further this trend. Greater conformity in hours when stores are open is also in evidence. As similarity trends in retail stores increase and markets change more rapidly, management will have to find new ways to appeal to consumers.

Price comparison of similar types of merchandise is a very difficult task, even for the informed customer. Faced with the options of trading stamps, private brands, and advertised cut-price inducements, consumers have additional difficulty in deciding where to stop and shop. While shopping choices of this kind are typical of a buyer's market, the impact of the total store image is becoming a more important facet of building and solidifying customer patronage.

MATCHING CONSUMER AND ORGANIZATIONAL GOALS

As pointed out, the store image influences and is influenced by merchandising policies. To be effective merchandising policies must conform to the dictates of the changing economics of trade. And the long-run success of any retail organization varies directly with the effectiveness of its merchandising policies.

In discussing the economics of trade, it should be pointed out that manufacturers attempt to mold the merchandising policies of retail firms. For example, manufacturers of highly advertised, branded merchandise feel that their products require little or no selling effort on the part of the retailer. In such cases, the producer looks at the retailer as merely a processing stock-keeper for presold merchandise. Thus, many brand-name manufacturers defend lower list-price mark-ons as fully justified—especially in the convenience goods areas.

Nevertheless, it is display and shelf space in high traffic areas that often determines the volume and extent of convenience goods sales. Convenience goods are available in almost all types of retail stores; growing availability of similar types and brands of merchandise has become commonplace. Consequently, low profit margins on goods readily available cause the retailer to shift emphasis to similar merchandise carrying higher mark-ons.

Again, when convenience goods are fair-traded, price cutting often comes into vogue, as hard-pressed retailers seek to bolster declining sales. In this case, the retail firm is provided with an "umbrella" pricing pattern that leaves adequate room for price cutting.[7] Such lines are generally sold by the manufacturer directly to the retailer. The manufacturer-retail cycle in these cases is very short, and sales feedback has to be much faster if it is to prove useful.

By-passing the normal channels of distribution by both consumers and retailers is another aspect of the changing economics of trade. Management, in attempting to be as flexible as possible in meeting new consumer wants, has had to adopt an almost completely functional approach in order to minimize channel by-passing. Warehouse sales to give a store a "discount" or "wholesale" flavor are examples of cyclical matching of store policies to consumer behavior through functional adjustments. Thus, management develops solutions to business problems by using general economic analyses in all functional areas. Generalized economic analysis in this context means matching needs to want-satisfying utilities within the framework of a total systems approach.

THE ROLE OF DECISION CENTERS

A new concept in meeting change on a continuing basis is the use of a systems approach to problem solving. The systems approach essentially involves the development and use of decision centers for most functional areas within the store. With this approach, policy formulation and administration are no longer based on narrow concepts of functional field specialization, because decision vari-

---

[7] "Fair-Trade" is "permissive" legislation which permits a contract to be entered into by a manufacturer of a branded good and a retailer. The retailer agrees to sell the branded good at a fixed "fair-trade" price. Legislation of this kind permitting vertical price-fixing was eventually passed by forty-five states under the Miller-Tydings Act in 1937; this Act was invalidated and repassed in essentially the same form by Congress, and is now known as the McGuire Act (1951). Many state courts have outlawed the use of such legislation for price fixing in the market place. Both fair-trade and unfair-sales legislation will be discussed in detail in later chapters on government and business.

ables that in the past were considered basic and fundamental no longer adequately serve as guides for problem solving, decision making, and managerial action.

Decision Centers Within the Retail Organization

Instead of considering the chain of command of the retail firm as a static organizational structure, the modern management systems concept regards each functional operation as either a single decision area or part of an over-all decision center. The size of the firm is deterministic.

Decision centers can lie on various levels, such as an over-all planning center, a merchandise management center, or a store coordination center, all associated with an over-all general management center for action. The industrial engineering staff is tied to these various centers in a staff capacity; the logistics involved in an engineering approach to departmental management and operation is constantly increasing in importance.[8]

The capabilities of computers can be extended to make decisions based on qualitative nonlinear data. This is carried out by simulating the thought processes of human managers on a probability basis. By this means, a heuristic nonlinear program is set up.

> There is now good reason to believe that the processes of nonprogrammed (heuristic) decision making will soon undergo as fundamental a revolution as the one which is currently transforming programmed decision making in business organizations. Basic discoveries have been made about the nature of human problem solving. While these discoveries are still at the stage of fundamental research, the first potentialities for business application are beginning to emerge.[9]

However, in retail distribution, a static market or a set framework must be assumed. As a result, a great deal of initial adjustment must be made. But since the retail structure is so highly volatile and dynamic, effective adjustments are rarely possible. In the past, the manufacturers of a product or a service were the ones to determine how it should be promoted and sold. Today, market segmentation and fragmentation has created an almost infinite number of avenues of approach to promotional and marketing policies—especially in the areas of demand creation, sales, and consumer satisfaction. This is the essential objective of basing a marketing plan on strategy developed not from a manufacturer's or a distributor's viewpoint but rather from the standpoint of the consumer.

By using more pertinent consumer-oriented information, the total marketing plan is likely to be set up on a much more productive basis. In a sense, the proper

---

[8] An engineering approach is one in which the tools, techniques, and methods of the industrial engineer are used in making policy decisions in plant layout, materials flow, storage, and warehousing. For example, a well-engineered layout permits a maximum exposure of goods to all possible customers at a single location. This approach is reviewed in detail in Chapter 8.

[9] Herbert A. Simon, *The New Science of Management Decision* (New York: Harper and Brothers, 1960), p. 21.

use of information technology and all its potential applications is one of the keys to efficient progress in making trade more economic.

Other volatile changes in the market place are taking place in the areas of management of merchandise and management of operations, both of which overlap in all sizes and kinds of stores. The net result of such overlapping is increased costs of operation. For example, supermarkets, which at one time had the lowest cost of operation of any type of retail establishment, now have, in many cases, uneconomic cost structures; this is the result of functional overlapping and expansion into marginally located stores. Supermarkets that expanded extensively into nonfoods have found that their over-all cost of operation increased because of lower turnover and the additional responsibilities of handling more specialized and less familiar merchandise lines. Decisions of these kinds will be reviewed in the section on over-all planning.

To overcome functional allocation problems in less familiar merchandise areas, supermarkets use "rack jobbers" (wholesalers) to operate unfamiliar merchandise departments and new classifications. Frequently, many of these foods firms, once they become familiar with the lessors' operating methodology, take over and operate previously leased departments themselves—often disadvantageously. Often the better equipped and more forward-looking of these wholesale rack jobbers, when dislocated by lessees, open competing stores.[10]

Managerial Action Through Decision Centers

In addition to providing a better means of practical economic analysis, decision centers serve as processing centers for managerial action. Such centers are needed because available information has grown at a far greater pace than any individual manager's ability to utilize such information for decision making. As a result, almost complete rethinking and redirection with respect to the scope of administrative management is taking place. Managerial decisions are being made to an increasing extent on the judgment of integrated groups of specialists. By such means new theories of communications, control, and human behavior are being created.

Within decision centers, functional specialization can still be creative and productive. Integrated decision making provides excellent feedback to functional specialists, particularly in conjunction with pertinent applications to over-all organizational problems. For example, when the sales of budget-type merchandise in a store are decreasing while sales of higher-priced "upstairs" store merchandise is increasing, the problem involves much more than one area of functional management. The availability of a decision center for solving interdepartmental problems facilitates an adequate solution.

---

[10] In Pittsburgh, Pa., the management of the independent White Cross discount "drug" stores was formerly geared to service supermarket chains on a rack jobber basis. Their competition with supermarkets has been so great, due to price cutting on standard national brands, that many markets exerted pressure on manufacturers either to stop selling or to uphold fair trade where applicable. Sunbeam, Zenith, and Gillette Safety Razor Company have been engaged in this kind of litigation.

SUMMARY AND CONCLUSIONS

In this chapter some of the more pertinent changes in consumer purchasing patterns and managerial effectiveness in meeting these changes were reviewed. The indispensable functions of exchange, supply, and facilitation in carrying out the work of retailing were reviewed with a reminder that, while the middleman could always be eliminated, his functions never could.

The role of the informal organizational structure was examined from the standpoint of its effect on informational flows, both upward and downward. At the same time, its influence on integrated decision making at all levels in the organization was reviewed.

The economics of trade in managerial decision making was also analyzed in light of its changing requirements for effective management performance. Problem solving, decision making, and actionable conclusions are the bases used in maximizing a firm's long-run market position. There is not, nor is there likely to be, a single theory on classical economics and management science, or a single theory of the firm which can be applied to all decision making. Nor is there likely to be a sufficiently conclusive single philosophy of management that can be universally applied.

The dynamic processes of production and consumption in a complex modern society require general rather than fixed economic concepts for maximizing organizational efficiency. The concept of adaptation to change applies to scholars, practitioners, and students in the field, as well as business leaders. More specifically, adaptation to change involves continuing critical evaluation and analyses of changing market structures, organizational processes, management techniques, and over-all goals.

A "rethinking" of formal organization charts listing chains of command and channels of communications is good review. By such means, optimal decisions can be generated and carried out. In the chapter that follows, the operation of functional management within the organizational structure is examined.

Part Three

The Internal Setting:
Organizational Structure
Areas of Flexible Management Control

Chapter 8: *Functional Management Within the Organizational Structure*

As reviewed in Chapter 4, the daily operations of management can generally be categorized into three elements—planning, organizing, and controlling. A business is composed of manpower, material, and money. It is the basic function of management to procure and combine these elements into the compound that will most effectively achieve the designated goal—realization of profit.

The management of all businesses performs these functions, but the variety and complexity vary with the size of the firm and product line. In retailing, the size refers to the extent of merchandise lines handled. It is obvious that the problems encountered by the management of the Bell Telephone System—a utility with 750,000 employees and two and one-half billion dollars yearly sales—are not the same as those facing the managers of a retail firm with a dozen to a few hundred employees; yet the organic functions of management of both types of firm are the same.

The functions of planning, organizing, and controlling are organic in nature because they are part and parcel of all managerial operations regardless of size. How well these functions are carried out determines whether the firm becomes a dynamic, living organism or merely an underutilized resource.

Management must be able to think effectively to arrive at effective solutions of business problems. Business problems in retailing are concerned with the movement and interaction of people, places, and merchandise. A philosophy of management based on individualized concepts of free enterprise, competition, and marketing strategy is a prerequisite to the continuing successful interaction of these elements. This is of special importance to retail management, because in no other field of endeavor does the long-run success of the enterprise depend so much on daily face-to-face relationships both within and outside the store.[1]

The internal organizational framework, of course, forms the basic framework for the successful economic operation of the firm. Only by thoroughly exploring the functioning of the basic organizational structure can the proper logic essential to the best solutions to retail problems be developed. Problems such as the continuing cost-profit squeeze faced by increasing numbers of retailers have to be resolved. The organizational structure should also reflect management philosophy in the automatic provision for leadership in depth at all times in order to assure constant and orderly pursuit of company objectives.

THE ROLE OF BUSINESS OBJECTIVES

Every business has primary, collateral, and secondary business objectives. As an economic institution, the retail store must be prepared to supply wanted goods and services to its customers at competitive prices. In the pursuit of its primary service objectives of creating public values and fair dealing with consumers, the payment and status of the store's personnel and the social acceptance of its executives are an important facet of successful operation. To achieve the corollary and secondary business objectives, a properly weighted payment scale must be set up along with a fair dividend policy for investors and a reputation for fair dealing with manufacturers and suppliers. In other words, the success of any retail enterprise is primarily determined by the total over-all image it creates and its resulting impact in the market place.

The organizational structure of the retail enterprise should also reflect the ethics of its merchandise and service ideologies. As concepts change in what the public wants, important amounts of time and money must be expended to maintain an effective desirable store image.

The responsibility for successful achievement of primary service objectives of creation of customer and public service values rests squarely with top management. It is management—the function of executive leadership—that breathes life into the firm and, by day-to-day reaction to the impinging forces of public opinion, competition, and legislation, maintains a profitable state of equilibrium of the elements composing the firm. Top management policy decisions furnish the rules of action

---

[1] New concepts in retail theory were explored on this basis in a series of seminars at the Marketing Science Institute, Philadelphia, Pa. (1962–1963). Their initial framework is called the "CRIM" model, or "Consumer-Retailer-Interface-Model." This will be reviewed in greater detail in a later chapter.

for the achievement of business objectives; these rules act as guides and constraints for orderly procedures throughout the firm.

PLANNING

Planning is the formulation of a course of action based on systematic and apt data gleaned from research information. This information is obtained from sources within and outside the organization. The ability of management to utilize available data effectively is determined to a large extent by whether or not management has planned for a free two-directional flow of information—both upward and downward within the firm.

Planning must be carried out on both short- and long-run bases. Short-range planning may be considered as the evolution of a scheme of action based on relatively well-established and inflexible facts. As longer time factors come into the picture, so also do the possibilities increase that the estimates upon which the plans are based will change. The future is never certain; consequently the forecasting of expected events is a matter of educated guesswork. Although its function is an internal organic one, planning, of necessity, tends to be concentrated in areas most susceptible to uncertainty—those external to the organization. Typical uncertainties exist in meeting changes in consumer tastes and style changes, predicting acceptability of new products or designs, and sales forecasting.

Short-Range

A typical short-range planning function is evidenced by the headline of a recent article in a leading business newspaper: "Many Factories Plan to Lift Output Without Adding More Workers." Such plans are based on the knowledge that automated plants can be more intensively used with no, or proportionately little, additional manpower, or, in other cases, by overtime work or by adding shifts. The same conditions hold for the retail store: sales areas can be utilized more effectively with greater resulting sales volume and with the same number of sales personnel.

Actually, the above plan would be only one facet of a series of plans, and, if viewed in isolation, is an oversimplification. A plan to increase output through more intensive plant utilization must include consideration of such things as increased and less convenient maintenance, inventory turnover and storage problems, customer service problems, internal and external transportation problems, effects on the channels of distribution and on image projection, as well as problems in the control of merchandise quality, layout flexibility, and public and community relations. This is by no means an all-inclusive list; subplans that contribute to the broad decision must also be set up.

Long-Range

As an integral part of functional management, the development of a five- or ten-year long-range plan requires a number of short- and long-term programs.

Such programs have a tendency to be interdependent, with the object of one program becoming the premise for planning another. Such planning requires a high degree of coordination and calls for exacting managerial skills. True, such planning requires much time and work. Over a length of time, effective planning becomes not only simpler and more interesting, but also more effective as a blue-print for "doing." [2]

An example of a six-year plan is the following integrated, coordinated forecast of sales with the "work plans" necessary to achieve the sales goal:

1965 Actual Sales: $10 million

	Projected Sales (millions of $)	Planned Implementation
1966	11	Improvements in customer relations and services
1967	13	Internal reorganization to sales management type of sales control
1968	16	Addition of new branch stores; more central warehousing
1969	22	Adding of budget-type operations with self-service and check-out
1970	32	Increasing use of market research in choice of new store locations
1971	40	Mergers and acquisitions to increase sales capacity and diversification

The modern manager is in the same position as a person who stands at the side of a still pond with a handful of stones of different shapes and sizes; upon casting these stones in the water one at a time in a random fashion, he is required to predict with some reliability the time and place of the intersection of the various concentric rings. The only certainty is that the rings, while of varying size and distance apart, eventually do intersect.

Because of eventual operating interaction throughout the organization, planning is one of management's most critical functions and is by no means reserved for top management exclusively. Generally, the amount of time that an executive spends in the planning function is in direct ratio to his level in the firm. In other words, the higher the echelon of the executive, the more likely he is to

---

[2] Some contend that even a ten-year forecast plan is too short to be considered a long-range plan. (From a speech by E. J. Cordiner, President of General Electric, to the Economic Club, New York City, March 1958.)

delegate authority and responsibility for "doing" and the more likely he is to concern himself with long-range planning and policy making. The lower the echelon in which an executive manager operates, the more likely he is to handle the more detailed and shorter-range planning functions. Functional management along these lines is one of the goals of the organizational structure.

ORGANIZING

The achievement of a given goal is best attained by first devising a precise plan of action; an effective organization is the foundation upon which a business plan is carried out by both administrative and operating management. Too often the organization is considered to be the end, rather than the means through which company objectives are realized. Through proper organization, any ineffective methods and functioning of top management are spotlighted. Faulty organizational structure and improper methods of interaction permit costly problems to arise. Firms with faulty organization often grew like Topsy—usually, but not necessarily, during wartime or periods of rapid product or institutional innovations when truly competitive environments put the firms to the test of fire. The Grayson-Robinson organization is typical of many firms that have failed to meet the competitive test and have had to be completely reorganized. In this case, reorganization of the firm took place under an eleven-year extension plan under Chapter XI of the Bankruptcy Act.[3]

In the Retail Organization

The retail organization is primarily an economic institution. As such it must create customer values. The greater the values created, the more effective and profitable the organization. In a one-man organization, organizing may consist only of rigid self-discipline, but for the most part, organizing in retailing implies a line-and-staff method of operation, with staff being a function of organizational size and growth. In effect, the retail organization may be described as a group of individuals cooperating toward the accomplishment of certain common objectives with an executive leader coordinating and controlling their efforts.[4]

A good organization facilitates operating relationships between functions, physical factors, and personnel, with assurance that the functions of the firm will be grouped wherever feasible. For example: business continuity depends upon long-run customer satisfaction, which in turn depends upon the extent of the total

---

[3] See Women's Wear Daily (February 8, 1963), p. 21. In 1962 there were 146 discount store failures with total liabilities of $74 million (Dun & Bradstreet). While discount stores accounted for only 2 per cent of retail failures, they accounted for 21 per cent of retail liabilities. 63 per cent of the failures had liabilities under $100,000, 30 per cent had liabilities ranging from $150,000 to $1 million, and 7 per cent had liabilities exceeding $1 million. Dun & Bradstreet's definition of a discount store is "an organization with a sizable dollar volume of sales or an important part of its business from discount store operations or leased units."

[4] See R. C. Davis, Fundamentals of Top Management (New York: Harper and Brothers, 1951), p. 327.

"packages" of customer conveniences. Customers evaluate their store experiences in terms of total satisfactions received from a store for money spent. The "packages" of satisfactions received by customers are determined by how well functional management operates within the retail organization.

Approaches to Effective Organization

There are today two general concepts of the organizational function of management: one may be called the traditional or formal organization approach; the other is known as the modern industrial organization or theoretical approach. The traditional approach to the organizational function of management places more emphasis on the role of the individual in the firm. The industrial organization or theoretical approach places more emphasis on the analytical tools developed by social scientists in their investigation of existing organizational structures in dynamic industrial complexes.

Purposes of Organizing

The purpose of organizing is to determine the scope and limit of persons or groups of individuals, with emphasis on the relationships of these groups through a "chain of command" or channel of communication. The primary reason for creating functional management within the organization is to achieve effective coordination and control throughout the company. It is a matter of planning to bring the basic assets of the firm together in a way that will result in the greatest possible productivity; at the same time, all planning must be flexible enough to meet the challenge of any changing business conditions.

In a small business, the problem of organizing is relatively simple; the manager and possibly a few other employees perform the functions of planning, organizing, and controlling as outlined in the organization charts of such giants as General Electric, General Motors, or Federated Department Stores. While the operations of small-business managers are essentially the same as those of the larger firms, the problems of coordination and control are obviously vastly greater and more complicated in the larger businesses, which may have hundreds of selling departments, many warehouses, delivery trucks, and workrooms and other ramifications. All of these organizational segments may operate with a high degree of autonomy, but functional management within each group must still work toward the common goal of the firm, within the range of established policies.

Procedures Involved in Organizing

The basic step in determining the kind of functional management necessary is to examine the needs of the particular business. In a manufacturing firm with a standard product, the organization will usually be quite different from a multiproduct firm or a broad-based department store chain sponsoring discount houses as a competitive weapon.

For example, the technique of grouping like or closely related activities and having them reported to a functional manager may be used. The obvious result of this idea is the advantage of specialization and of a division of work. This is the basic step in organizing—the determination of "the smallest number of dissimilar functions into which the work of an institution may be divided." [5] This procedure is often followed in branch-store organization in assignment of departmental manager responsibilities. Other steps in organizing include the selection of qualified personnel and delegation of the necessary authority and responsibility for attaining organizational goals.

The basic functions of a business enterprise also include production, sales, and financing. In the department and chain store, production becomes an extension of the sales function. To create an effective organization, direct labor employees, such as warehousemen, window dressers, maintenance men, and the office force, should be grouped into a single task force because they are all engaged in sales-supporting activities. The individuals manning these operations usually report to a manager of building services or operations manager, who coordinates his activities to the needs of the merchandising.

Once the basic organizational functions are established and managers chosen, the framework in which the subordinate activities are to be conducted is set up. In the case of retail organizations, the common functional operations secondary to sales are advertising, sales promotion, layout, display, stockkeeping, inventory control, departmental housekeeping, and general floor supervision. Provision for functional management in these areas becomes the second basic step in organizing.

A third step takes place when secondary departments develop as management finds the spans of control to be too broad. For example, in the smaller firm the store manager may have both selling and nonselling employees reporting to him. However, when the operation enlarges and the number of employees grows, other levels of supervision are injected between him and the hourly worker: thus, new functional areas must be provided for in the organizational structure. In the small independent general store the owner or manager is responsible for the entire buying and selling functions (and those of physical supply and facilitation); in the big-city department store the general merchandise manager performing the "basic line function" is in charge of only the exchange functions of buying and selling. The big-city merchandise manager has supervisory personnel reporting to him who perform secondary functions, such as inventory control; these middle-management executives in turn have fragmented their supplementary functions into all the selling departments in the store.

Aside from an organization based primarily on functions, management may decide on a form of organization based on price lines emphasis or a prestige emphasis, and mold the store accordingly. The differences in the organizational structure of retail firms are testimony to their interest in their customers and the satisfaction of their needs. Actually, the logical conclusion in evaluating man-

---

5 H. A. Hopf, *Organization, Executive Capacity and Progress* (Ossining, N.Y.: Hopf Institute of Management, 1945), p. 4.

agement in the organizational structure makes it apparent that any form of organization, to be successful, especially in retailing and marketing, must be customer-oriented.

Store Organization by Merchandise Classification

The decision to establish separate departments to handle the various merchandise needs of a firm's customers is dictated by the actual or potential percentage of sales attributable to each group of purchasers. The technical services needed in the sale of goods is a secondary consideration in organizing departments in a store. Goods may be departmentalized by type of product and often by age of customer —for example, housewares, youth shops, boys' and men's hats, and so on.

It would be well to point out that organization by merchandise classification does not imply that all functions in a firm should be oriented toward particular users. In a serialized type of manufacture (for example, automobiles) the units of product are generally tailored not to the needs of any specific customer but to requirements of a basic package to which extras can be added. In this case, the production function is organized on a product or territorial basis, raw materials, and/or manpower needs rather than on the prime basis of customer satisfaction. In the retail store, however, only the customer-oriented organization can be assured of long-run success.

Organizing to Meet Product and Trading Area Requirements

A product price-related firm represents another approach to organizational specialization. Many discount houses are organized on this basis. The product-related approach is found where the volume of sales of items offering dissimilar utilities warrants the establishment of separate stores or departments. Many department and specialty stores, in attempts to recapture dwindling shares of the market, have gone into more diversified operations such as budget stores (self-service type), where potential demand has remained at high levels. In such cases, success for the new, generally autonomous stores depends on the degree of support from the existing organization.

As product lines, price zones, or branch-store expansions become more diversified, it is not good policy to attempt to maintain a *status quo* in managing within previously developed sales and sales-supporting frameworks.

The trading-area type of organization is found in retail firms that have branched out in wide geographical regions. This kind of movement is justified on the grounds of "going to the customer." As distances from the parent store increase, branch stores have developed increasing autonomy in their organizational operation. In such cases, functional management becomes more general and less specialized throughout the organization.

In many cases increased effectiveness has resulted from decentralized management and autonomous branch store operations. Where good customer services are of the essence for optimum public relations and development of long-run patronage motives, the selection of local people for employment and management positions may be quite advantageous.

Other reasons for increased effectiveness of the organizational structure are improvements in communications, greater use of part-time people, more intensive use of specialized personnel, more stable purchasing policies, and more scientific data gathering for use in decision making.

The properly organized multistore retail firm often benefits greatly from more accessible suburban locations. From the standpoint of the firm itself, suburban locations generally boast lower tax rates, lower real-estate costs, lower labor rates, and also lower selling costs. Operating advantages of this kind accrue provided that the spans of executive and operating control are not violated.

In summary, then, the retail organization must be customer oriented. Functional management within this kind of organizational framework is naturally directed toward the establishment of good local relations. A corollary objective is the development of "pools" of junior and middle management echelons familiar with handling changing territorial problems. When economies of scale are sufficiently high to offset the generally higher costs accompanying greater decentralized controls, a firm foundation for organizational growth is provided.

CONTROLLING

This is the managerial function that relates the establishment of formal standards, measures, and procedures to observation and reappraisal in the applications of company policy.

Such standards, if they are to be enduring, cannot be originated without a great deal of planning and thought about the results to be obtained. When policies are equitably and thoughtfully established, the "exception principle" of management can come into being as an effective organizational tool. This principle of exception states that only problems which cannot be solved by application of past precedent or clear interpretation of policy are referred to higher levels of management. When this principle is correctly applied, many problems that arise in the course of a work day are automatically resolved by the general knowledge of past practice and policy; as a result, all levels of supervision are freed from the consumer's responsibility of making obvious decisions. Generally, use of this principle is considered an attribute of good organization.

In essence, the function of control refers to the activities undertaken to force events to conform to prearranged policy or plans. Since all activities in the firm are conducted by people, this function relates to the control of people. Even in the case of the completely self-service store or completely automated factory, someone must make decisions, see that customers are satisfied, and correct trouble should it arise. Activities such as sales control, inventory control, financial control, and quality control form the basic framework for analysis of the control function.[6]

---

[6] Each of these activities is examined in depth in later chapters.

Within the framework of this chapter, the discussion of control is limited to that of people, because of their basic contribution to any success that an organization achieves. In other words, people make up the organization, and functional management cannot succeed without the willing cooperation of these people. And willing cooperation depends on proper motivation. In this context, it must be kept in mind that the difference between control and manipulation lies in an understanding of motivational techniques and human-relations theory. First, let us examine what is involved in personnel motivation within the organizational structure.

Theories about Motivation and Control

There is a wide range of concepts dealing with motivating—from the theory that the exercise of control must flow from authority to the theory that employees can be best motivated by getting them to combine their goals with those of the organization. Both of these approaches have profound implications concerning personnel management and direction in retail firms. The authoritarian approach is founded on assumptions that people must be firmly directed and strongly controlled. This philosophy is so deeply imbued in many managerial echelons that any variation on the theme often appears too novel and untried to warrant the time, money, and effort necessary to experiment with it.

The strong control idea is based on the beliefs that the employee must be browbeaten, coerced, cajoled, forced, and pressured into conforming to company policy and practice, that he does not want to work and never will want to, except possibly after retirement. Adherents to this philosophy ridicule the opposing view that permissiveness and individual goal-setting processes lead to higher productivity and more placid and rewarding employee relations. Authoritarians state this is not possible, since the typical person resists individual action because, above all, he desires security. This managerial group feels that the employee will exploit the firm whenever possible and accept all financial and other benefits in the anticipation of more to come—although such rewards are not adequate to stimulate and maintain his cooperation. Therefore, they believe, rigid controls and disciplinary systems must be constant.

The above is a strongly worded point of view, but it expresses the sentiments of many business executives; on the other hand, many executives are willing to accept the newer motivational theory, but at the same time feel it necessary to retain "the prerogatives of management." [7]

The success of human-relations programs and a social research approach to functional management within the organization structure is contingent upon a revision of management attitudes toward employees. Leavitt outlines it well:

... Management has to worry about influencing people instead of assuming that people automatically want to do what is best for management. Influence, in turn, is not simply a matter of wielding authority but a much more com-

---

[7] Harold J. Leavitt, *Managerial Psychology* (Chicago: University of Chicago Press, 1958), p. 298.

plex issue that must take individual perceptions and interdependence into account. Responsibility becomes something people have to be influenced to accept and feel, not something that can be passed out like the pay check.[8]

Dr. Leavitt also points out that traditional organizational theory oversimplifies the complexities of human nature by assuming that people try to satisfy only physical needs at work and that there is no conflict in working motives between one member of a group and another—that traditional theory observes what people should do. and not what they actually do. In the numerous personal interactions in retail establishments, human-relations programs and their influence can be continually observed. The salesperson's interactions with customers can improve the store's total image where such programs are effectively carried out.

A good human-relations program in a firm gives the employee a sense of psychic fulfillment and of participation as a "recognized" individual in the company. If this desire for recognition is not fulfilled, symptoms of frustration will appear—usually aggression or apathy. Such manifestations cause management to apply more and more control, which only reinforces poor behavioral patterns and ineffective performance.

The Organizational Environment

It is the task of functional management within the organization to identify the needs and set courses of action that will best motivate employees. Whatever policies are accepted by management, they should be consistent.[9]

The greatest danger to effective management is an adoption of a middle-of-the-road, passive, "be nice" sort of leadership. This type of leadership is characterized by management that does not expect much from its executives and employees and molds store policies accordingly. When employees are given the "fair wage" for the community, with standard benefits, without any consideration for proper job motivation or strong executive leadership, their performance or productivity is far more likely to be mediocre than effective.

In this type of organizational environment, the employees become passive and disinterested, employee turnover and absenteeism increase, and attempts at cost

---

[8] *Ibid.*, pp. 298–330. Another assumption of traditional authoritarian theory is that man can never be satisfied and will always want more. This can be better expressed by saying that man is a creature of need—these needs ranging from physical appetite to aesthetic or psychic wants. When man's needs are fulfilled, they cease to be paramount to him, and therefore no longer cause him to act in a manner to satisfy them. This refers particularly to the easily defined physical needs. Thus, when a firm offers employees good wages with above-average job security and good working conditions to the point where the person is satisfied, these "needs" are no longer effective in motivating him.

[9] See Ernest Dichter, *The Strategy of Desire* (New York: Doubleday, 1960). Dichter points out that "motivations seldom consist of lists of reasons arranged in a linear manner to be added up arithmetically"; they are rather complicated structures which are best compared to machines with many moving parts, where every part has a very particular influence on the next and where the interaction takes place in a definite timely order. A practical problem of policy decision, whether in the political, commercial, or international field, therefore, cannot really be undertaken unless this functional principle has been understood and considered.

reduction or improved productivity generally fail. Such problems of lethargy are found in all organizations—military, church, manufacturing, wholesaling, and retailing. Further, as pointed out above, psychic and ego-centered fulfillment must be used by management to motivate personnel by blending their personal objectives with those of the firm. In other words, management within the organizational framework involves much more than fulfilling the basic needs of job satisfaction and adjusting to changing market requirements.[10]

There are some 65 million workers and their families and associates who represent the spending public. The attitudes and philosophy underlying their consumption patterns are of key importance. And projective methods and techniques have been developed by psychologists in an effort to decide what and, more importantly, why the public buys what it does. The same motivations underlie what it takes to create and manage an effective organization. Thus functional interaction in retailing organizations is a significant consideration.

Motivation research is a generally accepted technique and seldom considered by knowledgeable people to be the "mumbo-jumbo," black magic approach of the popular view. Few companies will base a major managerial or promotional decision solely on the findings of motivation research, but they do give proper motivation prime consideration in developing effective performance at the informal as well as the formal organizational level.

REAPPRAISING

One of the cardinal principles that must be observed in the controlling function is that of flexibility—the firm and its management must be capable of adjusting to constant change. Thus, a system of reappraisal must be developed and maintained as part of the central control process. Each day a manager makes decisions based on a vast amount of kaleidoscopic data provided from within and outside the firm. Since no business can remain static, especially in retail and market distribution, the need for constant reappraisal is obvious. The standard tools for reappraisal are personnel surveys, attitude surveys, market research, budget forecasts, and sales estimates. There is also an array of other information which the manager and his staff must assimilate and evaluate in order to choose a course of action consistent with the controls currently in use.[11]

---

[10] See Edgar Schein's article refuting the findings of W. E. Mayer's thesis on brainwashing in E. E. Maccoby, T. Newcomb, and E. L. Hartley, Readings in Social Psychology, (3rd ed., New York: Henry Holt and Co., 1958); and Albert D. Biderman, "Dangers of Negative Patriotism," Harvard Business Review (November–December 1962), pp. 93–99. In an address before the Freedom Foundation several years ago, Major William E. Mayer, an Army psychiatrist, reported the same problem in relation to our soldiers who were captured in Korea. He asserted that they were very susceptible to brainwashing because it was easy for the Communists to isolate the individual and prevent group solidarity. Because our soldiers had no sense of purpose and understanding of their goals, owing to passive lower-echelon leadership, there was little group loyalty. Thus, when called upon to meet the challenge of being a prisoner of war, the individual lacked the spirit and belief and knowledge of goals above the subsistence level and therefore was incapable of rising above this level.

[11] The specific research aspects will be discussed in detail in later chapters.

In the process of administration or group management, sizing up a situation and planning a program of action should be based on the conclusion and recommendations flowing from the reappraisal process. In summary, then, the accomplishment of the business objectives within the organization must be carried out through people who work together effectively along the planned lines of procedure. If the executive in charge finds that his objectives are being met, he is ready to tackle another problem. If reappraisal shows that what should have occurred has not, then remedial action should be promptly instituted.

INFORMATION FEEDBACK AND EFFECTIVE MANAGEMENT

The days when the retailer was free to manage on the basis of intuition and rule of thumb are long past. The days when the year's results were evaluated only after the annual physical inventory are also past. The tempo has increased, and organization needs are more immediate.

Retail management needs to know at all times if it is offering "the right goods at the right price, in the right selection, at the right time." Inventory results do not give him such guides soon enough.

In attempts to increase efficiency and productivity, many of the larger stores and chains have separated the buying and selling functions. Thus, where centralized authority and control once existed, there now are groups of autonomous people—one group in charge of buying and another group consisting of department managers in charge of sales. Others in charge of advertising, personnel, finance and budgets, maintenance, service, and inventory continue to operate on a semiautonomous basis. Unless such divisional operations produce proper informational feedback in time to be utilized, over-all effectiveness of the firm cannot be generated.

Management is a process that pervades the organization in that it must make certain that every last dollar invested in the business yields the maximum possible return. And it is in the area of merchandise offerings and pricing policies where the success or failure of the retail firm is determined.

THE ENGINEERING APPROACH TO FUNCTIONAL MANAGEMENT

The industrial engineering approach involves the improvement of efficiency in the operating plant by such basic procedures as a study of the flow of material in relation to efficient storage and warehousing needs, and effective shipment of merchandise sold to customers. For example, in examining the flow of customers and merchandise through the store, a layout should be planned which allows the shortest movement of goods possible, consistent with maximum exposure to customers. Special thought should be given to shortest possible movement of weighty or bulky packages by the buyer in self-service stores, with adequate plans for handling upon arrival. This approach will be reviewed in greater detail in Chapter 10.

Extending further the engineering approach to retailing and to the merchandise handled, Mortimer has described ten forms of convenience wanted by the buying public. As a standard of comparison, management should make certain that such conveniences can be extended through its organizational structure. They are:

(1) Form convenience—miniaturized or transistorized products
(2) Packaging convenience—disposable packages, storage lockers
(3) Time convenience—evening hours
(4) Place convenience—drive-in theaters
(5) Quantity or unit convenience—half-pint to one gallon package of milk
(6) Readiness convenience—instant coffee, dehydrated foods
(7) Combination convenience—do-it-yourself kits
(8) Selection convenience—various color combinations
(9) Automatic operations convenience—automatic transmissions, appliances
(10) Credit convenience—almost anything on credit.[12]

While the American public is finding more and more leisure time, there are more diversions competing for this time. For example, the dollar volume of sales generally has little or no correlation to the amount of time that the customer spends in a store. Actually, the time spent by customers in a store often correlates negatively to sales volume; generally, however, the less time the consumer spends in movement within or between departments, the more pleasant the surroundings, and the more available other services and conveniences, the greater the likelihood of his increasing his spending in a store. The goal of the organization structure should always be to enable the customer to spend his time in readily accessible merchandise display and sales areas—and not in walking through parking lots or underpasses, riding elevators and escalators, or awaiting service.

SUMMARY AND CONCLUSIONS

The retailing-marketing functions were reviewed with an eye to showing how they could best be employed to attain business objectives. Administrative management is largely group management, while operative management is generally project management that enters directly into the creation of utilities. The larger the organization, the more complicated and more specialized the marketing functions and degrees of specialization needed. The accomplishment of the organization's economic objectives is determined by external factors and constraints of the physical plant, its layout and location. Goal attainment is also determined by internal factors such as the personal or human ones involved in carrying out organizational objectives. Effectiveness in this case is determined by morale.

Morale generally depends on the "contractual" relationship or meeting of the minds between management and its employees. This is the basic responsibility of executive leadership. As a practical requirement, the organizational structure

---

[12] Charles J. Mortimer, *Two Keys to Modern Marketing* (Scarsdale, N.Y.: The Updegraff Press, 1955).

should provide built-in guarantees that personnel at all levels in the organization should be able to confer with management concerning both their social and economic well-being. This is basic to how well the work of planning, organizing, and controlling is carried out within the organization.

The degree of delegation of authority and responsibility is directly dependent on the philosophy underlying the organizational structure and the ability of the personnel manning it. An effective organization structure facilitates the attainment of the primary operating objective in the retail organization—the creation of values saleable to the public on a profitable basis.

The grouping of functions with similar characteristics forms the basis for an effective organizational structure. Functional grouping molds individuals into a team working towards the same common end. Thus, the functions of good organizational structure in retail firms may be summed up in the firm's ability to:

(a) Constantly improve service to the consumer and the community without increasing its total cost structure as a percentage of sales;

(b) Consolidate purchases and reduce shipments with consequent reduction of transportation costs and increasing purchasing efficiency;

(c) Reduce expenses to the manufacturer as well as to itself by correctly gauging customer demand and helping the manufacturer to plan better and smoother production runs;

(d) Provide for adequate funds through cash-flow analysis so that accounts payable may be discounted and so that customer accounts receivable may be handled more economically, thus building both supplier and customer good will;

(e) Above all, provide executive management with continuing knowledge of community development and change on a broad scale to be able to reduce problems in both areas as a matter of course.

In the chapter that follows, an analysis of the operations of the divisional segments of the retail firm will be reviewed from the standpoint of the more flexible factors of internal control.

Chapter 9: *Divisional Operations in the Retail Structure*

The larger the retail organization, the greater the number of specializations and the greater the need for inter- and intra-division coordination and flexibility. Also, the larger the firm the greater the proportion of nonselling to selling employees in the store. Scalar principles hold true in retailing as well as in other fields of endeavor.[1]

Multidivisional operations within the retail firm require high-level administrative management who must provide continuous policy coordination for autonomous divisional growth. Only by this means can effectiveness be maximized in terms of lower over-all costs. Unfortunately, applications of scalar growth principles occur only with coordinated administrative management. As a result, greater efficiencies that should accrue with growth fail to materialize because many organi-

---

[1] For a discussion of scalar growth, see R. C. Davis, *The Fundamentals of Top Management* (New York: Harper and Brothers, 1951), pp. 217–19; and James D. Mooney and C. Reilly, *The Principles of Organization* (New York: Harper and Brothers, 1939), p. 5. Scalar growth implies a ladderlike growth of magnitude within effective limits.

zations feed on themselves in terms of vested interests and institutional overlaps, as in Parkinson's description of staff duplications.[2]

IMPLICATIONS OF SCALAR GROWTH

When functional growth occurs naturally as the result of volume increases and carefully managed spans of administrative control, staff duplications are less likely to occur. During an organization's growth period, any inflexibility hampering functional growth generally adds supervisory costs faster than the ability of additional sales volume to absorb them. For the most part, excessive costs during periods of growth result from violations in the span of executive control. When top executives attempt to manage too many executives and too many divisional areas, expensive administrative gaps are created. These gaps occur because responsibilities associated with functional growth advance geometrically rather than arithmetically.[3] Thus, the larger the volume the greater the need for a large number of high-echelon administrative management executives. This is especially true in the case of geographical expansion, which often necessitates greater degrees of divisional autonomy. When management does not carry out organizational adjustments along these lines, then an uneconomic and often uncontrollable divisional structure develops.

CHANGING DIVISIONAL NEEDS

Executive growth should proceed naturally on a continuum from one degree of specialization to another, and rotate from line to staff echelons, as greater degrees of decentralization and specialization are needed. This kind of executive development policy calls for a flexible pool of middle management executives in which transfers, promotions, resignations, and temporary absences can be handled on an automatic basis. Such provisions also insure a vital and alert middle-management group and minimal degrees of departmental upsets. In other words, automatic provision for executive changes at all organizational levels is a basic attribute of good organization. Internal flexibility along these lines also permits the firm to adjust itself to both temporary and permanent changes in economic conditions without crippling losses in effectiveness. For example, provision for adequate managerial supervision can be quickly set up in the event of mass transit strikes or other emergencies.

Autonomy and Flexibility

To insure greater autonomy and flexibility, one of the largest department stores in the country reorganized its merchandise divisions into a so-called "buying line"

---

[2] C. Northcote Parkinson, *Parkinson's Law* (Cambridge, Mass.: Riverside Press, 1957), p. 2. "Work expands to fill the time available for its completion" is his basic thesis, with resulting staff duplication and higher costs.

[3] R. C. Davis, *op. cit.*

executive organization. The reorganization was set up to "handle functions cutting across all divisional operations with the firms." [4] Under the old approach, the buyer was also responsible for the selling functions within his department—in fact, his former departmental responsibilities were roughly equivalent to the general management of a specialty shop. In this context, he was also responsible for planning and control of buying as well as for pricing, gross margins, merchandise inventories, and departmental supervision of both the main store and branches. In essence, the buyer was an important factor in planning the total sales promotion program for the goods that he bought.

Under the new operating plan, the central buying concepts used by large retail chains and buying groups were adopted. Merchandise managers and buyers were responsible only for the buying functions, with a departmental manager type of organization responsible for the selling functions. The Macy change was an attempt to achieve greater efficiency through larger degrees of autonomy and specialized services for each branch store; in this case each store manager was responsible for merchandising management as well as store operation. It was also felt that, regardless of the differences in divisional operations of the branches and parent store, better understanding by the consumer of the character, personality, and image of the store would result if "specialists" in the selling and service areas were provided. While this concept of divisional operations was apparently successful, no accurate measure of its success is available.

On the other hand, Lit Brothers in Philadelphia, after trying out this same kind of organizational setup, divorcing selling responsibility from that of buying, found that it was impractical for their high-fashion, high-turnover departments. In these departments it was found that creating the proper merchandising image needed for good turnover and profitability required experienced, "all-around" executives rather than narrowly trained specialists. Buying and selling operations, after being separated, were again concentrated in the hands of buyers operating from the parent store.[5] It is clear that both types of divisional operations can be justified, depending on the particular needs of the firm and its philosophy of management.

Often, many stores lose management flexibility when unrealistic work rules are forced on them as the result of labor contracts. In such cases management is forced to delegate only specific areas of responsibility to supervisory executives. Organization flexibility as well as stability depends on having the proper number of junior and middle management executives always available to step into any job of greater responsibility, although care must be taken not to have an excessive number of such individuals lest low morale and executive obsolescence develop.

---

[4] *Women's Wear Daily* (November 9, 1962), pp. 1, 18. (Store noted was R. H. Macy & Company, New York City.)
[5] *Ibid.*, p. 18.

EFFECT OF THE SIZE OF FIRM

In retailing more than in other types of business enterprise, the one-man organization is quite prevalent. Also, "bigness" in retailing, per se, does not necessarily imply a lower cost–higher profit operation—either within the framework of a large centralized store or in a downtown store with all types of satellite branches. Large hierarchies of executives often cause rapid obsolescence in performance and over-all organizational efficiency. Even with increasing volume the expense ratio percentages tend to increase. With growth in volume, variable cost percentages should decrease as organizational efficiency increases. Otherwise, total average costs rise and level off at points higher than those found at lower volume levels, as illustrated in Figure V. Increasing rather than decreasing cost curves are evident in the growth of so many retail firms that their long-run average cost curves often resemble these of the extractive industries.

FIGURE V
DECREASING RETURNS TO SCALE AT THE RETAIL LEVEL

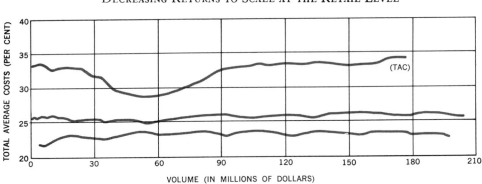

For this reason the small independent, because of his greater flexibility and better cost control, can not only survive but grow. The retention of internal flexibility in meeting organizational needs and marketing strategy is essential to achieving greater efficiency and profitability. When long-run costs in the smaller store increase, it is, more often than not, because of "undermanagement" and violations in the span of executive control.

PHYSICAL FACILITIES

The type of physical facilities available often determines the kind of services and operating procedures offered as well as the kind of organization developed. For example, a store with a small frontage in a downtown location may have a ready-to-wear or accessory division filling the dominant role for the entire store. Also, when perimeter stockrooms are available on the selling floor, there is less need for autonomous divisions in the store. Often, decisions to move completely from one location to another are based on inadequate physical facilities. In Houston, Texas, Joske's moved entirely out of downtown Houston because of limitations in physical facilities.[6]

Yet department layout must be set in terms of the best possible appeals to customers—not for ease in maintenance but for sales maximization. Customer service policies, not optimum engineering considerations, should determine the nature of the policies governing store operation. The new physical layout feasible in branches have provided downtown stores with the means for testing how new organizational structures can provide the basis for strategic action against innovators and price and merchandise competitors.

DEPARTMENTALIZATION

Departmentalization may be defined as the dividing of various lines and classifications of merchandise into separate merchandise and selling groups and the systemizing of their operation for optimum utilization of all sales-supporting activities within the store. In many cases, departmentalization is the only means of knowing exactly what controllable margin data are for many commodity classifications. Irrespective of size, some degree of segmentation and/or departmentalization in any business organization can prove helpful. In the smaller store, departmentalization still takes place, but on a more inclusive and informal basis.

The one-man organization can work efficiently only up to certain volume levels. Generally, it is not possible in the larger retail stores for efficient operations to be maintained unless new areas of responsibility are created for more positive controls. In addition, department budgeting is set up on the basis of operational planning of open-to-buy,[7] sales, stocks, and turnover goals.

Specific planning for both budgets and operations should begin at the departmental level and flow upward; more often than not both budget and operating policies devolve downward. For example, divisional separations of merchandise lines and classifications involve the provision of adequate selections of companion, interdependent, and complementary lines. In effect, the manner in which the merchandise offerings and sales transactions are developed in the store determines the store's fundamental image and its long-run success.

In addition to furnishing another basic framework for developing the store image, departmentalization provides a scientific basis for revealing profitable and unprofitable lines and permits the rapid assessment of initial mark-ons and gross margin requirements and results. It facilitates the use of the retail method of

---

[6] Joske's, an Allied store, experienced a great loss in its share of the market when it gave up its downtown location, and Allied finally acquired the Wolff & Marx store downtown. As a result, the entire procedure has been under close scrutiny by the Federal Trade Commission.
[7] O.T.B. (open-to-buy) means planned sales (merchandise on hand plus purchases); these procedures are detailed in later chapters on buying and merchandising.

inventory and pinpoints areas in which stock turnover can be improved. When management delegates authority and responsibility to divisional group managers, optimum control of shortages results.

ROLE OF FUNCTIONAL DIVISIONS

The four broad functional divisional operations—general management, control, merchandising, and publicity—must match in personal and organizational objectives and have an equitable distribution of work based on logical groupings of related functions; this minimizes duplication of activities and provides for organization growth. Every decision made in the business organization is generally carried out in the midst of conflicting views and forces. While philosophies of management among various personnel and divisional groupings within the same firm are rarely the same, their total organization objectives should be.

Managerial controls must be clear, constant, and determined, so that strong individuals within the organization will not ignore or by-pass lines of authority. If lines of authority are by-passed, divisional domination takes place within the firm; this can occur when a divisional segment boasts a strong leader. For example, some stores have a reputation of being controller managed and dominated; others are merchandise-manager controlled. The fixing of responsibility in all areas by general management facilitates control and forces concerned executives to coordinate effectively.

Cross-functionalization in the Expanding Organization

Line responsibility for divisional operations is set up as part of the policy procedures for the total store operation, as illustrated in Figure VI for a large department store. Roughly, these areas correspond to the major decision centers previously discussed.

In the area of middle management, the coordination of action is achieved primarily through smooth interrelationships of physical activities. The line and staff organization of the typical departmentized store tends to lag behind its expanding needs. As a result, excessive spans of executive control in administrative management open up. For example, a branch store may be opened some twenty miles from the main downtown store. A store manager and department group managers are appointed. Automatically, they assume responsibility for both the sales and sales-supporting functions. In many cases they also supervise the staffing function of the branch. At this point, they act in both staff and line capacities. For the most part, branch-store executives are generally subordinate to their opposite numbers in the main store. Department managers also engage in and suggest buying specific merchandise classifications while supervising the selling and operating functions in their areas of responsibility.

If the department manager is a dominant individual, he may suggest procedural changes in buying, receiving, and marking-room activities while performing his

FIGURE VI

Broad Functional Divisional Operations in a Large Department Store

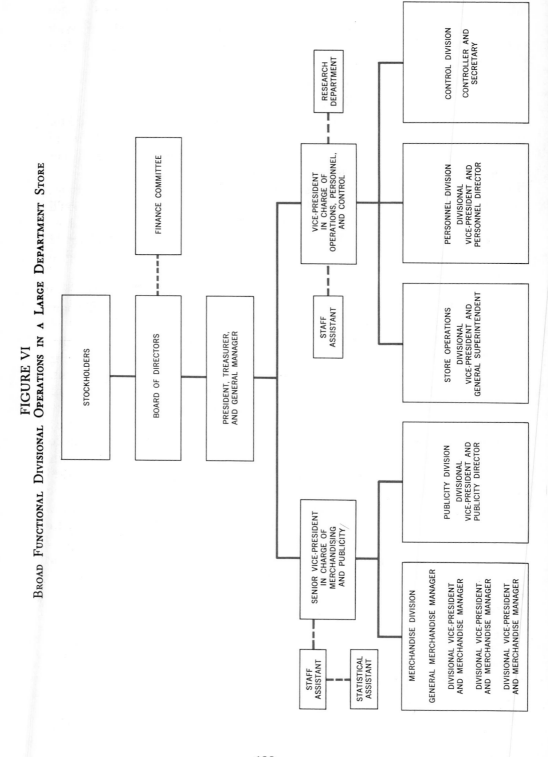

duties as floor manager. In addition, he often imposes merchandising and display changes on the branch-store superintendent or branch-store manager. In other words, necessity and expediency take the place of adequate planning and staffing for organizational growth.

Staff Planning

In the process of staff evolution into functional specializations such as director of personnel, publicity, or control, organization changes may not be set up in any formal manner. In theory, each functional division should have its own staff creatively developing policy procedures for consideration by the executive committee—for over-all store policy as well as on a divisional basis. For example, the determination of the kinds of charge-account systems that the store should use should be a function of the control division. The actual decision as to how to proceed would be up to the operating division, as would the training of personnel to man the system. However, the merchandising division must agree on the manner in which the charge-account systems should be applied.

Unfortunately, except for the very largest firms, coordinated research as a formal staff function is generally nonexistent or hidden within the control division. Where research is designated as a function, it has been narrowly confined to testing merchandise, comparison shopping, listing of complaints, and such activities. When any major research is needed for problem-solving, decision-making purposes, management consultants are often called in to carry out the analysis. For example, in forecasting, econometricians or forecasting specialists may be called.

As the volume and responsibilities of individual departments expand, the need for divisional assistants grows. For example, a buyer with ten full-time people on the floor may need a second assistant called "head of stock" to work with the assistant buyer. However, cost control needs may deprive him of this assistance, with the result that the entire department suffers.

In retailing, recognition of ability or the lack of it comes much sooner than in industry, where face-to-face contacts with top management are far less likely to occur. Further, the responsibilities of supervisory management grow in both circular and almost geometric fashion. As greater buyer and supervisor autonomies develop because of store expansions, the needs for staff planning and assistance become much more acute.[8]

GENERAL MERCHANDISING OPERATIONS

The merchandising division, as the sales and income-producing unit, is responsible for the setting of price lines, price zones, the determination of basic and model

---

[8] "Study Greater Autonomy for May Co. Units," Home Furnishings Daily (October 29, 1962). This is a discussion of how main-store buyers can be relieved of undue burdens, such as stock-keeping and some buying responsibilities which have been shifted to the branches.

stocks, and the carrying-out of open-to-buy plans and procedures on the basis of the sales forecast.

Among the major responsibilities of the general merchandise manager is the coordination of the various divisions and departments and their operating budgets. It is also the function of the merchandise division to formulate market strategy and have adequate stocks on hand to carry out the planned strategy. The planning needed for sales promotion and demand creation is carried out in conjunction with the publicity director.

As is evident from the above and from Figure VII, sales planning is also part of the merchandise manager's province. Developing the actual forecast is the task of the staff and statistical assistants of this division working directly with the research director or outside consultants.[9]

Contract Departments

Most modern large stores maintain a contract or wholesale sales department. The contract department is technically part of the merchandising division; it sells large quantities of furniture and furnishings to motels, hotels, and other institutions. Because of a retailer's wide knowledge of sources of supply, and its ability to contract quickly for large orders, the retailer often acts as a wholesale "drop shipper" [10] for bulk sales.

Separation of Buying and Selling Functions

The actual responsibility for developing sales volume levels is in the hands of the buyers in most retail organizations. The concept that the buyer should be responsible for his purchases is constantly being challenged—specially where wide geographical dispersions of physical units have taken place. Under the impact of expanding volume and changing market and productivity requirements, many technical aspects in the management of the selling function have had to be divorced from buyer responsibilities.

The basic question here is: Does a buyer, relieved of the responsibility of selling the merchandise he buys, have an automatic excuse for merchandise not selling? Also, does the type of organization that separates the buyer from the sales force and customer reduce efficiency in both areas? In the areas of high fashion apparel and accessory lines which require high turnover and experienced evaluative judgments, such decisions are critical.

There is a direct, integrated relationship between buying and selling in the

---

[9] The usual starting point is the sales data of the corresponding period of the previous year; these sales are then adjusted with the most recent sales trends and pertinent trading area forecasts. Mechanical adjustments are made for holidays that occur at differing times during the year, such as Easter Sunday. Fashion considerations and extent of selling season are also involved in such adjustments.

[10] A drop shipper is a merchant middleman who takes title to the goods but does not handle them; orders are sent to resource for shipment to the buyer. Usually, large bulky commodities are handled in this manner.

retail firm. Actually, the sales force is also a service force catering to the consumer. Some argue that selling should be the sole responsibility of the operations division, not the merchandising division. Yet when selling responsibility ends with contact of a salesperson with a section or department manager and not with the department buyer, inadequate feedback results. To insure proper checks and balances, merchandise knowledge must be part of the section managers' responsibilities; this is not now a requirement for most operating and supervisory managements at this level of the firm.

In the retail firm it is the effective functioning of the sales force that determines the extent of a store's profit. If the service aspect is emphasized over the selling one, long-run sales losses may occur; on the other hand, if selling is emphasized over service, then a reputation for being a "high-pressure" store may result.

PUBLICITY

In Figure VIII are shown the titles and operating responsibilities of the publicity division. Retail establishments are highly sensitive to all publicity generated by or attributed to the store. The publicity division encompasses advertising, public relations, display, sales promotion, selling management, and various combinations of these activities. In many stores, comparison shopping and research activities are also assigned to this division.

The publicity director works directly with the general and merchandise managers; he is responsible for initiating sales events and creating competitive breakthroughs. The areas of direct mail, mail-order sales, style shows, public relations, and "tryout" or new media activities are also in his province. The relative importance attached to this division varies with the organization's philosophy of management.

As coordinator for the store's merchandising offerings and sales promotion activities, the publicity division has store-wide duties. It is generally subordinate to the merchandising division in choice of merchandise to be advertised. Institutional advertising is an important part of this division's activities and of its public-relations work. The publicity director is, in effect, similar to the marketing director in the industrial organization.

In recent years, public-relations activities have become a much more important operating segment of the publicity division's responsibilities. Creating the desired store image in the minds of consumers and the community is of paramount importance for the store's long-run success; and, more often than not, such activities are handled by the publicity director himself.

CONTROL

In the smaller store, the manager or store owner generally acts as the controller-treasurer for the organization. Control functions in the larger firms are no longer limited to providing and safeguarding funds and keeping accounting records; the

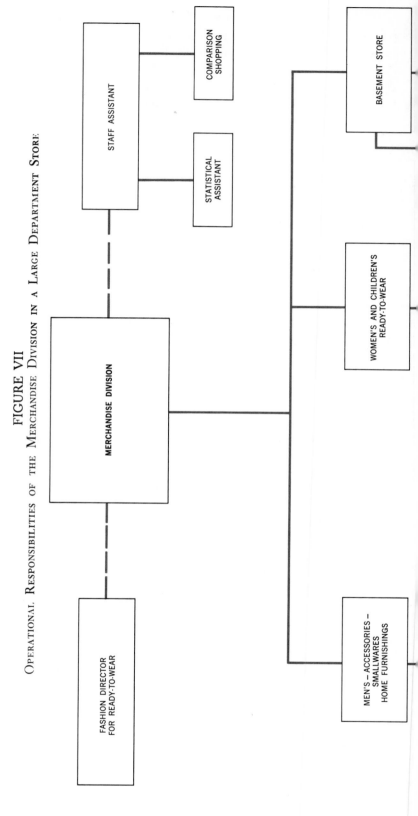

FIGURE VII

OPERATIONAL RESPONSIBILITIES OF THE MERCHANDISE DIVISION IN A LARGE DEPARTMENT STORE:

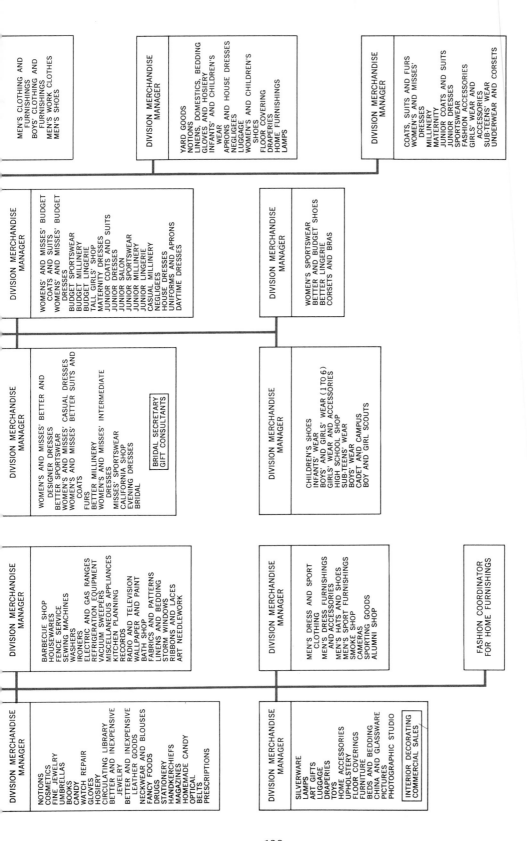

MEN'S CLOTHING AND FURNISHINGS
MEN'S CLOTHING AND FURNISHINGS
BOYS' CLOTHING AND FURNISHINGS
MEN'S WORK CLOTHES
MEN'S SHOES

DIVISION MERCHANDISE MANAGER
YARD GOODS
NOTIONS
LINENS, DOMESTICS, BEDDING
GLOVES AND HOSIERY
INFANTS' AND CHILDREN'S WEAR
APRONS AND HOUSE DRESSES
NEGLIGEES
LUGGAGE
WOMEN'S AND CHILDREN'S SHOES
FLOOR COVERING
DRAPERIES
HOME FURNISHINGS
LAMPS

DIVISION MERCHANDISE MANAGER
COATS, SUITS AND FURS
WOMEN'S AND MISSES' DRESSES
MILLINERY
MATERNITY
JUNIOR COATS AND SUITS
JUNIOR DRESSES
SPORTSWEAR
FASHION ACCESSORIES
GIRLS' WEAR AND ACCESSORIES
SUB-TEENS' WEAR
UNDERWEAR AND CORSETS

DIVISION MERCHANDISE MANAGER
WOMENS' AND MISSES' BUDGET COATS AND SUITS
WOMENS' AND MISSES' BUDGET DRESSES
BUDGET SPORTSWEAR
BUDGET MILLINERY
BUDGET LINGERIE
TALL GIRLS' SHOP
MATERNITY DRESSES
JUNIOR COATS AND SUITS
JUNIOR DRESSES
JUNIOR SALON
JUNIOR SPORTSWEAR
JUNIOR MILLINERY
JUNIOR LINGERIE
CASUAL MILLINERY
NEGLIGEES
HOUSE DRESSES
UNIFORMS AND APRONS
DAYTIME DRESSES

DIVISION MERCHANDISE MANAGER
WOMEN'S SPORTSWEAR
BETTER AND BUDGET SHOES
BETTER LINGERIE
CORSETS AND BRAS

DIVISION MERCHANDISE MANAGER
WOMEN'S AND MISSES' BETTER AND DESIGNER DRESSES
BETTER SPORTSWEAR
WOMEN'S AND MISSES' CASUAL DRESSES
WOMEN'S AND MISSES' BETTER SUITS AND COATS
FURS
BETTER MILLINERY
WOMEN'S AND MISSES' INTERMEDIATE DRESSES
MISSES' SPORTSWEAR
CALIFORNIA SHOP
EVENING DRESSES
BRIDAL

BRIDAL SECRETARY
GIFT CONSULTANTS

DIVISION MERCHANDISE MANAGER
CHILDREN'S SHOES
INFANTS' WEAR
BOYS' AND GIRLS' WEAR (1 TO 6)
GIRLS' WEAR AND ACCESSORIES
HIGH SCHOOL SHOP
SUB-TEENS' WEAR
BOYS' WEAR
CADET AND CAMPUS
BOY AND GIRL SCOUTS

DIVISION MERCHANDISE MANAGER
BARBECUE SHOP
HOUSEWARES
FENCE SERVICE
SEWING MACHINES
WASHERS
IRONERS
ELECTRIC AND GAS RANGES
REFRIGERATION EQUIPMENT
VACUUM SWEEPERS
MISCELLANEOUS APPLIANCES
KITCHEN PLANNING
RECORDS
RADIO AND TELEVISION
WALLPAPER AND PAINT
BATH SHOP
FABRICS AND PATTERNS
LINENS AND BEDDING
STORM WINDOWS
RIBBONS AND LACES
ART NEEDLEWORK

DIVISION MERCHANDISE MANAGER
MEN'S DRESS AND SPORT CLOTHING
MEN'S DRESS FURNISHINGS AND ACCESSORIES
MEN'S HATS AND SHOES
MEN'S SPORT FURNISHINGS
SMOKE SHOP
CAMERAS
SPORTING GOODS
ALUMNI SHOP

FASHION COORDINATOR FOR HOME FURNISHINGS

DIVISION MERCHANDISE MANAGER
NOTIONS
COSMETICS
FINE JEWELRY
UMBRELLAS
BOOKS
CANDY
WATCH REPAIR
GLOVES
HOSIERY
CIRCULATING LIBRARY
BETTER AND INEXPENSIVE JEWELRY
BETTER AND INEXPENSIVE LEATHER GOODS
NECKWEAR AND BLOUSES
FANCY FOODS
DRUGS
STATIONERY
HANDKERCHIEFS
MAGAZINES
HOMEMADE CANDY
OPTICAL
BELTS
PRESCRIPTIONS

DIVISION MERCHANDISE MANAGER
SILVERWARE
LAMPS
ART GIFTS
LUGGAGE
DRAPERIES
TOYS
HOME ACCESSORIES
UPHOLSTERY
FLOOR COVERINGS
FURNITURE
BEDS AND BEDDING
CHINA AND GLASSWARE
PICTURES
PHOTOGRAPHIC STUDIO

INTERIOR DECORATING
COMMERCIAL SALES

FIGURE VIII

TITLES AND RESPONSIBILITIES OF THE PUBLICITY DIVISION IN A LARGE DEPARTMENT STORE

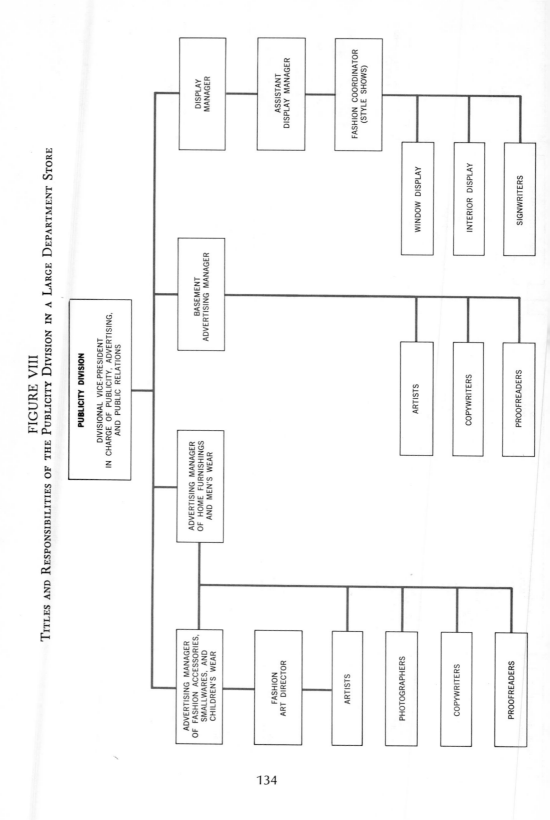

controller often takes the initiative in analyzing departmental as well as budgeting operations. Today, besides having the functional responsibilities shown in Figure IX, the controller is regularly called upon to interpret internal statistical data and make policy recommendations to top management.

Where a controller is research-minded, many new approaches to the improvement of organizational efficiency and market position are developed. It is through the control division, primarily, that new techniques in electronic data processing (EDP) systems and automated techniques are introduced in the store.

Expense and Work Centers

In recent years the concept of "expense centers" was developed by the AMC (Associated Merchandising Corporation) organization from factory cost accounting methods.[11] Working along very similar lines, the NRMA published an expense center and productivity unit accounting manual. It can be used as a tool to gauge the performance of individuals and to improve conditions in the control area. By setting up work centers and standard indexes of performance, units of productivity were developed as basic criteria.

It may be said that the cost rigidities at the base of the "profit squeeze" have been in a great measure responsible for rapid development of these techniques. The controller today is dealing to a greater extent with productivity as a measure of the over-all performance of the firm. In this regard it may be stated that employee efforts alone are seldom major forces in developing higher productivity. Rather, increased productivity is the result of many different factors—for example, better layout, better selling methods, and better customer appeals. However, the measurement of productivity changes is a very difficult process because of the complexity of the factors involved and the necessity of making estimates based on generally incomplete data.[12]

Use of Productivity Measures

An understanding of responsible accounting for improving productivity is part of every divisional executive's job. In many cases, taking periodic audits of the progress of his subordinates is as far as most executives can go. Such audits may be on a formal or informal basis through fixed deadlines for particular performances. Fixed deadlines are advantageous in that they provide freedom of action and high morale when success results. On the other hand, if the interval between audits is long, checking performance on specific assignments becomes difficult and may involve lost time and money if performance is not up to standards; therefore

---

[11] The AMC is a department-store-owned buying office, with many of the country's leading stores—such as Lazarus in Columbus, Bullock's in Los Angeles, and Carson, Pirie, Scott and Company in Chicago—as members.

[12] Productivity is a ratio of the sales to the input of resources in terms of merchandise and total operating costs which increase the over-all productive efficiency of the business. For a scholarly discussion in depth on productivity, see Bela Gold, *Foundations of Productivity Analysis* (Pittsburgh, Pa.: University of Pittsburgh Press, 1955).

FIGURE IX
TITLES AND RESPONSIBILITIES OF THE CONTROL DIVISION IN A LARGE DEPARTMENT STORE

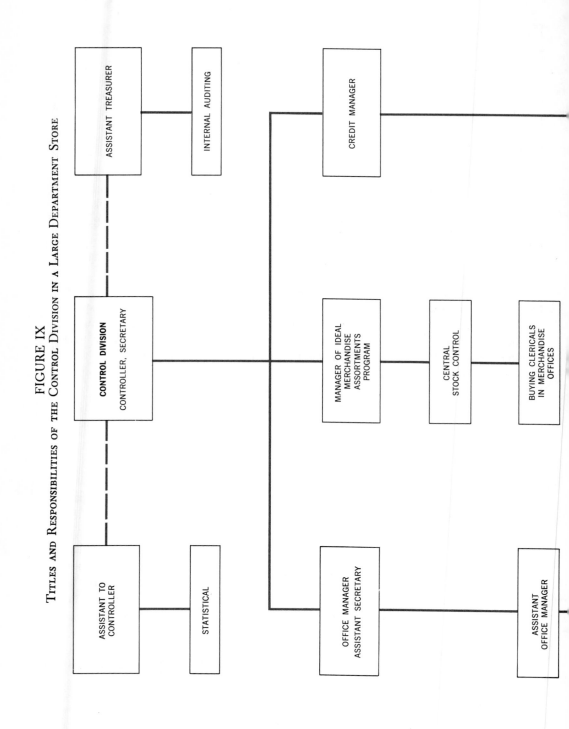

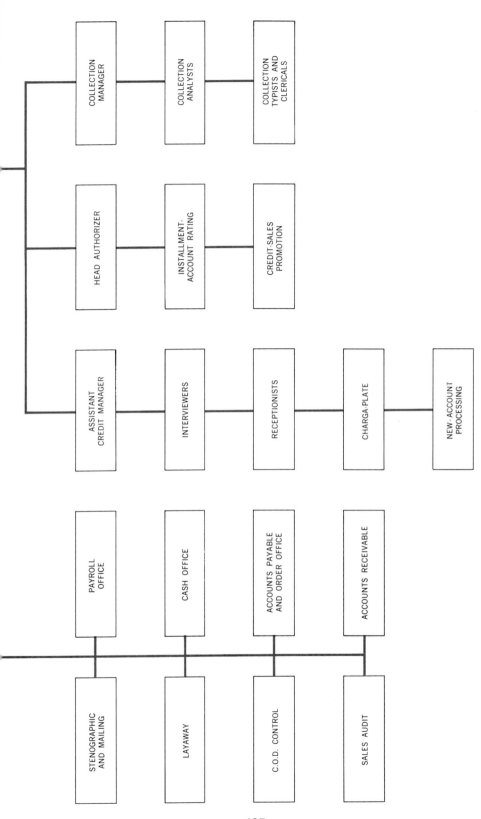

COLLECTION MANAGER — COLLECTION ANALYSTS — COLLECTION TYPISTS AND CLERICALS

HEAD AUTHORIZER — INSTALLMENT-ACCOUNT RATING — CREDIT-SALES PROMOTION

ASSISTANT CREDIT MANAGER — INTERVIEWERS — RECEPTIONISTS — CHARGA-PLATE — NEW-ACCOUNT PROCESSING

PAYROLL OFFICE — STENOGRAPHIC AND MAILING

CASH OFFICE — LAYAWAY

ACCOUNTS PAYABLE AND ORDER OFFICE — C.O.D. CONTROL

ACCOUNTS RECEIVABLE — SALES AUDIT

137

irregularly timed checks on managerial performance must be treated as a calculated risk.[13]

A more formalized method of measuring productivity changes is through regular reports on accomplishments worth measuring: e.g., comparative labor costs between one department and another, sequential investment in supplies for similar volume levels, cost related to materials-handling procedures, and quality standards for incoming merchandise as well as selling performance. Care must be taken that the comparisons correctly evaluate the factors to be measured, because many projects may be quite complex and involve other integrated cost elements that should not be considered. For example, where the completion of one project is necessary before the beginning of another, the project performance must be evaluated in terms of correct allocation of expense.

Another method of roughly checking productivity is direct questioning during group meetings on progress in recent developments. The more rigorous methods of productivity measures will be analyzed in Chapter 27 on control.

THE GENERAL MANAGEMENT AND OPERATIONS DIVISION

General management policy determines internal operating systems and procedures as well as the best form of organization needed to attain company objectives. The nature of the responsibilities and powers to be delegated within the firm are also stipulated. At the divisional level, policies and procedures are set up for store maintenance and engineering functions such as the provision of heat, light, power, ventilation, housekeeping, cleaning, sweeping of floors, and so on. (See Figure X.)

General policy also determines the type of customer services to be offered. It is not at all uncommon for many store general managers, although specifically charged with responsibility for sales-supporting activities, to supervise directly particular divisions within the store—either as a challenge or as a matter of keeping continuous contact. The general manager also systematically reviews customer services and their supervision by section managers. Section managers are also customer service managers in every sense.

The store-management division is responsible for processing merchandise upon receipt and for its handling, marking, and transporting to the appropriate departments. If merchandise has not been preretailed, it should be immediately called to the buyer's attention for price confirmation before being released for selling. The rapid processing of invoice OK's for discount payment is also this division's responsibility.

Workroom Operations

Department store workrooms are also in the province of the store-operating di-

---

[13] See *Expense Center and Productivity Accounting Manual*, rev. ed. (New York: National Retail Management Assoc., Controllers Congress, 1957), for applications of such methods to specific operations.

FIGURE X

GENERAL MANAGEMENT AND OPERATIONS IN A LARGE DEPARTMENT STORE

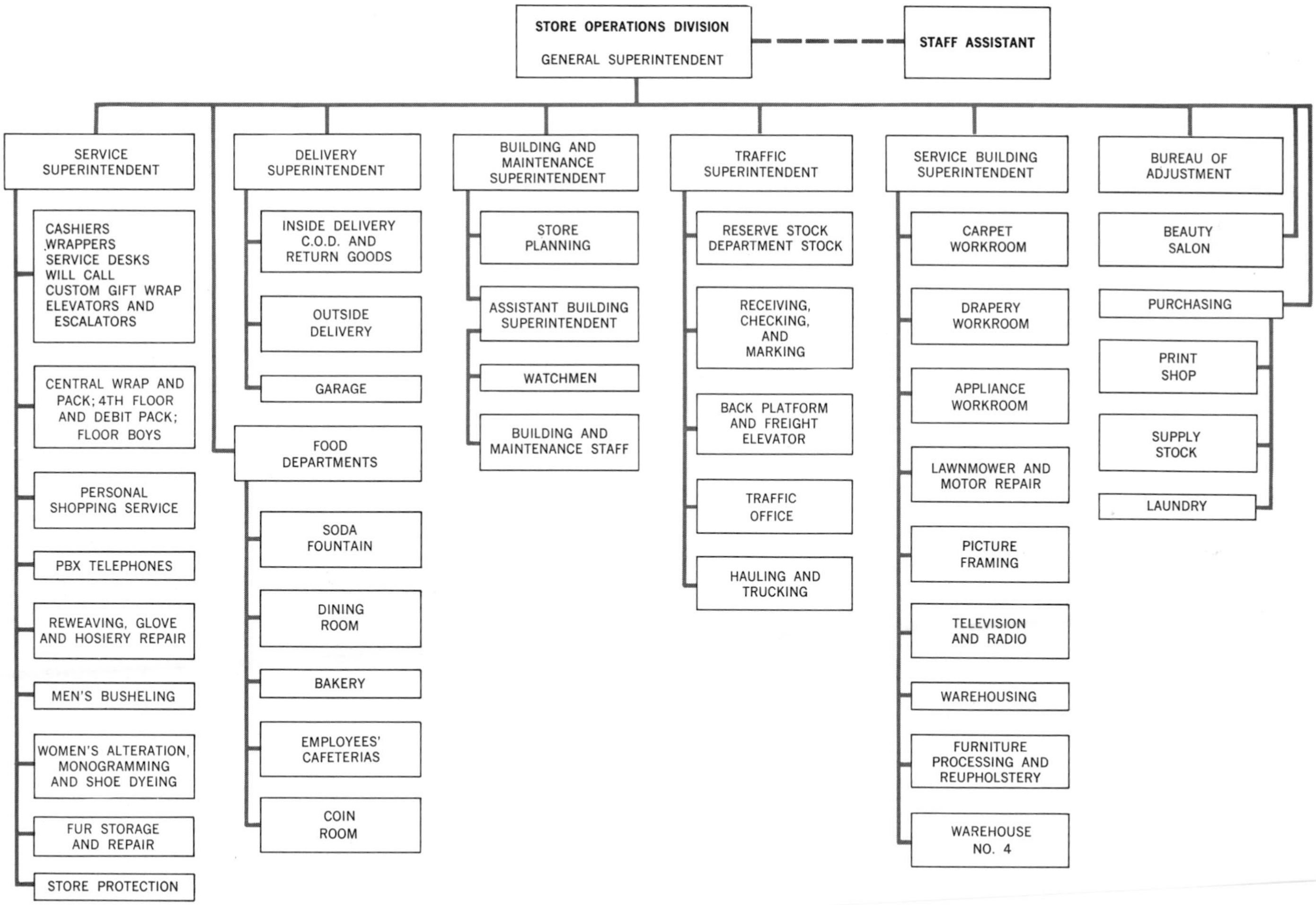

STORE OPERATIONS DIVISION
GENERAL SUPERINTENDENT

STAFF ASSISTANT

SERVICE SUPERINTENDENT
- CASHIERS
- WRAPPERS
- SERVICE DESKS
- WILL CALL
- CUSTOM GIFT WRAP
- ELEVATORS AND ESCALATORS
- CENTRAL WRAP AND PACK: 4TH FLOOR AND DEBIT PACK; FLOOR BOYS
- PERSONAL SHOPPING SERVICE
- PBX TELEPHONES
- REWEAVING, GLOVE AND HOSIERY REPAIR
- MEN'S BUSHELING
- WOMEN'S ALTERATION, MONOGRAMMING AND SHOE DYEING
- FUR STORAGE AND REPAIR
- STORE PROTECTION

DELIVERY SUPERINTENDENT
- INSIDE DELIVERY C.O.D. AND RETURN GOODS
- OUTSIDE DELIVERY
- GARAGE
- FOOD DEPARTMENTS
- SODA FOUNTAIN
- DINING ROOM
- BAKERY
- EMPLOYEES' CAFETERIAS
- COIN ROOM

BUILDING AND MAINTENANCE SUPERINTENDENT
- STORE PLANNING
- ASSISTANT BUILDING SUPERINTENDENT
- WATCHMEN
- BUILDING AND MAINTENANCE STAFF

TRAFFIC SUPERINTENDENT
- RESERVE STOCK DEPARTMENT STOCK
- RECEIVING, CHECKING, AND MARKING
- BACK PLATFORM AND FREIGHT ELEVATOR
- TRAFFIC OFFICE
- HAULING AND TRUCKING

SERVICE BUILDING SUPERINTENDENT
- CARPET WORKROOM
- DRAPERY WORKROOM
- APPLIANCE WORKROOM
- LAWNMOWER AND MOTOR REPAIR
- PICTURE FRAMING
- TELEVISION AND RADIO
- WAREHOUSING
- FURNITURE PROCESSING AND REUPHOLSTERY
- WAREHOUSE NO. 4

BUREAU OF ADJUSTMENT
- BEAUTY SALON
- PURCHASING
- PRINT SHOP
- SUPPLY STOCK
- LAUNDRY

vision. The most common types of activities in store workrooms are alterations of ladies' ready-to-wear and men's and boys' suits and clothing. Workroom operations are carried out in terms of necessary services, because most workrooms are operated at loss. Necessary services are often contracted out by retail firms; such operations include dry cleaning and shoe repair centers, manufacturing workrooms that make millinery, draperies, curtains, slipcovers, and spreads, and preparation and repair workrooms used with deliveries of furniture and appliances. The larger firms boast "general workroom operations" that make, adjust, or repair store fixtures and mechanical and refrigeration equipment, and can move store departments when required.

A high degree of technical competency is involved in workroom operations because of their "manufacturing" nature. As such they are operated under the cost method of inventory. Where volume in certain workroom areas does not warrant a full staff, work is generally contracted out on a piecework basis.

THE PERSONNEL DIVISION

Retailing is concerned with the interaction of people, places, and commodities; labor costs involved in these interactions can prove quite substantial.

As shown in Figure XI, the personnel division is responsible for recruiting, employment, training, counseling, executive development, and so on. Apart from the people in his own division, the personnel director is rarely given blanket authority to hire and fire other than rank-and-file employees. In effect, he is responsible for seeing to it that all divisions in the firm are properly staffed. The division also acts in an advisory capacity to all managerial echelons. The executive pay roll, however, is usually handled on a separate basis—generally by an assistant to the store's general manager.

While the core aspects of merchandising promotion and selling can be easily recognized and delineated, the activities of the personnel division seem to be only "understood" and are less clearly specified in most retail firms. One of the more clearly defined areas of responsibility for the personnel division, however, is the seeking out and development of executive talent for middle management. In this field, personnel also develops performance criteria for all store employees.

Many difficult problems are always present in executive development. For example, according to a personnel vice-president of a large eastern department store, no individual would be hired for the store's executive development program unless he was a college graduate, could pass the store's testing procedures, and could be classified as having top management potential. Individuals meeting such criteria have been scarce, because starting salaries in retailing have generally been lower than those of comparable openings in industry despite the fact that promotional opportunities in retailing are far greater. As a result, there is a continuing acute need for junior and middle management echelons in retail firms.

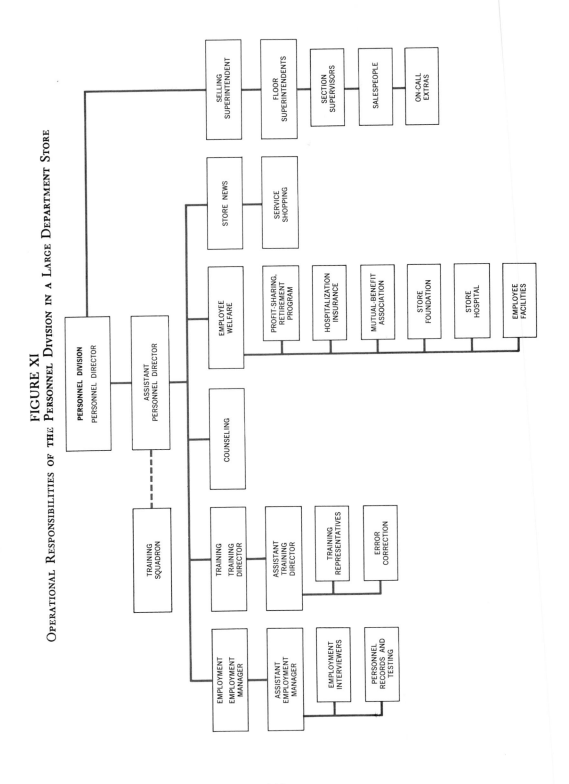

FIGURE XI
OPERATIONAL RESPONSIBILITIES OF THE PERSONNEL DIVISION IN A LARGE DEPARTMENT STORE

THE PRIMACY OF THE MERCHANDISING DIVISION

The needs of the merchandising division must supersede those of all others in the store. As the income-producing division, it must plan purchases and stocks in both dollar amounts and units so as to satisfy expected customer demand within budgeted allotments. As pointed out above, selling is guided by the department buyers and supervised by section managers from the management division; the control division supervises sales procedures so that financial, inventory, and budget goals are achieved.

The exact lines of authority and responsibility between the merchandising manager, the controller, the publicity director, and the store manager are difficult to delineate, as the latter are in reality a team with constant formal and informal interactions—often on a cross-functional basis.

Cross-functionalization within the retail store can be likened to an interdisciplinary approach used for the solution of a business problem. In a similar manner, engineering, sociological, and psychological considerations interweave within the broad organization structure. For example, in changes in store, departmental, and floor layouts the engineering approach is interwoven with behavioral considerations. The use of standards for merchandising management as well as operative management tasks is often introduced by the store manager. Where the merchandising and operating reports of the Controller's Congress are used to measure expenses and maximize gross margins, such standards facilitate reappraisals throughout the firm.

The function of merchandising management corresponds to the product engineering department of a manufacturing firm. For example, a fashion coordinator, in effect, determines the product, price, and style combinations needed for presentation of a complete offering. These combinations, set up in "theme" fashion, are carried out through coordinated purchases by various departmental buyers. The "themes" are based on prior understandings of consumer wants and the necessary technical competency and good taste to satisfy these wants at competitive prices.

When a strong merchandise manager pre-empts executive direction in both the management and control areas, the controller, if he is strong, may pre-empt many of the functions considered to be of a merchandising nature. Where the controller and merchandise manager are equally strong, there is often duplication of efforts in merchandise planning and inventory control. Only through exacting demands for teamwork under a single strong executive leader at the top can divisional operations be clearly defined for efficient coordinated operations.

SUMMARY AND CONCLUSIONS

In this chapter the divisional operations of the retail firm were broadly discussed so as to provide a framework for the more specific economic and managerial analyses that follow in later chapters. The functional areas of merchandising, control, publicity, and operations management were briefly reviewed in light of the personal nature of the retailing process.

The types of management decisions that are made throughout the store determine the way in which divisional operations are coordinated to attain company objectives. Thus, any change in the values or image concepts of any particular division would affect operations in all divisions of the firm. It was also pointed out that the totality of merchandise and service offerings through divisional coordination cannot be evaluated apart from the location of the offering and its market potential.

While market factors limit managerial actions in divisional operations, generalizations here should be summed up in terms of opportunity costs, as they often determine the types of decisions made by divisional managers. Such alternative cost considerations are also important to the individual, although they may appear transitory and hardly definitive. The real problem in divisional operations of the retail structure rests with management's ability to pinpoint operating inadequacies on a continuing basis.

In the following chapter, the internal layout and service procedures requirements needed for optimizing operations will be reviewed.

Chapter 10: *Internal Layout and Service Procedures*

Organizational policies determine not only the internal layout of the store, but also the general location of any new unit. The processes from site selection until the opening of a store are the responsibility of management, although practically all facets of new store development and internal layout modernizations are delegated to experts in the field. Of critical importance is the coordination of internal layout and space so that functional planning and the store's selling efforts can be effectively carried out.

FUNCTIONS OF INTERNAL LAYOUT

Internal design and departmentalization of the store are set up in order to facilitate the service and sales offerings made to the public. They are also indicative of the philosophy of the store management as interpreted by the architects and designers.

Store layout must furnish the most comfortable setting for triggering purchasing decisions and for maximizing in-store traffic to all sales areas. Whether "free-flow" or "grid-type" areas are used, the basic objective is maximum merchandise exposure consistent with the store image.

Store layout and service procedures must facilitate customer purchases and at the same time suggest other items. For example, some supermarket planners believe that the entering customer should be faced immediately with a display of the main portion of a meal; in stores so planned customers are always confronted with and must pass by the meat counter first. Other supermarkets force customers by means of their internal layouts, to travel through mazes of milk, vegetables, and canned goods before they can finally arrive at the counter displays offering main meal selections.[1]

By means of simulation techniques and depth interviews, one can achieve the best in design consistent with optimizing consumer behavior at the point of purchase.[2]

Optimizing consumer behavior at the point of purchase increases the store's over-all productivity as well as the shopping satisfactions of its customers. Customers, once in the store, should be led by its interior design and layout into "impulse" shopping areas as well as the sales areas they seek. Throughout the store at the various points of purchase, the store's service offer should take over to induce sales. Because of the many recent trends towards self-service and self-selection, the productive nature of the service offer is often hidden and difficult to evaluate. Also, most services are an integral part of the total sales package. While services such as delivery and personal sales efforts lend themselves to greater degrees of measurement, value alone is not the basic consideration. The extent of the services offered to the consumer is determined by competition rather than purely intrafirm economic considerations.

Stores strive to be all things to all people. The retail institution projects its basic image through its merchandise and service offerings and the manner in which these are presented to the public. For example, "easy in–easy out" sections are necessary with most stores having fast-moving departments. Credit and non-selling service departments which require time for completion of service are placed either on upper floors or in comparatively "dead" areas.

Ideally, the store should be so planned as to provide for the efficient functioning of all elements as a unit. Often, models are set up to structure simulations of different types of layouts. By such means, every aspect of space and traffic flows can be measured for adequacy and efficiency.[3]

INTERIOR DESIGN

The purpose of interior design in a store is to furnish the proper setting for selling and sales-supporting activities. At its best, the interior design develops a

---

[1] The A & P Supermarkets are among those planned in this fashion. Many of the Kroger stores are set up in the "meat-counter-first" type of layout.

[2] From an interview with J. Rogers Flannery, Jr. (President, Flannery & Associates), architect and store planner, Pittsburgh, Pa., May 1963. (The depth interviewing concept will be reviewed in greater detail in the chapter on research.)

[3] Some firms may insist on related merchandise being placed in adjacent selling areas; others do not feel this to be necessary. For example, hats, shoes, gloves, and handbags should be grouped for coordinated selling. However, in actual practice they may be located in many store areas.

congenial setting for customers and salespeople through appropriate layout and choice of fixtures.[4] In general, layout and interior design call for the use of restraint to allow maximum flexibility. Because of the costs and the inconvenience of business interruption involved in change, planning should be completed before proceeding further.

Fixtures should be simple, functionally designed, and constructed of inconspicuous wood with the outside painted to blend into the wall. As the building of new structures increases in cost, each square foot of selling area becomes a most expensive premium. Prefabricated fixtures and furnishings can be set up in a sectional system that can be easily changed in accordance with changing requirements. Often the variety of assembly alone will compensate for the lack of styling, and will fit quite well into a flexible arrangement. With this system, plans and service offerings can be tested and adjusted as needed.[5]

The Function of Interior Decor

Just as a store's organizational structure determines the type of selling service offered, so interior decoration provides the setting for the store's personality or image. Interior decor represents the sum total of the individual effects of background design and decoration, displays, entrances, and signs. Interior decor should be functional and should be an integral part of the store's personality. In Figure XII some of the influences of civilization on interior design are illustrated.

Customer entrances, the store front, the sales space inside, and all display areas should be coordinated into a predetermined theme. Signs and signature "cuts" of the store should be used as trade name backgrounds throughout the store. A well-designed store should have visible background displays representing the kinds of merchandise handled with appropriate directions for locating these companion items. Points of entry to various departments should be clear and unobstructed so as to facilitate merchandise selection. To be truly functional, interior decor should "frame" the buying situation as a natural entrance to all parts of the store. It should also create feelings of warmth and ease of shopping so that visits to all store sales departments are encouraged.[6] Well-designed guiding points indicating where related or other types of merchandise may be obtained within the store itself should be worked into the total scheme of decor.

Merchandise visibility invites more selectivity and creates pools of customer traffic which stop and buy. The entire theme should always be one of conven-

---

[4] Improper considerations of the internal physical distribution systems in the store and of delivery and/or storage layouts could create a major obstacle to efficient operations as well as inventory carrying costs. J. L. Heskett suggests that any physical distribution system should be viewed from a planning standpoint as a set of actual or potential inventory cells in network links. In this case the network would consist of the various store areas and departments. (From a paper presented to the American Marketing Association, Washington, D.C., September 1965.)

[5] Walter S. Sobotka, The Principles of Design, mimeographed (Graduate School of Retailing, University of Pittsburgh, 1961).

[6] Morris Ketchum, Shops and Stores, rev. ed. (New York: Reinhold Publishing Corp., 1957), p. 133.

FIGURE XII
THE AGES OF CIVILIZATION

(*As an influence on design*)

PRIMITIVE AGES

Need and art are closely related: homogeneous character of culture

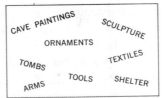

NEED AND ART
(AS SYMBOLS OF COMFORT)

AGES OF ART

Arts and crafts follow same principles; craftsmanship takes care of elaborate goods. Fashion has limited influence. Provincial developments are more structural in design; need of the poor stays outside.

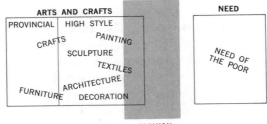

FASHION
(AS SYMBOL OF SECURITY)

AGE OF INDUSTRY AND DISTRIBUTION

Fine arts receding; applied arts spreading; needs, not taken care of, almost disappear, but new needs are added. Ever-growing influence of fashion.

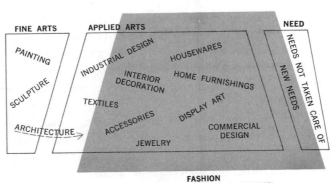

FASHION
(AS INFLUENCE FOR PURCHASING)

Source: Walter S. Sobotka, *The Principles of Design*, mimeographed (Graduate School of Retailing, University of Pittsburgh, 1961). Parenthetical material added by present author.

ience and fun in shopping. In the larger stores, comfortable benches and chairs can give the store a relaxed shopping atmosphere.

In the proper setting and when creatively set up, a store, regardless of size, can generate a feeling of intimacy at the point of sale. This objective is easier to achieve when there is full-service selling, when sales-supporting activities have been fully coordinated, and when forward stocks are always almost instantly available.

The Function of Design

Design is the key coordinating force of interior decor; it is the force that shapes and styles attitudes and indirectly but firmly fixes a store image in a customer attitude so that he is encouraged to be in a buying mood. The design of furniture and fixtures in a store should symbolize the merchandising policy and promotional impact of the entire store. Store furniture and fixtures should provide utility with a design theme, but the design must not be so outstanding as to overshadow the merchandise that is offered for sale.[7]

ROLE OF STORE EXECUTIVES

New concepts in store design flow from both necessity and fashion. Retail management, with the help of the merchandising executives, set up the guides for store planning and design. The store buyer, although chiefly concerned with buying and merchandising goods, is the key link between sales and profits, and his thinking should represent the funnel through which policy procedures for changing store layouts or departmental displays are carried out. Yet, buyers are rarely, if ever, consulted regarding such changes.[8]

The store architect is responsible for developing and coordinating the internal layout on the basis of planned in-store traffic patterns of customers and needs of all supporting departments such as sales, service operations, displays, and workrooms; he also suggests colors, texture, lighting consistent with building codes, contracting needs, and plot structure. The architect acts as the principal co-ordinator of the supporting agencies involved in the construction of any new store—principally the real estate firm, the landscaper, the store planners, and the logistics personnel of the store. The analysis of construction costs, the scheduling of operations, and assembly of the necessary materials are the responsibility of the builder.

When building costs are not excessive, it has been found that the split-level mezzanines and downstairs store arrangements adjacent to main-floor layouts prove quite efficient because of the ease with which customers move from one level to another without use of escalators.

Fashion appeal should be the first consideration in setting up the so-called "decorative" approach to store design. In the so-called "performance" approach

---

[7] Sobotka, op. cit.

[8] An excellent example of changing planning and design is the new 300,000-square-foot Fountain Square store of Mabley & Carew, Cincinnati. The aim of the operation is a specialty shop department store, definitely a fashion store aimed at enlarging its fashion market. However, it has a home furnishings floor—a new field for the former soft goods store in which performance, construction, and materials were the important selling considerations. Another concept is the new Neiman-Marcus hexagonal 70,000-square-foot suburban store recently opened in West Fort Worth, Texas. Clustered about the main store are additional wings plus shops rented to other merchants. The Neiman-Marcus shops include the Wine Cellar, Le Beau Chien (Poodle Salon), and the Bath Shop, specializing in fine bathroom accessories. (Grey Matter, Vol. 9, No. 3, May 1963.)

materials are basic while the decorative approach becomes secondary. Once a new unit is planned and set up on a rational functional basis, all subsequent decisions involved in opening a new unit are facilitated.

MODERNIZATIONS VERSUS NEW STRUCTURES

It is far more difficult to embark on a store modernization program than to build a new store. During modernization, sales areas must always be kept open with the least possible customer dissatisfaction. Any contemplated project must first be flexibly programed so as to set up objectives, means, methods, costs, and timing. The major factors to be considered are the definitions of sales space, forward reserve stock areas, customer service areas, cashier and wrapping facilities, and space allocation for receiving, marking, and employee conveniences. At least 50 per cent, and preferably as much as 70 per cent, of the total available floor area in any store should be used for sales activities. At least 70 per cent is recommended for branch stores; their needs for stock storage areas are generally less than parent units.

Store management must furnish the merchandising objectives in any modernization program. Goals should be set up in terms of needed floor area and should follow standards such as those published by the National Retail Merchants Association. The necessary floor space should be allocated into departments.

SPACE PLANNING

Space planning in retail stores begins with the customer. Therefore space must be set up for selling departments first and sales-supporting activities second. Customer traffic patterns determine display arrangements and the relative worth of various locations on the selling floor. Normally, locations nearest the store entrance and adjacent to open front window displays are the most valuable. Total rental cost allocations are charged on the basis of both square feet occupied and its relative value in terms of economic rent based on projected traffic patterns. The principle here is the same as it would be for a store renting a location in a business or shopping area. In a multifloor store, charges to the various departments for space are made on the same basis—customer traffic patterns.

In Table 11, an illustration of typical rental charges for various space allocations is shown. Space rental rates in retail stores have wide ranges in economic values. Normally, the higher the turnover and the less bulky the item in relation to its cost, the smaller the space allocation and the better the traffic location needed for the department. For example, women's hosiery, handbags, and cosmetics show a relatively high return per square foot of selling space, and are usually found in the most expensive main floor location. On the other hand, furniture and bedding have lower stock turnover, need much more space, and are generally found on much less expensive upstairs locations.

TABLE 11

APPORTIONMENT OF BUILDING RENT BY FLOOR

FLOOR	STORE NUMBER										
	1	2	3	4	5	6	7	8	9	10	11
	%	%	%	%	%	%	%	%	%	%	%
Basement	35	..	25	..	15	10	10	15	12½	15	15
Main	65	65	50	60	45	45	50	40	35	35	30
Second	..	35	25	30	25	25	20	20	20	20	19
Third	..	..	..	10	15	10	10	15	15	10	15
Fourth	..	..	..	..	..	10	10	10	10	10	8
Fifth	..	..	..	..	..	..	..	..	7½	5	6
Sixth	..	..	..	..	..	..	..	..	..	5	4
Seventh	..	..	..	..	..	..	..	..	..	..	2
Eighth	..	..	..	..	..	..	..	..	..	..	1

Source: Paul H. Nystrom, *The Economics of Retailing*, 3rd ed. (New York: Ronald Press, 1930), p. 229.

DETERMINING SERVICE REQUIREMENTS

The service requirements of any retail institution are determined by the store's objectives and by the degree of both price and nonprice competition in the trading area. Once determined, service offerings of the firm should be publicized by every promotional means possible. Because of the growing uniformity among stores, it is more important than ever before to stress nonprice differences. Essentially, this means institutional differentiation in terms of service offerings, so that brand-based patronage motives can be generated. The variations of services offered to the customer are almost limitless. From the standpoint of long-run maximization, service offerings constitute a meaningful form of sales promotion underlying the nature of the total appeal of a store.[9]

Unquestionably nonprice variables in the retail markets are of growing significance in the market place and serve to differentiate the image appeal of retail stores handling similar types of merchandise. It is conceivable that under the impact of greater service offerings and better image projections permanent volume increases would accrue not only to the offering store but to the total shopping area as well.

Utility is a function of total satisfactions received. The functional characteristic of the seller's offer is the extent of the total satisfaction received by the buyer in relationship to the demand structure of an area. While each store within a trading area has differing opportunity costs, service on a part of the seller's offer can either improve or decrease total customer satisfaction. In other words, both price and nonprice factors vary from one location to another in accordance with the opportunity costs of the seller. Physical accessibility to particular stores also differs; thus, the utility and demand function of similar stores vary from one location to another depending on their respective accessibility and grading area

---

[9] From time to time attempts have been made to measure some of the nonprice factors in store offerings—such as automatic doors, air conditioning, music, days and hours open per week, check cashing, postal and money order services, premiums, and extent and convenience of parking areas, and completeness of product lines. See Robert R. Holdren's text, *The Structure of a Retail Market and the Market Behavior of Retail Units* (Englewood Cliffs, N.J.: Prentice-Hall, 1960).

potentials. The more accessible a retail unit, the less the need for maximizing the nonprice offerings to equalize competitive effectiveness.

In the case of convenience goods stores—drugstores, supermarkets, and so on— it is obvious that movement from one location to another has great impact because the driving time that consumers are willing to spend for such shopping is relatively small. Also, relocations or new branches of drugstore or supermarket units are often faced with a completely different population mix with differing consumer expectations. On the other hand, shopping and specialty goods stores (such as women's ready-to-wear stores, department stores, and furniture stores) can relocate more easily because of their considerably larger geographical trading areas.

It cannot be assumed that the consumer is really aware of the alternative offering mixes of any one store. Price differentials would have to be quite significant for limited service stores to create the same "draw" of well-known, prestige service stores. In-store ease of shopping can induce customers to undergo the inconvenience of visiting many store selling departments in much the same fashion that ease of driving and convenience induce them to travel greater distances in order to shop at a particular store.

Basically, the total image projection of the store determines its effectiveness and patronage appeal. In Figure XIII an illustration of some of the underlying motivations determining consumer patronage and buyer are shown. In the minds of consumers, every store is characterized as either a prestige, promotional, semi-prestige or a convenience type of institution. Continual institutional advertising backed up with follow-through selling services can deliver better than average total package satisfactions.

DETERMINING THE TYPE OF SALES EFFORT

Today, even the highest-prestige full-service stores employ some modification of self-selection selling in specific areas. Convenience rather than the reduction of selling costs, per se, should be the criterion for adaptation to particular kinds of selling efforts. As a general rule it may be stated that the fewer the salespeople employed, the greater the need for ease of movement within the store and the greater the need for point of purchase informational displays throughout the store.

The kind and extent of sales efforts expended in stores is often determined by manufacturers of national brands who feel that their products and brands are "pre-sold" and hence require little sales effort and low mark-ons for the retailer. This is particularly true for convenience goods where self-service, check-out, and simplified selling procedures represent the gamut of the selling efforts. However, the salesperson is still indispensable in the long run regardless of the extent to which he is employed.[10]

---

[10] In a speech before security analysts in St. Louis, Mo., J. S. Mack, Board Chairman and President of G. C. Murphy, pointed out that the salesperson was still indispensable because "the customers like service and Murphy's will continue to operate its 510 stores with full complements of clerks." (*Women's Wear Daily*, May 21, 1963, p. 2.)

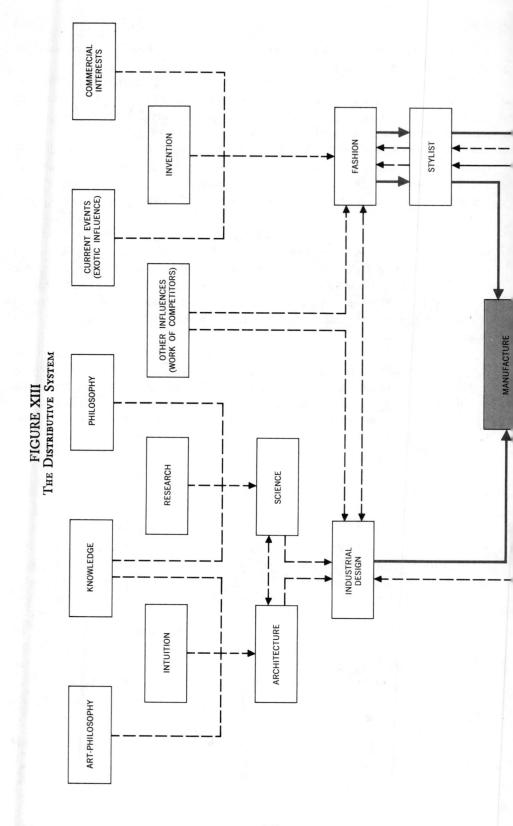

FIGURE XIII
THE DISTRIBUTIVE SYSTEM

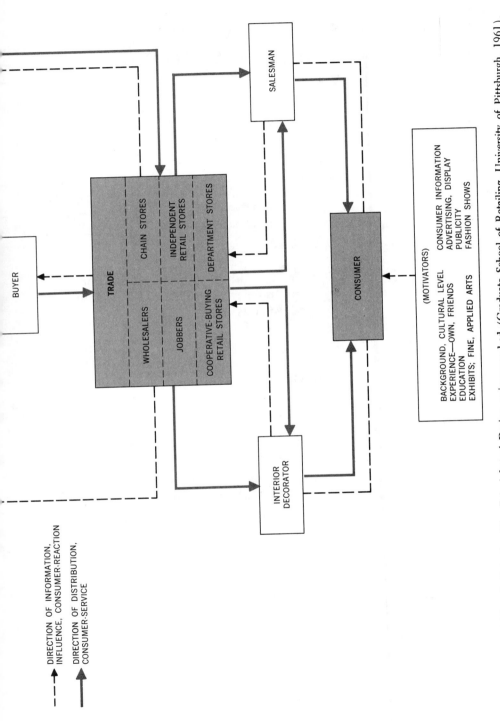

Source: Walter S. Sobotka, *The Principles of Design*, mimeographed (Graduate School of Retailing, University of Pittsburgh, 1961).

153

Full-Service Selling

Full-service selling, as the name implies, means actually assisting a customer in every phase of his or her buying effort—through greeting, creating rapport, personal solicitation and inquiry, suggestion selling, and closing and completing the sale. Advisory services and "plus" reassurances which many customers need are part of the package where warranted. When relative productivity per sale is high and the price of the merchandise is high in relation to bulk (with important fashion or technical elements), then full-service selling should be part of the sales offer. Departments such as men's and women's clothing, shoes, major appliances, services, and better furniture are in this category. While certain aspects of self-selection and self-service procedures are utilized in these areas, it is almost impossible to upgrade merchandise line sales with less than full-service selling.

Another aspect often overlooked is that far fewer sales are lost with full-service selling than with self-service, more than outweighing any additional expense involved. Of course, it may be wasteful to have full-service selling in departments where staple, well-known, branded products are sold. However, it is at the point of sale that customers are in a buying mood and can easily be "traded up" into buying other merchandise.

As long as the selling effort is carried out with intelligence and pleasant courtesy, a highly favorable image impact on customers is established. When full-service selling is properly used, personal sales efforts tend to become quite productive. There is a direct correlation between the availability of full selling services, good will, and volume increases. In repeated surveys, courtesy and merchandise knowledge were ranked first and second by respondents who stated that they were favorably impressed by a store's selling efforts.

The beneficial effect of personal attention on full-service selling can also be a highly detrimental store weakness. In answer to the question, "Have you had an unsatisfactory person wait on you recently?" respondents stated almost without hesitation that indifference and lack of merchandise knowledge were what they resented most.

Thus, where full-service selling is a factor in the store image, constant supervision must be maintained to insure a high level of service. In general, it may be stated that full-service selling is generally far more desirable for shopping and specialty goods and that self-selection selling is more economic for convenience and low-cost impulse goods.

Simplified Selling

Simplified selling and self-selection may be viewed as the midpoint between full service and the self-service check-out type of operation. Many large stores—among them Sears, Roebuck and Company and the J. C. Penney Company—have "quick-service cashier" systems. A central control register system is characteristic of a simplified selling system. Signs through the store advise shoppers to make their own selections and take them to a central wrap desk for payment. Proponents of limited-service selling systems (among them Mr. P. F. Prince, Sears' Merchandise Training Director), claim that self-selection and simplified selling service help increase sales to the point where many "walkouts" are salvaged and converted into sales.[11] Mr. Prince also pointed out that salespeople trained to "trade up" could increase sales to potential purchasers because the self-service, self-selection type of buying situations seemed to encourage customers to buy lower price lines. Simplified self-selection in many cases has been the answer to stores needing measures of extra service where self-service check-out failed and where full-service selling proved uneconomic. Despite obvious advantages here, it should be pointed out that self-service check-out should always be implemented with the use of "roving" salespeople in order to increase the sales of higher-price merchandise.

Self-Service and Check-Out

Actually, there is no exact line of demarcation between self-service and simplified self-selection. Only where complete display merchandise lines and assortments are available can the self-service check-out type of operation be installed. Employees who work in this latter type of operation are generally classified as checkers and wrappers. Self-service has been defined as having buyers who help themselves with the assistance of service clerks. It is claimed that all mass retailing is actually, "if not theoretically," self-service.[12]

In attempts to cut costs and become more competitive, retail management has been expanding the number of lines available on a self-service–self-selection basis; however, lower costs have not always resulted, despite wide customer acceptability.

Self-service check-out operations require specialized departmental layouts. For example, the more progressive hardware stores have merchandise display fixtures which encourage customer self-selection. Similarly, drugstores, variety stores, greeting-card shops, garden shops, and even grocery stores use self-service merchandising techniques to the fullest possible extent.

One of the main advantages of this type of operation is reduction in selling expense. Surveys have also shown a reduction in pilferage because the customer has to pass by a check-out lane or control counter. In a study of the budget store operation of a large department store in the Midwest, it was found that the check-out lane acted as a sentinel. The store, a prestige operation, found that they were getting far less pilferage in fitting rooms from professional female shoplifters than when they were on an open, simplified-selling system.[13]

Among the disadvantages of self-selection and simplified self-service is the necessity for a larger inventory investment and greater costs (such as interest charges,

---

11 "Quick Service Cashiers Halt Sears' Busy Hour Walkouts," Home Furnishings Daily (July 22, 1957), p. 6. Fifty per cent of the hardware items, 70 per cent of men's furnishings, 75 per cent of infant's wear, and 80 per cent of houseware sales were handled on simplified self-selection selling systems. Mr. Prince also stated that pilferage totaled approximately 0.25 per cent by the "quick-cashier" system.
12 Grey Matter, National Advertising edition, Vol. 23, No. 13 (July 1, 1952).
13 From research records of J. Rogers Flannery & Associates, Management Consultants and Store Planners (March 1963).

lower turnover, and more merchandise duplication). Such added costs must be weighed against any savings in selling expense. Unquestionably, mass displays properly controlled can encourage increased selling space productivity. Unless merchandise control is rigorous and constant, the benefits possible from this type of selling are quickly lost. Even in highly automated supermarkets, coffee grinding, meat service, and delicatessen departments are manned by service clerks. While complete robot shopping represented by vending machine operations will grow and become more important, they will continue to be tied to the sale of low-cost convenience goods merchandise.

Complete automation of the selling function will never be achieved, regardless of what facilities can be developed in the check-out type of self-service. Retailing is a face-to-face operation, and maximizing its effectiveness in a competitive economy requires elements of service. In effect, the savings per dollar in limited-service selling in many areas can be more than canceled out in terms of lost sales and lower price lines sold.

SELLING TECHNIQUES AND ORGANIZATIONAL OBJECTIVES

As previously pointed out, there is no one selling policy or technique that is best for all kinds of stores. The most efficient operating methodology may call for the adaptation and combining of all types of selling efforts—even for similar merchandise lines. For example, cosmetics, infant's wear, baby preparations, hosiery, phonograph records, hair preparations, and white goods are sold in varying degrees of efficiency by means of all kinds of selling efforts.

Salespeople can be either the best or the most doubtful asset for the retail establishment. At one end of the spectrum, there is no better "halo" effect possible than that developed by salespeople who are well trained and public-relations-minded, and who have merged their personal service objectives with those of the store. At the same time, there can be no worse detriment to a store's image than an indifferent salesperson.

In the final analysis, the key contact point between the store and the customer is the salesperson. Removing him for possible savings often backfires. A salesperson is needed to make an optimum offer from the store's viewpoint because self-service customers generally buy lower-priced items and cannot be exposed to suggestion selling on a personal basis.

Further, one of the problems in the cost-profit squeeze is that there are too many "one department" customers. Customers make only marginal use of the store facilities when self-service and limited-service stores fail to entice them to shop in more than one department. When layout and service requirements are formulated through the organizational structure, attempts are made to maximize the effectiveness of every square foot of selling area. For example, in setting up the store layout, the credit and accounts receivable departments are generally placed on an upper floor or in a section of the store which the customer can reach only by traveling throughout the store.

THE NEED FOR SERVICE SELLING

Customers want services and prefer to deal with stores that offer them. As pointed out previously and in Table 12, service expenditures have become an increasingly important market consideration. In the period from 1956 to 1965, consumer spending allocations for services increased by 65.1 per cent—more than for any other category of expenditures. Further, many of these services are readily adaptable for in-store selling.

TABLE 12

CONSUMER EXPENDITURE ALLOCATIONS
(billions of dollars)

	1956		1958		1960		1962		1964	
	DOLLARS	PER CENT	DOLLARS	PER CENT	DOLLARS	PER CENT	DOLLARS	PER CENT	DOLLARS	PER CENT
Total Goods and Services	269.9	100	293.2	100	328.5	100	356.8	100	399.4	100
Durables	38.5	14.3	37.3	12.7	44.8	13.6	48.4	13.6	57.0	14.3
Nondurables	131.4	48.7	141.6	48.3	151.8	46.2	162.0	45.4	177.3	44.4
Services	100.0	37.0	114.3	39.0	131.9	40.2	146.4	41.0	165.1	41.3

CHANGES IN CONSUMER EXPENDITURE ALLOCATIONS
(1956–1965)

	PER CENT CHANGE
Total Goods and Services	+48.2
Durables	48.1
Nondurables	34.9
Services	65.1

Source: *Survey of Current Business* (July 1961, Febuary 1963, and May 1965).

Thus, the closer store management can come to a total service concept, the better are the chances of attracting new customers and holding existing customers who do not mind paying for services. An over-all service concept permits stores to offer customers a total "package" of satisfactions rather than just a locale where a purchase can be made.

Thus, the continuing boom in service sales is a new conceptual market consideration for department and specialty stores. Regardless of the manner in which service sales are expanded or the types of services offered, the introduction and promotion of service sales will help improve over-all sales volume and customer patronage motives.

One of the more important facets of expanding service sales are the personal face-to-face relationships that they involve. This can go a long way in helping reverse the trend toward "sameness," which has grown alarmingly at the retail level. A re-emphasis of a quality-service image as "the place to shop," can induce more consumers to go longer distances. Regardless of how it is done—in dead spaces or in other nonproductive areas—selling more services can help in several ways in achieving product differentiation. One distinctive feature of selling services is that, unlike tangible goods, the product cannot easily be separated from the producer or the store. A second feature is that services are usually created and sold as wanted, so there is little if any problem of physical inventory handling and storing. A third feature is that services provide alert management the means for maintaining a more continuous, personal, and direct contact with customers.

Effect of Prestige Motivations

The desire for prestige and status has always been acceptable to most American consumers. In the past, to satisfy such desires, consumers in upper-income levels purchased exclusive, generally high-priced merchandise. In such cases status was translated in terms of difference in goods or purchasing habits. In recent years, however, increasing numbers of consumers have been financially able and willing to conform with the taste makers of the community. As a result, style leaders and community pace-setters have had to turn to other areas in which to differ in their consumption patterns.

These individuals—and their number is increasing—no longer seek prestige and snob-appeal satisfactions solely through the purchasing of differing commodities. As one young suburbanite says, "There's no fun in owning a super-duper wagon when everyone in the block has one." They don't want the sameness in merchandise offerings that they are seeing in too many of the better stores in which they shop.

Therefore, satisfying the desire to be different has translated itself into buying different amounts of services and in shopping in only certain stores. For example, some parents seek status through the purchase of particular educational services for their children—such as ballet and music lessons, or they spend more for travel. However, they are also willing to pay for services that are easily adaptable to retail operations.

Services Adaptable to Retail Firms

Of course, the purchase of services by consumers runs the entire gamut from "cooked dinners" to stenographic and duplicating services. Among some of the adaptable services in which tremendous sales increases have taken place are credit plans, all kinds of decorating services, television and appliance rental and repair services, beauty-shop and personal care services and products, stenographic, duplicating, and printing services, miscellaneous rentals such as reducing equipment, dress suits, and "drive yourself" automobiles. In many cases some of the rental charges can be applied to total purchase price when customers want ownership. As a matter of fact, the growth in the sale of services is presenting department and specialty stores with special renewed opportunities to tie their customers up on a strong patronage basis. For example, in-store chiropodists, optometrists, and druggists do create strong patronage motives for the entire firm as well as themselves when their services can be tied into a total service concept within a store.

As shown in Table 12, in 1964 consumers spent more than 165.1 billion dollars for services of all kinds. This means that the average consumer allocates more than 41 cents out of every dollar that he spends for services. Further, a growing number of consumers are not as price-conscious as they once were—a trend that started shortly after World War II when many consumers increased their standard of living. This large and expanding "middle majority group" is apparently more willing to pay for quality and services in all expenditure areas. The proper interior decor and store design help immeasurably in the institutionalizing of such sales.

Table 13 shows the growth of service sales by categories. Not included are the integral service components of expenditures related to the sale of apparel and accessories—such items as fur storage and repair, in-store millinery workroom, upholstering, and installations services are included in merchandise sales.

TABLE 13
SERVICE SALES GROWTH, 1954–1964[a]

KIND OF BUSINESS	APPROXIMATE PERCENTAGE GROWTH IN SALES
Motels, tourist courts	93
Trailer parks, camps	54
Industrial laundries	47
Linen supply	38
Diaper service	27
Beauty shops (including combinations with barber shops)	62
Barber shops	45
Photo studios and related services	40
Miscellaneous personal services (Turkish baths, massage, reducing salons, dress suit rentals, rug, furniture cleaning on location, checkroom concessions, and so on. (SIC729))	95
Credit bureaus, collection agencies	55
Duplicating, stenographic, blueprinting, statistical	55
Miscellaneous services to dwellings (Janitorial, floor waxing, maintenance and repair to buildings and homes)	80
Auto repair, services, garages	77
Auto and truck rentals	140
Auto parking	35
Radio, TV repairs	65
Electric repairs (including refrigerator)	73
Reupholstery, furniture repair	25
Dance halls, studio and schools (including children's)	75
Bowling alleys	110

[a] Based on Selected Services, *U. S. Summary 1958, U. S. Census of Business*, various *Surveys of Current Business*, Department of Commerce, and the writer's projected estimates.

As cut-price competition becomes less effective, more and more discount houses are turning to income-producing services for volume expansion. Thus we have today a trend to "scrambled services." Yet individuality is still a necessity. It is likely that demand for services will either stabilize or decrease somewhat as consumers in most cases are paying more for *less* service.

Management should always evaluate the amount and extent of the services offered and should determine what if anything should be "visibly" charged for such services. Wherever possible, the cost versus yield concept should be utilized. As long as there is a *net* yield—when marginal revenues exceed the marginal costs of any additional volume generated from service offers—a particular service should be continued. Should volume drop or costs increase to the point where marginal costs exceed marginal revenue (MC>MR), then a different type of service should be offered or the service should be eliminated.

SUMMARY AND CONCLUSIONS

In this chapter the internal layout and service procedures were analyzed as they affect the total operation of the store and its sales methodology. These are basic to the control of enterprise. Thus internal layout represents the physical structure through which organizational policies operate and company objectives are carried out. The service offer represents a flexible means of developing customer satisfactions and meeting competition on a nonprice basis.

While interior layout is generally determined by the kind of services offered by the retail firm, interior design is the foundation that endows the store with a "symbolic expression" and is representative of the total store image. The basic principle of interior design and fixtures is that it should stop short of the point where its total effect may detract from and conflict with the merchandise displays.

The various types of selling methods—full-service, simplified, and self-service selling—were analyzed in the setting of space planning and layout. The need for a productive service sales approach was also reviewed in this context.

In Part IV the internal setting with respect to the financial management of the firm will be discussed, beginning with a chapter on the economics of investment in retailing.

Part Four

The Internal Setting:
Financial Management
Determination of Financial Requirements

Chapter 11: *The Economics of Investment in Retailing*

Investment in an enterprise of any kind is determined by the potential return and risks attendant on the venture. The investment needs in retailing relative to sales are much smaller than in wholesaling or manufacturing; in the service industries a still smaller amount of initial capital investment is required.

In a manufacturing enterprise large initial outlays for investments such as plant, equipment, and supplies, are required before any finished goods inventories are produced and ready for sale. In retail distribution, allocation for working capital such as inventories and receivables is the major investment area; fixed capital requirements are much less. In general, the more efficient the retail firm, the smaller the inventory investment and corresponding working capital requirements.

In any investment, the factor-owner suppliers of capital attempt to maximize returns for the money units they supply to business. Although their goals may seem to conflict directly with those of consumers, happily, differences of opinion as well as of goals permit solutions. Thus directly opposed economic factor units, each feeling that points of individual satisfactions have been reached, consummate transactions.

THE FUNCTION OF NECESSARY RETURN ON CAPITAL

As pointed out, in retailing, probably more than in other fields of endeavor, most establishments are relatively small in size, with sole proprietorship and partnership as the predominating forms of organization. In these stores the element of both an implicit wage and an implicit return on capital are involved, because most of the firms are operated by the owner-entrepreneur type of management.[1]

The involvement comes from the fact that management and ownership of the firm are carried out without any directly earmarked compensation accruing to the owner-manager for the use of self-invested funds and for the "giving" of supervisory and operative assistance in conducting the affairs of the firm. As a result, a proportion of the net profit returns of the business do not include a deduction for entrepreneurial and investment costs.

In the calculation of the net returns on investment the questions must be asked: How much would the manager-owner have earned had he been employed in the same capacity by another organization? What would the normal rate of return have been if the entrepreneur had invested in fully insured savings or bonds?

While the Federal Bureau of Internal Revenue does not recognize implicit wages or other imputed costs as a deduction from net profit returns, such payments are or should be calculated as "real though imputed cost" in conducting the enterprise.

THE INVESTMENT DECISION

Firms operating in retail markets do so under conditions of monopolistic or imperfect competition. In the short run, under conditions of imperfect competition, savings in total average costs of the firm are not passed on to the consumer. Thus there can be no exact criterion of standards for retail firms. Comparisons have to be made with firms that are either "typical" or ideal to calculate the lowest possible costs and greatest profitability over time.[2]

In retail markets, there are no perfectly elastic demand curves. Because of market imperfections (inconveniences involved in the buying decision, such as driving time), and the lack of perfect or adequate information, both high-cost and low-cost firms exist side by side in the same markets. This is so because knowledge of actual total costs is so incomplete that prices have to be set at a "cushioned" level so as not to realize a loss.

The effect of a sloping demand curve on sales and the optimum size of store are still the most difficult factors to determine in the retail process.

Effect of the Return on Capital

Potential profit return consistent with safety standards is the basic inducement for the owners of capital to invest their funds and forego liquidity. More specifically,

---

[1] Small firms of the "service" type of establishment are also in this category. The legal forms of organization are further discussed in Chapter 12.

[2] E. H. Chamberlain, *The Theory of Monopolistic Competition* (Boston: Harvard University Press, 1933).

the promised return on capital must be equal to or greater than that attainable on the safest type of investment—a government bond or a fully insured type of savings. Essentially, an investment must promise a form of compensatory return sufficient to overcome the liquidity preference of the investor.

Part of the expected compensatory return in many cases may be the possibility of windfall profits, which would compensate the holder of loanable funds for his risk of loss. In all cases the decision to invest requires that the potential investment promise at least as great a return as that offered by minimum-risk securities.

In the field of retail distribution, where the proportion of total working capital to fixed capital is high, constant reshuffling of funds takes place as working capital is reallocated in order to maximize the effectiveness of the firm in a constantly changing market. A very flexible market strategy is standard operating procedure in the field; as a result many mistakes are likely to occur in the operating process. At the same time, the possibilities for a greater than normal return on investment becomes more likely because of continuing opportunities for windfall profits—in other words, "pure profits." Markets in which retail firms operate offer all kinds of opportunities as well as pitfalls for the investor of funds. Thus, individuals with a sense of adventure are much more prone to invest in retail operations.

The Element of Risk

Investment in the retail enterprise represents a business risk of capital. Net profit represents compensation for this risk and an economic return on capital. The greater the risks, the greater the potential net profits if investment capital is to be attracted. The retail firm, if it is to reinvest its funds in productive merchandise categories, must have full knowledge of the techniques that can measure the success of its offerings; only by this means is retail management able to evaluate its various investment opportunities. By this means also, the supplier of capital seeks to maximize his return with the greatest safety consistent with potential gain as his price for relinquishing liquidity. Stated alternatively, the greater the degree of security involved in the investment, the smaller the rate of return that has to be promised in order to secure the necessary venture funds in the market place.

Also, the greater the degree of liquidity that a firm possesses, given its sales and markup, the lower the expected rate of return. Too much liquidity may imply an ineffective use of invested funds which can be considered as idle plant time or capacity and indicate overcapitalization.

Financial Risks and Failure Rates

In every business enterprise there are two types of risks involved: transferable and nontransferable. Transferable risks are insurable: fire, theft, credit, liability, business interruption. Nontransferable risks are associated with market fluctuations and result directly and normally from any private-enterprise operation. Nontransferable business risks can be minimized but not eliminated.

Investment in any business enterprise should be measured on the basis of potential return and growth possibilities compared with the degree of security involved. Venture capital or common stock investors should be the ones to profit most from any returns, inasmuch as the business risks undergone are theirs.

Unsuccessful management of the financial risks in retailing is essentially due to failure to reach a satisfactory level of sales; the largest percentage of business terminations is succession by another firm.[3]

The field of retailing accounts for approximately seven out of ten business failures. This is due to the comparative ease of entry into the field. Many entrepreneurs enter the market on a "shoestring" basis. Yet, statistics on failures attribute poor management as the primary cause, not insufficient capital. Reconsideration of this element, differentiating the number of undercapitalized firms, would pinpoint poor management as significant, although managers of unsuccessful retail firms are often unwilling to admit this.[4]

TURNOVER AND FINANCIAL PLANNING

Managerial policy decisions can be immeasurably improved when measurements of profit are available. Two of the principal indicators of the economics of investment in retailing are capital and merchandise turnover. The turnover in any retail operation figure is critical in the determination of initial financial requirements. It follows also that these requirements will vary with different types of stores because turnover differs with the classification of goods handled. For example, a women's specialty store handling fashion cottons and daytime dresses could expect an average annual turnover of 10, provided that the store management has enough "know-how," a flair for fashion, and the promotional ability to do an effective job. If the store has a projected annual volume of $200,000 a year, the inventory at retail would average $20,000 (200,000 ÷ 10). With an average initial cumulative mark-on of 40 per cent, the inventory investment *at cost* would average $12,000 ($20,000 × .60 [100 per cent minus the initial mark-on]). Fixtures, equipment, and leasehold capitalization would be minimal and generally would not require an immediate capital outlay exceeding $5,000. Leasing the equipment would bring the initial costs down still further.

A qualified young man or woman with a minimum investment of approximately

---

[3] Warren W. Etcheson and James F. Robb, Management, Research Summary (Washington, D.C., Small Business Administration, 1963). In this study of business terminations in the state of Washington, about three fourths of the sample firms were sole proprietorships, nearly half had annual sales of less than $5,000, more than half had been in business for three years or less, and 70 per cent were engaged in retailing.

[4] Elizabeth Y. Deran, A Study of Retail Survival, Research Summary (Washington, D.C., Small Business Administration, 1963). In this study, retailers felt that poor management (lack of planning and overuse of vigorous operating and merchandising policies and related criteria) was a main factor in business failures. Further failures were attributed to failure to adjust to neighborhood changes, changes in personal affairs, chain-store competition, and excessive customer credit. Retailers themselves felt that the following (named in order of frequency) were potentially the most serious threats to business continuity: heavy price and chain-store competition, inadequate cash reserve and overexpansion, nonprice competition and lack of experience, nearby crop failures, movement of customers, and changing locations of customers.

$12,500 could open and operate a store of this kind. The $12,500 would be sufficient to cover 50 per cent of the inventory requirements ($12,500 × .50), a $2,500 down payment for $5,000 in fixed assets and $3,750 in cash for "miscellaneous and contingencies." On a projected $200,000 annual volume, the approximate average cash flow inward per month would be $16,666 ($200,000 ÷ 12).

With an average maintained markup of 35 per cent on sales (after customer discounts, markdown, and shrinkages have been deducted) and a burden for all operating expenses of 30 per cent, the "factor owner" entrepreneur could count on approximately 5 per cent net profit, or $833 monthly, for reduction of payables ($16,666 × .05). Of course, seasonal variations would require larger provisions of funds before the seasonal peak and smaller provisions after the peak.

In Table 14, changes in departmental turnover are shown for the period from 1950 to 1963. For the most part, individual stores handling merchandise lines

TABLE 14

VARIATIONS IN TYPICAL STOCK TURNOVER RATES IN DEPARTMENT STORES, 1950–1963

| DEPARTMENTS | ALL STORES | | | |
| | TYPICAL TURNOVER RATES | | | TURNOVER RANGE 1962 |
	1950	1961	1962	
Total store (including branches)	3.9	3.2	3.2	2.9–3.6
Selected departments:				
Fine jewelry and watches	1.7	2.1	3.4	2.7–4.4
China and glassware	2.0	1.6	1.5	1.2–1.8
Men's clothing	2.8	2.1	2.1	1.7–2.6
Furniture and bedding	3.1	2.4	2.5	1.8–3.2
Boys' wear	3.2	3.1	3.0	2.5–3.5
Notions, laces, etc.	3.3	3.1	2.6	2.1–3.1
Housewares, paint	3.3	2.8	2.6	2.1–3.1
Linens and towels (HH textiles)	3.6	3.1	3.2	2.6–3.7
Books, magazines, and stationery	3.9	3.5	3.6	3.1–4.3
Toys and games	3.9	3.3	3.3	2.6–4.2
Infants' wear	4.5	3.3	3.4	2.7–4.1
Major appliances	4.8	3.9	3.5	2.6–4.6
Aprons, house dresses, and uniforms	5.6	5.6	5.6	4.7–6.7
Women's hosiery	5.9	3.9	3.9	3.1–4.5
Television, radios, hi fi, etc.	7.0	4.8	4.2	3.1–5.5
Women's and misses' dresses	7.1	5.6	6.2	5.1–7.5
Millinery	10.6	9.9	8.7	7.1–9.9
Candy	10.7	11.1	8.9	7.9–10.3
Cosmetics and drugs	n.a.[a]	n.a.	3.1	2.6–3.6
Piece goods	n.a.	n.a.	2.5	3.5–4.6
Handbags and small leather goods	n.a.	n.a.	4.9	4.2–6.3
Basement store division, all depts.	5.2	4.2	4.0	3.5–4.6
Selected departments:				
Boys' wear	4.7	4.2	4.0	3.2–4.8
Dresses	10.0	7.8	6.1	5.2–7.8
Millinery	16.7	12.6	10.7	8.4–12.5

[a] not available

Source: *Departmental Merchandising and Operating Results of Department and Specialty Stores* (New York, National Retail Merchants Association, 1951, 1962, and 1963), Tables 1, 3, and 7.

similar to those of departments in larger stores generally have comparable turnovers and objectives. The data in Table 14 are used for initial financial planning. Without knowledge of turnover of merchandise inventories, valid financial planning cannot be carried out.

Importance of Turnover to Profitability

Stock turnover is also important from the standpoint of measuring profitability. Whether enterprise profitability is expressed as a percentage of net sales or as a percentage representing return on total investment, the turnover figure as a fluctuating constant represents a basic element in evaluative criteria of the firm, and an understanding of the turnover concept is of paramount importance.

There are three general aspects of turnover: (1) stock turnover at retail, which is sales divided by average inventory at retail; (2) stock turnover at cost, which is the cost of sales divided by the average inventory at cost; and (3) capital turnover, which is sales divided by the average stock at cost.

The first turnover relationship is the one most generally used as a measure of merchandising efficiency. Stated formally:

$$(1)\ \text{Stock Turn} = \frac{\text{Net Sales}}{\text{Average Inventory at Retail}}$$

For example: if net sales total $100,000 and average inventory at retail is $10,000, then the turnover would equal 10 (100,000 ÷ 10,000).

The second aspect of turnover in equation form is:

$$(2)\ \text{Stock Turn} = \frac{\text{Cost of Goods Sold (net sales at cost)}}{\text{Average Inventory at Cost}}$$

If the maintained (or final) markup on the $100,000 above is 35 per cent, then the cost of goods sold would total $65,000 (100% − 35%); if the *initial* markup on the goods was 40 per cent, then the average inventory at cost would equal $6,000 (10,000 × .60). Substituting in the above formula, the results are as follows:

$$\text{Stock Turn} = \frac{\$65,000}{\$6,000} = 10.83 \text{ times.}^5$$

The capital turnover concept (3) represents a measure of merchandising rather than a financial efficiency ratio. Capital turnover, in this context, measures the number of times during any given period that the inventory investment is returned in the form of sales: i.e.,

$$(3)\ \text{Capital Turnover} = \frac{\$100,000\ (\text{sales})}{\$6,000\ (\text{equity investment in the merchandise inventory})} = 16.67 \text{ times.}$$

As a measure of efficiency this latter turnover concept helps in determination of the cash flow of a business and is almost indispensable in performance evaluation.

---

[5] Stock turnover calculated on a cost basis is always greater than on a retail basis because the initial cumulative markup used (in this case 40 per cent) is based on inventories (not sales) and is always larger than a maintained or final markup based on sales. The difference between initial markup and maintained markup is due to markdown, shrinkages, shortages, and discounts. The total process is reviewed in detail in the section on merchandising.

The Capital Turnover Concept

Capital turnover as used above is an index of the merchandise efficiency of the firm and is of key importance to the financial analyst as well as to the merchandise manager, although each uses this ratio in a different manner. As used here, the capital ratio bears a direct relationship to the stock turnover. In accounting or finance, capital turnover represents the ratio of sales to capital investment in a business. Net worth is almost always larger than the inventory investment, hence capital turnover, in the financial sense, is a smaller ratio.

This figure bears a direct relationship to stock turnover. The relationship between sales and stock is used as a control device in maintaining the relationship of the inventory at retail at the beginning of the month (B.O.M.) to the estimated sales for that month. A stock-sales ratio concept always refers to a B.O.M. inventory unless specifically stated otherwise.

The chief usefulness of the stock-sales ratio lies in the fact that there is a causal relationship between B.O.M. stocks and sales for the month for which inventory has been acquired. It is a basis for planning stocks that should be on hand at a given time to meet particular sales. In this respect, the "average" inventory figure as used in merchandise turnover is of only moderate usefulness, but the B.O.M. stock-sales ratio provides a basis for planning as it pinpoints the financial needs of the business at particular times during the budget period. Also, stock-sales ratio data have been used as a continuing statistical comparison by the Board of Governors of the Federal Reserve System and now by the Department of Commerce. An illustration of stock-sales ratio indexes is shown in Table 15.

FIXED AND WORKING CAPITAL

Most firms in seeking to maximize their long-run profit potential attempt to limit their fixed-asset investments: buildings, for example, are no longer bought but leased almost on a perpetuity basis. Where it is necessary for the retail enterprise to build, buy, and/or underwrite a building or shopping center, the usual practice is to sell the premises when completed and lease back the facilities. In this manner retail management gets exactly what it wants in the way of location and space planning at a rental cost it can live with.

It is felt that by converting scarce investment capital into liquid form the long-run financial soundness and expansion potentials of the firm can be immeasurably enhanced. This is not always true, because in some cases it may lead to overexpansion and overextension of facilities. Failures such as Master's Discount Stores can be attributed to just such imprudent emphasis on liquidity and expansion at the price of higher fixed costs which require strong and continuing high volume levels. As can be seen from Tables 16 and 16A, the data from "typical" department-store firms show current ratios ranging from over 10 to 1 for mail-order firms to 3 to 1 for combination mail-order and retail firms such as Sears, Roebuck and Montgomery Ward, and slightly less than 2 to 1 for the "sample" stores of the group.

TABLE 15

Monthly Department Store Sales and Stocks 1961–1963

Summary by Selected Department Groups
(Based on retail dollar amounts)

| Month and Year | Main Store | | | | | | | Basement Store Total |
	Main Store Total	Women's Apparel and Accessories	Men's and Boy's Wear	Home Furnishings	Piece Goods and Household Textiles	Small Wares	Miscellaneous	
Sales Indexes (Unadjusted, 1947–49 average monthly sales = 100)								
Oct. 1961	124	132	122	128	91	123	99	115
Nov. 1961	150	145	170	147	97	166	190	134
Dec. 1961	231	213	319	170	119	327	386	190
Aug. 1962	109	112	99	114	112	108	94	103
Sept. 1962	116	128	105	118	84	113	84	106
Oct. 1962	128	136	124	135	94	125	104	116
Nov. 1962	154	149	174	152	99	168	196	131
Dec. 1962	235	217	328	176	122	327	389	190
Aug. 1963	117	121	109	121	120	111	100	111
Sept. 1963	120	131	110	126	89	117	87	109
Oct. 1963	129	136	120	138	96	128	105	112
Nov. 1963	147	143	170	147	97	158	170	126
Dec. 1963	253	232	358	189	132	352	419	205
Stocks Indexes (Unadjusted, 1947–49 average of end-of-month stocks = 100)								
Oct. 1961	172	193	196	143	134	176	194	146
Nov. 1961	178	198	201	145	134	197	204	151
Dec. 1961	142	150	147	132	133	151	119	115
Aug. 1962	155	181	166	135	122	150	144	129
Sept. 1962	170	198	192	142	133	161	166	146
Oct. 1962	185	211	213	152	138	187	208	156
Nov. 1962	189	212	218	153	138	207	214	160
Dec. 1962	150	159	160	140	135	159	126	121
Aug. 1963	162	187	178	139	127	157	150	133
Sept. 1963	178	208	205	147	138	168	174	153
Oct. 1963	197	226	231	159	145	195	221	169
Nov. 1963	202	227	234	161	145	219	236	170
Dec. 1963	158	168	170	145	142	165	137	128
Ratio of Stocks to Sales								
Dec. 1961	1.6	1.5	1.4	2.6	3.3	1.4	0.7	1.2
Dec. 1962	1.7	1.5	1.5	2.6	3.2	1.5	0.8	1.3
Dec. 1963	1.6	1.5	1.4	2.5	3.1	1.4	0.8	1.3

Source: Board of Governors, Federal Reserve System, Washington 25, D.C. (1964).

Use of Loan Capital

Retail firms generally use the merchandise credit extended by wholesalers, manufacturers, and other suppliers to the maximum. This is reasonable, since such credit is available at practically no cost. The terms of trade of various classes of commodities handled are generally set up in accordance with the turnover of the goods at the retail level. For example, in the case of bread and milk, which turns over daily, the terms of trade are on a receipt of goods (R.O.G.) basis, which is the same as cash. In the case of dry groceries (canned goods), payment is expected every ten days, which is the rate at which this stock is turned into cash (turn of approximately 36 times annually). Another facet of Table 14 (the turn-over rates of various kinds of merchandise classifications), is that these stock turn ratios are directly connected with their terms of trade and inventory investment requirements.

TABLE 16

DEPARTMENT STORE FINANCIAL DATA[a]

(AGGREGATE OF FOURTEEN LEADING STORES)

	1942	1947	1961	1962	1963
Balance Sheet Data:					
Cash and Equivalent	8.58%	14.95%	9.75%	8.57%	7.89%
Receivables—Net	19.34	20.37	28.82	29.12	27.89
Inventories	23.83	33.07	24.78	25.43	26.52
Other Current	0.44	0.86	1.48	1.69	1.71
Total Current Assets	52.19	69.25	64.83	64.81	64.01
Plant and Equipment—Net	44.01	26.68	29.45	28.88	29.42
Investments	1.74	1.71	3.57	4.16	4.51
Other Noncurrent Assets	2.06	2.36	2.15	2.15	2.06
Total Noncurrent Assets	47.81	30.75	35.17	35.19	35.99
Total Assets	100.00%	100.00%	100.00%	100.00%	100.00%
Notes Payable to Banks	1.89%	0.67%	0.15%	0.15%	1.08%
Accounts Payable	7.32	10.28	12.71	13.67	13.45
Accrued Federal Taxes	4.30	9.69	5.30	5.64	4.64
Other Current	4.20	6.92	3.86	3.84	3.94
Total Current Liabilities	17.71	27.56	22.02	23.30	23.11
Long-term Debt	19.83	7.41	16.07	16.58	16.39
Reserves and Other Liabilities	1.47	2.49	1.47	1.56	2.39
Preferred Stock	15.39	14.38	5.34	4.29	3.46
Common Stock and Surplus	45.60	48.16	55.10	54.27	54.65
Net Worth	60.99	62.54	60.44	58.56	58.11
Total Liabilities & Net Worth	100.00%	100.00%	100.00%	100.00%	100.00%
Operating Data:					
Net Sales	100.00%	100.00%	100.00%	100.00%	100.00%
Operating Expenses	93.67	91.38	94.47	94.28	94.59
Net Operating Profit[b]	6.33	8.62	5.53	5.72	5.41
Pretax Profit	5.77	8.22	5.21	5.38	5.00
Federal Income Taxes	2.63	3.62	2.62	2.72	2.53
Net Profit	3.14%	4.60%	2.59%	2.66%	2.47%
Ratios:					
Cash/Current Debt	0.48x[c]	0.54x[c]	0.44x[c]	0.37x[c]	0.34x[c]
Current Assets/Current Debt	2.95	2.51	2.94	2.78	2.77
Current Assets/Total Debt	1.34	1.85	1.70	1.62	1.53
Plant and Equipment/Net Worth	0.72	0.43	0.49	0.49	0.51
Sales/Receivables	8.34x[c]	11.58x[c]	6.79x[c]	6.68x[c]	7.09x[c]
Sales/Inventories	6.77	7.13	7.89	7.65	7.45
Sales/Net Working Capital	4.68	5.66	4.57	4.68	4.83
Net Worth/Total Debt	1.56x[c]	1.67x[c]	1.59x[c]	1.47x[c]	1.39x[c]
Net Profit/Common Equity	11.10%	22.52%	9.18%	9.54%	8.95%
Net Profit plus Interest/Net Worth plus Long-Term Debt	6.28	15.50	7.46	7.90	8.04

[a] For fiscal years ending January 31.
[b] Profit before interest, other income, and federal income taxes.
[c] x = estimated.
Source: Henry S. Kahn, *Comparative Financial Data* (Chicago, Harris Trust and Savings Bank, 1964).

TABLE 16A

FINANCIAL DATA, OTHER LEADING MERCHANDISERS[a]

Balance Sheet Data:	ALDEN'S	SPIEGEL	MONTGOMERY WARD	SEARS, ROEBUCK	FOURTEEN-STORE AGGREGATE
Cash and Equivalent	3.60%	7.60%	25.92%	6.15%	7.89%
Receivables–Net	67.44	79.72	8.35	44.65	27.89
Inventories—Net	18.38	6.35	37.26	23.38	26.52
Other Current	2.78	2.11	3.74	1.09	1.71
Total Current Assets	92.20	95.78	75.27	75.27	64.01
Plant and Equipment—Net	6.15%	2.61%	16.80%	16.22%	29.42%
Investments	0.98	0.94	7.93	8.42	4.51
Other Noncurrent Assets	0.67	0.67	—	0.09	2.06
Total Noncurrent Assets	7.80	4.22	24.73	24.73	35.99
Total Assets	100.00%	100.00%	100.00%	100.00%	100.00%
Notes Payable to Banks	6.00%	— %	— %	— %	1.08%
Accounts Payable	5.55	2.41	8.78	4.39	13.45
Accrued Federal Taxes	1.80	0.67	1.22	4.48	4.64
Other Current	4.35	30.10	5.44	7.37	3.94
Total Current Liabilities	17.70	33.18	15.44	16.24	23.11
Long-Term Debt	43.44	32.45	—	12.54	16.39
Reserves and Other Liabilities	6.75	13.40	1.01	10.34	2.39
Preferred Stock	2.63	1.83	2.63	—	3.46
Common Stock and Surplus	29.48	19.14	80.92	60.88	54.65
Net Worth	32.11	20.97	83.55	60.88	58.11
Total Liabilities & Net Worth	100.00%	100.00%	100.00%	100.00%	100.00%
Operating Data:					
Net Sales	100.00%	100.00%	100.00%	100.00%	100.00%
Cost of Sales	79.40	—	—	—	—
Gross Profit	20.60	—	—	—	—
Other Operating Expense	13.21	—	—	—	—
Net Operating Profit[b]	7.39	8.82	2.37	9.86	5.41
Pretax Profit	5.60	5.15	2.62	9.74	5.00
Federal Income Tax	2.77	2.58	1.19	4.67	2.53
Net Profit	2.83%	2.57%	1.43%	5.07%	2.47%
Ratios:					
Cash/Current Debt	0.20x	0.23x	1.68x	0.38x	0.34x
Current Assets/Current Debt	5.21	2.89	4.88	4.64	2.77
Current Assets/Total Debt	1.36	1.21	4.58	1.92	1.53
Plant and Equipment/Net Worth	0.19	0.12	0.20	0.27	0.51
Sales/Receivables	2.05x	0.96x	22.27x	3.69x	7.09x
Sales/Inventories	7.51	12.03	4.99	7.05	7.45
Sales/Net Working Capital	1.85	1.22	3.11	2.79	4.83
Net Worth/Total Debt	0.47x	0.27x	5.08x	1.56x	1.39x
Net Profit/Common Equity	13.23%	10.29%	3.29%	13.72%	8.95%
Net Profit plus Interest/Net Worth plus Long-Term Debt	8.64	9.09	3.18	13.55	8.04

[a] Fiscal year to January 31, 1963
[b] Profit before interest, other income, and federal income taxes.
Source: Henry S. Kahn, *op. cit.*

Business borrowers, especially retail firms, have always been highly important customers for commercial banks. In recent years, the increased internal cash flow of corporations has enabled them to reduce their dependence on almost all sources of external financing. Banks supply approximately 30 per cent of fluid commercial paper, which is used as a short-term liquid asset. Other businesses and the public supply the remainder.

Because of the uncertainties involved in a mercantile operation, the total capital needs must be set up with a high ratio of venture to loan capital. In other words, the owners' or stockholders' equity in the firm should be in a relationship of $3 to every $1 of borrowed capital (Tables 16 and 16A). For example: in a corporation with $120,000 in total assets, ideally the enterprise should have a minimum of $90,000 of venture capital invested in the business and no more than $30,000 in permanent loan capital. An industrial mercantile firm operating in a competitive market cannot "trade on equity" as do public utilities, because of the sales uncertainties in the market place.[6]

Through the extension of trade credit—the credit one nonfinancial business extends to another—businesses themselves are turning into major competitors of banks. Trade credit rose from $23.7 billion in 1946 to some $103 billion by 1963, an increase of more than 330 per cent. About 60 per cent of this credit represents financing within the corporate sector itself. The remainder is credit extended to noncorporate business and others. And most trade credit involves retail firms.[7]

Normally, the suppliers of venture capital should receive a larger rate of return than suppliers of credit capital. Because of the tax structure, the financial policies of corporations are set up so that common stocks today rarely pay annual dividends as high as 5 per cent of market prices. Investment in common stocks is made for value appreciation in market price in order to give the purchaser an option to sell on a capital gains basis.

Because of the unprecedented levels of expenditures in all areas, retail sales are continuing to increase. Because of the underlying economic stability and growth of consumer expenditures, equity investment in well-managed retail firms secures a very high rate of return. These rates of return on net worth are illustrated in Tables 16 and 16A. Many discount houses generate well over 20 per cent net profit on net worth.

Long-Term Financial Considerations

When the risks involved are relatively high, the demand for operating funds often becomes critical. During times of stress, even high-rated firms factor their accounts receivable in addition to going to banks. Cash is also acquired in order to take advantage of cash discounts available from merchandise vendors. In many cases the effective annual interest rate involved in cash discounts on merchandise purchases may run as high as 50 per cent per annum; such a return well justifies the payment of 10 to 20 per cent effective interest rate demanded by factors. As for seasonal needs for cash, it is neither economic nor efficient for any firm to retain year-round surpluses of cash on hand or in banks.

In evaluating any long-term investment, the prime considerations encompass cost, income, and risk:

---

[6] A corporation trades on equity when it is able to finance its business primarily by means of bonds or other credit instruments. In such cases as much as 70 per cent of the total asset investment in the business may represent loan capital.

[7] The Chase Manhattan Bank, *Business in Brief*, No. 55 (March–April 1964), pp. 1–3.

    a. *Cost considerations*: length of investment time, possible additional investment needed to maintain share of investment in firm, cash outlays chargeable to expense, working capital requirements, and estimated capital outlays required for framework units.

    b. *Income*: total cash earnings per annum, income taxes, and timing of firm's long-run growth potential.

    c. *Risk*: Are cost and earnings projections realistic?

Long-term debt of mercantile firms is limited generally to first mortgages and/or five-year bank notes. It is only on rare occasions that retail firms can secure long-term credit without such underlying tangible assets as plant and equipment for security. Only in the case of large, well-known, blue-chip firms such as the Federated Department Stores Corporation or Sears, Roebuck & Company would any preferred stock or debenture bond offer be effectively sold.

PROBLEM OF RISING RENTAL COSTS

Investment in retailing is not as attractive as it was formerly. The tremendous expansion of stores into both old and new suburban centers in response to population dispersions has made it more difficult for small stores to get started. In addition, leasehold costs in shopping centers are generally higher for the small independents, and they receive a favorable lease only as a final resort. As pointed out, first choice usually goes to national chains and the larger department stores who have to be enticed into a regional shopping center.

In other words, in order to attract the blue-chip stores whose presence can assure success, a center must give the larger, generally AAA-1 rated firms a highly favorable lease and choice of location. The small stores that occupy approximately 30 to 35 per cent of the available selling space must pay a higher rental in order to locate.

In addition, leases in centers are set up on a minimum rental basis plus a fixed percentage above a minimum sales volume guarantee. As a result, any additional volume generated above a projected minimum does not result in lower percentage rental costs and resulting greater profits, but continues on a fixed percentage basis.

In past years, independent entrepreneurs could locate in a secondary or neighborhood shopping area with a fixed dollar rental cost. By generating additional sales volume above that originally projected on a sales forecast, the total net profit of the firm could easily be doubled or tripled with increasing volume. With rental on a percentage basis, pure profits in an economic sense, and higher than typical profits in an accounting sense, become very difficult to achieve.[8]

---

[8] Accounting practice may be said to be a compromise between a logically based technique on one hand and expediency on the other—with a certain bias toward "expedient practicality." An outlay of $10,000 resulting in revenues of $12,000 does not necessarily mean a $2,000 net profit—if the outlay were insured in 1948. The 1964 dollar will not buy as much as the 1948 dollar; the net profit proceeds are much smaller. See *The Economist* (June 12, 1948), pp. 977–78.

THE ENTREPRENEURIAL DECISION

The entrepreneur is one of the principal "prime movers" in a capitalist society. He is often motivated largely by a desire to be his own boss. He not only invests his own funds and time but he promotes investment from outside sources to complete the financing of his enterprise. Should his methodology, business acumen, and timing be correct, then the rewards of his investment choice may be great. On the other hand, bad planning, poor organization, and marginal management may lead to financial impoverishment and loss of the enterprise.

Investment in the field of retailing commodities and/or services is often a highly desirable outlet for an entrepreneur with a minimum of capital funds to invest. By this means he becomes an investor-entrepreneur. This is not the same as buying common stock in a corporation, although technically it may be so construed. In common-stock investment the investor is merely supplying venture funds to a business without the excitement and rewards of managerial decision making. Theoretically, the owners of the common stock are the owners of a corporation. Technically, the executive officers of the corporation report to and are responsible to the board of directors who represent the owners of the enterprise. In actual practice, the common-stock investor is merely a loaner of venture funds to a corporation with little or no direct or primary determination of company policies and objectives. The investor, however, is free to sell out his interests in a firm of whose policies and procedures he disapproves and to reinvest his capital in other firms run more to his liking.

EFFECT OF SIZE OF FIRM AND SCALE OF PLANT

The cost of conducting any economic activity of a private enterprise depends on only a limited number of long- and short-run variables. The short run is that period of time in which some factors—such as store size and managerial organization—are taken as fixed. In the long run, all factors are able to change in response to market conditions. Returns to scale refer to revenue income per firm size, numbers, and size of plants in a growing market—i.e., on the basis of cost of operation per $1,000 sales as a firm grows.

The upward or downward financial pressures on the efficiency of firms undergoing mergers, branch store expansion, and other forms of growth are rarely clearly delineated, because of the many subtleties involved in characterizing the differences between the short- and the long-run returns to scale in retailing. As a result, many of the expenses incurred are capitalized for a long-run write-off instead of being immediately absorbed. It would be well now to examine more specifically the relationships between total operating expenses (costs) at a fixed scale of plant and those in which the scale of plant changes.

First, a firm is always more than a plant, regardless of the amount of time the owner or chief executive allocates to buying, merchandising, personnel, sales promotion, or general management. Also, it cannot be assumed that the most efficient (or lowest-cost) firm is made up of a group of lowest-cost retail outlets.

An outlet at the retail level is synonymous with a plant at the industrial level. At the retail level, a plant may be described as an integration of various fixed-asset factors housing the inventory offerings—typically the layout, furniture, fixtures, structure, and organization.[9] Therefore, any long-run cost curve which is drawn for any type of retail establishment (or plant) would be based on a series of short-run curves. These short-run curves are assumed to be consistent factor prices and representative of the various factor units. Full-service selling, self-selection, and self-service are examples of different technologies which generate varying cost results at different levels of operation. *Ceteris paribus*, the long-run cost curve is rarely *directly* relevant to the problems confronting any enterprise. This is so because prices of any input factors for any given scale of output in the form of sales will depend on the quality of the input factors; in this case, the "right" input factors would consist of having the right merchandise, at the right price, in the right quantity, and at the right time for optimum sales.

Effect of Integration

In other words, the price of any merchandise purchased by retail buyers is directly dependent on the volume bought; the cost of selling groups of merchandise is directly related to the volume generated. The scale of firm and size of plant would have to be assumed constant for comparison purposes. In effect, long-run returns to scale cannot be calculated unless the long-run cost function can be directly related to a series of short-run cost curves. A firm representing the integration of two or more store plants would have a combination of two different cost-size relationships integrated into a purchase-sales concentration in the same market.

Further, the merchandise costs of the horizontally integrated firm would be greater than the same generated volume for firms integrated vertically and utilizing the combination of manufacturing, wholesaling, and retailing. The criterion here is that the costs of large-scale firms such as Sears, Roebuck, J. C. Penney, and Montgomery Ward, who produce, distribute, and sell their own commodities, are less than those of firms acquiring wider ranges of products as they expand horizontally.

SELLING COSTS—A FACTOR DETERMINING PROFIT

The various cost functions associated with sales of specific merchandise classifications are basic determinants of the necessary initial markup. Indirectly, specific conditions of supply, demand, and competition also determine price.

Competitive prices, per se, can no longer guarantee adequate volume and market security. Attempts to increase efficiency by increasing the size of the firm and/or the scale of plant do not work out in retailing as they can in most manufacturing

---

[9] See *Cost Behavior and Price Policy* (New York: Committee on Price Distribution, National Bureau of Economic Research, 1943), p. 220.

operations. The generation of volume in or through various units cannot be balanced with the same operating framework setups as in industrial production. Even within the same market or within the same firm, the means for volume generation differ; this is true in terms of both an operating system and the coordination of merchandise offerings. Savings or reduction of unit costs in retailing do not accrue as they would through functional integration or increased production in manufacturing.

Even within the framework of a single plant, only by the integration of all costs and the relating of these costs to specific output can assessments of maximum efficiency be set up.

At present, sales per square foot of selling space are being used increasingly as a measure of comparative efficiencies within the store. Sales per square foot are treated by food supermarkets as one of the best direct measures of sales volume and store profitability. For example, in 1963, average sales per square foot in new supermarkets increased to $2.87, the highest since 1959, as shown in Table 17.

TABLE 17

WEEKLY SALES PER SQUARE FOOT OF SELLING AREA,
1957–1964

NEW SUPERMARKETS OPENED IN	SALES PER SQUARE FOOT	
	AVERAGE	MIDDLE HALF
1957	$2.93	$2.24 to $3.64
1958	2.63	2.10 to 3.30
1959	2.91	2.28 to 3.50
1960	2.62	2.02 to 3.24
1961	2.61	2.06 to 3.28
1962	2.69	2.10 to 3.33
1963	2.87	2.21 to 3.46

Source: Eleventh Annual Report, *New Super Markets, 1963* (Chicago, Super Market Institute), p. 7.

Manufacturing managers rarely feel that any production run is long enough. To a sales promotion manager, no sales volume is ever adequate; and limitations of efforts are rarely encouraged. At the same time, there are standard minimum points for guidance. Such points should be limited to the market potential that a firm can cater to.

Only by developing the maximum number of uses for its products can a firm approach the lowest unit costs possible. Yet products at the lower unit costs prove too costly if selling costs rise faster than the reduction of unit costs.

Thus, optimum size for the maximization of over-all profits of the firm in relation to investment is the point where capacity production would be lowest in cost. An operations research approach of this kind can generate the lowest total average costs for the entire firm and the highest possible profits. The same principles hold for retail management.

Once a store has been opened, there is simply insufficient time to make the necessary long-run adjustments for total optimization. The difficulty lies in the fact that the optimal plant located for the convenience of particular sets of consumers is constantly subject to locational displacement and change.

Restrictions on entrepreneurial freedom because of lags in adjustment to scale in single plants are often eliminated in multi-unit firms such as department or specialty stores with branches. In multi-unit firms, empirical determinations of minimum cost functions are far easier to make because continuing changes in various market places and differently situated stores can be easily pinpointed. A single, individual plant operating at an optimum level is easy to develop—but only for brief periods.

By establishing a "twig unit," a department store can expand via a specialty store route and restricted merchandise lines in order to take advantage of specific customer wants in an area. These smaller units, selectively planned and scientifically set up, are often far more efficient and profitable than larger existing units. At the same time, the firm's over-all market share and long-run profitability can be enhanced.

Thus, the efficiency of any store depends not only on the state of its technology in meeting customer needs but also on its ability to adapt to changes required in its cost structures due to market changes. Generally, the smaller the firm, the greater its flexibility; the greater its flexibility, the greater its ability to keep its costs in line and the greater the likelihood of increasing its market share in the long run.

MARKET FLEXIBILITY AND THE OPPORTUNITY FOR PROFIT

The maintenance and increase of market share depends directly on a firm's market flexibility and its ability to scale its variable costs as needed. For example, advertising expenditures, one of the important variable costs, varies with different types of retail operations and merchandise offerings. Continual experimentation in this area is the norm for firms at all economic levels. Experimentation continues because, except for rules of thumb and broad generalizations, there is no way for measuring the effectiveness of advertising on a short-run basis. Thus the nature and direction of advertising expenditures have a very strong bearing on a firm's profitability.

Policy flexibility with respect to variable and semivariable expenses within an organization also directly affects its profitability, as do costs such as:

a. implicit wages;

b. implicit returns to executive management who have loanable funds invested in the enterprise;

c. the consistency of annual returns in the form of earnings which exceed total costs of production in the economic sense (includes the coverage of costs in the economic sense and "normal" profits).

Effect of Price Uniformity

Retail firms operating in suburban communities adjacent to large cities generally enjoy lower than average operating costs. Higher costs of operations result from higher wages combined with older, less efficient plants located in the central business districts of "hub" cities. Yet, both downtown and suburban stores sell similar commodities and offer substantially similar services at essentially the same prices. As a result, the suburban plants enjoy a more profitable operation than those in urban areas.

The same type of analysis is applicable to branch stores of downtown department stores. The developing technology and know-how in the efficient use of regular and part-time sales personnel developed from branches have been applied to urban units with very profitable results. Generally, greater-than-average profits accrue to branch and suburban units. The additions to net profit are used as an offset to the lower net profits generated by urban units.

The greater the geographical dispersion of multi-plant retail firms, the greater the tendency for area-wide price uniformity on the part of all firms. At the same time, the possibilities of generating a monopoly profit are greater because of lower attendant costs in outlying areas. Thus, "umbrellas" rather than "floors" on prices exist in many suburban markets, and marginal operators are, in effect, subsidized because of the lack of price competition.

THE COMPETING AWAY OF PROFITS

In evaluating any economic or marketing policy, the classical precept of laissez faire implies that the system has more positive attributes than disutilities. In the complex field of retail distribution, the two most common types of monopoly are those of time and location. Yet, unlike industry, monopolies at the retail level tend to be short-lived because of ease of entry into the field. As a result, when profits tend to become "excessive" (above average), additional entrants come into the market generally with lower costs and often more efficient or innovational operation.[10]

In the field of market distribution, the elements of what constitutes "pure" profits are always in a state of flux. Two conventional yardsticks, of course, are pre-tax and after-tax earnings in relation to investment (capital stock and surplus). The weighted average of pre-tax earnings was 11.5 per cent of capital and surplus in 1958 and 12.0 per cent in 1957; and after-tax earnings on the same basis were 5.5 per cent and 6.0 per cent for 1958 and 1957, respectively.[11] The range of figures for these two ratios in 1957–1958 according to the several volume groups is shown in Table 18.

Since many concerns in the two smallest volume classifications are partnerships

---

[10] See J. A. Schumpeter, *The Theory of Economic Development* (Cambridge: Harvard University Press, 1955), especially pp. 74–94.

[11] These are revised weighted averages, excluding the over-$50 million firms.

TABLE 18

PRE-TAX AND AFTER-TAX EARNINGS IN
1957–1958 FOR VARIOUS SALES-VOLUME GROUPS

TOTAL NET SALES PER TAX REPORT (IN THOUSANDS)	PRE-TAX EARNINGS AS A PERCENTAGE ON CAPITAL STOCK AND SURPLUS	AFTER-TAX EARNINGS AS A PERCENTAGE ON CAPITAL STOCK AND SURPLUS
Less than $250	——	——
$250– $500	——	——
$500– $1,000	5.0%	3.0%
$1,000– $2,000	10.0	5.5
$2,000– $5,000	9.0	5.0
$5,000–$10,000	12.0	6.0
$10,000–$20,000	10.0	5.0
$20,000–$50,000	12.5	6.0
$50,000 or more	——	——

Source: Henry S. Kahn, *op. cit.*

or proprietorships, no comparable figures for earnings on investment could be developed for them. At the other end of the volume scale a different difficulty is encountered: namely, the fact that so many of these large stores are members of ownership groups and therefore in many instances do not have individual balance sheets which could clearly reflect the capital and surplus used. General experience in recent years, however, indicates that the usual after-tax rate of return on investment for such enterprises is distinctly higher than the general average, presumably in the vicinity of 8 or 9 per cent of sales.

In 1962, the data shown in Table 19 emerged in a sample survey of chain stores.[12]

TABLE 19

NET INCOME OF CHAIN STORES AS PERCENTAGE OF NET SALES AND OF NET WORTH

TYPE OF STORE	NUMBER IN SAMPLE	NET INCOME % NET SALES (AFTER TAXES)	NET INCOME % NET WORTH
Discount	11	1.5	14.9
Department and General Merchandise	6	2.6	11.0
Home Furnishings	5	2.0	5.6
Apparel	5	2.2	5.0
Mail Order	3	4.1	10.8
Supermarkets	4	1.2	11.5
Variety	4	3.1	6.9
Shoe	4	2.3	9.8
Drugs	5	1.8	9.5

The stress of competitive pressure shows up in the return on investment and sales data—and is usually first apparent in sales volume results. Other competitive pressures tending to upset long-run stability, in addition to changes in price and service, take the form of trading stamp giveaways, excessive or uneconomic advertising allocations, and unproductive innovations in the market place.

---

[12] Raymond S. Kahanes, "Discounters Look Better in Analysis of '62 Figures," *Women's Wear Daily* (June 18, 1963), p. 42.

Implications of Existing and Theoretical Market Competition

While the concept of pure competition in retailing exists mostly on a theoretical basis, it does exist to a far greater extent in the market for loanable funds. In financial markets, almost full information is attainable. In retail commodity markets, the details as to what constitutes the best market price of commodity groups is almost impossible to ascertain.

Total expenditures for consumer goods, regardless of price levels, is relatively income-inelastic in the long run. Yet, because of changing consumer preferences and changing forms of competition, total expenditures for consumption goods can and do change.[13]

In adjusting to changes in demand, prices of manufactured consumer goods, capital goods, and money available in capital markets generally adjust to a level which would clear the market. However, price adjustments in themselves do not always succeed in clearing the market. At the retail level, sellers have substantial control over market prices only in seller's markets. However, as pointed out, the normal condition of market operations in the American economy is a buyer's one; the lowest-cost firm can choose the basis on which it will compete and—*ceteris paribus*—flourish.

SUMMARY AND CONCLUSIONS

Mass production requires mass distribution. Mass distribution requires the stimulation or maintenance of adequate demand. Only by the effective maintenance of adequate demand can we approach the goal of full use of resources. Mass distribution on an efficient, low-cost basis is the objective of the marketing segment of our economy.

Effectiveness in the market place insures the highest possible return for equity investors and the greatest safety for those with loanable funds. Efficient distribution also means the highest possible packages of satisfactions available for consumers.

Estimates of profitability and security of investing in a firm are dependent on the estimated present values of pure profits in the economic sense—in essence the same factor as good will in an accounting sense. It has been pointed out that the profit or psychic satisfaction rule is the single most reliable assumption that can be made about buyer behavior or seller goals in the economic setting.

The limitations involved in achieving profitability and security result from inadequate knowledge of the market, uncertainty of present and future demand for a firm's products, varying unit costs of production, and lack of knowledge of points where maximum efficiency would be generated.

The single greatest difference in money allocations between investing in marketing and manufacturing institutions is that much smaller working capital to fixed

---

[13] Arthur F. Burns, *The Instability of Consumer Spending*, 32nd Annual Report (New York: National Bureau of Economic Research, 1952), p. 9.

capital requirements are needed in industry. The principal characteristic of the capital structure of mercantile firms is the preponderance of funds needed for working to fixed capital. The difficulties of financing a mercantile enterprise derive from the smaller size of its operations compared with industrial firms. Because of continuing change and intensive and extensive competition at the retail level, the potential returns on investment offered in the field have to be higher than those offered for similar investments in other ventures.

The field of retail distribution will always remain attractive for the small-scale entrepreneur with managerial acumen and limited capital. In the chapter to follow, the functions of the legal forms of organization in carrying out the work of retailing are analyzed.

Chapter 12: *Matching the Legal Form of Organization with Financial Requirements*

Assuming that the goal of any business enterprise is that of long-run profit maximization, the attainment of this objective is dependent upon an optimum legal framework. When a business has a legal framework sufficiently flexible to meet any and all changes that may occur in the market place, long-run profit maximization becomes feasible.

LEGAL FRAMEWORK AND ORGANIZATIONAL FLEXIBILITY

It follows that the nature and scope of any business are directly influenced by the particular legal form of organization under which it operates. For the marketing firm, this generally encompasses operation as a sole proprietorship, a partnership, or a corporation. The sole proprietorship and partnership forms of organization are common law in character and formation, while the corporation is a "creature of the state" and is formed under statute law.[1]

The over-all operating policies of management are also influenced by the legal structure. For example, departmental organization within a firm is influenced by

---

[1] The common law, English in derivation, is the unwritten law developed and handed down by custom and usage; statute law is the written law as developed by governing bodies.

its legal structure. Mercantile firms differ from those in manufacturing in that changes in the product or merchandise line offerings can take place with little or no change in capital investment, institutional structure, and channel of distribution.

Any decisions as to the legal structure of a business organization should never be final. The changes that occur in the environment of the firm, its owners, and its directing officers may necessitate periodic examination of all aspects of the legal structure. This is especially important in the small and middle-sized firms where personal estate problems might have a direct bearing on the effectiveness and continuity of the firm.

Relative Importance of Various Organizational Structures

As can be seen from Table 20, the proprietorship form of organization predominates in retailing in number. But, in industry, growth, mergers, and acquisitions

TABLE 20

INCOME OF BUSINESSES, 1961–1962

(From Income Tax Returns)

LEGAL FORM OF ORGANIZATION AND INDUSTRIAL DIVISION	TOTAL NUMBER OF RETURNS[a] (IN THOUSANDS)	PER CENT OF RETURNS	NET INCOME (IN MILLIONS OF $)	PER CENT OF INCOME
Sole Proprietorships				
All Divisions	9,242.0	100.0	170,981	100.0
Wholesale and Retail Trade	1,943.0	21.0	85,639	50.1
Retail Trade	1,564.0	16.9	65,158	38.1
Active Partnerships				
All Divisions	940.0	100.0	73,954	100.0
Wholesale and Retail Trade	277.6	29.5	37,389	50.6
Retail Trade	228.8	24.3	23,421	31.7
Active Corporations				
All Divisions	1,190.0	100.0	820,773	100.0
Wholesale and Retail Trade	364.6	30.6	265,484	32.4
Retail Trade	230.0	19.3	129,408	15.8
Retail Trade Only				
Sole Proprietorships	1,564.0	77.3	65,158	29.9
Active Partnerships	228.8	11.3	23,421	10.7
Active Corporations	230.0	11.4	129,408	59.4
Total Retail Returns	2,022.8	100.0	217,987	100.0

[a] Number of returns exceeds number of establishments listed by the Census of Business, Retail Trade (Bureau of the Census), because establishments with receipts of $20,000 or less are not included, nor are any retail businesses without a "recognized place" or establishment for conducting business.
Source: Developed from *Selected Financial Data*, 1961–1962, for Corporate and Non-Corporate Business (Statistical Division, U. S. Treasury Department, Internal Revenue Service, May 1963), Tables 1, 2, and 3 (Two-Sigma Level of Selected Frequency Estimates).

are making the corporate form of organization increasingly important from the standpoint of income. Corporations classified as retail generate the bulk of retail sales. In 1962, retail corporations, while comprising only 11.4 per cent of all retail organizations, generated approximately $129,408 million, or some 59.4 per cent of retail sales volume for that year.

FUNCTIONAL NEEDS IN ORGANIZATIONAL GROWTH

When a young, vigorous organization wishes to pursue a policy of expansion, the corporate form of organization is indispensable. A shift to the corporate form of enterprise does not necessarily mean either a closely held corporate management or loss of control. When new financing becomes indispensable—as when going into an "all phases" credit policy—the financial and operating policies interact. Because of strategic complexities, an interdependent systems approach in financial planning becomes highly desirable in setting over-all store policy.

The kinds of demand on the generally limited financial resources of a retail firm more often than not determine whether an organization is in a position to expand. Further, the many areas where new financing can be utilized determine also the type of expansion that takes place. In addition to the basic requirements for operating the business, funds may be needed for real-estate transactions and the possible development of subsidiary holding companies for advantageous mergers and/or acquisitions.

Generally speaking, when any firm is in the process of growth through mergers or acquisitions, recourse must be made to outside investors and both short- and long-term creditors. This means that any growth firm must be prepared to present a favorable profit figure not only in relation to sales, but also in terms of total investment and equity investment. The amounts and rates of return are all evaluated in relation to the risks involved. In effect, the legal form of organization determines the freedom of movement under which management can build up operational effectiveness.

RANGE IN AND CONSTRAINTS OF LEGAL FORM OF ORGANIZATION

The legal framework of the firm should not only implement the financial objectives open to it but should also maximize the effective interaction and coordination of all phases of store operations. The legal structure is independent, and at the same time indirectly deterministic, of the firm's internal organizational structure, in turn, the internal organizational structure fixes the external responsibilities in all its personal, business, and public relationships.

The internal organizational structure—divisions, groups, branches, departments, and so on—is the vehicle through which company goals are achieved. The legal framework encompassing this structure forms the limits in which increases in net sales, net profit, and market share are generated. Success in achieving these objectives depends not only on the legal framework but also on the restrictions imposed on it by the market in which it deals—i.e., the degree of competition, the receptiveness of the public agencies, and the personnel and financial resources available to it. Suppliers of trade credit and funds evaluate both the range **and** constraints of the legal organization of the firm, as well as its market potential, before making any commitments.

ANALYSIS OF LEGAL FRAMEWORKS

The Sole Proprietorship

The simplest form of organization is the sole proprietorship. This type of organization is relatively easy to start and generally requires small investments of capital funds.

The sole proprietorship is a common-law legal organization, generally with a single owner-manager; thus an individual may have sole authority and responsibility for the success of the enterprise. The principal advantage of the single proprietorship is that there is no division of authority. On the other hand, the sole proprietorship can acquire relatively little capital or credit extensions, and its size always is limited. The business continues only as long as its owner can operate; turnovers and liquidations of this form of business are common. Also, the owner-manager's liabilities are unlimited; this means that any tangible personal property in the owner's name is subject to any liens resulting from the business enterprise. Of course, the prudent individual upon going into a noncorporate business generally places all personal property, such as his home, savings, etc., in his spouse's name. Thus, the assets underlying the solvency of the firm are reduced. Such procedures, of course, also serve to reduce the amount of credit extended by suppliers and banks. The income of a sole proprietorship is taxed as ordinary income at the marginal rate of the proprietor.

Advantages	Disadvantages
Ease of formation	Unlimited liability
Single control and freedom of action by authority	Dependence upon a single individual
Secrecy and economy of operation	Difficulty of raising capital for either operations or expansion
Federal and state aid (Fair Trade laws, chain store taxes, FTC Act, Unfair Competition laws, Antitrust laws)	Single responsibilities attended by personal difficulties
	Lack of delegation for large operations
Personal incentive	Limited life

Partnerships

Partnerships have most of the advantages and some of the disadvantages of the sole proprietorships. The major weakness of partnerships is that they divide managerial authority and responsibility. All business decisions are the prerogative of any of the partners. For example, the act of one partner regardless of agreed areas of managerial responsibility binds the firm. Further, partnerships have **a** high turnover, as either the death or withdrawal of any one of the partners dissolves the business. On the other hand, it is evident that the partnership can secure capital financing generally on more favorable terms than the sole proprietorship because of the unlimited liability of more individuals who would be responsible for any unpaid debts of the firm. However, as a business grows, it is likely to move into the corporate form of organization.[2] For example, a well-to-do partner may own only a 25-per-cent partnership interest in a firm; he could be held liable for the total losses of the firm if the other partners do not have sufficient personal assets to satisfy their pro rata shares of any outstanding judgments.

In the case of either of the common-law forms of organization above, business transference and inheritance taxes also have relevance in setting up policy programs under which to operate. Payment of such taxes by the heirs of a business often force its liquidation. Despite such disadvantageous tax and legal considerations, the small unincorporated business in our retailing-marketing complex persists.

Partnerships and proprietorships with small earnings have many tax advantages, generally, over a corporation. The double taxation feature is not present; i.e., a corporation distributes profits in the form of dividends after paying a corporate income tax. Recipients of corporation dividends (shareholders) are also taxed on the same earnings, at present for all amounts in excess of $100 per recipient. However, the corporate tax may be less, because the remunerations of executive management in corporations represent part operating expense and not a withdrawal from corporation earnings; this feature reduces the taxable revenues of the corporations.[3]

Advantages	Disadvantages
Ease of formation	Unlimited liability
Division of profits and separate rewards (different capital investments and different returns for service and ability)	Limited life (easily dissolved by death or withdrawal of a partner)
Flexibility of operation	Division of responsibility and control
Increased sources of capital acquisition (more than proprietorship but less than corporation)	Possible lack of coordinated goals and policies
Retention of individual control	Limitations of capital
Personal relationships and promotional advantages for key employees in the larger firms	Any partner can dissolve partnership
	Single lines of authority and responsibility difficult
	Needs well planned and mutually agreeable provisions for business continuation

[2] Even, it seems, in the case of brokerage and, to a smaller extent, accounting firms.
[3] Although corporations have limited liability, in the case of a "closed" corporation owners will occasionally be made liable for total liabilities; this is especially true when proof can be presented that the corporate form of organization is merely a subterfuge for a partnership.

Corporations

Corporations are separate legal entities—"artificial creatures of the state" which can sue and be sued, and in whose name businesses can acquire large sums of capital with which to operate. The corporate form of organization was introduced during the nineteenth century in England to circumvent the unlimited liability provisions of the law of partnerships.[4] Thus the basic weakness of proprietorships and partnerships is solved by limiting the liability of the owners (equity shareholders) of the business to the amount invested in the stock or share of the business which is owned.[5]

The corporation also circumvents another serious weakness of common-law forms of legal organization—that of business continuity. As pointed out, the death or withdrawal of any partner or of a single owner of a business dissolves the enterprise; not so the corporation. The length of life of a corporation is a stated length of years usually renewable upon application or amendment, depending on whether it is a state or federal corporation.

Each state has its own laws regarding the formation of corporations. These require slightly different legal procedures regarding taxation and the structure of the organization. The larger publicly held corporations are usually owned by absentee owners and run by professional managers. This is often true of large business enterprises. Professional management in the field of retail distribution has become very commonplace.

Advantages	Disadvantages
Limited liability	Difficulty of formation
Continuity of management	(must be formed under statute law)
Skill and flexibility of management	Charter limitations must be observed
Easier growth through mergers and acquisitions	Greater government control and regulation
Acquisition of new capital	"Double" taxation of distributed income
Personnel advantages (executive salaries are expenses, not profits)	Little voice for minority stockholders
Power to bind corporation must be specifically designated	Generally separate ownership and management
Ease in transfer of ownership interests	
Can command large volume of funds	

---

[4] The uniform partnership act defines a partnership as "two or more persons to carry on as co-owners of a business for profit." Although this definition has not been adopted by a majority of the states, the act has served to codify the common-law concept of this form of legal organization.

[5] This is true for most corporations with the exception of banks, where the liability is double the amount invested, and to mutual stock companies of the assessable type (joint venture), where the total liabilities of the corporation may be prorated among the stockholders.

The Choice of a Legal Framework

The legal organization through which business is conducted supplements the environmental framework in providing a model. In addition to the considerations mentioned above, all businesses are influenced to some extent by government control affecting their legal organization. Other legal forms of organization not mentioned above include limited partnerships, joint stock companies, joint ventures, syndicates, and trusts. In general, the corporate form of organization may not be economic when profits are not expected to exceed $25,000; on the other hand, when profits are reasonably projected to exceed $100,000, it generally pays to incorporate. "Taxes, unfortunately, can sometimes overcome economic or managerial advantages. Also, disregard of tax penalties may offset the best financing and the best type of management." [6]

SUPPLIERS OF FUNDS

Once the legal form of organization has been chosen, the next step is the acquisition of the necessary capital. Suppliers of capital fall into two classifications: creditors and owners. The amounts supplied by each grouping are readily found in the balance sheet. Assets are separated according to the manner of use, such as working capital, fixed capital, or deferred charges to expense—in other words, roughly according to their liquidity. The various owners of equity in the corporation and the amount of funds supplied are added to the "liability side" along with classifications of debt capital; these are offsets to balance the assets on the left-hand side of the balance sheet. These items are listed according to kind of suppliers, such as financial, merchandise, or fixed investment. Such moneys are extended with the expectations of repayment under conditions of expected business continuity. The remaining funds, balancing off the total assets of the firm, are the amounts of equity capital. The funds supplied by the owners or shareholders of the corporation represent the remainder of funds invested in the business.

Balance sheets, income statements, and other formal accounting reports are restricted by law and custom to certain "generally recognized principles" which bias the reported values conservatively and tie current accounting values to historical costs and receipts. These are useful in determining income-tax liabilities and are interesting to arbitrators in the event of merger or dissolution. But accounting values should not be taken as conclusive of either current going-concern or liquidation values.

Venture Capital

In retailing, especially in the smaller concerns, the suppliers of venture capital generally take an active part in the management of the business. This is not usually true in the larger corporate form of organizations. The suppliers of permanent

---

[6] J. K. Lasser, *Business Management Handbook*, rev. ed. (New York: McGraw-Hill, 1960) p. 4.

venture capital funds invested in a business have valid equity holdings or claims to proportionate management control only as long as the firm is a "going one." In a proprietorship or partnership the investment or venture capital outlay on the part of the owners is generally a basic part of their *risk* in return for possible profits. This invested sum is increased by profits and assessments or decreased by losses and withdrawals. This fluctuating investment in a corporation is known as retained earnings—earned surplus—and becomes part of the investment in the corporation.

Funds supplied by share buyers in a corporation are in the form of either common stock or preferred stock, the latter nonvoting in nature; preferred stock secures only a limited and fixed proportion of any possible profits. Equity shares (common stock) representing venture capital in an industrial or mercantile corporation usually comprise 65 to 70 per cent of the total funds invested in the retail firm. Of course, the more that can be financed through bonds and other types of credit investments, the greater the possible return to equity investment. However, the greater the interest payments on bonds, the greater the need for stable earnings to pay the interest, because payment cannot be deferred; thus the greater the risk attached to balancing equity investment.

Non-Equity Capital

Merchandise suppliers generally represent the largest class of creditors for retail firms. Extensions of ninety-day commercial loans by banks are also commonplace. In mercantile firms, fixed liabilities are generally restricted to suppliers of mortgage bond moneys. Banks, in recent years, have been the suppliers of intermediate credit (one to five years) to business firms. The government, through the Small Business Administration (SBA), has also been extending intermediate loan funds.

In the case of the smaller retail firms, a secured mortgage is often the only means of securing long-term funds. This means that the business must put up some marketable security such as land, buildings, or equipment as the basis for the loan. In the larger businesses, debenture bonds may be sold.[7]

Other Suppliers of Capital Funds

Other suppliers of debt capital besides banks are sales finance companies, insurance firms, Small Business Administration, and independent investors. Sales finance companies (such as the Commercial Credit Company of Baltimore, Maryland) generally concern themselves with the furnishing of cash to retailers for their receivables. "Their rates, which fluctuate from 8 to 10 per cent per annum and up, are competitive with those charged by banks for this type of financing." [8]

---

[7] A bond is a promise to pay a certain sum at a definite maturity date with a stated amount of interest; bonds are generally issued in denominations of $1,000 each, and each bond generally has a fixed maturity date. A debenture bond is in reality a long-term promissory note based on the general credit of the corporation.

[8] William Clyde Phelps, *The Role of the Sales Finance Companies in the American Economy* (Baltimore: Commercial Credit Company, 1957).

The sales finance company as an institution arose in response to a great social need. While primarily used by the automobile industry at the retail level, its financial services have been used by all kinds of retailers. Many sales finance companies also handle "investment plans" offered to consumers by retailers.

Furnishing funds for investment in marketing institutions involves financing at both the wholesale and retail level. Funds for the completion of installment sales are most critical in the case of automobile and major appliance sales because of the large unit sales, large volume of trade involved, and relatively long-term credit needed. Sales finance companies differ from the ordinary finance or loan companies in that they engage primarily in buying consumer purchase contracts from the seller; at the same time they provide wholesale financing for these dealers on various types of "floor plans." They charge rates which are competitive with those charged by banks or other lenders for equivalent services. Often they take great risks in serving their dealers through practically all stages in the distributive channel in which consumer durables move from the factory to the ultimate consumer. Keen competition exists between independent sales financing firms as well as with agencies in the buying of commercial paper.

Wholesalers and manufacturers who sponsor individually owned retail chains offer them practically complete financing. Included in this grouping are chains sponsored by Butler Brothers (Ben Franklin Stores), Western Auto, Firestone, and Goodyear Stores.

Insurance firms, either directly or through loans to real-estate operators, also finance large amounts of the fixed assets of retailers. Many suburban shopping centers and downtown retailing properties are owned or financed by life insurance companies.

THE INTERACTION OF FINANCIAL AND OPERATING POLICIES

The ratio of venture to permanent loan capital in an organization indirectly influences its operating policies. When a company has sizable fixed indebtedness, promotional and expansion opportunities may not be undertaken or even considered. Adequate equity financing means that the financial and operating goals of the firm can be carried out effectively through the existing organizational structure. In this case, the organization serves as the medium through which management plans and directs teamwork by flexible communications.

Retailing is a high-risk business because it must deal in uncontrollable market variables. Overexpansion often creates self-competition that reduces investment returns on established locations. Even when a new store location has been selected, there is always a "dilution" potential present. Dilution can occur at the executive levels also, as financial policies often determine the specific activities of both line and staff executives. Projected earnings of 10 to 12 per cent per annum should cover the amortization and interest on the debt capital of the company without strain.

Operating policies interact also in the type of financing underlying the business.

Smaller retailers should seek outside financing only as a last resort. If outside nonequity financing becomes necessary, most banks and other lending agencies would require first mortgage financing before considering any other type of debt structure. The result is that investment by retailers in new locations may never achieve a return equivalent to that of investments of similar size in low-risk, high-grade corporate bonds.

Some commercial banks will grant and extend term loans for periods up to five years. If debt service depends upon earnings, a retail location should provide repayment for any term loan in its entirety within a five-year period.

Among other sources of long-term capital funds is "landlord financing," which can be classified into two types: tenant allowances and direct loans. The first enables the company to complete retail space; the second represents an opportunity to obtain additional working capital without affecting the balance-sheet relationships.

In recent years, the small business investment companies (SBIC) have greatly benefited small businessmen by providing capital financing on reasonable terms. In 1958 Congress created a "fourth banking system" by permitting the SBA to license private financial institutions. The system parallels in many respects the Farm Credit System and the housing and home finance system, as well as the commercial banking system. "Typically, SBIC's lend money to small companies in return for debentures running from 5 to 15 years to maturity. These debentures are convertible into common stock of the small company at a predetermined price." [9]

In securing funds from the SBA, a five- to ten-year forecast giving the nature of the present and proposed market structures, as well as the organizational structure of the business, is needed. The qualifications of the principal executives as well as the long-run financial objectives of the business must be stipulated.

Under the requirements of the Act, the total assets of the firm seeking such financing must not exceed $5 million and net worth must not exceed $2.5 million. An average net income after taxes must not exceed $250,000.

Where a retail firm seeks to shift from a cash to a credit policy or to a larger, more inclusive credit policy, where present "bank plan" charge-account services are unsatisfactory, or where a decision is made to expand the number of stores, the SBIC has proved of inestimable value. [10]

---

[9] Neil H. Jacoby, "Getting Money for Long-Term Growth," Management Aids (March 1962), p. 2. SBIC's also make loans that are not convertible into common stock. Such loans to small unincorporated companies often carry stock purchase warrants or options. These warrants give the SBIC a right or privilege to convert all or part of the debt into stock under certain conditions—for example, should the small company become incorporated during the life of the debt. The average rate charged by SBIC's for supplying such long-term capital is competitive and relatively low—in many cases about 8 per cent a year.

[10] An example of the use of this plan for expansion purposes is the Paul Harris stores of Indianapolis, Ind., where dissatisfaction with an existing bank charge-account service prompted management to set up its own charge plan with the SBIC furnishing the necessary capital. See Earl Harris, "Financing for Growth," Credit Currents (July 1963), p. 8.

SUMMARY AND CONCLUSIONS

In this chapter the functions and limits of some legal forms of organizations were analyzed. The legal structures examined were sole proprietorships, partnerships, and corporations. Compared to the requirements of industry, a much lower ratio of fixed to current asset investment is needed in the financing of retail firms.

All financial and operating policies of a firm should be geared toward its objectives. From the financial standpoint, this means a perfect balancing of investment funds with loan funds without creating hazardous, high, fixed expenses.

The amount available for the initial investment is often the basic factor in determining not only the size of the enterprise but the legal form that the organization takes. At the same time, suppliers of funds (both equity and non-equity) initially examine the legal structure as well as the debt-paying ability of the firm before investing. Sources of funds were discussed in the framework of the resulting circular effects on over-all store profitability. Planning for financial requirements from the standpoint of the firm and within the framework of these constraints forms the subject matter of the chapter that follows.

Chapter 13: *Planning for Financial Requirements*

Once the legal form of organization and the kind of business wanted have been determined, the successful operation of the firm depends on the sufficiency of the capital funds available to the enterprise—the basic assumption being that management's capacity to manage is adequate.

As discussed in Chapter 5, the choice of a suitable location and an estimate of its potential become the basis for the amount of rental or lease guarantee that can be paid. Once the basic minimum volume that must be generated in a particular location is determined, an additional amount should be projected to allow for a margin of safety. At this point the location should be reappraised to make certain that the total projected volume can be generated in that location and with that size of store.

For example, an individual wishing to open a family shoe store finds what he believes to be a suitable location in a moderate-sized shopping center. The store has a 60-foot front and a 100-foot depth—6,000 square feet over-all. The renting agent asks for a minimum leasehold guarantee of $6,000 a year with added rental charges of 6 per cent of all net sales in excess of $100,000 annual sales volume. (An annual volume of this size is necessary to cover fixed leasehold costs.)

Upon checking Dun & Bradstreet's median figures, let us say the prospective owner finds that a 6 per cent rental is usual for the type of family shoe operation that he has in mind. If, upon examining population, income, competition, and other economic factors, he feels that this volume can be easily obtained in the location, he can give serious consideration to signing the lease. Of course, the entire operation must be profitable at the projected level of sales volume for the businessman to prosper at this location. He should also consider other locations at other rentals before choosing. If he feels that a minimum $100,000 annual volume would be difficult, the entrepreneur should either attempt to negotiate lower rental charges or drop the location from further consideration.

PROVIDING THE INITIAL INVESTMENT—WORKING CAPITAL

Capital investment consists of both fixed and working capital. In the case illustrated, let us assume that a $100,000 annual sales volume seems reasonable for that location. An initial amount of $6,000 will be needed for rental during the year. Business prudence would dictate having at least one-fourth of this amount, or $1,500, for three months' operation.

The next phase in financial planning is the determination of average inventory requirements. This depends directly on projected sales and estimated merchandise turnover. The turnover ratio of any marketing firm varies according to merchandise lines handled and the type of store handling it.

Let us assume that a family shoe store median should turn over four times annually. By dividing the total estimated sales volume by the turnover figure ($100,000 ÷ 4) we arrived at an average inventory figure of $25,000 at retail.[1]

Assuming a 40 per cent initial, cumulative mark-on based on retail sales, the cost of an average inventory for this type of operation would amount to $15,000 at cost. (This cost figure is calculated by multiplying the average inventory at retail by 100 per cent minus the initial mark-on, in this case 60 per cent × $25,000.[2])

Assuming further that the owner has a 60-day period in which to settle his merchandise payables, he can probably shift the cost of handling one-third of his average $15,000 inventory, or $5,000, to suppliers. However, in accordance with conservative practice, he should not attempt to shift more than one-fifth of his average inventory at cost, or $3,000, in the form of merchandise. This would leave additional working capital requirements for inventory at $16,500. He will also need a certain amount for out-of-pocket expenses (such as salaries, heat, light, taxes, insurance, advertising) and contingencies always present in any business venture. Summing up, the projected working capital needed for this shoe store with a projected $100,000 volume would be as follows:

---

[1] Inventory, as well as merchandising and sales planning concepts, will be taken up in detail in later chapters.

[2] Every retail inventory consists of two portions—a mark-up portion and a cost portion. The cost portion is always the balance between the mark-on at retail and 100 per cent—in this case, 100 − 40, or 60 per cent.

Three months' rent	$ 1,500
Average inventory at cost (4/5 of total)	12,000
Contingency reserve	3,000
Total working capital needed	$16,500

This is the kind of planning that must be undertaken in order to determine the amount of working capital needed. A useful way of checking the consistency of plans and the sensitivity of projected needs to possible errors of estimation is to prepare pro-forma accounting statements for conservative and expected median levels of sales volume.

FIXED CAPITAL ALLOCATIONS

As previously pointed out, the proportion of fixed to working capital is relatively small in retail distribution. In this example, funds would be needed for furniture and fixtures (such as shelving, footstools, chairs, cash register, safe, adding machine, typewriter, rugs, and interior decor); these are depreciable items and can generally be obtained on long-term purchase plans or on many available leasing plans. In any case, almost all fixtures can be obtained with as little as 10 to 15 per cent down, with balances to be paid in periods ranging from three to seven years.[3]

Assuming the estimated cost of the fixed capital requirement to be $10,000, then $2,500 would probably suffice: $1,500 for down payment (15 per cent), and $1,000 for contingencies reserved.[4] At this point, a total of $19,000 in fixed and working capital is needed for this venture.

Another provision must also be made for the first year of operation. It is very rare, indeed, for any new store to open and show a normal profit the very first year of operation. In planning financial operations, it is usually sound to plan on no better than breaking even during the first year.

Except for a few rules of thumb in financial planning for furniture and fixtures, each store unit presents differing problems depending on the store image desired in a particular locale. Chain stores with generalized and similar layout policies merely follow pre-existing patterns. In new branch department stores, it has been estimated that the cost of carpeting, fixturing, furniture, and so on, runs about ten dollars per square foot of selling space. Again, in many instances there is always the possibility of leasing out certain departments and areas. In such cases the lessee furnishes the financing for the space occupied.

---

[3] The acquisition of new capital seems in the past to have been a prime requisite for manufacturing as well as nonmanufacturing corporations. In attempts to stay in step with the constantly increasing demands of a high-level and expanding economy, a substantial part of new capital obtained was directed toward geographic expansion, the carrying of larger inventories, and the underwriting of greater amounts of accounts receivable. Where certain economies of scale and other competitive advantages were realized, such new capital inputs proved most economic. (*Monthly Business Review*, Federal Reserve Bank, Cleveland [February 1962], p. 3.)

[4] This reserve should not be confused with a depreciation reserve, which is not a fund that can be used to retire debts.

Where equipment is leased for management's own use, it represents a form of long-term debt and should be so illustrated on the balance sheet. In fact, a lease involves the same type of obligation as a purchase, especially if the equipment is to be leased for a period of longer than three years. Yet leasing equipment is a good method of obtaining furniture, fixtures, and equipment not otherwise obtainable. Maintenance costs should be programed in the permanent expense structure and provided from a cash budget outlay.

Thus, venture capital should be sufficient to underwrite working capital needs and that portion of the fixed assets which cannot be financed on a long-term basis at a reasonable rate of interest. A sound financial plan set up in this manner means that seasonal financial needs or borrowing for expansion purposes become relatively easy to negotiate. A creditor looks favorably on the management of any business firm that can forecast its seasonal needs well in advance. The failure to establish a permanent "line of credit" for seasonal purposes is one of the great weaknesses of managers of small businesses.

Store policy procedures determine the adequacy of the firm's financial requirements and capital investment. In the shoe store example, all sales were assumed to be cash, with merchandise delivered to customers upon completion of transaction. If credit were extended as a service and delivery of goods offered, the financial needs of the store become greater. Stores under simplified service, self-service, or full-service basis have differing kinds of financial needs.

LINES OF CREDIT

In negotiations with a private investor or promoter for lines of credit, the papers should be drawn by an attorney. For large-scale enterprises, it may be wise to place the problem before an investment banker. Such bankers can generally arrange private issues of securities or small public issues. Issues of $300,000 or less and those offered within a state do not require registration with the Securities and Exchange Commission (SEC). Costs of dealing with investment bankers may run as high as 15 to 20 per cent. On the other hand, dealing directly with individual investors may only be carried out by promising large interest rates and sizable blocks of stock.

In planning for lines of credit, the total amount of working capital should be sufficient for normal business operations, with additional financing needed only for peak inventory build-up periods. For most general merchandise stores, such periods occur during January and February—inventory build-up for spring selling and spending and accounts receivable from Christmas sales; July and August—build-up for fall; and October and November—for Christmas selling.

All current assets generally represent the minimum working capital required. Of course, before seeking outside help, possible retrenchment should be carefully reviewed.

The "four C's of credit" considered by a potential creditor are character, capacity, capital, and conditions. A good accounting system and regular audits by a Certified Public Accountant are the best bases of information for a line of credit. Also, filling in confidential survey reports of agencies such as Dun & Bradstreet is another important prerequisite in setting up adequate lines of credit—especially from merchandise resources. For this reason, as well as for more effective management, financial planning forecasts should include projected budgets of sales, expenditures, and investment.

Lending institutions and merchandise suppliers are more impressed by the trend of a business than by static figures at any one point in time. These illustrate community acceptance and are much more indicative of maintaining competitive position than day-to-day sales. Table 21 indicates banking views on desirable characteristics of small firms.

TABLE 21

IMPORTANCE OF VARIOUS CHARACTERISTICS OF SMALL FIRMS AS PROSPECTIVE BORROWERS FROM BANKS

CHARACTERISTIC OF FIRM	PERCENTAGE OF BANKS RATING EACH ITEM AS:		
	VERY IMPORTANT	FAIRLY IMPORTANT	OF LITTLE OR NO IMPORTANCE
Profit trend	85.1	14.9	0.0
General business experience of management	79.4	20.6	0.0
Ratio of current assets to current liabilities	78.6	20.8	0.6
Willingness to furnish security[a]	73.1	25.4	1.4
Experience of management in present line of business	72.5	27.2	0.3
Ratio of equity funds to liabilities	69.7	29.4	0.8
Ratio of current profits to assets or net worth	67.9	31.8	0.3
Ratio of inventories to sales	66.4	31.6	2.0
Willingness to amortize loan fully[a]	64.2	32.3	3.5
Depth of management	62.2	36.9	0.8
Ability to furnish collateral	61.6	35.9	2.5
Changes in liquidity and equity—debt position	61.5	37.6	0.8
Ratio of inventories to size of business	61.5	37.0	1.4
Growth rate in sales	55.5	42.8	1.7
Age of the firm	53.7	43.2	3.0
Willingness to sign a formal term-loan agreement[a]	53.2	32.6	14.2
Growth rate in assets	47.2	49.7	3.1
Prospective depositor	45.5	48.3	6.1
Maturity wanted	40.3	46.2	13.4
Borrowing relationship with any other bank	33.0	49.3	17.7
Credit rating given by credit rating agencies	27.1	55.6	17.3
Period the firm has been borrowing from your bank[b]	23.6	56.7	19.7
Prospective outlet for loanable funds[b]	23.3	43.0	33.7
Average deposit balance[b]	18.1	63.9	18.1
Period the firm has been a depositor of your bank	13.9	57.9	28.1
Size of the firm	9.6	59.6	30.9

[a] If a term loan is desired.

[b] The questionnaires were sent out before the issuance of SBA's Simplified Bank Loan Participation Plan on September 1, 1961. Later reactions would probably be more favorable.

Source: Based on decisions of 364 Wisconsin bankers in "Attitudes of Bankers Towards Small Business Financing," R. W. Hooker, *Management Research Summary* (Washington, Small Business Administration, December 1962), p. 3.

EFFECT OF OPERATING POLICIES ON FINANCIAL REQUIREMENTS

Customer Credit Policies

In the smaller store it is generally inadvisable to assume credit risks because of the expense involved and the often more limited financial resources available. For example, any store offering 30-day charge accounts must expect an average collection time of 45 to 60 days. Most smaller stores are rarely in any financial position to support the extra financial requirements of such credit policies. To aid smaller stores, banks have come along with "credit plans"; in some cases the customer initiates the credit application at the bank, and charges from the store are automatically accepted and discounted by the bank.

However, the plans are very costly, with the bank charge to the store often approximating 4 to 6 per cent of sales. Because the accounts are accepted without recourse, the bank discounts from purchase price may represent a substantial gross margin loss. In addition, the customer also pays interest on the account—a negative patronage factor. As a means of generating additional volume, the use of credit is indisputable. The desirability of pursuing credit extensions must be evaluated by comparing the total sales increase with the increase in costs in attaining such sales. Such costs should be examined from the standpoint of overall reduction in percentage operating expenses because of the increase in total sales.

In order to raise capital for financing receivables, some of the larger department and chain stores have initiated group efforts to develop jointly owned, receivables financing subsidiaries. Such subsidiaries could also furnish small stores with a vehicle for financing their accounts receivables at relatively low cost.

This technique could attract companies now, or considering, financing receivables through sale to banks. All joint setups would permit stores to have enough money for their needs with greater flexibility and economy than is generally possible when banks dictate the borrowing terms. Bank loans would continue to be used on top of these inside funds.

"This program opens to independent stores a source of long term money that would impart strength in this respect comparable to that possessed by big chains with unlimited access to this avenue of financing."[5] Among others, Paul M. Mazur, Harold J. Szold, Morris Natelson, and Stephen DuBrul, Jr., from Lehman Brothers, have taken a teamwork approach to setting up this kind of financing program for retail firms. Sears, Roebuck and Company, May Department stores, Montgomery Ward, and R. H. Macy and Company have all set up subsidiary financing companies along these lines.

It should be stressed that, insofar as credit policies are concerned, the largest costs associated with credit sales are administrative and clerical costs, not losses from bad debts. However, credit sales must be sufficiently diversified and not so great in total that losses from bad debts cannot be easily absorbed.

---

[5] Samuel Feinberg, Women's Wear Daily (June 6, 1962), p. 16. Mr. Feinberg also mentions jointly owned financed affiliates, such as Appliance Buyers Credit Corp., which purchases paper from distributors of Whirlpool, RCA-Whirlpool, and Carrier Corp. products. The equity of ABCC is owned 80 per cent by Whirlpool and 20 per cent by Carrier. He writes, "Allied, Federated, and May are not using their finance companies other than in a nominal sense. Allied and Federated sell their receivables to banks. May doesn't sell its receivables at all."

Selling Policies

The type of selling policy that a store pursues bears a direct relationship to the financial requirements of the store. For example, in simplified service and self-selection procedures the customer is expected to complete the processes of merchandise selection and acquisition. Under such self-serve operations more will have to be expended in the form of fixturing and self-service displays because of display elasticity of demand.[6] This kind of selling also involves more financing for "classification detail" registers and for channeling customers through certain checkout or register areas. On the other hand, such additional costs can be offset by the necessity for fewer clerks and fewer supervisors. In the case of full-service selling, the necessity for registers and more elaborate fixturing is often less. At the same time, the salaries and overhead of a larger sales force would represent an additional cost in over-all financial planning.

Even though total costs under these plans may not be very different, the avoidable (as opposed to "fixed") costs may be markedly different and important to the planning and financing of a new store.

Other Service Policies

Depth and width of merchandise line assortments as a basic policy involve varying capital outlays for inventory requirements. Meeting the competition of merchandise assortments handled by business rivals may take such decisions out of the control of financial planners. In other areas, it may be necessary to limit the lines of goods carried to meet over-all financial budgets. Each time additional lines are introduced, not only space availability but the extent of permanent capital investment must be considered.

Other service policies dictate decisions as to how to compete in price and quality. If the decision is to compete on a price basis, then further commitments in capital resources may be necessary. Length of store hours is another type of policy that may involve additional capital for pay-roll and fixed maintenance expense.

A store furnishing delivery services can lease out such operations either to firms such as the United Parcel Service or to any number of locally owned firms who specialize in deliveries. The extent of financial planning in this direction depends directly on how delivery costs are absorbed—by the customer or the store.

The total costs involved in the manner in which sales are actually transacted in retail establishments were investigated by P. G. Herbst,[7] a British economist. He argues that the fundamental difference between small stores and large stores lies in their relative dependence upon an explicit administrative function—the small store being "intrinsically regulated" and therefore not needing administrative

---

[6] Here demand is determined by the effectiveness of the displays in the traffic aisles.
[7] "Measurement of Behavior Structures by Means of Input-Output Data," *Human Relations* (1957) 10, pp. 335–46.

specialists, thus operating at lower costs than larger firms. On this basis, the smaller firm can actually offer more services than a larger firm, absorb relatively smaller amounts of capital, and still remain competitive!

COMPETITIVE FACTORS IN FINANCIAL PLANNING

In any economic analysis of the retail firm, there is some evidence that the short-run cost curves and long-run envelope curves (described in economic theory) are appropriate to the retail trade only up to certain points—depending on the line of trade. The firms themselves do not know what points represent their most efficient operating peaks. And profit ratios alone are not a sufficient basis for evaluating firm size from the social point of view. Because retail firms operate in imperfect or monopolistically inclined competitive markets, charges of misallocation of resources when profits seem high are not necessarily true.[8]

Often, the economic conflicts found in the competitive structure of the market tend to be quite intense. Severe competitive stress forms a special kind of drain on financial resources. Such drains take the form of subsidies of certain merchandise classifications which are subjected to keen price competition and which must be carried regardless of profitability or economic feasibility.

As often as not, in many such cases there is little, if any, increase in over-all sales to help reduce operating expense ratios. For example, harsh competition often forces stores into uneconomic sales promotion and advertising expenditures. Moneys allocated merely as a means of maintaining an existing competitive framework within a trading area tend to become wasteful, and require additional financial commitments. Promotional devices such as trading stamps, special discounts, or give-aways often fall into this uneconomic category when additional volume is not generated.

CIRCULAR EFFECT—COSTS OF EXPANSION

In planning for expansion, the U-shaped average unit cost curve for the long-run situation represents a series of points and is wider than a U-shaped average unit cost curve for the short run because the former represents the envelope of all short-run cost curves.

Geographic or merchandise line expansion represents new inputs, depending on the state of technology. When store management decides to operate an additional unit of expansion, a different service and promotional cost may be involved.

An equilibrium position for an industry operating under conditions of external economies of scale would never result in a single firm supplying the total retail market. At the retail level the growth and limit of the size of firm and scale of plant are not determined solely by the planning activities of its managers, but the

---

[8] See Edna Douglas, "Size of Firm and the Structure of Costs in Retailing," *The Journal of Business*, Vol. XXXV, No. 2 (April 1962), pp. 158–90.

nature of the planning activities is determined by the competence and experience of the planners.

As a firm nears the limit of its borrowing power, it must expect to pay a risk premium in the form of higher interest rates or lower prices from the underwriter of any bond issue. Further, as the business risk becomes higher than the premium interest rate, only very limited additional funds can be produced. Once a firm accepts loans beyond its "prudent" borrowing power, capital becomes rationed, pursuit of maximum advantage is restricted, and expansion possibilities are usually minimized or become nonexistent.

The test for feasibility of a financial plan is simple. The amounts demanded for each type of security and time rate of interest mutually determine the cost of capital to a particular firm. An organization's ability to expand is thus determined by the cost of capital to the firm. And the financial plan of the retail enterprise is subject to processes of continuing adjustment to both internal and external changes.

Real-Estate Costs

In downtown locations, where real-estate costs are higher than in suburban areas, land and building costs often require separate financial planning. Businesses which have signed leases in downtown locations—before traffic dilution took place—had to absorb heavy rental expenditures. Thus, real-estate costs in downtown shopping locations determine the kind of financial planning that takes place.

Ownership of a store building in a downtown area represents a sizable capital investment by many retail firms. In shopping centers, however, ownership is held by promoters with major financing coming from insurance companies, real-estate companies, and banks. Also, leases in the development of centers are generally handled by real-estate brokers and shopping center developers. In each case, a different type of financial planning is involved.

When a firm purchases a site and/or building on a long-term amortization basis, only that portion of the monthly payments which represents interest and real-estate taxes is deductible as rental expense. The balance of the monthly payments are additions to the firm's fixed asset capital holdings. Where such transactions are not handled separately, they enter into the financial operation of the firm. In determining the business's true profitability, interest and taxes plus "economic rental charges" should be entered separately as an "imputed" rental cost of conducting the enterprise.[9] Generally speaking, if investment and tax considerations are important in determining true profitability, it is always better to take the rental as a cost. In fact, it is always good procedure wherever possible to invest in a "tax deduction."

---

[9] In computing a fair charge for one's own property, total rental cost should be the amount a second party would demand for rental of the same location. The difference between the amount paid for interest, taxes, and depreciation of the building and the fair rental value would represent the imputed rental cost addition.

Rental Charges

Retailers operate in highly competitive environments. The smallest kinds of stores compete side-by-side with multi-million-dollar corporations. Only by having the proper degree of managerial control of prerogatives can stores hope to stay in business. Yet, the usual type of lease signed in a shopping center is on a percentage of net sales. This eliminates certain courses of action by store management, especially in the area of financial planning, to maintain the efficiency and profitability of volume increases. When shopping-center developers demand percentage leases plus guaranteed dollar amounts above certain minimums, they feel that they have a bona fide interest share in the merchant's business; the value of their property will increase with an increase in the lessee's sales and provide an automatic hedge against inflation.

However, the retail enterprise operating in a normal buyer's market depends upon its buying policies, selling and pricing policies, promotion and advertising effectiveness, the extent of the services offered, and the competency of its personnel and financial management in order to increase its value—not just on the economic value of the property.

A more equitable arrangement would be the periodic reappraisal of the property value; a clause in the lease to this effect should result in a fair return on the changing economic value of the property itself. This would remove many constraints now being undergone by many lessees because increasing sales can only be generated on an increasing cost basis. A retail store with a percentage lease tends to be a high mark-up operation.

Off-price sales and loss-leader selling as promotional devices tend to be uneconomic in locations where a landlord with a percentage lease shows a higher return per dollar of investment than does the retailer. A fixed rental expense allows an organization to develop productive and efficient merchandising policies. Thus, increased volume results in increased financial strength, increased profits and growth potential, rather than "monopoly" profits for the owners of the site and the building.

Today, most expansion by retail firms is geographical. Numerous small "independents" have expanded into planned shopping centers. However, national chains or store ownership groups or large independent department stores of unquestioned drawing power usually have to take leases before any large regional center can be assured of success as a shopping hub. As a result, the larger firms can negotiate extremely favorable lease arrangements.

The smaller stores are able to acquire leases in the center only on a high charge basis because their contribution to the "draw" of the center is minimal. When competing merchandise lines are carried by many outlets in a center, the high rental costs can result in only slight profit by competing smaller stores.

In such cases, expansion by smaller firms becomes quite difficult because of inadequate financing. Some managements, in order to expand, may take the "SBIC" route as discussed in Chapter 12. Others may resort to self-liquidating commercial loans.

A serious problem with so-called self-liquidating or commercial loans is that, if the purpose of the loan is fulfilled, the firm will be relatively more profitable and inclined to expand its business. Increases in sales volume require increased investments in working capital and increased needs for further borrowing, and so on. This is one reason why so often success can spoil a business firm.

USE OF LEASED DEPARTMENTS FOR FINANCING AND EXPANSION

Leasing departments within large stores is generally negotiated because of the inability of stores to secure specialized personnel for optimum operation of particular departments. Another major reason for leasing departments is that the management feels the required capital investment in inventory, fixed assets, and space allocations of particular departments would not prove economic if handled by themselves. Thus in order to expand, many firms may take the leasing route because this represents a means of going into a major business enterprise without being pressed for additional capital outlays. Many discount houses are expanding by just such means.

Yet, on the basis of empirical evidence, there is no direct relationship between the percentage of leased department sales and total volume and profitability of the entire store. "The lack of relationship between store profit and income accruing to the store because of leased department volume is surprising—especially since commission rates paid by lessees generally are less than the contributions to net profit usually reported for the same departments when operated by the store itself." [10]

The types of leased departments that have been common in department stores since 1945 are millinery, beauty salons, photographic studios, sewing machines, lending library, watch repair, shoe repair, optical, "in home" sales items (such as vacuum cleaners), and automobile supplies and accessories. In supermarkets, non-foods such as housewares, toys, drugs, and sundries may be leased to wholesale rack jobbers. In each of these cases specialized personnel are needed for optimum management and sales.

While in some cases median lease charges may range as high as 15 to 20 per cent, such charges will average from 9 to 12 per cent. If credit services are extended, then the average would be higher. There is definitely a place in the retail structure for leased departments of all kinds in almost any store, especially to

---

[10] Based on interviews conducted with controllers of large department stores in Eastern United States, 1962–1963.

In evaluating the profitability of the lease, it is important that all direct expenses such as selling and advertising, rentals, supplies, services purchased (i.e., local telephone), prorated insurance items, as well as charges for depreciation on fixtures and equipment (when furnished by the store) be included. Otherwise the lease's contribution to over-all store efforts will be overstated.

specialists. Such departments can represent one of the means by which stores can offer their customers more complete service and merchandise assortments without any recourse to added financial investment. Because lessees are often owner-managed and more specialized, they may be much more efficient in their buying, selling, and merchandising than many store-owned departments. However, most leased departments need continuing lessor management supervision to make certain that over-all store policies are being maintained.

USE OF "BREAK-EVEN" POINTS IN PLANNING

Before finalizing any plan for financial requirements, the various departmental or store "break-even" points should be calculated. As previously discussed, the break-even point is the amount of volume that will provide coverage for total average operating costs of the firm. Again, a break-even point may be defined as the volume necessary for a business to continue without undue strain and the application of additional capital funds.

To carry out the break-even projection, all operating expenses (such as salaries, heat, light, rent, insurance, taxes, and depreciation) are separated according to whether they are fixed or variable costs, and are projected separately. To illustrate with an example, a supermarket that has a projected volume of $1 million a year, a total expense budget of $180,000, and an estimated 20 per cent gross margin would generate a 2 per cent net profit on sales if the projected volume is achieved. On the other hand, should only $900,000 of volume be generated, then the operating expense of $180,000 will rise to 20 per cent (180,000/900,000); thus, $900,000 would be the break-even point of the company. Any smaller volume would result in an operating loss.

Figure XIV illustrates the method of setting up a break-even chart for the shoe store discussed earlier in this chapter. Expenses are on the y axis and number of sales on the x axis.

Although knowledge of the break-even point solves no problems, it is an invaluable aid to management in furnishing a minimum operating criterion and acts as a warning device in budgetary control and sales evaluation. The break-even-point analysis treats sales volume as a variable and helps management keep a continuing check on the proper ratios of fixed to variable expenses at any volume level. Such minimum operating volume requirements should be set up on a monthly or quarterly basis. Break-even charts are valid in terms of costs and profits only under the set of conditions prevailing when the chart is set up.

SUMMARY AND CONCLUSIONS

In this chapter the basic factors in planning for financial requirements were set forth. These included considerations in providing for the initial investment and its allocation into fixed and working capital. It was stated that the adequacy of the

FIGURE XIV
BREAK-EVEN CHART FOR SHOE STORE

(*Based on average sale of $9.00*)

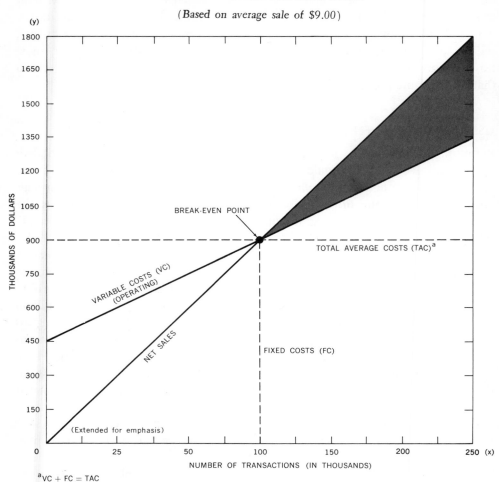

^aVC + FC = TAC

location and appropriateness of store size in generating the necessary volume for success were basic to planning for financial requirements and the success of the venture.

Once the location's adequacy is assured and initial financial requirements provided, the next step is judicious planning for profitable operation and growth. This depends on being able to project a realistic flow of funds as a basis for growth.

Problems involved in fund flow are discussed in the following chapter.

Chapter 14: *Flow of Fund Analysis*

It is evident that the long-range financial resources of the business must be adequate if the organization's goals are to be effectively attained. Continuing adequacy of financial resources is provided by the flow of funds within the firm. Planning for a continuing flow of funds means having funds available when needed and in the amounts needed; this is generally the responsibility of the treasurer and/or controller.[1]

THE INTERACTION OF FUND SUPPLY AND EXPANSION POLICIES

A firm's ability to secure funds internally is a basic part of business and marketing strategy. Whenever a retail firm has too high a turnover or an unusually high level of total fixed costs, then it must either expand or be acquired. If a firm operates with too high a stock turn or too high a return on total investment, this may be indicative of either lack of capital or over-rapid growth rather than a high degree of efficiency. When fixed costs represent too high a proportion of

---

[1] In essence, the treasurer is responsible for providing over-all financing for the business, while the controller is responsible for the use of funds in the day-to-day operations of the firm. This distinction between the treasurer and controller tends to narrow and disappear in smaller stores where the functions are unified in one person.

total costs, an inefficient plant or operation or a deteriorating situation may be indicated.

Firms following fixed expansion policies often have a high ratio of inventories to total debt. Firms with relatively high inventories have low stock turnover; such firms may be able to carry basic stock without additional financing. In every case, before any expansion is carried out sales forecasts and budgetary plans should clearly demonstrate that sales goals can be easily attained at profitable levels. It is not well understood that once a business begins to operate effectively, capital requirements for optimum operation may increase sharply with its increasing effectiveness. Discount houses such as Korvette and Zayre, for example, fall into this category. In some cases, enough treasury stock may be held by the company itself so that it would not be too costly to acquire additional capital.[2] Thus, expansion policies depend on and interact with the flow of funds as well as the cost and availability of additional fund acquisitions. As firms expand, money becomes "tight" and relatively expensive. When this happens, the treasurer-controller becomes the decision center for over-all policy planning as to how best to assure an adequate supply of funds. This is essentially the situation today.

Another type of capital expenditure is the allocation of funds for promoting a definite corporate image in the face of constantly changing complexities in the market place. Store expansions and main store modernizations—the most common types of capital expenditure—require justification for the necessary investments involved on an "expected cash flow and capital recoupment" time basis.

THE CONCEPT OF CASH FLOW

In planning for financial requirements it must be kept in mind that profits do not necessarily produce cash. Some cash can be expected from sales and noncash expenses resulting from depreciation of fixed assets.[3] In the latter case, actual decreases in cash occur when sinking funds have been set up for replacement of wasting assets. (See the discussion later in this chapter on depreciation policies.)

The first step in developing a cash budget is to set up a preliminary sales forecast, usually on a six-month basis. Then an over-all income and expenditure budget is formulated for the entire firm before any specific allocations by category and division are developed.

This budget begins with estimates of cash accruals resulting from gross margins less out-of-pocket costs. Of course, provision must be made for pay-roll and other recurring costs such as heat, light, taxes, insurance, and advertising; suitable fund

---

[2] Treasury stock is common stock, authorized but either unissued or repurchased by the firm itself. It is used for both expansion purposes and for sale to executives (through stock option plans) or to the public for acquiring additional capital.

[3] A "noncash" expense means that no actual payout is made by the firm. This type of book expense is a legitimate business expense, although no cash is paid out at the time when the transaction is recorded. Thus depreciation expense represents an additional cash accrual to the firm. Technically, this cash accrual should be invested in order to provide for replacement of the asset being depreciated. (More often than not such "cash" funds are used for immediate contingencies.)

provisions must also be made for the discounting of merchandise accounts payable. The latter represents a major area of nonoperating income.[4] The control of costs must be related to projected gross profit, out of which all cash payments must eventually be made. Discounting invoices for trade credit is a must within the framework of the merchandise plan, which is coordinated with the sales forecast for the same six-month periods.[5]

The merchandise plan includes the open-to-buy budget, which is set up and timed for particular delivery periods during the course of the six-month planning period. All arrangements for additional money requirements should be made in advance by establishing lines of credit (generally with banks) so that there will be no undue costs involved when credit is needed. As long as the differential amount returned to the firm in the form of attained gross margin is sufficient to cover total operating costs (including imputed costs of entrepreneurial investment) and leave a margin for profit, the basic requirement for continuity is met. How well the firm does with its gross margin return is then determined by the effectiveness of its budgeting procedures and organization control.

USE OF BUDGETARY PROCEDURES

Correct budgetary procedures facilitate operations analysis and can be of key importance in predicting cyclical input-output flow of funds. The analysis of variance between what the expected fund flow actually is and what it was planned to be will test the quality of the budgetary procedures. And these influence the buying behavior of the firm and the manner in which it prices its asset acquisitions, their use, and their disposal.

All budgets are based on the sales forecast and the estimated cost conditions necessary to attain the forecast goal. Also, each budget contains a statement of goals in terms of levels. A standard cost is set up in the budget plan and a place for the actual levels of attainment is set up. The differences between the actual operations and the planned forecast budget, regardless of what area or division is involved, should be analyzed so that future budgets will be more realistic. Overall planning budgets should result in adequate flow of funds as needed by the firm.

PREPLANNING THE SALES FORECAST BUDGET

As a firm seeks to maximize profits, the sales goals should be set up in such a way that the total costs involved in producing the forecast sales are at a minimum; i.e., the marginal productivity of the last dollar spent should be equal to its manner of use. The sales output of the firm is planned on the basis of what is believed possible. This means that equilibrium within the firm would not necessarily be

---

[4] The nature and extent of trade credit supplied by wholesalers and manufacturers often determine the success of a business establishment. Merchandise suppliers want cash discounts to be taken, and their terms of trade in reality penalize firms that do not discount their invoices.

[5] These plans are discussed in detail in the chapters on merchandising and buying.

at the point where marginal costs equal marginal revenue. Also, the marginal value productivity of each inventory input does not necessarily produce its goal maintained markup.

Obviously, the sales forecast process does not proceed without consideration of the nature, the mix, and the cost of the marketing efforts needed to achieve the sales goal. The selection of sales promotion methodology and determination of the "optimum" merchandise mix are part of the over-all task of budgeting in the retail firm. It is thus essential that both qualitative and quantitative analyses encompass more than just the limited area traditionally envisioned within the framework of budgetary control.[6]

The sales budget is, in itself, the most important single planning device for any business firm. From this flows profit and provision for new working capital—the basic ingredients for the growth of the enterprise.

In sales planning, all pertinent economic indicators and variables should be taken into consideration. For example, sales during corresponding periods of the previous year should enter into the calculations in proper perspective, as should price trends, fashion changes, industry changes in the community, and so on. Price changes involve not only the total dollar sales but the number of transactions as well. Projected changes in business conditions, changes in degrees of competition, and differences in the number of selling days per month must also be considered. Other items that can enter the calculations are changes in store policy, departmental or store space allocations, and changes in dates of holidays such as Easter and Labor Day.

Short-term sales are generally planned for periods of six months or a year. Forecasts should be completed at least six months in advance of the initial application date, and sales projections broken down on a monthly and weekly basis. The sales budget as a functional plan is coordinated by the controller, who prepares estimated balance sheet and income statements for each month or for each quarter. Upon approval of the sales forecast by the general merchandise manager and the store's executive committee, each division (including nonselling) prepares budgets of operating, marketing, and administrative expense so as to arrive at either contributions to profits and flow of funds inward, or contributions toward facilitating the merchandising process.

As pointed out, the necessary lines of credit for seasonal needs are established in advance. The success of forward planning for the critical periods of seasonal cash needs may range from two to three months. When enough cash is on hand to operate smoothly the year round, it generally means that the financial planning has been uneconomic. Recourse to short-term bank financing during the year should be a normal operating procedure for any business firm.

---

[6] As will be illustrated, the details of determining the marketing efforts needed to achieve the sales goals underlie operating and financial budgeting. The controller's familiarity with the latter areas places him in an important position to provide the necessary balance of output-input flows of funds. The sales, merchandise, expense, and cash budgets as well as some initial capital budgeting procedures are discussed more specifically in the chapters on merchandising, sales promotion, accounting, and control.

THE MERCHANDISE BUDGET

Cash flows directly from the sale of merchandise. The merchandise budget, generally called the merchandise plan, is the blueprint for the acquisition and handling of inventory needed to meet sales goals. An effective merchandise plan is essential to the successful operation of the store because it is the base from which is derived the operating income of the organization. The merchandise plan itself is the result of the combined efforts of the controller, the merchandise manager, and the department buyer, and evolves from their judgment as to external market needs and internal effectiveness in supplying these needs.

The merchandise plan requires the utilization of total market information about what the store's customers want, when they want it, and at what price. It is a flexible plan of action and should always be adjustable to actual conditions; it is also flexible in that different kinds and quantities of merchandise mixes are associated with different prices. It includes operating variables such as initial markup, markdowns, cash discounts, alteration and workroom expense, total operating expenses, maintained markup, and gross margin goals. The goal turnovers for each department in the store are also initial considerations in setting up the complete merchandise plan.

In preparation, merchandise plans do not vary much from one store to another, and in all of them sales, stocks, purchases, and reductions are coordinated. Seasonal stock turnover and initial markup goals are key figures in the plan. In many cases stores include expense items which also appear in the expense and sales budgets. Usually, these are variable and somewhat controllable expenses that are technically under the control of the buyer and/or departmental manager. Direct departmental expenses such as selling, salaries, and advertising fall into the "controllable" classification.

THE CASH BUDGET

The primary purpose of the cash budget is to allow management to project the amount of money that would be available at any given period of time in the future. Net cash flow inward is often at a minimum before Christmas, Easter, or school openings because the cash paid for inventory accumulations is generally highest when cash received from sales are at relatively low levels. In other words, the need for merchandise accounts payable for Easter, preschool, and Christmas occurs some two to four months in advance; thus cash for inventory bulges outward and cash flow inward do not coincide. Credit extensions to customers further accentuate these cyclical changes.

For example, the inventory build-up of a large department store from mid-March through mid-April, depending upon when Easter occurs, generates many merchandise accounts payable to vendors. At the same time, charge-account sales to customers may represent a major portion of the total sales of the stores, creating a sizable "sales-cash-income" due, as customer payments may not be made until fifty to seventy-five days after sales. It is during such seasonal variations that critical cash-accrual periods arise. Thus, the cash position of a department store would generally be adequate from the middle of May through August because of the excess of cash income over payments for merchandise inventories. The store's cash position again begins to decline from the middle of August to approximately December 1, when inventories and customer accounts receivable again begin to grow, culminating in January, with probably the highest amount of customer receivables of the year. Customer payments for Christmas purchases do not begin coming in until mid-January, with the result that generally additional funds may be needed from outside sources during this time.

Planning for Seasonal Fluctuations

Seasonal requirements represent fluctuations of varying length during the course of the year. In formulating a cash budget, two columns may be set up for guidance, as follows:

Cash flow inward *tends to increase when:*	*Cash flow outward* *tends to increase when:*
Customer receivables increase (receivables turnover ratio constant)	Accounts payable decreases (payments constant)
Inventory decreases	Turnover decreases[7]
Stock turnover increases[7]	Credit sales proportion increases
Cash sales increase	Current liabilities are increased
Nonoperating income increases	

The above illustration shows in a general way the effect on a firm's cash position of various operating and seasonal changes. In effect, the sales mixture of cash and the kinds of credit extended (regular charge accounts, revolving accounts, regular installment accounts, etc.) all have a bearing on cash flow estimates. Standard percentage repayment of customer accounts receivable by type can be estimated along with projected cash sales.

By evaluating the total sales breakdowns by type, cash needs can be efficiently planned. This kind of advance planning is necessary because lines of credit are usually choked at similar times during the year and banks and other sources of funds themselves must forecast their needs for loan funds in much the same fashion as marketing enterprises forecast their merchandise needs.

THE EXPENSE BUDGET

Because of the many regularly recurring patterns of expenditures (such as rent, heat, light, taxes, insurance, administration, and occupancy costs), expense budgeting is not a difficult process. The scheduling of expense payments by months can be forecast quite accurately. This kind of cash flow outward can be easily provided for in advance through the expense budget; such allocations are classified as,

---

[7] Assuming that sales forecast budget goal is achieved.

and are part of, the firm's working capital requirements. In addition, provision must be made for having available sufficient cash for pay roll, petty cash expenditures, and any emergency that may arise.

For example, donations to charitable organizations must also be provided for in the expense budget—usually grouped in a miscellaneous category. This ties in with a sort of reciprocity selling basis for the same organizations when they find that they need merchandise on a large scale. In such cases, charitable organizations often buy merchandise from forward-looking stores on a wholesale contract basis. Another miscellaneous fund need is performance guarantees for cash payments to technicians and servicemen who install storm doors, storm windows, building materials, and interior-decorating merchandise such as carpeting, drapes, or home improvements which are sold by the store. Workmen have to be paid immediately, although the total amount of service and merchandise costs may be and often is charged by the customer for repayment on an installment basis.

In calculating cash outlay requirements, it must be kept in mind that there are more months during the year when an excess rather than a shortage of cash may exist. Short-term investments such as treasury bills or commercial paper may be made with excess cash. Purchasing bills or notes with varying maturities help schedule the proper amount of cash when needed. Banks often require that a minimum balance be on deposit at all times as a form of "additional service" charge for their extension of funds. (Of course, there may be a wide gap between what banks consider sufficient for a deposit balance and what is economic from the standpoint of the business firm.)

Once the over-all expense budget has been determined, fixed allocation of funds on a weekly or monthly basis should be made for pay roll, pension funds, taxes, unemployment compensation, and other types of payments that recur regularly during the year.

The supply of cash adequate to discount merchandise purchases is one of the major sources of nonoperating income for the store. It is axiomatic that all cash discounts on merchandise should be taken wherever possible; it is too costly not to.

Merchandise discounts computed on an annual basis may range from 18 to 55 per cent. For example, terms of trade stating "3/10, net 30" would be equivalent to an effective annual interest rate of 54 per cent. In this example, when the invoice is paid in ten days, it is prepaid by 20 days (net $30 - 10$) after which a 3 per cent cash discount is given; and there are eighteen 20-day periods in a year ($360 - 20$) resulting in a 54 per cent effective rate maximum (18×3). Needless to say, the taking of the cash discounts by prompt-paying firms may very well represent the difference between a successful and an unsuccessful venture.

EFFECT OF DEPRECIATION POLICIES

One of the least understood factors in business operation, both at the retail and manufacturing levels, is proper evaluation of the effect of depreciation policies on competitive procedures and market strategy. Depreciation expense is a legitimate expense although, as pointed out, it is of a noncash variety. It is a return of a prior capital expenditure outlay for buildings, equipment, and other depreciable assets, and in a very real sense represents a means whereby stores can set aside funds with which to expand and provide for contingencies. The cost of buildings, fixtures, and equipment may thus be written off over the years of their useful life. For example, if office equipment in a store had an initial purchase price of $10,500 with $500 salvage value, writing the equipment off over a 10-year life period would give the firm a *cash* return of $1,000 annually, using straight-line depreciation.

In a sense, the purpose of depreciation is to provide the means of replacing existing fixed assets as they wear out. Because of the general rising price levels in the economy, depreciation returns rarely are sufficient to cover full replacement of the depreciated asset. Further, many firms may continue in business for years on the basis of cash from depreciation expenses when their marginal revenues do not equal their marginal expenses.

CAPITAL BUDGETING

Capital budgeting is a top management responsibility and one of the top jobs of management; it is the formulation of an explicit and systematic approach to capital allocation and its management. The capital budget is a framework for the assembly of relevant information for the measurement of investment opportunities and is set up in a series of fixed processes to aid decision making and facilitate action.

For example, in opening a new branch store the treasurer would first set up a financial plan in terms of a wholly individual economic unit. Initial inventories and other requirements would be ordered and planned for in the same manner as the store itself. Such allocations would represent a very high capital outlay for an extended period of time in which no reimbursement of funds can flow inward.

The cost of furniture, fixtures, and equipment represents long-term capital needs, as do the advertising expenses required in publicizing the opening and solidifying the position of the establishment. For budget purposes these are long-term capital funds—not current expenses. In addition to funds allocated before the store opens, an additional two or three months of excess cash needs over income should be planned for. Application of funds of this nature—stated as "preopening expenses"—must be provided for out of a capital, *not* an expense budget.

The determination of methods of financing, the control of expenditures, and the assessment of profitability of investment are part and parcel of the capital budget. Thus, capital expenditure decisions form the framework for a company's over-all efficiency and growth.

The capital budget is usually on a long-range forecast, generally for a period of ten years. Internal cash flow for the capital budget is produced by profits or by noncash depreciation expense. Should additional funds be needed, the costs of obtaining funds from various financial institutions are investigated. As previously discussed, depreciation expense accruals provide, in theory at least, replacement funds for capital equipment, and profits provide the operating funds for working capital, taxes, dividends, and so on. The term "surplus" in a capital budget is a misnomer in that it is rarely in the form of cash but generally represents money reinvested in the business. But this theory assumes—somewhat unrealistically—zero growth, constant capital structure, and dividends equal to the difference between accounting income and income taxes.

Cost of Capital and Return on Investment

Top management must evaluate the cost of capital and return on investment *before* any decision to expand is made. Some of the factors to be considered are these. In which departments will there be a sufficient return on investment to justify their establishment from solely financial considerations? Will underwriting costs for new funds be justified by the potential return on planned expenditures? (Actual underwriting costs are rarely less than 12 per cent for the stock issues.) In other words, on the basis of such costs, will the return on the investment be sufficient to cover nonrecoverable promotion expenses and still leave necessary funds for return for senior securities and common stock? Most retail stores earn from 2.5 to 4 per cent on sales after taxes. The Federated Department Store group generally has the best showing, with an approximate return of 7 per cent on sales.[8]

For example, a new branch store incurs costs of approximately $10 per square foot merely to equip. This includes such equipment as cash registers, carpeting, and fixtures; these are allocated expenditures *before* any merchandise is brought in. A store with 100,000 square feet of selling space would typically involve a fixed capital outlay of $1 million and a total investment of over $2 million before the doors are opened for business.

Investment Return

Many investors feel that the field of retail distribution generates too small a return on invested capital. Many retail store managers also feel that consumers are getting a tremendous advantage from the nature of competition at the retail level. Some of these statements are based on the fact that gross margins have not changed significantly in the last thirty years. But we must be careful not to confuse gross margins with rates of return, which depend not only on gross margin but equally on the turnover of assets or capital investment.

In any forward planning, conditions of high labor costs, high rentals, and high advertising costs must be carefully evaluated in the store's over-all policy

---

[8] In core studies of four typical department stores, the average rate of return on total investment for the 1951–1960 period (including adjustment for leases) ranged from 7.69 to 11.50 per cent (Gregory M. Boni, "Actual Case Study of a Store's Financial Program," *Retail Control* [January 1962], p. 22).

procedures. A low rate of profit does not mean that the control division should dominate the organization. Too often, the blanket use of the return on investment concept as a yardstick to evaluate the need for any particular department or merchandise line can result in loss of customers.

While a plan may be financially feasible, it may not be sound from a total institutional and merchandising standpoint. The true profitability of a department to the firm must be interpreted in terms of secondary effects on the profitabilities of other departments, as well as on the direct or primary profitability of the given department itself. Each department should be evaluated from that standpoint of necessity and also from the standpoint of presenting a total-service store image to the customer. Of course, it may be argued that adequate return on investment insures a continuity of management, improved vendor relationships, and greater ability to borrow money under more favorable terms. However, operating evaluations solely from the standpoint of adequate return on investment and continuing low-cost supply of funds as needed may not be sufficient for the achievement of long-run organizational goals.

At Woodward & Lothrop's ready-to-wear department in Washington, D.C., return on assets ranged well above the store's average, as did the children's departments, although they were not ranked with the highest group.[9] The study also showed that many departments in the downstairs store operated at a loss despite reasonably good turnover, that first-floor departments were above average, and that the rate of return on home furnishings departments ranged from twice the store average to some that actually produced losses. It was the conclusion of the store that the return on investment is an important, but certainly not the only gauge for executive action.

SUMMARY AND CONCLUSIONS

Analytical systems for the provision of adequate flow of funds to a firm are based essentially on input-output relationships of converting assets into cash and back into assets. Cash on hand and in banks should be sufficient for the major portion of the year, but at the same time not "over-liquid" in character.

The financial management of the firm can be deemed efficient only if a fair return on investment is earned. When it is too low, the doorway to oblivion opens. Should return on investment be too high, hosts of competitors would be induced to enter the market should they suspect easy operations and lack of competition.

For many retailing firms, a return of 15 per cent on assets is an adequate goal. However, there are many successful retail organizations that earn only 8 to 11 per cent annually on total invested capital. Notable exceptions are Sears,

---

[9] Mr. C. Robert McBrier, vice-president for finance of Woodward & Lothrop, stated: "The twenty best departments in the store had return on investment from 90 to over 487 per cent and the 20 worst departments ranged from losses to 16.6 per cent." Women's Wear Daily (January 13, 1960), p. 18.

Roebuck and J. C. Penney Company, whose statements indicate returns of approximately 15 to 22 per cent.

Interest and amortizations on long-term debt (bonds) and short-term notes represent a critical outflow of funds that must be provided for along with merchandise costs and operating expense. Prompt payments in such areas are basic to the continuity of the firm and its potential for growth.

An integral part of the financial plan of the retail marketing firm is fund analysis, which is essentially a blueprint-budget of the spending and income of the firm and the effect on its working capital. Working capital in the form of merchandise inventories is the single largest investment allocation in the retail firm. The correct evaluative analyses of changes in these operating assets are basic to the achievement of the retail firm's long-run goals.

In the next section a comprehensive analysis of basic merchandising and strategic market planning will be presented.

Part Five

Merchandise and Merchandising Management

Chapter 15: *Merchandise Management*

Successful merchandise management requires the effective integration of buying, selling, and sales-supporting activities to meet the constantly changing requirements of the socioeconomic environment and to provide optimum conditions for making a profit. Marketing management at the retail level can be considered interchangeable with both merchandise management and sales management.

THE PERVASIVE NATURE OF MERCHANDISE MANAGEMENT

More specifically, merchandise management involves all the activities directly involved in planning, organizing, and controlling the selection, buying, price-setting, and promotional and selling policies of the firm's merchandise and service offerings. Regardless of size, the success of the firm depends on the primacy of the merchandising division as the income-producing segment of the operation.

The merchandising division is also responsible for recognizing and introducing new products and services, and the anticipation of shifts in demand. It is also the task of the merchandising division to help develop and utilize the sales forecast budget as the basic planning device for buying and merchandising as well as for stock planning and control. The general merchandise manager, in addition to setting buying and selling policies, must determine the marketing strategy needed to guide the total planning efforts of the organization. For example, where new fashion trends are forecast, the merchandising division is responsible for evaluating their scope, volume, potential, and importance. In effect, the general merchandise manager is responsible for meeting the store's sales volume and gross margin goals.

Relationships of Sales, Merchandising, and Marketing Management

Sales management within a firm is considered a complete economic function. Its functions may be defined as the selection, supervision, and administration of a sales force in order to attain a firm's sales objectives. In this context, the functions of the sales manager are similar to the sales functions of the merchandise manager in the retail firm. Both sales management and merchandising management involve the planning and coordination of merchandise inventories so as to optimize selling.

Marketing management differs little from merchandise management. The latter also includes, in a formal manner, all the internal and external marketing functions in addition to those of exchange, physical supply, and facilitation. For example, the "open-to-buy" budgets are planned and completed many months in advance of actual purchase and delivery. Included in these plans must be a built-in flexibility to adjust to sudden changes, such as any new forms of competition or any new products that may enter the market during the stages between planning, execution, and delivery.

Strategic planning for any possible eventuality within a dynamic framework is the task of market planners and analyzers. While marketing analysis and evaluation has always been carried out in the past by merchandise managers, such activities are not considered as a formal, necessary activity of the merchandising division for the success of the organization.

In recent years the term *management* has developed a sort of omnipotent, prestige meaning in business applications. Management as the function of executive leadership still involves decision making under uncertainty. Decision making in the merchandising division involves high degrees of staff planning and coordination in order to minimize the attendant risks. New concepts in retail merchandising should combine the utmost in creativity along with scientific control and reappraisal. In the larger retail organizations, the operating, publicity, and control divisions serve as the staff to the merchandising divisions. In the smaller store, the merchandising functions are generally combined and carried out by the store manager.

Under normal operating procedures the divisional merchandise manager has delegated to him the authority to buy within predetermined quotas the necessary merchandise to meet sales goals. Buyers, in turn, have the authority to consummate the actual purchases of merchandise from vendors. Selection, buying, and price setting of purchases are part of the buyer's merchandising responsibilities, as are most markdowns and clearances.

CHANGING ROLE OF THE STORE BUYER

As pointed out, the buying and selling functions are a single responsibility under store buyers in most retail firms—the theory here being that the buyer should assume the selling responsibilities of his purchase judgments. Also, the buyer should have the authority to determine what he believes to be an efficient use of the variable and somewhat controllable selling expenses in his department. This also means responsibility for the selling functions in a buyer's assigned department.

Buying merchandise for resale must conform to certain predetermined standards of control within the framework of the merchandise plan. Judicious planning of buying requirements should permit enough flexibility for the firm to remain in a continual "open-to-buy" position.

Today, with the increasing number of branch stores and multi-unit firms, less time is being spent on buying and merchandising. In many cases, buyers are charged with the visiting of branch units. As a result, more top managements in retail firms feel that a buyer should function only as a buyer and not be concerned with the myriad details of promoting and selling merchandise and supervising sales personnel within his department. This policy has led to a "departmental sales manager" type of organizational framework—a segmentizing of the buyer's responsibilities.

Thus, there are constant re-evaluations of the role of the buyer in retail stores. Chain-store buyers operate centrally and are responsible for the buying functions for all retail outlets in their firms. In chains and branch stores, store managers are responsible for the selling functions; in multi-unit firms, the department manager has these responsibilities. Departmental specializations are not the rule, of course, in small independent retail stores.

Regardless of the organizational framework of the merchandising division, both advantages and disadvantages accrue. The advantages of using buyers in a specialized capacity are:

1) Better merchandise coordination of related departments;
2) Higher salaries, as buyers can buy for more departments and broaden their salary base;
3) Greater opportunities for better product knowledge and greater operational skills for the buyer; and
4) Elimination of departmental sales supervision by buyers, often indirect at best.

The disadvantages of specialized buying are:

1) Lack of communication and coordination in the store's total merchandising efforts;
2) Buck-passing in purchase and sales responsibilities (the buyer need no longer be fully responsible for the sale of his purchases and the department manager can claim that his merchandise offerings were inadequate);

3) Narrow and insufficient executive training for the department managers as future top management potential for the firm;

4) Fewer top management jobs with less attractive promotional possibilities for qualified personnel;

5) Lack of full concentration on coordinating both buying and sales efficiency at departmental levels.

DETERMINING MERCHANDISING POLICIES: BASIC FACTORS

The buyer's basic responsibilities revolve around a thorough understanding of the conceptual relationships between initial cumulative mark-ons and average mark-ons as they evolve into maintained markup and gross margin.

The maintained markup and gross margin figures are two of the three key "pay-off" figures upon which the merchandising operations of the firm may be evaluated.[1] The other key figure is the amount of store volume generated, which must be at a level sufficiently above the break-even point to reach the profit goals of the firm.

Thus, merchandising to a profit involves planning and control of inventories by store buyers. Another basic principle of merchandising management is to insure that the net return per investment dollar will bear a reasonable relationship to return on capital compared with investment in other forms of enterprise. The philosophy of store management determines the actual control methodology used, such as the basic stock method, percentage-change (variation) method, stock-sales ratio method, or the week's supply method.[2]

The plan that blueprints the store's buying and selling activities is called the merchandise plan. It is the guideline by which merchandise inventories are projected so that the right merchandise will be on hand when needed. In effect, this plan is the basic strategy on which the success of the retail enterprise is determined. It is the result of the store's operating philosophy and store image.

THE FUNCTIONS OF STORE IMAGE

The merchandise plan of the store represents the store's basic means of projecting itself to its public. Any firm or enterprise that deals directly with the public must be prepared at all times to accept and meet the challenge of effective public relations. Each retail establishment attempts to project itself as a personality, as

---

[1] Maintained markup is the amount of money above cost that was actually generated by actual merchandise sales. Or, stated as a formula, maintained markup is the amount of money above cost actually received for the merchandise over the actual sales prices:

$$\text{Maintained Markup} = \frac{\text{Actual Markup Dollars}}{\text{Actual Net Selling Price}}$$

Gross margin includes nonoperating income and nonoperating expense and can be either larger or smaller than the maintained markup.

[2] Each of these is analyzed in detail in Chapter 20, as is the analysis of the merchandise plan.

"a place to shop." One store may be known as a prestige store; another as a popular price store; another as a semi-promotional store. In each case, the store personality or image is basically the result of the merchandising policies regarding price lines, assortments, depth of lines, merchandise coordination, services, and the concern of the store with pleasing its clientele. In effect, the store's merchandise policies represent the framework of its public image.[3]

In attempts to develop a desired image, each retail firm must decide what its merchandise offerings should be and stress constant coordination of strong, weak, and marginal departments. This is not necessarily confined to general merchandise stores, but applies to supermarkets, variety, and specialty stores—in fact, all types of stores. Of course, the same departments are not necessarily the strongest or weakest in similar types of stores. For example, in any community one supermarket may be known as having the best quality meats; another, the best buys in dry groceries; a third, the best in produce. In the case of department stores, one may have a reputation for carrying the best selection of women's handbags and at the same time be known for carrying only fair assortments and styles in shoes. Stores with such failings, not consciously coordinated on accessories, have many "one-department" customers who "store hop."

MARKET ANALYSIS AND EXECUTIVE ACTION

The formulation of store policies so as to achieve the desired store image is market analysis. This begins with the delineation of the store's trading area into primary and secondary zones of the store's customers.[4] After delineation into "zones of attraction," the trading area itself should be analyzed and segmentized into population and income groups. Area segmentation may be developed from average monthly rentals, price of owner-occupied homes, types of industry and jobs in the community, and the household formation rate in the particular trading area.[5] The demographic groups are then analyzed in terms of transportation type, driving time, distance, shopping frequency, and open hours preferred. From that point, all facets of consumer tastes peculiar to a community are considered so as to arrive at a final decision on what primary service, pricing, merchandise, and promotional approaches will be profitable. If necessary, the desired store

[3] Andrew Goodman, of Bergdorf Goodman, sums up the impregnable position of the country's Bergdorfs and Neimans with this counsel: "Successful stores cannot be one kind of store this year; another kind, next. They must decide where they're going, what they want to be, and stay on that well-defined straight road. Of course, retail stores must be flexible and modernized, but always within the basic framework. Success will come from strength—stressing what the store can do best—not from weakness."

[4] For an interesting report of the effects of marketing research upon the individual firm and upon the economy as a whole, see Stewart H. Rewoldt, "The Economic Role of Marketing Research," *Planned Marketing—Managements' Responsibility*, fourth of the "Marketing for Executives" series (Chicago, American Management Association, 1957), p. 17. See also "Bringing Precision to Market Analysis," *Business Week* (April 28, 1962), p. 90.

[5] A. G. Auble shows that the number of households formed is closely correlated with the number of men in the 20–24-year age group in "A Note on the Demographic Base of Household Formations in the 60's," *The American Statistician* (February 1961), pp. 25–26.

image should be changed to conform more closely with market requirements.

In attempts to broaden their basic appeals, many retail organizations set up competitive departments handling essentially the same types of merchandise. The most common forms of competitive departments are found in "downstairs" and "upstairs" stores. The downstairs "budget" operation offers differing price lines of similar merchandise offerings and often operates on a self-service or simplified selling base. Branch units of the same firm may offer different merchandise assortments and prices, depending upon the results of market analysis of the individual trading areas. While broadening the basic appeals of a multi-unit firm may prove quite profitable, extremes should be avoided. No retail firm can be all things to all people.[6]

In planning storewide merchandising policies at the department level, there must be a continuing line of communications and executive rapport and cooperation between all merchandising divisions. Executive action must provide an affirmative answer to the question, "Are our merchandise offerings compatible with the store image we wish to project?" Otherwise, the merchandising policies of the branch, downstairs, and upstairs segments of the organization will prove ineffective.

POLICY PLANNING AND MARKET STRATEGY

Branch Store Policies

Suburban and geographic expansions have become nationwide. Many firms have found that to attempt a unified merchandising policy for the whole organization, patterning their branch-store policies after their main downtown stores, results in marginal stores. The underlying error in such cases is that location in urban peripheries rather than in central business districts often involves a completely new merchandising approach. Even locations in fairly close proximity may differ markedly in consumer purchase motivations. This means that the merchandise lines handled in branch units may have to differ not only as to size and scope but more particularly from the standpoint of emphasis and special promotions because of dissimilar trading areas. At times, branches may have to be operated as completely separate, independent units based on the "want indicators" in the trading

---

[6] Much criticism is being leveled at marketing research because so much of it is said to aim at solving specific problems. In other words, say the critics, there is too much digging and too little dreaming in marketing and advertising research. To quote Jay W. Forrester, Professor of Industrial Management at Massachusetts Institute of Technology: "...it seems to me that most research measures the composite result of campaigns and does not establish enduring principles to guide future work. Much stands to be gained by changing the emphasis of research, by asking different questions and seeking different answers. We have, or are rapidly acquiring, the know-how. Will we get the right direction and support from top management? In time, the answer is certain to be yes. Already some companies are beginning to put research programs into the pure nature and purpose of advertising (and marketing). Also, some consulting organizations and academic institutions are beginning to delve into the basic market forces and their interactions rather than being content with gross over-all measurements of sales changes." *Grey Matter* (June 1959).

Research needs more of the adventurer, the explorer of uncharted social and economic seas. Then we can develop marketing plans that will anticipate and then make capital of changes in our society and in our economy.

area.[7] Thus, the merchandising policies for new branch units should be the result of careful analysis of the site location rather than be based on the strengths and weaknesses of buyer opinions within the parent store.[8]

Mail and Phone Order Selling

Because of increasing expenses and comparatively static gross margin returns, marketing institutions are faced with a "cost-profit" squeeze. As a result, there are constant pressures to seek new ways of improving sales, competitive position, and the use of plant and resources.

Mail-order and telephone selling have become increasingly important. Unlike branch stores, such efforts represent opportunities to expand sales within the framework of the existing plant. The mail-order and telephone sales operations of Sears, Roebuck and Company and Montgomery Ward, among others, are carried out in conjunction with the operations of their multi-store and multi-warehouse centers located in almost all regions of the country. Featured in these operations are a general line of shopping and specialty goods in moderate-price zones.[9] There are also small mail-order houses that feature specialty and novelty goods not generally available in most local stores.[10] Many small companies, espe-

---

[7] Sanger Bros., Dallas, is an example of expansion variation. Sanger operates two full-line branches in major suburban shopping centers, a limited-line branch concentrating on apparel and other soft goods in a smaller shopping center, and a very small branch carrying children's apparel and accessories.

The J. L. Hudson Company, Detroit, has been operating a basement store in a shopping center in a working-class community for more than two years. Thalheimer's, Richmond, has a children's wear branch. Snellenburg's, Philadelphia, owns several automobile accessory "twigs." Lit Brothers, Philadelphia, has opened a roadside store devoted entirely to shoes for the family. It will be in a shopping strip in the Camden, N.J., area.

Likewise imbued with the total-market concept, Allied Stores Corporation is experimenting with a shop for children operated by its Maas Brothers subsidiary in a suburb of Tampa, Fla. Perhaps ten miles from the children's shop, Maas has a complete home-furnishings store in which the assortments are appreciably greater than in the mother store.

These innovations are cited by Samuel Feinberg in his column, "From Where I Sit," Women's Wear Daily (September–October 1965).

[8] These principles should also be applied to "twig" or "convenience" stores, which are usually located between the downtown and branch stores or in well-frequented areas such as hotels or airports. The twigs range in size from 30,000 to 50,000 sq. ft. The advantages of this type of store are:
   1) Flexibility;
   2) Mobility;
   3) Small investment;
   4) Obtaining a larger share of the consumer market as a result of convenience shopping in a store near the customer's activity.

[9] Mr. Cullinan, vice-president of Alden's, Inc., Chicago, points out that the national trend toward self-service merchandising is continuing to grow and that the selling of goods through mail-order catalogues is the quintessence of self-service.

The annual catalogue business has declined perhaps 30 per cent since the 1930's in terms of the volume done through the mails alone. However, the total national volume of goods sold by catalogue in stores and other outlets, as well as by mail, has increased impressively in the past two decades and is still rising.

The eight biggest mail order houses, which sell about $2 billion a year, earn profits ranging from 4 to 10 per cent of sales and work on markups of 35 to 37 per cent. Sam Gottesfeld, "Mail Business Seen Headed for Golden Age," Women's Wear Daily (May 16, 1956), pp. 1, 115.

[10] For a further discussion see "Discount Selling; Saving through the Post," Economist, (July 20, 1963).

cially manufacturers and wholesalers, sell by mail to dealers and industrial users as well as to consumers. Wholesalers also handle retail orders within their normal sales coverage areas as part of their total selling program. Exporters, importers, salvage and service firms, book publishers, and so on, handle great volumes of mail-order sales at retail.

Today, most large departmentalized stores have mail-order department promotions in all store areas. Effective mail-order promotions within the retail store generally require that the products have some novelty or special appeal. They should also carry a higher than average markup, because mail-order and catalogue selling are high in cost on account of the low rate of response and high mailing costs. Yet, although mail-order and catalogue sales represent high-cost selling, a better utilization of assets and facilities results. Where high fixed costs tend to impose an uneconomic burden, mail- and phone-order selling should be seriously considered, much as geographical expansion. When set up on the basis of utilization of idle plant time and capacity, mail and telephone selling definitely becomes a valuable consideration because it permits "sunk costs" of indirect expenses to be spread over a greater sales volume.

Nonstore Selling

Another aspect of merchandise management is "nonstore" retailing. This is a sort of "drop shipper" or "rack jobber" [11] type of operation, so familiar at the wholesale level. Many discount houses with little or no stock and door-to-door salesmen operate from lists and catalogues. Many have no recognized establishment or place of business from which they operate. They function by taking title to the goods, furnishing credit on an occasional basis, and selling on an order basis. Their mark-on policies include freight plus 10 per cent. Technically, if they cater to groups on a continuing basis, they also handle the guarantees on the merchandise sold. Carload, freight yard, and warehouse sales may be considered other forms of nonstore retailing.

Semi-Jobbing, Contracting, and Horizontal and Vertical Integration

Other types of merchandise policies are often set up by retail firms so that they may take advantage of vertical integration. The first of these merchandising policies involves a contract department in charge of wholesale specialty selling to hotels, motels, and religious and other institutions. Organizations of this kind require large quantities of bedding, beds, uniforms, carpets, and other items, and can

---

[11] Rack-jobbing in essence is the merchandising of an item in a high traffic area through the use of display cases calculated to provoke impulse buying. The jobber selects the merchandise for sale on the rack and is responsible for keeping fast-moving items on hand and regularly replenishing supplies; the owner of the premises on which the rack has been put up actually sells the products and receives a percentage of sales.

The rack-jobber claims that: 1) he is reaching a segment of the population which may never before have had easy access to the particular merchandise; and 2) he is creating an avenue for impulse buying by great numbers of people who regularly visit these high traffic shopping areas.

See Henry Brief, "Disc Rack Jobber Vital Industry Cog," *Retailing Daily* (April 4, 1956).

justifiably be given wholesale discounts. The gross margin results of such operations should not be included with the gross margin results of the normal retail operations. In other words, contract operations should be evaluated on a "contribution" basis and handled separately. In effect, contract department sales represent quantity purchases and the firm becomes to that extent a wholesale "semi-jobber." Most contract departments in department and specialty stores are quite profitable in that the relevant fixed-cost burdens have already been allocated to regular selling departments and only direct variable costs have to be recovered.

The effects of vertical integration are illustrated in Figure XV. Vertical integration into manufacturing allows many of the larger retail firms to subsidize, determine production planning, and set up specifications for various products which they will in turn sell as private brands. Many retail firms have bought into appliance or other manufacturing firms so as to guarantee themselves a relatively fixed and low-cost source of supply.[12] Whenever vertical integration by retail firms into manufacturing and wholesaling takes place, great care must be taken to see that violations of the Robinson-Patman Act do not occur. The Act stipulates that "like" prices must be given to "like" buyers for "like" quantities in interstate commerce. The legal aspects of retailing are discussed in the chapter on government.[13]

Vertical integration is very much a part of the operations of the large supermarket chains. Bread, canned groceries, butter, oil, and bulky, relatively standardized products are manufactured and wholesaled by many retail food chains. Gen-

---

[12] While Sears, Roebuck is often held in awe for its achievement of low cost of merchandise, the company says it doesn't arrive at this point by taking it out of the hide of the resource. "We get cost down by maximum efficiency. Buying and operation of the factory are tied in for maximum efficiency." Often Sears helps the factory obtain efficiency in material procurement through long range production scheduling. At other times the firm will retool at what might appear to be enormous costs with the definite objective of achieving further economies.

Under Sears' specification, buying costs are mutually agreed upon by Sears and the factory. Savings effected are passed on to the customers in lower prices. A factory's cost of selling to Sears is almost negligible compared with the traditional manufacturer-wholesaler-retailer setup with its higher costs for salesmen, sales promotion, and advertising.

Sears' work with producers makes for a "linear situation" wherein its factories avoid many of the peaks and valleys in orders and production that eat away at the efficiency of so many manufacturers who deal only with independent merchants.

In general, Sears prefers an arrangement wherein the factory sells goods to other customers in addition to the big retail-catalogue firm. The reasoning behind this is that factories working with both types of merchandisers are constantly fighting the battle of the market place at large, and must always be razor-sharp competitively in order to survive.

"Uniformity of Production Opens Door to Efficiency," Home Furnishings Daily (February 1965).

[13] A Senate antitrust investigation of a giant United States corporation explored how a company's large size and vertical integration affects price competition in other industries. The Senate investigators were told that the automobile industry is so dominated by a few big producers that price competition has been disappearing. Price competition still prevails in the electrical appliance field, but it is strongest among distributors and dealers and it is all subject to what the few leaders will allow. John T. Norman, Retailing Daily, (Nov. 8, 1962).

Reports of vertical integration can be found in the following articles: E. B. Weiss, "Will Manufacturers Go into Retailing," Advertising Age (December 31, 1962), pp. 35–36; E. B. Weiss, "Is Manufacturer-Retailer Cooperation Entering a New Stage?," Advertising Age (March 25, 1963), p. 80; T. L. Stevens, "Here Comes Vertical Marketing," Industrial Marketing, (September 1963), pp. 123–27.

FIGURE XV
VERTICAL INTEGRATION

(Showing financially or contractually established relationships)

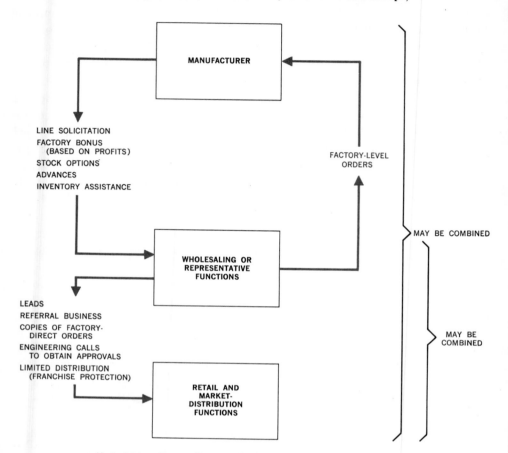

Vertical integration can be economic. As the brackets indicate, the bottom two "layers" can be easily combined into a two-stage marketing organization. . . . In fact, the development of such combinations is usually the first step in the evolution of vertical marketing. . . . Completion of the cycle is accomplished in one of two ways, either: (a) a manufacturer merges with an existing two-level organization, or (b) a marketing firm initiates or acquires its own manufacturing operation.

Source: "Here Comes Vertical Marketing," *Industrial Marketing*, September 1963, p. 125.

eral merchandise and specialty store firms may manufacture millinery, do reupholstering, or handle radio and television repair as part of their over-all merchandising policy.

COMPETING IN CHANGING MARKETS

Merchandising policies represent the over-all strategic weapon of the retail firm, and the weapon upon which its economic well-being depends. Merchandise line assortments, price lines, and price zones are the basis of the store's promotional efforts. Price and nonprice competition are the tools used by a firm in formulating its marketing strategy. T. H. Barton stated in a recent interview:

> Intelligent pricing is scientific. It starts with sound marketing facts, and sound cost data. It is neither a guessing game nor a pseudo-solution to cost problems.... Pricing [should not be] a mere concession to cost or competition.... If the price can't be held—after due consultation with everyone involved—take steps to soften the increase and prepare for possible lost business.[14]

As pointed out earlier, a basic marketing principle is that in any competitive framework no economic unit can continually and generally undersell all its competitors. Underselling or price competition can occur on specific items but not on all items and rarely at the same time in meeting similar consumer needs. Where price competition does occur at the retail level, it is generally quoted in comparison with "fair-trade" or list prices or where price differences tend to bring immediate price comparisons with similar products.[15]

Trading stamps, a form of discount for the payment of cash, may also be considered a form of price competition, even though the giving of stamps is primarily a promotional device for cementing store loyalties. Giving stamps as part of a store's competitive, promotional policy is largely relegated to stores that handle convenience goods, are visited often, and offer merchandise roughly similar to those of hosts of competitors. At times, trading stamps are also used as a form of competition on "big ticket" items such as appliances, refrigerators, and television sets. In such contexts, stamps represent a veiled form of mild discounting. The amount for "trade-ins" on big ticket items also represents price competition. Where manufacturers police the pricing of their products at the retail level, price cutting through trade-ins often assumes importance.[16]

PRICE POLICIES, LINES AND ZONES

Another basic and early consideration in merchandise management is the determination of price policies, price zoning, and price lines. For example, a store's

---

[14] "Take Guesswork out of Pricing Decisions," *Business Management* (May 1963), pp. 48–53.

[15] For further views on pricing, see: W. H. Peterson, "Divergent Views on Pricing Policy" (discussion of books and ideas), Bibliography of *Harvard Business Review* (March 1963), pp. 20–22; J. Backman, "1963: How to Price for Tomorrow's Competition," *Nation's Business*, (January 1963), pp. 36–37; T. Wilentz, F. Michelli, "How to Survive in a Price-Cutting Age," *Publisher's Weekly* (June 18, 1962), pp. 29–32.

[16] The establishing and policing of retail prices by manufacturers and government elicited this comment by Irwin D. Wolf:

> The manufacturer is entitled to decide what price we shall pay for his goods because he alone knows how much it costs him to make them.
> We (the retailers) are entitled to set the retail price of the merchandise we sell because we alone know what it costs to distribute them.
> The tendency of manufacturers to usurp this basic price setting element of the retailers' job can have deplorable consequences. Margins are narrowed. Needed services are curtailed. Unscrupulous dealers do not observe such prices.
> This situation is analogous to what happens when government tries to use superficial methods such as price and wage controls to run the economy. Or it is like a child

merchandise policy may stipulate that a $10.95 price line of women's shoes **must** be available in a good assortment in the store. Any other price line of $10.95 women's shoes or any other price would not cost the same—nor would they be likely to come from the same source. As a result, mark-on percentages must be averaged so that goal maintained markups can be realized.

At the retail level, having a series of retail prices with fixed-percentage initial mark-ons would necessitate a new retail price with every change in cost. But this would be virtually impossible; the system of record-keeping alone would create chaos. Therefore, one function of the buyers and the merchandising divisions is to *average* merchandise mark-ons so that they conform with the store's pricing and competitive policies. For example, a buyer may have to purchase shoes at costs ranging anywhere from $5.50 to $6.50 a pair to provide a $10.95 assortment of women's shoes for his customers. Assuming a $6 average cost, a $10.95 retail price would represent an approximate 45.2 per cent initial cumulative mark-on $[(10.95 - 6.00)/10.95]$.

Variety of styles and colors does not usually cause pricing complications. What is important in pricing strategy is that price lines that appeal to the store's customers must be available. When a consumer intends to make a purchase, consciously or unconsciously he has a certain price range in mind. At the retail level, this potential demand would be defined in terms of price zones, which thus represent a range of prices that appeals to customers in various income groups. The individual who pays $10.95 for a pair of shoes may have a price range between $9 and $12 in mind. If this is the case, the $10.95 purchase price would represent consumer satisfaction with the basic price offer. On the other hand, the store may also have price offerings of substitutable merchandise at $8.95, $10.95, and $12.95; this range would represent the store's price zones for this department—with lines of coordinating merchandise departments similarly priced.

Stores can readily establish sound price lines by listing sales by departments on a price basis. Sales at original prices should be separated from sales at reduced prices. Specific sales at each price should also be totaled along with the total amount of stock available at each price in order to evaluate price lines. This kind of separation gives a sound indication as to whether or not specific price lines should be continued and/or promoted. Also, "want slips" [17] tallies for mer-

---

who tries to make a balloon smaller by squeezing it. When he pushes it in here, it comes out there. Of course, he may also break it. And of course, manufacturers may do serious harm to the gross margin percentages needed to run a sound retail business.

(From "Men's Clothing for Mass Retailing," *Department Store Economist*, [May 1953].) See also: "Proposed FTC Rules Draw ARW, Wholesalers' Fire" (Price lists at issue in deceptive pricing fracas), *Air Conditioning, Heat & Refrigeration* (June 17, 1963).

[17] A "want slip" system is a customer demand feedback process to department buyers. In this system, any merchandise or size requested by a customer that is unavailable is listed by the salesperson on a "want slip" and turned in to the buyer at the end of the day. This system is detailed in the chapter on market information.

chandise at particular prices should be included in the evaluation, as well as promotional efforts and results at particular prices. But price research of this kind is not the sole criterion by which to evaluate competitive effectiveness. It is sometimes possible that the price line producing the largest amount of volume may not necessarily be the most desirable or profitable. In some cases, had more merchandise been available at another price, better sales might have resulted.

A second step for existing stores and a first step for new stores in the setting of price lines should be the checking of median family incomes within the store's trading area. By this means, customers' needs and what they can afford to pay can be initially projected. To optimize customer offerings, each merchandise classification should be represented by three different price categories. What may be an expensive item for one customer may be an average item for the median-income customer and a cheap item for the high-income customer.

The final step in price-line setting should be the coordination of price lines within the store—in other words, a coordinated price throughout the store. This is especially important regarding men's and women's fashion clothing and accessories. In the case of supermarkets, pricing policies may vary widely, with more expensive or gourmet items correlated with the availability of the "best" in meats, poultry, and vegetables.

Function of Price Endings and Price Spread Offers

It is a function of store policy to determine the price endings. Before the advent of sales taxes in most states it was a major pricing policy that no "even" dollar-and-cents price endings should be used. The theory here was that this forced the ringing up of cash sales in order to give the customer his change and, at the same time and less obviously, insured receipt of the cash and a record of the transaction in the register. Another facet of odd price endings is the psychological effect on the customer ($4.98 seems so much less than $5). With today's sales taxes, prices with odd cents ending are less common.

The lower the actual dollar prices, the smaller the spread that is necessary between price lines. Similarly, the higher the price, the wider the spread that is necessary to carry any significance in the differentiation of prices. For example, in a $2 item, a 50-cent price reduction may be quite significant because this price cut would represent a 25-per-cent off-retail reduction. To have a similar impact, a $20 commodity would have to be reduced by $5 to $15.

Another important consideration in price lines is the actual "landed cost" of imports. In such items, the price averages of all wholesale costs (including transportation inward) must result in a satisfactory cumulative markup—a predetermined planning function of the merchandise plan.

Although price level forecasts from one year to another are not a difficulty, they must be considered in setting any price lines. Again, decisions must be made regarding quality and pricing policies in periods of rising or declining prices. There is always the choice of raising prices and maintaining the quality in periods of rising prices or lowering the quality or amount and keeping the same price. These choices are discussed later under specific aspects of basic merchandising.

Function of Nonprice Competition

In the retail setting, nonprice competition is an important managerial policy when competing stores handle similar and clearly substitutable products. In the total "goods-framework concept" very few direct price comparisons can be made, because of product differentiation, multiple brands, and the difference in service functions attached to the sale of various products by different types of stores. In other words, it is the total "package" concept that determines the actual price paid by consumers for particular commodities. Nonprice competition can be seen in services, extra courtesies, better deliveries, better scheduling in the case of transportation agencies, better wrapping of merchandise, and so on. In states having Fair Trade laws and Unfair Sales Acts—or in the case of public utilities or transportation agencies where charges are approximately the same—competition, of necessity, is generally nonprice in character.

SUMMARY

In this chapter, preliminary considerations regarding the functions of merchandise management were broadly analyzed. The elements of marketing and sales management as a prerequisite to successful merchandising were reviewed. The importance and methods of trade area analysis were discussed as necessary prerequisites to the formulation of merchandising policies with a view to developing a particular store image. Merchandising policies in branch, mail-order, nonstore, and contract departments were analyzed with reference to the merchandise policies of the main store. In addition to offering broad merchandise lines in depth, many of the basic elements of the store's over-all marketing strategy were found to lie in price and nonprice competition.

A deeper study of the use of market analysis and the effect of merchandising techniques on the determination of merchandising policies forms the subject matter of the next chapter.

Chapter 16: *Effect of Market Analysis on Merchandising Policies*

Merchandising policy should result from a careful market analysis of a store's local trading area, and not merely reflect hunches, value judgments, and haphazard market evaluation.

Successful merchandising requires the application of techniques taken from the behavioral sciences as well as those of mathematical and quantitative analysis to identify the structural changes that have taken place and to contribute common definitions that are useful in describing these changes. Also, the application of such techniques can indicate areas where further research is needed.

MARKET AND TREND ANALYSIS

Market analysis is that phase of market research having to do with the determination and evaluation of an area's size and potential. Good analysis takes account of socioeconomic conditions, the changing composition and size of the population, and all other demographic factors that bear on the area's economic future.

Since World War I retailing costs have risen between 24 and 33 per cent. It is doubtful that cost decreases can be anticipated; therefore additional profits must be generated from better merchandising. If distribution efficiency is to be increased, more effective sales promotion and selling methods must be employed. If market sales are totaled by merchandise lines within definitive trading areas, marketing and retail organizations can readily assess their competitive positions by comparing their own merchandise line sales to these criteria.

The direction and scope of business trends are always more important and revealing than static figures taken at one point in time. A realistic merchandising policy can be formulated when a trend analysis of population, income, types of merchandise bought, ethnic preferences, potential merchandise lines, volume by types of goods, and the assessment of local economic trends form the basis for planning. Such analysis must also consider the changing effectiveness of national and local advertising and the turnover ratios of merchandise classifications.

A clear-cut trend in customer preference can help establish such policies as the type of selling for various departments—i.e., self-selection, self-service or simplified, or full-service selling. Trend comparisons of fixed and operating cost ratios, markup and inventory turnover, and other data with standards for the industry serve as control indicators for merchandise managers.[1]

A planned research program designed to seek out and reveal change will make certain that pertinent information is brought to the attention of management. Three items which should be included in such a program are: 1) a continuous analysis of the sales records of the company and the industry; 2) periodic surveys of consumer purchasing behavior and attitudes; and 3) periodic surveys of retail outlets to reveal variations in operating methods and attitudes.

NEW COMPETITIVE CHALLENGES

In any retail framework there are efficient, moderately efficient, and inefficient managers operating the same types of businesses. As a result there are many ranges in price for the same kinds of merchandise, possible because of inefficiency and/or charging "all the traffic will bear." Pricing situations of this kind can continue because of imperfect information in the market place and convenience appeals, such as differences in driving time. In some metropolitan areas it is customary for the larger stores to do "competitive shopping" and thereby avoid a competitor having a price edge on a given item: i.e., in New York, Macy's shops Gimbels regularly throughout the day.

When top prices are charged because of location monopolies rather than need, pure profits result, and additional competitors are encouraged to enter the market.[2] Among these, in recent years, have been discount-house operations of all kinds, revival of house-to-house selling, and increased use of "scrambled" merchandising techniques.

---

[1] M. Mellman, in "Marketing Cost Analysis: Development and Current Practices," *Accounting Review* (January 1963), pp. 118–23, provides a good discussion of this method as applied particularly to manufacturing. See also *Merchandising and Operating Results of Department and Specialty Stores* (Controllers' Congress, National Retail Merchants Association; annually).

[2] See R. Triffin, *Monopolistic Competition and General Equilibrium Theory* (Cambridge: Harvard University Press, 1940), Chapter 3; in this chapter Triffin analyzes competition and competitive markets.

Innovators and new competitors can cause previously established retailers to operate more efficiently. When attained gross margins are lower than planned without accompanying increases in efficiency, profits disappear and incentives to continue in business or to handle specific merchandise lines become marginal. For example, in 1948 and 1951 when home appliances became plentiful in supply because of overproduction, discount selling and discount-house competition increased tremendously. Such policies lowered gross margins still further. When demand for hard lines declined, discounters cut prices still further and attempted to increase their merchandise appeal by handling shopping and specialty goods of all kinds "at a price." Many existing stores dropped "hard line" departments as being uneconomic.

Appliance and furniture dealers had to revise their pricing and merchandising policies or go out of business. This new competition plus lack of sustained demand resulted in the closing of many departments in departmentized stores and, in some cases, conversion to a "discount-house" type of operation—the philosophy in the latter case being "if you can't beat them, join them."

In many cases, once an establishment developed an image of being a "discounter," its off-price selling was reduced to a minimum and the initial psychological image of minimal pricing seemed to sustain itself in the marginal efforts only. Other psychological assumptions of low prices were formed by the interaction of all kinds of unrelated merchandise line offerings. Such policies, termed "scrambled merchandising," tend to give consumers the impression of a vast array of diverse merchandise offerings in depth.

Effect of Scrambled Merchandise Operations

Scrambled merchandising techniques received their tremendous impetus during World War II, when many types of merchandise, especially durable goods, were unavailable and retailers and wholesalers, regardless of commodities previously handled, purchased all manner of merchandise in order to have goods to sell.

From an internal operating standpoint, the broader base of merchandising operations tends to "smooth out" periods of slack by creating more uniform sales patterns throughout the year. Supermarkets are still using scrambled merchandising techniques as a means of expansion. They have also used rack-jobbers extensively in the handling of nonfood categories such as drug items, housewares, and soft lines—all merchandise lines with which supermarket executives tend to be unfamiliar. An interesting study of nonfood sales in supermarkets has recently been published by W. T. Bonwich of the University of Notre Dame. Some pertinent results of this study are shown in Table 22.

Discount House Problems

Innovations in the market place are generally the result of economic forces that cannot solve the marketing problems so as to "clear the market." One of the more important institutional trends evolving from such forces has been the discount house.

TABLE 22

RATIO OF NONFOOD SALES OF SELECTED SUPERMARKETS

STORE CHARACTERISTICS	STORE I	STORE II	STORE III	STORE IV	STORE V
Geographic location (region)	W. S. Central	New England	Mountain	W. S. Central	Pacific
Average wkly. $ sales volume	30,000	57,500	50,000	62,000	80,000
Average wkly. $ nonfood sales	2,100	4,600	4,500	4,500	6,400
Nonfood Sales: per cent of total sales	7.0	8.0	9.0[a]	7.3	7.9[a]
Store size: total area (sq. ft.)	18,500	18,000	42,500	35,500	36,000
Size of selling area (sq. ft.)	14,000	12,000	22,000	23,100	24,000
Size of nonselling area (sq. ft.)	4,500	6,000	20,500	12,400	12,000
Number of checkouts	7	9	15	11	12
Total number of items carried: food & nonfood	9,000	6,000	15,000	18,000	10,000
Number of nonfood items	4,100	1,600	8,500	7,100	2,500
Nonfood items: per cent of total items	46.0	27.0	57.0	39.0	25.0

[a] More recent studies indicate that nonfood sales in Mountain and Pacific areas exceed 12 per cent of all supermarket sales (Research Division, University of Denver, October 1964).
Source: W. T. Bonwich, "Non-Food Operation Studied in Model Units," *Food Topics* (March 1960).

In 1948, for the first time since 1941, production of manufactured consumer goods again began to exceed market demand. Intensive competition at the retail level and overproduction at the manufacturing level resulted in the back-up of inventories in appliances and other hard goods, rapidly changing the sellers' market into a buyers' market.

Manufacturers, in attempts to unload inventory, made indiscriminate sales to wholesale and retail jobbers of all kinds. These functionaries sold the "jobbed" durables direct to consumers or, by means of transhipment, directly to discounters and drop-shippers. This made the stocking and selling of brand-name merchandise on an "off-list" basis a continuing operating possibility. At the same time, because of the pressure of high inventory backlogs, manufacturers who had "fair-traded" their products did little—in some cases nothing—to police their stipulated prices at either the wholesale or retail level. Thus chaotic pricing was encouraged.

Discount stores range from the small open showroom and catalogue order office all the way up to full-line limited-service stores which closely resemble and, in actuality, can be classified as promotional department stores. Also included within this grouping is the closed-door or membership type of discounter which supposedly caters only to homogeneous groups such as union members, government employees, or teachers.

Some observers claim that price is the sole reason for the success of discount houses, yet that is too simple an answer. Although price has a strong appeal, these stores have also grown because they have created a shopping excitement not seen in existing stores since the end of World War II.

There are approximately 12,000 retail establishments included in our discount-house definition. These stores handle almost every category of merchandise and generate approximately $10.5 billion of sales a year. It is further estimated that an additional $32 billion of some $284 billion in retail sales in 1964 was made on a "discount basis" by conventional retailers and wholesalers. This does not refer to clearance items but to new merchandise only. These estimates also exclude the sale of new automobiles, which, except in the 1946–1948 period, have usually been sold on a discount basis.

Examining these figures in the broader framework of the national economy, we find that a little more than one-half of 1 per cent of all retail establishments can be classified as discount houses, and these outlets are presently absorbing a little more than 3.5 per cent of all retail stores' sales. With this comparatively small market percentage, it is revealing that discount houses have created such a furor. On closer examination, it is clear that their impact lies not so much in the proportion of the market they have captured, but in what they have accomplished as innovators in shaking the complacency of existing firms. In other words, the discounter's impact has not been in the actual growth of the discount houses themselves, but rather in the triggering of discount selling and other defensive measures by previously established competitors.

The growth of these new types of competitors has forced department stores, supermarkets, specialty stores, chains, and other conventional retailers to re-evaluate their store policies, services, pricing, and over-all methods of doing business. Because of reluctance to change, organizational inflexibility, and dwindling percentages of family income being spent in retail stores, a competitive struggle of panic proportions has been taking place.

The result is that many stores have completely changed their methods of doing business; some, ignoring the discounter as a temporary innovation, have re-emphasized their previously developed store images and institutional appeals. Others have met the new competition head on and have become discount houses themselves. Many conventional retailers merely dropped lines of merchandise in which they felt chaotic pricing conditions existed, while many others met the challenge of competitive prices in key merchandise areas only. Some stores cut services and formalized selling efforts in attempts to lower both expenses and prices. At the same time other established retailers undertook strong measures of nonprice competition by improving their basic operating policies.

Many of the retail firms that are presently classified as discount houses will continue to grow either through mergers, acquisitions, or other expansions such as leased departments. So will their operating expenses, regardless of their scale of plant or size of firm. There are simply too many built-in cost factors that accumulate over time. Most discount houses will gradually become more traditional, higher priced, and less competitive. As this happens, a new competitive cycle will begin and another stream of innovators will doubtless take their place.

Other Competitive Challenges [3]

Variations of the cut-price store are catalogue stores, salvage stores, and "closed-door" discount houses where admission to buy is through purchase of membership cards by consumers. Many "closed-door" discount houses have been able to expand by means of a $2 card fee and leased departments.

---

[3] This section taken from R. D. Entenberg, "Retail Competition: New Problems," *Pittsburgh Business Review* (December 1961 and Spring 1964).

Table 23 presents the financial aspects of leased departments, indicating how this type of operation can immeasurably assist the total organization. The primary strength of a leased department is that it is generally run by a smaller entrepreneur who has special know-how as well as financial resources in buying, merchandising, and supervising specific merchandise categories. This enables him to perform far more effectively than the landlord or supervising firm.

TABLE 23

COMPARISON OF FINANCIAL RATIOS OF DISCOUNT STORES,
DEPARTMENT STORES, AND LEASED DEPARTMENTS[a]

FINANCIAL RATIOS	LEASED-DEPARTMENT OPERATORS			DISCOUNT STORES, MEDIAN	DEPARTMENT STORES, MEDIAN
	UPPER QUARTILE	MEDIAN	LOWER QUARTILE		
Current Assets to Current Debt (times)	2.00	1.44	1.19	1.49	3.49
Net Profits on Net Sales (%)	2.99	1.83	0.55	1.42	2.00
Net Profits on Tangible Net Worth (%)	29.32	16.76	7.90	14.98	5.30
Net Profits on Net Working Capital (%)	38.93	24.89	5.38	18.63	6.98
Net Sales to Tangible Net Worth (times)	12.46	8.95	6.27	9.94	2.76
Net Sales to Net Working Capital (times)	24.61	10.47	7.94	14.85	3.66
Net Sales to Inventory (times)	7.5	4.6	3.9	6.5	5.3
Fixed Assets to Tangible Net Worth (%)	16.4	25.6	40.2	28.7	26.4
Current Debt to Tangible Net Worth (%)	112.8	172.1	268.6	145.7	29.4
Total Debt to Tangible Net Worth (%)	180.3	313.8	379.7	182.1	69.5
Inventory to Net Working Capital (%)	172.7	284.9	477.6	208.5	66.2
Current Debt to Inventory (%)	75.9	97.0	128.1	95.1	61.5
Funded Debts to Net Working Capital (%)	144.2	72.3	84.1	43.5	31.3

[a] No proprietorships are included in this tabulation.

Note: *Profits* on both net worth and working capital are excellent—even ahead of all discount stores whose median is substantially above the department-store level.

Profits on sales fall about midway between department stores and discount stores, further emphasizing the profitability of leased departments.

Inventory Turnover. In all 3 quartiles the rate is surprisingly small but is one reason why some discount department stores prefer to have an outside lessee in certain departments. Despite this slower turnover rate the leased department can obtain an excellent profit, which is an acknowledgment of its management skill.

Debt position is very heavy and *liquidity* is weak by normal standards. As a further indication, over 50 per cent of the concerns in the sample were running past due with suppliers or had obtained special terms.

Source: D. Kessler, "Discount Retailing and Leased Departments," *Financial Analyst's Journal* (May 1963), pp. 99–102.

The catalogue store mentioned above is a form of discount wholesaler, with or without stock, which sells from manufacturer's brand-name inventory lists. This represents an uneconomic form of channel by-passing. In many cases, the customer "shops" the regular item and may obtain the stock number, style, and price. Then, the customer takes this information back to the discounter who orders the item at a fixed percentage above cost. The retailer carrying the "branded item" performs all the marketing functions, yet becomes a mere display house.

ANALYSIS OF FUNCTIONAL BY-PASSING

The margins taken by the various merchants participating in a marketing system may be regarded as the cost for getting a portion of the marketing task completed. It is, in essence, the price offered an outside functionary for creating values. Of course, a store or potential user may exercise the option of not paying the functionary's price and performing the middleman's task. Should higher over-all costs result, they could be justified only if the quality of performance is greatly improved. Merely retaining control of a vital function would not be justified unless the "value added" to the ultimate buyer was improved psychologically or materially. Where a higher price results (assuming a competitive market) because of overhandling by market functionaries without an increase in consumer values, then a long-run loss in demand is likely to occur.[4]

Another situation that has an impact upon margins is vertical integration by the assumption of marketing functions by the manufacturer. Figure XV (p. 230) shows some of the typical vertical integration now taking place. The lines of demarcation between traditional manufacturer and traditional retailer are becoming blurred. At present we have a vast number of marketing arrangements wherein the manufacturer performs so many of the traditional retail functions that it is not a simple matter to determine who actually performs the key retail functions.

For example: General Electric has a program whereby the retailer carries only floor samples. When the customer places an order, it goes to a General Electric warehouse; the purchase is then delivered (drop-shipped), installed, and serviced by a General Electric subsidiary. The Keystone Express Corporation (which warehouses furniture) estimates a tenfold jump in factory-to-consumer furniture traffic as the result of these kinds of sales.

Because of space limitations, warehouse costs, servicing, storing, and handling problems within plants, and union problems with delivery—not to mention the increase in stock turnover and lower costs involved—many retailers thoroughly approve this factory-to-consumer procedure. Department stores that have a traditional free delivery policy find that drop-shipping gives them lower competitive costs.

The appliance and furniture businesses have moved decidedly toward the factory-to-home delivery; there is no reason to assume the movement will stop with these industries. Two trends in this area seem to be indicated:

1), manufacturers are taking over more retailing functions, resulting in store ownership or control by manufacturers; and

2), manufacturers are integrating vertically into food retailing, and the larger retail firms are also integrating upward vertically into manufacturing and wholesaling to a greater extent.

As retailers receive greater manufacturer discounts for performing fewer functions, a change in discount structure is now taking place.[5] Because of the fast pace and growth of supermarkets, retail firms are following many of their retail innovations. In fact, many home furnishing, appliance, and automobile accessory outlets

---

[4] *Cost and Profit Outlook*, Alderson and Sessions-Marketing and Management Counsel (October 1954).

[5] E. B. Weiss, "Manufacturer Gets Closer to the Consumer," *Advertising Age* (August 12, 1963), p. 64. See also E. B. Weiss, "Lot of the Trend Spotter," *ibid.* (July 29, 1963), p. 60.

now call themselves "supermarkets." Discount outlets have also borrowed extensively from food supermarket innovations. Supermarkets have been very quick to spot trends within their own affiliated industries as well.

However, no matter what the extent of borrowing or channel by-passing, it must be remembered that a market functionary may be able to eliminate the middleman but never his function.

SALES TREND EVALUATION

Evaluation of sales trends is one of the basic methods of market analysis. Sales may be analyzed in terms of volume, kinds of merchandise sold, type of store or department doing the selling, location, method of operation, and so on. But institutional sales trend analyses become difficult to assess because of the almost continuous combinations at almost all levels of industry, in which firms set out to free themselves from the effect of unrestrained competition and at the same time secure possible tax advantages.[6]

In discussing the effects of market analysis on merchandising policies, one must take into consideration over-all sales trends. Retail sales increased from some $130 billion in 1948 to $170 billion in 1954, $284 billion in 1965, and will approximate $304 billion for 1966. This means there is a total over-all increase in retail sales of some 54 per cent generated during the ten-year period from 1954 to 1964.[7] This increased business was done by approximately the same number of establishments. Yet, there have been significant changes in the kinds of stores remaining. For example, in the food-store category alone there has been a decrease of over 100,000 establishments, with most of those disappearing being the smaller grocery stores and candy, nut, and confectionery stores. The smaller corner grocery and convenience stores have decreased because of consumer predisposition toward "one-stop shopping," where wide ranges of merchandise offerings are available.

Of course, some kinds of smaller stores can and do compete with larger ones when their merchandise offerings are the result of merchandise and market analysis and not individual preferences.

Trend analysis of changing markets and purchase preference in various types of establishments can be projected so that merchandise policies can keep pace with changing consumer buying patterns. W. R. Davidson has said, "Retailers who fail to properly evaluate their merchandising policies in the light of their existing and potential market conditions may end up walling themselves off from a considerable portion of their potential market." [8]

As an example of what he meant by trying to live with outmoded concepts, Davidson cited Woolworth's persistence in adhering to a 5- and 10-cent policy

---

[6] *Mergers in Industry* (New York: National Industry Conference Board), p. 1.

[7] For 1963 sales influences and trends see "Doing Fine and Better Days Ahead," *Business Week* (August 24, 1963), pp. 25–26.

[8] W. R. Davidson, Ohio State University, Pierce-Phelps Institute of Appliance Management, as reported in *Home Furnishings Daily* (May 31, 1960).

long after it might have added a great deal of volume by dropping it. He also said that J. C. Penney's long delay in using credit cost that chain much possible added volume.

Sales Trends in Terms of Changing Consumer Shopping Habits

Today, with a resurgence in movement back to the cities, even greater changes in consumer habit and expenditure patterns are developing. Part of these changes are the direct result of an increase in spending units and an increase in the discretionary income of these units. For example, since 1940 there has been approximately an eightfold increase in the discretionary spending power of individuals. There are today eight and one-half times more spending units with incomes in excess of $3,000 than there were in 1941.[9]

The American consumer is undergoing substantial changes in his philosophy of spending—especially in the area of credit. The changes in spending habits are having wide repercussions on certain types of installment and consumer credit as well as on the American manufacturer and retailer. There are many indications that home improvements, home expansion, clothes, vacations, and traveling—to mention just a few items—are attracting more of the consumer dollar.

Among underlying changes in spending attitudes are new social desires, new purchase patterns, and new shopping motivations. Changes in environmental factors include higher educational levels, greater readership by more people, more leisure time, increases in home ownership, more three- rather than two-bedroom houses, movements to both urban and suburban areas, more two-home families as well as two-car families, and a changing composition of the population, with great percentage increases in both older and younger persons, and smaller and more mobile families.

Analysis by Type of Operation

Sales trends by type of operation are often difficult to analyze because stores bearing similar census classifications change their operating and merchandising policies without their store classification being changed. Changes from cash to credit selling, merchandise-line shifts, and changes in methods of customer service to self-selection or to simplified selling often make substantial differences in sales volume. For example, during 1962 the J. C. Penney Company changed from a "cash-credit" policy and broadened its merchandise offerings to include durable-goods lines.

One continuing merchandising trend is the "trading up" policy introduced by many stores to meet the demand created by higher real incomes. Variety stores such as W. T. Grant, G. C. Murphy, and F. W. Woolworth, among others, all offer expanded choices of merchandise classifications with apparently no upper limits on price lines handled. These former low-priced and cash-only stores now

---

[9] R. D. Entenberg, *The Changing Competitive Position of Department Stores in the United States by Merchandise Lines*, rev. ed. (Pittsburgh, University of Pittsburgh Press, 1961), p. 36.

also offer delivery and credit. At the same time, variety stores such as J. J. Newberry Co. and Kresge's have gone into opposite directions with expansions into discount stores, although many of their existing stores that are tied up with long-term leases continue to operate in the old manner.[10]

MERCHANDISING MANAGEMENT ACCOUNTING

Another tool of analysis in setting merchandise policies is merchandising management accounting (MMA), which seeks to determine the exact cost involved in handling and carrying certain merchandise categories so that better item profitability can be determined. In effect, MMA is an extended form of factory cost accounting.

It has been stated that this accounting method was developed because merchandise managers and buyers did not fully understand the retail system and focused their attention too much on gross margin and planned mark-on percentages as major operating tools. Malcolm P. McNair, one of the sponsors of MMA, charges also that too many merchandise executives assumed "average costs" for all merchandise categories with practically no attention paid to differences in possible elasticities of demand. He also concluded that when gross margins determine a significant portion of the buyer's compensation, the buyer becomes reluctant to handle merchandise lines carrying mark-on percentage figures lower than those set as his operating goal.[11]

Essentially, there is need for considerable re-education of buyers and merchandisers, and a reorientation toward some new philosophies of management in store operation. Retailers who get away from the heavy emphasis on department-wide gross margin, particularly in its percentage forms, and away from regarding total departmental expenses as applying in a fixed manner "across the board," can immeasurably improve their total over-all operations. In the opinion of this writer, the need here is not so much for new concepts as for thorough training in the use of existing tools of analysis.

Nevertheless, for most merchants the retail method of inventory is still a more satisfactory tool of merchandise control and evaluation; this method not only furnishes scientific data for analysis, but, more importantly, has proved to be an excellent common denominator for data interchange.

The retail method, as a system of merchandise control, provides data in the form of averages; in this framework, management is able to gauge demand and provide means for unit and dollar control of the firm's operations through its provision of automatic "open to buy" by merchandise categories. The more specific details of the methodology will be found in the chapter on stock planning and control.

---

[10] The F. W. Woolworth Co. has also gone into discounting with its "Woolco" operations.
[11] From a speech given at the Merchandise Division Session during the 47th Annual Convention of the National Retail Merchants Association (January 9, 1957). Arthur Anderson and Co., Chicago accounting firm, is also a sponsor of MMA.

THE MERCHANDISING POLICY SYNDROME

Thus the determination of merchandise policies cannot be solely the result of "delivered cost" of the merchandise. With the increasing size of stores and area specializations, the necessity for keeping detailed records has become a major concern for business—in too many cases deterministic of policy rather than a basis for it.

Until 1914 and the passage of income tax legislation, the keeping of accurate records was not a necessity in business. In the 1920's standard expense and markup data were developed in the form of "typical" figures by the then National Retail Dry Goods Association (now the NRMA). The publication of these figures represented one of the first attempts to determine profitability scientifically by merchandise lines. These compilations also furnished a firm base for scientific merchandise analysis; it was at that time that the use of the "retail base" for all operating and merchandise ratios was recommended.

It was around this retail sales base idea that a comprehensive accounting and merchandise system was structured and correlated on an establishment basis by volume categories. This structure culminated in a formalized accounting system known as the retail method of inventory. Although this method has been used in some form or another for almost seventy years, the scientific applications of the retail method did not really acquire wide acceptability until the decade of the twenties. In effect the retail sales base idea became the basis for measuring market position and merchandising policies.

SUMMARY AND CONCLUSIONS

In this chapter the importance of market analysis in formulating merchandising policies and market strategy was reviewed in relation to new competition, scrambled merchandising techniques, innovistic changes, and consumer demand in the market place.

Consumer expenditures can no longer be regarded as stable, so merchandise policies must be constantly reviewed. More than ever before, the basic motivations underlying the changes in consumer purchasing patterns must be clearly identified and utilized if long-run profits of the firm are to be maximized.

It is within this framework also that the changing nature of consumer preferences must be analyzed—especially those revolving around the much narrower breakdowns of preference shifts with respect to specific merchandise lines.

Also reviewed in this chapter was merchandise management accounting (MMA). Despite the many benefits in assessing exactly the cost of each item, cost alone should not be the only basis for pricing or handling particular merchandise lines. Gross margin goals based on "average costs" should not be the sole policy determinant in these areas.

Chapter 17: *Determination of Merchandising Policies*

Merchandising policies are subject to constant change. This means that pricing policies and techniques must also be subject to change. These variable merchandising policies can result in an optimal utilization of resources. Developing a higher stock turnover, provided it is not excessive, or doing more business with the same turnover are examples of better utilization of resources and hence greater returns to scale. This is the primary function of merchandising policies as molded by organizational goals and pricing techniques.

In addition, merchandising policies are planned to foster long-run growth, which can be generated only when total revenues equal total costs in the economic sense. At the same time, merchandising policies should not create "pure profits" so that the store image can be maintained and enhanced over time.

DETERMINATION OF GROSS MARGIN REQUIREMENTS

In planning, the first step is the determination of the gross margin requirements. Since 1954, one of the most pressing problems of retail firms is that net profits have been decreasing as a percentage of net sales. Management has been re-examining the productivity of all its selling and nonselling departments in looking for a solution, especially in terms of merchandise lines handled. In many instances it found that attained profits had been the sole determinant of the specific merchandise lines handled.[1]

The use of the net profit approach as the primary evaluative criterion in considering the desirability of retaining or dropping particular merchandise lines is far too narrow a base; customer wants and the coordination of merchandise offerings are equally important. Yet the importance of the net-profit gross-margin expense for departmental evaluation should not be underestimated. Perhaps more operations research approaches are needed to maximize the effectiveness of the total store system; this does not imply that each segment of the operation must exist at a maximand. The return on net sales after federal income taxes, or the "bottom line," is the final determinant of the success and continuity of any private business enterprise.

Examples of returns on net sales are illustrated in Table 24. Although it does not show the actual gross margins attained by these firms, this table does illustrate

TABLE 24
Net Profits on Net Sales, by Kinds of Business[a]

Type of Store	Median Figure	Range (up to Lower Quartile)
Clothing, Men's and Boys'	2.07	0.21–4.69
Clothing, Men's and Women's	4.06	1.83–8.47
Department Stores	1.83	0.65–3.01
Dry Goods	3.53	0.27–11.10
Furnishings, Men's	3.03	0.39–5.44
Furniture, 50% or more of volume	1.49	0.09–3.19
Groceries and Meats, Chain	1.40	1.15–1.59
Groceries and Meats, Independent	1.01	0.54–1.38
Hardware	1.12	0.07–2.56
Lumber and Building Materials	1.66	0.58–4.56
Shoes	2.44	0.34–6.12
Women's Specialty Shops	1.90	0.27–3.74

[a] After taxes, 1957
Source: Roy A. Foulke, *Current Trends in Terms of Sale* (New York, Dun & Bradstreet, 1958), p. 59.

the significance of the cost-margin profit squeeze in many retail organizations. It is evident, also, that the narrowness of the "spread" between gross profit and total costs is so small that little or no margin for error in operations remains.

Any sudden loss in volume and/or failure to meet sales goals would almost automatically push operating costs above attained gross margins. In addition, any volume losses would decrease planned gross margins because of stocks "backing up," becoming obsolete, with resulting increases in markdowns. Further, any decreases in sales volume would automatically decrease the stock turnover rate and

---

[1] The net profit accounting method means that all indirect expenses and proportionate "burden costs" of such expenses are charged to a selling department's operation.

increase merchandise handling and storage costs, thus increasing the cost of goods sold. The process can be easily analyzed from the following relationships:

Sales (S)	− Cost of Mdse. Sold − (C of M Sold)	= Gross Profit or Gross Margin = (GP) or (GM)
GM (GM)	− Total Operating Costs − (C)	= Net Margin or Profit = (NP)

THE ECONOMICS OF ENTERPRISE

In effect retailing may be said to be a social process system externally and an applied economic one internally. If sales increase, then cost of merchandise sold decreases and merchandise turnover increases as average inventory decreases and handling and investment costs decrease. Thus net profit tends to increase both in terms of dollars and as a percentage of sales and investment when volume increases. That is:

If (S) increase (↑), then (C of M sold) decreases (↓), then merchandise costs (↓), and turnover (↑); Result: Net Profit (↑).

If sales decrease, then cost of merchandise sold tends to increase as stock turnover decreases and inventory, handling costs, investment costs, and markdowns increase; thus net profit tends to decrease on a greater than proportional basis (as compared with sales):

If (S) (↓), then (C of M Sold) (↑), and turnover (↓) and merchandise costs (↑); markdowns (↑), investment costs (↑); Result: Net Profit (↓).

The merchandise manager is responsible for the attainment of the necessary gross margins in the firm. Attainment of the necessary gross margin is dependent upon sufficiently high initial mark-ons so as to provide for the normal inventory processing and sales. Not only must gross margin needs be directly related to operating expenses and merchandise costs, but the resulting prices must be evaluated externally by competition. Regardless of whether a net profit or contribution plan of accounting is used to help formulate pricing policies in terms of internal organizational goals, the generation of adequate volume remains the primary underlying goal for any store or department.

In illustration, a hypothetical case of a children's wear store will be used. Size is not a factor, as the operating averages and motivations are not significantly different. The illustrations below use the net profit plan of accounting.[2]

In this first case the sales volume forecast is $200,000, and projected operating expenses are as follows:

---

[2] Both the contribution plan and the net profit plan of accounting are explained in detail in the chapter on accounting. The contribution plan includes the allocation of only indirect expenses.

Rental (fixed)	$16,000
Depreciation (noncash)	4,000
Salaries (incl. executive)	32,000
Advertising	4,000
Light, Heat, Taxes, Insurance, Miscellaneous	4,000
Total Operating Expenses	$60,000

$$\frac{\text{Total Operating Expenses}}{\text{Sales Volume Forecast}} = \frac{60,000}{200,000} = 30.0\%$$

Assuming further a 36 per cent maintained markup and 6.67 per cent in markdowns and shrinkages, a projected minimum initial cumulative markup of 40 per cent would be needed.[3]

Illustration A

IM = *Initial Markup*
MM = *Maintained Markup*   (Assuming nonoperating expense and nonoperating income are equal, MM is used interchangeably with gross margin.)

Thus: MM (or GM) Goals = Net Sales − (Cost of Goods Sold + Total
    (34%)   Operating Costs) = Net Profit

    Sales − MM   = Cost of Merchandise Sold

    ∴ 100% − 34   = 66% = Cost of Sales (or Merchandise Sold)

and Sales − Cost of Sales = MM
    (100%)   (66%)   (34%)

or Cost of Sales + Total Oper. Costs = Total Cost of Sales (TC of S)
    (66%)   (30%)   (96%)

and Sales − (TC of S) = Net Profit
    (100%)   (96%)   (4%)

As long as the projected volume of $200,000 is generated, operating expenses will not "squeeze" the gross margin figure and the following profit picture would result:

---

[3] When a markdown is taken only the *cost of the markdown* represents a loss to the store. The markdown has both a cost portion and a markup portion. In this case, with a 40 per cent initial mark-on only 60 per cent of the markdown would represent a cost: specifically, .60 × .0667, or .040020, or 4 per cent, and the cost of markdown would be:
$$\text{MM} = \text{IM} - \text{Cost of MD, or}$$
$$40\% - 4\% = 36\%$$

Sales		$200,000	(100%)
Gross Margin (actual amount above cost received from sales)	34% × 200,000	68,000	(34%)
Less Operating Expense	(30%)		

$$(\text{GM} - \text{Op. Ex.} \times \text{Sales}) \text{ or } 60,000 \quad (30\%)$$

(4% × 200,000)	or 8,000	(4%)
(68,000 − 60,000)		
Net Profit	$8,000	

Illustration B. Let us see what happens if, instead of generating $200,000 in sales, the volume drops 10 per cent to $180,000. In this event, it is not likely that fixed expenses would be reduced concurrently with the 10-per-cent loss in volume. Any short-run change in volume along these lines would not be considered permanent or "nonrecoverable," although there may be some accompanying decrease in variable and semivariable expenses. In this type of situation dollar expenditures would tend to remain relatively the same in the short run.

However, this means that instead of $60,000 in operating expenses representing a 30-per-cent overhead, percentage expenditures would increase by 3.3 per cent to 33.3 per cent ($60,000/$180,000) instead of 30 per cent ($60,000/$200,000).

In addition, as pointed out above, any decrease in projected volume tends to depress attainable gross margins as well as increase total costs.[4] For the sake of simplicity, let us assume that maintained markup remains as in Illustration A and gross margin remains at 34 per cent; on this basis, the gross profit decreases to $61,200 (.34 × $180,000, instead of .34 × $200,000), resulting in a net profit of $1,200 ($61,200 − $60,000) instead of $8,000—a decrease of $6,800 in net profit.

As the result of a 10-per-cent decrease in projected volume, net profits decreased 85 per cent. Vividly illustrated here is the importance of the margin-cost-volume relationships in any business enterprise. The illustration also explains the constant stress on volume and the importance attached to market penetration concepts by business firms. For these are the basic motivating forces behind the setting and meeting of sales objectives for the firm. Business survival is at stake.

Illustration C. On the other side of the picture, it is also quite conceivable that with the same dollar operating expenses a 10-per-cent increase in volume is also quite possible. On this basis, using the same basic data, a 10-per-cent increase in volume would result in sales of $220,000.

With approximately the same $60,000 in operating expense, because of the short-run increase, the "expense-volume" ratio percentage then becomes 27.3 per

[4] The reason for the downward pressure on gross margins when sales do not come up to expectations is that an "overbought" stock condition ensues. Generally, the only means of correcting this condition is by clearances at markdown prices. Failure to attain sales goals may result in the decrease of gross margins to the point where they are insufficient to cover total average costs (TAC). Then marginal revenues do not equal TAC and the firm is in danger.

cent ($60,000/$220,000), instead of 30 per cent ($60,000/$200,000)—a decrease of some 9 per cent in operating expenses.

With dollar operating expenses constant, the generation of a larger-than-projected sales increase would result in fewer markdowns, a smaller relative inventory, and a higher turnover. In this case, management should have little or no difficulty in achieving a maintained markup in excess of the 34-per-cent goal; however, for purposes of illustration this figure will still be used.

When the same maintained markup of 34 per cent [5] is applied to the new volume of $220,000, a dollar gross profit return of $74,800 results (.34 × $220,000). Subtracting $60,000 in operating expense from the gross profit of $74,800 gives a net profit of $14,800. Thus, a 10-per-cent increase in volume results in a net profit increase of some 68.25 per cent!

As can be seen from the above examples, the setting of any merchandising policies and pricing policies must be based on market competition as well as cost of operations, with primary emphasis on sales volume. The number of inflexible costs and external considerations attached to the business enterprise determine the strategy that must be used by management if gross margin "squeezes" set by inflexible market factors are to be minimized or eliminated.

MERCHANDISING POLICIES AS A FUNCTION OF GROSS MARGIN REQUIREMENTS

The planned initial mark-on of any merchandise line handled by a marketing firm should cover all direct costs in the short run but not necessarily its total average costs (TAC); TAC includes indirect as well as direct costs. Admittedly, planned gross margin attainable on each individual merchandise line is a factor in setting up the over-all merchandising policies of the firm. Nevertheless, for maximum effectiveness, markup policies should also be more strongly guided by strategems dictated by market requirements regardless of specific returns. In other words, if a lower-than-average markup on a particular line helps to maximize the effectiveness of the firm as a whole, it should be maintained.

For example, merchandise lines in a department store with an average operating expense ratio of 33 per cent should have an over-all return in excess of 33 per cent if it is to continue in business. MR must exceed MC (in a business sense). [6]

On the other hand, major appliances and television sales normally receive initial mark-ons of only 22 to 28 per cent. Assuring a 33-per-cent overhead for the store as a whole, the use of a strict standard yardstick of comparison such as this overhead figure would preclude the handling of such lines.

In the first place, major appliances boast a stock turnover of 6 to 7 times

---

[5] In this case the same gross margin also, in all likelihood a greater than forecast gross margin, would result.

[6] Note: marginal costs (MC) in the economic sense included "normal profits"; stated in an "economic sense" MR (marginal revenues) must equal MC.

annually; compared with the average department store stock turns of 3.5 to 4.3 times annually, the higher attainable stock on these lines more than compensates for the lower-than-average gross margin. The greater the turnover, the lower the margins needed. When the turnover of a merchandise line significantly exceeds that of the firm as a whole, simple percentage comparison and analyses of operating costs and planned gross margins do not reveal item profitability. In addition, the factors of market requirements and total store image and increased traffic also enter the picture.

Thus, it is of utmost importance that departments be carefully evaluated on the basis of contribution as well as net profit dollars.[7] The contribution plan of accounting also evaluates to some degree the intangibles of desirability from the standpoint of customer conveniences, of presenting a complete store and the proper "service" image to the public.

Evaluation of Profitability

The mere limitation of a low initial markup does not mean that a merchandise line is an uneconomic consideration. With all kinds of stores carrying all types of merchandise, regardless of generic relationship, the application of over-all standards of comparison to specific merchandise lines would not generally be effective. The problem of profitability evaluation is still present because of complicated adjustments involved in the comparison of handling costs—MMA applications notwithstanding.

To illustrate, greeting cards, dry foods, and groceries are generally sold on a simplified, self-selection, or complete self-service basis; on the other hand, curtains, draperies, custom upholstery, women's better ready-to-wear, millinery, and accessories are generally sold on a full-service basis. Lines such as these are carried within a single store plant and at times adjacent to each other. A standard allocation of overhead costs would involve unscientific bias. Comparison of the relative merchandising efficiency ratios, such as turnover and gross margins, cannot be the sole criterion of what specific merchandise lines cost to handle. Of course, sales per square foot of selling space and in-store location are important specific considerations.

Net Return Requirements

To be economic, the net profits accruing to the business firm must exceed total operating costs as well as the imputed costs of invested capital. The cost of capital may range anywhere from 4.7 to 6 per cent annually, depending on the specific kind of business in which the firm is engaged, the security offered, and the market demand for money in relation to its availability.

---

[7] As pointed out, contribution dollars are the income dollars generated by a department above direct fixed and variable costs, but not including indirect costs.

For example, before a department or section is leased within a store, the potential return is capitalized by projecting the minimum rental guarantee in relation to the cost of the space to be leased. Then the profit potential of the section, were it to be operated by the lessor, is used as the standard of comparison to determine the profitability of renting versus operating.

Net profit returns on capital invested by equity shareholders should exceed the return of fully secured interest investments. Equity returns in well-managed concerns should approximate 6 to 9 per cent on investment; this includes the projection of both dividend returns and growth.[8]

MERCHANDISING POLICIES AS A FUNCTION OF WORKING CAPITAL AND TURNOVER GOALS

Major working capital needs consist of cash on hand, cash in banks, provision for merchandise inventories, accounts payable, and recurring cash expenses. The permanent working capital invested in a business must be adequate to provide for sufficient inventories to conform with planned merchandising policies; otherwise sales goals cannot be attained effectively.

The planning of merchandising policies is also a function of the availability of working capital and turnover goals. The turnover figure (and resulting inventory) is planned by executive management as one of their policy projections. Once sales have been forecast, the projected retail sales figure is divided by the firm's planned turnover goal. Sales divided by the average turnover equals the average inventory at retail.

$$\text{Average Inventory} = \frac{\text{Sales}}{\text{Stock Turnover (times)}} \qquad \begin{array}{l}(\text{dollars}) \\ (\text{funds})\end{array}$$

Stated Alternatively:

At Retail
$$\text{Average Inventory} = \text{Sales (S)} \div \text{Stock Turnover (S.T.)}$$
or:
$$\text{A.I.} = \frac{S}{S.T.}$$

At Cost
$$\text{Average Inventory} = \frac{\text{Cost of Sales}}{\text{Stock Turnover at Cost}}$$
or:
$$\frac{(\text{Retail})}{\text{Stock Turnover (times)}} = \frac{(\text{Sales})}{(\text{Average Inventory at Retail})}$$

---

[8] From an examination of various market reprints regarding common stock returns on invested capital (1960–1964).

$$\therefore \text{Average Inventory (at Retail)} = \frac{\text{Sales}}{\text{Stock Turnover}}$$

and: Permanent Working Capital Needs = (Average Inventory at Retail) ×
(for Merchandise Inventory)   (Reciprocal[sa] or Cost Complement
of Initial Markup)

For example: in a millinery shop with an estimated annual sales volume of
$50,000 and a turnover figure of 10, the average investment at retail would be
$5,000 ($50,000 ÷ 10). As millinery has a high initial markup (some 45 per
cent based on retail), the cost complement or reciprocal of the initial markup
would be 55 per cent. The permanent working capital needs for inventory purposes in this operation would be $2,750 at cost.

Illustration. Given:

Planned Annual Sales	$50,000
Planned Turnover (times)	10
Planned Initial Markup	45%

$$\therefore \frac{\text{Sales}}{\text{Turnover}} = \text{Average Inventory at Retail (A.I. at R.)}$$

$$\frac{\$50,000}{10} = \$5,000$$

$$\therefore \frac{\text{(A.I. at R.)} \times \text{(Reciprocal of I.M.)} = \text{A.I. at Cost}}{\$5,000 \times .55 \qquad = \$2,750}$$

In effect, lower merchandise inventories may mean a smaller likelihood of
markdowns and would release working capital for the adding of other merchandise
lines or assortments. However, should turnover be too high, the resulting condition
might result in "stock-outs" and loss of sales because of the insufficient merchandise assortments, not to mention loss of customer satisfaction. Also, when too
many "special orders" of staple merchandise result from too high a turnover,
higher sales costs result. Merchandising policies along these lines would endanger
long-run organizational goals. It should also be kept in mind that stock turnover
is a function of pricing policies. In all cases, price theory, real or implied, is
applied in an operations research format so the "total store concept" is promoted.

THEORY OF THE FIRM AND PRICING

Up to the early thirties, scant attention was given by many economists to applying
the tools of analyses developed in related disciplines to pricing. Empirical work
in price theory up to that time consisted primarily of marginal analysis and the

---

[sa] The term "reciprocal" is used here in sense of $(100\% - x)$, and not in the strict mathematical
sense of $1/100$.

examination of the changing relationships of prices of broad groups of commodities and services as segments of a "price system." Much of these data were developed on the basis of government data, using almost continually changing commodity specifications as the bases for analysis. Nevertheless, many indexes of broad significance did result and economic data did become better understood.[9]

During the late thirties, significant pricing studies were carried out by many economists and government agencies in attempts to explain the underlying causes of price changes and fluctuations in the market and the relationship of these changes to the volume of sales generated.[10] The results of these studies showed that any better understanding of price-sales relationships would have to be directly related to the demand function in specific markets. To be effective, the criterion used would have to be a standard product sold to an ultimate consumer.

As for the price-output relationship—that of the supply function—a realistic statistical approximation was often possible for agricultural products such as lumber, cotton, textile fabrics, and bituminous coal. In these areas, production is very closely related to conditions of pure competition because price acts almost automatically as the regulator of supply.

This is not so for most other commodities sold in retail markets, as each individual firm plans its own market share percentage as an organizational goal. Thus, firms produce consumer products whose total exceeds more than 100 per cent of total demand. Market gluts and off-price clearances result.

Price theory has been used increasingly with respect to the operation of the individual firm under assumptions of various demand and cost schedules. While the exact pinpointing of market demand as a tool for price determination is generally broad based, market demand over time can be measured in terms of particular products and product categories. A basic assumption underlying demand calculations by specific product lines is that consumer purchases are made on predominantly rational bases; but such is not the case.

Purchases in retail markets are based on emotional as well as rational motives. Many consumers often cannot explain their actions at the point of purchase. Much empirical research demonstrates that a large proportion of purchase decisions at retail are made on an impulse basis—"pre-sold" concepts notwithstanding. In no other area of economic thought and inquiry is there as large a gap as exists between economic theory and theories in buyer behavior. Reasonably accurate and useful measures of effectiveness have been obtained in studies of the effect of price policies on sales showing how psychic value and utility estimates are made by consumers in their purchase decisions. The net results of these studies show that there is no one type of merchandise policy that is the best in all cases—not even in the same market![11]

[9] Frederick Mills, *The Behavior of Price* (Washington, D.C.: National Bureau of Economic Research, 1927).

[10] Henry Shultz, *The Theory and Measurement of Demand* (Chicago: University of Chicago Press, 1938).

[11] R. D. Entenberg, *Marketing Studies of Purchase Motivations* (Retail Research Center, Graduate School of Business, University of Pittsburgh, 1961–1964); papers given before the annual meetings of the NRMA on decision processes.

SUCCESSFUL AND DIFFERING MERCHANDISING POLICIES IN SINGLE COMPETITIVE MARKETS

In Pittsburgh three major department stores prosper in the central business district.[12] Here, three firms boast three different types of pricing policies in a highly competitive market. Each is exposed to the same conditions of demand; because of central unified bargaining policies, their labor costs are roughly similar. Each of these firms generates net sales in excess of $60 million annually, yet they operate under three almost completely different philosophies of management with regard to merchandising and pricing policies. Their store character and store images differ. All are successful. Kaufmann's, with a reputed volume approximating $100 million annually, is known by consumers as a prestige-promotional store with price ranges for every income range; the Joseph Horne Company, with a reputed volume approximating $85 million, is known as a prestige store; and Gimbel Brothers, with a reputed volume of over $60 million, is known as a highly promotional store.

Here is the apparent (but nevertheless not unusual) paradox of three completely different firms operating successfully in the same market with three different sets of merchandising policies, which nevertheless interact at certain levels of similarity.

All three stores offer relatively the same services, stress customer satisfaction, and attempt to offer the same degree of shopping ease and convenience. Each of the present store images was developed as the result of three vastly different merchandising and pricing approaches.

Even in their downstairs and budget operations, pricing policies differ. In one firm, markdowns from upstairs merchandise departments are cleared semiannually "at a price." In another, the downstairs store handles completely different lines of lower-priced, first-quality merchandise, appealing to a completely different group of customers than would normally shop their upstairs store. The highly promotional store boasts a downstairs operation where "job lot" and "distress" merchandise is continually promoted on a strong basis. Yet, in many areas, especially in soft goods, similar lines and even similar brands are priced and promoted differently and successfully.

In the aggregate, the total operating expense ratios of these stores are roughly similar. The wide differences of consumer buying appeals used for promoting similar merchandise departments has apparently not affected each firm's success. It is no wonder that simple analysis of pricing policies in similar competitive market situations tends to be overgeneralized at the retail level.

THE PRICING DECISION—ESCAPABLE COSTS

The character and make-up of market factors and economic conditions in the market place are, in essence, the basic over-all determinants of selling price. Al-

---

[12] Kaufmann's (a May Department Store affiliate), Gimbel Brothers, and the Joseph Horne Company (a member of the Associated buying group).

though manufacturers and suppliers suggest initial cumulative markups for their products, these remain only suggestive in nature unless they are "fair trade."

The concept of escapable expense is often used as justification for the elimination of specific lines and as a basis for influencing merchandising policies. For example, one aspect of escapable expense for the retailer may be the extent to which he depends on the manufacturer for cooperative advertising allowances and special point-of-purchase materials. When suppliers or manufacturers underwrite these costs, selling costs are pushed upward in the channel. These expenses can be considered escapable in the sense that they do not become a part of the store's functional operating costs. In the case of discount houses, where customers make their own deliveries and handle factory warranties directly, the attached costs have become escapable in the sense that they are pushed downward in the channel to consumers. While such policies tend to reduce retail costs, these savings have not generally been passed on to consumers.

A third type of escapable expense is involved in selling bulky and awkward-to-handle goods on a drop-shipment basis. For example, furniture purchases may be sent directly from the factory to the individual purchaser, with demonstrating, selling, and giving title to the goods remaining the seller's functions.

Escapable expenses must be considered from the standpoint of whether or not prices are lowered to reflect the differences in handling costs. If not, the tendency to by-pass the middleman is created. The elimination of a normal functional responsibility of the middleman in the marketing channel should be reflected in the price to the buyer.

Sunk Nonescapable Costs

Contrasted with escapable expenses, the additional "cost" of merchandise replacements due to increasing price levels represents sunk nonescapable costs. Because of obvious lags in consumer acceptance of merchandise of the same quality at higher prices, the initial increase in the wholesale cost of goods is generally not immediately passed on to the consumer. This represents a form of sunk nonescapable costs.

On the other hand, were the wholesale prices of a merchandise category to decrease with an immediate decrease in the selling price, the loss in market cost value would represent a sunk nonescapable cost.

EFFECT OF SPECIALIZATION ON MERCHANDISING PLANNING

The degree of specialization within an organization determines the nature of its sales-supporting activities. The larger the firm, the more decentralized its activities, the greater the delegation of authority and responsibility, the more decentralized its decision-making functions, and the greater the likelihood that the same merchandise classifications are offered for sale under differing price policies. A multi-unit firm, geographically dispersed within one trading area, has cost differential considerations to evaluate before formulating merchandising and pricing policies for the entire organization. Regardless of sizes, policies should be uniform and at the same time adequate to cover total costs. Pricing policies must also be competitive and rationalized to the public for purposes of justification as a wanted business entity.

A centralized firm is, of course, much more likely to have uniform merchandising policies and closer supervision. In decentralized operations the buying and selling functions are apt to be separate functions with somewhat looser direct managerial controls.

In the more specialized organizations, where functions are separate yet interact, executives with buying responsibilities often blame executives responsible for selling activities when merchandise purchases fail to move. At the same time, the selling organization finds fault with the merchandise purchases.

ROLE OF EXPECTATIONS

Sales expectations depend on consumer buying intentions, which are always in a state of flux. Merchandise plans are set up six to nine months in advance to make certain that the necessary inventories are available to carry out the sales plan. Pricing flexibility is needed in order to meet the sales goal when expected sales do not materialize. In other words, pricing policies are a definite function of sales expectations, a continuing variable.

A second type of expectation is often referred to as market anticipation. Such anticipations "revolve about the interplay between the firm's actions and its environment." [13] A sales forecast with the accompanying pricing and strategy to insure its attainment is, in effect, market anticipation.

A third classification of expectations upon which market anticipations and intentions are based is "outlook." This is a form of expectations about conditions which a firm cannot perceptibly influence. However, "conditions" do shape the size and draw potentials of a market. This class of expectations includes forecasts of the general economic situation—the level of gross national product, the rate of government expenditures, foreign market potentials, changes in tax rates and regulations, and so on. "Conditions" also include forecasts of the position of the industry in the economy for which the actual forecast is a part.

For example, a petroleum firm's estimate of total gasoline sales is referred to as "outlook"; its estimate of its share of the market is termed "market anticipation"; and its projected sales campaign for realizing its share of the market is called "intention."

Outlook estimates, market anticipations, and intentions may be formulated within the firm or contracted out to reliable marketing experts or business economists. If formed within the firm, they may be the result of expert value judgments;

---

[13] *An Appraisal of Data Research on Businessmen's Expectations About Outlook and Operating Variables* (Washington, D.C.: Board of Governors, Federal Reserve System, September 1955), p. 8.

e.g., estimates of industry prospects are made on this basis by a competent staff of economic and market analysts. Such groups provide external guiding points for many large firms. Federated Department Stores and Sears, Roebuck and Company are examples of large retail firms who base expectations on formal research departments.

Intuitive sales forecasts are often made by experienced executives who "have the feel of the market," or forecasts may result from "opinions on matters the estimator cannot really judge." [14] Because of the nature of market uncertainties and the suddenness with which they occur, any inflexibilities in the merchandising or forecast plan would prove uneconomic over time.

DISCOUNTING AS A MERCHANDISING POLICY

Cut-price policies cannot be relegated solely to discount houses. Discount selling, in one form or another, takes place in almost all retail firms on either a regular or an occasional basis.

Discount outlets generally attempt to handle "brand name" hard lines where direct price comparisons with list prices can be easily made. This is a far easier type of merchandising policy to establish and follow in hard lines than in soft lines. In the latter case, direct price comparisons are often impossible—not to mention comparisons of selection and fit, which are also a factor in the sales transaction. The use of competitive prices by discounting firms is often mitigated by the limited-service nature of their offer, which is generally a basic part of their operating philosophy.[15]

For example, discount stores often charge for "normal" delivery and "free" thirty-day credit; these charges are rarely included in the advertised purchase price. Many also require trade-ins, stipulated in abnormally small type as "w/t" in their advertisements. For the most part, the customer is expected to absorb the cost of these functions in order to take advantage of a lower price. On the other hand, traditional stores such as department stores generally absorb such service costs in the normal course of their business operation.

The "price-volume-minimum-service" approach has enabled discounters to move tremendous volumes of hard goods. As a result, many manufacturers are apparently willing to assume many additional functional costs in pricing, delivery, terms, datings, and consignment selling which they would not normally extend to their "regular" distributors. Such practices result in indirect price discrimination, which permits a lower cost operation by price-volume sellers.

Many traditional stores are apparently effectively meeting such cut-price challenges. Others have dropped highly competitive hard-line merchandise; Bloomingdale's, New York, for example, stopped handling all major appliances in 1954

---

[14] *Ibid.*, pp. 8–9.
[15] Stipulated price comparisons may be real price cuts or only simulated through "bait" promotions.

because of this type of competition—a complete change in merchandising policy and pricing strategy.[16] This is a perfect example of a change in merchandising policy due to severe and perhaps unfair competitive practices.

FLEXIBILITY VERSUS RIGIDITY IN COMPETITIVE PRACTICES

As a result of such competitive stresses, many retail firms have revised their market strategy and now work with a "totality" conceptual approach. An Operations Research (OR) approach means that departmental goals are set up to maximize the effectiveness of the firm and the system under which it operates. This policy implies the underwriting of departments affected by competitive pressures. On this basis, a housewares department handling small electric appliances would meet all cut-price competition regardless of resulting profitability. The balance of the store's merchandising line offerings would be used to offset the probable resulting losses. The over-all results, in most instances, generally improve the effectiveness of the entire store.

Supermarkets, gasoline stations, and other types of convenience establishments often give stamps or prizes with purchases in lieu of a price-cutting merchandising policy. By such means they hope to avert "price wars." In the short run, customers benefit from these types of competition, especially in revisions and liberalization of customer services and return policies. With shopping center expansions and suburbanization a nationwide fact, it behooves retail management to evaluate their market strategy carefully and constantly to see if their competitive effectiveness is being maintained. It is not at all unlikely that changing merchandise policies may follow one another as the nature of consumer demand changes in trading areas.

EFFECT OF CHANGING COST-PRICE MOVEMENTS

As pointed out, attempts to formulate merchandise policy decisions solely from a cost or MMA standpoint would be inadequate. In determining the character of any merchandise expenditures, the flow of capital inward must be planned. Sales must provide the funds for merchandise inventories, expense, disbursements, contingency funds, profits, taxes, and dividends. Such expenditures involve continuing and prudent allocation of current income for business continuity and growth.

A business organization generates long-run profits through the creation of customer values. In distribution, just as in industry, maximizing potential returns is generally the underlying goal of executive decision making. Because of the rapidity of change, no executive can be thoroughly acquainted with all the changing cost-price relationships. Also, there is simply insufficient empirical evidence on the nature of cost-price movements for prediction of such changes to be economically

---

[16] R. D. Entenberg, *The Changing Competitive Position of Department Stores in the U.S. by Merchandise Lines* (Pittsburgh, Pa.: University of Pittsburgh Press, rev. ed. 1961), pp. 110–11.

possible. Yet, this is the key area on which net profits depend. The changing cost-price relationships also directly affect depreciation policies, plant utilization, product obsolescence, inventory investment, turnover requirements, and markdown policies.

In order to minimize the effect of market changes, many firms have a "death-rate" system of operation so as to force markdowns and speed turnover with lower and fresher merchandise inventories. In this system, an automatic selling life for every merchandise classification is determined. This list, once approved by the general merchandise manager, is then used as a merchandise policy guide-line.[17]

For example, if a line of misses' dresses is received in August for fall selling at an invoice cost of $10 and a retail of $17.95, any remaining unit in the group which is still on hand in January (six months after receipt) would be inventoried at either 50 per cent or 33 per cent of the original cost, depending on store policy. Should any units still be on hand at the end of the subsequent six-month period, the dresses remaining would be credited as a "unit credit" at "zero" cost. This kind of policy forces buyers constantly to seek to eliminate dated items and speed turnover.

SUMMARY

This chapter has been primarily concerned with merchandise planning and the techniques of pricing and market strategy used to achieve organizational goals, as applied by retail and market managers in their operations.

The management of enterprise on an applied economic base was illustrated in a simulated retail operation. The role of management expectations and the need for flexibility in market application were analyzed from the standpoint of formulating optimum market strategy.

---

[17] See W. Burston, "A Death-Rate System to Force Markdowns and Speed Turnover," *Stores Magazine* (November 1959), p. 17.

Chapter 18: *Basic Merchandising*

The prime need in good buying is to have enough wanted merchandise at competitive prices so that forecast sales-volume goals can be met. But good buying also entails meeting customer requirements without an unnecessarily large inventory investment. Efficient stock turnover then becomes the key variable to be "averaged" in the merchandise plan.

BUYING TECHNIQUES AND INTERNAL RESEARCH

There are at least four generally accepted methods of setting up the open-to-buy schedules and initial buying plans. The first, the basic stock method, may be defined as providing the minimum amount of merchandise which a department should have on hand at all times so that an adequate reserve is provided for customer selections; this means protecting the department against loss of sales from "stockouts." [1] The basic stock for the month may be defined as being equal to sales for the month plus the average stock for the season minus the average monthly sales.

---

[1] See Bernard P. Corbman, *Merchandising* (New York: Ronald Press, 1952) p. 208 ff., for an excellent discussion in stock-control plans.

262

Expressed in the form of an equation, the basic stock needed for the beginning of the month (BOM) inventory (for the six-months' season) is:

BOM stock = sales for the month + average stock for the season − average monthly sales.

Other methods of stock control and planning, such as the stock sales ratio method, will be discussed under planning and control of merchandise inventories.

A good start in optimizing buying decisions is the development of a functional bookkeeping system wherein operating costs are allocated and maintained in terms of merchandise classifications. This system results essentially in a "cost of handling" statistical product relationship which can be used for merchandise management accounting. In other words, a functional bookkeeping system can pinpoint the store's most profitable merchandise lines as well as those sold at markdowns. A system of analyzing buying functions along these lines, coupled with a review of past open-to-buy (OTB) budgets, clearly indicate the effectiveness of buying and merchandising decisions.

Other internal research can be developed from budgets. Budgets, per se, are essentially planning documents. When compared to pertinent balance-sheet and income statements they can be used to measure the results of prior open-to-buy plans. Then transaction and sales analysis can be used in conjunction with over-all analyses to do a more informed job in buying.

THE DEMAND SCHEDULE AND PRICE CUTS

In any six-month forecast budget, futurity and uncertainty must be channeled into the pattern of expectations through the firm's pricing policies. It is not necessary that all assumptions on which the forecast is made be valid. When products are not homogeneous—and especially when knowledge of consumer expectations of particular products is limited—reaction to price changes cannot be as predicted.

Sales forecasting is based primarily on the projection of current market demand. Retail stores handling diverse commodities have a difficult time in sales forecasting because of the necessity for interpretation of many segmented series of individual demands under varying prices and fluctuating competition. The demand for various commodity lines that consumers buy varies with existing prices at particular times and with particular market conditions—especially where commodities are homogeneous.

Merchandise planners and buyers state that they do not think in terms of economic theory in evaluating demand. Yet they act on just such bases in the market place. For example, a buyer acting on the basis of a simple demand schedule would consciously or unconsciously use either a marginal utility concept or an indifference-curve technique. In merchandise planning, potential shifts in demand are taken into consideration. Table 25 points out in graphic form the kind of advance planning that should take place to estimate changing demand as a result of change in price.

As can be seen from Table 25, when the price of a homogeneous product such as percale sheets of a fixed size is reduced, the law of diminishing marginal utility does not seem to affect market demand, especially when the sheets are

TABLE 25

INCREASE IN DEMAND DUE TO CHANGE IN PRICE[a]

UNIT PRICE AFTER CHANGE	QUANTITY DEMANDED	QUANTITY DEMANDED AFTER CHANGE (FROM $2.20)
$2.00	4,000	5,000
1.80	6,000	8,000
1.60	8,000	11,000
1.40	10,000	14,000
1.20	15,000	25,000

[a] Product here was full-size, first-quality, percale sheets, 81 x 108 in., sold in establishments located in a central business district or a regional shopping center. (Based on studies in price-quantity relationships of standard products, 1964, at the Retail Research Center, Graduate School of Business, University of Pittsburgh.)

offered for sale at a price well below that of total average cost (a genuine bargain). Demand, under these circumstances, apparently does not subside because there will be a tendency to hoard.

CONSUMER MOTIVATIONS

In buying for merchandise requirements, the store buyer must assume that the consumer will seek to maximize his satisfactions in terms of available income. In maximizing satisfactions, the consumer consciously or unconsciously applies a sort of "satisfaction utility" concept in his purchases. The cost of acquiring additional units of a similar item can be measured in terms of marginal (and hence convenience) costs. The possession of an additional unit of an item always adds fewer utilities and satisfactions than the original acquisition. This concept is especially important in the case of replacement or additional demand for high-priced, big-ticket items such as automobiles, houses, refrigerators, freezers, and washing machines. Without an offset trade-in of an existing high-priced item, the consumer may find an additional purchase of a similar item uneconomic.

In the case of most soft-goods purchases, however, the law of diminishing returns tends to become inoperative, because product and price substitutability cannot be fully achieved; in these areas commodities are much less likely to be substitutes for one another. However, buyers behave as if products are fully substitutable, and most retail managers merchandise their stores accordingly. Normally, the intensity of demand diminishes with the possibilities of being able to "store" an item; the intensity of consumer demand also diminishes whether or not the need for the item is postponable.[2]

---

[2] K. E. Boulding, *Economic Analysis*, rev. ed. (New York: Harper and Brothers, 1948), pp. 616–17.

The purchasing power freed by price reductions will not necessarily be used by the consumer for other goods. More often than not, spending on bargains may come from savings as well as from the reallocation of freed income. This is directly related to the substitution effect in consumers' purchasing. Consumers not only find it advantageous, but also derive psychic satisfactions from the purchase of "off-price" goods, especially when they are nonperishable and can be used later.

Each consumer, while attempting to maximize total satisfactions, has varying utility scales for all goods. Thus the triggering of purchases is basically a function of overcoming the consumer's indifference scale of utilities in terms of his liquidity preferences and available funds.[3] It is on the basis of such motivations that price cuts are formulated as part of the merchandising strategy of functionaries in the market place.

ANALYZING THE MARKET

For retail organizations, as well as for manufacturers and distributors, the first step in evaluating merchandising policies is to classify the customers for whom the merchandise is intended. Customers must be analyzed in terms of buying behavior and social motivations. As a first step in customer analysis, sales are grouped by merchandise classifications. Customers in the store's trading area are then grouped by zones of residences. This is relatively easy for charge-account customers when a random sample of the accounts is used. Randomized samples can furnish this information with respect to cash customers. From zones of residence, consumers are further classified into income groupings and general social strata.[4]

If research uncovers the fact that certain income groups are not making purchases in the store, merchandise and pricing policies should be re-examined for reasons why these particular groups are not patronizing it. This may involve customer analysis by geographical areas; contacts can be made by either telephone or mail. Objective questions can be asked discreetly as to what could be done to increase sales. Such questioning can also lead to improved performance in advertising copy, promotional appeals, and sales. In other words, this kind of research will reveal whether the department buyer is keying his purchases to the groups representing the greatest potential in terms of over-all, long-run sales. In the chapters on research and communications macro- and microanalytical procedures will be reviewed.

---

[3] J. M. Keynes, *The General Theory of Employment, Interest, and Money* (New York: Harcourt, Brace, 1935).

[4] From an evaluation of the price of houses in an area, total upkeep costs may be determined from average monthly payments of interest, taxes, insurance, amortization, heat, light, etc. The totals of these payments give a general measure of family incomes in a neighborhood. The average wage earner spends approximately one-fourth of his family income for household expenses and maintenance.

Vendor Analysis and Wholesale Price Movements

In the evaluation of suppliers, it should be kept in mind that wholesale prices fluctuate more often and more widely than do retail prices. Wholesale prices fluctuate on identical merchandise purchases during the same season. At the same time, retail prices for the same merchandise in the same season generally remain constant.

Mark-ons therefore vary constantly, as do costs of handling, storage, promoting, and selling the same merchandise during the course of the year. Fashion changes and improper size or style purchases, as well as other mistakes in buying, must be provided for in the determination of initial markups.

In any analysis of merchandise resources, evaluation should be made of pricing and delivery policies, terms of sale, response to complaints, dependability, and the creativity of the merchandise values offered. Normally, pertinent comments about suppliers should be listed on duplicate invoices and recorded on vendor analysis cards. Vendors should be listed alphabetically and cross-referenced to another file by product categories. Thus, any shifts in store buyers will not leave the organization without a file of basic information on merchandise resources.

ELEMENTS OF MARKUP

In essence, markup is the difference between the cost and the selling price of the merchandise handled. The management of buying, pricing, and basic merchandising depends on an understanding of the specific elements of merchandise markups. Mark-on or markup refers to the actual amount above cost that the merchandise inventory has been priced. Gross margin (GM) or maintained markup (MM) represents the actual amounts above the cost of goods sold. Although both gross margin and maintained markup are used interchangeably, GM differs from MM in that it also includes nonoperating costs and income. Mark-on represents an initial merchandise price; no sales are involved at this point. On the other hand, a gross margin designation cannot be applied unless a sale has been made. (Whenever markup or gross margin is used in this or later chapters, per cent will always be implied unless stated otherwise.)

Relationships Involved

Most retail stores use markup based on the retail or selling price, although many retail firms still base their markup on cost. The effects of such differences are illustrated as follows. A bedspread retailing for $20 with a $12 cost would carry a 40 per-cent markup based on retail:

$$\frac{\$8 \text{ (difference between cost and selling price)}}{\$20 \text{ (selling price)}} = 40\%.$$

The same $8 markup expressed as a percentage of cost would carry a 66.7 per-cent markup:

$$\frac{\$8 \ (\text{difference between cost and selling price})}{\$12 \ (\text{cost})} = 66.7\%.$$

The markup per cent based on retail sales is *always* smaller than the same markup per cent based on cost, as the cost-base denominator would always be smaller.

As pointed out above, markup, markdowns, salesmen's commissions, salaries, rental costs, and so on, are all based on net sales as the standard of comparison. The use of retail price concepts in markup and control standards makes it possible to use the retail method of inventory system as a form of profit and merchandise accounting. Many firms base markup on cost because of processing activities or the perishable nature of the merchandise categories handled, such as fruits, vegetables, or meats. Other firms, predominantly smaller ones, feel that markup on retail is merely a method of averaging and would not produce significantly accurate results for their firms. For example, a millinery shop which "creates" its own hats would be set up on the cost method of inventory. While markup based on cost is not used by most retail buyers and organizations, the concepts involved should be part of every buyer's fund of knowledge.

Markup based on retail rather than on cost has a better public-relations connotation, because the stated percentage is always smaller than the one based on cost.

Because markup, expenses, net profit, and all other data are expressed as a percentage of retail sales, the most meaningful measures of comparison result from use of markup on retail and the retail method of inventory. Essentially, the retail method of inventory is a system of averaging markups, retail deductions, and net profits. It is easily the better systems approach to retail operations.[5]

Use of Selling Price as a Markup Base

In any determination of markup based on retail, the basic formula is:

$$MU = \frac{(SP - Cost)}{SP}$$

where:

MU = Markup (initial or maintained)[6]
SP = Selling price or retail
C = Cost

Thus, if a misses' wool suit sells for $90 and the cost is $50, the markup in dollars ($SP - Cost$) is $40 and the initial markup would be 44.4 per cent.

$$\frac{\$90 - \$50}{\$90} = \frac{40}{90} = 44.4\%$$

---

[5] A full discussion of the retail method of inventory will be taken up in Chapter 27.
[6] Initial, or cumulative or average markup, is based on inventory stock on hand, and maintained markup (gross margin) per cent is based on *actual* net sales. The difference would be clear from data supplied.

If the cost is known and the desired percentage markup is known, another version of the basic formula is used:

$$\frac{\text{Selling price}}{\text{(in dollars)}} = \frac{\text{Cost of item (or purchase)}}{\text{Complement of desired initial markup}}.$$

For example, if a furniture buyer purchases some occasional chairs at $22 each, and has an initial markup goal of 45 per cent, his initial selling price would be $40:

$$SP = \frac{\$22}{(1.00 - .45)} = \frac{22}{.55} = \$40$$

When the selling price and percentage markup are known and the cost is to be found, the following formula can be used:

$$\text{Cost} = SP \times (\text{complement of markup per cent}).$$

If the list price of a portable 19-inch television set is $120 and the initial planned markup is 30 per cent, then the cost would be $84:

$$\begin{aligned}
\text{Cost} &= SP \times (\text{complement of markup per cent}). \\
&= \$120 \times .70 \\
&= \$84
\end{aligned}$$

Use of Cost as a Markup Base

Only on markup based on cost is it possible to have a 100-per-cent markup, because the basic markup formula is:

$$\text{Markup (on cost)} = \frac{SP - \text{Cost}}{\text{Cost}}.$$

Thus, if a sewing machine costs $40 and a markup of 80 per cent (based on cost) is desired, use of the formula projects a $72 retail price ($x = SP$):

$$.80 = \frac{x - 40}{40} \quad \text{or} \quad (.80 \times 40 = x - 40)$$
$$x = \$72 \text{ (the retail price).}$$

As another example, a tie selling for $3 has a 50-per-cent markup on cost. To find the cost, the base cost (100 per cent) has added to it the 50-per-cent markup, totaling 150 per cent as the base cost plus markup, which totals the selling price of $3. Dividing this figure by 150 per cent would give us a cost of $2. Any 50-per-cent markup based on cost is equivalent to a 33⅓-per-cent markup based on retail:

$$\begin{aligned}
SP &= \$3.00 & \$1 \div 3 &= 33\tfrac{1}{3}\% \\
\text{Cost} &= \$2.00 & \$1 \div 2 &= 50\%
\end{aligned}$$

The proportionate differences between a cost base and a selling price base are constant ratio percentages.

Conversion of Data

Where the retail markup is known, equivalent markup on cost is figured by dividing by the reciprocal of the retail markup percentage. For example, if the retail markup is 40 per cent, the equivalent markup per cent on cost would be 66⅔ per cent (40% ÷ 60%) (the reciprocal of 40 per cent).

On the other hand, where the markup based on cost is known, it can be converted to a markup based on retail by dividing by 100 per cent (the cost base) plus the given cost markup; i.e., if the markup on a television set is 40 per cent (on a cost basis), the equivalent markup per cent on retail would be 28.6 per cent.

$$40\% \div [100\% \text{ (base of the cost)} + 40\%]$$

$$\frac{.40}{1.40} = 28.6\% \text{ (equivalent retail markup based on markup cost of } 40\%).$$

The handling of such markup elements is needed for a basic understanding and management of price policies and the economics of enterprise.

In the normal course of business operations, management is not primarily interested in actual individual or cumulative markups. However, management is concerned with the total average markup on merchandise groupings and classifications. The buyer also operates in terms of averaging his multiple costs into price lines appropriate for his customers.

THE MERCHANDISING PROCESSES

Planning Purchases with Inventory

In the planning process, the buyer regards the projected inventories on hand before he plans his purchases. For example, in a paint and wallpaper store, a planning calendar for buying might appear as follows:

September 1

	Cost	Retail or SP
July 1 inventory	$ 40,000	$ 70,000
July–September planned purchases	60,000	90,000
Total merchandise handled	$100,000	$160,000
Initial cumulative average markup	$\left(\dfrac{60,000}{160,000}\right) = 37.5\%$	

Obviously, it is impossible to obtain the same markup on every classification or subclassification when a markup goal is planned. Therefore, merchandising is an averaging process. Even within similar price lines or within similar price zone groups, averaging always takes place, although actual price lines must be few and psychologically sound, otherwise confusion is created.[7]

The Pay-off Markups

Because maintained markup and gross margin are based on actual sales, they are the "pay-off" markup of any business enterprise. Initial, average, and cumulative markups are always based on purchases and inventory and *not* on sales. Thus, the base on which the various markups are computed is not the same as actual sales. As a result, conversion of initial to cumulative markup requires adjusting factors. This adjustment is one of the merchandising processes least understood—even by practitioners in the field. At the same time, it is probably the single most important process in the field.

For example, a buyer purchases three dozen shirts for $4 retail each at cost of $2.30, for a total cost to the department of $82.80 ($2.30 × 36) (not including cash discount which generally accrues to the store). With an initial selling price for the purchase of $144 ($4 × 36), the initial cumulative markup would be 42.5 per cent [($144 − $82.80) ÷ 144].

In setting this markup the buyer must include provision for markdowns, employees' discounts, and stock shortages and unforeseen contingencies. For the purposes of this example, let us assume the shirts have been priced in the marking room and are on the way to the selling department. Should the stock boy damage one of the shirts in the delivery process, only 35 shirts would be delivered for sale.

In the selling process, 20 shirts may be sold at the original retail price of $4, generating an $80 revenue.

Let us say that the remaining 15 shirts are "promoted" at a special sale price of $3.50. Five shirts sold at this price would bring in an additional $17.50. The remaining 10 shirts might then become dated, soiled, or shopworn, necessitating a price reduction to $2.50 each. Assuming 8 of the 10 remaining shirts are sold at the $2.50 price, the remaining two shirts may then be "cleared out" for $1 each, bringing in an additional $2. The above example is not far-fetched but truly represents a "normal" merchandising process in a competitive framework!

Summing up the above process:

Initial Cumulative Markup

Total Cost	Original Retail
36 @ $2.30 = $82.80	36 @ $4.00 = $144.00

$$\frac{(SP - Cost)}{SP} = \frac{\$\ 61.20}{\$144.00} = 42.5\% \text{ initial cumulative markup.}$$

---

[7] "Psychologically sound" means that price differences in similar merchandise categories must be clearly evident to the potential buyer on an intrinsic value basis.

Actual Retail

$$20 \times \$4.00 = \$\ 80.00$$
$$5 \times\ \ 3.50 = \ \ \ 17.50$$
$$8 \times\ \ 2.50 = \ \ \ 20.00$$
$$2 \times\ \ 1.00 = \ \ \ \ \ 2.00$$

$\$119.50$ = actual net selling price of the lot.

$\$144.00$ (original retail) − $\$119.50$ (net selling price) = $\$24.50$.

Total retail deductions for merchandising process in this case is $\$24.50$. Actual maintained markup is *not* based on $\$144$ (the original selling price of the shirts), but on the actual selling price of $\$119.50$ (net sales). This means that the projection of $\$61.20$ margin above cost resulted in only $\$36.70$ net realization on all the purchased items, or $\$24.50$ less than projected. The maintained markup percentage then becomes:

$$\frac{\$\ 36.70\ \text{(actual money realized)}}{\$119.50\ \text{(actual selling price)}} = 30.7\%.$$

In other words, if 30.7 per cent was the buyer's maintained markup, this buyer provided for an "off-retail" percentage of 17 per cent:

$$\frac{\$\ 24.50\ \text{(total retail reductions)}}{\$144.00\ \text{(initial markup retail)}} = 17\%.$$

The markdown percentage in this case is:

$$\frac{\$\ 24.50\ \text{(markdown)}}{\$119.50\ \text{(actual selling price)}} = 20.5\%.[8]$$

In calculating the gross margin, the difference between nonoperating income and nonoperating expenses is included with the pay-off markup.

OTHER PRICING CONSIDERATIONS

For the most part, prices are set by individual sellers with strong influences from competition and resources. Resources which "fair trade" their products and "suggest" a retail price are usually interested in a minimum price—not a maximum.

Price management entails the formulation and carrying out of a policy of selective judgment in a marketing strategy sense. It is an area which does not have a set framework, and hence a great deal of intuitive judgment is needed. Markdowns, shortages, and proposed net profit goals are all included in any initial mark-on determination.

Many customers prefer to buy certain goods at or near customary prices. This in itself creates additional variations in actual markup policies. Also, legislation

---

[8] The markdown percentage always represents the amount of retail deductions expressed as a percentage of the actual selling price.

in such areas as "fair-trade" pricing, unfair sales acts, and fixed pricing in certain commodity areas also influence pricing policies and practices.

In the merchandising planning process the following averaging of markups takes place:

1) on two or more purchases;
2) on merchandise classifications when purchases or inventories have the same cost but differing retails;
3) on merchandise classifications that have the same retail but different costs; and
4) on two or more classifications of merchandise handled in the same departments.

A great deal of judgment must be used in connection with the mathematical computations. The arithmetical computations are only a guide for formulating a pricing and marketing strategy. It should be kept in mind that in the final analysis the only difference between a good buyer and a bad buyer is that the good buyer makes fewer mistakes.

SHORT- AND LONG-RUN PRICING FACTORS

"Nonprice" as well as "noncost" considerations enter into the price decisions. In the short run, off-price reductions from list may take the form of giving trading stamps, accepting trade-ins, granting "extras"—furnishing more than customary services and easier credit terms.

The most profitable price is not always the highest. To maximize profits, sales must be maximized at a price which can generate the greatest amount of total volume. In a monopolistic-competitive market of imperfect competition such as a retail market, it is neither possible nor desirable to change prices constantly in accordance with short-run demand curves. As pointed out, this is characteristic of wholesale markets where prices fluctuate often and rapidly from day to day.

At the retail level, consumers expect customary and relatively stable price levels. Only in the aggregate and over a season can total demand be a factor in relation to supply and price. The aggregates of total demand are felt in wholesale rather than retail markets.

Cross-elasticities of demand in the form of substitution of different products as well as direct product substitutability tends to lower high pricing policies. Total costs are made up of cost of goods sold and all operating expenses, including noncash depreciation expense. Gross margins obtained may not be sufficient to cover total costs. In the long run, however, pricing must provide for complete coverage of total costs.

Basically, every firm has some degree of discrimination in its pricing structure, depending on the exact character of its merchandise line offers. Price policies may vary from specific merchandise lines with complete freedom in price to merchandise lines where suggested "list" prices exist.

Pricing policies are generally determined by an executive committee consisting of the merchandise manager, the controller, the promotion director, and the firm's general manager. Within the business entity, the controller strongly emphasizes the need for full coverage of total costs. The sales promotion manager attempts to maximize the effectiveness of available media through the full use of the firm's price strategy as a base. The general manager attempts to coordinate the lines of both short- and long-run pricing at the market and at times above the market.

The gross margin "squeeze" (where "total costs" force a "squeeze" on the income generated) often forces arbitrary decisions which may not be appropriate either for short-run or for long-run profit maximization.

ROLE OF PRICE THEORY

Price theory in managerial economics is generally stated in terms of a firm producing a single product and confronted by several alternatives in its pricing. These alternatives are analyzed in a combined classification of markets containing a varying number of sellers with differentiated products.

At the retail level, where the normal environment is that of a buyer's market, price discrimination is minimal. Competitive prices often determine the long-run cost of particular products because of long production runs, rather than cost determining price. Actual prices, because of lack of full market information and the heterogeneity and substitutability of commodity offerings, are thus not determined on the basis of economic equilibriums. At the retail level, price theory is used informally only in order to justify pricing decisions that may seem inconsistent with the merchandising policies of the store.

In the application of price theory at the retail level, every action of the entrepreneur in determining price is aimed at achieving the firm's long-run objective of profit maximization.

In retail markets, total maximization of satisfactions by means of price is only theoretically attainable. For example, branded items with fixed prices continue to be carried by retail firms on a "constant-price" basis regardless of changes in market conditions. When total costs of the firm rise and prices remain constant in specified branded lines, prices on the other items handled must of necessity be raised. No store can continually and generally undersell all its competitors on all items in a competitive market.

Also, decreases in price do not automatically increase sales, because of seasonal demand variabilities. For example, attempting to promote sales of antifreeze in June would not result in many sales.

In markets where there are a few larger sellers, retail firms generally have paid much attention to Federal Reserve Board merchandise-line statistics in determining whether or not they were maintaining their share of the market.[9] The tendency is for firms to retain existing price policies as long as their share of the market is either stable or increasing. As a result, actual measurements of the cause and

---

[9] In 1965 the Federal Reserve Board stated that it would transfer the compilation of such statistics to the Department of Commerce.

effect of price changes are, at best, difficult to ascertain. What is now needed in price theory is research of an empirical nature which would provide a definite eclectic approach.

VENDOR DISCOUNTS AND CHANNEL BY-PASSING

Despite the paucity of underlying motivations on prices, there are many obvious considerations in the price-setting process; among these are terms of trade, legislation, and service considerations.

In terms of trade, cash discounts from vendors are not generally regarded as price offsets to merchandise costs in determining selling price. The control division feels that cash discounts from vendors are a form of nonoperating income; thus, such discounts are used to reduce the total store operating costs.[10] On the other hand, invoice datings, combined orders, and seasonal and trade discounts are considered in the actual price-setting situation.

There have always been tendencies to by-pass retailers and buy directly from a resource or manufacturer. This is especially true in the case of high-priced specialty goods where strong brand identification exists. Resources that engage in such practices are in effect competing with their own retail customers. Often, such channel by-passing is carried out by public merchandise warehouses and manufacturer's agents used by distantly located resources.

Basically, resources should be evaluated in terms of merchandise suitability, quality and breadth of assortments, brands offered, mark-on potentials, services offered, and dependability. Often, all these requirements cannot be provided effectively, especially in foreign purchases. Foreign resources, despite their potential for larger markups, are much more likely to by-pass the normal channels of distribution.

EFFECT OF LEGISLATION ON PRICE

Among the various types of legislation affecting price formulation at wholesale and retail is the "Fair Trade Law." This is federal "permissive" legislation which, when passed by a state, permits horizontal and vertical price-fixing of branded products by a manufacturer. In states where Fair Trade Laws are legal, a manufacturer may enter into an agreement with a retailer not to sell his brand except at the minimum fixed price agreed upon except for clearances. Only one signed contract in any state binds all sellers of that product within the state. The Miller-Tydings Act and the McGuire Act were known as Fair Trade Laws. The present proposal before Congress is known as the Quality Stabilization Approach. The effect of such legislation is to restrict competition.

---

[10] In such cases the buyer must consider the discount from the vendor as a loading charge—an addition to his billed cost. A loading charge is the "fixed" cash discount expectation of many department stores. Management of these stores feels that its cash position and credit ratings are so good that its departmental buyers should be able to secure a 4- to 5-per-cent discount on all purchases, regardless of usual terms of trade on particular classes of goods.

Unfair sales legislation on pricing is enacted by states. These Acts prohibit pricing below cost, or cost plus a minimum operating percentage. In this context, unfair sales Acts are not permissive in that minimum-price-fixing agreements within the framework of antitrust legislation are permitted. Such legislation is in effect in at least thirty-five states. It was enacted to prevent the "footballing" of many items or the unfair promotion of "loss-leader" pricing policies. Chambers of commerce and better business bureaus often sponsor such legislation in attempts to prevent "unfair" competition and perhaps raise the ethical standards of trade practices.

The Robinson-Patman Act of 1936 also affects selling prices indirectly. The Act restricts the practice of giving to large buyers unfair price advantages. More specifically, it states that purchases by retailers or wholesalers from manufacturers or suppliers must be made at prices on a proportionately equal basis. In other words, in interstate transactions suppliers must offer like prices to like buyers for like purchases of like quantities.

EFFECT OF SERVICE OFFERINGS AND NONPRICE COMPETITION

The services offered by any store must be underwritten by sales revenues. Also, "customary" prices as well as competition set an upper limit on prices which can be charged. And no store can continually and generally undersell all its competitors.

Thus, business firms seek in every way possible the development of product and store differentiation. Only by such means can pricing strategies be made effective in the market place. Where the store image has been built up to garner wide customer acceptance, competitive pricing becomes a less important factor in market strategy. Thus, a "specialty" concept of commodity or style differentiation enters as the more important shopping consideration. In such cases, management considers the demand curve based on price alone as secondary in nature.

Development of a prestige image is merely one form of nonprice competition. Locational and time monopolies (Sunday and late-hour openings) are other forms of nonprice competition. For example, independent grocery "superettes" which compete with chain supermarkets may choose dissimilar business hours or days in which to stay open so as to acquire a temporary monopoly situation based on convenience.

SUMMARY AND CONCLUSIONS

In this chapter some of the basic buying, pricing, and merchandising functions of the enterprise were reviewed, including the more important elements of initial and maintained markup.

The unforeseen elements of enterprise should always be reflected in the *normal* course of merchandising events in which the initial selling prices are set up. "Normal" events are markdowns, stock shortages, breakage, spoilage, fashion changes, employees' discounts, alteration expenses, and cash discounts. All these are considered in setting up the store's pricing strategy and initial markup goals. These are the *expected* occurrences that are normal for any selling season. Unless these operating norms are provided for, the firm's maintained markup goals cannot be attained.

Initial markup must be great enough to cover all operating expenses (cash as well as noncash) so as to leave an adequate net operating profit; at the same time, the initial selling prices must be low enough to be competitive. The merchandise plan is the principal means for achieving these goals.

The merchandise plan is also a basic requirement for fashion promotion, as well as merchandising and inventory management. These analyses are detailed in the next two chapters.

Chapter 19: *Integrating Fashion Promotion into Basic Merchandising*

Fashion merchandising differs from other types of merchandising because fashion is ephemeral—a quality encouraged by fashion designers and society leaders. Thus, a high initial markup is necessary to cover the higher-than-average markdowns and to produce an adequate final maintained markup. In some cases, where department and specialty stores handle high-priced, high-markdown fashion merchandise, the markup goal may be secondary to the prestige and status value of the merchandise to the store.

THE SOCIOECONOMICS OF FASHION

Fashion may be defined as "innovistic" custom in the guise of a departure from custom. Most individuals consciously or unconsciously attempt to break away in some measure from blind acceptance of what is customary. Fashion also offers a discrete solution to conflict between the individual and the society to which he belongs. In a powerful society which constantly supresses the individual's ego, the individual can assert and rediscover himself by departure from social norms.

The desire for prestige or notoriety can be satisfied by making changes in existing fashion. Through imitation, fashion bridges the gap between the taste makers or the social classes that set fashion and the followers of the so-called "smart set." The logical results of any general acceptance of a fashion by most members of a society is the cyclical disappearance of consumer satisfactions with existing goods and services and a desire for change.

From a historical viewpoint, fashion is simply a variation in a recognized sequence; it can also be termed a departure from an immediately preceding mode. A change in fashion and its recognition, upon which the effectiveness of a firm can depend, is the result of the prevailing culture and the social ideals of the society. For example, the tremendous current demand for the Ford "Mustang" model is an excellent illustration of what happens when a fashion is accepted.

Under what appears to be a stable culture there are always strong psychological drifts to which changes in fashion immediately respond. For instance, in the United States there is a continuing unacknowledged drift toward class distinctions; fashion has found many ways of giving symbolic form to such subliminal desires. Often these ways are quite devious and subtle.[1]

Social Position and Fashion Acceptance

All factors in a society become important determinants in its manner of dress. Status symbols of the past continue to disappear, and individuals who possess them usually find it much more difficult to display other signs of uniqueness which can be regarded as replacements. The reinforcement of the vogues found in national fashion magazines by television and movies has served to break down some of the lags in fashion acceptance found in certain sections of the country. However, time lags in acceptance still exist. In such cases, the social position of the individuals who adopt a new fashion plays an important part in the fashion's acceptance by the community and the firm's success in its promotion.

It is no longer possible, however, to recognize the country bumpkin of the past. More often than not, the young lady from a rural area is much better dressed than her supposedly sophisticated sister who dwells in the city. In our society today the "poor" career girl has actually become much more fashionable and fashion-conscious than her contemporary in the higher-income group. While the career girl may always be dressed in the height of fashion, the well-to-do girl differentiates herself by using less makeup, less jewelry, plain pumps, and simple tweed things with plain sweaters. Such taste trends toward simplicity continue until the career girl begins to acquire the same look and the cycle begins anew.

Effect on Market Management

Mass production, mass distribution, higher incomes, television, and rapid communications of all kinds have helped to equalize somewhat the psychological and

---

[1] Edward Sapir, "*Fashion and Sociology Theory*," in Edgar K. Borgatta and Henry J. Meyer, eds. *Sociological Theory* (New York: Alfred A. Knopf, 1956). See also C. F. Phillips and D. J. Duncan, *Marketing Principles and Methods* (Rev. ed., Homewood, Ill.: R. D. Irwin, 1964), Chapter IV.

economic class differentiations in our society—at least outwardly. Theoretically, our society presupposes that all individuals are equally entitled, insofar as their budgets permit, to the insignia of fashion, both in dress and the interior decor of their homes. An example is the new vogue in "original" paintings for all income levels. As a result, fashion change has become quite rapid.

This universalizing of fashion in all areas shortens its cycle and lessens its profitability. The very impetus that forces rapid changes in the fashion cycle creates difficult and hazardous problems at all levels in the channels of distribution—designing, manufacturing, wholesaling, and retailing.

Women's fashions show greater variability than do men's because the woman is the symbol of man's social and economic stature. The young woman who is not yet married attempts to express herself as a symbol of the status she would like to achieve with her future husband. Thus, the American woman is in the always hopeful and exciting position of emphasizing extravagance upon the slightest provocation or impulse.

Marketing managers and store buyers who understand the psychological impulses of the individual in the social milieu often depart successfully from the accepted "scientific method" in buying for their customers. When creative merchandising of this kind takes place, greater profitability results.

FASHION BUYING AND MERCHANDISING STRATEGY

Central resident buyers as well as buyers from all manner of retail units are always seeking novel designs. In the field of women's ready-to-wear, design is still greatly influenced by Parisian designers of the *haute couture* class. However, houses such as Chanel, Dior, and Schiaparelli no longer enjoy a dictatorial influence on American design and fashion, despite the increasing influx into Europe of fashion buyers from North America. New designs are today being created by stores such as Bergdorf Goodman, Saks Fifth Avenue, and Bonwit Teller, and by fashion advisers to buying offices.

Buying and merchandising fashion goods have much the same general characteristics as design creation and promotion. And the selection of fashions involves the same coordinating procedures as in the selection of a basic stock. For example, in planning buying strategy, a sizable proportion of commitments are made six months in advance of a selling season, with 30 to 40 per cent of total purchases remaining on a monthly open-to-buy basis. During the selling season, continuing review of resources and costs in various markets is made.

UNDERLYING MOTIVATIONS IN FASHION PURCHASES

In motivation research studies on fashion acceptance, it has been found that individuals buy in accordance with the class preferences of the socioeconomic group with which they identify themselves. Individuals, consciously or unconsciously, also classify themselves with a certain image or rank. Such self-classifications become evident in the types of merchandise purchased by specific groups.

For example, appliances and better high-style furniture purchased in discount houses involve little, if any, reflection on personal status if particular national brands have achieved a high degree of acceptance. This is not the case with respect to better ready-to-wear fashion apparel, which has still not achieved any high degree of acceptability for consumer purchases through either discount houses or medium-sized promotional department stores. Most fashion-conscious men and women still prefer to purchase their clothes in "acceptable" specialty and department stores.

From the merchandise standpoint, the purchasing patterns of the American family are middle class. This middle majority often introduces and follows particular fashions with modifications of their own. While the so-called taste makers may be leaders in setting fashion acceptability, they represent less than 12 per cent of American consumers; and, with respect to buying behavior and underlying motivations, a rich family is not a poor family with more money.

At the poverty end of the scale, lower economic groups generally prefer heavy trimmings, heavy furniture and fabrics, and high-priced active sporting goods. Such purchases are easily displayed as "in-home" evidences of security.

Maximizing profits, especially in fashion promotion and merchandising, is generally achieved through the medium of snob-appeal symbolism and other emotional appeals. The tools of analysis developed in psychology and sociology are used continuously in attempts to motivate and adapt consumer behavior to wanting available merchandise offerings. Only by such continuing efforts, it is argued, can the mass capabilities of our manufactured consumer goods industry be fully utilized.

Because fashions change and styles do not, only certain styles are in fashion at any one time or place. Thus, if a fashion is rejected by buyers and the public, it may not be entirely discarded, merely stored in the event of a revival at another point in the time-space continuum.

From a managerial standpoint, it must be stressed that better material, values, or workmanship in themselves do not promote and give the store a fashion image. Knowing and presenting good design and maintaining constant contact with customers and creative resources are basic to all long-run economic fashion promotion.

Emulation and Other Appeals

When well-known persons whom the public admires adopt a fashion, its success is highly probable because of the tendency to imitate. Such individuals have been labeled the taste makers of the public. The emulation appeal may not always be representative. In designing men's clothing, Elizabeth Hawes found that changes in men's fashions were often first accepted by the blue-collar working man; in this case, the desire to be comfortable rather than a desire for change was the motivating factor. The blue-collar worker was the first to wear the soft knitted shirt open at the neck. However, the Madison Avenue executive does not feel that he can risk his social and economic position for comfort. Thus, emulation in such cases carries doubtful prestige. Fashion acceptance also depends on public judg-ment, personality traits of radicalism and conservatism, and the degree of changes occurring in general.

Fashion compatibility also involves matching accessories such as handbags, shoes, and hats. The basic question facing retail and marketing managers is how well can all accessory items be promoted along with new fashion so that over-all sales volume can be maximized. This becomes the function of complete, coordi-nated control within the store.

Fashion Coordination

In the larger department and general merchandise stores, the fashion coordinator furnishes specialization and simplified control within specific fields. Within the total store framework, the fashion coordinator acts in a staff advisory capacity to the ready-to-wear merchandise manager. The organization of such a store is shown in Figure XVI.

FIGURE XVI
MODIFIED ORGANIZATION SEGMENT
SHOWING RELATIONSHIP OF FASHION COORDINATOR

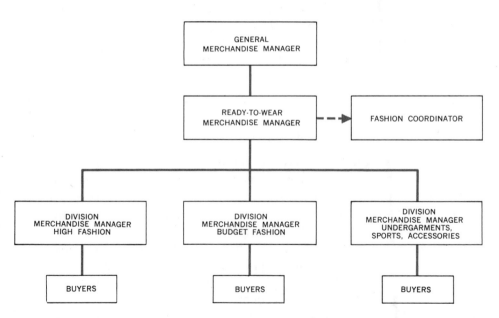

Within this framework, the principal function of the coordinator is to forecast fashion and its demand, to spot "runners," to serve as the major channel of fashion communications and promotion within the store, and to represent the store to manufacturers, designers, and fabric creators. This is not an easy matter. For example, high-priced fashion imports from European resources and *couture* copies are ballyhooed to an extent far above what their dollar sales might appear to warrant. They do have glamour, news value, and snob appeal, which endows the store and related departments with added attractiveness. Nevertheless, it is difficult to find a store that generates more than 3 to 4 per cent of its total soft-goods volume in imported merchandise.[2]

In the United States, the setting for fashion creation and promotion differs almost completely from that in France. In our socioeconomic system, the designer is merely recognized as another artistic professional in the market place. The American designer must pay for his materials, has high labor costs, and does not have a sizable upper class devoted to chic and leisure—the pace in the United States is too rapid. Women of wealth are busy attending board meetings and/or working for charity. Because of such basic differences between the European and American groups of women who initiate fashion, there is a definite need for the American designer.

The American designer performs an important function in expressing the American way of life in such things as clothes, automobiles, homes, and furnishings. Elizabeth Hawes, Claire McCardell, Hatti Carnegie, Mainbocher, and others create clothes that satisfy the casual and suburban tastes of the wealthy American woman.

American designers may be *couturiers* who make only custom-made clothes, such as Morris of Bergdorf-Goodman, whose clothes are featured in the high fashion salons found in the better retail stores. The names of Clare Potter, Evan Picone, Vera Maxwell, and McMullan are associated with the sportswear market. Mr. Mort is very popular in the junior market. The casual way of life in Arizona, Texas, and California has produced a distinctive style of dress for both men and women.[3]

THE FASHION MERCHANDISING CYCLE

The understanding of the fashion cycle is indispensable in buying, merchandising, and coordinating the store's offerings. Fashion acceptance may be a slow, selective process. However, once a style is recognized as being in fashion, it enters a cycle.

During the first stages of acceptance, an incoming fashion is generally very costly. In the case of a misses' garment, fashion at this point interests women who are patrons of the exclusive *couturière* shops and boutiques in department and specialty stores. The original is soon copied line for line by manufacturers of better ready-to-wear, generally in the $75 to $150 retail-price range. In these first two stages the fashion is highly publicized.

By the time the fashion reaches the general acceptance stage, it is generally

---

[2] *Women's Wear Daily* (Feb. 9, 1960), p. 10.
[3] See also Edith F. Hayter, *Fashion Merchandising* (New York: Pageant Press, 1965); Bernice G. Chambers, *Fashion Fundamentals* (Englewood Cliffs, N.J.: Prentice-Hall, 1947); David Ogilvy, *Confessions of an Advertising Man* (New York: Atheneum, 1963); and Stanley C. Hollander (ed.), *Explorations in Retailing* (East Lansing, Mich.: Michigan State University Press, 1959).

modified to meet the demands of mass production and carried by most fashion retailers on a "regular" price line basis. When a style is good, it is good at any price—anywhere from $17.95 to $100. At this point also, lines may be simplified, less expensive materials may be used, patterns can be cut with standardized sizes, and the cost structure becomes lower. Merchandise managers are in a position to profit from fashion inventories. When "special purchase" offerings of the silhouette appear, this is an indication the fashion is nearing its decline.

Changes in any one element of fashion will cause modifications throughout, because all fashions are interrelated and interdependent. The acceptance of a dress style causes changes in the whole realm of accompanying accessories from handbags to foundations. The acceptance of a specific color will likewise call for complementary colors in accessories.[4]

Buyers must be very discerning in separating fads from fashion, as their cycle of obsolescence may be rapid. Fads are offspring of particular fashions which have no discernible utility, compatibility, or prestige. Fads find a special acceptance among teen-agers. Unfortunately, they cannot be forecast; buyers must guess on a fad's geographical spread and be prepared to introduce the merchandise when appropriate in their particular trading areas.

Fashion acceptance and subsequent use may also have far-reaching effects in hard-goods design and merchandising. For example, the acceptance of the short skirt and sheath style has prompted certain automobile manufacturers to introduce the swivel front seat and rising roof flaps for easy entrance and exit.

The department buyer must be extremely careful of his reorders when "special purchase" offerings of a silhouette appear. When it enters the obsolescence stage, it becomes a "clearance item" on which markdowns must be taken. Figure XVII illustrates the cycle.

This cycle is illustrative of all types of fashion merchandise, although certain lines of fashion goods and in some cases new products have differing length of popularity once they are accepted. This model is applicable to the women's ready-to-wear dress market. In general, color is more rapid in movement through the cycle than line, design, or silhouette. Several colors may have a rise and fall within one season. New fashions in jewelry, handbags, scarfs, and other accessories become obsolete within a single selling season. Fabric designs typically endure for a year. A silhouette generally lasts from seven to eight years.

In analyzing the fashion cycle model, it should be kept in mind that the total curve is made up of hundreds of roughly similar curves superimposed over short periods of (usually) less than two months. Local area preferences which vary over time and in scope create lags in various geographical areas of the country. Styles that may be "successes" in New York and Dallas may not reach stages of acceptability in Pittsburgh, Kansas City, or Denver until many months later—perhaps not at all.

[4] John B. Swinney, *Merchandising of Fashions* (New York: Ronald Press, 1942). See also "Development in Consumer Goods," *Federal Reserve Bulletin*, pp. 1–9 (Washington, D.C., January 1966) for development of background information into projective techniques.

FIGURE XVII
MODEL OF THE FASHION CYCLE

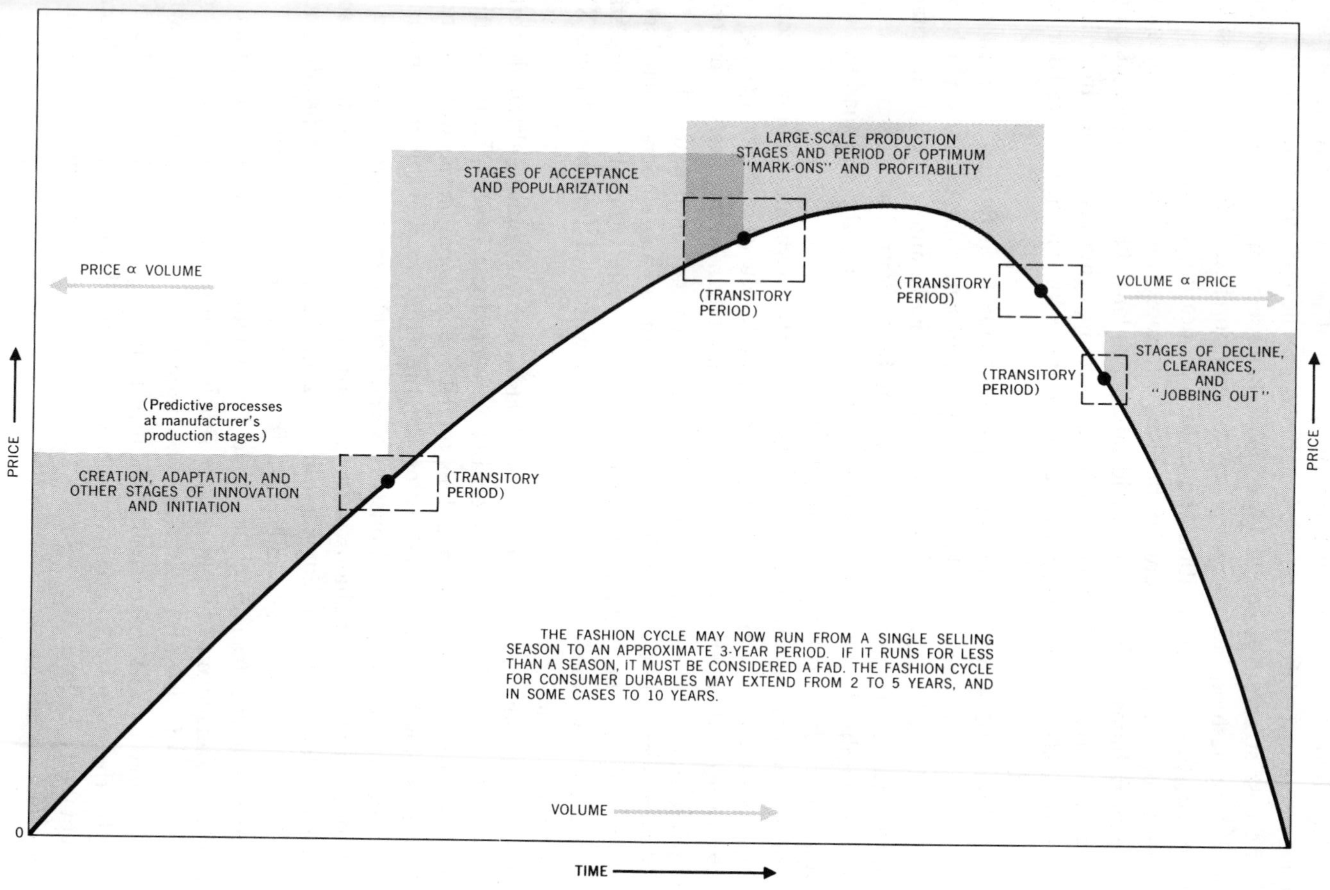

PRICE →

VOLUME ∝ PRICE

STAGES OF DECLINE,
CLEARANCES,
AND
"JOBBING OUT"

(TRANSITORY PERIOD)

(TRANSITORY PERIOD)

LARGE-SCALE PRODUCTION
STAGES AND PERIOD OF OPTIMUM
"MARK-ONS" AND PROFITABILITY

(TRANSITORY PERIOD)

STAGES OF ACCEPTANCE
AND POPULARIZATION

THE FASHION CYCLE MAY NOW RUN FROM A SINGLE SELLING
SEASON TO AN APPROXIMATE 3-YEAR PERIOD. IF IT RUNS FOR LESS
THAN A SEASON, IT MUST BE CONSIDERED A FAD. THE FASHION CYCLE
FOR CONSUMER DURABLES MAY EXTEND FROM 2 TO 5 YEARS, AND
IN SOME CASES TO 10 YEARS.

(TRANSITORY PERIOD)

(Predictive processes
at manufacturer's
production stages)

CREATION, ADAPTATION, AND
OTHER STAGES OF INNOVATION
AND INITIATION

PRICE ∝ VOLUME

PRICE →

VOLUME

TIME →

O

284

FASHION IN DURABLE-GOODS MERCHANDISING

Customer acceptance of innovations in hard lines is more deliberate and more enduring than fashion goods. "Tooling up" for new designs in appliances and house furnishings can be more risky than in soft lines. In these merchandise categories market managers must research continuously on contemporary social changes because of lower turnover and, generally, higher costs and inventory commitments.

Customer tastes, especially in hard lines, are more sophisticated and individualized than in the past. No longer does the "middle majority" want a "ready-made" room. Consumers today prefer to express their own personalities and style of life in the interiors of their homes. This is especially evident in the rising sales of original pop art.

This expressionistic trend can be traced, in part, to the standardization of house and floor plans in the majority of medium- and lower-priced homes. If one's home is practically identical to his neighbor's, then interior furnishings and decor become the vehicles for distinguishing features. Also, emphasis by fashion magazines and manufacturers on "do-it-yourself" items has accentuated customer tastes for individuality. Today, most furniture sales are made on an item or individual-room basis, and individual tastes and needs can thus be fulfilled.

More than ever before, a store's ability to satisfy its customers depends on its interior decor services, as reliance is placed on the growing style sense of the consumer. The average homemaker has her natural creativity in the kitchen stifled by the easy availability of frozen foods and modern cooking devices. Thus she uses her free time in developing novel ways to decorate their home. Accentuating this sense of individuality in the home has been the trend toward a more casual and informal living. Such choices are illustrated by the growing number of family rooms, living-dining-room areas, and combination spare bedroom-den areas being utilized to the greatest possible extent. However, there is also a growing desire for elegance and refinement as expressed in the growing number of requests for a second and more formal living-room in new residential construction.

In merchandising home furnishings, provincial may gain at the expense of modern, or vice versa. Provincial fills a need for casual elegance in furniture wanted by certain groups of consumers. Comfortable, durable individual pieces may be used in the family room regardless of style. Modern or contemporary styles can be found at either extreme of the price range. Custom-made Swedish modern and originals by American furniture designers are found at the high-priced ranges.

THE IMPORTANCE OF IN-STORE COORDINATION AND IDENTIFICATION

Continuing research at the University of Pittsburgh and the University of Denver indicates that the average homemaker ranks style first in selection of home furnishings, with comfort and price following in that order. Management, in analyzing its sales potential, must include current social changes if its forecasting is to be sound.

In no other aspect of merchandising is the prestige of the retailer more at stake than in the realm of fashion. Department and specialty stores, such as the Joseph Horne Company of Pittsburgh and Neiman-Marcus Company of Dallas, are representative of retail firms which base their total store acceptance on fashion, prestige, and status. At the same time, it must be kept in mind that prestige and status for the retail firm is of limited desirability unless these attributes can be transferred into strong patronage and purchase motives. Continuing this kind of motivation is basic to the maximization of a merchandising profit and return on net investment.

ROLE OF BUYING OFFICES

The closer the fashion buyer is located to the market, the greater the number of market visits that should be made. For the most part, buyers are not in any position to visit the market as often as needed; they generally use resident buying offices, which supply continuing market information and assistance to stores throughout the country. Buying offices, whether classified as independent, merchandise brokers, "store-owned offices," or private, associated, or syndicated, essentially perform similar functions.

The independent resident buying office services buyers of many stores, usually on a contract basis. Charges may be as low as $100 or $125 a month or on the basis of .25 to .5 per cent of the store's sales. Also included in this group are merchandise brokers who buy fashion in central markets for retailers who operate similarly merchandised stores in various parts of the country. Because of continuing merger patterns at the retail level, independent resident buyers are becoming relatively less important than store-owned offices. Examples of store-owned buying offices are those of firms such as Marshall Field and Company, the Associated Merchandising Corporation (AMC), and Frederick Atkins.

Buying offices are in a unique position to gauge fashion acceptability. Working with individual store buyers, they are able to make effective analyses of customer demand adjustments and/or returns. Shipments of wrong colors, garments with poor fit and/or poor styling are quickly fed back to the manufacturer. The resident buying office, in effect, operates in much the same manner as a merchandise manager, but on a far larger and more inclusive scale. Because of daily market trips and the performance of a continuous information function, the resident buyer is in an excellent position to help individual buyers achieve better stock assortments, higher turnover, and increased departmental profitability. By coordinating local and central market information and furnishing this directly to retail firms, he helps promote a more effective fashion image for a store.

SUMMARY AND CONCLUSIONS

Applying the fundamentals of good design is important not only for fashion merchandise but also for all the merchandise lines and classifications in the store.

Style and fashion considerations are a must for all retail firms—food, appliances, autos, specialty, or general merchandise.

The store image and its patronage appeal is determined by its highest-priced merchandise classifications. The importance of a department store's fashion acceptability far exceeds the weight of the 15- to 20-per-cent proportion of sales that may be generated in the ready-to-wear and accessory departments.

In terms of long-run stability, fashion promotion for suburban as well as downtown stores means the development of a definite program aimed to appeal to the fashion leaders of the community, to the growing number of teen-agers, and to career women. A completely different fashion approach is also needed for the young homemakers who have only marginal inclinations to "dress up" and shop downtown.

Finally, fashion promotion is fundamentally the key aspect around which a store's merchandising policy should revolve. Fashion sells more women's, men's, and children's ready-to-wear than any other single factor. Therefore, when a buyer finds a manufacturer who produces good designs that meet his customers' wants and his markup requirements, the buyer should cultivate and utilize that source to the fullest possible extent.

Chapter 20: *Inventory Planning and Control Systems*

The primary goal of any merchandise control system is to have what customers want when they want it, with minimal inventories and minimal loss in sales due to "stock-outs." Effective planning and control of merchandise inventories are basic to increasing the over-all productivity of the firm.

In stock planning maximum coordination between a parent store and its branches is essential for effective assortments at all selling points. Otherwise, uneconomic imbalances in inventories result. Branches may and often do cater to different clienteles and will thus need different merchandise. The branch store cannot be expected to carry the same assortments, depth, or even the same price lines as the parent store.

VARIATIONS IN MERCHANDISE CONTROL SYSTEMS

Because of the wide range of single- and multi-unit firms in retailing, control methods vary from systems using calculated risks to very rigid and costly operations involving total control. In the latter cases, the cost of control may exceed the potential savings. Regardless of the system used, all control procedures should be periodically reviewed on a cost versus potential-savings basis.

Multiple and branch stores also have control problems in shipments, transfers, and warehousing. As a planned, calculated risk these organizations may decide not to carry a book inventory for branch stores or to exercise more than a nominal control on merchandise transfers between stores. Other types of calculated risks that could lower the effectiveness of inventory management are 1) the acceptance of customer merchandise returns without sales check, 2) no formal control of the issuance of sales and/or credit books, 3) prepayment of invoices to earn discounts and anticipations, and 4) skip-marking merchandise.

Merchandise Planning as a Management System

Management plans, organizes, and controls its human and nonhuman resources so as to produce the maximum value added to the goods and services that it offers. To carry this out, risks in the form of inputs are processed into the firm in order to reap long-run profits. The key nonhuman resource for the retail firm is the merchandise inventory. The best means for maximizing its usefulness is processing it through the use of the retail method of inventory. In this inventory system, gross margin, net profit, and inventory on hand can be determined easily and "on the spot" at any time during the year. In this way management can achieve an unparalleled means of merchandise control with minimum calculated risks.

As will be shown, the retail method of inventory is a total system of merchandise control through maintenance of perpetual inventories at retail. The mechanics of the retail method of inventory are detailed in the chapter on accounting and control.

Effect of Merchandise Planning on Productivity

Output per worker is one of the measures of productivity in any firm, achieved indirectly in retailing by the maximization of sales. Thus, sales increases represent the single most important means of increasing productivity in the retail firm. The incremental input per unit of labor becomes most significant when sales increases accompany the addition. Even where a full-service system of operation has been changed to either a self-service or a simplified selling system, resulting sales and productivity increases cannot be improved without an accompanying increase in the effectiveness of the total merchandising system.

The productivity in both marketing and retailing has not increased significantly in the last three decades, as shown in Table 26. Loss of sales from inappropriate or inadequate merchandise offerings directly affect the productivity of the total organization.

CONTROL PROCEDURES

Essentially, merchandise control may be carried out by either a dollar- or a unit-control system. Operational reappraisals are developed from weekly or monthly summaries of merchandise open-to-buy (OTB) reports. Many firms schedule such

TABLE 26

AVERAGE ANNUAL RATES OF LABOR PRODUCTIVITY CHANGES, 1929–1958

(All Industries, Goods-Producing Industries, Retail Trade, Wholesale Trade)

	OUTPUT, %	PERSONS ENGAGED, %	AVERAGE WEEKLY HOURS, %	OUTPUT PER PERSON ENGAGED, %	OUTPUT PER PERSON ENGAGED HOUR, %	OUTPUT PER WORKER,[a] %	OUTPUT PER WORKER HOUR, %
All Industries[b]	2.72	1.17	−0.75	1.55	2.30	——	——
Goods[b]	2.74	0.39	−0.49	2.35	2.84	——	——
Wholesale Trade[c]	3.11	2.05	−0.20	1.05	1.24	——	——
Retail Trade[c]	2.89	1.85	−0.32	1.03	1.35	1.11	1.43

[a] Workers include persons engaged plus unpaid family workers.
[b] From V. R. Fuchs, *Productivity Trends in the Goods and Service Sectors. 1929–1961: A Preliminary Survey*, Chaps. 2 and 3.
[c] Output and persons engaged from *Census of Business, 1930, 1958;* hours from *Census of Population, 1940, 1960*.
Source: David Schwartzman, *Some Tables from the Study of Productivity Growth in Distribution, 1929–1958*, National Bureau of Economic Research (New York: Columbia University Press, 1964).

reports to coincide with the turnover of the particular classifications handled. Where the retail firm is on a self-service or simplified selling basis, the control reports may coincide with changes of merchandise displays.

The merchandise OTB summary represents the merchandise needed until the next order is received; this forms the basic operational control factor. The sum of all departments' OTB represents the total amount of funds needed to carry out the firm's merchandising policies. The OTB is calculated as follows:

Total Merchandise Needed	Total Merchandise Available
Planned EOM (end-of-month) stock	Merchandise available BOM (beginning of month)
Planned sales for the period	Purchases to be delivered in current stock period
Planned markdowns	

Merchandise needed − Stock available = OTB (open-to-buy for the period)

The OTB has a flexible built-in policy permitting various methods of increasing or decreasing the "open" amounts. Some are positive methods, such as 1) realistic increases in planned sales, 2) reducing the stock on hand by valid returns to vendors or transfer-outs to other merchandise departments, 3) canceling outstanding orders, and 4) postponing delivery on outstanding orders to later periods.

Other methods of increasing the OTB may be opportunistic—such as attempts to cover errors in buying or planning. Unwarranted increases in planned markdowns or planned closing stocks would represent negative methods of obtaining additional OTB.

In all methods of merchandise control, a basic reserve of units must always be on hand at all times so that a minimum of sales will be lost because of inexact delivery schedules or unforeseen order delays. Most OTB plans are based on a system of maximums and minimums. A minimum stock is based on an "equal to" or a safety factor which insures an adequate selection of merchandise at all times. Or the "minimum" stock is based on a reserve which is calculated through an estimate of the number of weeks' supply needed on hand and the average delivery period of the particular merchandise category. Once the minimum has been determined, the frequency of reorder would depend on the predetermined maximum and the relationship between the reserve, the delivery period, and the reorder period. Expressed in equation form:

Maximum stock (in terms = Reserve factor (which must always be on hand)
    of week's supply)   + delivery period + reorder period (in terms of
                                     week's supply)
Then, Unit OTB = Maximum stock factor (in terms of week's supply)
                    (times) average weekly rate of sales

In a like manner, the development of the dollar OTB budget begins by multiplying the total number of units needed by the average price of the individual transactions. This method also furnishes the buyer indirectly with a unit OTB. The dollar-control system will be reviewed in conjunction with the development of the merchandise plan later in this chapter.

PLANNING THE MODEL STOCK

The basic purpose of a model stock plan is to be sure that the store gives the customer a suitable assortment of items in line with effective demand. In planning and formulating an optimum system, it is not only necessary to merchandise the product offerings within the store, but it is also necessary to merchandise the price lines themselves. Each merchandise classification can then be set up in a model stock plan.

In setting up a model stock plan, records of past seasons and results of the curent season to date, along with analyses of current consumer demand, are utilized. Merchandising a stock with the proper price lines for the most effective customer appeal within a trading area generally necessitates a minimum of three price lines within each major classification. An ideal system for a model stock along these guidelines is illustrated in Figure XVIII. The principles set up in this format have needed very little change over the years. In developing the merchandise plan and resulting model stocks, inventory is planned by classification so as to have the proper number of items at each price by material, size, and color in order to provide the basis for maximizing sales. Thus, a model stock represents the final planning budget of a unit control system by price lines and merchandise classification.

Stock, as well as information, is provided for by unit control systems. However, the amounts of stock are not necessarily proportionate to sales. More often than not, some merchandise offerings necessitate much larger assortments than would be warranted by their sales. For example, in furniture, occasional chairs selling at $59.50 would not require as large an assortment as women's coats or

FIGURE XVIII
MODEL STOCK PLAN*

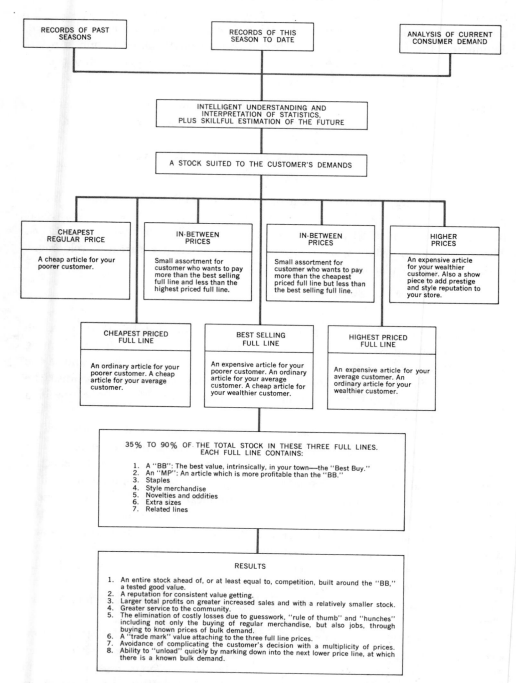

RECORDS OF PAST SEASONS

RECORDS OF THIS SEASON TO DATE

ANALYSIS OF CURRENT CONSUMER DEMAND

INTELLIGENT UNDERSTANDING AND INTERPRETATION OF STATISTICS, PLUS SKILLFUL ESTIMATION OF THE FUTURE

A STOCK SUITED TO THE CUSTOMER'S DEMANDS

CHEAPEST REGULAR PRICE

A cheap article for your poorer customer.

IN-BETWEEN PRICES

Small assortment for customer who wants to pay more than the best selling full line and less than the highest priced full line.

IN-BETWEEN PRICES

Small assortment for customer who wants to pay more than the cheapest priced full line but less than the best selling full line.

HIGHER PRICES

An expensive article for your wealthier customer. Also a show piece to add prestige and style reputation to your store.

CHEAPEST PRICED FULL LINE

An ordinary article for your poorer customer. A cheap article for your average customer.

BEST SELLING FULL LINE

An expensive article for your poorer customer. An ordinary article for your average customer. A cheap article for your wealthier customer.

HIGHEST PRICED FULL LINE

An expensive article for your average customer. An ordinary article for your wealthier customer.

35% TO 90% OF THE TOTAL STOCK IN THESE THREE FULL LINES. EACH FULL LINE CONTAINS:

1. A "BB": The best value, intrinsically, in your town——the "Best Buy."
2. An "MP": An article which is more profitable than the "BB."
3. Staples
4. Style merchandise
5. Novelties and oddities
6. Extra sizes
7. Related lines

RESULTS

1. An entire stock ahead of, or at least equal to, competition, built around the "BB," a tested good value.
2. A reputation for consistent value getting.
3. Larger total profits on greater increased sales and with a relatively smaller stock.
4. Greater service to the community.
5. The elimination of costly losses due to guesswork, "rule of thumb" and "hunches" including not only the buying of regular merchandise, but also jobs, through buying to known prices of bulk demand.
6. A "trade mark" value attaching to the three full line prices.
7. Avoidance of complicating the customer's decision with a multiplicity of prices.
8. Ability to "unload" quickly by marking down into the next lower price line, at which there is a known bulk demand.

* Source: Edward A. Filene, *More Profits from Merchandising* (New York, A. W. Shaw, 1927), pp. 152–153.

suits selling at the same price and generating the same volume. In the latter case, size, fit, and color would all be inventory and buying considerations and samples would not suffice.

In the case of staple merchandise, the maintenance of a model stock merely involves keeping of unit inventory up to a required plan. Periodic reorder times would depend on a predetermined reorder-point minimum; as pointed out above, this minimum would depend on the average rate of sale and the delivery and reorder periods. The model stock in such cases merely requires a review of current trends for adjustments.

The important underlying consideration in merchandising any price line is that each item carried for sale is regarded differently by various customers. For example, the middle-price full line as shown in Figure XVIII should represent the best-selling price line; at the same time, this middle-price range would represent an average price line for the average customer, an expensive line for the lower-income customer, and an inexpensive article for the store's high-income customer. The objective of merchandising the offers of the store is to price the merchandise at the most popular price ranges for the store's middle majority group, or for approximately 65 to 70 per cent of all of the store's potential customers in a trading area.

THE MERCHANDISE PLAN—PRELIMINARY CONSIDERATIONS

Regardless of the merchandise and operating-control systems in a store, merchandise plans must be based on a realistic sales forecast. This, in turn, must be based on an understanding of the economics of the trading area and its customers—what they are willing to accept in the way of goods and services and where and how they are willing to buy them.

Retailers as well as manufacturers must thoroughly understand the "whys" of changing customer demands as these changes directly affect the regional production-consumption functions. The forecast enables the merchandise manager to make effective purchase allocations among durable goods, nondurable goods, and services. Decisions based on local economic analysis tend to be more effective. The divisional merchandise managers must also go one step farther within the firm; they must allocate OTB among the much narrower breakdowns of departments and specific merchandise line categories. The buyer, in turn, has to make similar decisions regarding the forecast demand for the classifications that make up his department's merchandise lines.

A dynamic programing output model provides the department manager or buyer with expected sales and average inventory for the planning period. It is then management's problem to allocate the total sales to the various months, calculate the desired inventory levels for each month, and plan departmental purchases. The buyer is expected to adjust to changes in sales volume in such a way as to maintain the desired inventories. The technique for carrying this out is called a merchandise plan; in some cases rigid mathematical methods are used. Both techniques are illustrated in this chapter.

The Economics of Cost-Price Analysis

Prior to pricing, the first step is to know the general economic analysis of the cost structure of the firm. A visual diagram can be set up to represent cost structure. In Figure XIX the firm receives P for each unit it sells and can sell all the units it buys or produces. The cost function is U-shaped. The rise at the left results from a constant fixed cost allocated to fewer sales units. The rise at the right of the diagram is the result of the law of diminishing returns or to the institutionalization of cost over time, due to built-in rigidities which accompany age in most firms.

FIGURE XIX
MARGINAL ANALYSIS OF A FIRM'S COST-PRICE STRUCTURE

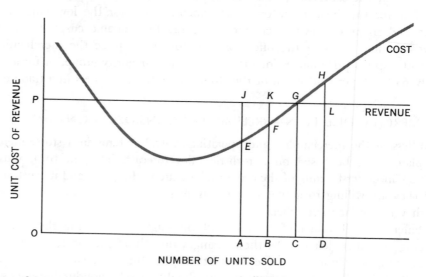

From this graph it can be seen that selling B units is more profitable than merely selling A units. In fact, the increased profit is the area $EFJK$. Similarly, the sale of C units is more desirable than B. Note that the two curves cross A when sales are equal to C. Any increase in sales above C results in a decrease in profits, as in the triangle GHL. This is exactly what happens when a "profit squeeze" occurs—when additional volume is secured but only at decreased profit.

Thus, in any plan to maximize profits, sales must be increased to the point at which the unit cost equals the unit revenues. This point is determined by the best combination of total fixed costs matched to various scales of variable costs.

Dynamic Inventory Programing for Determining Optimum Scale

This is best carried out by testing data to a dynamic programing output model to determine the most profitable inventory level. The following is a model from which to start:

Inventory	Profit	Incremental Profit
$125,000	$20,000	$2,000
130,000	22,000	1,000
135,000	23,000	500
140,000	23,500	300
145,000	23,800	200
150,000	24,000	

The selection of an optimum inventory level depends to a great extent on the cost of maintaining an inventory. If the inventory carrying costs are 8 per cent of the retail value, then it would cost $400 to carry an additional $5,000 in inventory. An increase in total profit will result as long as the incremental profit is above $400, the incremental cost. In this case, the optimum inventory is found to be $140,000.

For example, a shoe department intends to carry an adequate inventory in all sizes stocked, but wishes to stock only those sizes that are profitable. Obviously, some index of profitability must be generated.

Let $\triangle S_k$ = expected sales of a given size k
M_k = markup anticipated on size k
a_k = variable sales expense rate on size k
r = inventory storage expense rate
$\triangle I_k$ = inventory of size k required

If size k is stocked, contributed profits, P, can be increased by

$$\underset{\text{(gross profit)}}{\triangle P = M_k \triangle S_k} - \underset{\substack{\text{(selling} \\ \text{expense)}}}{a_k \triangle S_k} - \underset{\substack{\text{(inventory} \\ \text{expense)}}}{r \triangle I_k}$$

Size k should be stocked if $\triangle P$ defined above is positive. Therefore,

$$(M_k - a_k) \triangle S_k - r \triangle I_k \geq 0$$
$$(M_k - a_k) \triangle S_k \geq r \triangle I_k$$
$$\frac{\triangle S_k}{\triangle I_k} \geq \frac{r}{M_k - a_k}$$

If the last relationship is satisfied, size k should be stocked.

In addition, if the model levels to the decision not to stock, it is possible to compute the minimum markup required to stock that size profitably:

$$M_k \geq r \frac{\triangle I_k}{\triangle S_k} + a_k$$

The above is a quantitative approach suitable for machine solution; the more comprehensive and general merchandise plan approach follows.

THE MERCHANDISE PLAN—PROCEDURES

The merchandise plan represents a coordinated approach to a dollar-control budget of merchandise inventories, generally for a six-month or annual period. Once the period of time involved is determined, it is then subdivided into weeks or months. In shopping and specialty-goods stores the plan usually covers two time periods: February 1 through July 31, and August 1 through January 31. The termination dates are when inventories are generally at their lowest and the firm's cash position at its highest. This facilitates the taking of physical inventories and insures a more accurate planning of OTB purchases. In addition, the seasonal pattern of merchandise transitions usually takes place at these times, i.e., from winter merchandise to spring, and summer goods to those needed for fall. The beginning and termination dates as well as the actual time periods involved in the merchandise plan may vary depending on the kinds of goods handled.

Nature of Plan

More specifically, the merchandise plan is a budgetary method for the coordination of sales, stocks, purchases, markup, and markdowns. The plan may also include controllable expenses such as selling salaries and advertising, alteration expenses, and initially maintained and net-profit goals. In fact, any facet of the departmental operation may be included. A general format and layout of a merchandise plan is shown in Table 27 (p. 303).

While the forms and specific inclusions may vary from one organization to another, the principles and methods used are generally similar. The forecast average sales and number of transactions are also included.

In general, the over-all merchandise plan for the store is the result of the sum of coordinated plans set up by the merchandise manager and controller in conjunction with the individual department buyers. The departmental merchandise plan for the buyer is likewise the result of a series of individual merchandise plans made up for each of a selling department's merchandise classifications.

Planning Procedures

As pointed out, the initial entries in any merchandise plan begin with an estimate of sales and a net-profit goal for the coming period. The total estimated operating expense dollars are subtracted from the gross margin dollars to arrive at the net profit in dollars and per cent for the period.

Maintained markup is that markup or margin difference resulting between the actual cost and the selling price of any merchandise. The net differences between the maintained markup and gross margin of a department or firm represent the nonoperating facets of the merchandising cycles. Gross margin is used more often in connection with the firm as a whole. Maintained markup includes all prior provisions for markdowns, shortages, and employee discounts. Thus, the gross-margin figure includes *all* operating and nonoperating facets of the department or the firm. The gross margin is derived by adjusting the maintained markup for nonoperating income and expense, such as discounts from vendors and workroom costs.

Determining Initial Markup

These maintained markup figures as objectives of the firm cannot be generated unless a sufficiently high initial mark-on is placed on incoming inventories. This means that the price setter must have a thorough knowledge of the inventory-to-sales processes and the accompanying shrinkages to margins. Planning for these attritions must include estimates for markdowns, shortages, breakage, shrinkage, and obsolescence. Once these are estimated, an initial mark-on requirement can be calculated.

In order to calculate this, estimates of the total markdowns, employee discounts, stock shortages, and planned net-profit percentages must be made. This means that the initial selling price must be large enough to cover all operating expenses and profit, as exemplified in the following estimated margin percentages to be covered:

Planning Considerations	Per Cent
Net profit	4
Stock shortages	1
Cash discounts, employees	2
Markdowns	7
Operating expenses	30
	44

As initial markup is always based on the original selling price of the merchandise inventory *before* markdowns, shrinkages, shortages, and discounts to employees, 100 per cent would always represent the final, actual selling price of the merchandise classification being priced. The original 44 per cent needed for planned coverage must therefore be applied to a base greater than a 100 per cent figure, which represents the final sales figure *after* markdown, shrinkage, shortages, etc., have been taken. Thus, the original selling price of the inventory must be 100 per cent plus all planned reductions. In this case, it would include the following planned figures:

markdowns 7%,
cash discounts to employees 2%, and
stock shortages 1%; or 100% + 10% = 110%.

$$\therefore \text{IM} = \frac{44\% \text{ (operating expenses, profit, \& retail reductions)}}{110\% \text{ (100\% + retail reductions)}},$$
or 40%; and
40 per cent becomes the average initial markup (IM) for the period.

Once this initial markup has been determined, its cost complement is determined by subtracting the markup from 100 per cent. In this case, the cost complement is 60 per cent (100 − 40). This means that the cost of the inventory will average 60 per cent of the selling price during the season.

Every markdown and retail reduction or loss actually consists of two elements: a markdown portion and a cost portion. In this case, the 10 per cent retail reduction will result in only a 60 per cent reduction in margin, as no loss occurs on the markup portion of the selling price or markdown for the

10% retail reduction	markup portion	40%
	cost portion	60%

Thus, to the 40 per cent initial markup only a 6 per cent loss in markup would occur, and 34 per cent (40 − 6) maintained markup on sales results. With a 30 per cent operating expense ratio, a 4 per cent net profit (34 − 30) would result.

STRATEGIC CONSIDERATIONS

The planned markup and turnover goals are formulated in conjunction with re-appraisal of the results of prior years. If the planned original markup and turn-over goals of prior years were not met, why were they not met? Were they realistically planned? Were internal operations consistent? Did bad buys or over-buying occur? Or were the goals limited by external factors such as new competitive policies by existing firms or new competitors? If the reasons cannot be pinpointed, then a complete review of merchandising and sales policies might be in order. On the other hand, if failure to achieve gross margin and turnover goals was due to unpredictable events such as fire, earthquakes, floods, and so on, then are existing policies still valid? Are improvements possible?

Thus, planning takes on many facets. Five-year trend analyses of all variables can often bring out new considerations. Also, pricing and merchandising executives are strongly influenced by trade association data for prior years and Dun & Bradstreet figures, with slight adjustments in the light of local competitive conditions. For example, the smaller the trading area and the greater the degree of competition, the larger the inventories needed.

Responsibility for developing and carrying out the merchandise plan is ultimately that of the merchandise manager. At the same time, the buyer has operating accountability for the attainment of the sales, markup, inventory, and turnover goals.

THE TECHNIQUES OF MERCHANDISE PLANNING

In developing a departmental merchandise plan, the various classifications carried in the department are first divided into needed assortments. For example, a line of merchandise such as men's and boys' shoes and slippers can be broken down to delineate boys' loafers, scout shoes, oxfords, etc., and men's dress, sport, casual, and athletic footwear, moccasins, riding boots, sandals, ski boots, etc. Regardless of the merchandise line—sporting goods, appliances, furniture, or coats—the same principles apply. And the basic stock contains any item that a customer has the right to expect to find whenever he comes into a department. The price lines chosen are the heart of the stock in the department. The price lines must have sufficient dollar differences between them, the difference being larger as the price increases. This tells the customer that there is a difference in intrinsic value between the merchandise lines.

The total dollar value of basic stock should be less than the total dollar allocation for the smallest month. This allows for prestige, promotional, and fill-in merchandise, should it be needed. In the case of lingerie, a fashion item, outstanding and timely styles, colors and materials might be needed. Fashion information from lingerie manufacturers, central buying offices, and New York market trips have to be supplemented by new suggestions from *Women's Wear Daily*, *Harper's Bazaar*, *Vogue*, *Seventeen*, etc. In other merchandise areas, pertinent trade journals along with manufacturers and salesmen supply information on market novelties.

The lingerie department of a department store generating more than $50 million a year will illustrate merchandise planning. The department's volume approximates $1.5 million annually and is made up of six classifications: slips, petticoats, gowns, pajamas, gown and robe sets, and panties and small items. The developing plan follows:

The Initial Breakdown

The most important aspect of any merchandise plan is the breakdown of each department's needs by classifications. In the selected lingerie department the classifications may be broken down as follows for the planned six-month period from February through July 1967:

Sales Apportioned to Classifications (Lingerie Department)

Classification	% of Sales	$ Sales
1. Slips	30	216,600
2. Petticoats	20	144,400
3. Gowns	25	180,500
4. Pajamas	8	57,700
5. Gown and Robe Sets	4	28,900
6. Panties and Small Items	13	93,800
		$721,900 (approx.)

This is further broken down by sales estimates by months, as follows:

	February	March	April	May	June	July		Total
1.	$ 26,900	$ 33,600	$ 33,100	$ 45,000	$ 47,700	$ 30,300	=	$216,600
2.	17,900	22,400	22,100	30,000	31,800	20,200	=	144,400
3.	22,400	28,000	27,600	37,500	39,700	25,300	=	180,500
4.	7,200	8,900	8,800	12,000	12,700	8,100	=	57,700
5.	3,600	4,500	4,400	6,000	6,400	4,000	=	28,900
6.	11,500	14,500	14,400	19,700	20,500	13,200	=	93,800
	$ 89,500	$111,900	$110,400	$150,200	$158,800	$101,100	=	$721,900 (approx.)

Justification for Data Breakdown. The above classifications of merchandise have been broken down as to percentage of sales that each contributes. Previous percentages are about the same as those given in each class except for one classification, petticoats. This classification is estimated to contribute 20 per cent of the total lingerie sales volume because of the tremendous increase in petticoat sales over the past decade. With new patterns in all new colors and print designs, petticoat sales are estimated to increase to over 18 per cent proportionate sales of the current year; also, special promotions, color newspaper advertising, and a large floor area given to the display of petticoats should increase sales for the spring season. This firm is also known for its complete sizes in staples and latest fashions. The peak month for slips and petticoats is generally June.

Division of Planned Markdowns

Estimated markdowns for the merchandise plan can be set up along the following general lines:

Markdowns	% Sales	% Markdowns	$ Markdown Total
1. Slips	30	35	$12,600
2. Petticoats	20	22	8,000
3. Gowns	25	25	9,000
4. Pajamas	8	6.8	2,500
5. Gown and Robe Sets	4	3.7	1,300
6. Panties	13	7.5	2,700
	100%	100.0%	$36,100 (approx.)

Markdown by Months and Classifications

	February	March	April	May	June	July	Total
1.	$2,300	$1,500	$2,300	$1,300	$2,000	$3,300	$12,700
2.	1,400	1,000	1,400	800	1,300	2,100	8,000
3.	1,600	1,100	1,600	900	1,500	2,300	9,000
4.	500	200	500	200	400	700	2,500
5.	200	200	200	100	200	300	1,200
6.	500	300	500	300	400	700	2,700
	$6,500	$4,300	$6,500	$3,600	$5,800	$9,400	$36,100

Sales	$721,900
Markdowns	$ 36,100
Markdown %	5%

Justification. Markdowns in this example total 5 per cent of sales. The peak month for markdowns in this case would be July at 26 per cent. That is because July is the last month of the season and all new stock received for the spring season that has not sold will be marked down. Also, July is generally a slow month, and markdowns increase as business decreases. A comparison with (typical) MOR standards will appear as follows:

MOR Figures for Department Stores over $50 Million Volume

	Markup	Typical	Markdown	Typical	Gross Margin	Typical
1966	37.7–39.0	38.3	3.6–5.4	4.8	38.4–39.4	39.3
1967	37.9–38.9	38.3	3.4–5.7	4.8	38.5–39.9	39.3

	Stock Shortages	Cash Discounts	Workroom Cost
1966	1.1	4.9	0.1
1967	1.2	5.0	0.2

Planning the Open-to-Buy (OTB) Requirements

Open-to-buy and planned purchases represent the amount of merchandise that should be received into the store during the stipulated buying period. The planned purchases should be sufficient to supply the stock needs not already provided for as of the beginning of any particular month. Also, the buyer must be able to determine his OTB at any time during the month. Naturally, outstanding orders and purchases during the month reduce the OTB. In this case, let us assume that the basic stock method for computing the OTB is used. The formulas that can be used in computing the OTB are:

BOM Stock = Sales for the Month + (Average Stock for Season − Average Monthly Sales).

$$\text{Average Stock for the Season} = \frac{\text{Sales for the Season}}{\text{Stock Turnover for the Season}}.$$

Basic Stock = Average Stock for Season − Average Monthly Sales.

EOM = BOM for following month.

Ending Stock July 31st = (7 × Actual Average for Season − Total BOM for the Season).

(OTB) Planned Purchases = Sales + EOM Inventory + Markdowns = BOM Inventory.

Stock Turnover: 2.2 times
Initial Markup: 38.6 per cent
Average Stock: $98,500 (approx.)
Basic Stock: $62,400

The OTB is then calculated for each of the merchandise classifications that make up the department. The computational data needed are illustrated below for the slip classification within the lingerie department:

Slips

Month	Sales	BOM	EOM	Markdowns	Planned Purchases Retail	Cost
Feb.	$ 26,900	$ 89,300	$ 96,000	$ 2,300	$ 35,900	$ 22,000
March	33,600	96,000	95,500	1,500	34,600	21,200
April	33,100	95,500	107,400	2,300	47,300	29,000
May	45,000	107,400	110,100	1,300	49,000	30,200
June	47,700	110,100	96,700	2,000	36,300	22,300
July	30,300	96,700	94,200	3,300	31,100	19,100
Totals	$216,600	$595,000	$599,900	$12,700	$234,200	$143,800

Data Justification

The department does an excellent slip business and therefore, a markup of 38.6 per cent is established. Competition is strong in the city on slips. A turnover of 2.2 is adequate to maintain a good profit through maximum sales and a minimum of investment.

In each classification, the initial markup, the average stock, the basic stock, and the stock turnover are computed. Only the total average data will appear on the merchandise plan for the department for control and reappraisal by the divisional merchandise managers. Similarly, a division's merchandise plan would consist of the total plans developed for each of its departments. The combination of all these plans thus becomes the blueprint for the line operation of the firm.

Sales by price lines and units are also important considerations in the over-all plan. In the lingerie department, the basic price lines could be $4, $6, and $9, with variations of the $6 basic line going as high as $8, and that of the $9 retail price having a variation of $3, or a high of $15 for the normal selling seasons. Further division in this case is made of styles, colors, materials or set up within the framework of the plan. The merchandise plan for this lingerie department appears in Table 27.

RESTATING THE MERCHANDISE PLAN

The Quantitative Approaches

In the realm of the newer business theories, quantitative approaches, such as mathematical programing, have had a great deal of impact on traditional marginal analysis. The principles of linear programing are similar to those used in marginal economics but much more useful if the data are set up for programing into a computer. For example, in a mathematical programing approach for planning and control of merchandise inventories, a combination of matrix algebra and a computer can be used.

Originally, marginal analysis was used to determine the optimum size of a firm under conditions of perfect knowledge and perfect competition with a goal of marginal revenues equal to marginal costs. Today, marginal analysis revolves primarily around the factors of present values and discounted cash-flow "rates of return" on investment; it is used to a great extent in capital budgeting.

In seeking solutions to merchandise planning and control through a more mathematical framework, a systems concept can be used. Some of the concepts involved in the quantification of data follow:

Estimating Required Profit Goal

Let S = expected sales volume
C = expected costs
P = desired profit

Then, minimum markup $(\%) = \dfrac{C + P}{S} \times 100$

Example: A department expects to sell $350,000 worth of merchandise during the

TABLE 27

MERCHANDISE PLAN, LINGERIE DEPARTMENT

DEPT.: LINGERIE		No.: 100		FROM: FEBRUARY 1967 TO JULY 1967			
% of Initial Markup		39.01		% of Workroom Costs		0.1	
of Markdowns		5.0		of Maintained Markup		35.96	
of Cash Discounts		3.9		of Gross Margin		38.86	
of Shortages		0.9		Turnover (season)	1.950		

SPRING	FEBRUARY	MARCH	APRIL	MAY	JUNE	JULY	TOTAL
Sales							
Planned	$ 89,500	$111,900	$110,400	$150,200	$158,900	$101,100	$722,000
Revised							
Actual							
BOM							
Planned	337,300	369,700	368,200	408,000	416,500	366,900	2,266,600 (Average Stock, $377,766)
Revised							
Actual							
EOM							
Planned	369,700	368,200	408,000	415,900	366,900	379,700	2,308,400 (Average Stock, $384,733)
Revised							
Actual							
Markdowns							
Planned	6,500	4,300	6,500	3,600	5,800	9,400	36,100
Revised							
Actual							
Retail Purchases							
Planned	128,400	114,700	156,700	161,700	114,900	123,300	799,700
Revised							
Actual							
Cost Purchases							
Planned	78,100	69,900	95,600	98,800	70,200	75,100	487,700
Revised							
Actual							

selling season. Operating costs, including space, utilities, sales force, and advertising, but excluding cost of goods, are expected to be $120,000. Management desires 8 per cent return on sales.

$$S = \$350,000$$
$$C = \$120,000$$
$$P = (.08)(\$350,000) = \$28,000$$

Therefore, minimum markup $= \dfrac{\$120,000 + \$28,000}{\$350,000} \times 100 = 42.3\%$

Regarding the basic break-even point calculations in the same vein, the following can be applied:

Let S' = minimum expected sales volume

C = expected cost

Then, minimum markup $(\%) = \dfrac{100C}{S'}$

Example: Although the department in the previous example expects to sell $350,-

000 worth of merchandise, if there is a downturn in the regional economy sales may only reach the $300,000 level. In this event, there will be no opportunity to reduce costs in proportion, since they are fixed in the short run. In order to break even, the minimum markup should be

$$\frac{\$120,000 \times 100}{\$300,000} = 40\%.$$

Should analysis of the competitive situation show that the maximum markup to be considered would be greater than the minimum allowed, the problem then becomes one of setting initial and sustained (maintained) markups such that

$Mmin \leq Msustained \leq Minitial \leq Mmax$,

where $Mmin$ = minimum markup

$Msustained$ = sustained markup

$Minitial$ = initial markup

$Mmax$ = maximum markup.

The difference between initial and sustained markup represents markdowns. Experience provides a satisfactory estimate of R, the per-cent markdowns. Therefore, the problem becomes one of selecting Minitial, subject to the restrictions

$Minitial \geq Mmin + R$

$Minitial \leq Mmax$

While the above is set up in algebraic and, therefore, quantitative terms, only a systems concept would find such calculations economically useful.

The marginal analysis approach given in the first part of the chapter would, of course, be much more useful for most practitioners and students in the field; especially where an EDP system is not available. Because of the increasing impact of computer technology, the above type of analysis is becoming more important.

Continuing the estimate with respect to the turnover criteria: The firm attempts to allocate its scarce resources in such a way as to maximize profits; this necessitates turnover to sales volume as the most important factor in optimizing profits; this means strict inventory planning.

The problem is defined as:

(Turnover) = (Sales) ÷ (Average Inventory at Retail)

From this it can be defined that the retailer's goal is to maximize turnover; yet, too high a turnover can result in stock-outs and lost sales.

Therefore the retailer sets turnover goals based on composite industry figures such as the "typical" statistics of the MOR of the NRMA. Since retail managers set their own goals on how to be best, this means striving to be at least "typical" within the mid-quartile range of data. By using high-speed computers and mathematical programing to handle various sets of results, depending on choices of inventory assortments, management hopes to optimize resource allocation and long-run profits.

Dynamic Programing

This is a mathematical technique for the solution of multistage decision processes. In such processes economic resources are allocated to activities so as to maximize total return.

Prior to dynamic programing models, seeking an optimum approach required the testing of various types of combinations. However, even consideration of ten alternatives per stage in a four-stage process would mean the evaluation of 10,000 combinations. A ten-stage process would require so many combinations that, if 10 combinations per second could be evaluated, it would take more than 30 years to find an answer.

Dynamic programing reduces the merchandise planning problem to a linear one. Thus, for the first time, multistage problems can be solved economically. The solution for each stage depends on the results at the previous stage, as is shown in the following table:

Resources at Stage N	Return from Stage N	Resources at Previous Stage	Return at Previous Stage	Total Resources	Total Return
$800	$900	$10,400	$14,900	$11,200	$15,800
700	880	10,500	15,000	11,200	15,880
600	850	10,600	15,100	11,200	15,950
500	800	10,700	15,200	11,200	16,000
400	700	10,800	15,295	11,200	15,995
300	600	10,900	15,385	11,200	15,985
200	300	11,000	15,475	11,200	15,775
100	100	11,100	15,550	11,200	15,650
0	0	11,200	15,600	11,200	15,600

From this analysis, it can be seen that the most effective use of $11,200 in resources is to allocate $500 to Stage N and $10,700 to previous stages.

In order to apply dynamic programing to determine the optimum allocation of inventories, the relationship between inventory in a given department and the resultant sales and profits must be calculated.

But a relationship of this kind cannot be determined experimentally because the uncontrolled variables cannot be held constant. Therefore, the relationship between sales and inventory would exhibit the following characteristics:

1) at relatively low inventory levels, turnover will be low because sales are low. This is due to inefficiencies inherent in maintaining an inadequate inventory;

2) turnover will increase up to a maximum value even as inventories increase because sales would tend to increase also;

3) at relatively high inventory levels, turnover will again decrease as the "law of diminishing returns" takes effect.

This relationship is illustrated by the following graph:

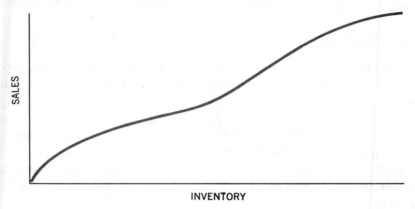

In order to represent such a relationship, Bellman and Dreyfus [1] propose the following mathematical function:

$$R(x) = V[1 - (1 - e^{-a/x})^x], \text{ where}$$

x = resources expended
$R(x)$ = return on resources expended
V = maximum potential return
a = scale factor reflecting level of competition
e = base of natural logarithms $(2.718\ldots)$.

This function can be used as a model to predict the effect of inventory level on sales or gross profit. We know the following:

x = current inventory level
$R(x)$ = present return
V = estimated maximum return.

From these we can compute the scale factor (a) using the formula

$$a = -x - (1 - \frac{R(x)}{V})^{1/x}.$$

Since our goal is to maximize profits, the first step is to define:

$$R(x) = MM(\text{sustained}) \times S(x), \text{ where}$$

$MM(\text{sustained})$ = sustained markup
$S(x)$ = sales volume (\$) generated by \$x in inventory.

Policy may require the allocation to maintain a minimum inventory in each department: profit maximization may not coincide with the full-service store concept.

---

[1] Richard Bellman and S. Dreyfus, *Applied Dynamic Programming* (Princeton, N.J.: Princeton University Press, 1962).

The data required for the computer program would be as follows:

> Department Identification
> Minimum Inventory Value
> Present Inventory Value
> Present Sales Volume
> Potential Sales Volume
> Sustained Markup (Maintained)

The output would contain the optimum allocation of inventory for each value of total inventory, along with the resultant sales and gross profit figures.

Thus, the technique of economic analysis would also be needed to find the level of total inventory which maximizes profits.

QUANTITATIVE INVENTORY PLANNING AND CONTROL

A periodic physical count of inventories is a prerequisite to inventory planning, because: 1) the buyer must know his current inventory in order to adjust his proposed purchases to the merchandise plan; 2) it is necessary in management's evaluation of the effectiveness of a given operation; and 3) it is required for various accounting purposes.

Since inventory figures may often be required on a weekly or monthly basis, a book inventory is used, as a physical inventory count would be prohibitively expensive.

The retail method of inventory system can be used. Again, this is based upon the mathematical relationship of:

Ending Inventory = Beginning Inventory + Purchases − (Sales + Markdowns)

Losses due to markdowns, shrinkages, and discounts are easily computed. Losses due to shortages show up when the annual or semiannual physical inventory is taken. The difference between the ending book and physical inventories represents the shortages.

Inventories may be expressed in any of the following units:

> Dollars at retail price
> Dollars at lower of cost or market
> (Under the retail method, multiplying the ending physical
>   inventory at retail by the reciprocal of the initial
>   markup gives the same result.)

Inventory expressed in terms of item count is of little value either to management or to the accountant, since this means adding apples and oranges. Such an inventory is, however, of considerable value to the buyer in planning new purchases or marking down slow-moving goods.

SUMMARY AND CONCLUSIONS

In this chapter, methods used in the planning and control of merchandise inventories were analyzed and reviewed from the standpoint of the line operation of the firm. Both a merchandise system based on easy-to-grasp marginal analysis and a system based on quantitative methods were analyzed and detailed. The variations in stock buying, merchandising, and control were also analyzed from the standpoints of all sizes and kinds of firms.

Within the framework of planning and control of pricing, sales, and merchandise inventories, the merchandise plan was shown as the key planning document in the operation of a mercantile firm.

Part Six

The Framework for Communications and Sales

Chapter 21: *Publicity and Market Management*

The publicity division in the retail firm acts in a staff capacity to the merchandising division and in a line capacity in setting the over-all sales promotion policies of the firm. The final links in the promotional process, personal selling, and customer service policies are also within the purview of the publicity division.

Publicity management includes all the activities of the firm involving and influencing its public image externally and its private image internally. More specifically, the function "can be defined as any form (paid-for or free) of nonpersonal presentation of the facts about goods, services, or ideas—or of the goods themselves—to a group." It includes advertising, display, the special-purpose publicity —all of which are methods of presentation that do not involve individual, personal contacts with customers.[1] The publicity director generates the creation of time, place, and possession utilities by coordinating and directing the activities involved in stimulating goodwill and getting goods into the hands of the ultimate consumer. The functional responsibilities of the publicity division are illustrated in Figure XX.

[1] Charles M. Edwards Jr., and R. A. Brown, *Retail Advertising and Sales Promotion* (Englewood Cliffs, N.J.: Prentice-Hall, 1959). See also pp. 43–47.

FIGURE XX
The Publicity Division Model

Functional Management Within the Retail Organization *

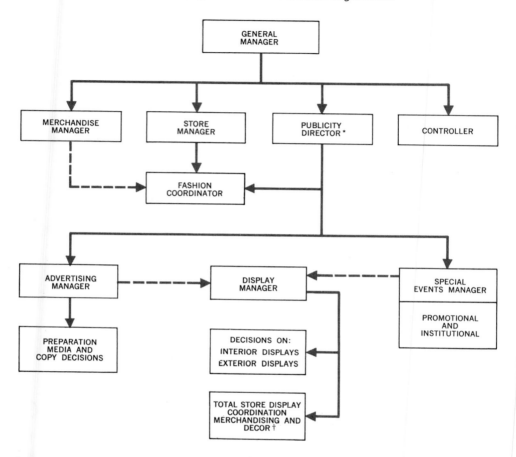

* THE PUBLICITY DIRECTOR IN MANY INSTANCES MAY REPORT DIRECTLY TO THE GENERAL MERCHANDISE MANAGER, IN WHICH CASE HIS RANK AND IMPORTANCE WOULD APPROXIMATE THAT OF A DIVISIONAL MERCHANDISE MANAGER.

† (A) EVALUATE AND PROMOTE FIRM FROM CUSTOMER'S POINT OF VIEW.
(B) INITIATE, CARRY OUT, AND EVALUATE SALES EVENTS.
(C) COORDINATE PRESENTATIONS AND PROMOTIONAL WANTS OF MERCHANDISING DIVISIONS.
(D) PRESENT STORE POLICIES AND SERVICES IN ORDER TO BRING CUSTOMERS INTO THE STORE IN A RECEPTIVE MOOD FOR BUYING.

Thus the publicity division is in reality the organizational vehicle for retention and expansion of the market share of the retail firm. By determining the manner in which each advertising dollar is allocated, the publicity manager is responsible for the total store image and its impact on encompassing trade areas. The director is generally a divisional vice-president of the organization. And so publicity and public relations are in reality part of the marketing management activities of the firm. As such, the division is responsible for the allocation of relatively limited publicity dollars among hosts of various media; the expenditures are critical, and will become even more so because markets are becoming more segmented in character, thus forcing a larger spread for expenditures. For example, it was estimated that by the end of 1965

> ...72% of the total population or 141,915,900 will be living in metro areas. Even more important, 80% of the country's buying power, or $350 billion, will be represented in these markets. And 76% of consumer spending in retail outlets will be done in metro territories ...[2]

This means that the publicity director must create demand for literally hundreds of merchandise classifications and price ranges in ever-widening markets. In many cases, buying attitudes will have to be aggregated with more current data in order to project the firm's marketing strategies.

Advertising procedure is provided for in the publicity budget. In determining the amount of expenditures to be allocated to the publicity budget, the age of the store, its size, its merchandising policies, location of the store, size of trading area, competition, and costs of various media are all considered. Generally, past experience and business conditions form a standard of comparison. Naturally, stores want to maximize their output per dollar expenditure.

IMPORTANCE OF MERCHANDISE LINES HANDLED

The merchandise lines and classifications offered by a store underlie its promotional policies. For example, the tremendous range and importance of merchandise offers are clearly illustrated in Table 28, which lists the changes in sales of department-store merchandise line classifications. The illustration shows data from the Fourth Federal Reserve District. The merchandise lines and classifications depicted here clearly illustrate the inter and intra merchandise line competition that exists and which should be analyzed on a trading area basis. In developing standards and goals for measuring sales performances, the means for re-emphasizing the store image as well as its promotional policies is clearly indicated.

For example, in the case of high-priced specialty shops such as Saks Fifth Avenue or Bergdorf Goodman, their publicity approaches through advertising, copy appeal, and layout differ markedly from those of popular-priced dress shops such as Lerner's or Three Sisters. This copy would differ even more from supermarket advertising, which utilizes a minimum of sales promotion activities from a publicity division standpoint. Very little (if any) white space would appear in the latter's advertising.

PUBLICITY BUDGET

It is clear that the store image and its controlling factor, the publicity division, touches on every facet of store operation. Through the use of the publicity budget, advertising is planned along with and in much the same fashion as sales. Once a sales budget is forecast for a six-, nine-, and twelve-month period, a proposed

---

[2] "Metropolitan Area Projections—1965," *Sales Management*, November 10, 1964, p. 163.

TABLE 28
Department Store Sales and Stocks by Departments
(Fourth Federal Reserve District, Year Ended January 1965)

DEPARTMENT	SALES	STOCKS [1]
11 SILKS, VELVETS, AND SYNTHETICS	+ 3	
12 WOOLEN YARD GOODS	- 5	
13 COTTON YARD GOODS (Including linings)	- 5	
11-13 PIECE GOODS	- 1	
14 LINENS (Including towels)	+ 6	
15 DOMESTICS (Muslins, Sheetings)	+10	
18 BLANKETS, COMFORTERS, AND SPREADS	+ 5	
14-18 HOUSEHOLD TEXTILES	+ 6	
1X PIECE GOODS AND TEXTILES NOT REPORTED SEPARATELY	- 1	
10. PIECE GOODS AND HOUSEHOLD TEXTILES	+ 4	
21 LACES, TRIMMINGS, EMBROIDERIES, AND RIBBONS	+13	
23 NOTIONS	+ 5	
24 TOILET ARTICLES AND DRUG SUNDRIES (Excl. prescriptions)	+ 9	
25S SILVERWARE AND CLOCKS	+10	
25C COSTUME JEWELRY	+ 3	
25F FINE JEWELRY AND WATCHES	+ 4	
25 SILVERWARE AND JEWELRY	+ 5	
27 ART NEEDLEWORK (Excluding artists' supplies)	- 2	
28B BOOKS AND MAGAZINES	+ 9	
28S STATIONERY	+ 9	
28 BOOKS AND STATIONERY	+ 9	
2X SMALL WARES NOT REPORTED SEPARATELY	+16	
20. SMALL WARES	+ 8	
31 NECKWEAR AND SCARFS	+ 6	
33 HANDKERCHIEFS	+ 4	
34 MILLINERY	+ 3	
35 WOMEN'S AND CHILDREN'S GLOVES	+ 4	
36 CORSETS AND BRASSIERES	+ 6	
37 HOSIERY	+ 5	
38 KNIT UNDERWEAR	+ 9	
39 SILK & MUSLIN UNDERWEAR, SLIPS, AND NIGHTGOWNS	+ 3	
42 NEGLIGEES, ROBES, AND LOUNGING APPAREL	+ 6	
38-42 UNDERWEAR, SLIPS AND, NEGLIGEES	+ 5	
43 INFANTS WEAR (Including infants' furniture)	- 2	
46 HANDBAGS AND SMALL LEATHER GOODS	+ 4	
47C CHILDREN'S SHOES	+ 3	
47W WOMEN'S SHOES	+ 6	
47 WOMEN'S AND CHILDREN'S SHOES	+ 5	
3X READY-TO-WEAR ACCESSORIES NOT REPORTED SEPARATELY	+ 4	
30. WOMEN'S & MISSES' READY-TO-WEAR ACCESSORIES	+ 4	
51C WOMEN'S AND MISSES' COATS	+ 8	
51S WOMEN'S AND MISSES' SUITS	+11	
51 WOMEN'S AND MISSES' COATS AND SUITS	+ 8	
52 JUNIORS' COATS, SUITS, AND DRESSES	+13	
53I WOMEN'S AND MISSES' INEXPENSIVE DRESSES	+ 5	
53B WOMEN'S AND MISSES' BETTER DRESSES	+ 6	
53 WOMEN'S AND MISSES' DRESSES	+ 6	
54 BLOUSES, SKIRTS, AND SPORTSWEAR	+ 8	
55 GIRLS' WEAR	+ 7	
57 APRONS, HOUSEDRESSES, AND UNIFORMS	+ 2	
59 FURS	+10	
5X READY-TO-WEAR APPAREL NOT REPORTED SEPARATELY	+ 3	
50. WOMEN'S AND MISSES' READY-TO-WEAR APPAREL	+ 8	
61 MEN'S CLOTHING	+12	
62 MEN'S FURNISHINGS AND HATS	+ 7	
66 BOYS' WEAR	+ 4	
67 MEN'S AND BOYS' SHOES AND SLIPPERS	+ 5	
6X MEN'S AND BOYS' WEAR NOT REPORTED SEPARATELY	+14	
60. MEN'S AND BOYS' WEAR	+ 8	

DEPARTMENT	SALES	STOCKS [1]
71M MATTRESSES, SPRINGS, AND STUDIO BEDS	+ 8	
71R UPHOLSTERED AND OTHER FURNITURE	+15	
71 FURNITURE AND BEDDING	+14	
73R RUGS AND CARPETS	+ 6	
73L LINOLEUM	+ 9	
73 DOMESTIC FLOOR COVERING	+ 6	
74 DRAPERIES, CURTAINS, UPHOLSTERY, AWNINGS, AND SHADES	+ 4	
75 LAMPS AND SHADES	+ 4	
76 CHINA AND GLASSWARE	+ 6	
77 MAJOR HOUSEHOLD APPLIANCES (Including cabinets)	+12	
78 HOUSEWARES (Pots, pans, cutlery, toasters, percolators)	+ 7	
79 GIFT SHOP	+12	
82R RADIOS, PHONOGRAPHS, AND TELEVISION	+18	
82S RECORDS, SHEET MUSIC, PIANOS, INSTRUMENTS, ETC.	+ 9	
82 RADIOS, PHONOGRAPHS, TV, RECORDS, SHEET MUSIC, ETC.	+15	
7X HOME FURNISHINGS NOT REPORTED SEPARATELY	+ 9	
70. HOME FURNISHINGS	+10	
91 TOYS AND GAMES	+ 2	
92 SPORTING GOODS AND CAMERAS	+14	
91-92 TOYS, GAMES, SPORTING GOODS, AND CAMERAS	+ 7	
93 LUGGAGE	+11	
96 CANDY	+ 3	
9X ALL OTHER MERCHANDISE DEPTS. NOT REPORTED ELSEWHERE	+ 8	
90. MISCELLANEOUS MERCHANDISE DEPARTMENTS	+ 7	
MAIN STORE TOTAL	+ 7	
BASEMENT STORE DEPARTMENTS		
110. DOMESTICS AND BLANKETS	+ 5	
131H HOSIERY	+37	
131U UNDERWEAR, NIGHTWEAR, ROBES, CORSETS, ETC.	+ 4	
131X INTIMATE APPAREL NOT REPORTED SEPARATELY	+ 9	
131 INTIMATE APPAREL (Incl. hosiery, nightwear, corsets, etc.)	+ 3	
150C COATS AND SUITS (Incl. juniors)	- 0 -	
150D DRESSES (Incl. juniors)	+ 2	
154 BLOUSES, SKIRTS, AND SPORTSWEAR	+12	
155 GIRLS' WEAR	- 0 -	
156 INFANTS' WEAR (including infants' furniture)	- 0 -	
157 APRONS, HOUSEDRESSES, UNIFORMS	- 0 -	
WX WOMEN'S&MISSES' READY-TO-WEAR NOT REPORTED SEPARATELY	+ 2	
130. WOMEN'S AND MISSES' READY-TO-WEAR	+ 3	
161C MEN'S CLOTHING	+ 3	
161F MEN'S FURNISHINGS	+ 5	
161 MEN'S WEAR	+ 4	
162 BOYS' WEAR	- 0 -	
160. MEN'S AND BOYS' WEAR	+ 3	
170. HOMEFURNISHINGS	- 0 -	
190. SHOES	- 1	
BX BASEMENT STORE DEPARTMENTS NOT REPORTED SEPARATELY	+ 3	
BASEMENT STORE TOTAL	+ 2	
NON-MERCHANDISE DEPARTMENTS		
NI BARBER AND BEAUTY SHOP	+ 6	
NX ALL OTHER NON-MERCHANDISE DEPARTMENTS (Fur storage, photo studio, restaurant, optical, shoe repair, etc.)	+10	
NON-MERCHANDISE TOTAL	+ 9	
GRAND TOTAL – ENTIRE STORE [2]	+ 8	

1. End of month, retail value.
2. Includes data from some stores which do not report on specific departments.

Source: Federal Reserve Bank of Cleveland, Research Department, G.7.3(D), April 8, 1965.

publicity budget to carry out the forecast is set up. Following this allocation is an evaluation of how much, to what extent, and in which media expenditures of the publicity budgeting dollars will take place. (The development of the budget itself is closely related to and coordinated with the merchandise plan as detailed in the previous chapter.)

The purpose of the publicity budget is to allocate various sums from the sales promotion budget among the different merchandise departments and divisions. Through the effective control of the publicity and sales promotion expenditures, the long-run sales of the firm can be maximized. Included in the allocations would be the publicity division pay roll of advertising and display expenditures, special research appropriations, and contingency funds for special events and professional services. The budget is determined by either a "percentage-of-sales" method or an "objective-task" method, whichever is likely to be much more productive and economic. Total expenditures can be determined by either a "break-down" or "build-up" method of appropriations.

This publicity budget must be carried out in terms of immediate as well as long-run goals. Once the total to "do the job" is deemed adequate, and if the "break-down" method is used, the budget should then be broken down by seasons, months, days, departmental classifications, media to be used, and types of advertising to be handled. In stores giving stamps, the redemption value of the trading stamps issued should also be included as part of the publicity budget expenditures. (Stamps in stores are generally utilized as a promotional expenditure.)

The publicity division as a specialized function initiates selling events and presents the store's policies and services from the customer's point of view.

IMPORTANCE OF STORE IMAGE

Publicity and marketing management mold and are guided by the store image. Furthermore, all advertising and promotional activities, whether paid for or sponsored as news, must develop a coordinated approach for the most effective store image. This is the intangible attribute which forms the public's attitude toward the store and the degree of patronage that it receives. The clientele and sales volume generated is the resultant "sum total" effect of the firm's market impact and image. The maximizing of sales volume may be considered the primary goal of all the publicity efforts of the organization.

The creation of effective demand represents the merging of the consumer's ability and willingness to buy. The desire to buy in particular stores—customer response—may be the result of publicity efforts being applied with full use of the tools of analysis developed in the social, behavioral, and quantitative sciences.

Because there is no longer a fine dividing line between necessary immediate purchases and those that are postponable, most categories of manufactured consumer goods do not have significant price demand elasticity. Despite protestation to the contrary, expansion of demand and intentions to purchase on the part of consumers often result from attempts to "keep up with the Joneses" and expectations of good economic conditions rather than from price stimulants.[3] For example, in grocery sales,

> ... one new chain unit developed over twice the sales of a new competing store of the same size and description. To determine the reason, research showed that the women of the community characterized the new store as "clean and white," "the store where you see your friends," "the store with helpful personnel," etc. ... In short, shopping in this store was a pleasurable experience instead of a routine chore. It is significant that not once did any of the shoppers interviewed mention lower prices, better bargains, or greater savings. ...[4]

Thus, the store image, character, and/or personality is a matter of continuous change and is literally everyone's business; the store image is a "public image" and a "communicating" device to and for all of a firm's public.

Stores cannot be all things to all people. Yet, they should constantly strive to publicize and keep abreast of changing wants and attitudes of the public. In attempts to enhance this concept of predicting and utilizing change, Carson Pirie Scott & Company of Chicago, under the aegis of a continuing store public relations approach by its president Virgil A. Martin, asked all its executives:

FIRST, IF YOU OWNED CARSON PIRIE SCOTT & COMPANY WHAT ONE THING WOULD YOU DO TO ENHANCE ITS "MERCHANDISING POSITION" IN THE COMMUNITY?

The answers given by store executives covered all the store functional areas. Specific references were made to:

1) Image
2) Parent store
3) Personnel training
4) Special events
5) Basic stocks
6) Sales promotion
7) Branch stores
8) Merchandise research
9) Department establishment, location, and/or relocation
10) Basement budget floor
11) Mark-down merchandise
12) Branch store
13) Buyers department manager
14) General
15) Leadoff
16) Expansion, economic outlook
17) General management
18) Merchandising, sales promotion operations
19) Buying fashion
20) Demands of time on buyers
21) Recruiting
22) Figures; operating, statistical, Federal Reserve data
23) Branch store accounting

All of these items would be illustrative of the all-embracing role of this division.

---

[3] See also "Consumer Income, Spending and Saving," *Federal Reserve Bulletin* (Board of Governors. Federal Reserve. Washington, D.C., April 1965); also *Consumer Buying Indicators* (and *Expectations*), "Current Populations Report" Series (Series P-65, No. 10, May 25, 1965).
[4] Pierre Martineau, "The Personality of the Retail Store," *Harvard Business Review* (Cambridge, Mass.), Reprint (January–February 1958, Vol. 36, No. 1, pp. 47–55).

DETERMINATION OF BUYING APPEALS

Consumers buy goods for many different reasons. However, some of the reasons are bound to be more prevalent than others. When any promotional plans are developed, the distinctive motivational features of the offered merchandise should be emphasized in "one action." The advertising and market managers must determine the motivational appeals that are held in common by the greatest number of consumers. The motives appealed to are generally of low intensity. Therefore, refined statistical analysis should be applied before conclusions are drawn and acted upon.[5] Merchandise classifications once evaluated as to appeal should be promoted towards a definite market if economic results are to be generated. Nevertheless, many merchandise classifications have broad appeal to more than one kind of customer group. Thus, the delineation of merchandise purchase appeals into specific groupings results in more effective and pertinent promotional efforts.

In attempts to predict buying behavior on a more consistent basis, many descriptive models for use in digital computers have been generated. An example of such a model is shown in Figure XXI. Analysis of buyer behavior is simplified greatly through the use of such models.

MASS VERSUS CLASS APPEALS

When appeals are categorized by merchandise classifications, the proper stimuli can be promoted by economic groups and social classes (the characteristics of each class, their age groupings, their manner of life, and their interests). Through motivational appeals of this kind, the publicity director can develop the maximum consumer interest.

Most publicity directors operate on the basis that there is no longer a mass market, only a "class" market. Therefore, they program their advertising expenditures toward the particular classes of customers which are most likely to patronize their stores. The various social classes in a community have differing psychological expectations and seek different measures of satisfactions in the marketplace. As a result, only particular appeals will be effective.

For example, the homemaker in the lower income group looks at goods in a functional sense; she is generally concerned with the practicality and dependability of goods. She will seek to identify herself with the store whose image reflects her values of concreteness and economy. In contrast, the homemaker in the upper income group is generally most interested in the labels on the merchandise and whether or not the symbolic meaning of the store personality reflects her status and style of life. Successful sales promotion managers thoroughly understand such concepts and maintain and reinforce symbolic values in all their promotional activities.

Technically, copywriters are guided by working backward from known con-

---

5 See also Alfred Politz, "Motivation Research from a Research Viewpoint," *The Public Opinion Quarterly*, Vol. XX, No. 4, Winter 1956–1957, p. 672.

FIGURE XXI
Individual Consumer Purchasing Decision *

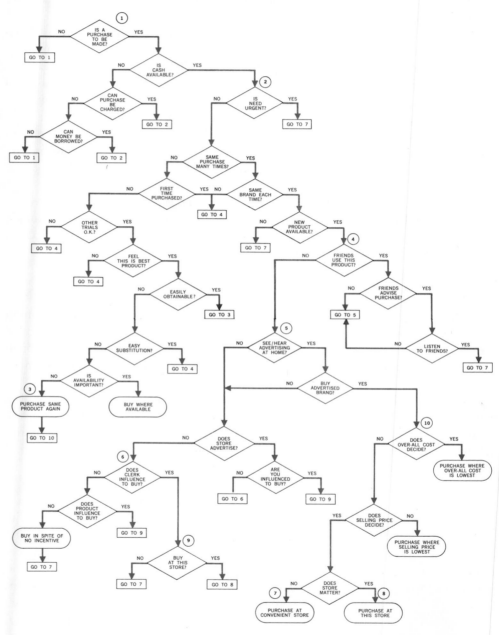

* Model developed by author in conjunction with graduate marketing management seminars. This model submitted by R. A. Schultz.

318

sumer interests and income levels of each group of individuals within their trading areas in order to create an optimum approach.[6]

The management of each retail firm must determine what the market position of the store should be, who its customers are within the trading area; management can then proceed on the basis of logical, orderly promotions and marketing management.

Once the customers have been defined and categorized, the store is in an excellent position to project the most effective promotional appeals and competitive strategy. Every shopper tends to patronize the store whose image is most congruent with the image they have of themselves. The closer the "tie-in," the more effective the store's promotional efforts. Unless the store's image is acceptable and consistent with those of its potential customers, publicity efforts tend to be only marginally economic with respect to the generation of sales. However, it was earlier pointed out that it is rarely (if ever) possible for a store to be all things to all people. And consumers tend to shop only where they feel most comfortable. Thus, each business institution must determine its own individual niche in the market place and project this concept through its sales personnel and public relations activities.

Once each marketing firm knows how many present customers contribute significantly to profit and how many marginal customers can be converted into profitable customers, the optimum market buying appeals can be projected. In many cases, the existence of a well-run public transit system adjacent to a store determines the kind of image appeal which it develops. Unquestionably, a great many value judgments are deterministic; these judgments are generally based on continuing statistical analysis of both internal and external data molded by the consumers in a trading area.

Although there seems to be some question as to whether or not there is a "mass" market in particular trading areas for most retail firms, there is no doubt that the more specific the motivational buying appeal and the broader its base, the greater the number of sales transactions that can be generated.

SELECTION AND EVALUATION OF MEDIA

All publicity department expenditures are generally planned and budgeted on a planning chart similar to the one shown in Figure XXII. On this chart, the more specific appeals are projected on a media basis.

Transmitting the appeals on a mass basis then becomes the task of concen-

---

[6] See also sociological community studies—such as August B. Hollingshead, Elmtown Youth; W. Lloyd Warner, The Social Life of a Modern Community; and Helen and Robert Lynd, Middletown—as helpful sources in clarifying the extent to which one can delineate customers in a community. These authors have taken a community, studied it intensively as participant observers, and classified the entire population into classes. They then proceeded to describe in detail the behavioral characteristics of each class, thereby demonstrating the interrelationships between existing social classes and their behavior. Knowledge of such relationships is of immense value to retailing. Yet, only marginal use is made of such studies in promotion and merchandising to particular communities and community segments.

trating consumer information in public media, primarily newspapers. Newspapers receive the greatest portion of the retail firm's publicity dollar. Because of its ephemeral nature and fast turnover, daily newspaper expenditure allocations are generally quickly assessed, but only in a broad general way. Measurement is generally relegated to immediate returns per space used correlated to specific advertising dollars spent.

FIGURE XXII
PLANNING CHART

(NRMA—Sales Promotion Calendar)

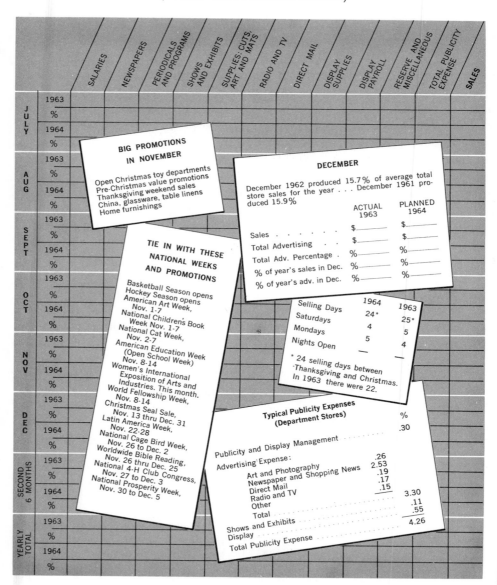

The methodologies used today to measure advertising effectiveness provide only general indications, not specific measurements. Nevertheless, many attempts to measure advertising effectiveness are continually advanced. For example, in Figure XXII, it is shown that daily and shopping newspapers absorb approximately 76.4 per cent of the total publicity dollar although precise measures of the effectiveness of these media are not generally available.

Advertising impact is difficult to measure accurately; many rules of thumb are used. Regardless, where advertising expenditures are cut or eliminated, an almost immediate over-all depressing effect on sales results. This is especially apparent in the smaller stores which utilize special sections of daily newspapers or local "shopping newspapers" as their primary advertising efforts. Weekly and semiweekly "shopping newspapers," circulars, and radio advertising are generally the best for local and minimum area purpose advertising.

Very little is known about creating sales by advertising. More must be known about the relationship between audience and exposure data and sales with workable degrees of accuracy. Results may very well ensue from experimental techniques, because what is being sought is causation.

In general, the experimental method rather than the survey method is a more powerful tool for the analysis of causation, because of better control over extraneous variables—in this case, the relation of advertising expenditures to sales.

For example, a test campaign run in a metropolitan trading area may use medium A for one merchandise category group; in another group, medium B, and so on. At the check points, the sales increase in each group could be taken as a measure of specific effectiveness.

The assumption of approximate equality in all factors other than media must also be made in any such measurements. This means that the merchandise advertised with various markets and media would have to be comparable and of similar price range and appeal. Area competition would vary from one area to another; however, adjustments would not necessarily be too difficult. The model of resulting sales in each area would depend on the effectiveness of the following variables.

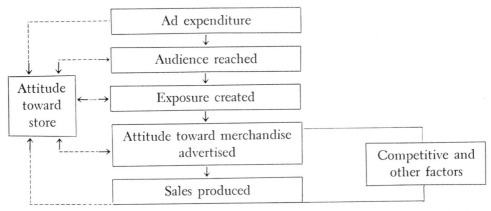

In other words, advertising creates and emphasizes the store image and then the merchandise. These cannot be separated. Also, this is both its objective and true measure of accomplishment. The extent to which these attitude changes are translated into actual purchase of the merchandise advertised depends on competition as well as timing.[7]

In the case of food chains and other types of multi-store operators, the advertising expenditures in daily newspapers tend to be economic and well directed. Nationally and regionally advertised brands can also be a good publicity factor when promoted.

Because newspaper rates are lower for local advertising, nationally sponsored advertising is often displayed under a local heading on a "cooperative" basis with local firms. By channeling their answers to retailer and wholesaler "pressures" for extra discounts on merchandise purchases, they further their own interest as well as the interest of their customers. In effect, the real advantage of newspapers as a mass communication medium is their strong local and regional appeal in depth.

In all firms, especially the middle-sized and smaller ones, the historical concepts of the store image are directly related to the personality of the owner-operator; in turn, the medium used to project this image often becomes a matter of habit rather than continuing analysis.

In the larger establishments, executive management is so far removed from actual customer contacts and transactions on the floor that both projected and incoming feedback are superficial. Today, face-to-face communications between top management and store customers are generally illusory with the result that there is a widening gap between the store, its customer, communications media, and professional retail management. The result—media selection and evaluation are more haphazard than scientific.

It may be stated, however, that the greater the store emphasis on moderate-to-high-priced shopping and specialty goods, the greater its trading area and the longer the driving-time distance that a customer will undertake in order to shop at that store. Thus, high-priced specialty and department stores have relatively large geographical areas from which to draw.

Conversely, the greater the proportion of "convenience goods" that a store offers, the smaller its trading area and the shorter the distance that a customer is willing to travel in order to shop at that store. Supermarkets, dry cleaning establishments, drugstores, variety stores, and shoe repair shops all fit into this category and have relatively small geographical areas from which to draw. Stores like Neiman-Marcus of Dallas and Lord & Taylor of New York draw on both statewide and national populations.

Newspapers

For speed and good market coverage of a local area, newspaper advertising is the ideal medium. Constant use of daily newspapers helps give the retailer continuity for most promotional activities. Newspapers, especially in a "one-paper"

[7] Alan S. Donnahoe, "A New Direction for Media Research," *Richmond Times Dispatch* (Richmond, Va., 1961), pp. 1, 7.

town, possess enough general characteristics to attract most population segments of a community. Newspaper advertising generally provides more local market coverage per dollar of expenditure than any other single medium.

Direct Mail

Direct mail is a medium that can be highly selective; however, it can be no better than the quality of the address listing used. In cases where direct mail enclosures are sent to charge-account customers, mailing costs can be minimized as the "stuffers" can be included with the monthly billings at no extra cost. The principal disadvantage of the direct mail is that it has a high "throw-away" factor—*before* being read. Despite its high selectivity and personalized approach, an 8 to 10 per cent sales return on mailings is rare.

Radio and TV

Radio advertising as a medium has become primarily local in character. Radio network hookups today are at a minimum except for newscasts of major broadcasting outlets. To survive, most radio stations must rely on local spot advertising, especially in connection with sports, weather, and news programs. Through radio, however, the small store can sound just as impressive as the larger one. This is unlike the use of newspaper or catalogue media, where space-cost differences are immediately apparent. Also, radio is extremely flexible; changes may be made right up to broadcast time.

Television, to date, has not had the impact hoped for by retail management. High costs per viewer for particular departments and its inability to sell fashion item merchandise in volume have been the chief complaints. Only on novelties and specialties have item promotions been successful. Despite the rapid expansion of use of TV on network combinations, its use in local markets by retailers is still limited.

Advertising media themselves also have a public image indicative of an index of acceptability of the products, institutions, and services advertised therein. It is rare indeed when a message can be separated from the communications medium. There is a continuing "subtle interaction" between the two. In studies of such interactions, it was found, for example, that radio and television seem to have a "show business" public image while that of newspapers is a "more creditable" type of image.[8]

INSTITUTIONAL VERSUS PROMOTIONAL APPEALS

Most advertising can be classified as institutional or promotional. The type of advertising used depends directly on the stage of community knowledge and acceptance of a store, its service, and its products.

---

[8] Alan S. Donnahoe, "The Public Image of Advertising Media," *Business and Economic Review* (University of Missouri, January–February 1960, Vol. 1, No. 1).

Institutional advertising can be characterized as that used primarily for the developing and retaining of store acceptance through personification of an "image." Institutional advertising is used to enhance the prestige of a selling organization to the point where merchandise acceptance is greatly facilitated. The build-up of consumer attitudes and promotion of patronage motives can also be referred to as indirect advertising. Smaller stores cannot afford, for the most part, to invest very heavily in institutional advertising. Promotional advertising is very closely related to—and is often called—direct action, product advertising.

As pointed out, stages of community acceptance are built up in much the same fashion as new product introduction. For example, in opening a new store or branch, the initial advertising phases must reflect a pioneering, "hard-hitting" tone. This phase should continue until the new facility is well known. Once the store has been generally accepted as a going concern, the firm's advertising can then enter a competitive stage where the cementing and expansion of market position is attempted. The competitive stage is the one in which all firms in the market place should consider themselves. Should the firm feel that it has achieved its goal market position and community acceptance, then retentive institutional advertising may be carried out. Retentive, low-pressure advertising should not be carried out during the firm's pioneering and competitive stages. Only in the retentive stages should institutional advertising be used extensively, and then not for any long period of time. Otherwise unwise organizational rigidity and uneconomic results ensue. (See Figure XXIII.)

FIGURE XXIII
THE ADVERTISING STAGES *

Spiral Affects Institutions and Products

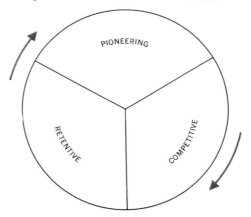

*Otto Kleppner, *Advertising Procedure*, 4th ed. (Englewood Cliffs, N.J.: Prentice-Hall, Inc., 1950), pp. 8–20. Kleppner also makes some interesting points about the transition form one stage to another.

It follows then that the first stage of any institutional cycle in opening a new store or developing a new product is a pioneering one, wherein all the attributes of the store and the merchandise are strongly promoted for the widest and most immediate type of acceptance. Then the other two stages of appeal follow in a wheellike pattern.

In the pioneering stage, every product, price, and feature offered should be strongly promoted and justified in order to be consistent with the organizational attributes to be projected. The competitive stages should include a broader and more active role in total market competition. When the "final" or retentive stage in the cycle is reached, it should be brief and should entail the institutional projections of assured success and recognition. This should then be followed by a resumption of the cycle into the pioneering and competitive stages.

Cyclical changes in consumer attitudes in trading areas determine advertising stages of both marketing institutions and product offers. The stages constitute the result of a spiral of policy decisions concerning "repetitive situations" which at times are difficult to distinguish. Thus, a "set" model for the maintenance of a parameter framework for "guiding" decisions in advertising procedure should be instituted. Within this framework, an "operations research" approach towards problem solving can be set up.

COOPERATIVE ADVERTISING

Cooperative advertising is generally sponsored by a manufacturer or wholesaler of nationally branded products carried by a retail firm. By this means, the advertiser is able to take advantage of the lower local rates, and the store involved benefits from greater advertising impact. Another type of cooperative advertising is that generated by wholesale- or retail-sponsored voluntary chains, such as Associated Hardware Stores, IGA Stores, Firestone Tire Stores, and Western Auto Stores.

Manufacturers and suppliers also furnish "cooperative" advertising allowances to stores in return for use of display space and for the purchase of certain quantities of particular items.

Suppliers often grant price concessions by such means in order not to violate the Robinson-Patman Act in which it is stipulated that like prices must be given to like purchasers of like quantities for like merchandise shipments in interstate commerce.

DISPLAY MANAGEMENT

Because of the increasing trend of self-service, self-selection, and simplified selling, point-of purchase advertising displays and creatively designed in-store directories have become a more important part of the over-all sales promotion plans of the retail firm. An example of a well-designed shopping guide is illustrated in Figure XXIV.

The visibility and effectiveness of in-store displays must be such as to attract and hold customer attention and generate impulse sales. Impulse goods are purchased in volume when displays in high traffic areas can arouse subliminal emo-

FIGURE XXIV
EXAMPLE OF WELL-DESIGNED SHOPPING GUIDE AS TIE-IN FOR IN-STORE PUBLIC RELATIONS AND SUPPLEMENT TO INTERIOR DECOR *

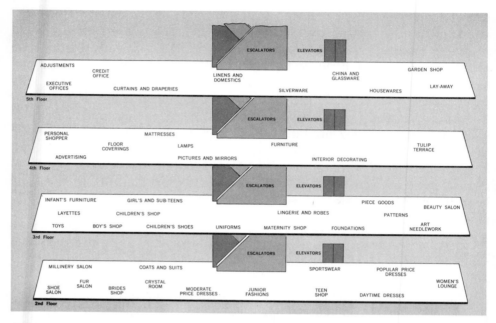

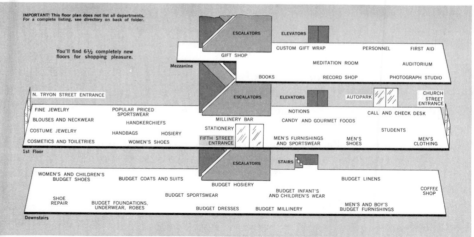

° J. B. IVEY CO., CHARLESTON, S. C.—"HANDY SHOPPING GUIDE" AVAILABLE TO ALL CUSTOMERS AT STORE ENTRANCE.

tional desires of possession in the consumer. Goods such as artificial flowers, knickknacks, imported delicacies, men's and women's hosiery and footwear, table radios, and even small portable TV sets and cameras can be sold as "impulse" purchase items when properly displayed. Even within the same display, items at eye level sell better than those at other heights. There are hosts of studies available in display management, a field more generally referred to as "visual communications."

Only by pertinent "impulse" displays can the demand elasticities of various categories of goods be exploited and coordinated with marketing strategy. Thus, displays must be used in coordinated fashion so as to assure continuity in the projection of the all-important store image as part of the total publicity effort.

In recent research studies[9] concerning the relationship of store display to store image and resulting sales impact, it was found that:

1) Downtown stores concentrate more on exterior displays, while stores in the shopping centers concentrate more on interior displays, uniqueness of the building structure, and the projection of parking availability.
2) Consumers have little difficulty recognizing the store advertising and displays without any "logo" or signature cut.
3) The larger stores in the downtown area feel that product knowledge, selection, and price are the major determinants of a store's image along with the quality of sales personnel.
4) The more exclusive and more specialized the store, the older, more knowledgeable, and more congenial are the salespeople. In fact, this plays as important a part in the store image as do the displays and advertising.

THE MANAGEMENT OF PUBLIC RELATIONS

For most levels of consumer-goods manufacturing and distribution, the retailer is the direct, sole contact with the ultimate consumer. In no other field of endeavor is success or failure so critically dependent on public attitudes developed on a "face-to-face" basis. The merchandise offerings and all selling and nonselling activities in the retail organization influence public attitudes in the trading area. Regardless of internal conflicts, the public view of the firm should always be a favorable one. It follows that the better the employee-management relations of the firm, the higher the organization morale, the more likely that the firm has courteous, informed, and friendly salespeople, and the more likely that store management can build volume and maximize profits.

The continuing boom in service sales is a new conceptual market consideration to be included with the public relations activities of the store.

Customers want services and prefer to deal with stores which offer them. The closer department and specialty store management can come to a total service concept, the better the chances are of attracting new customers and holding existing customers who don't mind paying for services and the merchandise that is for sale with them. An over-all service concept permits

[9] From current studies, Division of Research, College of Business Administration, University of Denver, 1965.

stores to offer customers a total "package" of satisfactions rather than just a locale where a purchase can be made.[10]

Another aspect of a store's public relations is that concerned with vendors. Regardless of market conditions, vendors should always be dealt with fairly and statements discounted wherever possible. Continuing good relations with suppliers can result in optimum cooperation in times of shortages or when "special" merchandise offerings are available. Employee and supplier relations also could be deemed representative of good internal sales promotion activities. When employees are convinced that what they are offering the public are the best values available, the feelings are easily transferred into good selling and good employee-customer relations.

With respect to community relations, retail managers should serve as leaders in civic movements and especially in public transportation and urban development. Supporting the operations of the Better Business Bureau, the Chamber of Commerce, United Fund, and other civic campaigns would be other examples of essential community participation.

ADVERTISING MANAGEMENT

In the larger stores there is a separation of functions in preparing and completing advertising. First, there is a schedule of "due dates" for advertising requests, depending on deadlines. The request for an ad should originate with the buyer. Once the ad has been set up, it is generally checked for accuracy and value through the comparison department; at the same time, proofs are arranged. Once the copy and layout have been approved, final production is set.

More specifically, the four principal aspects of advertising management can be stated in terms of merchandise, means, price, and timing. Along with this, consumers respond to physical appearance, tone, style, and more often than not to subtle qualities in a store's advertising. For example, the liberal use of white space in a store's advertising can indicate an offer of gracious elegance by the store.

The Copy Mix

Selling and distribution management cannot be divorced from advertising management with maintenance and expansion of demand. Today, social scientists employ the tools of scientific research in discovering new concepts of buying behavior and integrating these concepts into the firm's advertising. Borrowing eclectically from psychology, sociology, anthropology, and other related disciplines is a common denominator in all consumer communication processes.

The appropriate "mix" of merchandise, means, timing, and price is the basic

---

[10] Robert D. Entenberg, "Customer Services: A New Look at an Old Technique," *Department Store Economist*, June 1963.

policy-planning feature in advertising management. In addition, copy may be slanted toward:

1) the shopping reader who reads all ads, buys bargains, and is generally a regular customer of the store;
2) specific purchasers who look for particular bargains and may eventually be made into regular, profitable customers;
3) the casual reader who may be sold the store as well as the merchandise advertised. These individuals make intelligent discrimination among stores and can make advertising profitable;
4) the regular customer who is the store's best asset. These customers believe in the store and look for the ads. They also buy *unadvertised* merchandise on a regular basis. And,
5) the "individual who never reads advertising." When the "house" is full of brands, this individual may be drawn by interest, humor, honesty of advertising, or by good public relations activities.

Often, the only points of customer contacts with the larger firm are sales personnel. Courtesy and consideration at the points of customer contact reinforce attitudes initiated by the appeals promoted in the advertising media. In addition, attention paid to specific details helps develop favorable customer attitudes towards a store's merchandise offerings. Where budget and upstairs store departments appeal to differing classes of customers, advertising layout, signature cuts, use of white space, and price emphasis must be set up into differing yet conforming patterns.

In upstairs and higher-priced departments, the elements of high style, restraint of tone, greater formality, and snob appeal must be readily apparent in all advertisements; this often means a precise linkage of fashion emphasis and price de-emphasis in advertisements. On the other hand, in popular-priced or shopping-goods stores and/or discount operations, large bold-face type is often used to convey the price character of the appeals. While most retailers claim that they do not think in terms of economic factors, they do act in exactly such terms as they respond to sales feedback from customers. In effect, sales promotion strategy represents a key part of any sound merchandising technique. Use of research evaluations, experience, resource information, and customer feedback underlie the decisions as to how, what, and where to advertise—and the kind of pricing structure that will be undertaken. Such processes are all part of the market and selling strategy.[11]

---

[11] Regardless of the dictates of marketing strategy and competition, all firms should adhere to a fair practice code at all times. Its pervasiveness is clearly demonstrated in the text that follows:

The Fair Practices Code, which was formulated in 1952 by the Better Business Bureaus, requires advertisers to:
1) Serve the public with honest values.
2) Tell the truth about what is offered.
3) Tell the truth in a forthright manner so that its significance may be understood by the trusting as well as the analytical buyers. [footnote continued on next page]

SUMMARY AND CONCLUSIONS

The emphasis in this chapter has been on the unity of publicity and market management. No market or retail manager should look upon publicity as a subordinate responsibility. Publicity is rather the coordinated efforts of the total firm to accomplish its objectives.

Decisions as to what appeals are used and how promotional funds are allocated and spent have been analyzed. Selection and evaluation of media "mix" have been reviewed and analyzed within the framework of implementation of marketing strategy. Because most manufactured consumer goods have price as well as "status" demand elasticity, there is no longer a fine dividing line between necessary wants and postponable purchases. As a result, a wider range of buying appeals and advertising strategy should be utilized to expand sales.

To expand demand, mass communication media have, in a measure, contributed to consumer dissatisfactions with goods on hand. It is the task of market research to uncover latent demand as well as to identify new consumption patterns. Research must then project a measurement of these expenditure patterns so that management can decide on the best way to utilize them. Thus, the management areas of advertising, communications, and research are complementary functions. Further examination and analysis of the functions of communication and research form the subject matter of the chapter that follows.

[Footnote 11, continued]

4) Tell customers what they ought to know, what they have a right to know, and what is offered, so they may buy wisely and obtain maximum satisfaction from their purchases.

5) Be prepared and willing to make good as promised and without quibble on any guarantee offered.

6) Be sure that the normal use of merchandise or services offered will not be hazardous to public life or health.

7) Reveal material facts, the deceptive concealment of which might cause consumers to be misled.

8) Advertise and sell merchandise or service on its merit, and refrain from attacking competitors or reflecting unfairly upon their products, services, or methods of doing business.

9) If testimonials are used, take only those of competent witnesses who are sincere and honest in what they say about what you sell.

10) Avoid all tricky devices and schemes—such as deceitful trade-in allowances, fictitious list prices, false and exaggerated comparative prices, bait advertising, misleading free offers, fake sales and similar practices—which prey upon human ignorance and gullibility.

The code has been instrumental in helping to remove unethical gimmicks, such as the fictitious list prices and misleading offers in advertising mentioned above.

Chapter 22: *Research Methods and Communications*

A firm communicates with its public on a mass basis through sales promotion and advertising. To be sound, advertising should be based on continuing research of the trading area. Research findings can also lead to more effective operations by providing the optimum basis for staff advice and coordination. Thus research methods and communications are complementary guides for action.

All retail firms should use market and business research in order to keep up with change. In all firms, also, there is a wealth of material in company records. For example, the Controller of Gimbel Brothers, Pittsburgh, Pennsylvania, pointed out that some of the changes resulting from internal organizational research included a saving of 1,000 square feet of selling space. This was achieved by re-arranging the credit department and accounts receivable sections into a more modern reception area and by the use of "stand-up" interviewing. Needed space also resulted from the introduction of a single eight-year ledger card to replace extensive and cumbersome files.[1]

Credit department inquiries as well as general customer comments can be

---

[1] From a speech by Harry Margules to the Controllers Congress, NRMA, New York City, January 11, 1961.

used as an excellent means of guiding the sales promotion and communications activities of the store.

Internal research can also find answers to operational problems of lost sales checks, and can furnish more equitable bases for salary adjustments and better personnel relations. In the case of lost sales checks, research at Gimbels indicated that salespeople were instructed to treat sales checks as money; to implement this idea, the sales slips were kept in registers. The result was fewer lost checks.

Some of the more specific research studies upon which advertising decisions are made consist of Consumer Panels whose actions measure customer buying habits; Service Shopping Reports of competitors' merchandise offers; analysis of Complaints and Returned Goods Reports; and Organization Communications Reports as to media acceptability.

Another function of research and communications is to furnish the base for improving market and marketing strategies. In actuality, the mechanics of research and problem solving are much easier to develop than the problem of overcoming the reluctance of management to change. Management generally is also more adaptable to major rather than minor changes.

ADVERTISING AS A MASS COMMUNICATION MEDIUM

The daily newspaper is the most effective medium of mass communications for the retail firm, where (as analyzed in the previous chapter) quick action, last-minute changes, and high visual impact are needed. Other printed media, such as shopping newspapers and mail-order catalogues, can then be used to round out a program. Radio and television are generally used by retailers on special-purpose, experimental bases. Research procedures used in measuring the efficiency of retail advertising rarely measure the attributes of the ad itself, but rather attempt to measure the results in terms of sales volume.

Newspaper advertising receives the largest allocation of the retail publicity dollar. Effective advertising creates primary demand and expands existing demand. In other words, the functions of advertising specifically and sales promotion generally are to "trigger" potential into effective demand and to expand markets.[2]

MARKET MEASUREMENT

The determination and definition of the market and marketing facets of a retail firm's trading area are key aspects of market and management research. Analysis of the zones to which the store's package deliveries are made helps to measure and define the store's trading area. Any analysis of a store's charge accounts by zones of residence would be another method of defining trading area. An example of the factors which must be taken into consideration is shown in Table 29, a "Master Plan for Research Study for Market Definition and Expansion." By means of such master plans, pertinent market indices can be developed which

---

[2] *Potential demand* may be defined as the willingness or the ability to purchase a product or service, while *effective demand* would be the willingness *and* the ability to purchase.

TABLE 29
MASTER PLAN FOR RESEARCH STUDY FOR MARKET DEFINITION AND EXPANSION
(Department Store)

I. TO MEASURE SIZE OF POTENTIAL MARKET

a. Subdivide geographical area into primary, secondary and other sections.

b. Determine income and money available among the households in the area. Determine pattern of characteristics of merchandise line expenditures.

II. HOW IS THE MARKET DIVIDED AMONG PRINCIPAL COMPETITORS?

a. Your store's share.

b. Share for each major department store.

c. Share for each other major type of outlet; subdivided between downtown, secondary, neighborhood, and suburban locations.

1. Specialty stores
2. Variety stores
3. Mail-order branches
4. Others: drug stores, super-markets, etc., depending on the merchandise line.

III. DETERMINE CUSTOMER CHARACTERISTICS BY EACH TYPE OF COMPETING STORE
What is exposure to each type medium?

a. Social.
b. Economic, purchasing habits.
c. Aesthetic, literary, etc.
d. Stability.

IV. CHARACTERISTICS OF THE CONSUMERS EXPOSED TO EACH MEDIUM
(In terms of appeals, study each of the characteristics in III for readers, listeners, or observers of the following)

a. Each newspaper, each radio and television station.
b. Billboards, car cards, window and interior display.
c. Direct-mail and bill enclosures.
d. In-store personal selling, in-home sales, telephone selling.

V. CHARACTERISTICS OF EACH STORE'S APPEAL TO CUSTOMERS

a. Prestige; social.
b. Economic; price, value, quality, assortment.
c. Aesthetic; style.
d. Consistency of policies, personal services offered.

Sections III and V must be studied simultaneously and the results analyzed by comparison. Once the appeals which succeed most often with each group of customers are known (III), the appeals of the sponsoring store can then be critically examined to decide whether or not management is appealing to those segments of the market which it wishes to dominate.

---

furnish the guides through which the potential demand for a store's merchandise and services can be fully exploited.

In market measurement also many new terms such as "megalopolis" and "inter-urbia" are appearing more frequently. These concepts have not replaced standard metropolitan statistical area (SMSA) definitions but are being used more frequently to pinpoint sales areas. The concept of "Interurban Market" has been delineated by Jerome R. Pickard, Research Director of the Urban Land Institute. He defines an interurban market as "an urban region with a majority of its population urban, made up of a continuous series of adjoining urban counties, with the inclusion of a few transit counties (not to exceed one-fifth of the total counties in the region)." He set two qualifications for urban regions: "1) population must total at least one million, 2) average density must be at least 180 persons per square mile, which is three times the conterminous U. S. norm." There are twenty-one such markets in the United States.

These markets have 56% of the population, 65% of all Effective Buying Income, and 61% of total retail and "rate extra sales planning." Specially favored by migratory population shifts and industrial relocation trends, these urban groupings will continue to expand at an above-average clip.[3]

In conjunction with the "Master Plan" research study shown in Table 29, provision for recording changes in traffic arteries, roadways, signal lights, and size and composition of traffic flow should be a continuing supplement.

For example, the existence of rivers, lakes, and mountains in a trading area limits lateral transportation facilities in a community, thus limiting the scope and drawing power of any proposed shopping center. Uneconomic transportation and parking along with lack of civic and social attractions and communication facilities also tend to limit retail trading area potential.

Traffic congestion rather than population density in central cities and in adjacent surrounding suburban areas tends to limit the trading area of central business district hubs. Analysis of daily telephone calls from specific zones on average business days compared with such calls made to competing trading areas also helps to delineate trading areas within a city or suburban area. Charting the circulation distribution of daily newspapers and driving-time distances from the particular shopping areas via isochronic maps also helps to define a trading area. Any changes in existing patterns should be recorded immediately in the master plan. For example, whenever a larger shopping center opens competitively close to a smaller one, the drawing power of the larger center will draw away a large percentage of the shopping and specialty-goods sales from the smaller one.

MANAGERIAL AND ECONOMIC ANALYSIS OF PROMOTIONAL POLICIES

As a basic policy, promotion expenditures should generate enough sales volume to more than offset allocated expenditures. For example, if a store is generating a $1 million volume annually and spends a total of $280,000 for operating expenses made up of $30,000 or 3 per cent of its net sales for advertising and an additional $250,000 or 25 per cent for all other operating expenses, the total operating expenses of the firm would be 28 per cent. Should management decide to allocate an additional $15,000 for promotion expenditures, then the firm's projected resulting sales increase, if it is to be economic, should approximate $500,000, bringing the sales volume up to $1.5 million. An increase of this magnitude would be needed if advertising expenditures are geared not to exceed 3 per cent (45,000/1,500,000).

Assuming a maintained markup of 35 per cent, then a 7 per cent or $70,000 net profit resulted with a $1 million volume (.35–.28). Should an additional $15,000 be spent for advertising with a resulting $1.5 million volume, far greater profits would ensue because the total expense percentage would not rise proportionally.[4] To illustrate: The prior over-all operating expense of $250,000 would

---

[3] From "Interurbia," *Sales Management*, November 10, 1964, pp. 60–77.
[4] As pointed out in Chapter 17, the maintained markup is the actual amount above cost of merchandise sold/received as part of total sales.

not increase an additional $125,000 (25 per cent) as a result of the incremental sales. It is far more likely that as a result of increased volume with existing plant that while the dollar operating costs would rise somewhat, they would not rise proportionately with increased volume. Pertinent to the illustration, however, let us assume that operating expenses increased by $55,000, exclusive of advertising. The new total expense figure would appear as follows:

Advertising Expenditures	$ 45,000
($30,000 + $15,000)	
Balance of Operating Expenses	
($250,000 + $55,000)	305,000
Total Operating Expenses	$ 350,000
Projected Volume	$1,500,000

Thus the new total operating-expense percentage figure would be 23.3 per cent instead of 28 per cent and the resulting net profit on sales before taxes would then be 11.67 per cent on a $1.5 million base ($175,050) instead of 7 per cent on $1 million or $70,000. Under such circumstances, the use of advertising becomes most economic.

On the other hand, should the additional $15,000 in expenditures result in only a moderate increase in sales revenue, then total operating-expense percentage could rise well above 28 per cent with a resulting lower dollar and percentage profit.

Budgeting significant increases in advertising expenditures should not be undertaken unless substantial incremental sales volume can be reasonably projected. In effect, promotion expenditures can be offset by increased volume. The increases in volume should be programed to result in a reduction of total operating-cost percentages. Greater profits accrue to a business entity whenever management can widen the spread between operating-cost percentages and relatively fixed maintained markup percentages on greater revenue income. In the above case, the maintained markup can be assumed to remain at 35 per cent while the total operating-expense percentage dropped.

Evaluating Promotional Policies

Most stores located in downtown areas have relatively little waste circulation in their advertising because of their accessibility to all parts of the central city peripheries. Thus, chain or multi-unit firms in the same trading area, as well as those in the central business district, can maximize their advertising expenditures.

The retail firm must depend on continuing customer satisfaction for long-run volume and profit maximizing. To carry this out, the retail firm must deliver "psychological" as well as "real" satisfactions on a continuing basis through well-planned and well-run promotional policies. Included must be constant restatements of store policy concerning delivery, credit, a fashion image, the courtesy of sales-people, and a quality image of all merchandise offerings as part of a total "package" of value satisfactions. Promotional expenditures represent a "controllable" variable expense which tends to increase customer traffic and consequently merchandise exposure.

Unfortunately, promotional advertising expenditures are the expense factors most generally curtailed in times of stress or declining sales, when additional sales and income increments are vitally needed. The very means by which sales can be improved is the variable expense that is most generally cut back when volume slackens.

In advertising, "values" offered by the firm must be clear-cut and have utilitarian as well as psychological appeal to prospective purchasers. When the various forms of advertising are fitted into an optimum media pattern, both the short- and long-term profit outlook can improve because of a resulting better utilization of existing plants.

THE NEED FOR RESEARCH CORRELATIONS

When advertising is planned in three- to six-month sequences, timing is of critical importance and is carried out on the basis of selectively applied continuing research. Naturally, sales increases can be measured, but correlating cause and effect on sales is not possible generally as differing philosophies of management exist in respect to how advertising effectiveness should be measured.

And, for like reasons, many research methods are needed to pinpoint information for management. For example, do higher income-level families require greater expenditures or a different type of advertising to create primary demand for new items? Does a community have "tastemakers" who set standards for the entire trading area? Do changing economic patterns in the community change on linear or nonlinear bases? Is research analyzing and correlating into meaningful patterns the significant impact of social, economic, and technological changes taking place in the trading area? How much "lead time" information does research furnish the merchandise and general publicity managers so that effective sales projections can be planned?

The underlying elements in the sales promotion activities of any retail firm should be based on research-oriented marketing strategy. In addition, research can determine how appeals must differ within the same geographical areas for similar merchandise categories. Even staple classifications such as sheets, pillow-cases, daytime dresses, uniforms, saddle oxfords, and men's white shirts may require differing advertising to the same individuals during various times of the year.

By using the pertinent elements of the methodological concepts underlying the research parameters of Figures XXV and XXVI, market and marketing strategy and communications research can be effectively formulated.

FIGURE XXV
New Concepts for Retail and Market Measurements *

Economics
Retailing — RESEARCH — Sociology
Marketing Psychology
Anthropology

A. "Value added" terminology—$100 billion (1965 estimate)
   (Average 27% of total selling price)
   Represents approximately 15% of GNP (value added to economy)

B. *Two fields or approaches*
   1. Environmental influences—or Behavioral Sciences
   2. Quantitative analysis

C. *Terminology differs over time but same knowledge*
   Applied Economics at consumer level
   roughly equates Retailing
   Applied Economics at distribution level } Marketing
   roughly equates Wholesaling
   No real difference in thoughts or concepts; primarily language differences and introduction of more logical measures of cause and effect of predictive purposes

D. *Concepts*
   1. *Measurement*—types of:
      a. *Physical*—Institutional and physical movement aspects;
      b. *Communications*—Forms of sales, buyer behavior, consumer impact (return customers), media exposure. and feedback;
      c. *Financial*—long-range planning, capital budgeting, short-run budgets, credit, dynamic factors of change, pressures;
      d. *Control*—measurement of social change to pressures and movements—circular dynamics into input-output models;
      e. *Management*—changes in organization structure and retailing functions due to horizontal and vertical integration; and
      f. Social role of retailer as community and patronage symbol.
   2. *Concepts of Social Exchange Functions:*
      The standard of living has risen directly in proportion to cost of distribution (personal research of author—1959–1965).

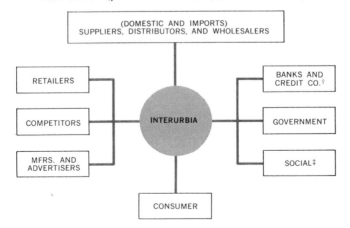

* (Developed in conjunction with Marketing Science Institute
   Seminars and the author's own research)
† Banks calling selves retailers
‡ Interactions here—social function (moving in and out of public)

FIGURE XXVI
THEORY OF THE FIRM *

Market Distribution Model

CRIM Model	(M.S.I.)	Consumer-Retailer-Interface-Model

	↓	↓	Linear Programing
↓ Retailer	↓ Model	Input-Output Analysis of Dollar
Consumer	Interface	Control Values in Exchange Function

Theory

Purpose of theory is to predict consumer behavior; therefore, to be effective, predictive results must be measurable.

A. Consumer attempts to predict what value satisfactions he can obtain from various retailers or suppliers.

B. Retailers, to be effective, must predict what the demands of the consumers will be.

C. Points of interchange indicate mutual efficiency. Mass communications media are the catalytic agent and the personal selling functions are the cementing transfer agents.

D. Concepts based on game theory; game model is a strategy process involving the transfer elements of normative, descriptive, and predictive models depending on competitive situation in the trading area; and, strategy changes, motivational changes, and availability of funds on an economic base.

(a) *Vector Model*

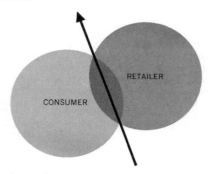

(1) **The closer the circles are or the more they overlap, the better will merchandise assortments fit needs of consumers, and the better will consumers be able to determine where and from whom to purchase.**

(b) *Structural Model*

Measures over time, the various measures of "satisfactions" that a consumer gets on a "market-basket" basis; gross the margin that a retailer can obtain without the store having an accurate forecast of consumer demand would form the "standard." The more stores that a consumer shops, the wider the band of evaluative criteria that a customer would utilize before making a purchase.

* *Ibid.*, Figure XXV.

DETERMINATION OF ADVERTISING EFFECTIVENESS

The social scientist is faced with a host of highly volatile and unpredictable social, economic, and psychological factors that cannot be changed at will. On the other hand, the researcher in the physical sciences has direct control of the major variables contributing to the outcome of a particular experiment. This does not generally hold true in biological and social science experiments, as can be seen from the market distribution and measurement models previously mentioned (Figures XXV and XXVI). However, this does not rule out the possibility of isolating the influence of key factors, for example, to determine advertising effectiveness.

In recent years, mathematical models have been used experimentally to determine advertising effectiveness. Such models have been used successfully in military weapons systems, production and inventory control, traffic scheduling, routing and dispatching, and queue line control of dock-loading usage in operations research control experiments. However, in marketing and advertising, mathematical models have not been too successful for actionable conclusions because of failure of the "builders" to understand the retail merchandising and processing systems. Without understanding a total process or knowing its frame of reference, any hypotheses or models are likely to be questionable in value.

For instance, advertising measurement should include degrees of customer carry-over and habit formation of previous direct or indirect advertising. Yet, these variables are rarely known or stipulated. Within this framework, assumptions, *ceteris paribus*, of important causative residual factors of consumer choice will help but will have a high degree of risk in terms of a calculated error! Because the "error" impulse of choice can be in either direction, a re-emphasis of previously used rules of thumb or intuitive administrative judgment can be set up.[5]

The measurement of advertising effectiveness is also an *ex post facto* measure because current "inputs" have been allocated; yet the advertising inputs may still be at work, especially in printed media. Thus, planning and timing as well as measurement are key blueprints for maximizing sales. Again, in testing advertisements there is no clear general agreement as to what constitutes effective copy. While it is difficult to predict in advance the results of any particular advertising, the tone of the ads, the copy appeal, and the extent of the trading area to be covered can be deterministic.

It is evident that the difficulty in predicting sales arises from the lack of verifiable pragmatic evidence needed for evaluation. Risk is a business investment that must be justified. And risk is involved in every aspect of store communications.

Problem of Nonlinear Measurement

Advertising copy is intended to perform a function beyond the mere development of familiarity with the institution, brand name, or product that is its subject. Copy is also intended to shape motives and desires and to build believability into the merchandise offer and the institution making the offer.

The problem is that a specific sales increase or a reversal of a declining sales trend cannot be related to a specific advertising action, or to one of its parts

---

[5] See also Alfred A. Kuehn, "How Advertising Performance Depends on Marketing Factors," *Journal of Advertising Research*, March 1962, Vol. 2, No. 1, pp. 2–10.

(copy treatment, a sound effect, a headline, or an effective sales quotient). "Indeed, it is almost naive to imagine that any relationships can be established between specific advertising actions and sales." [6] Yet, this is exactly what should be done and/or constantly attempted. As a result of such efforts many effective principles have evolved. For example:

1) The ads which have proved most successful are those emphasizing a single idea or those having a strong focus on a single objective.
2) Furthermore, when promotional communication makes a product or store look different from all others without violating the truth, "measures" of sales effectiveness result.
3) To be effective consumer advertising must give the consumer a "channel of action"—as to where, how, and at what price a product may be purchased; and advertising must give this "action choice" to the consumer at a time when he is psychologically prepared to buy that product.

To accomplish this objective, a "media mix" and known marketing relationships of merchandise line sales by seasons must be utilized in conjunction with "single fact" results of continuing research.

RESEARCH PLANNING

Research analysis, in a micro-economic sense, deals with specific or individual situations of people, income, and/or trends. It deals with trading area problems and furnishes the means for evaluating commodity flows and channels of distribution. An example of research areas for investigation is illustrated in Table 30. This kind of research furnishes the basis for conclusions on which action can be taken.

Analysis within the firm deals primarily with merchandise classifications, control, turnover rates, and acceptability of price ranges. When properly conducted, internal research provides the needed impetus for managerial creativity which should be able to "budge" the many productivity blocs that constantly arise.

Internal records also form the basis for over-all analysis of the firm's market operations. Such investigations lead naturally to analytical guides for management as to what should be researched. The first step in any research requires a pinpointing of the problem area and a statement defining a particular problem. A knowledge of how to gather the necessary facts to solve the problem and a basic knowledge of fundamental statistical techniques is also a must. A knowledge of such techniques is needed in order to be able to quantify and evaluate any discovered facts into meaningful patterns with a view toward developing the basis for conclusions leading to action. While it is not necessary for the business manager to understand the actual techniques involved in research, it is necessary that he should be able to evaluate and apply the results.

---

[6] Alfred Politz, "The Dilemma of Creative Advertising," *Journal of Marketing*, October 1960, Vol. 25, No. 2.

TABLE 30

RECENT RESEARCH AND REPORTS[a]

Principal Conclusions and Areas of Investigation

1. "Drawing power" of institutional advertising. (One out of four claimed it resulted in going downtown to shop.)
2. Ability of customers to recognize the advertising format of the stores without a signature cut. (Most were able to do so.)
3. Changing acceptability of compact cars. (Key difference was originally "distinction at a price," then savings of gas; evidently, both were sufficient to overcome smallness in size.)
4. Effect of delivery charges on store purchases. (In many cases reduced impulse buying of lower-price bulky items.)
5. Urban renewal: Next large growth in geographical expansion will be in secondary business districts and stable string-street locations. (Indicates increased emphasis on renewal of central-city decay.)
6. The influence of business conditions on consumers. (Less influence on purchases of durables than commonly supposed.)
7. Recent trends in food-store pricing philosophy. (Food prices vary directly with wages in particular zones and communities for nonperishable items. Space permitting, all supermarkets are increasing nonfood items in an effort to maintain sales and margins. Supermarkets are therefore representing competition to an increasing number of nonfood retailers. The larger food chains carry national brands but promote private brands. Smaller chains will stick to national brands except where mergers and cooperative buying greatly expand present volume. Volume that has been built on trading stamps can be maintained only by continuation of this promotional device; many are trying alternatives.)
8. Acceptability of foreign-made goods by the American public. (Novelties and gifts of quality have been the most "suspect.")
9. In purchases of many appliances, most customers mention Westinghouse but more often buy General Electric or other brands.
10. Fashion lag and degrees of acceptability of innovations by various cities can be measured.
11. Men's hat survey. (Most apparently like them but don't wear them.)
12. Millinery. (Casual suburban living no longer makes the wearing of hats a routine "must.")
13. What happens to fashion ready-to-wear sales when a major store closes in a downtown area? (Total fashion business downtown decreases and "acceptable" shops near home take over.)
14. Effect of in-store restaurants and tearooms. (Serve as a drawing power for customer traffic; effect is measured by the increase in customer traffic, and impulse sales of fashion accessories and ready-to-wear.)
15. How do sectional and regional shopping centers affect the shopping habits of customers in the immediate surrounding areas? (Immediate effect is to cut downtown shopping traffic; the long-run effect is to change shopping habits with approximately 40% of residents in 10-minute-driving-time distance, cutting downtown trips by 50% and more.)
16. Sunday store openings. (Public opinion varies by zones and regions.)
17. Mass transit. (Habit is greatest factor; continuing re-education needed for success.)
18. Consumer acceptability of "value-added" concept in marketing and retailing. (Slow, but gradually attaining acceptability.)

[a] All the above surveys and capsule results are taken from research carried out under the supervision of the author from 1955 through 1964 at the Graduate Schools of Retailing and Business, University of Pittsburgh. Methodologies used were Stratified Quota Samples and Stratified Random Samples representative of the "populations" of the SMSA's of Pittsburgh, Washington, Baltimore, Philadelphia, Cleveland, Chicago, St. Louis, Indianapolis, Denver, and Los Angeles.

Another aspect of research planning involves the application of change into innovation for meeting change. Innovation is one of the key factors in market strategy, and thereby the long-run competitive position of any firm may be enhanced. Its starting point is the programing of a policy of continuing research for predictive purposes. For example, during World War II consumer-goods shortages continued to mount and inflationary pressures ensued. While many firms attempted to handle lines of merchandise with which they had no experience but which were available during the war emergency, most firms were apparently either unprepared or unable to change. This inability to adapt to change was and still is a causative factor in the failure of many firms.

A great many research planning applications are needed in "cost of distribution" studies, as costs in retail distribution have grown at a much more rapid rate than productivity. Many retail firms are still caught in cost-profit squeezes with resulting marginal profits.

Even less is apparently known about the kinds of functional cost analyses that can be applied, especially in the publicity areas and in productivity unit accounting. Many research attempts to solve cost problems are being made through Expense Center Analyses, which are discussed in Chapter 27.

MARKET MANAGEMENT RESEARCH

By definition, market strategy should be based on valid research predicting demand of specific commodities in particular markets. Consumer demand includes patronage motives, locations in which to shop, types of merchandise desired, and types of services wanted.

Manufacturers, suppliers, the many stages of government agencies, newspapers, and other media furnish informational reports of a research nature to business firms and executive management. In order to improve their image and volume, advertising media furnish research reports of comparison shoppings, customer and trading area analysis, fashion acceptability, and ideas of interest to women shoppers. Many of these reports, when properly used, can help a firm's advertising strategy.

In sum total, the publicity director (through the feedback from store displays, public relations, fashion coordination, and comparison shopping), furnishes executive management with the basis of marketing actions, adaptation to change, and problem areas that need to be researched.

Market planning and research involve the interaction of two or more executive opinions into a single strategic decision. Uncertainty is always involved, and a plan is needed to provide for whatever alternatives are present. The alternatives revolve around competitors and customer reactions to changes in market strategy. The "probable" action of either competitors or customers—or both—is forecast on a probability basis set up through planned research studies. In effect, these types of research studies are a form of pretesting through experimental design. Thus research management may at times appear more intuitive than scientific. In a decision model of marketing research expenditures, it is suggested that a priori formal analysis within a design parameter would provide management with decision areas more germane to executive talents.[7]

FORECASTING

Forecasting sales on both a short- and long-run basis is one of the focal points of research planning. The forecast projection forms the basis for the sales budget and the "control" vehicle for future plans. Economic indicators, often called business barometers, form the basis for most forecasts. Most of the business indicators are published by the National Bureau of Economic Affairs and the Office

---

[7] See also Frank M. Bass, "Market Research Expenditures—A Decision Model," *The Journal of Business*, University of Chicago, January 1963, Vol. XXXVI, pp. 77–90.

of Business Economics of the United States Department of Commerce and appear in the monthly "Survey of Current Business." There are only general, not specific, interpretations as to their use.

Because of the growing technical complexity of the statistical data used in projecting the future, management should have an understanding of the manner in which the indicators are used as well as the nature and significance of the indicators themselves. The economic indicators may be separated according to particular functional field applications and may be further classified as to whether they are leading, concurrent, or lagging in nature. For example, a leading indicator would be one whose change would precede or be influential in determining a future economic trend. A concurrent indicator would help recognition and analysis of incipient trends; a lagging indicator would help in "just past" evaluations.

In Appendixes F through I are lists of economic indicators, business cycle and trend fluctuations, and sources for many of these statistical data. These data are classified according to financial, distribution, and industrial areas and further delineated into components of prices, profits, inventories, employment, and unfilled orders data. Irrespective of what indices are used, they should be summarized according to their particular economic implications for the firm. The forecasting approach should be from the macro (the general), to the micro (specific) basis, utilizing both the theoretical and practical. To illustrate: Table 31 shows the four basic component indicators making up Gross National Product.

Gross National Product (GNP)

The most widely used economic indicator is that of Gross National Product (GNP).[8] GNP is estimated on a quarterly basis by the Office of Business Eco-

TABLE 31

FOUR COMPONENT INDICATORS BY TYPE MAKING UP GROSS NATIONAL PRODUCT

(in billions of current dollars)

ITEM	1929	1933	1939	1950	1955	1960	1962	1964
Gross National Product	104.4	56.0	91.1	284.6	397.5	502.6	476.4	516.0
Personal Consumption Expenditures	79.0	46.4	67.6	195.0	256.0	328.2	356.8	399.3
Durable goods	9.2	3.5	6.7	30.4	39.6	44.9	48.4	57.0
Nondurable goods	37.7	22.3	35.1	99.8	124.8	151.8	162.0	177.3
Services	32.1	20.7	25.8	64.9	92.5	131.5	146.4	165.1
Gross Private Domestic Investment	16.2	1.4	9.3	50.0	63.8	71.8	79.1	87.7
New construction	8.7	1.4	4.8	24.2	34.9	40.7	44.2	48.9
Producers' durable equipment	5.9	1.6	4.2	18.9	23.1	27.6	29.0	35.1
Change in business inventories	1.7	−1.6	.4	6.8	5.8	3.5	5.9	3.7
Net Exports of Goods and Services	0.8	0.2	0.9	0.6	1.1	3.0	4.0	7.0
Govt. Purchases of Goods and Services	8.5	8.0	13.3	39.0	75.6	99.6	116.3	128.6
Federal	1.3	2.0	5.2	19.3	45.3	53.1	62.9	65.5
State and local	7.2	6.0	8.2	19.7	30.3	46.5	53.5	63.0

Source: Office of Business Economics, U. S. Department of Commerce, and *Survey of Current Business*, for various years and for May 1965, Vol. 45, No. 5, pp. 4–7.

Seasonally adjusted quarterly estimates at annual rates are available from 1939, and annual estimates from 1929. The series is also published in constant (1954) dollars which makes available the measure of "real" GNP after correction for price changes.

---

[8] Statistically speaking, it should not be a valid measure as it represents an "average" of "averages."

nomics of the United States Department of Commerce. It is the sum total of expenditures by consumers, business firms, and government, and includes the sales of net exports of goods and services.

The forecast of total GNP is generally made by first estimating consumer expenditures which account for approximately two-thirds of GNP. These consist of durable goods—primarily household equipment and autos—nondurable goods —mostly clothing and food—and service outlays—which would include rent, domestic help,[9] and medical care.

The largest segment of consumer expenditures is still for nondurables, although it has declined from 51 per cent to approximately 45 per cent in 1965. Durable-goods spending approximates 13 to 15 per cent of consumption expenditures. Gross private domestic investment represents some 15 per cent of GNP. Change in business inventories, new institutions, and producer's durable equipment expenditures make up the balance of this component.

The most volatile segment in this group is the change in business inventories, which may fluctuate as much as $3 billion annually. The smallest component of GNP is the "net profit figures" which account for less than 1 per cent of the total, except for war and periods of emergency.

"Net expenditures of goods and services" measures the excess of foreign sales over imports; such expenditures are included in the "spending" within the other three sectors. This does not include imports bought by Americans overseas. The figure is significant as it shows the relative importance of foreign trade to the United States economy. Net exports of goods and services reached peaks of $9 billion in 1947, in 1953, and in 1959.

The second largest component of GNP is "Government purchases of goods and services"; this segment includes all the expenditures of the Federal, State, and local governments, except for national defense. Only spending for goods and services is counted in the GNP series. Thus the Federal government expenditures are higher than those included in any segment of the GNP totals. In recent years, expenditures by government have represented a far greater proportion of the nation's output. In 1929 Federal expenditures were less than 2 per cent of GNP. Today such expenditures exceed 20 per cent. State and local government expenditures have been rising at a faster rate than those of the Federal Government. In fact, from 1959 to 1961, Federal Government expenditures declined by 1 per cent in contrast to a 7 per cent increase in expenditures by other governmental bodies.

While it is beyond the scope of this text to analyze completely a forecasting methodology, it is felt that an understanding of the business cycle by component indicators and their general effect on the economy is necessary. The managerial-economic approach to effective distribution necessitates a basic understanding of these barometers. With this objective in mind, some of the key forecasting components of the economy are—namely, reviewed national income, personal income, the

[9] It is a strange commentary that outlays for domestic help are part of the Gross National Product, while the work that the individual homemaker performs in her home is not considered as "work" and hence has no "value."

labor force, unemployment, industrial production, wholesale prices, consumer prices, and seasonal adjustment and business cycle interpretations.

National Income. National Income measures the total income to the factors of production: interest and rent for the owners of land, total employee compensations for labor, factor interest and income to the owners of capital equipment as factor capital, and compensation for executive management as the reward for making the other three factors of production work in producing economic values.

In effect, national income represents the "factor cost" of the nation's output, whereas GNP represents expenditures in terms of the "market value" of the output—in other words, the sale price to purchasers. "Nonfactor" costs spread throughout the National Income Accounts are chiefly: depreciation on buildings and equipment and indirect business taxes, such as excise and property taxes.

The most closely watched and most volatile component of this series is corporation profits, because these are indicative of structural changes in the economy. Individual estimates are made for corporation profits, both before and after taxes and before and after dividends and retained earnings. Inventory valuation adjustments are reported separately, so that profits reflect the value of any real changes in inventories rather than merely changes in book values, which are carried out in accounting statements.

Proprietor's income includes sales of the balance of the nation's business enterprises; sole proprietorships, partnerships, and noncorporate businesses are shown in individual comparisons.

Personal Income. Personal income is obtained from national income by subtracting contributions made for social insurance and adding dividends, net interest paid by the government, and transfer payments. Transfer payments include payments not resulting from current production (social security benefits, veterans' bonuses, and corporate gifts to nonprofit institutions). Personal income includes not only money payments but nonmonetary income as well—chiefly, net rental values of owner-occupied homes and "the value" of food produced and consumed on farms. Personal income statistics are available on a monthly seasonally adjusted basis for the nation, and annually by states. They are one of the few measures of over-all economic performance available at the state level.

The amount of income available for spending or saving is "disposable personal income"; it is found by deducting "taxes" from total personal income. Taxes in this case include personal taxes, such as income and estate taxes, and nontax payments, such as fines, but excludes property and commodity taxes. Contributions to social insurance funds are also deducted.

Consumption expenditures subtracted from personal income equals personal saving; this includes not only changes in cash holdings and bank deposits but changes in reserves of life insurance companies and equity in real property, farms, and other unincorporated businesses.

Since personal savings estimates are the difference between two much larger "estimated" totals (consumption expenditures and personal income), the estimates are subject to large relative errors.

The importance of personal income is shown by the fact that "consumer purchases" in 1964 were approximately 65 per cent of GNP, and "compensation of employees" accounted for 70 per cent of national income. Thus, in both the expenditure and receipt side of the nation's economic accounts, the labor force is the most dominant factor.[10]

The Labor Force. The household survey on the *Status of the Labor Force,* the survey *Nonfarm Business Establishment,* and the official records of the unemployment insurance programs are the three complementary series which furnish the data on the labor force and its composition.

While the three series are complementary, interpretations and parameters differ. For example, in the monthly survey "Sample of Households," each individual fourteen years of age and over is classified as employed, nonemployed, or not in the labor force according to his activity during the week of the survey.[11] On the other hand, in the Sample of Households, an unemployed person in the labor force is one who is not working in the week ending nearest the fifteenth of the month and who is looking for work.

The unemployment rate, which is a "leading" indicator, is given as a percentage: the total unemployed in relation to the total civilian labor force for that month. The unemployment rate covers "insured" individuals only, and is based on the unemployed *covered by state programs only* and then related to the average covered employment for the most recent twelve-month period. The Bureau of Labor Statistics adjusts the data for seasonal variation. However, the weekly rates are not adjusted.

Industrial Production. The Federal Reserve Index of Industrial Production "sums up" specific industry development and forecasts economic growth. In Figure XXVII the market and industry components of this index are shown. The index measures changes in the physical output of the industrial sectors of the economy: manufacturing and mining establishments and gas and electric utilities. This index does not include agriculture, construction, wholesale and retail trade, foreign trade, finance, transportation, and service trade data. Thus, the index is not a measure of general business activity but does account for slightly over one-third of GNP. It is more important as a forecast tool than as an index, as it is very sensitive to changes in over-all demand and business activity. For example: its components include the relative measures of minerals extracted and processed, manufactured and semimanufactured goods output, and utility outputs which are used by *all* sectors of the economy. Because it is published monthly, with a time lag of only about fifteen days, it is one of the most useful barometers of changes in over-all business activity.

---

[10] Elizabeth W. Angle, *Keys for Business Forecasting,* Federal Reserve Bank of Richmond, Va., April 1964.

[11] *Ibid.* See also E. W. Angle's series of articles on business fluctuations, published by the Federal Reserve Bank of Richmond, Va.

FIGURE XXVII
Economic Indicator of Industrial Production by Industry and Market Groupings *

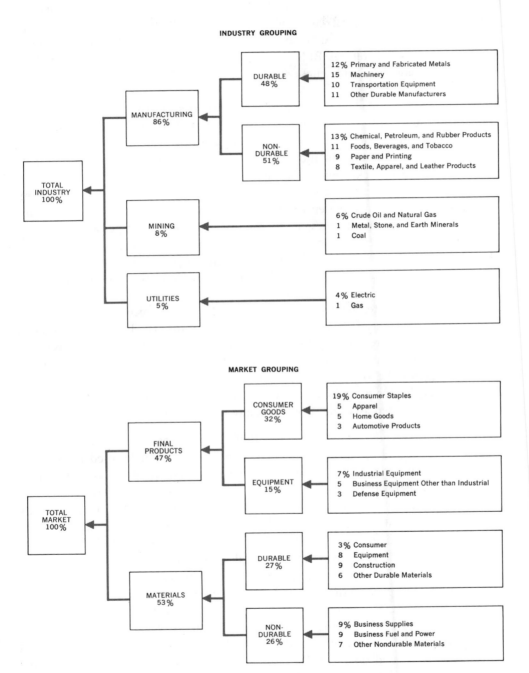

INDUSTRY GROUPING

TOTAL INDUSTRY 100%

MANUFACTURING 86%

DURABLE 48%
- 12% Primary and Fabricated Metals
- 15 Machinery
- 10 Transportation Equipment
- 11 Other Durable Manufacturers

NON-DURABLE 51%
- 13% Chemical, Petroleum, and Rubber Products
- 11 Foods, Beverages, and Tobacco
- 9 Paper and Printing
- 8 Textile, Apparel, and Leather Products

MINING 8%
- 6% Crude Oil and Natural Gas
- 1 Metal, Stone, and Earth Minerals
- 1 Coal

UTILITIES 5%
- 4% Electric
- 1 Gas

MARKET GROUPING

TOTAL MARKET 100%

FINAL PRODUCTS 47%

CONSUMER GOODS 32%
- 19% Consumer Staples
- 5 Apparel
- 5 Home Goods
- 3 Automotive Products

EQUIPMENT 15%
- 7% Industrial Equipment
- 5 Business Equipment Other than Industrial
- 3 Defense Equipment

MATERIALS 53%

DURABLE 27%
- 3% Consumer
- 8 Equipment
- 9 Construction
- 6 Other Durable Materials

NON-DURABLE 26%
- 9% Business Supplies
- 9 Business Fuel and Power
- 7 Other Nondurable Materials

* Source: Office of Business Economics. U. S. Department of Commerce, and E. W. Angle, Federal Reserve Bank of Richmond.

347

Wholesale Price Index. The most comprehensive measure of the general commodity price levels is the monthly index of wholesale prices compiled by the Bureau of Labor Statistics (BLS). The Wholesale Price Index is designed to measure price changes of all commodities sold in the country's primary markets wherein are found the first large-volume classes of buyers.

The index is not designed to measure prices received by wholesalers, jobbers, or distributors. The official BLS index of wholesale prices is available back to 1890. There have been only slight modifications since that time in the calculation methods used.

The index is divided into two principal categories: firstly, farm products and processed foods with separate indexes for each; and secondly, all commodities other than farm products and foods. The latter is subdivided into thirteen major industry groups. The current index has a 1957–59 base period (as one hundred) and is published weekly and monthly.

Price changes influence every phase of the economy. Commodity flows by means of transactions are generated either easily or haltingly through the price mechanics of the market. Price measures at all transaction levels are especially important at the production level. The changes in this index with the Federal Reserve Bank's index of Industrial Production generally vary directly with business activity. Retail managers, by graphing the changes in these two barometers, would have a ready springboard for action.

Only marginal interpretations of economic fluctuations can be made without measurements of price movements. Three of the most widely used measures of price movements are the comprehensive implicit price deflators for GNP. Of major importance are the Wholesale Price Index, the Consumer Price Index, which measures the purchasing price of the dollar, and the Retail Price Index (which is no longer published by the Department of Commerce but the projection of which is used as a "deflator" by many in forecasting retail market change).

Consumer Price Index. The Consumer Price Index measures the changes in the prices of goods and services purchased by consumers. It can be used to correlate the effect of price changes on any closely defined group of workers. From its inception in 1913 through December 1963, the index applied to goods and services bought by wage-earner and clerical-worker families. With the January 1964 index, weighting was revised and coverage extended to include purchases by single workers living alone. The 1957–59 period is now the index's base period. A separate index on family purchases is also published.

The index includes approximately four hundred commodities and services, priced in a sample of retail outlets located in fifty-six metropolitan areas and cities. The index represents the market-basket purchases of the thousands of commodities and services made by wage earners and clerical workers living in all United States urban areas. The sample and the weights used to combine the individual price series are based on the 1960–1961 consumer expenditure surveys conducted in sixty-six cities. The "old" index, based on 1950 expenditure patterns, was continued through June 1964.

The BLS also publishes a series with a 1957–1959 base which indicates the current purchasing power of the dollar. Because of the wide publicity given to this series, it has important psychological implications to consumers.

Seasonal Adjustments. It is characteristic of retail markets to have widely fluctuating seasonal, cyclical, and irregular trends. These fluctuations are dynamic, very volatile, and are classified according to time intervals, but they must be dealt with on an automatic and continuing adaptability basis. These fluctuations are known as time series; when properly interpreted, these series indicate whether an upward or downward movement will take place in the near future. These data are both long-run and short-run in nature.

When time series are periodic and recurring, they are to a degree measurable statistically, and any individual movement can be isolated for assessment. The movements that are measurable are the secular, cyclical, and seasonal. The irregular trend must be expected but cannot be projected. These curves are illustrated graphically in Figure XXVIII.

Thus there are four primary time series components which should be considered in forecasting: the secular trend, the long-term trend over time; the cyclical trend, which may range in 8- to 12-year cycles; the seasonal, which usually represents two to four repetitive movements within a year superimposed on the cyclical; and the irregular trend, which reflects random movements of unusual events, "acts of God," and which cannot be forecast. The four types of changes—secular, cyclical, seasonal, and irregular—vary in importance and relationship. Management may be interested, for example, in only the trend-cycle component. This is carried out by reviewing the seasonal and irregular effects on the business cycle.[12]

Seasonal patterns vary in amplitude from series to series, and also over time as social customs and market competition alter underlying conditions. Seasonal changes may be gradual, as in the case of "summer electricity" sales adjusting to the spread of air conditioning, or they may be abrupt, as in the case of a change in the timing and introduction of new fashions.

Irregular adjustments should be identified and removed and corrected before computing seasonals. Adjustments for the irregular patterns should be made for changes in the number of working or trading days, the number of weekends in a month, and the patterns as to when Easter or Christmas falls. It is also possible to adjust a series for the greater relative importance of some days of the

---

[12] In adjusting a statistical series to remove the effect of a trend component such as "seasonal," the original series is divided by the measurement of the seasonal. Thus, secular and cyclical movements are clearly discernible. For example: before any seasonal adjustments take place, the original series is generally termed O; in any data units this is the resultant of ($T \times C \times S \times I$).

$$O = T \times C \times S \times I, \text{ where}$$

O = original series (sum total of all trends),
T = secular long-term growth trend,
C = cyclical alternating upswings and downswings of various length and amplitude,
S = seasonal (fairly regular movements within a year),
I = irregular random movements and unpredictable "acts of God."

To adjust for seasonal variation; for example: $O/S = T \times C \times I$, or to adjust for cyclical, for example: $O/C = T \times S \times I$, etc. (Other computational details of this method are described in most textbooks on economic statistics.)

FIGURE XXVIII
Changing Combinations of Business Fluctuation Patterns

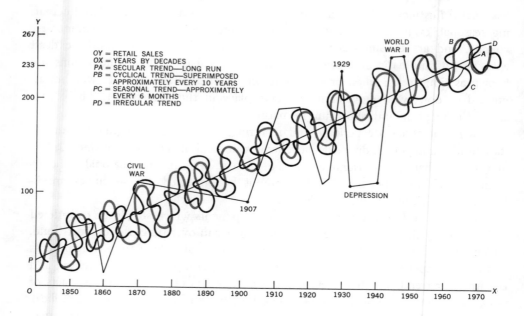

OY = RETAIL SALES
OX = YEARS BY DECADES
PA = SECULAR TREND—LONG RUN
PB = CYCLICAL TREND—SUPERIMPOSED
    APPROXIMATELY EVERY 10 YEARS
PC = SEASONAL TREND—APPROXIMATELY
    EVERY 6 MONTHS
PD = IRREGULAR TREND

week which show the greatest relative sales importance. At all times, whatever statistical adjustments are made must be clearly designated.

For instance, apparel sales tend to show larger increases in months with five Saturdays than in months with only four, although the number of actual trading days may be the same. The effect of holidays may also vary from year to year. For example, special adjustments are made in forecasting retail sales to account for the shifting dates of the Easter season when increased shopping activity takes place.

Business Cycle Barometers

The indicator approach to defining and analyzing the business cycle was originally developed by the National Bureau of Economic Research (NBER), whose definition states that the business cycle consists "of expansions occurring at about the same time in many economic activities, followed by similarly general recessions, contractions, and revivals which merge into the expansion phase of the next cycle." Business cycles are those alternating and recurring movements relating to aggregate economic activity, as distinguished from the cycle of any individual statistical series. There are two essential ingredients in the NBER definition: first, it is a composite picture of the economy; and second, it delineates the indicator forces which can induce forces working directional changes in the total economy.

There have been twenty-six "peaks" and "troughs," turning points of business cycles which have been reference-dated from the 1854 to 1961 periods by the NBER. The last dated turning point was the trough of February 1961.

Turning-point reference dates are set up with lead or lag labels, or coincide with the turning points in general business. Individual series whose peaks and troughs roughly parallel those in general business are termed the "roughly coincident series." Among the nine most commonly used "coincident indicators" are GNP, personal income, industrial production, nonagricultural employment, the unemployment rate, and the index of wholesale prices of commodities other than farm products and food.

The turning points of any of these individual series do not always coincide with the NBER reference dates, which are chosen on the basis of how the turning points of the coincident series are clustered. For decision making, management prefers to have peaks and troughs designated on the basis of the behavior of a single indicator, particularly GNP or the industrial production index. The "leading indicators" refer to any of the twelve major series in this category relating primarily to future production and employment. Included in this group are manufacturers' new orders for durables, the average workweek in manufacturing, new housing starts, corporate profits after taxes, common stock prices, and spot market prices of industrial materials.

Indicators which generally "follow" the turning points in general business activity designate business investment costs. Included in this group are five major services: plant and equipment expenditures, changing manufacturers' inventories, and bank interest rates on business loans. As pointed out, the number of months an individual series precedes or follows the cyclical turning points varies as does the average length of lead and lag times at differing peaks. The reason for the difference in forecasts is that there is no valid, short-cut method of predicting business cycles. Management must be certain that careful, detailed analysis of the aggregated data has been made before reliance is placed on any forecast.

THE RESEARCH PLAN

In forecasting, which is a specialized aspect of market research, the process flows from the general to the specific. In a like manner, the research plan flows from the over-all general problems of the firm to the specific defining of the problem to be researched. Once defined, this is followed by a situation analysis which sets up the factual data in a cause and effect relationship, so that any ambiguity in the objectives of the plan is cleared up. Before proceeding, all data sources are examined, and pertinent research on similar problems are first investigated.

In setting up a research plan, any phase of store operations or market definition would be a valid research area. For example, balance sheet and operating statement analyses would represent significant areas for internal research. Balance sheet ratios, such as current assets to current liabilities, or the ratios of fixed to working capital, would be static in nature and representative of the firm's instant position. Profit and loss (P & L) or income statements ratios, such as sales to operating expense or gross margin to sales, would be dynamic in nature and be illustrative of the effects of changing market strategy to competition. Again, by correlating the various budgets with operating results, evaluative criteria are furnished to administrative management. When similar ratios are set up over five- to ten-year periods, changes become readily apparent and can make evident research areas.

Consumer Analysis

Once a survey is decided upon as a research methodology, the "situation analysis" becomes the starting point. This would correspond to personal observations and previously noted conditions subjectively supplemented by "ideas" and hunches. Usually, the situation analysis consists of "observing" the behavior patterns of existing and potential customers.

There are only three broad classes of information that can be developed from consumer surveys:

1) *Who a person is* (through observation and determination from sex, age, educational level, zone of residence);
2) *What he does* (behavior); or
3) *What he knows* (how he feels—knowledge, attitude, etc.).

Within this framework, the zones of residence and trading areas of potential customers can be pinpointed, along with their income ranges, social characteristics, and known buyer behavior.

Buyer behavior—besides being of key importance to the firm from a promotional standpoint—is vital in characterizing buyer attitudes (which include the particular individual's concept of the store). Thus, knowing what a customer thinks and who he is gives management an indication of his probable behavior in the market place.

The Questionnaire Survey

To discover consumer attitudes, knowledge and behavior questionnaire surveys can be set up. Fundamental to the development of any research survey are the definition of the problems and the formulation of an outline of the subject matter. Survey findings, especially at the retail level, can often indicate whether or not a company, idea, or location will be successful.

The most common type of consumer survey is the kind carried out by the objective "conversational" questionnaire which requires no "depth interviewing" experience.[13]

In the first drafting of any objective questionnaire, the introductory question "addressed" to the respondent must create rapport—confidence on the part of the

---

[13] Where motivations below the level of awareness are sought, experienced interviewers with psychology backgrounds and/or experience would be needed.

respondent that the interviewer is really interested in his views on a "nonpersonal" basis and is not there to sell him something. In all cases a pre-test of the questionnaire should be made to "typical" residents, so that all possible hidden bias or improper phrasing can be eliminated.

Also, questions must be carefully arranged in sequence in order to be psychologically sound. The final draft of the questionnaire, once "pilot tested" for objectivity, completeness, and psychological concreteness, is then used in accordance with the determined sample with every question being asked *exactly* as written.

In general, questions to consumers on future actions or behavior should be kept to a minimum, as should questions having prestige content. Whenever possible, only simple, direct, one-part questions should be used. In a like manner, questions which might reflect on a person's intelligence should be avoided.

Sampling

Ideally, to learn about the operating characteristics of an economic unit, one would have to observe the reactions of all dependent variables to various input stimuli; first one at a time, and then in various combinations. Given enough such experiments, it would be possible to discover the important stimuli, as well as how their variations are related to a dependent variable such as buyer behavior.

For example, how important to volume are pre-Easter price cuts on garments as compared to similar price cuts after Easter? Should garments in a ready-to-wear department be put on racks according to price ranges, colors, or sizes? Or, possibly, in combination, with "sizes" predominating? What is the relationship of parking charges to limiting downtown shopping traffic? Or is downtown shopping traffic more a function of "driving-time distances" and availability of easy parking at peak periods.

The key to the validity and reliability of any sample survey depends on the choice of the correct "universe" and the manner in which the sample is drawn. The most reliable and statistically valid samples are the pure random sample or the stratified random sample, in which every element in the "universe" has an equal chance of being chosen. A random sample, once its size has been deemed adequate, can be relied upon and can be mathematically verified as to its reliability and representativeness.

Telephone interviewing via random or stratified random sampling is relatively simple. The telephone directory of most areas would represent a valid "universe," as the vast preponderance of households in most metropolitan areas have telephones. Telephone directory listings are valid also in that the characteristics of the population listed are independent of their position in the directory.

A third method of sampling would be the controlled or stratified quota sample. In this method a sample is set up to conform to the socioeconomic characteristics of the "universe"; age, sex, income, education, ethnic background, and marital status—all would be included. This method of sampling necessitates knowing in advance the specific characteristics of the population to be sampled.

Probably the most accurate method of a mass sampling procedure is the random method with stratification; this is also referred to as "area sampling" and is the method employed by the Bureau of the Census. In Census procedures, once the choice of the area or region to be sampled is made, the sampling unit within the zone is randomly selected and the size of the cross-sections determined. This might be a city block, a political ward, or any clearly defined geographical area. In other words, every element or unit must have an "equal" chance of being chosen. Because the data have been chosen randomly, the permissible sampling error can be determined statistically.

Research Evaluation

With a basic understanding of statistics as a working guide, masses of data can be transposed into simple, understandable terms. Many survey conclusions would be couched in terms of measures of central tendency or averages called a mean, a mode, or a median.

The mean is an arithmetical summation of values of the raw data divided by the total number of cases in the sample universe. The median, another measure of central tendency, is the midpoint of a series of measurements arranged in numerical order. (The median may or may not represent an actual case, since the number of cases in any group may be even.) The third average or measure of central tendency, the mode, is the point of cluster or maximum frequency in any data array. Unless the use of the average is accompanied by an exact identification and a range or tolerance limit of the data, its meaning is clouded and ineffectual for any conclusions by management that might lead to action.

For example, the purpose in using an average is to present more readily an over-all meaning to data.

The range or tolerance limit attached to an average is a necessary measure of variability which quantifies any sets of data. Measures of variability, also a type of tolerance limit, indicate the spread of a series or the scatter of data around an average. For example, in evaluating the authenticated average annual income in a trading area, only limited applicability would be obtained from knowing that household income averages $6,000 per household without knowing the range or "skew" of the data about this average. In other words, just how high and how low are the incomes making up this income average of $6,000? Such measures define the range; classifying the average defines its meaning. Classifications of this kind are essential in using research findings. For example, a $6,000 average resulting from a range of incomes from $4,000 to $30,000 annually is a far, far different communications pattern problem than a range of $5,000 to $7,000 annually. In effect, the simplest method of measuring dispersion is to show the range or difference between the highest and lowest numbers—in this case, income groups by size.

Other measures of central tendency are the standard deviation (SD) and the standard error (SE). The former is related directly to the variability of the data, the actual data, and the total number of cases. In order to derive such data, they must be actual or have been randomly selected. The standard deviation is equal to the square root of the sum of the deviations (from the mean) squared, multiplied by the frequency divided by the number of individual cases. For example, the standard deviation is given by:

$$ SD = \sqrt{\frac{\Sigma\,FD^2}{N}} \qquad\qquad observed = \sqrt{\frac{\Sigma\,FD^2}{N}} $$

where F is the frequency, D is the deviation of the individual scores from their arithmetical mean, and N is the total number of scores. (Σ is the common summation operator.)

If class intervals are not used, the frequency is always *1*, since each piece of data is handled separately.[14] If class intervals are used, the frequency for each interval is the total number of data points falling within that interval.

In the sample shown in Table 32, the raw score data are 1 to 15; the SD as developed is ± 3.572 with a mean of 7.28. This means that approximately 68 per cent of all the cases in this sample are within ± 3.572 of the mean. In this case, 10.852 (3.572 + 7.28) and 3.708 (7.28 − 3.572). Where two standard deviations are used it would cover approximately 95 to 98 per cent of all cases in the sample or survey. The standard error (SE) is another measure of variability and is closely related to the standard deviation ($SE = \sqrt{PO/N}$).[15] It is used where it is not possible to measure the actual variability of the individual cases. Another evaluative statistical measure is that of reliability. When more than one measure of central tendency is used, the comparison of both to each other becomes a test of homogeneity and reliability of the data.

CORRELATION

Another measurement concept—and probably the most important from the managerial standpoint—involves correlations or measures of relationship. Correlations immediately point out to management any significance between the findings of a survey and real applications. For example, when a particular type of store can establish a mathematical relationship between sales and one or two of the "leading" economic indicators, then there is a basis for general forecasting.[16]

Again, market studies, especially those on changing consumption patterns, are of maximum usefulness when they can be used to measure or predict behavior. In this regard, correlation techniques become extremely useful because the relationships explain a degree of relationship of one set of data in terms of another.

---

14 Where meaning is desired from great masses of data, the data are grouped into equally spaced intervals or groups for processing as units. This facilitates the computations (which are essentially the same, if not "overgrouped"), without severely biasing the results.

15 P = value of percentage wanted; O = value of actual percentage subtracted from 100; N refers to the total number of cases. Because samples have to be large the "−1" part of the denominator is generally omitted.

16 Perfect positive correlation would be stated as 1.0; perfect negative correlation would be −1.0.

TABLE 32

DEVIATION OF THE MEAN, MODE MEDIAN, AND STANDARD DEVIATION[a]

X	F	FX	D	D²	FD²
1	1	1	6.28	39.4384	39.4384
2	2	4	5.28	27.8784	55.7568
3	1	3	4.28	18.3184	18.3184
4	3	12	3.28	10.7584	32.2752
5	1	5	2.28	5.1984	5.1984
6	4	24	1.28	1.6384	6.5536
7	2	14	0.28	0.7840	1.5680
8	1	8	0.72	0.5184	0.5184
9	3	27	1.72	2.9584	8.8752
10	2	20	2.72	7.3984	14.7968
11	1	11	3.72	13.8384	13.8384
12	2	24	4.72	22.2784	44.5568
14	1	14	5.72	32.1784	32.1784
15	1	15	6.72	45.1584	45.1584
	25	182			Σ319.0312

F = Frequency
X = Raw data (cases)
D = Deviation from mean

Total FX 182
Total Cases   25

$$\therefore \text{Mean} = \frac{FX}{X} = \frac{182}{25} = 7.28 \qquad \therefore SD = \sqrt{\frac{\Sigma FD^2}{N}}$$

Mode—(Points of cluster) 6.28 $\qquad SD = \sqrt{\frac{319.0312}{25}}$

Median—(Midpoint)   7 $\qquad SD = \sqrt{12.761248}$

(13th case) $\qquad SD = \pm 3.572$ or range of data about
the "average" (mean).

[a] Developed by Author.

Correlations may be either quantitative, where the relationship may be expressed in terms of numbers, or qualitative, where the variables cannot be expressed numerically.

While it is the function of research to indicate to management the significance of purported correlations, caution must be exercised by both research and management not to confuse chance or spurious correlations with actual causative relationships. Relationships which are likely to change should be so indicated.

Thus, no assumptions should be made in any comparisons that a high correlation, for example a +.75, necessarily indicates a cause and effect relationship. For example, a high "readership" of magazine advertising or a high "median" viewing index does not necessarily indicate a high ratio of the product sales per space bought or program viewed. Also, it may be entirely false to assume that purchasers of particular brands or that shoppers in particular stores have noticed particular ads, or that they acted on direct impulse as a result of action triggered by prior subconscious exposures from particular directions.

SUMMARY AND CONCLUSIONS

In this chapter, policy and managerial technique procedures regarding communications, forecasting, and research methods were analyzed. Both analytical and survey illustrations were used. The role of research was developed from the standpoint of its basic usefulness as a basic management staff function.

Communications and research represent the methods for the marketing firm. Advertising and the use of the mass appeal represent its public image; selling represents the results of that image.

Chapter 23: *Management of the Selling Functions*

The success and business continuity of the firm depend directly on efficient management of the selling functions. The supervision of this function is essentially one of sales management and cannot be minimized. Customer contacts at point of sale are critical in nature. The nature and importance of the selling function is reflected in the strong institutional policies in this direction. Regardless of whether selling is carried out on a full-service, simplified, or self-service basis, the transactions made reflect the sum total of all the coordinated activities of the firm.

As it has been pointed out, and as was described by J. A. Hobson, with only two-thirds of the manufactured consumer-goods capacity absorbed since 1948, the economy has been (and is) in an overproduction-underconsumption cycle. The basic difference today is that consumption is no longer subordinated to production. With an excess supply of manufacturer's consumer-goods capacity in the American economy and with rising imports, consumers will continue to have an unparalleled freedom of choice of how, what, and where to shop.

INSTITUTIONAL DECISION-SALES POLICIES

Each type of firm institutes the kind of selling procedures and sales methodologies most consistent with its philosophy of management and the requirements of the goods classification which it offers. Selling methods at the retail level range all the way from complete self-service check-out to full-service selling. Thus, one of the firm's major decisions concerns the determination of its sales policies. These were previously described. There is rarely any one best method of selling for an entire store. What may be an optimum sales approach for one classification or department can be detrimental in another. In managing the sales functions of a firm, the choice of the most effective selling method determines its degree of success.

Retail management deals in a great measure with intangibles as well as tangible goods; the former usually defy accurate measurement and lack immediate economic visibility to the consumer in terms of value added! Yet qualitative as well as quantitative utilities are of key importance in the buyer-seller relationships in the process of satisfying consumer wants.

There has, however, been a continuing decrease in institutional acceptance of psychological values attendant to in-store sales methodologies. Furthermore, the emphasis today is mostly on "ringing registers" and procedural inventory accounting rather than on selling. Many "in-store" areas which have been changed over from full-service selling to simplified or self-service operations have not shown significant increased productivity results.[1] Nevertheless, there is strong customer acceptance for self-service and simplified selling procedures in many areas.

In the larger stores, interdepartmental selling, because of the dispersed physical locations for similar and coordinated classifications in the store, becomes largely ineffective. Furthermore, each goods classification and each type of establishment generally has its own selling policies and procedures regardless of selling methods.

STRUCTURAL PROCEDURES IN THE SELLING PROCESS

In full-service selling, each transaction contains "the approach," "the informative procedures," and "the closing." In the case of self-service check-out, the approach and the informative procedure are carried out passively by means of creative packaging of wanted merchandise with prices clearly marked; implementing these functions, there is the direct assistance of point-of-purchase materials. The great weakness in self-service is that the customer has to "sell" himself—in other words, a "self-closing" sales function. The only way that he communicates with management is through his purchases.

The principal advantage of full-service selling over simplified selling is found in the availability of a salesperson, who can furnish customers with answers to their questions, volunteer suggestions, and act as management channels for informational feedback. When properly motivated, roving "missionary" sales supervisors can assist customers in "selling themselves." The customer approach even in an indirect manner, such as in self-selection, determines the rapidity and extent to which sales are made.

---

[1] Research studies of "What Happens Where Store Selling Procedures Are Changed," unpublished research memorandum, Graduate School, University of Pittsburgh, 1963.

A pleasant greeting and immediate recognition of the customer's presence in a department store is encouraging to customers. This is part of the store's service offer and is an intangible "value" which marketing generates in the form of time, place, and possession utilities.[2]

With respect to the service offer, as long as the marginal net yield of the additional volume generated is positive (cost of services versus contribution dollars), particular services are economic and should be continued, since the likely results of all efforts show up as additions to existing volume. The yardstick of "volume added" can be a good one because it lends itself to a qualitative evaluation in terms of a quantitative measurement. For example; if volume decreases and attendant service costs increase to the point where marginal costs become greater than marginal revenues $(MC > MR)$, then a different type of service effort or a revision of merchandise policies should be instituted.

SALES MANAGEMENT AND MARKET STRATEGY

The importance of this type of marginal analysis is that there are significant differences in sales productivity even among similar departments within a store. In evaluating effectiveness, many types of sales-productivity ratios have been developed. Many techniques consist of gauging the percentage of walkouts to total departmental or store traffic shopping.[3] Interviewing individuals leaving the store without a package is an excellent means of gauging advertising effect and pinpointing symptomatic problems as to whether the salesperson, the merchandise, or the service offered is at fault.

In addition to walkout analysis, there are many positive quantitative analytical approaches set up on models of disaggregative probabilities. For example, some of the ratio standards of comparisons which may be used are:

$$\frac{\text{Units sold}}{\text{Total traffic}} = \text{Traffic Productivity Ratio (TPR)}$$

$$\frac{\text{Transactions}}{\text{Traffic}} = \text{Per cent of traffic sold}$$

$$\frac{\text{Walkouts}}{\text{Traffic}} = \text{Per cent of walkouts}$$

$$\frac{\text{Units sold}}{\text{Transactions}} = \text{Units sold per customer}$$

$$\frac{\text{Planned traffic}}{\text{Traffic-sales}} = \frac{\text{Planned volume}}{\text{(TPR)}}$$

---

[2] See also J. A. Hobson, *Work and Wealth*, rev. ed. (London, George Allen and Unwin Ltd., 1933), p. 6.

[3] George Engel Associates, management consultants now merged with Amos Parrish & Co. of New York, have developed many ratios of this kind.

$$\text{Salesman ratio} = \frac{\text{Traffic}}{\text{"Salesperson"-days}}$$

$$\text{Profit per unit of traffic} = (\text{TPR}) \times \text{Gross Margin}$$

In order to determine which market mixes, including selling approaches, would best maximize sales, many models of the way in which "interacting" individual households behave in particular market situations were set up and observed. For example, in Markov chain "model experiments" several thousand hypothetical individuals representing choice "types" were observed and classified by various demographic and economic variables. A stochastic selection of media appeals and selling methods for the various groups of individuals was then projected, measured, and aggregated to determine the best grouping. The variables involved in determining an optimum run in the total product-service of the firm are shown in Figure XXIX.

In this model, "a randomly determined *number* of customers in a randomly determined 'dollar-size' of individual sales" are formulated. Because of the many hundreds of interacting data, this kind of quantitative analysis requires a computer for solutions. Thus, such analyses cannot be used by management without research assistance supplying the results in terms of actionable conclusions.[4] In Appendix L are shown management applications which can be used to improve off-season sales.

Managers of the selling functions should make certain that all sales and sales-supporting personnel are kept informed of the basic qualities of all the merchandise lines handled; this must include any basic changes in merchandising or marketing policies. The dissemination of product information as well as sales training are integral parts of the sales manager's supervision of the selling function. In any managerial-economic approach to selling management, the basic objective is to maximize sales. The system processing of functions must precede any actual managerial applications to selling.

Personal selling per se represents the sum total of all line and staff efforts within an organization furthering the exchange function. Management agree that the importance of effective sales personnel cannot be underestimated; yet, when a new person is hired and "put on the floor," formal training of the salesperson is often overlooked. With increasing geographical dispersion of multi-unit, highly departmentized firms, such procedures make effective selling management marginal at best.

For example, although the device of weekly floor sales meetings has proved effective, the vast majority of retail stores neglect to employ even this elementary device. Most top salesmen in retail organizations can be used as teachers or even as "on the job" examples for new sales personnel.

---

[4] See also Haskel Benishay, "A Disaggregative Model for the Generation of Sales," *Journal of Market Research*, September 1965, Vol. II, No. 1, pp. 74–79. In effect, Benishay presents a stochastic two-stage random process (a-number-of-customers stage, and a-size-of-sale stage) as a disaggregative approach for the representation of sales for analyses.

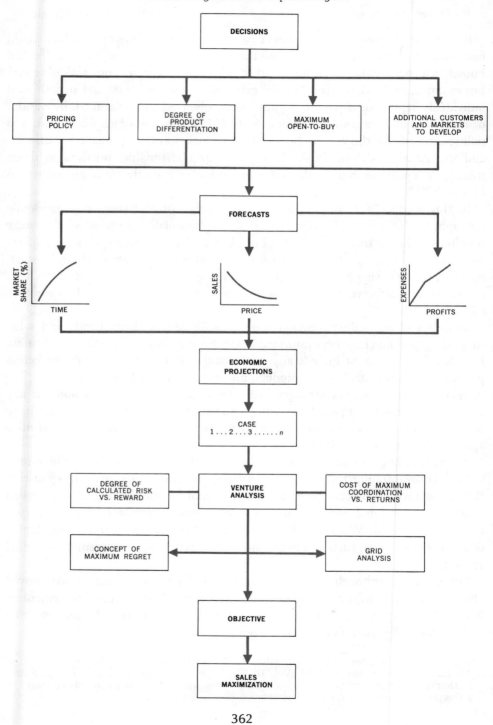

FIGURE XXIX
SEQUENTIAL POLICY APPLICATIONS FOR MANAGEMENT OF THE SELLING FUNCTIONS

A Flow Diagram for a Computer Program

There are exceptions, however; since 1963 the personnel division of Allied Stores Corporation has been using selectively applied programed instruction for training retail sales personnel. They have developed a self-instructional programed text which teaches the fundamentals of courtesy and the techniques of suggestion selling. The criteria used by Allied Stores sales personnel development are, 1) sales dollars per hour, 2) number of transactions per hour:

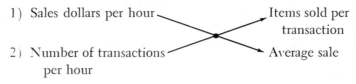

1) Sales dollars per hour   Items sold per transaction

2) Number of transactions per hour   Average sale

In their first experiment with their "program-trained" group, their sales-dollar revenue per hour increased over that of the "not-so-trained" control group by 25 per cent. To supplement the training, Allied also used self-instructional manuals in courtesy and suggestion selling—especially in training part-time and seasonal employees. The manuals are also used for introductory training of sales personnel in their branch and smaller stores. By providing the best "mix" of classroom and other instruction, the corporate personnel department feels that sales performances are being improved.[5]

For sales training to be effective, it should also be accompanied by proper incentives. When sales personnel are paid on a straight salary basis, proper motivation ensues only if the salary or working conditions are of a "high reward" nature. The salary to be earned should provide the correct motivation in developing good salesmanship in the organization. The most productive salespeople are generally those who work on a straight commission or a realistic quota-bonus basis.

Most buyers or assistant buyers are so busy with merchandising and routine details that they are not very effective sales supervisors. With many store executives believing that management of the selling function is automatic in nature, they often "go out to lunch" from 11 A.M. to 2 P.M., when the store is busiest. During these most important periods of the day, except for technical "blue-pencil" overviews, functional selling and its management are left to fend for themselves.[6]

EFFECTS OF CIRCULAR INFORMATION FLOWS

One of the most serious shortcomings in maximizing the sales function of stores is failure to transmit adequate merchandise information. Information emanating from comparison shopping services, trade papers, resident buyers, and bulletins rarely gets to the salespeople on the floor where such information would be of maximum value. This lack of a communications channel to the selling personnel

[5] See Frederick Finegan, "Programmed Sales Training," *Department Store Economist*, April 1963, pp. 33–34.
[6] Based on observation and research by the author of selected retail firms throughout the country, 1959–1965.

results in a companion lack of feedback upward to management. Thus, the prime "built-in" sources of information remain bottled up on the floor.

Adequate and timely communications and information flows help reinforce job security concepts and raise morale. Formal information passed to employees dispels rumors and fears, and gives them confidence in the organization. Furthermore, formal communications on a continuing basis also give employees a real understanding and appreciation of store practices, policies, and procedures. Such a program also personalizes the store and builds the type of image that management desires. Understanding of organizational goals by rank-and-file employees helps in cutting down absenteeism and lateness. This is more important than ever before, because the growing scale of firm and size of plants have created "personal touch" vacuums not prevalent in the past.

For example, before any advertisements are run, the opinions of regular salespeople in the department should be polled. Salespeople should be a major source of buying information; they develop a knowledge of a store's customers as well as a thorough knowledge of merchandise wanted as part of their stock in trade.

One of the best methods of compiling feedback information is the customer want-slip system illustrated in Figure XXX. Any items asked for by customers are listed, and the list handed in to the buyer at the end of the day. Additional items which should be added to the want-slip system are customer comments on service as well as on merchandise and prices. A well-planned want-slip system is the principal means by which management can actually evaluate its performance in terms of merchandising effectiveness.

Records or lists of all advertisements should therefore be sent to every selling department in the store. It should always be kept in mind also that each salesperson is a promotional unit of the entire store. Since sales personnel serve in a continuous customer contact capacity, they are in an excellent research position to know what customers want and what merchandise should be promoted. Should their knowledge be channeled, merchandising offerings could be more effectively geared to demand, insuring easier and more effective selling.

In branch stores, the store manager is also a selling executive, as many of his managerial functions parallel those of his counterpart, the sales manager in industry. As a sales executive, the branch-store manager should be alert to "best sellers" or "runners" very quickly; he should also have a place on the store's merchandising-policy committee. As the branch store's sales manager, he is in an excellent position to evaluate customer requests and opinions of salespeople.

COORDINATION OF THE SALES AND SALES-SUPPORTING FUNCTIONS

Each member of the firm can be classified as either a sales or a sales-supporting agent. Every individual member of the retail and market organization, regardless of his assigned responsibilities, must be considered an integral part of the firm's total sales and public-relations organization.

FIGURE XXX
TYPICAL WANT SLIP USED FOR COMPILING FEEDBACK INFORMATION

```
            DEPARTMENTAL WANT SLIP


   DEPARTMENT _____   DATE _____

   EMPLOYEE # _____ NAME_____

   INSTRUCTIONS: PLEASE LIST ALL CUSTOMER REQUESTS WHICH COULD
   NOT BE FILLED FROM AVAILABLE STOCK. . . . LIST ANY PERTINENT
   CUSTOMER COMMENTS REGARDLESS OF CLASSIFICATION OR PRICE.
   HAND IN WANT SLIPS TO DEPARTMENT BUYER OR MANAGER AT THE
   END OF EACH SELLING DAY.



       ITEM REQUESTED AND
       CUSTOMER COMMENTS              PRICE RANGE
   _____   _____


   _____   _____


   _____   _____


   _____   _____


   _____   _____


   _____   _____


   _____   _____


   _____   _____


   _____   _____

            EMPLOYEE'S INITIALS _____
```

The total institutional framework should be set up for maximum coordination of the selling and nonselling functions; this means that the service, merchandising, and sales-promotion activities must be thoroughly meshed towards a single goal.

In attempts to improve selling effectiveness, the rapidity of sales transactions and to increase the probability of sales, attempts are made to measure the changes in customer attitudes toward the total selling organization. Various scaling devices are used, such as the "Thurstone" Scale, which attempts to measure attitude to sales.[7] In marketing analysis this is sometimes referred to as "longitudinal analysis."

More specifically, when scaling measures are only marginally conclusive, sales

[7] L. L. Thurstone, The Measurement of Values (Chicago: University of Chicago Press, 1959).

demonstrations are used to measure changes in attitudes of prospects over time.[8] In the case of retail firms, the changes induced by all the firm's public relations programs and selling functions are constantly being measured.

In evaluating the human-relations aspect of coordinating the selling and sales-supporting functions, Professor McNair of Harvard feels that the human-relations aspects in selling have been blown up too greatly. In coordinating varying functional divisions within an organization, Professor McNair stresses that management must make certain that the productivity gains "turn out to be net gains"—not just losses in one area to make up for gains in another.[9]

INTERNAL COORDINATION—SALES AND SUPPORTING FUNCTIONS

A fast, effective internal communications system is the most powerful single management tool in any business or retail organization. A well-engineered, administrative sales-control system can provide the answers to such important questions as:

1) What percentage of present customers contribute to profit?
2) What distinguishes profitable from unprofitable customers?
3) How much money, if any, is being lost on unprofitable customers?
4) How many market areas can become profitable if cultivated?
5) What selling patterns are most likely to convert greater ranges of trading-area residents into customers?
6) How many sales dollars are being spent on unproductive media?
7) How effective are department managers and the store's sales force, and what are the strengths and weaknesses of each? [10]

It should be kept in mind that the mechanical phases of sales supervision and control are generally handled by the operating division through its service and by floor managers as part of the line function of store management. In fact, every functional division within a retail firm works in a staff capacity in furthering the selling functions of the merchandising division; these functions are carried out as supporting activities. For example, line responsibilities of the publicity division include fashion introduction, coordination, fashion shows, and public-relations activities which provide the aeges for effective sales promotion of the total fashion and institutional image of the store. These functions serve to enhance the total sales of the firm, as they coordinate supporting activities for the merchandising division.

---

[8] G. David Hughes, "Comparing Three Scales Under Field Conditions," unpublished memorandum, Graduate School of Business and Public Administration, Cornell University.

[9] Malcolm P. McNair, "Thinking Ahead, What Price Human Relations," *Harvard Business Review*, March–April, 1957.

[10] See also the memorandum, "Marketing Intelligence for the 'Pace-Setting Sixties,'" Al N. Seares, President, National Sales Executives-International, for a similar discussion on a broad market managerial base.

Store Services

The publicizing of free services available to customers is another aspect of the public-relations activities of the store; store services are managed directly by the operating division. In attempts to cut expense, many stores have been eliminating services, although the availability of "service" has been one of the department store's strong competitive points over discount-house competition. For example, in promoting curtains and draperies, storm doors and windows, television sets, upholstery fabrics, and other items in a semifinished or "yet to be installed" fashion, the easy availability of accompanying services is essential and is part of the sales package.

In many cases, internal research can guide management in exploiting the sales-promotion aspect of the store's service offers. A follow-up research of customer opinions of alterations of women's ready-to-wear apparel and men's suits brings with it many significant verbatim responses regarding the entire store.

Every one of a store's service offers should be continually researched and publicized, both from an institutional and a promotional standpoint. When promoted properly, greater over-all sales result. On an institutional basis, the availability of store services should be a part of the continuing public-relations build-up of the store image itself. Firms featuring a wide range of store services can build high prestige patronage motives.

Stores operating on self-service bases can have "stock-out" cards attached to the various registers for want-slip recording. Another method of internal research for determining current customer demand can be researched on a random on-the-spot, conversational interview basis.

The greater the degree of communication and interaction between line and staff executives in an organization, the more important the effectiveness of the store's impact in a community. With respect to advertising specifically and sales promotion generally, management often uses informal simulation techniques and game strategy in determining the optimum promotional strategy and selling methods to be used at the point of sale.

Suggestion Selling

Management in the area of suggestion selling has had only marginal success. Inadequate interdepartmental informational exchanges may be said to be an important cause. Also, if a salesperson does not know what merchandise is on hand or on order, or what new items the store has obtained, it is impossible to pass such information along to customers. In some stores, this lack of information is the result of poor administration; in others, it is a direct result of inadequate store policy.

Suburban branch stores, in particular, have had little success in getting their employees to engage in suggestion selling. In these areas most of the sales personnel are drawn from the ranks of suburban housewives who apparently feel too "genteel" and uncomfortable about engaging in suggestion selling for fear of forcing sales. However, the notion that suburban customers just want to browse and don't want to be assisted can be discounted as just not so.[11]

Another inhibiting factor in the success of suggestion selling is that too few incentives (such as bonuses, extra discounts, and prizes) are offered to the sales force. The difference between a very profitable operation and a mediocre one can often be the degree of suggested sales. When sales personnel are highly motivated toward suggestion selling, more productive sales patterns result. The sales schedule, set up from the sales forecast budget, should take such potentials into account. For as pointed out, sales increases without additional inventory stock result in a higher stock turnover, better service for customers, fewer losses from markdowns, lower handling and storage costs—and generally without increases in selling costs. The total effect: additional sales volume and customer service.

It is important to motivate an entire staff, both selling and nonselling, toward suggestion selling; also, it is a promising way in which fewer selling days per month and per season may be made more productive. The mounting cost-profit squeeze is also helped. For example, if a firm that has 10,000 transactions a day engages in a full-scale suggestion selling program, an important increase in sales results, even if only one out of every twenty selling suggestions bears fruit. And generally the "extra" sale is made at no extra cost.

Merchandise Perishability

The more perishable the product the more fashionable or novel the merchandise, the greater the need for extreme coordination of the total sales promotion function. Merchandise line coordination plays a major role in the sales of perishable and seasonal merchandise. To achieve a minimum perishability and obsolescence of merchandise, there must be complete interdepartmental communications especially among those handling similar or complementary lines. Perishability in itself denotes the need for speed in handling, processing, and selling. The more perishable the product, the greater the turnover that should be generated by the merchandise, as its prime selling-time period is short in duration. This is another volatile element in the management of the selling function.

Only fresh, new merchandise should be on display, and these items should be featured just before and during the optimum selling periods only. The minute that merchandise does not meet the criteria of freshness or newness, it should not be displayed; nor should such items be shown to customers as regular price, regular stock merchandise. Once perishable merchandise loses its optimum sales appeal, it becomes "para-obsolescent," [12] and it should be "jobbed out" or relegated to an EOM clearance. Although such policies are part of the merchandising function, they are directly related to optimizing sales on the selling floors.

Merchandise classifications as well as the packages themselves can be prone

---

[11] Based on unpublished motivational research studies, Graduate School of Retailing, University of Pittsburgh, 1960–1962.
[12] Incipiently oriented toward a downward trend.

to obsolescence—for example, fountain pens, coffee tins with "plastic tops," soda in cans, new package holders for six or eight bottles. Failure to have the latest affects the selling function directly and must be considered, in effect, a "methodological perishable."

PACKAGING AND PRODUCT DIFFERENTIATION

Because of the great mass of roughly similar product offers, distinctive packaging and the creative use of private brands have assumed a greater role than ever in the selling function. Likewise, the increased use of mass displays, open selling, and particularized self-service systems have become more significant: these have made point-of-purchase visibility of key importance. The stimulation of impulse and "directed" sales depends directly (as well as indirectly) on the merchandise offered, its brand, its package, the manner in which it is displayed, as well as its location within the store or department. For example, one would not look for a budget-priced dress in an upstairs department of Saks Fifth Avenue. Without proper "locale" merchandising and sales, effectiveness can only be marginal. For example, food, gasoline, garden supplies, hardware, and children's apparel will continue to be bought primarily at stores located adjacent to zones of residence in suburban areas. Specialty and shopping goods such as fashion apparel, accessories, and home furnishings, as well as men's clothing and shoes, will continue to be bought primarily downtown, where selections are more complete.

The psychological effects of skillful, creative packaging should never be underestimated in any promotional plan or any venture. The stimulation of impulse and directed sales through a dynamic packaging policy must conform to and be consistent with that of the store image.

Private Branding

Thus, private branding and creative packaging are functions of market and marketing strategy. Skillful packaging assists in the selling function by furnishing customers with additional merchandise choices, both real and implied. When the package attracts a customer's attention to a firm's private brand, the firm's competitive market position and gross margin can be enhanced. Private brands generally furnish the sponsoring organization with higher than average mark-ons and give customers wider action choices.

Many of the larger retail and marketing organizations have flexible private branding policies depending on the degrees of institutional and sectional competition. The flexibility is needed for marketing strategy. Applications in merchandising areas where national brands tend to predominate (such as in drugs, cosmetics, dry groceries, and traffic appliances) would be examples of such merchandise areas. For example, The May Company has an Arcross brand for its drugs and an Armaid brand for its appliances; Sears has an All State brand for its tires and a Kenmore brand for its major appliances. The Federated Department Stores have an AMC brand on many of their offerings, and the A & P Tea Company has an Ann Page brand for its top dry grocery lines and Sultana and Iona brands for the balance of its private-brand, dry grocery lines. Even when a private branding policy has been undertaken merely to create psychological rather than product differentiation, it can be a potent sales factor.

For example, in an Elmo Roper beer study of 5,000 consumers, conducted for the Continental Can Company, it was shown that the packaging of beer may at times be more important than the brand or, possibly, than the retail institution handling the product. In this study:

> ...45% of the respondents said they would switch stores rather than take their beer in a different package.
>
> If their favorite container were dropped by their brand, 42% of those who prefer bottled beer would switch to cans. Among those who prefer canned beer, 40% would change to another brand, while 42% would be willing to accept the brew in bottles.
>
> Says Roper: "Beauty may be only skin deep, but in these days of decreasing product differentiation, skin deep is often deep enough when digging for pay dirt." ...[13]

In essence, packaging—especially when used in conjunction with mass displays and self-service selling—represents the ultimate "sell" to customer communications in self-service stores.[14]

The major areas of stress by management on packaging have been in problems of prewrapping, premarking, and the need for varying corporate identities of the resources involved so as not to detract from the store image. Usually, the manufacturer has his package designed to reflect his corporate identity; this is carried out through the use of a "corporate" color or combination of colors, a trademark, symbol, logotype, or a particular shape. Without a private label program to broaden its merchandise offer, retail management more often than not promotes the manufacturer's image rather than that of the store.

EFFECT OF TRADING STAMPS

A classic question that often enters into any evaluation is the effect of trading-stamp plans. Recent studies show that stamps generally help convenience-goods stores (such as supermarkets, grocery stores, and drugstores), and primarily at the time when they are initially introduced into the firm's operation. They do help in product differentiation, may improve a firm's competitive position, but will rarely expand the over-all market size in terms of "driving-time distances."

There are over 2,000 trading-stamp distribution centers throughout the country, with S & H, Top Value, and Gold Bond redemption centers the most numerous. More recently, in surveys taken at eight large Eastern and Midwestern metro-

---

[13] See also "Sales and Distribution," *Dun's Review and Modern Industry*, November 1959, p. 87.
[14] See also David Breedon, "Packaging," *Store Magazine*, June 1965, Vol. 47, No. 6. First of a six-part management series on packaging and packing: materials, techniques, dimensions, and graphics; also, "Special Report on Packaging," *Business Week*, February 20, 1965, #1851, pp. 90–114.

politan areas, it was stated by eight out of ten respondents that they saved trading stamps because "they are given to me anyway." Six out of ten respondents felt that they paid more for merchandise when shopping in the store giving trading stamps; the most frequent reason given was, "the store has to pay for the stamps."

Almost all respondents in similar consumer surveys stated that they would continue to shop in the same stores even if the store stopped giving stamps. Nevertheless, the popularity of trading stamps is a potent competitive weapon, but will continue to show cyclical variations in popularity.

PRODUCT ACCEPTANCE

Merchandise creatively bought, coupled with skillful management of the selling function, is one of the most effective ways to maximize the over-all productivity of the firm. In effect, the point of sale represents the pay-off points of the total store operation. It is at these pay-off points that institutional acceptance becomes deterministic.

Most retail establishments have a tendency to move slowly with respect to new products; nevertheless, it is unquestionably a competitive advantage to be the first to introduce a new product or fashion. At the same time, there is always the risk of losing money on new product introduction. Extraordinary losses of this kind should be considered promotional expenditures in much the same manner as the costs of trading stamps.

In the acceptance of any new product, difficulty often lies in getting the consumer to try it under normal conditions.[15] Similarly, in gasoline marketing, the introduction by Sunoco of a "multi-grade" system in 1956 represents a classic example of applied, pretested market strategy in new product introduction in a framework of both price and quality competition.[16] Leaders in retailing offer both novelties and goods that have proved their worth. For instance, the purchase of a color television set may satisfy the wants of many consumers from both a "status" and a practical standpoint. During the initial period of introduction, the stores offering color TV achieved a leadership role at a higher average cost. Once prices on the color sets began to drop, market demand increased to profitable levels. At this point, the stores handling the initial introduction generally had measurable competitive advantages.

Generally speaking, a store's corporate image is better than its corporate look; in other words, the public's impression of a store is generally better than the sum total of all its visual manifestations. Being first with new items or operations continues to enhance a store's corporate image.[17]

---

[15] See also research studies on "Product Acceptance Testing" conducted by A. J. Wood & Co., Philadelphia, Pa., as found in their publication, Wood Chips, Ed Hafler, ed.

[16] James B. McNallen, "A New Concept in Gasoline Marketing," The Journal of Marketing, January 1958, Vol. XXII, No. 3, pp. 273, 281.

[17] Developed in a series of research interviews with the major executives of Kaufmann's, the Joseph Horne Co., and Gimbels, Pittsburgh, Pa., 1960–1964.

SUMMARY AND CONCLUSIONS

The management of sales is not a single activity but the integral part of the retail firm's total promotional efforts. Thus, effective management of the selling function requires maximum coordination of total store efforts if sales objectives are to be met. The management of sales is the final cycle of the merchandising efforts and is part of the firm's service offer.

Management of the selling function is also molded by competition. Retail establishments rapidly acquire reputations of being easy, pleasant, or difficult stores in which to shop. The image of a "good place to shop" is the direct result of customer satisfaction in all store contacts. Such contacts can be enhanced by the store's tone or morale.

Managing the selling functions involves the coordination of the different departmental ideas within the framework of store policies and the funneling of these patterns into over-all selling policies. This results in ideal informative guidelines as to organizational procedures.

Effective organizational guides improve managerial performance and store operations, and form the basis for growth: this will be the subject matter of the next section.

Part Seven

The Management of Enterprise:
The Operating Structure

Chapter 24: *Store Management and Operation*

The store management-operation division is responsible for the complete coordination of the sales and the sales-supporting functions. More specifically, operations management under the store superintendent supervises personnel management, store workrooms, store protection, shopping services, in-store and external traffic management, central wrapping, housekeeping, building and equipment maintenance, leased departments, and store adjustments. Expense and control-systems management are also under his purview. All these functional areas are operated to improve the effectiveness of the merchandising operations.[1]

In large firms a separate personnel division with a vice-president in charge is commonplace; he generally handles the labor relations and executive development.

OPERATING POLICIES

In small and medium-sized stores, the store manager is not only the operating executive but also serves as the store's general and, even, its merchandise manager.

---

[1] In many larger stores, as well as in marginally financed smaller stores, departments such as millinery, shoe repair, beauty salon, photograph studio, and travel-service centers are often leased out to specialists in the field.

In larger stores, the store manager is the line executive in charge of all store operations and reports to the president of the firm. Essential to proper management is the formulation of policy in every area where the delegation of authority and responsibility is feasible and economic. Delegation does not mean abdication of responsibilities.

Thus, the manager delegates authority and responsibilities to individuals and helps set up operating policies to facilitate the attainment of company goals. The purpose of a policy is to clarify management's viewpoints and philosophy throughout the organization. This is especially critical on the selling floor, where policies must be designed to cover all transactions, regardless of the differing variables that exist. Operating policies must be flexible if they are to be effective. They do not consist of directives, orders, or comments.

Over-all store policies should be set in terms of basic objectives—generally long-run profit maximization. Operating policies must serve to facilitate and improve the merchandising function, which is the basic income-producing segment of the mercantile organization. It is important also that each policy or system that is put into effect remains simple to understand and apply. With changing technology and continuing innovation, selling and nonselling activities must be constantly reviewed for adequacy. For example, merchandise-management accounting, productivity-unit, and expense-center accounting have been developed to measure departmental performances. Operating policies have to be formulated for parking and easy access roads and buildings, so that the greatest number of persons can be encouraged to enter the store. Included in parking policies must be adequate provision for vehicle circulation within the parking areas. Shopping-goods stores need maximum ease of access as well as maximum encouragement of pedestrian traffic movements.

Such policies may involve traffic counts at entrances, evaluation of ratio and timing of parking accumulations, of parking lot turnover and duration, and of the "demographic" analysis of automobile occupants—such as age, sex, or zone of residence. It is assumed that a family group occupies each vehicle; this being so, the more individuals there are per vehicle, the lower the sales volume per person. For instance, in the purchase of food and home furnishings items, made primarily for the family and household, sales are apt to be the same no matter how many individuals in the purchase or shopping group.[2]

HANDLING IN-STORE TRAFFIC PROBLEMS

Further complications to the operational problem arise because most customers as well as competitors feel qualified to advise the retail firm. Some individuals, for example, believe that there should be a salesperson for every single customer. The aim, rather, is to have salespeople available for the average peak periods.

---

[2] Kenneth C. Welch and Bruno Funaro, "Parking Plans for Shopping Centers," *Traffic Quarterly* (Eno Foundation, Saugatuck, Conn., October 1952), pp. 416–426.

Transaction studies reveal wide variances in the number of shoppers in different departments during the day and during particular seasons. For instance, women shop certain departments by day when their children are in school; in other departments the evening is more important—the boys' department, in particular; and on school holidays, departments like girls' and boys' are generally very busy.

In effect, the basic selling organization should be just enough to handle the slowest business periods during the entire year. In this respect a full-time salesperson, working forty hours a week and entitled to all company benefits, may cost as much as $1.15 an hour more than a part-time assistant. However, there is a tremendous turnover of part-time personnel; it is ten times that of full-time employees.[3]

Many store managers feel that department managers should sell as well as supervise, and often give them "modified quotas," to make certain that they spend part of each day in customer communications. Mr. Kulle, a store manager for Sears, Roebuck, pointed out that he instituted a "no-overtime policy" in the marking room. His marking-room staff consisted of twenty-six full-time people and, depending on the season, as many part-time people. In some cases slow-downs on Thursday and Friday had occurred before the "no-overtime" rule had been instituted.

Projecting in-store traffic is especially important during periods of significant price changes. The recorded number of sales transactions forms a rough index of the physical volume of merchandise being sold. At times when dollar sales volume is being influenced by price change, dollar and percentage figures alone may obscure cost per transaction and the meaning of changes taking place.

When both the number of transactions and the average size of sale are climbing to higher levels, two influences are contributing to increased dollar volume—namely, larger physical quantity of goods sold and higher value of the average sale; under such conditions expense pay-outs, as percentages of net sales, should drop. Thus, comparisons in a dollar and percentage basis may well conceal an over-all rising costs average.[4]

SYSTEMS—NATURE AND SCOPE

Policy must be part of a total systems framework within any organization. The purpose of any system is the establishment of sound, orderly procedures for attaining the firm's objectives. Thus, the merchandising division depends on the store management group for departmental supervision of all facets of reappraisal and control needed to maximize the effectiveness of the selling system. To this end, store management must also decide on which of various kinds of calculated risks should be taken in operating methods and procedures. For example, calcu-

---

[3] John Kulle, "Comments of a Store Superintendent," *Retail Control* (June 1964), pp. 43–50. (Reprint of a presentation to the Arizona Retail Controllers Association, October 19, 1964.)

[4] See Malcolm P. McNair, "Operating Results of Department and Specialty Stores" (Graduate School of Business, Harvard University, Cambridge, Mass., 1960–1965).

lated risks in procedures such as the acceptance of merchandise returns without accompanying sales checks, clerk wrap of "sends" or "take withs," use of self-service or "quick service" booths, and so on must be appraised in terms of "possible cost savings" against "possible losses." If the cost saving is clearly greater than the probable losses, the less expensive action should be instituted. For instance, when salespeople are permitted to calculate their own sales and returns for bonus purposes without a thorough sales audit system, a calculated risk is involved. (When bonuses are calculated and paid weekly, it is a relatively simple matter not to deduct for merchandise returns.) In such cases, the cost of the comprehensive audit is likely to be far greater than a salesperson's "oversight."

Calculated Risks versus Savings

A calculated risk under a cost-versus-savings sales-audit system is taken when some control—even informal control—over the issuing of sales books permits the oversight of shortages or overages of $2 or less; when employee discount costs and parcel post services are estimated on a historical basis only.

Calculated risks are also involved in the use of common cash register drawers or single fund operations of multiple clerk cash registers, and in the elimination of a cash count or "listing" of monies by sales personnel when money is turned into the cashier's office. Additional examples of calculated risks are failure by branch stores to carry a "charged" inventory, "skip" marking of merchandise, no marking of any merchandise selling for $1 or less, and failure to mark hard-line items of $2 or less. All such risk considerations must be systemized and routinized through operational policy procedures. For instance, there are many management systems which can inform supervisory management of errors, which can check postage, double-check deliveries, traffic charges, and postings on a regular basis.[5] By such means a systems complex facilitates the goal attainment processes of the business organization.

Simplicity versus Suitability

Complex systems in themselves do not indicate suitability. Mercantile firms deal basically with human beings, and so retail and marketing organizations are subjected to wide ranges of customers' requirements and complaints. Store operating policies and procedures must be stated as simply and broadly as possible, so that administrative decisions and action can have the widest possible application. Otherwise, decisions are made with too much lag between the recognition of problems and any action directed toward their solution. For example, in the case of a customer complaint, operating management would have the authority to solve the problem to the customer's satisfaction. Adjustment policy techniques are set up

---

[5] For example, the Moss "Key-Rec" operation system of Dayton, Ohio, is an example of a process procedure that speeds and controls merchandise through in-store handling systems.

as general management policies and are generally handled on a routinized systems basis. When a systems approach for operating management is developed, greater confidence in both the staff and line organization results.

Effect of Interacting Networks

When decision making is facilitated, it makes executives more productive and does produce effective action at all levels.

Of major importance, the operating division is the focal point for the interaction networks within the store. Although he may not be a party to any, the store manager should understand the natural interactions of the informal organizational structure which is not delineated in the company organizational chart. For example, business organizations must strive for an economic market share in order to survive and grow. Inconsistencies in internal communications must be balanced. Often this takes the path of strategic "teams" within the organization meeting naturally and frequently and on continuing ad hoc bases—for example, during coffee breaks. For instance, the general manager may meet with the personnel manager (operations), the comptroller (finance), and the merchandise manager (market and sales).

The personnel manager interacts continually with all echelons and divisions in the firm—more often than not on general store matters rather than just personnel management. The store manager may meet with the controller, department managers, and the receiving, marking, and warehouse supervisors. These are examples of natural interaction networks not represented on any formal organizational charts. Still more common interactions are the networks of personnel interacting with their opposite numbers of similar rank in other divisions in the firm. Within these interacting networks are found the nuclei of the informal organization in which morale plays a vital role.

The basic structure of a systems analysis can be greatly simplified by classifying systems into three divisions: deterministic, probabilistic, and heuristic.

Systems which are deterministic are generally linear in nature and for the most part relatively simple; examples of models are window cables, a model for billiards, and a machine-shop layout for process production. Within the complex type of deterministic systems is the use of electronic digital computers in concurrent evaluations and automated feedback communications, such as those needed by departments having insufficient personnel on a selling floor. The deterministic system with the most immediate applications is in the accounting and control areas.

Of greater importance to market management in this area are the probabilistic systems of control. This was illustrated in the functional management operation of calculated risks. In effect, in any organizational system probability applications are constantly used. In administrative theory, for example, management systems are synonymous with (a) "influence," such as structuring, manipulating, or influencing available means in order to achieve a desired objective, and (b) the feedback concept, used in the automatic control concepts of cybernetics. Both of these concepts deal with the way in which a system using two processes can coordinate resources to attain objectives. All systems have both administrative and operational inputs and mechanized and semimechanized outputs. The systems approach to operations management is very useful because inefficiencies can be pinpointed on an input-output basis of similar units.

DELIVERY SYSTEMS

Full-service stores and most limited-service stores include merchandise deliveries as part of their service offer. Most full-service stores charge a nominal sum, perhaps 25¢, for purchases of $3 or less. Along with credit availability, delivery of merchandise is one of the more important kinds of service which help to maintain a store's competitive image.

Included in the framework of delivery systems should be the supervision of incoming merchandise deliveries as well as the maintenance of physical plant and docking areas. In and out systems from receiving and selling areas are easily formulated. (Fashion and perishable merchandise would receive priority.)

Also under the supervision of the store superintendent is traffic management. The use of freight forwarding and car pools often helps to minimize delivery costs and to speed shipments. When incoming merchandise is received from resources, notification is sent both to the appropriate buyer and to the accounts payable section of the control division. An immediate check and confirmation are made so that cash discounts and any permissible "anticipation" discounts may be taken. One of the weak points of internal communications in many retail organizations is the lack of immediate information of merchandise deliveries to the department concerned. Instead of "stockouts," many sales could be generated by "instant" receiving-room communications of "order receipt" to pertinent selling departments.

Operations management in internal traffic includes the processing and movement of merchandise between various departments, stockrooms, and workrooms, and its necessary protection in transit. Such merchandise includes radios, TV, furniture, appliances, draperies, and carpets, along with items needing repair or "make-ready" services before being sent either to customers or to the selling floor.

Among the other important protective responsibilities of the store's operating management are those in the highly sensitive areas: cashiers, packers, porters, and people who work at night. Further protective checks should be made concerning cash sales.

When the sales audit department samples, on a tickler file basis, fast-turning selling departments such as cosmetics, hosiery, and drugs, the average cash sales per salesperson over three-week periods can be determined. From the comparative averages, any salesperson low in cash sales may be suspected of irregularities because he may be taking cash from sales. In such areas, the individual should be shopped three or four times to test his honesty.[6] Another protective test is a

---

[6] C. C. Curtis, *Modern Retail Security* (Springfield, Ill.: Charles C. Thomas, Publisher, 1960)

baling-room test carried out at least twice a year once the bales have reached the carting truck.

WAREHOUSE AND TRAFFIC MANAGEMENT

The key to efficient warehousing is to minimize the movement of merchandise, people, and "things." The smaller the store or the firm, the more centralized the warehousing and receiving facilities should be. In the larger multi-unit store organizations with outlets in adjacent trading areas, incoming merchandise, once checked and marked, can be processed through a centralized warehouse unit before transshipment. Service warehouses located in core-centralized areas lend themselves readily to automation. In effect, successful warehouse management means that the logistics of internal distribution involve minimum movement and maximum service.

To increase productivity, electric trucks with fork lifts, planning of palletized loads of various sizes, roller conveyers, gravity belts, and monorail systems for the hanging, pressing, and marking of ready-to-wear merchandise are widely used. Inefficiency of internal merchandise movements can often be traced directly to lack of forward stocks on the selling floors. Thus, the efficiency of the store's internal traffic system varies inversely with the movement and distances traveled as well as with the number of merchandise movements made from point of receipt to point of sale or disposal.

In addition, merchandise movement should be scheduled for slack periods during the day and not during peak selling periods. From the time merchandise is received until it is delivered to a customer, the cost of the merchandise increases with each movement. This is why policy planning in these areas is of such vital importance.

For example, in Figure XXXI is illustrated a service center containing some 370,000 square feet. This is a classical example of the "minimum movement" principle. This center was planned so that a two-pronged flow would enable bulk goods, furniture, and small wares to move to their respective delivery areas in an independent flow process through wrapping and packing to package delivery. Other affiliated activities were set up on a lower level of 50,000 square feet. Here space was provided for clerical and administrative staff, employee cafeteria, recreation area, storage space for the firm's display props and material, selling fixtures and supplies, radio, television, and major appliance workrooms, and mechanical equipment such as the center's heating plan and incinerator facilities. The center itself is located on a seventeen-acre site, eight miles from the downtown store, five miles from the suburban Westroads store, and five miles from the site of the new suburban North St. Louis County store, with a railroad siding adjacent to the building.[7]

---

[7] William E. Shamski, "Service Center Geared to Merchandise Processing," Stix, Baer and Fuller, Inc., of St. Louis, Mo. (formerly a member of the AMC group and now a member store of the Associated Dry Goods Chain). Diagram is from the Store Manager's Bulletin, NRMA, First Quarter, 1961.

FIGURE XXXI

Service Center with Individualized Merchandise-Flow Capabilities *

INDICATES GUIDE-O-MATIC LOOP

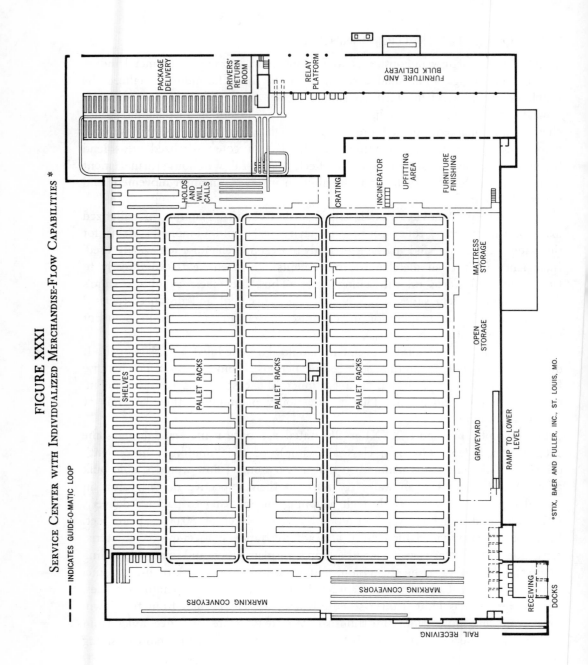

*STIX, BAER AND FULLER, INC., ST. LOUIS, MO.

In many of the newer branch stores, perimeter forward stockrooms and inter-floor storage sections are located behind or adjacent to the selling areas. By such means, it becomes possible to store reserve merchandise and maximize its effectiveness. Workrooms and other service areas necessary for optimizing the merchandise sales mix are generally centralized in the warehouse itself, and deliveries are made from there.

While there are many differences of opinion so far as merchandise movement and warehousing are concerned, there are many standards which have found general agreement:

1) Most warehouses for retail firms may employ from 0.3 to 1.8 persons per 1000 square feet with a concentration of 0.7 to 0.9 persons, depending on the extent and variety of the work.

2) In warehouse design, ceiling heights may vary from 10 to 13 feet; high ceilings are efficient only to the extent that they are used for specialized operations. For example, a clear stacking height under sprinkler clearance calls for a maximum of 13½ to 15 feet height as the most that can be justified from an economic standpoint. In multistory warehouse buildings, variable column spacing depends on driveways and loading docks, width of the truck dollies, and merchandise requirements, as well as available truck driveways and loading docks. The choice of column spacing is a definite cost factor, as are ceiling heights.

3) For general merchandise use, storage racks and bins have been found economic. Unit loads and palletized storage are very advantageous where merchandise is stable, well boxed, and durable. Forward thinking in warehouse storage methods features wider applications of movable storage units: For example, jumbo-sized pallets for mattress receiving and storage.

4) When hand movement of storage is used, less aisle space is required. In most manually operated warehouses, aisle space usually takes up to 35 to 40 per cent of the gross stock space. Warehouses with fork-lift operations have aisle space totaling as much as 60 per cent of gross stock space.[8]

Within the standard framework of dynamic comparisons and control, process-flow charts are set up by operation and supervisory management for both sales and sales-supporting activities. A process-flow chart of this kind is shown in Figure XXXII.

PERT–CPM: GOALS AND APPLICATIONS

The principal objective in developing a mechanized receiving and marking system is for accuracy, speed, and efficiency. This requires optimum planning, scheduling, and coordination of all inanimate and animate movements within the firm. In the case of store operations, the development of a systemized routing of all the goods handled and processed must be coordinated within existing plant and equipment; i.e., goals matched to capacities. Within this area would be found

[8] See R. D. Tatlow (President, Abbott, Merkt and Co.), "Merchandise Movement in Department Store Warehousing."

FIGURE XXXII
PROCESS-FLOW CHART

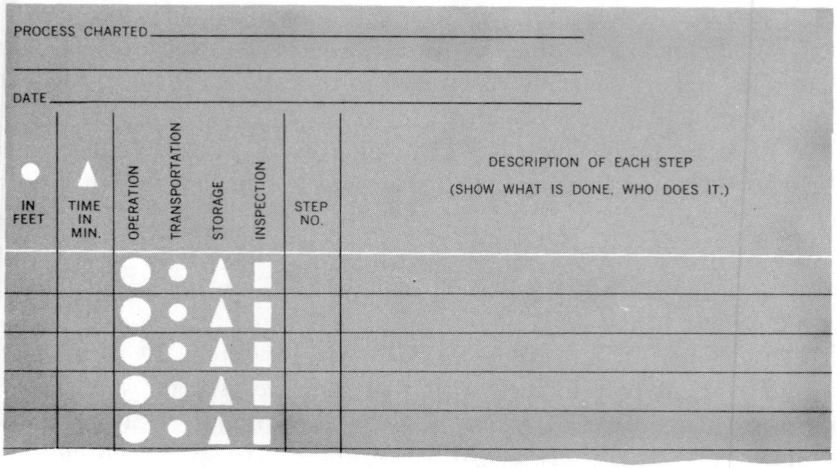

many of the planned movement concepts of PERT (Program Evaluation and Review)–CPM (Critical Path Method).[9]

Basically, PERT–CPM is a managerial tool of analysis in which graphic displays of a flow-process network system are applied. The graphic displays of a flow process form the necessary guides for planning and scheduling highly complex operations. Of even greater importance, the use of PERT–CPM permits the total systems network to be built up on an independent basis. This means that progress of total project toward the goals is not impeded by delays in most operational segments. Such procedures insure the utmost managerial coordination and effectiveness without loss of time.

In connection with the use in the development of a PERT–CPM system, the preplanning needed in process charting is generally set up as illustrated in Figure XXXIII, which illustrates a combined approach to networking.

FUNCTIONAL STORAGE

Regardless of the size of the firm, merchandise flow from the moment of receipt to delivery either to sales floor or to the storage area is essentially "live." The utilization of dead storage by any modern retail distribution center can be very costly because of attendant disutilities. Only when large purchases are made in advance of the season at substantial seasonal discounts can dead storage be economic. Toys and antifreeze are representative of products suitable for short-run dead storage.

Consumer commodities are adaptable to automatic routing and handling, as

---

[9] See Bruce N. Baker and René L. Eris, *An Introduction to PERT–CPM* (Homewood, Ill.: Richard D. Irwin, Inc., 1964). These concepts were originally developed by E. I. du Pont de Nemours & Co. and the Sperry-Rand Corp. as a joint venture to improve planning, scheduling, and coordination of highly complex projects.

FIGURE XXXIII
A Combined PERT–CPM Approach to Network and Development of Specifications and Evaluative Criteria for a Central Buying Program *

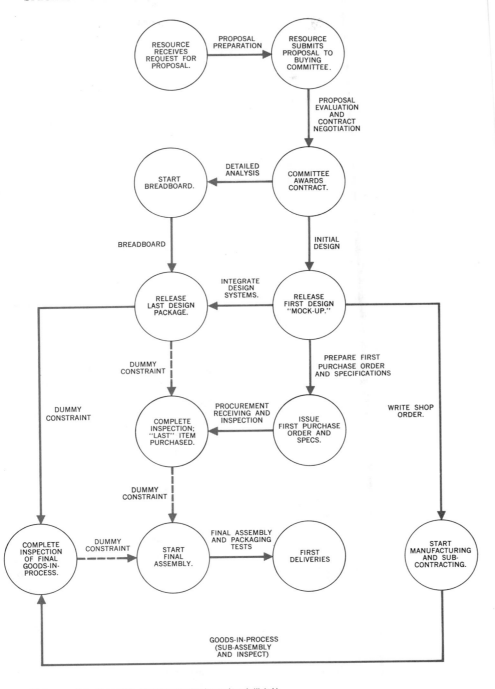

* Events are symbolized by a circle. (A square or rectangle may be substituted.)
/Activities are symbolized by lines.
An Event is an instantaneous occurrence which must be accomplished at a point in time—all milestone considerations of the time
program. Solid lines represent real activities connecting one PERT event with another. Dotted lines are imaginary.

their traffic and storage functions are repetitive in nature. As a result, traffic management has many areas for cost reduction applications—premarking, pre-packaging, and warehouse sales from floor samples are realistic examples of efficient functional storage requiring minimum movements.

Stores located in downtown areas deal primarily in vertical rather than horizontal movements because of high land costs. Vertical movement of merchandise requires elevators, because automatic lifts and vertical conveyers have many limitations. For example, in the movement of furniture, the lack of uniformity of many bulky, one-of-a-kind variety items requires adjustable racks or bins.

EFFECT OF SYSTEMS INSTALLATION

The installation of EDP systems in the framework of the operation of business firms tends initially to push fixed costs upward. Once a new installation is integrated into the firm's total operation, costs will then decrease.[10] EDP installations have found increasing acceptance in retailing in the handling of accounting data such as withholding and social security taxes, insurance, hospitalization, sales, pay roll, excise and use taxes, withholding of union dues, government-bond purchases and credit-union dues. The more important cost-saving possibilities would be within the elements of expense-center and productivity-unit accounting, data processing, and distribution cost analyses. Thus, the need today is in the area of integrating and correlating machine-system capabilities rather than in the addition of "machine hardware."

Of greatest possible importance is the development of "software" programs for information retrieval through which managerial decision making can be facilitated. The automatic sorting, posting, accumulating, and control of all sales data can be converted to classifications and summarization for instant use by management when wanted.

This is an example of effective information retrieval. Automatic input-output systems of this kind facilitate the work of merchandising and market strategy. Automatic inputs today are possible through the use of magnetic-tape systems; sounder company decisions result where almost instantaneous actions are constantly needed.

The availability of EDP systems has furthered the organizational trend in separation of the buying and selling functions in the larger retail organizations. In this respect, "central buyer" systems have been greatly simplified because of almost instantaneous retrieval of sales and stock information. This is not too

---

[10] Malcolm P. McNair, "The 1961 Operating Results of Department and Specialty Stores" (Graduate School of Business, Harvard University, Cambridge, Mass., 1961) shows that sales audit costs represent only .18 per cent of sales, a decline since 1957. Accounts receivable and credit costs represent 2.30 per cent of sales. The bulk of this represents credit sales costs. Accounts-receivable costs alone for a three-year period represented only .60 per cent of sales. Hence, the total for control and accounting functions, including accounts receivable, represents 1.55 per cent of sales. This framework of potential cost savings is all that most department stores can expect in justifying the cost of computers and peripheral equipment. With additional nonaccounting usage of the equipment, the installation becomes highly economic.

different from methodologies used for years by many chain and multi-unit organizations having homogeneous price lines and merchandise classification.

The quick identification of the most profitable merchandise lines and best sellers is also easier for firms having a "total systems" approach to store operation and merchandise management.

Self-service and self-selection selling methods are also forms of mechanized systems at the point of sale. Where customer service is the basic policy upon which the store image and reputation has been built, the expansion of these kinds of automated procedures is limited. However, EDP systems in inventory movement, record keeping, and information-processing systems are commonplace today in firms of almost all sizes. However, "slowdowns" in processing sales transactions create the greatest disadvantage of processing systems at the point of sale.

In systems formulations, the quantification of a problem is usually in the form of indexes. Indexing systems are valid only when a real relationship exists between the numerical values assigned and the actual operation. All properties, of course, cannot be assigned a reliable number in the early stages of development of an analytical system. Hence, there are analogous operations which suggest a judicious approximation which justifies the use of a formal system model. At first, the system is only an indicator. Once the quantitative relationships between the model and actual performance are tested, the indicators take on real significance and become tests affirmatively measured.

THE OPERATIONS RESEARCH (OR) APPROACH

Whether so named or not, most firms use some sort of Operations Research approach for managerial decision making; OR applications are used by retail and market managers to measure advertising effectiveness, to check the best type of sales efforts (both for "in-the-store" and "in-the-home" selling), to determine the best mix of floor space for particular stores, to decide on night openings (length, duration, and specific days), and to determine the best standards to be used for optimum inventory management.[11]

Operations Research is not susceptible to any precise definition; it is primarily concerned with the analysis of operating systems. The basic technique is to create a realistic (hypothetical) model of any operational process. Such models usually contain numbers of complex variables; thus the solutions must be approached by the application of mathematical techniques such as linear programing, probability applications, Monte Carlo methods, and game theory strategy. All these methods attempt to duplicate in statistical form the operation to be analyzed.

The creation of a mathematical model permits the simulation of a variety of conditions and situations within certain confined but, nevertheless, useful, limits.

---

[11] Other uses of OR in retail management are to determine the best varieties of merchandise lines to be offered, to route and schedule delivery trucks, to predict fashion silhouette types, to achieve better control in piece-goods purchasing, to carry out better inventory balancing, and to determine the most effective number of check-out counters for self-service establishments.

However, the results obtained from any model are only as good as the input data and the degree to which the model represents the real-world situation.

Thus OR presents a *special* point of view toward decision making—it is not an "end in itself," for it runs the gamut of all types of integrated approaches. The basic OR formula is:

$$E = F\ (c,\ u)$$

E = Effectiveness of the System
F = Function
c = Controllable Variables
u = Uncontrollable Variables.

Although individuals using this type of programing analysis may be interested in only a "single-action" phase of the total operation, the OR process is valid only when considered from the standpoint of a total systems concept—improving the effectiveness of the "whole."

All management and marketing systems are essentially of an input-output character. The underlying motivator of the system is the information handling process which insures the proper "feedback." This procedural process improves over-all effectiveness, insures market position, and tends to maximize long-run profit.

For example, manufacturers and advertisers are constantly seeking fast, up-to-date information on both wholesale and retail inventories, nationally and by market areas. This information is of a prime importance in production planning and raw materials purchases. An OR approach which included variables such as accurately estimated sales, inventories, business forecasts, turnover, general market conditions, and price levels could provide acceptable answers in the planning stages.

Problem Quantification

The basic technique used in OR is the development of heuristic (nonlinear) models including both the controllable and uncontrollable variables pertinent to the problem. For problems having direct cause and effect or proportionate relationships, linear programing techniques can be used in the simulations. This involves the development of solutions through a series of a finite number of linear equations which have "more unknown" variables than equations. Game Strategy techniques and Monte Carlo methods would be used for probabilistic, heuristic problems. They are based on Bayesian rather than the orthodox Fischer solution parameters.[12]

---

[12] T. Bayes, "Essay Towards Solving a Problem in the Doctrine of Chances" (1763). This work by Bayes and its expansion by Laplace form the basis for much of the probability theory in use today. R. A. Fischer, along with J. Neyman, E. S. Pearson, and A. Wald among other "orthodox" statisticians for many years rejected the methods of inference and concepts used by the Bayesian school.

See also F. J. Anscombe, "Bayesian Statistics," *The American Statistician* (February 1961, pp. 21–23). Professor Anscombe points out that "the Bayesian Statistician shows how the

Thus, when Operations Research is set up to solve a difficult problem, it is first generally translated into a simple mathematical form where analysis and synthesis facilitate setting up an optimum model. Once the solution is reached, the complex problem is then re-translated into simple terms so that management can determine the necessary decision.

Setting up a mathematical model permits the simulation of a finite number of solutions with varying conditions and situations (as in the case of any computing or analytical "machines"). As pointed out, the results are only as good as the input data and are valid only to the extent to which the model represents actual or potential situations.

All possible variations in data or phenomena should be assigned a "related" number, with the numbering system values closely describing and approximating the real-world relationships. Once the quantitative relationships between the "model" and actual performances have been checked and validated, the indicators become reliable and sensitive measures of performance and are adaptable to computer processing.

Operations Research results tend to limit the role of intuitive decision making. While creative intuition has an important place in executive decision making in business as well as in the field of pure science, intuitive management is short-run in character and limited in scope.

Because OR analyses are based on a framework of a total systems concept of the firm "as a whole," management can base its decisions on something more than a *single* function of segmented operation. In other words, OR develops any set of actions about which a policy decision can be made.

At all levels and in all types of industries, both centralization and decentralization are rapidly taking place. Decentralization, for example, depends upon a coordinated system operating and furnishing adequate and timely reports. This does not mean that the introduction of OR reports through high-speed computers would automatically furnish solutions. Too often, much extraneous and inconsequential data is introduced into the system. Not yet fully developed is a performance-measuring system which can be used quantitatively in conjunction with exist-

---

evidence of observation should modify previously held beliefs in the formation of rational opinions" upon which value judgments can be made between alternative actions. . . . Ramsey conceived of a theory of consistent behavior of decision making under uncertainty (F. P. Ramsey, *The Foundations of Mathematics* (London, Routledge and Kegan Paul, 1931).

"The orthodox statistician, during the last twenty-five years or so, has sought to handle inference problems (problems of deciding what the figures mean and what ought to be done about them) with the utmost 'objectivity.' He explains his favorite concepts, 'significance level,' 'confidence coefficient,' 'unbiased estimates,' etc., in terms of what he calls 'probability,' but his notion of probability bears little resemblance to what the man in the street means (rightly) by probability. He is not concerned with probable truth or plausibility, but he defines probability in terms of frequency of occurrence in repeated trials, as in a game of chance." (Reprinted with biographical note by G. A. Barnard, "Studies in Histories of Probability and Statistics," *Biometrica*, 45, 1958, pp. 293–315.) See also R. Schlaifer, *Probability and Statistics for Business Decisions: An Introduction to Managerial Economics under Uncertainty* (New York: McGraw-Hill, 1959). This text further elaborates on the calculation of risks of actionable conclusions resulting from probability analysis.

ing reporting procedures. There is still too great a gap between the two: the performance-measuring system and reporting systems procedures.

The complexities and rapidity of change in market competition will continue and with it, high obsolescence factors. This makes it highly improbable that sound executive decisions can be arrived at without the increasing use of more scientific methods and techniques. Even if an enterprise has the "ideal" top executive with a "computer for a brain" and an equally talented replacement, both would still need scientifically developed ranges of decision choices to maximize their efforts. The use of OR processes can develop the necessary information as the basis for actionable conclusions.

Problem Constraints

All problems, whether business or personal, represent conflict. Once, problems might have been the equating of customer services versus economy of operation, or seasonal discount economies from senders versus a higher inventory level and storage cost. These are merely two forms of constraints.

Constraints involve the "cost-effectiveness" principle. In this, costs must always be related to the "effectiveness" which is being "bought." A classic example of a customer-imposed constraint was a change in policy on the part of one of the largest supermarket chains in this country. The grade of its shopping bag was changed on a "cost-control" program. What was not taken into consideration was the fact that shopping bags are also used by housewives for temporary garbage storage prior to placement in disposal areas for removal. The cheaper bags disintegrated when used for that purpose—not to mention the frequent tearing, which scattered the grocery purchases before arrival at home. There were so many losses in patronage due to this unknown factor, that whatever savings had been anticipated by the firm disappeared in lost business.

In the discussion of management decisions to automate, potential savings in labor costs were shown to be a prime motivator in system research. The attainment of efficient cost control is motivated by management's attempting to lower the cost factor in the so-called "profit squeeze" dilemma. Retailing as well as industry is faced with so many built-in, "fixed" constraints that optimum relationships between price, cost, timing, and the best mix of merchandise are rarely achieved. These are the kinds of areas where OR can be most effective.

THE DECISION TO AUTOMATE

Management makes many decisions to automate; whether it is in the form of an EDP system, the installation of numerically controlled machines, or automated order-selection and conveyor systems in warehouse management. The large investment usually involved in this type of decision is generally substantial.

In small firms, the large capital outlay involved—especially in relation to the firm's total assets or sales—apparently may act as a deterrent. However, the smaller the firm, the larger the potential savings—i.e., the greater the potential decrease in total operating costs. In the smaller firm, also, the largest capital outlay can be almost immediately authorized by management; management is more general and close enough to operations for all aspects of support for the investment to be processed quickly. In the larger firm, the automation of even a single operation brings a much smaller reduction in total operating costs.[13] While the necessary investment in the larger firm may not be large relative to the firm's total resources, it generally requires high level approval.

Cost reduction, to be effected primarily by higher productivity, appears to be a major objective in decisions to automate. The benefits calculated to warrant change are deemed to result from lower man-hour requirements for both existing or prospective workloads.[14]

Other benefits seen by management in automation are the following: (a) processes produce less scrap, fewer rejects, and fewer damaged goods, and require less reworking; (b) less plant space is required because of fewer rejects; (c) there is less loss of goods-in-process and raw materials; and (d) automation increases "fixed" relative to "variable" costs in the short run and tends to stabilize costs in the long run, regardless of volume generated.

In a study of companies installing automation, it was found that increases in fixed costs were minimized, because most automatic equipment was not purchased unless it could be written off within a five- to twelve-year period. Because of employee turnover, expected savings in labor costs from automation took longer than expected. The work force, however, grew less rapidly under automation, as fewer part-time employees and fewer man-hours of overtime were needed to cope with seasonal fluctuations of volume.

Automation also helps alleviate work-force problems such as excessive turnover, pilferage, unsatisfactory performance of temporary employees, shortages of skilled workers, and restrictions on women's working hours.

Aside from the competitive aspects of automation, the evidence shows that operations problems to which no acceptable solution has previously been found can often be solved or mitigated by automation, especially in the area of store operating management.

SUMMARY AND CONCLUSIONS

The operating policies and sales-supporting activities of the management division were analytically reviewed. The efficient conduct of these activities facilitates the work of merchandising and ultimately determines a firm's fixed cost structure and its ability to compete over time.

Essentially, the function of the store's management division is to devise a bal-

---

[13] *Management Decisions to Automate,* Manpower-Automation Research Monograph No. 38, U. S. Department of Labor, W. W. Wirtz. (Richard S. Roberts, Jr., Project Leader [Stanford Research Institute, Menlo Park, California], Contract No. OAM–4–63.)

[14] *Ibid.,* pp. 1–13.

anced store operations program so as to utilize effectively the fixed, inescapable costs of the firm. By carrying this out, all variable expenses subsequently incurred would be highly productive. One approach from the managerial-economic point of view is the use of a comprehensive, calculated risk program. In this kind of program, points of diminishing returns for various operations can be quickly assessed, as can the desirability of continuing particular customer services or other facilitating functions. The "cost-effectiveness" principle would be the basis for action.

In essence, effective store management operates in a model framework that balances "controllable" variable expenses and "uncontrollable" fixed expenses. Within this framework, the organizational goal is the maximization of the effectiveness of the total system. To carry this out, management can also use various OR approaches to problem solving.

By furnishing alternative decision choices, OR offers measurable solutions to such problems as the allocation of floor space, night openings, hours of operation, inventory management, vertical and horizontal transportation, scheduling, determining optimum market mixes, routing and scheduling, and determining the proper number of check-out counters in self-service stores and departments. All functional operations in this division furnish the basic material needed by the management in their decision whether or not to automate.

Chapter 25: *Personnel Administration and Management*

In most retail firms the personnel director administers his division in a line capacity and helps in formulating administrative and personnel policies of the entire firm; he also acts in a direct staff advisory capacity to each of the divisions in the firm. In the smaller firm, recruiting, selecting, training, and the supervisory aspects of personnel management are likely to be part of each line manager's responsibility. The development and maintenance of good organizational morale would be part of any line management's responsibilities, regardless of the size of the organization.

The recruiting of suitable management personnel for retailing is particularly challenging because starting salaries are only marginally competitive and in many cases comparatively low—also, the required hours of work are generally drawn out over the course of the entire week. In attempts to be more competitive "special underwriting" funds have been provided to supplement starting salary offers. This has helped, but only to a limited extent because of long hours and the comparatively "low-status" effect attached to being a junior executive in the field.[1]

---

[1] In a further comment on this "status-prestige" aspect of not only retailing but marketing and selling, Herman C. Nolen, Chairman of the Board of McKesson & Robbins, Inc., stated in an interview: "It's due in part to the impression that selling and marketing don't contribute to the general well-being, and in part to a reaction against such abuses as deceptive ads, and sharp marketing practices." (*Sales Management*, June 4, 1965, p. 26.)

It is within this marginal environment that the work of personnel managers must be performed. In general, personnel administration and management in the field is no longer, "a sort of staff office boy to the rest of the organization."[2]

EFFECT OF ENVIRONMENTAL AND POPULATION CHANGES

Management's basic problem is still people. Unfortunately, many employers still regard labor as a commodity to be bought in the market place in the classical economic sense along with a rationalization of work as an incentive tool to greatness. Such "feudal-paternalistic" employer attitudes are giving way to new techniques and tools of analysis developed in the behavioral and social sciences.

The most significant changes that have taken place in the labor force during the last two decades have been in those groups where skills are at a minimum and wage rates the lowest. And, because of automation and mechanization, the relative number of unskilled jobs available has been and. is still shrinking.

In 1956, for the first time in history, white-collar jobs exceeded the number of blue-collar jobs. This trend is still continuing, as can be seen from Table 33. This table shows the changing relative number of workers by categories, numbers, and percentage.

An increasing number of men under twenty-five are either in school or in the Armed Forces. In the older age group—sixty and over—nonworkers are those who are somewhat disabled or on enforced "retirement." [3]

The most significant and continuing change—and the most important for retail firms—has been the steady movement of women from the home into labor markets.

Labor force participation among women ranges from a peak when individuals are in their late teens and early twenties (the school-leaving age and the period immediately after marriage). This peak tends to decline to disappearance as the birth of children removes them from the labor market. As children reach school age and women pass age thirty-five, the proportion employed outside the home

---

[2] P. F. Drucker, *The Practice of Management* (New York: Harper & Row, 1954). See also M. D. Dunnette and B. M. Boss, "Behavioral Scientists and Personnel Management," *Industrial Relations*, Vol. 2, No. 3 (May 1963), pp. 115–30.

[3] Bureau of Labor Statistics and Bureau of the Census. These data show that "the total number of nonproduction workers rose 19.3 per cent from 1952 to 1957. Percentage increases within this group: professional and technical, 45.4; managerial, 8.4; clerical, 10.8; sales, 25.3." The writer sees a host of problems posed by this historic change in the realignment of white- and blue-collar workers in the United States labor force. The job revolution affects: (1) income differentials among occupations; (2) workers' psychology; (3) the base of union power (as the change is heavily weighted toward middle-class workers, even hourly rates may become a thing of the past, according to a senior economist of the Federal Reserve Board):

> The upheaval of employment patterns could conceivably help extend Federal minimum wage legislation to all of retailing, increase State minimum wage rates in smaller communities and in labor surplus areas, and cause unions to ask for wage increases to permit the differential between minimum salaries in small stores and higher ones in larger stores to be held at status quo. Big stores might then be beset with demands for higher wages and greater fringe benefits.

Commenting on these charges, Samuel Feinberg, columnist of *Women's Wear Daily*, quotes excerpts from a research memorandum on "The Job Revolution" (R. D. Entenberg, University of Pittsburgh, 1959).

TABLE 33

EMPLOYMENT IN NONAGRICULTURAL ESTABLISHMENTS, BY INDUSTRY DIVISION

(*in thousands of persons*)

	1959		JANUARY 1965	
Manufacturing	16,675	31.29%	17,689	29.83%
Mining	732	1.37	634	1.07
Contract construction	2,960	5.56	3,223	5.44
Transportation & public utilities	4,011	7.53	3,939	6.65
Trade	11,127	20.88	12,424	20.96
Finance	2,594	4.87	2,980	5.03
Service	7,115	13.35	8,684	14.65
Government	8,083	15.17	9,707	16.38
Total	53,297	100.02	59,280	100.01
Unemployment rate	5.5%		4.8% (January only)	

Note—Bureau of Labor Statistics; data include all full- and part-time employees who worked during, or received pay for, the pay period ending nearest the 15th of the month. Proprietors, self-employed persons, domestic servants, unpaid family workers, and members of the armed forces are excluded.

Source: *Federal Reserve Bulletin*, February 1965, p. 314. Data include Alaska and Hawaii, beginning with 1959.

again rises. The rise continues until age fifty-five, when labor force participation rates for women tend to drop off.[4]

It is estimated that young women over twenty and women thirty-five years of age and over will continue to account for an increasing percentage in the total work force. Also, the addition of the large number of young people and married women to the labor force has resulted in an unusually large increase in the number of individuals seeking part-time work. Because of such socioeconomic changes, personnel managers have been able to optimize their efforts through greater flexibility in allocating and scheduling employees for the needs of peak periods.

In no other field of endeavor are there such great opportunities for women as there are in retailing. Retail management represents a realistic opportunity for the attainment of executive level careers for women. It is also an area in which women can go into business for themselves on a competitive basis. One in every six proprietors of retail stores is a woman. In 1958 there were more than two million men self-employed and more than 336,000 women in the same category.[5]

POLICY FORMULATION

Personnel managers set up policies that clarify management viewpoints regarding personnel in all operating areas. Such policies provide an effective pattern for the delegation of authority and responsibility, and serve as guides for facilitating strategic action in the achievement of company goals. All policies should be formulated within the legal framework of existing labor legislation; at present, the Manpower Development and Training Act (MDTA) of 1965, which amends

[4] Sophia Cooper and Stewart Garfinkel, *Labor Force Projection for the U. S., 1960–1975* (U. S. Department of Labor Statistics, Bulletin #1242, Superintendent of Documents), p. 20.

[5] See *Statistical Abstract of the United States*, 1959, Tables 278 and 283, pp. 218–26; 1964, Tables 306 and 310, pp. 228–35. (It is interesting to note that in France almost half of the businesses are run by women.)

the MDTA of 1962, applies. The principal changes in the Act are shown in Appendix J.

In effect, the basic objective of all personnel policies is to insure the full utilization of employees. The goal is to increase the executive management processes and the total impact and competitive effectiveness of the firm. Management of the human element is basic to successful personnel management policies.

Technically, once an individual has been selected for association in the firm, the function of personnel management is to assign him to the position for which he is most suited. This decision should be made with the participation of more than one executive. Personnel must also make certain that each executive with delegated responsibility has authority commensurate with his assigned responsibility.

The personnel division formulates policies for recruiting, interviewing, selecting, and testing; also for employment, industrial relations, fringe benefits, training, and explanation of company policies, and, where necessary, lay-off procedures. Other functional responsibilities of the personnel division include employee in-store discipline, supervision of adherence to work rules, compensation plans, executive development programs, and the maintenance of morale.

Legislative Constraints

Until 1963, retailers were generally exempt from the provisions of the Fair-Labor Standards Act which presently stipulates time and one-half pay for all overtime work in a store. More important, the retail industry objected strenuously to the salary tests in the definition of "an executive." The writer, in testimony before the Lundquist Committee at Department of Labor hearings, testified that:

> The wage-hour white-collar regulations applicable to retailing should not be made too restrictive, lest the drive to improve retail productivity and executive development be severely hampered.... An individual managing a store or a department meets the executive test when he has line authority in any aspect of the business.... A department or store manager is an executive if he is delegated the authority to plan, organize, and control the activities of his area of responsibility within a broad policy framework....
>
> Because buying situations are fluid and, once lost, are gone forever, maximizing managerial effectiveness actually involves "doing phases" of executive performance because of nonrecurring situations. These functions must be carried out, not on the basis of programmed planning but on a discretionary "as needed" basis....
>
> Often, executives have to pitch in during peak periods or when regular sales personnel are absent or at lunch.... Store executives, regardless of salaries, are interested in promotion and advancing the interest of management and themselves, rather than being disposed to "quibble over a few hours overtime."

During the hearings it was pointed out, in a study of remuneration received in retailing prepared by Perry Meyers, economic consultant, that 56.8 per cent of the previously covered executive employees in retailing were paid $125 and over per week. In specialty stores, 70 per cent of the previously covered executives in the survey were paid $125 and over, while 41.9 per cent of those in exempted stores were in that pay bracket.

COMMUNICATIONS POLICIES

The key policy area with which personnel management is increasingly concerned is effective communications. This is the lifeline of any organization. Adequate communications include effective horizontal communications between functional areas and vertical communications of the superior-subordinate type. Management must communicate its directives and ideas throughout the organization and must, in turn, receive communication feedback. Otherwise it is handicapped. At the retail level, the primary source of customer-contact reaction is through its sales and operating personnel.

Thus, from the management viewpoint, two questions arise: 1) Are employees receiving the message necessary for their work and at the same time being satisfied in their need for information; and 2) Do employees know how to or want to communicate needed information to management? In numerous research studies conducted in 1964 under the direction of the writer, the communications networks of multi-unit departmentized stores were investigated. The job classifications sampled for opinions included personnel from the selling (both downtown and branches) operations control, buying, warehouse, promoting, and display departments.

Approximately half of the employees felt policies and procedures rarely changed. In every case studied, more than half of all employees questioned stated that they did not and would not express their opinions on policy changes. When asked why, the reply was generally, "I'd better not mention my opinions, or I would go out the door."

Of the remaining employees who stated that they did express opinions on store policy, half expressed such opinions to their immediate supervisors; the remaining personnel interviewed (approximately one out of every five employees) expressed their opinions to "friends" but not to store executives!

This means that in the average retail firm, only about one-fourth of all employees and middle managers give any kind of feedback to management; the balance don't do so because of "'fear." Thus, any policy formulations by the personnel division should include the encouragement of employee communications upward in a "feedback without fear" process.[6]

JOB AND INDIVIDUAL EVALUATIONS AND SPECIFICATIONS

Job evaluation and specifications are formulated from productivity requirements and time and duty studies, and are influenced by the supply and demand for

---

[6] The surveys were titled, "Communications in a Departmentized Retail Store" (Retail Research Center, Graduate School of Business, University of Pittsburgh), 1963–1965.

labor in an area. Thus, the setting of job specifications is basically affected by availability and quality of local labor. Nevertheless, labor as a factor of production is still treated by many managements in much the same manner as by classical economists—a commodity to be bought at the lowest possible price with the fruits of the labor inputs sold at the highest possible price.

Job evaluations and specifications must be set on economic considerations as well as various standards of performance rather than merely on job demands and abilities required. A mere rationalizing of work in terms of monetary income incentives must be supplemented by psychic rewards in terms of status, prestige, self-development programs, and fringe benefits—all part of the "packaged rewards." [7]

Aside from senior executives or owners, scales generally range from "most unskilled duties requiring no special education" to "most complex, with both general and special education and experience."

The immediate job supervisor, department, or division head and the personnel manager should each evaluate the job itself in order to develop a job profile. The profile can then be used as the measure of comparison with the profile of the individual occupying the job.

In effect, all jobs in the firm should be classified into broad groups requiring similar degrees of skill, training, experience, and responsibility; every job classification may run the entire gamut. While there is no one best way of appraising the job performance of any individual, there are many approaches. Within the framework of quality control of the job and the individual, there are many valid approaches to the appraisal processes from the engineering as well as the behavioral standpoints.

Rating Methods

The evaluation and specification of a job assignment should include the relative measure of its productivity in relation to that of the total organizational framework. Along with the productivity measure requirements, a brief personality profile of the individual who would best carry out the total job assignment should be included.

Within this framework, also, a rating assessment chart should be developed so that both personnel and supervisory management may have a better means of measuring and evaluating the job classification itself and an individual's performance in relation to it. By measuring employee performance against what the job requires, a valid "promotion" standard can be made. In other words, job and individual evaluative procedures along those lines would pinpoint both "dead-end"

---

[7] H. J. Leavitt, "Toward Organizational Psychology" (Graduate School of Business, Carnegie Institute of Technology, Pittsburgh), March 1961. While basically referring to decision making within the organization, Dr. Leavitt uses the psychological aspects of organizational theory as part of an evaluation technique.

jobs and "dead-end" people in the firm. Increasingly, engineering and quantitative approaches to personnel evaluations are being used. A suggested framework for this kind of evaluation is shown in Table 34.

TABLE 34
JOB AND INDIVIDUAL EVALUATIVE SCHEDULE

CRITERION	HIGHEST OR VERY BEST	TO GREAT EXTENT	TO MODERATE EXTENT	SOME	LITTLE OR NONE
1. MANAGEMENT INVENTORY					
(a) To what extent does the job assignment call for planning, organizing, controlling, etc.?	___	___	___	___	___
(b) To what extent does individual plan, organize, and control (manage) in his area of responsibility?	___	___	___	___	___
(c) To what extent does individual make a cognitive relation along the following lines?[a]	___	___	___	___	___
2. SALARY ADMINISTRATION					
(a) To what extent do total payments of the job relate to its productivity?	___	___	___	___	___
(b) To what extent is individual receiving the proper remuneration in accordance with payments scheduled for job?	___	___	___	___	___
3. PROMOTABILITY					
(a) To what extent can an individual in this assignment be promoted to jobs needing roughly similar abilities and skills?	___	___	___	___	___
(b) To what extent does individual possess qualities and attributes to be considered for promotions?	___	___	___	___	___
4. EMPLOYEE DEVELOPMENT					
(a) To what extent is it evident that the job has a function within the framework of company goals?	___	___	___	___	___
(b) Is the job "noticed" by executive management?	___	___	___	___	___
(c) To what extent is individual noticeable in achieving job objectives?	___	___	___	___	___
5. JOB PERFORMANCE					
(a) To what extent can the actual performance requirements of the job be measured quantitatively? How?	___	___	___	___	___
(b) Does the individual match these requirements?	___	___	___	___	___

[a] See Martin Patchew, *The Choice of Wage Comparisons* (Englewood Cliffs, N. J.: Prentice-Hall, 1961), pp. 9–14. (Ford Foundation Doctoral Dissertation Series, 1960 Award winner.) Dr. Patchew's basic formula for this evaluation is:

$$\frac{\text{My pay}}{\text{Pay of other similar job categories}} \quad \text{(Compared to)} \quad \frac{\text{My position or division related to pay}}{\text{His (their) position on dimensions related to pay}}$$

Throughout, an engineering approach to measures of qualitative controls is used continually in job and personnel evaluation.

Quality may be defined as the inherent characteristics of an individual or product, and can be measured along the above lines or on a "quality scale," as illustrated at the top of the next page:

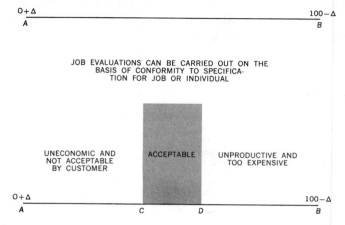

Job evaluations based on such rating schedules can regulate, within limits, the quality control of both job and the individual in it. This involves adjusting any variables at either end of the scale into the "normal" distribution curve pattern (C to D), as shown in Figure XXXIV. The tolerance limits of the quality control procedure are certain to fit the person and the job approximately 68 per cent of the time. The "normal frequency distribution" curve is based on the assumption that rational procedures in matching the "job and the individual" have been used. The quality scale control also assumes that all assignments carry with them the proper measures of interaction between people and merchandise. By listing the job "contact interactions" and the extent to which they should be carried out,

FIGURE XXXIV
FREQUENCY DISTRIBUTION (NORMAL CURVE) *

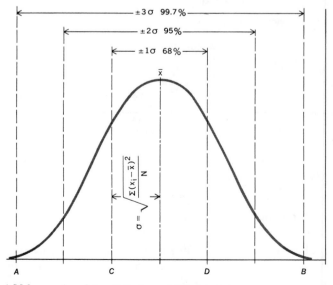

* Values assigned to attribute variables on scales.

the departmental, individual, and organizational effectiveness can be greatly enhanced.

In graphic form, the qualitative processes of the interpersonal network of the individual reacting in the job within the total organizational framework would look like a closed loop or circular flow as shown below:

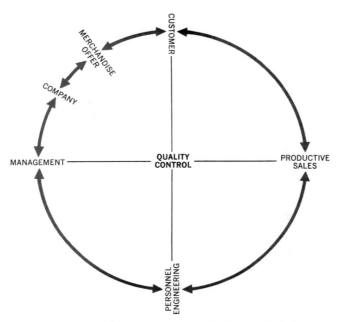

When a smooth flow results, an economic and better-than-average management is indicated. The alternating current (AC) concept is that of continuous quality control of a human-oriented job cycle. The systematizing of operating processes in this manner is termed "personnel engineering."

FUNCTION OF PROMOTION POLICIES

Realistic policies of promotion from within can assure capable management of replacement as executive obsolescence or retirements occur. Utilizing existing personnel resources wherever possible but not on an "ad-hoc-good-fellow" basis does not necessarily create "inbred" or "chaotically" appointed individuals.

However, promotional policies from within must be logical and consistent with the organic functions of control and reappraisal. The underlying concepts in the firm's advancement policies must be thoroughly understood throughout the organization; any deviations from a stated policy must be adequately explained.

The need to hire bright young people at the junior executive level is paramount. Too often, training and development of such people fall short of their personal service objectives and those of the firm. Yet most trainees feel that they are prepared to take over in productive supervisory capacities far sooner than the store's time stipulation. As a result, low morale ensues.

In any executive training program, length of preparation should be varied according to individual needs—not according to any preset, formalized schedules. Inflexibility here also lowers organizational morale, tends to be wasteful, and creates loss of loyalty and an uneconomic turnover of junior executives.

If recruiting for junior management is carried out with the primary purpose of creating a reserve pool rather than immediate placement in a supervisory capacity, then the individuals hired should be so told in advance.

MANAGEMENT OF EXECUTIVE DEVELOPMENT PROGRAMS

Executive development is a means of insuring future progress in an organization. The build-up and continuous advanced training of junior and middle management is vital to personnel administration. The primary goal of such programs should be the development of company-oriented executive echelons. Any composite self-portrait of top management reveals individuals who are primarily concerned with decision making and policy formulation. Good management must at all times be adaptable to change, and where feasible should judiciously delegate responsibility and authority to at least one supervisory level. This is only one setting.

An effective program must teach adaptability in other settings, too. In other words, a framework of projecting attitude reactions by type, in order to develop an effective philosophy of management is a primary goal. Achievement of a goal system and hierarchy of life values develops a management back-up at the ethical and social value levels; such attributes make for success.[8]

Thus, management development programs develop attitudes and motivations toward rational explanations of work behavior of the group. An additional objective is learning how to adapt administrative planning to executive action within the framework of the organization.

Thus, the determinants of selection for executive training should be systematic and related to a standard of character and behavior—for example, psychological testing of ability, industry, and integrity.[9] Before the initial interview—when recruiting and selecting individuals from outside the organization for the executive training programs—evaluations of candidates are generally obtained from university placement offices. An illustration of this type of evaluation is shown in Appendix N.

The need for potential executive management in retailing is great. For example, F. W. Woolworth alone needed 400 new store managers and additional district managers in 1965; Woolworths also increased the number of its executive trainees to 3,000—or more than one trainee for every existing store. The May Department Stores Company has a programed management executive development plan to cover obsolescence.[10] (Executive retirements can be planned and structured, but not obsolescence.)

---

[8] See also Dale Yoder, *Manager Attitude Studies, Clue to Manager and Organization Behavior* (Graduate School of Business, Stanford University, Berkeley, Calif., November 15, 1964).
[9] *Executive Evaluation in the Corporation*, American Institute of Management, New York, 1959.
[10] "How Top Retailers Build Executives," *Business Week* (June 5, 1965), pp. 89–92.

At the F. & R. Lazarus Company, executive management trainees are evaluated on the basis of personal drive and determination. Mental alertness and capacity, the ability to plan, to participate in a team, business ability, and the ability to lead, delegate and be "people minded" are also sought. Sensitivity to other people's thinking and behavior and capacity to communicate, of course, underlie such qualities.[11] In the long run, well-planned programs such as these can be economic and self-liquidating.

MIDDLE MANAGEMENT FUNCTIONS AND ADMINISTRATION

Consistently, the middle managers who are most productive generally boast the ability to allocate a minimum amount of energy to personal confrontations and the capacity to save time. In essence, the better "man-in-the-middle" has learned how to communicate through behavior as well as orally and in writing.

One of the problems in the personnel administration of middle management is adequate reward for achievement (such as *additional* opportunities for personal growth and not overt recognition only). "It is likely that small inputs of opportunities for achievement, rewarded through supervisory recognition by means of larger and more difficult opportunities for achievement might lead to a highly motivated, productive employee."[12]

In a well-adjusted business it is probable that all managerial echelons have enough "back-up" management to adjust promptly and automatically to any changing situation with minimum losses in effectiveness.

The opportunity for growth of the individuals making up middle-management echelons helps mold a firm's effectiveness. Such opportunities should provide the individual with the means for securing his personal service objectives.

The merging of company and personal service objectives is basic to good organization morale. This is the principle of continuity on which organizational performance depends.

One of the real problems in retaining middle management is the problem of not having higher echelon positions readily available. Promotable middle managers, through no fault of their own, must be given special notice that they have been "recognized" and that a tentative schedule for advancement has been set by management. In fact, in Montgomery Ward & Co., manpower and training needs are budgeted two years in advance for this purpose. But it is of vital importance that promotable personnel know at all times where they stand.[13]

In a study on "Simulating the Man-in-the-Middle," five well-defined factors

---

[11] Samuel Feinberg, columnist, Women's Wear Daily (May 24, 1963), p. 7.

[12] B. Watson, *Employee Needs, Perception, and Motivation: A Study of Selected Employer Work Groups and Their Supervisors* (Research paper presented to Western Division Academy of Management, San Diego, Calif., April 9, 1965). See also two studies concerned with achievement and recognition: Frederick Herzberg, Bernard Mausher, and Barbara Bloch Synderman, *The Motivation to Work* (New York, John Wiley & Sons, Inc., 1959); and Scott Myers, "Who Are Your Motivated Workers?" *Harvard Business Review*, Vol. XLIII, No. 1 (January, February 1964), pp. 73–78.

[13] From conversations with Philip J. Lombardi, Administrative Personnel and Development Manager, Montgomery Ward & Co., Inc.

were developed as needed for the success of the individual and a more effective organizational contribution.[14] These are:

1) *Consideration for subordinates:* same as in Ohio State Leadership Studies.
2) *Concern for authority:* consults others on important policy decisions.
3) *Regard for self:* but feels capable of making effective decisions by himself when warranted or when time factor is significant.
4) *Regard for reward:* evaluates his contribution in terms of return—but has total picture and realistic scales of measurement.
5) *General organizational concern:* must receive and give a rational approach to receiving and passing out directives—in the Pittsburgh study.

In several recent studies, the analyses of variance yielded significant differences in concern for authority. Those who showed an extremely low regard for authority also evidenced a general lack of concern about other organizational matters. Consistently, those in higher organizational echelons reported the least amount of consulting with boss and rulebook, while those at the lower levels reported the most. Those in operating departments (engineering operations) seemed more considerate of subordinates.[15]

SELECTING, TRAINING, AND MAINTAINING EMPLOYEES

In the hiring of supervisory and management executives, the personnel department functions as a staff agency. This is much more challenging and important than appears on the surface. Personnel's line authority is generally limited to salespeople, clericals, and other rank-and-file employees. One of the more serious problems of retail firms is the fact that most employees are nonskilled, and they are generally the store's only "contact" with customers. Thus their selection and training is of far greater importance than their rated jobs in the organization indicate. However, because of costs involved, such processing and procedures have been rather neglected in most stores.

Choosing the most appropriate test for each hiring situation has been and continues to be problematic. There are various groups of tests which are constructed to determine general aptitude and personality traits; another group of tests has been developed for determining specialized skills. One of the more effective tests is the Nonverbal Reasoning Test which purports to measure a

[14] Paper read at the American Psychological Association Meetings on September 16, 1963; based on a study by James Vaughan, University of Pittsburgh.
[15] Bernard M. Bass, James A. Vaughan, Jr., Louis Pondy, "Behavior in Groups," *First Annual Report,* Contract N ONR 624 (14) (November 1963).

person's ability to deal with new and unusual problems. It is also claimed that this test can furnish clues regarding the prospective employee's reaction to 1) supervisory relations: the ability to understand and to follow through on directions from supervisors; 2) customer relations: the ability to deal with unusual customer problems in a friendly, sensible manner; 3) relations with fellow workers: the ability to get along well with associates.[16]

Of critical importance in employee selection is that of management. Actuarial and clinical approaches are used: the actuarial tests include psychometric tests and personality inventories, and the clinical tests rely on interviews and projective testing and techniques for evaluations.[17]

Employees, properly selected and placed, need minimal attention except for follow-up training. Every employee should be classified into a general "behavior-pattern" category so that the personnel manager has an effective guide for solving any personal conflicts that might arise.

For example, in studies of behavior patterns of the individual in a group, the individuals are generally willing to classify themselves as being self-oriented, inter-action-oriented, or task-oriented.[18] The study was based on the manner in which an individual attempts to lead a group. More specifically,

1) Self-oriented individuals are those who expect reward for effort or identification—regardless of task accomplishment or effectiveness of their group interactions.

2) Interaction-oriented individuals reap rewards from psychic satisfactions of interaction with others; they too are interested in achieving task objectives, but not at all costs. However, they strive to solve the group's external problems but will make every attempt to avoid internal conflicts.

3) Task-oriented individuals expect success and rewards for their group leadership efforts; they are persistent and have no hesitation in attempting to solve problems outside the group.

Employee and executive classifications, once carried out through the orientation inventory process (Ori) described above, can assist personnel management in solving most organizational conflict that might arise. For example, research re-

[16] Developed by the National Cash Register Co., Dayton, Ohio. Presented to Personnel Meetings, NRMA, June 1, 1962, pp. 11–12.

[17] For further comparisons and correlations of both methods, see Maurice O. Burke, "The Clinical Method of Managerial Selection," *Business Horizons*, Vol. 8, No. 1 (Graduate School of Business, Indiana University, Bloomington, Ind., Spring 1965); and Paul Meehl, *Clinical Versus Statistical Prediction* (Minneapolis: University of Minnesota Press, 1954).

Various batteries of tests and testing equipment are continually being used experimentally and practically by all personnel management in continuing attempts to improve their selection procedure. Organizations such as The Psychological Corporation, N.Y.C., Science Research Associates, Chicago, and E. F. Wonderlic of Northfield, Ill., are representative.

[18] B. M. Bass et al., "Self, Interaction, and Task Orientation Inventory Scores Associated with Overt Behavior and Personal Factors," *Educational and Psychological Measurement*, Vol. XXIII, No. 1 (1963), pp. 101–21. See also support of this position by the work of McClelland, Atkinson, et al. (1953); French (1956); and Fouriezos, Hutt, and Guetzkow (1950).

sults showed that task-oriented individuals were most successful as technically trained supervisors, as first-line foremen, and as research and design engineers. Interaction-oriented individuals did better in consultative, supervisory, and administrative tasks.[19]

UTILIZING PART-TIME EMPLOYEES

The average work week for department-store employees has dropped from 37.5 hours in 1939 to 34.4 hours in 1963. It is also estimated that approximately 7.5 million individuals were working fewer than 35 hours per week. It is also estimated that from the period 1960 to 1965, part-time employment has grown at a rate four times that of over-all full-time employment.

The use of part-time employees in retailing is still growing because of longer store hours, varying peak selling periods, greater availability of people (particularly women) who only want part-time employment, and lower over-all costs.[20]

A part-time employee is a regular employee who works a predetermined schedule of usually 20 hours or more per week, but less than a full work week. The term "part-time" may be a misnomer, because part-timers are usually present during "the highest customer traffic periods and thus reflect to a majority of the shoppers the caliber of service" that a store offers.[21]

Thus, a new concept of personnel utilization has been developed in the use of part-time employees; this has been a much more economic process in suburban areas than downtown. In the suburbs, many young marrieds are available on a part-time basis as they are anxious both to supplement the family income and get away from the house. Effective training of part-timers, while relatively easier than that of full-time employees, is apt to be carried out on a "skimming basis," except for routine store policies and procedures.

Because of the growing importance of part-time employees in relation to total store employment, increasing emphasis has been placed on determining their attitudes, motivations, and productivity in relation to those of full-time employees. One of the more comprehensive studies of this kind was carried out under the direction of the writer; the results are summarized in Figure XXXV.[22] Most significantly, it was found that part-time and regular employees seek work for different reasons. Although methods of selection and training were generally the same, the methods of compensation differ. Different also was each group's understanding of organizational goals.

---

[19] Bass et al., "Self, Interaction, and Task Orientation Inventory Scores Associated with Overt Behavior and Personal Factors," op. cit., p. 120.

[20] George Plant and Lise Knudsen (eds.), Utilizing Part-time Employees Effectively (report of the Personnel Group of the NRMA, January 1964).

[21] Jean H. Sisco, Assistant Vice-President Personnel, Woodward & Lothrop, Inc., Washington, D.C. (Chairman of the Personnel Group Session).

[22] William E. Clark, What Part-Timers Think About Their Job (New York, The Retail Research Institute, NRMA, 1962).

FIGURE XXXV
SUMMARY OF RESULTS OF OPINION SURVEY GIVEN TO PERSONNEL EXECUTIVES *

AREAS	COMPARISON OF AREAS OF PART-TIME EMPLOYEES TO FULL-TIME EMPLOYEES		DIFFERENCES CAUSED BY AREAS TO MOTIVATIONS		DIFFERENCES CAUSED BY AREAS TO PRODUCTIVITY	
	REGULAR PART-TIME	EXTRA PART-TIME	REGULAR PART-TIME	EXTRA PART-TIME	REGULAR PART-TIME	EXTRA PART-TIME
REASONS EMPLOYEES SOUGHT WORK	DIFFERENT	DIFFERENT	SMALL	MODERATE	SMALL	MODERATE
METHODS OF SELECTION, TRAINING, AND COMPENSATION	SAME SAME SAME	SAME SAME DIFFERENT	NONE NONE NONE	NONE NONE SMALL	NONE NONE NONE	NONE NONE SMALL
UNDERSTANDING OF ORGAN. GOALS	SAME	DIFFERENT	NONE	SMALL	NONE	SMALL
BENEFITS AND INCENTIVES	DIFFERENT SAME	DIFFERENT DIFFERENT	SMALL NONE	SMALL SMALL	SMALL NONE	SMALL MODERATE
METHODS OF RATING EMPLOYEES	SAME	DIFFERENT	NONE	MODERATE	NONE	MODERATE

* Source: William E. Clark, *What Part-Timers Think About Their Job*, The Retail Research Institute, NRMA, 1962.

The three hypotheses and the results of their testing follow:

Hypothesis 1. "Part-time store employees do not feel that their jobs are meaningful in themselves and therefore do not use and develop their full potential in their work." Hypothesis as stated is invalid except for "extra" part-time employees.

Hypothesis 2. "Part-time store employees do not understand or identify themselves with the organizational goals." Valid. Store employees generally do not have concepts of organizational goals in order to maintain growth and maximize profits.

Hypothesis 3. "The productivity of part-time store employees is generally less than that of full-time store employees." Valid. Regular part-time employees are as productive as full-time employees provided "extra" part-timers are not included in evaluations.

MORALE AND ORGANIZATIONAL STABILITY

Morale is directly dependent on good channels of communication—both forward and backward within the organization. Good morale can be defined as an attitude of employees conducive to willing cooperation, interest, and loyalty toward management and other employees. Although the basic requirements for a high morale may differ for both operative and executive personnel, the basic motivations remain the same. When personal and organizational objectives are not merged, poor morale results.

MANAGEMENT OF HUMAN RELATIONS

Good human relations is the creation of continuous ultimate satisfactions of human, economic, and social desires. It is basic to the merging of the objectives of employees and the organization. The management of human relations in some cases may have to evolve on more than just routine administrative skills. For example, if an organization or group feels that it is operating as a closed society, better interactions within the group are easier to develop. With the fostering of "togetherness," the output can increase.

Proper selection and training and good promotional potentialities all contribute to good employee relations. The placement of individuals in jobs for which they are suited and from which they can rise to higher echelons is basic to an effective human-relations program.

Favoritism is an uncontrollable variable in the development of good morale. Where nepotism, unwarranted favoritism, or executive obsolescence occurs, executive management is faltering and poor morale ensues. In other words, an organization's morale can be no better than that reflected in the "capability image" of its executive manager.

Good morale is a basic line responsibility of the personnel division and a management criterion for measurement of its success. The attainment of high morale is one of the leadership requirements of successful management. Good morale is an index of the effectiveness of human-relations activities in the firm.[23]

Human-relations problems result most often from blocked communications channels and tend to limit the effectiveness and implementation of decisions made in the firm. Studies based "on rather extensive experience with psychological phenomenon" show that business effectiveness depends on group effort; and "group effort" depends on what may be termed the "interpersonal underworld" of the "informal" organization structure.[24] This is where poor morale shows up first.

Morale Index—Employee Turnover

Good morale is also dependent on job flexibility and the ability of personnel to adapt. Job and personnel flexibility mean lower employee turnover. Because of its general costliness—not to mention the attendant high unemployment insurance cost—a low turnover ratio is a key objective to the personnel division. Generally, the higher the turnover rate, the lower the organizational morale.[25]

Employee turnover can be reduced through functional differentiation in line and staff activities as volume increases. For example, as work loads increase, the manner in which delegated responsibilities are set up to accomplish increased and specialized performance requirements vitally affects employee turnover.

Whenever any type of functional differentiation becomes necessary, it should, wherever possible, be confined to jobs requiring the least intelligence, training, skill, and experience. When practically anyone can do a specified job, little re-

[23] F. L. W. Richardson, "Managing Man's Animal Nature," *Pittsburgh Business Review*, Vol. 34, No. 11 (Graduate School of Business, University of Pittsburgh, December 1964).

[24] See also W. C. Schutz, "Interpersonal Underworld," *Harvard Business Review*, Vol. 36, No. 4 (July–August 1958), pp. 123–35.

[25] The ratio should not be used by itself as a morale index unless specific variables of job terminations are evaluated with the index.

sentment is apt to follow split assignments. However, when a better employee is put in a low-requirement job, he soon becomes dissatisfied and looks for a move.

The Prestige-Status Syndrome

Every task or assigned job, regardless of real or apparent discrepancies, acquires relative degrees of status. The status level, in effect, determines the prestige of job and of the individual performing it. While these are primarily "psychic" attributes, they are nevertheless important as a vital morale factor. Thus, another important function of personnel management is to develop realistically significant and definite measures of prestige for every job wherever possible. The problem here is that development of status may be more intangible than real, as some changes may only be "titular" ones.

Over time, an assignment tends to acquire certain prestige levels generally consistent with its economic contribution and its "strategic" measure of power or usefulness in the firm. The nature of the work, type of experience required, pay involved, and promotional possibilities are all deterministic. Thus, when a particular job lacks a definite status level, it should be identified, wherever possible, with the position considered to be the next highest.

Importance of Organizational Flexibility

Low morale is a factor in high operating costs. Salaries paid in all store divisions should approximate the average wage rates paid in one area. With minimum wage regulations now also applying to retailing, this is more easily carried out than in the past. Low morale reflects itself in high labor turnover and organizational instability. There is generally a direct correlation between organizational stability and profitability and labor turnover. Stability does not mean organizational stagnation, which results from overindoctrination, naive brainwashing, and excessive inbreeding. It is for the sake of avoiding this type of inbred stagnation that companies seek flexibility in executive selection outside of the firm.[26]

One of the greatest hazards in maintaining morale is the tendency for long-time employees to feel that they have vested interest in their jobs and to act accordingly. Such complexes can be corrected only in the earlier stages of employment. Also, there cannot be too many differences in the departmental performance requirements of similarly classified employees.

Great care must be taken in consideration of the proper variables in evaluating organizational performance. For example, one department may have a very able and efficient manager, with a resulting low employee turnover; at the same time, another department may have a mediocre manager with good employees and with the same over-all departmental performance. Thus promotion and/or movement of employees within the firm is a valid means of reducing vested interests.

---

[26] See Henry Fayol, *Industrial and General Administration* (London: I. Pitman & Sons, 1924), p. 31, for discussions on these considerations.

Correlating Human Relations and Organizational Morale

In essence, applied human-relations programs mean that management recognizes the basic principle that all employees are subject to economic and social change. They should be regarded and supervised as "thinking beings." Otherwise, both employees and customers are apt to suffer in face-to-face contacts.

Essentially, good human relations emanate from a sense of duty created through moral obligations.

EFFECTS OF UNIONIZATION-LEGISLATION AND FRINGE BENEFITS

Retailing, as an industry, has the lowest ratio of organized to unorganized employees. Labor unions in retailing have developed at a much slower pace because of the almost daily face-to-face contacts of rank-and-file employees with those in supervisory, middle, and top management positions. In addition, many consider themselves employed either on a temporary or a stop-gap basis and thus avoid, when possible, the inconvenience of organization.

Until 1933, management often refused to meet the representatives of union and at times obtained injunctions to prevent organization. Until the passage of the Taft-Hartley Act of 1947, which amended the National Labor Relations Act of 1935, unions had practically a *carte blanche* in organizing. In amended form, this is still the basic legislation under which industrial and labor relations operate and are administered today. The industrial relations aspects of personnel management have become so important that a top executive, usually a company vice-president or a permanent management consultant, is generally in charge of these functions within the firm.

Civil Rights and Equal Opportunity Legislation

In 1965, many social and economic changes resulted from the enactment of the Civil Rights Bill. In some firms a paperwork revolution occurred. Almost every application blank and other pre-employment form had to be revised, and drastic changes were made in "help wanted" advertising. Re-examination and some revision of pre-employment testing and additional record keeping on all points involving employment also had to be instituted.

Under the Civil Rights Act, a Federal Equal Opportunity Commission initiated proceedings to develop a unified procedure between the federal and state governments. The Act was not fully operational until early in 1966. Initial emphasis has been on mediation and conciliation techniques, rather than on court actions for enforcement.

One of the most significant decisions to emerge from the NLRB was permission for "splinter groups" to organize and seek recognition. In the past, the majority of all employees in a store had to favor a union before recognition and bargaining rights were accorded. This decision may very well serve as a catalytic agent for increased unionization in retailing. However, the union's first attempts to utilize the "splinter" decisions failed.[27] Another focal point for unionization is the seeking of recognition for the whole store on a "branch-by-branch" strategy. This was a "splinter bid" recognition attempt by Local 65 of Retail, Wholesale, Department Store Union at Lord & Taylor and Arnold Constable; the union also failed in its initial bid in this direction at Bloomingdale's.

Many of the new moves in unions seek means of assuaging the "security mindedness" of the organization man. Management and employees are apparently both seeking permanent career relationships—a new concept in employment. The private income security programs cover such fringe benefits as group pensions, life insurance, unemployment benefits, accident and health insurance, and profit-sharing plans.

In the ordinary course of competition, these wage supplements differ from the regular monetary wage increases—benefits are not paid steadily and not to all workers, as in the case of wage changes. Also, costs of providing these benefits depend on many complex and highly uneven developments.

The cost of fringe benefit programs varies between companies, and from time to time in any one company. Furthermore, the accumulated reserve funds influence the financial markets as well as business and government decisions. The medical and hospital industries and the aged are also strongly affected. Also, the income security benefits have adversely affected the system of collective bargaining (by centralization, the reliance on experts, and inflexible long-term agreements); both unions and management have shown a sense of responsibility and social innovation to meet real needs, which has made income security primarily a co-operative effort.[28]

Fringe Benefits

Fringe benefits may be classified as belonging to a whole gamut of extras. In effect, fringe benefits are taking the place of immediate income. Regardless of whether or not a store is unionized, benefits gained by any worker group in a community tend to spread to adjacent competitors. In some cases, the threat of unionization often forces favorable negotiations for fringe-benefit additions.

Of growing importance in this area are vacation payments, plans for retirement income, profit sharing, and purchases of company stock. These are also important incentives for reducing employee turnover ratio. The fringe benefit cost in retailing is approximately one-fourth of the stipulated salary compensation paid. In Table 35 the combined total cost of fringe benefits for both retail and wholesale trade is 23.6 per cent. A significant addition to this is employee discounts for in-store purchases, which range up to 20 per cent off the stated retail price.

---

[27] Women's Wear Daily (March 1, 1965), p. 1.
[28] Benson Soffer, "The First Decade of Private Income Security for the Worker in the American Economy," unpublished memorandum emanating from study directed by Sumner H. Slichter on the Brookings Institute's Project on Union Management Relations (Graduate School of Business, University of Pittsburgh, 1958).

TABLE 35

FRINGE PAYMENTS AS A PERCENTAGE OF PAY ROLL BY INDUSTRY GROUPS, 1963[a]

			PER CENT
Total	All Industries		25.6
Total	*All Manufacturing*		24.2
		Range	
(Low)	Textile Products and Apparel		20.2
(High)	Petroleum Industry		28.9
Total	*All Nonmanufacturing*		27.8
		Range	
(Low)	Trade (Wholesale and Retail)		23.6
(High)	Banks, Finance, and Trust Companies		32.9

[a] Developed from p. 45, Table 2, "Briefing Sessions Workbook on Collective Bargaining" (February–March 1965), The Bureau of National Affairs. (Data based on survey of 1,150 companies carried out in 1963 by U. S. Chamber of Commerce, Washington, D.C.)
The Chamber's report covers the cost of employers of (1) legally required payments for social security contributions, unemployment compensation, and workmen's compensation; (2) pension, insurance, and employee meals; (3) rest periods, lunch periods, and wash-up time; (4) payments for time not worked, including vacations, holidays, and sick leaves; and (5) such items as profit-sharing payments, bonuses, and employee education.
In 1963 fringe costs rose to 25.6 per cent of pay roll. In comparison, the 1961 survey, covering 1,120 companies, showed costs of 24.9 per cent of pay roll (BNA, p. 44).

By including the "income from the fringe benefit cash discounts" for retail employees, the proportion of total benefits to total pay-roll costs is above the over-all average for all sectors of the economy.[29] There is no evidence that the trend in the proportionate increases of value of fringe benefits will diminish.

WAGE AND SALARY ADMINISTRATION

One of the problems in the economic aspects of job evaluation and remuneration arises from the many imperfections in our wage-price system. This is an important influencing facet of tying the proper monetary incentive to a job and its requirements in terms of its relative contribution to the firm's goals. Due to the erratic and unpredictable behavior of individual prices, their fluctuations are factors beyond company or government control. Such force generally have lead to "upward pushes" on the wage-price structures of the firm.

In wage administration, total wages and remuneration must be tied to produc-

---

[29] This estimate is based on a 20 percent discount of an average additional yearly purchasing power of retail employees. The estimate of yearly purchasing power of $2,080 is based on the discretionary income increase based on an average weekly salary of $75 for all retail employees. Multiplying 20 percent (discount) × $2,080 = $416, the average annual income in purchasing income.
Adding $416 to the average value of $1,431 per year per worker in fringe benefits received by workers in all industries (see BNA Data quoted above), the average return to retail employee exceeds $1,800 annually—or more than 25 percent greater than the $1,431 average fringe benefit return listed by the Bureau of National Affairs (BNA).
This average purchasing power estimate is from Weston P. Figgins, Vice President, Operations, Woodward & Lothrop, Washington, D.C. The data were published in the article on the "Sales Management News Bulletin," NRMA (First Quarter, 1961).

tivity, otherwise competitive long-run operations cannot continue. In the field of retailing, because of the "personal" face-to-face nature of its selling processes, productivity increases have been minimal. Whatever changes in productivity and efficiency have occurred have resulted for the most part from upward changes in volume rather than improvement in efficiency; vis-à-vis, as volume increases, output per man-hour tends to increase. Thus, during periods of increasing volume, the output per man increases substantially within limits.[30]

Compensation Plans

Compensation plans are a tool of management for providing proper direction and control of the firm's personnel. An effective compensation plan provides sufficient earnings so that proper incentives will result. Obviously, there are infinite varieties of compensation plans; most can be classified under the straight salary, salary and commissions, hourly, or quota-bonus plans. In the long run, regardless of method of payment, compensation plans must be tied to some measure of productivity. They must be fair and reasonable to all echelons in the organization and to the organization itself. Furthermore, they should be subject to constant review if good organizational morale is to be maintained.

The ideal compensation plan should be flexible and provide proportionate reward and incentive. It should be easy to understand and framed so that both company and individual goals are furthered. Other attributes of an ideal plan are low operating costs, recognition of good performance, and equal opportunities for additional earnings.

When sales personnel are employed on a regular basis, their basic "income-draw" should provide a wage sufficient to meet family expenses at an adequate level of living. ("Adequate" is defined as the average of the community.) In addition, whatever wage is offered should be competitive, not only within the industry, but in the community.

Under the commission plan of payment, if the minimum salary guarantees are properly set, there is far less likelihood of the development of higher than average selling costs than under the straight salary method. Men's clothing, women's ready-to-wear, shoes, furniture, and appliances are typical of merchandise areas where compensation is based primarily on commission.

When salary plans offer too little in the way of direct incentives for productive performance, over-all results may not measure up to expectations. With the advent of productivity unit accounting and "expense center" work units of measurement it is now much easier to engage costs to performance.

In the larger stores and chains, there has been a strong movement toward the straight salary method of compensation. The advocates of this plan claim

---

[30] "Recent Changes in Output Per Man—Total Private Economy and Major Sectors," Ewan Clague, U. S. Department of Labor, paper submitted to Joint Economic Committee (January 29, 1959), p. 3.

that this makes for greater interdepartmental flexibility, less hostility among employees, and more stabilized earnings, and is far less costly to administer than commission plans.[31]

Of greater significance in generating employee incentives are "profit-sharing" opportunities for all employees—not just executives. "Small companies are finding that profit sharing when properly handled, provides incentives which can help to bring about better employee teamwork, reduced labor turnover, high productivity, better product quality, and lower costs." [32]

A modified aspect of the commission plan is the salary and commission, or quota-bonus, type of payment. In such cases, the salary or "draw" should be sufficient to meet an adequate level of living; the opportunity for supplementing the "guarantee" serves as the additional incentive. When commissions are not paid until a given minimum volume has been generated, this is known as a quota-bonus plan, which is essentially the same as the salary and commission arrangement.

Pay Differentials

Different rates of pay for men and women existed in most industries until the Equal Pay Law was passed by Congress in June 1963; this became effective in June 1964.[33] Under the Act, area of administration that is probably the most difficult is the definition of equal work. "The jobs of the man and the woman whose wage rates 'are compared' must require equal effort, equal skill, equal responsibility and they must be performed under equal working conditions." [34]

Many retail firms no longer hire young women over 20 for their executive development programs because of the high attrition rates from marriage; and any potential benefits of hiring women because of pay differentials no longer exist. As a result it has become more difficult for young women to obtain a start in "career jobs" in retailing despite store protestations to the contrary.

---

[31] Samuel Feinberg, "Straight Pay Trend Is Growing at Big Stores," Women's Wear Daily (August 12, 1963), p. 21.

[32] B. L. Metzger, "Will Profit Sharing Help Your Firm?" Management Aids for Small Manufacturers. Small Business Administration, Washington, D.C. (October 1963).

[33] Eugene F. Rowan, Personnel Relations Manager, J. C. Penney Co., on "The Law on Equal Pay for Equal Work," Stores, Vol. 46, No. 3 (March 1964), pp. 11–13.

[34] Personnel is now concerned with application of the Equal Pay Law passed by Congress on June 10, 1963. The principal facets of the Act are: (1) Coverage: The law covers all employers and employees currently covered under Section 6 (minimum wage) of the FLSA (Fair Labor Standards Act). For retailers, this means that all retail enterprises with an annual sales volume of $250,000 or more are covered. (Stores with sales volume of less than $250,000 are exempt.) (2) Exemptions: Retail employees meeting the wage-hour standards for executive, administrative, and professional employees and outside salesmen are also exempt from coverage under the law. In addition, employees working primarily in a restaurant operated by a retail store are exempt. (3) Discrimination: The law prohibits wage differentials based solely on sex within any "covered" establishment—in other words, equal pay for equal work requiring equal skill, equal effort, and equal responsibility when performed under similar working conditions. (4) Differentials: The law permits wage differentials where the payment is based on: (a) a seniority system; (b) a merit system; (c) a system which measures earnings by quantity or quality of production; or (d) any factor other than sex alone.

Executive Compensation

Executive compensation in department stores is comparable to patterns of general industry. In general merchandise and variety chains it is substantially lower.[35]

In a McKinsey survey, the following data emerged from stores with sales volumes of $25 million, $70 million, $100 million, $300 million, and $970 million. In this study, the chief executive earns the following per cent of the total organization sales.

Department Stores	.212%	.111%	.086%	.037%	.017%
General Mdse. and Variety	.128	.006	.052	.026	.013

In a comparison of the remuneration of the second, third, and fourth highest paid executives in relation to that of the "chief executive," the ranking was as follows:

Rank	Department Stores	General Merchandise	All-Industry
2nd	74%	75%	71%
3rd	63	66	59
4th	60	59	54

SCOPE OF TRAINING—GENERAL

Adequate training is economic and can enhance the effectiveness of management —especially in the flow of information and communications within the organization. In terms of improved efficiency, training is well worth the resource allocation.[36] The scope of training in the store should cover every part of company policies and procedures, whether or not the individual's job assignment is directly involved. Sales-supporting personnel whose activities are adjacent to or on the selling floor should also be given training on customer services.

In most retail stores, training is held to a minimum in attempts to save expenses and because many top-management officials question the value of formal training beyond the initial basic stages. Where minimal formal training takes place, it consists merely of indoctrination in store policies, systems, and procedures. In the smaller store, the manager or owner does the training—usually by means of "on-the-job" instruction.

In many cases, the fundamentals of selling are taught by observation only. In medium-sized organizations the personnel director may also double as the training

---

[35] From author's article, "The Job Revolution," op. cit., 1962; David Caulkins of McKinsey & Co., Management Consultants, supplied the data frame ("1961 Eighth Annual Survey on Executive Compensation"). The survey included twenty-seven department store chains and independents and thirteen general merchandise and variety store chains. In their estimate of the total compensation received, salary, bonus, and deferred incomes were included.

[36] Under the provisions of the Manpower Development and Training Act (MDTA) of 1965, many personnel managers are attempting to get support from the federal government on training in EDP-systems installation and operations on how best to meet customer demand for services on a profitable basis.

director. Generally, a minimum of five hours of formal training is given to all employees who will be floor representatives of the store.

Even within a minimum program, stress should be placed on the art of being a good listener. Also, *all* personnel should be able to answer customers' questions or know where correct answers can be delivered. This is indispensable for becoming an effective link in the "store-contact-interaction" promotion of good will. The questions most often asked by customers are relatively simple; they generally concern merchandise and department location, hours open, deliveries, adjustments, credit and personal services, and specific conveniences available.

More recently, "programed instruction" methodologies have been introduced into personnel training. Programed instruction originated in part in psychological studies of human behavior. It is now being used for training store employees in areas where factual knowledge is a prerequisite to specific job performance. The immediate challenge to personnel executives lies in applying programing methods where warranted, in their training procedures: in effect, an analysis of the repertoire for a trainee, taking into account what he already knows.[37]

Among the several principles which come from the behavioral model and which are basic to programing are:

1) A clear statement of the behavior desired of the student or trainee at the conclusion of the program.
2) A clear statement of the behavioral repertoire of the student prior to taking the program.
3) A precise analysis of the material to be learned.
4) Instruction programed in such a way as to:
   a) require active responses on the part of the learner;
   b) provide immediate feedback to the student as to the correctness of his response; and
   c) introduce new material through gradual progression to establish a complex repertoire.

Training systems are still being evaluated. The quest for identification of the variables that motivate school learning begins anew with programed instruction. With longer programed materials, employee motivation has become a crucial variable.[38] Boredom occurs if sessions are too long; employees' failure to pay attention to what is being said, rejection of the communicator's statements, and attempts to ward off subsequent exposure to the anxiety-arousing content result.[39]

---

[37] George Plant and Carol Miller (eds.), "Programmed Instruction in Retailing," Personnel Group, NRMA. January 1963 report, p. 5.

[38] Lawrence E. Schlesinger, et al., "The Effect of Relevant Emotional Content on Performance and Learning in Programmed Instruction," final report of Media Research and Dissemination Branch Office of Education, Title VII, Grant No. 7–18–0100–197. See also, I. L. Janis and S. Feshbach, "Effects of Fear Arousing Communications," *Journal of Abnormal and Social Psychology*, Vol. 48 (1953), pp. 78–92.

[39] *Ibid.*, "Personality Differences Associated with Responsiveness to Fear-Arousing Communications," I. L. Janis and S. Feshbach, *Journal of Personnel*, Vol. 23, 154–66, December 1954.

Follow-up Training

Formal follow-up training is generally scheduled only for those with promotional potentials. Other follow-up training is carried out on a do-it-yourself basis. On the selling floor the buyers, assistant buyers, and department managers help whenever possible. In nonselling departments, section supervisors and operations managers also help.

For example, executive trainees who have been in the store for a period of six months or more should be given the opportunity to attend regularly scheduled executive management sessions.

Follow-up training becomes most economic and productive when it includes courses in:

The Competitive Framework of the Business

Management of Communication

Employer-Employee Relations

Human Relations Aspects of Executive Supervision

Measuring Results of Interdepartmental and Intra-Store Change

Evaluating and Rating Employees

How Personnel Reviews Employee Progress

Theory of Wage Payment Plans

How the "Totality" of the Organization Can Be Greater than the Sum of All Its Parts

SUMMARY AND CONCLUSIONS

In this chapter, the scope of personnel management both as a line and a staff function was reviewed. The role of executive development and increasing competition for bright young people for junior management was analyzed from a socio-economic standpoint.

Within this analysis of productivity requirements, corporation plans and quantitative approaches to personnel evaluation were analyzed, as well as new techniques in the behavioral sciences for promoting human relations and organizational morale.

Chapter 26: *Credit Management as a Sales and Control Operation*

One of the greatest assets facilitating the process of merchandising is a productive credit system. The basic purpose of credit management in any business organization is to maximize sales and to minimize losses. These functions are complementary.

Credit systems involve a balancing of calculated costs and profits, which is the responsibility of the credit department. The credit system evolves from the interaction of outside competitive influences and internal organizational goals. In final form, store objectives are balanced in terms of economic pressures, organizational goals, and current operating policies. When a strategy is developed, a credit policy results. The policy should be flexible and able to be adjusted. It should be capable of serving both the customer and the store. In many large retail stores, credit sales may represent as much as 80 per cent of the total sales; in the cases of automotive and major appliance stores, credit sales may approximate 100 per cent of all sales. The liberal use of both charge-account and installment credit has been receiving greater acceptance by increasing numbers of consumers.

Although the credit department of retail firms is operationally part of the control division, it should in fact be considered within the purview of the marketing management activities of the store.[1]

All credit transactions involve three elements: futurity, risk, and a debtor-creditor relationship. It is in this last element that credit management finds a key role in maintaining the continuity of the customer's relationship with the store. Although much of the work of granting credit is technical, the credit manager works very closely with the publicity division in order to develop maximum sales from the monthly mailings to customers.

In the industrial field, marginal credit applications are constantly being reviewed with the sales manager to make certain that no potentially valuable customers are being ignored. At the retail level, the credit manager works with the publicity and merchandising divisions in seeking new charge-account customers and in keeping existing charge customers happy. Also, the credit manager is generally charged with encouraging customers to shop frequently and make payments in person if possible.

The store's good will and its total economic impact on the community can be related directly to the effectiveness with which the credit function of the store is carried out. The credit department can enhance the store's public image by publicizing the store's available services. Throughout its operation, the credit department's records and coordinated promotions represent the single most important source of internal research materials for the entire store.

Within this framework, credit promotions, when coordinated within the advertising plan, are especially effective in the sale of high-priced durable goods and home furnishings. For example, direct mail circulars used in conjunction with monthly credit billings generally have a high impact on sales return. Actual inquiries from direct mail inserts may run as high as 14 per cent with actual resulting sales approximating 4 to 5 per cent of all mail stuffings.[2]

CREDIT AS A "POWER" AND PROCESS

Credit is a "power" extended to the consumer by the store so that he can obtain goods or services by a promise to pay at some future specified date.[3] The basic assumption underlying credit transactions is that there will not be any significant change, either upward or downward, in the nature of the credit risk during the credit period. Thus, continuous observation of the account during the credit period by the creditor should not be needed. The amount of credit that is extended at the retail level is determined by consumer demand. In turn, the amount

[1] See also T. H. Beckman and Robert Bartels, *Credit and Collections in Theory and Practice* (6th ed., New York: McGraw-Hill, 1955), p. 46. "Not only do both charge account and installment credit increase with general prosperity," it is here stated, but they increase the proportion of total expenditures made by customers with stores having a full range of credit facilities.

[2] Based on research studies conducted by writer, 1963–1964, Graduate School of Business, University of Pittsburgh.

[3] In effect, this is an extention of John Stuart Mill's definition as "permission to use another's capital."

of credit extended to retailers is determined by the amount of business activity. Business activity determines the demand for capital and current policy of the Treasury and the Federal Reserve System. The flow of savings and investments into capital markets furnish the bases for total debt.

Credit is sound only to the extent that the promises to pay underlying it are sound. Credit does not represent a tangible economic good as does wealth, and "from the standpoint of society, credit transactions do not in themselves increase wealth." [4]

Business activity and interactions have over-all circular effects on the total economy to the extent to which cash and credit transactions interact. The liberal use of credit throughout the economy has been a very real factor in the constant growth in National Income and Gross National Product. [5]

Buying on credit has always been highly acceptable in defined regions of the country—for example, in the South, the Midwest, and in many small communities.

Both independents and national chains, who in the past had nothing but cash policies, have turned to the use of credit in order to maximize their growth and competitive position. The J. C. Penney Company, which first started offering credit in 1961, is an example. Only in the large supermarket chain is credit generally not part of a firm's operating policies. The smaller stores have instituted and expanded their use of bank plans of various kinds which assume the risks involved on a "set fee" cost basis to the retailers and to the consumer. Others will extend credit on the basis of "issued" credit cards by nationally known firms or service agencies.

RELATIONSHIP OF CREDIT TO BUSINESS CONDITIONS

The extension of credit by retail firms is a result—not a cause—of business conditions. Thus consumer credit differs from government or business credit in the nature of its effect on the economy. The volume of consumer credit in the economy is the result of a variety of circumstances—chiefly the willingness and the ability of the population to pay for a constantly increasing standard of living. This is quite independent of the functioning of credit management itself. Our unparalleled and effective system of communications and credit interchange is a definite contributing factor in this direction. [6] In monopolistic competition, the roles of credit, savings, financing, and government operations are molded by business's philosophy of management and the nation's planned system of loose economic controls. With every economic crisis, real or imagined, come vociferous demands for additional government controls. This is the direct result of the failure

---

[4] *Ibid.*, p. 7.

[5] See Roy L. Reierson, *Credit Expansions and Interest Rates* (Bankers Trust Co., New York, 1960), pp. 1–5.

[6] R. D. Entenberg, "The Relationship of Credit to Business Conditions," *Credit Currents,* July 1957.

of those interested in such legislation to differentiate properly between the varying impacts of the credit used by the government, business, and consumers.

Business and Consumer Credit

The types of credit that are determining factors of business conditions are primarily government and business credit, not consumer credit. Consequently, any policy adopted regarding the expansion or contraction of credit must, if it is to achieve maximum effectiveness, apply chiefly to controls at both the government and business levels. There are no built-in guarantees that the arbitrary institution or omission of credit will result in either inflation or deflation. Although the market significance of consumer credit has been widely recognized for some thirty years, its true functions and import are still not clearly understood.

There has been a trend toward increasing government administrative controls of general credit, installment credit, and nonbanking, institutional credit. Consumer credit today is not excessive. However, to state the amount of consumer credit would be meaningless unless it is tied to a repayment factor. Consumer credit should always be related directly to disposable personal income, which furnishes the principal means for repayment. Using this ratio as a guidepost, consumers have not overextended themselves. The rate of savings by the same consumers who have taken advantage of installment and other credit facilities has increased, not diminished.

Ratio of Credit to Income

More specifically, disposable personal income—the income after taxes which an individual may choose to spend or to save—totalled some $432 billion in 1964 and $448 billion for the first quarter of 1965. Consumer credit outstanding at the end of 1964 was $76.8 billion and personal savings totalled $32.5 billion.

The consumer credit data given here are year-end figures, when credit extension is at its highest level. Yet the total amount of these outstandings represented only 17.8 per cent of disposable personal income for 1964 (DPI $43.8 billion),[7] despite an unprecedented sales expansion of new automobiles, as well as a repayment ratio on installment debt of 14 per cent during 1964.

Advocates of consumer credit controls cannot justify their arguments in the face of such national income and economic data. If there is any degree of pessimism in the economic picture, it certainly cannot be attributed to the volume or the manner in which consumer credit is being used.

CIRCULAR EFFECTS—CREDIT POLICIES AND STORE IMAGE

The availability of credit is probably one of the most important services that a store has to offer. Competition is today coming from commercial banks through

---

[7] From *Survey of Current Business*, Vol. 45, No. 5 (May 1965); also *Federal Reserve Bulletin* (June 1964), p. 870; and "Eleven Developments in Consumer Credit," p. 787.

their credit plans; as a result, this has equalized competition among all manner of stores in this respect. At the same time, the decision as to whether or not to grant credit or to decide on the kinds of credit policies that will be offered must fit in with over-all store policies.

Some of the general considerations determining the type of credit policy offered are: size of the community, the region and the trading area, competitive store policies, purchasing patterns of potential purchasers, income levels, the class of trade, the line of goods, sectional preferences, and, of course, the availability of capital on economic terms for the extensions of credit.

In effect, the price, quality, style, and service offerings of the retail firm determine the store policy with respect to charge and cash sales. In turn, the charge policies offered affect the store policy which led to their initiation. Thus, the store credit policies directly influence the merchandising offers of the store and the store image. In the convenience-goods field, with the exception of the full-service grocers and neighborhood pharmacists (among others), who offer charge and delivery services, a cash policy is usually followed. In the smaller shopping and specialty-goods stores, charge accounts are opened for "top-rated" customers only. It may be categorically stated that the lower the price of goods, the more likely the store is to have a cash only policy rather than cash-credit type of operation.

In effect, the retail credit offered by the store represents extension of private credit in the economy. Another form of private credit is "trade credit"; this is the "power" extended to wholesalers and manufacturers by retail firms. A third form of credit is that extended by commercial banks; this is essentially cash credit arising primarily from investments and demand deposits. Commercial bank credit is extended generally for ninety-day periods and for use as temporary working capital to meet seasonal needs. Mortgage funds are used primarily for permanent capital investment, such as in the development of new shopping centers, refurbishment of existing facilities, and initiating or expanding the extension of credit. With respect to retail firms operating in particular trading areas, consumer credit policies must be "merchandised" and managed in much the same manner as are the other goods and services offered by the store.

CREDIT POLICIES AND WORKING CAPITAL REQUIREMENTS

The credit department is a key part of the control division, and its operation is important in flow, utilization, and acquisition of funds. Many retail firms "factor" their accounts receivable during the peak months.

Thus, the type of sales and credit policies offered by a retail firm determines the over-all working-capital needs. The initiation of credit granting by a retail firm necessitates greater amounts of working capital and additional real and imputed costs. The amount of working capital needs involved between a cash and credit policy can be substantial. Credit increases volume and triggers sales which would not accrue under a straight cash sales policy. The additional sales which result from the extension of credit more than pay for its costs, regardless of whether or not interest charges are made on credit extensions for merchandise purchases.[8]

For example, in the use of a thirty-day charge account for convenience, the average receivables turnover generally runs for 45 to 60 days. The major costs involved in these accounts receivable are in the administration of the credit extension. While losses from bad debts may run as high as 3 per cent on credit sales of less than 1½ per cent on total sales, the additional volume generated through the credit extensions serves to reduce over-all expenses to a greater extent than those resulting from the credit department operation.

In a normative model of the above analysis, let us assume that the average collection period for a 30-day charge account is 60 days. The receivables turnover rate would then be 6 ($360 \div 60$). If the total charge sales for the year are $120,000, the additional working capital needed to finance this amount of credit sales, based on an average collection period of 60 days, would be $20,000 ($120,000 \div 6$). The imputed or actual interest involved would approximate $1,200 annually (20,000 $\times$ 6.0%). This amount would be the total additional operating costs of the additional working capital needed. In the case of big-ticket items such as major appliances, furniture, and automobiles, where purchases are generally made on the basis of budget and installment accounts, the interest-rate return more than offsets not only the cost of capital but total credit costs as well.[9] Where a valid credit plan is offered, additional sales are generated. Where a store is in a position to underwrite this additional capital requirement for credit sales, it can generally earn some 6 to 8 per cent on its credit sales—assuming an imputed or real interest cost of 6 per cent and an 18-per-cent effective interest-rate income per year, estimated on the basis of 1½ per cent per month on any unpaid balances.[10]

Even if the cost of credit administration were as high as 5 per cent on credit sales (which it is not), then the additional costs involved in this model would be $7,200 ($1,200 cost of capital plus $6,000, cost of credit operation (5% $\times$ $120,000). This amount would still be less than the usual 8 to 10 per cent return (before taxes) that accrues to most well-run retail firms. This percentage

---

[8] In a study of credit costs by the NRMA in 1963 ("Study of Customer Credit Costs in Department Stores 1963"), an unrealistic and misleading accounting approach to credit costs was published. For example: "The sixth cost category covers the cost of the additional sales people required to handle credit customers. . . . Added sales people would not be required if the credit function were discontinued." (p. 5). Their argument (Touche, Ross, Bailey & Smart, CPA's) for inclusion of this variable expense—despite the "self liquidity" of the nature of the selling function—demonstrates an unrealistic or a biased concept of selling in the relation of selling to total store sales.

The basic study, except for incidental interest, is not valid—even for the stores surveyed, because the basic assumption under which the study was conducted is not valid; i.e., "The basic criteria for identifying costs of credit was to identify for each participant these costs which could be eliminated if the credit function were discontinued assuming no change in total sales volume." This assumption is highly questionable for any supposedly objective study of this kind.

[9] Purchases of this kind are generally secured by means of chattel mortgages or conditional sales contracts so the resulting paper can readily be discounted for cash if necessary.

[10] *Op. cit.*, NRMA Study.

return on sales would tend to be even greater with credit, because the additional volume generated would tend to reduce over-all operating expense and increase gross profits.

CREDIT FUNCTIONS AND CLASSIFICATIONS

Functional management of the credit department involves the obtaining of "signed" credit applications, conducting the interview, and making the credit decision; other line functions of the department are soliciting new accounts, setting up "floor limits" for charge purchases not needing verification, and setting up policy for aging accounts receivable. The credit manager also formulates the store's collection policy and makes certain that the collection system has both "persistence and promptness" automatically built into it.

In checking the credit application, the credit manager must be certain, in order to determine the exact responsibility, that the name *in full* is registered. Various clues may be indicative of the credit-worthiness of the individual. For example, addresses or former addresses show the applicant's income expenditure patterns and level of responsibility. Residence in a rooming house or in a furnished apartment, or in a slum area, or young single persons living away from home in ultra-luxurious surroundings without visible means of support may be signs of an inferior credit risk.

Other areas of questionable risk would be those in occupations such as waitresses, entertainers, or taxicab drivers who have only marginally reliable sources of income.

Personal interviews, personal references, credit reporting agencies, and credit bureaus are the principal sources of credit information. The personal interview is probably the most effective source of information.

Consumer credit can be classified into three broad groups, depending on the purpose for which it is used: firstly, *convenience credit*, generally called the 30-day charge account (which in reality averages 45 to 60 days for repayment). The assumption here is that the customer can well afford to pay cash and uses this credit only for convenience. Then *installment or revolving account credit*, a deferred payment account that is used by consumers primarily to improve their standard of living (perhaps for the purchase of appliances, automobiles, ready-to-wear, home improvements, or for vacations). This kind of credit is self-liquidating, in that the cost of the credit to the store is more than offset by the interest charges. The third type of consumer credit—*cash credit*—is necessity or emergency credit, and perhaps belongs more properly in the area of personal finance rather than in distribution. However, with the substantial entry of banks into retail as well as consumer cash credit, the separation of classifications has become less important.

While there is generally no interest charge to customers for 30-day charges, it is still, in the long run, the most productive kind of charge.

Thus, users of "convenience" charge account credit are the most preferred because they are more loyal long-run patronage customers, are in a better position to purchase the higher-priced store offerings, and are also important cash customers of the store during the course of the year.[11] Despite store desires to sell on "deferred" credit plans in order to increase interest revenues, charge account credit is being used on a much more widespread basis than has heretofore been common. With the advent of credit cards of various sorts, the use of this kind of credit is vigorous and growing in importance.[12] For example, American Express Company cards are now being accepted for charge-account credit by all kinds and all sizes of firms, whether or not they are members. The nonmember companies operating in this manner use the card for identification purposes only; they then bill the individual directly, in order to save the average 7 per-cent service charge.

CREDIT INTERCHANGE AND COOPERATION

Probably no other form of business activity is so dependent on collective acts of cooperation as in the extension of credit. Credit departments cooperate with the credit departments of other business organizations through credit information interchange. This represents a mutually beneficial and vital use of information gathered by credit bureaus and agencies in the course of their business activities.

The development of good working relationships with a central credit bureau and credit agencies is basic to successful credit management. Credit bureau information is set up on the basic framework on which credit is extended. All retail and service establishments which sell on credit—including beauty parlors, physicians, dentists, commercial banks, and government agencies such as the Federal Housing Administration—seek information from credit specialists.

Used increasingly is the Association of Credit Bureaus with more than 1,700 members affiliated with the National Retail Credit Association located in Atlanta,

---

[11] See Robert D. Breth, "Cash-Buying Habits of Customers with Charge Accounts," *Stores*, Vol. 46, No. 8, September 1964, pp. 41–43. Mr. Breth is Vice-President of A. J. Wood Research Corporation and has conducted studies showing that "charge accounts influenced women to prefer and make purchases in stores where they had accounts by a 3.8 to 1 ratio over the same behavior by cost shoppers."

[12] See "Developments in Consumer Credit," *Federal Reserve Bulletin*, Washington, D.C., June 1965, p. 793; for example:

...The expansion in instalment credit has dominated the consumer credit picture, but charge accounts, single-payment loans, and other types of noninstalment credit have grown as vigorously in percentage terms. At the end of April, 1965, total noninstalment credit was about $1 billion or 8 per cent higher than in 1964 and about $4 billion or 35 per cent above what it had been 4 years earlier.

The impact of noninstalment credit on changes in total consumer credit outstanding is most noticeable in recessions, when such credit continues to increase while instalment credit tends to decline. Thus, during the first quarter of 1961 when instalment credit was declining at a seasonally adjusted annual rate of close to $400 million, noninstalment credit was rising at a rate of more than $750 million. Because noninstalment credit is often used for small and routine purchases, it is much less responsive to cyclical forces than instalment credit, which finances the larger, more cyclically variable expenditures....

Georgia. The association has on file over 50 million credit reports, representing more than 25 million individuals.

The most general source of credit information is references from other stores that have extended credit to the consumer in the past. Banks are another source of credit information, as is Dun & Bradstreet Co., Inc. Dun & Bradstreet is probably the best-known and largest credit reporting agency in the world. These sources are known mostly however, for their work at the wholesale and manufacturer level.

Usually the most important sources of credit information are the retail credit bureaus, who are primarily concerned with the exchange of ledger information among their customers. The more important service rendered by the credit bureau, apart from credit checking, is the publication of reports, bulletins, and ratings. When a credit report on a potential account is requested from the credit bureau, its costs should not exceed the amount that can be earned from the account being checked. To this extent the National Retail Credit Association has sponsored a goal of consistent uniformity in credit extension.

CREDIT PLAN TRENDS

The fastest growing type of credit plan is the revolving, flexible charge-account plan. These plans are adaptations and extensions of installment credit plans; the interest or service charge is generally 1½ per cent per month on the unpaid balance, or an 18 per cent effective rate per year. Many firms encourage such optional plans in place of 30-day charge accounts, which bear no interest on service charges. Nevertheless, under many revolving plans, consumers can clear a budget account every 30 days without interest or special assessments. Also, in many such plans, the consumer may elect to repay the account in as many months as he wishes, simply by paying a service charge on any remaining balance.

Sears, Roebuck and Company, Montgomery Ward, and the J. C. Penney Company offer variations of this plan with a 1½ per cent per month service charge on outstanding debit balances. Many of these plans have certain refund options for major purchases when accounts are repaid within a period of 90 days. In a similar manner, no interest is charged on 30-day charge accounts for "major" hard-line purchases repaid within 90 days.

In Figure XXXVI is shown a typical promotional "self-mailer" credit plan offered by the Woolco Department Stores, a division of the F. W. Woolworth Company. The reverse side has been designed for easy folding and sealing, is addressed, and has postage affixed. Most prefer to use the time payment or revolving type of charge account with a 1½ per-cent interest payment per month on any unpaid balances.

In effect, customers are given the choice of paying a minimum, a portion, or the full amount owing with the opportunity to vary payments each month. In this manner, the customer is not committed to a pre-set payment of an account. The correctness of this approach is borne out by many credit studies in which it was found that interest rates, downpayments, and durations of loans are more

FIGURE XXXVI

"SELF-MAILER" CREDIT-PLAN PROMOTION OF WOOLCO DEPARTMENT STORES

There's a Credit Plan for you at WOOLCO . . .

Complete Signature Card and Charge Agreement NOW. Your Account will then be ready for your use when you want or need it.

1. WOOLCO CREDIT PLAN—A 30 DAY CHARGE ACCOUNT with option terms. You decide after you receive your monthly statement how you wish to pay. No service charge if paid in 30 Days or, if you prefer, pay the small minimum payments for just a small monthly service charge of 1½%. (See Payment Chart below)

2. WOOLCO TIME PAYMENT ACCOUNT. Charge your major purchases such as Furniture, Home Furnishings, Appliances, T.V., Mowers, Sporting Goods, Camera Equipment and take up to 24 months to pay. NO DOWN PAYMENT . . . just sign for it and take it home.

3. Hold it on LAY-A-WAY with a small deposit and small regular payments. Take your LAY-A-WAY purchases home at any time by simply transferring your unpaid balance to your WOOLCO CREDIT PLAN ACCOUNT.

FOR STORE USE ONLY

TRADE LINE	A/C OPENED	HIGH CREDIT	DATE OF LAST SALE	AMOUNT OWING	MANNER OF PAYMENTS	TRADE LINE	A/C OPENED	HIGH CREDIT	DATE OF LAST SALE	AMOUNT OWING	MANNER OF PAYMENTS

STORE NUMBER	FIRST NAME	INITIAL	LAST NAME	ACCOUNT NUMBER

WIFE	STREET ADDRESS	CITY	ZONE	STATE	LIMIT	DATE OPENED

HUSBAND'S EMPLOYMENT	NAME OF COMPANY	ADDRESS	POSITION	HOW LONG

WIFE'S EMPLOYMENT	NAME OF COMPANY	ADDRESS	POSITION	HOW LONG

CREDIT REFERENCE   1.   2.   3.

WOOLCO DEPT. STORES   (A Division of F. W. Woolworth Co.)

In consideration of your selling merchandise to me on Woolco's Revolving Charge Plan, I agree to the following regarding all purchases made by me or on my identification plate:

1. You are to send me a statement each month which will show the unpaid balance on my account, your regular credit service charge thereon, and the amount of the monthly installment then coming due. The amount of such monthly payment shall be computed according to the following schedule:

2. I will make the monthly payment as computed above within 15 days after the receipt of your statement. If I fail to make any payment in full when due, you may declare the full remaining unpaid balance immediately due and payable.

3. I will pay the time sale price for each item purchased consisting of . . .
   (a) the cash sale price, and
   (b) an amount of credit service charge computed by applying the rate of 1½% of the previous month's ending balance (such charge not to exceed the lawful maximum) per payment schedule shown, until all purchases are paid in full.

4. It is agreed that the Credit Identification Plate issued to me remains the property of the Woolco Dept. Stores and may be reclaimed at any time.
5. I have the right to pay in advance.

WOOLCO CREDIT PLAN ACCOUNT PAYMENT SCHEDULE

If Your Balance Is	$5 - 70	$71 - 120	$121 - 180	$181 - 240	$241 - 300
Your Payment Is Check (✓) Amount Desired	$5	$10	$15	$20	$25

SIGNATURE   DATE

the result of individual negotiations than any standard policies.[13] Thus, when a customer feels that he wants to settle his account and save interest charges, he can do so without penalty.

Another type of "revolving" account permits the customer, within predetermined limits and without any increase in monthly payments, to continue to purchase as he wishes. This kind of revolving account satisfies the needs of customers, keeps the account on an "acceptable" credit basis, and enables a customer to concentrate his purchase with a single organization.

Other Types of Changes

In the past, credit planning in most retail organizations was concentrated primarily with the 30-day, (noninterest cost) charge accounts. Today, most retail firms attempt "to sell" the all-inclusive interest-bearing type of deferred credit plans: the installment plan, the revolving account with a "perpetual floating" bal-

---

[13] See also Norman Nybroten, et al., "Credit Practices in Furniture and Home Appliances Retailing," *Management Research Summary*, SBA, Washington, D.C., June 1963.

ance, and the "budget account." These are all variations of installment selling, and are used by the customers to increase their standard of living through "forced savings."

Among the initiators of the budget type of retail credit plans were the Chase Manhattan Bank of New York City and the Bank of America of California, the largest commercial bank in the country.

The Chase Manhattan Bank, which has since disposed of this phase of their operation, had in 1962 some 300,000 card holders, with 5,300 participating retail firms having some 6,700 stores in the city. Their administrative and operating costs were uneconomic because of insufficient volume.

The Bank of America, which initiated its plan in 1959, was more successful. By 1962 their plan included some 30,000 stores and had more than one million active card holders. It was not until 1961 that the Bank's credit-card system finally got out of the red and began "contributing to earnings." [14]

> In 1965 nearly 1.3 million individuals now carry Bank Americards, and in 1964 they drew cash and charged goods and services totaling $144 million—up 30% from 1963. Bank of America won't say how much it made on Bank Americards last year, but one finance industry man estimates the sum "very conservatively" at $4½ million before taxes. B of A does concede that operating profits on the card hit a record in 1964.
> In 1964, besides the 30% gain in volume, the number of active cardholders—those using their cards at least once during the year—rose by 20%, and another 2,500 stores, motels, and the like came into the fold. [15]

Consumer credit plans of various kinds had to be adopted by discount houses in order to stay competitive, especially on big ticket items. After the "first flush" of having effectively absorbed much of the "hard-line" business from department stores and small appliance dealers, the neccessity of credit services for adequate promotion became apparent. Many attempted to carry their own paper. Those that were inadequately financed soon failed to take advantage of cash discounts from vendors as their paper piled up. Those that factor their accounts receivables lost their merchandising profits through increasing costs and loss of supplier good will and cooperation. Today, most discount houses have working agreements with sales finance companies to finance their "big ticket" credit sales, in the hope that they can remain low-cost competitors. Thus, on one hand they attempt to sell at the lowest possible cost; on the other hand, they cannot avoid the somewhat costlier credit selling without raising prices and losing significant measures of competitive effectiveness.

Today, approximately one-third of all retail establishments and almost all wholesale firms sell on credit. In Figure XXXVII, the growth of installment credit

---

[14] "Chase Bank Mulls Sales of Its Credit-Card Operations," *The Wall Street Journal*, January 22, 1962, p. 24; see also *Business Week*, "The Charge Plan that Really Took Off" (February 27, 1965), p. 58 (quote as shown).
[15] *Op. cit.*, February 27, 1965.

FIGURE XXXVII
Changes in Consumer Credit by Shares Among Lenders
and by Volume Composition

(1960–1965)

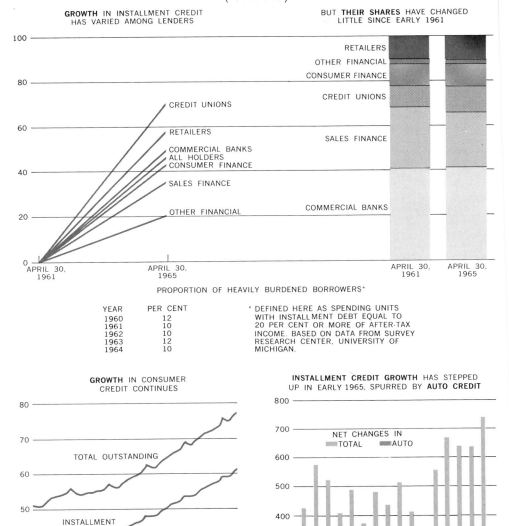

GROWTH IN INSTALLMENT CREDIT
HAS VARIED AMONG LENDERS

BUT **THEIR SHARES** HAVE CHANGED
LITTLE SINCE EARLY 1961

CREDIT UNIONS

RETAILERS

COMMERCIAL BANKS
ALL HOLDERS
CONSUMER FINANCE

SALES FINANCE

OTHER FINANCIAL

RETAILERS
OTHER FINANCIAL
CONSUMER FINANCE

CREDIT UNIONS

SALES FINANCE

COMMERCIAL BANKS

APRIL 30,
1961

APRIL 30,
1965

APRIL 30,
1961

APRIL 30,
1965

PROPORTION OF HEAVILY BURDENED BORROWERS*

YEAR	PER CENT
1960	12
1961	10
1962	10
1963	12
1964	10

* DEFINED HERE AS SPENDING UNITS
WITH INSTALLMENT DEBT EQUAL TO
20 PER CENT OR MORE OF AFTER-TAX
INCOME. BASED ON DATA FROM SURVEY
RESEARCH CENTER, UNIVERSITY OF
MICHIGAN.

GROWTH IN CONSUMER
CREDIT CONTINUES

TOTAL OUTSTANDING

INSTALLMENT

NONINSTALLMENT

1960   '61   '62   '63   '64   '65

NOTE.—END-OF-MONTH FIGURES, NOT SEASONALLY
ADJUSTED. LATEST FIGURES SHOWN, APRIL.

INSTALLMENT CREDIT GROWTH HAS STEPPED
UP IN EARLY 1965, SPURRED BY **AUTO CREDIT**

NET CHANGES IN
TOTAL   AUTO

1964   1965

NOTE.—SEASONALLY ADJUSTED DATA, LATEST
FIGURES SHOWN, APRIL.

Source: "Developments in Consumer Credit." *Federal Reserve Bulletin*, Washington, D.C., June 1965, Vol. 51, No. 6, pp. 787–98.

429

is shown along with the various changing shares among lenders by volume composition. The growth in installment credit since 1962 has been spurred largely by automobile debt.

As pointed out previously, the J. C. Penney Company, which has always had as its slogan and its image emphasis "cash sales," shifted to a credit as well as a cash policy when it entered into the hard-lines field. As a result, its competitive position in the industry advanced markedly.[16] Here is an excellent example of how credit availability increases sales, attracts a better class of trade, develops greater patronage motives, and helps level off sales during slack periods. A credit policy aggressively pursued can reduce many other operating costs—more than offsetting the credit costs of 2½ to 3 per cent of total sales.[17]

While credit sales do increase, the cost of generating sales invites complaints and ties up working capital. Good credit management, nevertheless, more than pays for itself. Furthermore, irrespective of attendant costs, charge-account availability for customers is not a privilege but a competitive necessity.

QUALITATIVE AND QUANTITATIVE FACTORS IN CREDIT EXTENSION

The extension of credit is based on the Four C's: Character, Capacity, Capital, and Condition. The "condition" evaluation, which is based on local economic factors, serves either as a limiting or as an expansive factor in helping to determine credit limits. In consumer credit, "character"—what a person is or his willingness to repay—generally rates as the most important single determinant of the credit evaluation of the individual; the ability to pay ranks second; "capital," the funds with which to repay, is third in importance, followed by "condition" as fourth.[18]

1) A person's *character* is said to be of a high level when the individual is governed by integrity, fairness, responsibility, and willingness to repay his debts as they become due.

2) *Capacity* is primarily a question of earning power or ability to repay. An individual has "capacity" when he is capable of fulfilling a contract; therefore, capacity may also be judged in the line of ability within existing circumstances.

3) *Capital*, on the other hand, is a measure of a person's equity or net worth. It represents the measure of tangible assets which an individual has, and in the case of extreme necessity, can be seized.

4) On the assumption that the first three C's are satisfactory for the purposes of granting credit, the fourth, that of *condition*, becomes the final measure of decision. It helps determine in a final analysis the true credit-worthiness of the individual. Condition, in effect, is dependent upon the economic setting in which

---

[16] See "Cost of Operating Department Store Credit Departments as a Percentage of Credit Net Sales," *Credit Management Year Book* (New York: NRMA) 1953–1954.

[17] In the most recent NRMA Survey, even with "overstatement" of expenses as discussed in Footnote 8 of this chapter, it was stated that it costs department stores an average of 2.55 per cent of credit sales to operate a credit department.

[18] In commercial credit extensions, "capital" ranks first in importance.

both the credit grantor and the individual credit receiver interact to form a final basis for judgment.

The Credit Equation

Thus the store's merchandising and operating policies determine the basis for the extension of credit. In turn, credit management determines which of the Four C's of credit should receive the greatest relative weight. The extension of credit and its attendant risk are not vague intangibles but definite, measurable amounts revolving around definite sets of circumstances.

As long as the risk can be measured, the extension of credit can be carried out on a sound statistical basis. But the credit grantor must be capable of assessing the calculated risk in terms of willingness to pay and ability to pay within the time limit set by the debtor.

The Final Evaluation

Once the credit attributes have been "scaled," the credit-worthiness of the individual can be measured quantitatively. For example, the Federal Housing Administration some years ago developed the following rating chart, which still has much to commend it.[19]

	Rating
Character	30%
Attitude Toward Obligations (character)	15
Associates (character)	5
Ability to Pay (capacity)	15
Prospects for Future (capacity)	12
Business History (capacity)	10
Ratio Value of Property to Annual Income (capital)	7
Ratio Monthly Mortgage Obligations to Income (capital)	6
TOTAL	100%

In the above equation, character is rated at 50, capacity at 37, capital at 13; although condition is not rated, per se, it would be deterministic in the total values assigned to capacity and capital. In the above also, when the individual's rating totals a minimum of 70, credit is usually granted. However, the type of risk involved as well as the policy of the house would have a bearing on the credit decisions. In the extension of consumer credit, character is the prime determinant for consideration; thus, all credit risks differ in terms of quality.

In retail firms, the proper evaluation of credit must result in decreasing costs. Otherwise, credit extension and the effectiveness with which it is managed assist only marginally toward the total success of the enterprise.

---

[19] See G. J. Martin, "Evaluating the Credit Risk," *The Credit World*, December 1940, p. 21.

PRODUCTIVITY AND COST OF NEW ACCOUNT DEVELOPMENT

The credit totality of a community or a nation is no better quantitatively than the soundness of the individual transactions making up the whole. Credit investigations should be impersonal. The majority of credit customers are generally acceptable risks. Furthermore, it is not good credit management to have prolonged investigations, which would negate the possible earnings involved in opening the account.

On the whole, when the trading area pattern is composed of high-income households, the manner in which charge account credit is promoted and available becomes a highly competitive process, especially for stores handling shopping and specialty goods.

This brings up the question of costs in the promotion of new accounts. In a four-year study conducted by the A. J. Wood Research Corporation of Philadelphia, the high-low estimated cost-range of acquiring a new credit customer was $5.35 to 0.39 cents with a $2.61 over-all average cost. Of the accounts opened, 76.5 per cent were used continually and productively. Thus, the total acquisition cost of $2.61 per new account resulted in the generation of $128.24 over the 4-year period. More importantly, the study showed an average net income ratio of cost to acquisition of approximately 7 to 1.

The conclusions of the A. J. Wood study were: 1) that new credit accounts should not be sought if the account saturation was at a maximum, as acquisition costs would then be too costly; 2) because of greater store loyalty, charge customers prefer to shop for specific merchandise and services in a single store in a ratio of 5 to 1 as compared to cash customers of the same store. This is especially true in stores carrying medium- to high-priced women's ready-to-wear fashions and men's clothing.

In other studies it was found that the availability of a charge account increases a customer's buying ratio in a particular store from 1 to 1 to 3.8 to 1; the assumption on which this ratio is based is that approximately 40 per cent of the average shopping and specialty-goods store's business is on a cash basis from charge-account customers.[20]

Figures of these kinds are indicative of most trading-area patterns. Saturation ratios of credit accounts and competition for existing business by all other sellers must be taken into consideration. With these factors being evaluated, the cost of new account development "lines up" with the U-shaped cost curve: namely, the higher the saturation of accounts the less likely it is that a 7-to-1 income ratio potential is likely to occur, as cost ratios would increase faster than volume and income. In other words, the law of diminishing potential is a consideration when high acquisition costs are likely. Nevertheless, with proper merchandise offerings at competitive prices, a high credit elasticity of demand can be generated.

In developing studies of the buying habits of customers with charge accounts, Mr. Robert D. Breth, Senior Vice President of the A. J. Wood Research Corpora-

---

[20] From A. J. Wood Corporation Research as reported in the *Women's Wear Daily*, May 10, 1960, p. 1ff.

tion, bears out the real value of charge-account customers. He also concludes that 60 per cent of the customers on a store's inactive account list still buy in the store for cash.[21]

This meets the cost criteria developed in the study "On the Idea of a Market" by the author and Professor A. James Boness. The long-run relation of development costs of new credit-account procurement in relation to resulting sales volume resembles that of a new firm moving from an initial pioneering stage into a highly competitive survival stage.[22] In Figure XXXVIII, the resulting long-run cost-time-volume relationships are shown.

FIGURE XXXVIII
LONG-RUN RELATION OF COSTS TO SALES VOLUME *

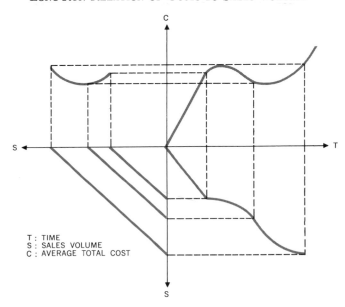

T : TIME
S : SALES VOLUME
C : AVERAGE TOTAL COST

* Robert D. Entenberg and A. James Boness, "On the Idea of a Market," *Journal of Industrial Economics* (Oxford, England), November 1964, Vol. 13, No. 1, p. 48.

This curve results when firms successfully meet and overcome the initial pioneering stage and move into a highly competitive survival stage. Then, as volume increases, higher than proportionate expense increases occur with the extreme portions of the resulting curve rising rapidly. This is the same type of cost variable encountered when approaching 100% area saturation in the development of new accounts.

For example, when a new store is opened, the firm's fixed cost structure generally inches upward on a continuum as the "competitive" stage is reached

21 Robert D. Breth, *op. cit.*, pp. 41–43.
22 Robert D. Entenberg and A. James Boness, "On the Idea of a Market," *Journal of Industrial Economics* (Oxford: November 1964), Vol. 13, No. 1, pp. 43–52.

—succeeding short-run equilibriums show costs "creeping in" thus decreasing competitive effectiveness. Factors such as uneconomic wage rates due to seniority factors, etc., excessive management salaries, under-utilization of space allocations, the furnishing of unwanted services or poor merchandising management increase total expense and reduce management's ability to compete.

As pressure builds up to reduce expenses, aggregates of static equilibrium result in "normal" operating volume ranges at less than maximum attainable volume levels—unfortunately, a triumph of mediocrity over efficiency.

Even when demand in certain markets is relatively elastic, expense to sales ratios tend to increase as competitive vulnerability grows and additional firms are "encouraged" to enter the market. With this type of volume-expense pattern, the advantages of scale of firm and size of plant in retail markets become more illusory than real as profits and market position are often "competed away." [23]

THE ECONOMICS OF INSTALLMENT SELLING

The demand for credit correlates directly with market demand—that is, expands and contracts to product demand. As purchasing power increases, greater volumes of durable and so-called luxury goods are purchased. Installment credit permits medium- and low-income families to acquire automobiles, high-priced musical instruments, household appliances, and new homes without long waiting periods. The use of installment credit unquestionably encourages a fuller life by channeling small units of spendable income into forced payments on costlier articles. Approximately 50 per cent of all spending units in the United States have some form of installment debt.[24]

The normal credit charge for deferred accounts ranges from 1 to 1.5 per cent per month on the unpaid balance, totaling an effective interest rate per annum. On straight installment contracts for items such as home remodeling the effective interest rate per annum might run as low as 7 per cent; in such cases credit increases the elasticity of demand.

The Basic Principles

One of the basic principles of installment credit is that the goods or services bought should not fall into the category of "immediate consumption" or "temporary use." The complementary principles of installment credit extension are: a

---

[23] Ibid., pp. 43–52. The appearance of great numbers of "off-price" and discount houses handling almost all product categories is an excellent example of such market realities. See R. D. Entenberg, "The Discount House—Panic or Panacea," Georgia Business, University of Georgia, Athens, Ga., October 1961. In this case it would be the almost limitless availability of retail credit from competitive firms.

[24] George Katona (Survey Research Center, University of Michigan), "Attitudes Towards Installment Credit," Credit Currents (July 1962), p. 6. In Table 1, the number of spending units with installment debt averaged from 43 per cent to 46 per cent between 1954 and 1961. In 1960, the number ranged as high as 49 per cent.

reasonable down payment, a minimum sale, and scheduling the frequency and amounts of repayments with customer income receipts; an adequate service charge should also be part of the total sale. Because of the rapid upward strides in the economy, these principles are being violated, apparently with no greater losses than normal. For example: pre-charged vacations and a three-year repayment period on new cars are being offered with practically no downpayments.

Most manufacturing operations are of a decreasing cost nature when operating toward capacity or higher levels. As volume increases, their total average costs decrease, and the cost of producing commodities also decreases. Thus, the availability of installment credit enables manufacturers to plan more continuous production, eliminate peaks and valleys in production runs, and in the long run, decrease the total cost of the consumer durables and nondurables that they make. The decrease in the cost of goods far outweighs the installment credit costs to the consumer. And the increasing standard of living is proof that the advantages of installment buying far outweigh its costs.

Cost Determination

Unquestionably, cases of misrepresentation and illegal use do occur. For example, additional charges are often made which raise the interest costs above legal limits. Also, many fly-by-night firms are diligent in hasty repossession. Charging for "unwanted" credit insurance protection, having inadequate methods for refunds, and failing to give credit for payments before due date are other examples of excessive charges.

For example, should the cash price of a used car be $300 and the installment price $350, $50 would be the cost of the credit. Under no circumstances should the cost of the credit be included in determining the total effective interest rate, as the $50 additional (for the cost of the credit) would not be needed if the cash were available.

In the assessment of credit charges, the first step should be the determination of the nominal rate of the credit charge. This is carried out by dividing the cost of the credit by the amount of credit used. In the example above, the nominal rate of the credit charge would be $50 ÷ $300, or 16.7 per cent.

Assuming an 18-month period for repayment, the normal rate per annum of 16.7 per cent would be prorated onto an interest rate per annum basis; the following formula would be used: [25]

$$\frac{16.7}{18} = \frac{r}{12}$$
$$18\ r = 200.4$$
$$r = 11.33 \text{ nominal interest rate per annum}$$

A relatively simple formula for estimating credit costs was developed by Dr.

[25] Beckman and Bartels, op. cit.

Theodore N. Beckman in 1924. It appeared in the second edition of his book on credits and collections in 1930:

Where:

R = annual rate of actual or effective interest per annum

r = nominal rate of simple interest per annum

n = the number of payments required to pay the principal (not the interest charges).

$$R = \frac{r(2n)}{(n+1)}$$

Rephrasing the above in terms of dollars and cents, the total costs involved in the use of the credit are as follows:

$$R = \frac{r(2n)}{(n+1)}$$

$$= \frac{16.7 \times (2 \times 16.7)}{(16.7 + 1)}$$

This 16.7 is the actual time needed to repay the credit used; and under no circumstances should any other figure apply for this computation.

$$= \frac{16.7 \times 35.4}{17.7}$$

$350 \div 18 = 19.44$ (payment per month)

$300 \div 19.44 = 16.7$ (months to repay actual amount of credit needed).

$$= \frac{601.18}{17.7} = 33.9\%$$

33.9% is the effective annual interest rate per annum —quite a high interest cost for this contract.

A contract to pay 1/12 of a given sum at the end of each month in 12 months is equivalent to a contract to pay the entire amount at the expiration of 6½ months; this represents one-half of installments of one-half the total amount of the loan. Thus, 6½ would be equivalent to $(n+1)$.[26]

Installment credit charges should be expressed in many ways: as a percentage carrying charge, as a dollar-and-cents carrying charge, or a "difference" between the credit and cash prices. Unfortunately, too many sales-promotion and selling firms are quoted in terms of a stipulated amount per week or per month. The ensuing confusions and misrepresentations have been instrumental in motivating congressional action to make it mandatory to have all charges for credit extensions listed in terms of simple interest per annum, although most customers prefer charges stated in terms of dollars and cents.

MANAGEMENT OF INSTALLMENT AND DEFERRED CREDIT

Mass production is not economic without mass distribution. Mass distribution has succeeded because of the general availability of commercial and consumers credit

---

[26] Beckman and Bartels, *op. cit.*, pp. 94–98.

over short and extended periods of time. Installment selling is still increasing in importance. Also, it is self-liquidating from a cost standpoint, because a service interest is generally part of the contract. In addition many firms offer the consumer a no-cost credit option if the contract is paid within 90 days.

There are generally three bases on which installment sales are made: firstly, on a signature "unsecured" basis; secondly, by means of a conditional sales contract (where title to the merchandise does not pass to the buyer until the final payment is made); and thirdly, by means of a chattel mortgage (whereby title passes immediately to the purchaser, but the merchandise purchased is not cleared of the mortgage encumbrance until final payment has been made). In the case of a revolving account, a "line of credit" is established, based on the signed application contract in which the customer stipulates the amount per month that he wishes to pay.

This amount is then multiplied by either six, nine, or twelve, depending on "conditions." The resulting total then becomes the credit limit or line of credit. Once the credit limit has been used and the customer begins his monthly payments he has a line of credit "open" to the extent of the balance between the amount owing and the total amount permitted to be charged.[27]

Management of installment and deferred credit is more than a mechanical process. Installment credit is the largest and most sensitive component of total consumer credit and economic activity. As pointed out, the rise in installment credit during the first half of 1965 was the most rapid experienced since mid-1961, several months after the rise in other major measures of economic activity.

> The pace of consumer borrowing usually corresponds to consumer purchases of an assortment of durable goods, particularly autos. Such large expenditures tend to increase strongly in periods of recovery when personal income is increasing; and conversely, they tend to be postponed during recessionary periods when income ceases to expand or decline.[28]

Policies and procedures in the management of installment credit should be flexibly set so as to conform to increases and decreases in income in the retail firm's trading area. The levels of repayment-income ratios depend directly on earnings which furnish the increase to repay debts. Income levels in a trading area thus, determine the evaluation of "conditions" as a precursor of consumer demand and credit evaluation and extensions.

FINANCING CONSUMER CREDIT

In the first part of the century, commercial banks were the only institutions to finance the movement of goods from producers to consumers. Because these

---

[27] To illustrate: Assume that the amount that the customer wants to pay is $30 and his credit limit is 6 months, $6 \times 30 = \$180 =$ line of credit. Once the $180 limit is reached, his credit limit again opens to the extent of repayments. Thus, credit payments for 2 months of $30 each or $60 would open up an additional $60 credit.

[28] "Recent Trends in Installment Credit," *Business Trends*, Federal Reserve Bank of Cleveland, June 5, 1965.

loans were made on too modest and too conservative a basis, sales finance companies came into being, gaining their real impetus as consumer durables became mass produced.

Sales finance companies have enabled the average consumer to own automobiles and durables and have enabled retail firms to grow and prosper.[29]

Thus, in any discussion of credit extensions and accounts-receivable financing, the role of sales finance companies is an important one. These agencies serve retailers, wholesalers, and manufacturers. They should not be confused with finance offices, which engage primarily in lending money to consumers under State Small Loan Laws, which permit rates of interest in excess of that charged by commercial banks. In Table 36, the source of funds for installment credit outstanding is shown.

TABLE 36

INSTALLMENT CREDIT OUTSTANDING BY SOURCE OF FUNDS*

(in billions of dollars)

	END OF PERIOD					
	1958		1960		1964	
TOTAL	100%–$33.6		100%–$42.8		100%–$59.4	
Total Financial Institutions	85.4%–28.7	100%	86.9%–37.2	100%	87.5%–52.0	100%
Commercial Banks	12.8	44.6	16.7	44.9	23.9	46.0
Sales Finance Companies	8.8	30.7	11.5	31.0	14.8	28.5
Credit Unions	2.7	9.4	3.9	10.5	6.5	12.5
Consumer Finance[1]	3.1	10.8	3.7	9.9	5.1	9.8
Other[1]	1.3	4.5	1.5	4.0	1.7	3.3
Total Retail Outlets	14.7%– 5.0	100%	13.0%– 5.6	100%	12.4%– 7.4	100%
Department Stores[2]	1.9	38.0	2.4	42.9	3.9	52.7
Furniture Stores	1.1	22.0	1.1	19.6	1.2	16.2
Appliance Stores	.3	6.0	.3	5.4	.3	4.1
Automobile Dealers[3]	.5	10.0	.4	7.1	.4	5.4
Other	1.2	24.0	1.4	25.0	1.7	23.0

*Figures will not total 100.0% because of rounding.
[1] Consumer finance companies included with "other" financial institutions until Sept. 1950.
[2] Includes mail-order houses.
[3] Automobile paper only; other installment credit held by automobile dealers is included with "other" retail outlets.
Data: Board of the Governors of the Federal Reserve System, Washington, D.C., Federal Reserve Bulletin, Consumer Credit, June 1965, p. 870.

As pointed out in Figure XXXVII (page 429) and in Table 36, the sources of consumer credit have not changed significantly. While lenders have changed their sources, their shares have not changed significantly since 1961.

Like all social institutions, those handling the financing and extensions of

[29] Clyde William Phelps, The Role of Sales Finance Companies in the American Economy, Commercial Credit Company, Baltimore, 1958, p. 9. See Appendix K for detailed functions of diversified sales finance companies.

credit contribute to the economic structure. In a free, democratic society, individual consumers also have certain choices in the allocation of their income; these allocations in turn determine the type of social and economic institutions that exist. More specifically, the sales finance company puts the distributors, wholesalers, and retailers in a position to settle their accounts payable quickly. In turn, market functionaries can offer their publics wider and more diversified purchase choices and plans on which to buy them.[30]

THE COLLECTION PROCESSES

When a new account is opened, the customer is classified as a good, fair, or marginal risk with appropriate credit limits. The good risk is one who has a previous record of a high credit limit and is reliable in paying promptly. (Such customers are highly sensitive and must be treated tactfully in any questions of repayment of a lagging account.) A fair risk is one who is classified as being "good but slow." The fair risk may postpone his obligations when he undertakes financial commitments that involve him in regular payments over a long period of time (for instance, when he buys large ticket items on impulse without planning).

The poor or marginal risk, on the other hand, is one who has just enough ability to pay and enough character to want to pay but not enough capital to pay rapidly. Such customers must be given smaller credit limits. It is evident that not every overdue account represents a collection problem.

Credit and collection policies are determined by the classification of debtor and the nature of the business. When the term *collection* is used, it refers basically to efforts used to gain payment *after* a debt has become past due. The signed application for the charge account is the basis for the institution of any collection procedures. The credit manager sets policy on collection procedures. Persistence and promptness are the two chief attributes of any collection system.

It is indispensable to good credit management and collection to keep up to date on new laws and on amendments to statutes. These are found in the annual editions of the *Credit Manual of Commercial Laws*, published by the National Association of Credit Management.[31]

Generally, there are four stages in any series of collection efforts: firstly, formal notification; next, a reminder, still gentle and persuasive; thirdly, discussion, where the tone of the collection effort becomes firmer; and finally—the last stage—

---

[30] See also J. M. Baskin, "Spiegel's Handles Own Receivables," *Women's Wear Daily*, and D. C. Luckett *et al.*, "The Factor Markets for Small Firms," *Management Research Summary*, SBA, Washington, D.C., 1963.

[31] The *Manual* digests, analyzes, and interprets state and federal laws of particular concern to the management of business credit. In addition, it includes a section on federal liens and creditors' rights, including analyses of recent cases, decisions, and rulings by the general council of the National Association of Credit Management.

compulsion, when the debtor is written off as a potential customer of the firm if the situation becomes unpleasant.

STANDARDS IN EVALUATING CREDIT MANAGEMENT

Any credit plan must be geared to the store image and the attendant conceptual goals of the selling organization. Methods for the proper employment of funds must also be developed. For example, a high credit-sales index results when the credit-management division is effective in maximizing sales.

The credit-sales index expresses the relationship of net credit sales to total net sales. By comparing this credit-sales index from month to month or from year to year by type of credit extended (installment, charge-account, deferred, and so on), an excellent evaluative measure can be developed.

For instance, in 1960 53.4 per cent of all Sears' sales were generated on credit. In 1963, Sears' credit sales accounted for 55.5 per cent of total sales. Again, shortly after the J. C. Penney Company went into credit selling, in March of 1961, 17.12 per cent of their total sales volume was on a credit basis. By the end of 1963, their credit sales approximated 28 per cent of all sales. Such indices can represent effective employment of funds.

The only known, identifiable and "reachable" customers of a store are the "charge" customers. Any other person is only a "cash shopper," whose loyalty is based primarily on price. Charge customers buy anywhere from two to four times as much in goods and services as do cash shoppers, and react to store advertising and promotion efforts more quickly and in greater numbers than do cash shoppers. Charge accounts among career girls become most valuable as they marry and rear families.

Charge customers also contribute substantially to the cash sales volume of any credit-granting store. Even inactive or charge customers who are presumably lost make substantial contributions to cash sales volume and have a more favorable image of "their" stores than they do of cash-only operations. This is one of the main reasons why they buy more. Thus, when any decision is made to open more new accounts, attempts to revitalize inactive accounts should also be made.

Other evaluative criteria for credit management are a "net profitability" income figure of the monthly service and interest charges on budget, revolving, and installment credit and on "lay-away" plans. These profits are not generally exactly identified but should be included with "other income from operations." This "nonoperating" income is estimated at 1.25 per cent of credit sales.[32] Other criteria are: new accounts opened, a fund reinvestment index, and a credit transaction index.

The other broad function of the credit division is that of minimizing losses. Here a bad debt loss index, a delinquency index, a collection percentage index,

---

[32] Fred Eichelbauin, in the "Focus" section of *Women's Wear Daily*, September 17, 1964, pp. 1, 10.

and a carrying cost index of accounts receivable are useful for measuring the performance of the department.

LEGISLATIVE CRITERIA—INDIVIDUAL BANKRUPTCIES

One of the more important problems in the granting of credit has been that of the increasing number of consumer bankruptcies. While most bankruptcies are valid, many may have been initiated unnecessarily.[33]

The problem of consumer bankruptcies arises from the fact that the bankrupt individual immediately becomes an acceptable credit risk again for many retail firms, as they cannot again go into bankruptcy within the succeeding seven-year period. On this basis, individuals might be tempted to undergo such proceedings when severe economic pressures are encountered.

"Truth in Lending" Legislation

In process at the present time are many so-called "truth-in-lending" bills introduced as part of the Administration's policy of protecting the consumer. The most publicized bill at present is labeled as the Douglas Credit Disclosure Bill, or S 1740. The bill would require a stated "full disclosure attachment" to all merchandise purchased. The disclosure would state, on a simple interest per annum basis, any interest or service charges. Opponents of the bill state that such statements would only confuse the consumer, not help him. This is borne out by research studies conducted under the direction of the writer, at the Retail Research Center, Graduate School of Business, University of Pittsburgh between 1962 and 1965.[34]

---

[33] See also: Charles J. Kushell, Jr., "Consumer Bankruptcy Question." Mr. Kushell, Vice President-Credit, Montgomery Ward, Chicago, Illinois, presented this paper at the Credit Management Division Session, NRMA convention, January 9, 1963. It was reprinted in *Credit Currents*, February 1963, pp. 1–7:

> The two basic functions of personal bankruptcy proceedings, simply stated are: The collection, liquidation, and equitable distribution of assets among all of the creditors of the debtor bankrupt.... The granting of a discharge to a debtor who has qualified under the Act in order to give the debtor a new financial start in life.... There are two ways to initiate bankruptcy proceedings: Involuntary proceedings—bankruptcy is initiated by the creditors to protect themselves against preferential treatment of selected creditors, or to prevent waste of assets that should be promptly distributed to the creditors.

[34] See, for example, Raymond P. Loftus' study of consumer "Awareness of Credit Costs," which answers the question, "If you made a large purchase, would it mean more to you if the service charge were stated in terms of actual dollars and cents, or in terms of simple interest per year, or both?" The stratified quota sample of respondents answered as follows:

Dollars and cents	77%
Both	1%
Simple interest per year	17%
Other	3%

By far the overwhelming majority—77 per cent—preferred to have the service charge expressed in terms of dollars and cents. "Many of the respondents felt that service charges in terms of interest were meaningless to them." Further conclusions of the study were as follows: "credit users" in general were satisfied with charge-account facilities and looked upon

Tax Criteria

Credit management also involves familiarity with tax implications. These revolve primarily around which kind of installment sales income is eligible for deferred tax treatment and which charges are not regarded as part of the sale. Generally, the two types of revolving or installment sales eligible for deferred tax treatment are: 1) Sales in which terms and conditions contemplate payment in two or more installments; and 2) a sale charged to an account on which the filed payments are made after being recorded, indicating that the sale is being paid in installments.

SUMMARY AND CONCLUSIONS

Credit is probably the most important single service which can be furnished by a store. This is no longer just a customer privilege, but a competitive necessity for most market segments. Credit extension requires an increase in the permanent working capital needed by a firm. However, many sales-finance companies and other lending agencies are ready to absorb the store's credit extensions.

Effective credit management results from good coordination with the merchandising and publicity divisions in maximizing sales—and with credit reporting agencies in evaluating credit risks. This function is consistent with minimization of losses.

While it is very difficult, if not impossible, to measure the actual "income value" of a single charge-account customer, the availability of credit generally more than pays for its cost because of the additional sales generated.

---

them as a beneficial service provided by the retail store; most consumers stated that they did not know exactly what their installment purchases were costing, despite the fact that the service charge was stated on the monthly statement or account book; two out of three respondents believed that the credit charges were fair; and finally, as stated above, most respondents felt that "a service charge in dollars and cents would be preferable since it is something they could think of in familiar terms and use as a basis of comparison."

Chapter 27: *Budgetary and Work-Center Accounting—Techniques for Managerial Control*

The controller is the line executive in charge of accounting, which has a vital function in managerial control. He is concerned with the interpretation of accounting reports.

Any accounting system must provide an up-to-date record of the way in which a business operates. The purpose of managerial accounting is to allocate financial responsibility and to pinpoint areas where improvement could be made.

The efficiency of managerial accounting can be gauged by the existence of an adequate net profit. Effective performance means a net profit output in relation to effort and financial inputs of the business. Net profit is the result of a relationship or the percentage spread between gross margin and total operating expenses. When the resulting percentage is applied to the firm's net sales volume, it represents the net profit of the firm, before taxes, in terms of dollars.

Financial planning, procurement of capital, conservation and allocation of funds, auditing of the financial operations and the control of the firm's total operation generally take place in a preplanning concept known as work and profit centers. The treasurer, however, is usually responsible for flow of funds management, and for provision of the financial needs of the firm.

The control function of the store includes the collection, classification, and analysis of all data pertaining to the operation of the firm. The controller, in effect, manages expense as an underlying framework for the success of the entire store system.

Systems design should have both specific and general applications to the total organizational structure. The most certain characteristic of any business organization is that it will always be subject to change. That is why systems design should be set up in conjunction with staff recommendations from all divisions in the store. The system should also furnish management with the proper analytical feedback so that proper reappraisals can take place.

USE OF MANAGERIAL ACCOUNTING IN CONTROL SYSTEMS

In the management of expense control, the most effective data for the development of standards are the many thousands of records originating within the organization itself. Unfortunately, the usual accounting classifications set up for recording purposes are only marginally useful for managerial analyses. They do not serve to keep track of records in terms of functions. For example, in the natural classification of expenses, total wages and salaries are lumped into a payroll category. Such aggregations preclude any penetrating departmental analyses. When such costs are directly allocated to the originating department a whole new concept in the use of existing data begins. A functional bookkeeping system and the use of expense centers with costs assigned on the basis of functions performed gives the controller a basic methodology for performance improvement.

For these reasons all accounting data should be recorded in such a way that they can be quickly summarized in monetary terms and readily compared with industry standards and with similar operations for the same periods of time. In fact, the accounting procedures that a company uses should serve as a total information system for managerial control, not just a means of tallies for income tax computations.

DEVELOPING AND MANAGING STORE SYSTEMS

It is the function of a properly designed store system to provide meaningful feedback and compilations on all the merchandising and non-merchandising activities of the store. This means that cost compilations and classifications by departments should be on a functional basis wherever possible. There is no one method or solution of determining the optimum means of controlling expense variables. Thus, it is in systems design that organizational flexibility can be introduced into the firm.

System flexibility is one of the main determinants of successful control. Organizational rigidity stems directly from inflexibility in store systems; the greater the degree of rigidity in the firm, the less its ability to plan and adjust. For example, in the area of budgetary planning and control, the expense stems directly from the estimated sales forecast, which is not fully controllable. Thus, all dependent budgets must be flexibly set.

Generally, the greater the organizational flexibility, the smaller the percentage of variable to fixed expenses and the lower the firm's total average costs. This is because flexible organizations find far greater opportunities for more productive measures of control in expense management.

There are many differences in the underlying scope of retail accounting as contrasted with that of other industries. Primarily, most transactions are for comparatively small amounts, and these transactions have to be related to hundreds of merchandise classifications. In a department store alone, for instance, there are generally more than one hundred different broad merchandise classifications which include tens of thousands of items.

Retail distribution involves essentially dealing with people on a face-to-face basis; this entails a great deal more "self-supervision" by the average retail salesperson than in most other fields. Therefore, the movement of merchandise and people often forces loose controls because of the self-delegation of authority and responsibility. Thus, the controller must function as a policy maker in the sorting and resorting of assets.

These assets represent the conversion of:

	into		into	
cash	————————→	merchandise	————————→	cash

as the firm acts as the purchasing agent for its publics.

Other important facets in accounting procedures are the sales-audit and unit-control systems, which represent daily compilations of sales and transactions correlated with cash receipts and customer charges.[1]

The most highly developed forms of retail accounting procedures are found in department and specialty stores and in supermarkets. With relatively small changes, these techniques can be applied to any type of retail operation.

CRITERIA FOR SYSTEM DETERMINATION

It is conceivable that there could be as many accounting systems as there are types of stores. Thus the initial step in evaluating any accounting system is the determination of its suitability for the type of store involved.

The first step in this decision is the choice of the form of legal organization (discussed in Chapters 11 and 12), whether or not the business should operate as a partnership, proprietorship, or corporation.

Two sets of books may be needed—one for inclusion of items needed only for income tax determination; the other for assessing the true profitability of the organization. In the latter set are included items such as imputed interest on "self-furnished" funds, imputed rent on "owned" premises, and a "salaries" that would have to pay for outside professional management, were it needed.

For example, if an organization owns the building that it is using, only "out of pocket" taxes, insurance and depreciation are charged for income-tax purposes.

---

[1] See also Herman F. Bell, *Retail Merchandise Accounting* (New York: Ronald Press, 2nd ed., 1956).

However, an additional expense should be imputed to these occupancy expenses. In other words, the imputed amount would be the rental difference that the subject firm would be forced to pay in a competitive market. Another factor is an imputed interest charge, which should be made for the total funds invested in the business. The amount of potential interest that the invested funds could earn (consistent with maximum safety) should be subtracted from the actual profit returns from the business. Only by such means can the firm's true profitability be assessed.

CONTROL MANAGEMENT—OBJECTIVES AND SCOPE

Accounting systems, like conceptual changes in economic development, experience changes in the philosophy of handling variables and estimating "going-concern" values. When a social scientist attempts to explain the behavior of individuals in a social milieu, he generally uses social institutions and cultural patterns to explain their actions. The most natural explanation for a social fact is further elaboration in terms of a second social variable. With accounting systems, management must rely on the system for furnishing the basis for decision making and for planning for the future. The accounting system should furnish the means by which pertinent correlations must, wherever possible, replace or supplement intuitive judgments.[2]

The controller depends upon interpretation of the profit-and-loss and balance-sheet statements, which are—as already pointed out—a basic framework for formulating store operating policies.

The second tool of control is that of budgeting. Budgets provide management with material by which they can control operations through regular cycles of anticipation of financial needs. It follows, then, that both accounting standards (which are developed from past experience) and budgetary standards (which are blueprints for future actions) interact directly. The result is a managerial control system.

Accounting procedures may vary from a simple cost system to the retail method of inventory. The assumption is that any private business enterprise is set up with the purpose of earning a profit. A further assumption is that each firm attempts to maximize long-run profits. These two assumptions are axiomatic and inseparable. Further, the element of risk in private business is such that there is a definite placebo effect in the risk-bearing function of the entrepreneur.

Managerial Applications—Budgeting

The accounting system helps to determine the profitability of the firm. Year-end statements by themselves are only indicative, not conclusively deterministic, of a firm's profitability. In fact, it is generally agreed that accounting statements indicate a firm's approximate level of profitability and show whether or not it is a "going concern."

---

[2] See also John C. Harsanyi, "Explanation and Competitive Dynamics in Social Finance," *Behavioral Science*, Vol. 5, No. 2, April 1960, pp. 136–145.

Managerial philosophy determines the manner in which an organization is operated. For example, the policies with respect to sales, pricing, personnel, audits, and expense management are so determined. Management policy also determines the manner in which the accounting statements and budgets are presented. For instance, the balance sheet is really a formally condensed presentation of the "real accounts" in the ledger. In most cases, the supporting data and footnotes are really the basis for analysis. A budget, in effect, is a plan involving futurity with the objective of promoting organization stability.

Once the forecast of expenditures is projected, the amounts involved are dovetailed into a projected accounting statement in order to make certain that the necessary funds are on hand. The expense budget itself should cover a period long enough to include seasonal fluctuations, so that at least one complete turnover of merchandise is included.

In Table 37 the interrelationships of budgets, work center, and functional classification of expenses are illustrated. The form provides the means whereby an objective can be formulated and a standard basis of comparison used. Once

TABLE 37
TYPICAL BUDGETING CHART RECORD
Basic Work Center Forms

| NO. | DEPARTMENT | COMPARATIVE MONTHLY BUDGET—MONTH _____ YEAR _____ | | | | |
		PAY ROLL	NUMBER OF UNITS	COST PER C UNITS	STANDARD COST PER C UNITS	VARIANCES
121	CONTROLLERS					
122	STATISTICAL					
123	MGR. & ASSTS. ACCT. REC.					
124	CLERICALS					
125	BILL ADJUSTERS					
126	BILLERS					
127	C.O.D. BKKGS.					
128	MGR. & ASSTS. CREDIT DEPT.					OTHER SAMPLE AREAS

(OTHER DEPARTMENTS ARE, FOR INSTANCE, INTERVIEWERS, COLLECTION, AUTHORIZERS AND REFER CLERKS, CREDIT PROMOTION, MANAGER AND ASSISTANTS ACCOUNTS PAYABLE, BOOKKEEPING MACHINE AND COMPTOMETER OPERATORS, MANAGER AND ASSISTANTS AUDITING, CASH AUDIT, CHARGE AUDIT.)

SAMPLE OPERATING BUDGETS COVER:*

DISTRIBUTION COSTS BUDGET—
COST TO PROMOTE AND DISTRIBUTE THE PRODUCTS DURING THE GIVEN PERIOD;

ADMINISTRATIVE EXPENSES BUDGET—
COVERS EXECUTIVE SALARIES AND OVERHEAD COSTS, SUCH AS RENT AND INSURANCE;

MERCHANDISING BUDGETS—
BASED ON THE NUMBER OF UNITS THAT ARE PLANNED TO BE SOLD;

RESEARCH AND DEV. COSTS BUDGET—
DOLLAR AMOUNTS NEEDED AND TIMING. R AND D WORK CAN THEN BE CHECKED IN SAME MANNER AS MERCHANDISING BUDGET;

CAPITAL BUDGET—
SUMS UP PLANS FOR MAJOR INVESTMENT EXPENDITURES AND THEIR TIMING;

CASH BUDGET—
SHOWS HOW MUCH ACTUAL MONEY WILL BE NEEDED, AND WHEN, TO PAY OTHER OPERATING BUDGETS; SHOWS ALSO HOW TRANSACTIONS AFFECT WORKING CAPITAL.

* SEE ALSO HARRY M. KAISER, "GETTING RESULTS FROM YOUR BUDGET," *MANAGEMENT AIDS*, SBA, WASHINGTON, D.C., SEPTEMBER 1961.

all the budgets are combined for top management, a complete blueprint for action and control becomes available.

Retail control generally sets budgets up on a six-monthly basis to coincide with the merchandise plan; this is longer than required for a single turnover for any selling department. Provisions for losses due to bad debts, for accrual and deferred items, and for credit extensions to customers must also be included. Once expenses are estimated on the basis of amounts spent in prior years, adjustments can be easily made, provided that no changes in store policy have occurred.

Expense breakdowns should be set up into three general categories: fixed (those that remain constant), variable, and semivariable. Semivariable expenses tend to increase higher than proportionately as volume increases. For example, when an additional salesperson has to be added to a selling unit, it may take some time until sufficient additional volume is generated for the added expense input to become productive.

INTERRELATIONSHIP OF EXPENSES AND WORK CENTERS

In the area of budgetary control, effective criteria can be applied to administrative expenses. The relative size of administrative expenditures is a good preliminary guide in the determination of a firm's total budget. Administrative expense includes the management and supervisory salaries of the individuals included on the executive pay roll.

Total selling expenses are segmented by months and are correlated to sales for that month. In this manner, frequent comparisons can be made of actual selling expense-profit ratios. The theory behind these comparisons is that it is the single best "quick ratio" for instant evaluation to progress.

Where the scale of plant is large and departmentalized, selling expenses are set up in a schedule form so that allocations of indirect expense may be conveniently handled.

For example, in Table 38, changing expense data by expense center groups are shown for both selling and nonselling departments. In all cases, total pay-roll expense is at least half of total expense. The important feature here in planning the budget is the changing relationships which occur from one year to another.

Sam Flanel, General Manager of the Controllers' Congress of the NRMA, points out: "Generally, the principal thrust of stores' expense control and reduction efforts is directed at each department head, who has already wrung every drop of fat out of his operation, and has in fact often lopped off a good bit of muscle as well."[3]

Within the framework of the natural classification of expenditures are pay roll, taxes, advertising, and so on, as shown in Table 39. Another widely used type of classification is the functional grouping which further subdivides the

---

[3] Sam Flanel, "An Approach to More Effective Expense Control," *Retail Control*, December 1963.

TABLE 38

EXPENSE DATA BY EXPENSE CENTER GROUPS

(for the year February 1962–January 1963)

	DEPT. STORES $10–20 MILLION		DEPT. STORES $20–50 MILLION		DEPT. STORES OVER $50 MILLION		SPECIALTY STORES OVER $1 MILLION	
	THIS YEAR	LAST YEAR	THIS YEAR	LAST YEAR	THIS YEAR	LAST YEAR	THIS YEAR	LAST YEAR
100 General Management								
Payroll %	0.68	0.67	0.59	0.58	0.30	0.36	1.70	1.69
Total Expense %	6.24	5.96	6.06	5.86	5.66	5.61	7.74	7.68
200 Control & Accounting								
Payroll %	1.08	1.05	0.84	0.85	0.82	0.83	1.28	1.28
Total Expense %	1.23	1.22	0.97	0.99	1.00	0.99	1.50	1.52
300 Accounts Receivable & Credit								
Payroll %	0.82	0.80	0.76	0.80	0.74	0.75	1.05	1.03
Total Expense %	1.77	1.77	1.50	1.56	1.51	1.50	1.85	1.89
400 Sales Promotion & Display								
Payroll %	0.73	0.71	0.70	0.71	0.61	0.60	0.96	0.98
Total Expense %	4.90	4.88	3.77	3.88	3.77	3.74	4.59	4.72
500 Superintendency & Bldg. Operations								
Payroll %	1.45	1.45	1.42	1.47	1.55	1.55	1.43	1.40
Total Expense %	3.41	3.42	3.27	3.30	3.32	3.25	3.78	3.75
600 Personnel Administration								
Payroll %	0.27	0.27	0.24	0.25	0.25	0.25	0.27	0.32
Total Expense %	2.14	2.17	2.02	1.91	2.05	1.92	2.03	2.16
700 Material Handling								
Payroll %	1.24	1.20	1.06	1.05	1.35	1.35	1.02	1.02
Total Expense %	1.90	1.89	1.91	1.89	2.29	2.27	1.70	1.70
800 Direct & General Selling								
Payroll %	8.95	8.95	9.11	9.07	9.10	9.16	9.00	8.93
Total Expense %	9.83	9.83	10.04	10.01	9.96	9.92	9.90	9.78
900 Merchandising								
Payroll %	3.70	3.66	3.72	3.76	2.95	2.97	3.79	3.77
Total Expense %	4.90	4.83	4.54	4.65	3.45	3.44	4.75	4.73
Total Payroll & Operating Expenses								
Total Payroll %	18.92	18.76	18.44	18.54	17.67	17.82	20.50	20.42
Total Expense %	36.32	35.97	34.08	34.05	33.01	32.64	37.84	37.94

Note: a. Data shown for this year and last year were derived from a sample in which each store reported operating ratios for the two fiscal periods and, therefore, are comparable. However, any data previously published are not comparable with the data shown above, since the former were derived from a different sample of reporting stores.

b. Supplementary Payroll Benefits are included in each center's payroll expense.

Source: Controllers' Congress, NRMA, 1964.

natural classifications into five broad functions—administrative, occupancy, publicity, buying, and selling. This approach, of course, represents functional groupings similar to work centers. The principal problem involved here is the unit of measure to be used in analysis (for instance, unit costs of sales transactions, number of invoices handled, number of adjustments, and so on), in order that a pertinent basis for expense allocations may be developed.

Thus expense-center and productivity-unit accounting have also been introduced as a tool of analysis. This type of accounting involves the use of "work areas" or centers, in which relative productivity and efficiency can be measured and compared from one accounting period to another. In effect, expense-center accounting represents a further extension of the NRMA's functional classification system (Table 39).

TABLE 39

Natural and Functional Classifications of Expenses*

	EXPENSE ITEM	NATURAL CLASSIFICATION — ILLUSTRATION OF COSTS INCLUDED
01	Pay roll	Salaries, bonuses, prizes, pensions, retirement, allowances
02	Rentals	Warehouse, garage, buying offices
03	Advertising	Direct mail, radio, TV, style shows
04	Taxes	Local, State, Federal exc. income taxes, pay roll, license fees
05	Interest	On cost value of inventories, owned lands, bldgs., equip., fixtures
06	Supplies	
07	Services purchased	Heat, light, power, outside delivery service
08	Unclassified	Bad debts, donations, cash shortages, etc.
09	Traveling	Trans., meals, tips, taxi, hotel
10	Communications	Postage, telegram and telephone
11	Repairs	Bld. equip., and furniture
12	Insurance	Fire, glass breakage, etc.
13	Depreciation	
14	Professional services	Legal, buying assn., credit bureaus, special surveys

FUNCTIONAL GROUP	FUNCTIONAL CLASSIFICATION — ILLUSTRATION OF COSTS INCLUDED
Administrative	All general administrative including executive offices, accounting, credit office, and general store expense.
Occupancy	Rental or interest on owned premises, taxes, depreciation, heat, light, power, housekeeping.
Publicity	Sales promotion office, newspaper, radio, TV, direct mail, interior and window displays.
Buying	Buyers' salaries and traveling expenses, buying offices and resident buyer, receiving and marking, returns to vendors.
Selling	Salespeople, floor managers, stock men, wrappers, cashiers, delivery.

Expenses may be allocated according to sales, transactions, invoices, adjustments, average weekly number of employees, average cost of stock, area occupied, directly, indirectly per package cost, etc. Trend today is toward production-unit accounting and use of expense centers.

* These classifications have been set up by the Controllers' Congress, National Retail Merchants Association (NRMA), New York City.

Function of Expense Analyses

In expenditure analysis procedures the first question should concern the type of expense involved—is it fixed, variable, or semivariable? Then the proportion of fixed to variable expenses or vice versa, and whether this ratio is comparable to in-store or other typical averages, should be determined.

Each record has an input source and an output resultant. Thus, a degree of relationship between the expense involved and the function of performance in terms of output is always present. Such relationships furnish the performance criterion on which a scientific analysis of its utility can be made.

In ratio analysis strict comparability of data in each case may not be possible, as records may not have been set up on similar bases. For example, in financial statement analysis, ratios may be used either as a percentage figure or as raw ratio—in the form of a fraction. If the average inventory at retail is $4 million and net sales for the year are $12 million, then the inventory turnover is 3 (12 ÷ 4). Often ratios such as the merchandise inventory turnover ratio are used to measure the capital turnover ratio because of their apparently close relationship and the implied concept of a return of assets in the form of cash. But a merchandise turnover ratio figure should not be compared to a capital turnover ratio, which involves cash flow of funds for the firm as a whole.

As pointed out previously, it is not possible to assess the actual profitability of any going concern because of lack of consideration of imputed costs and the lack of firm standards in the allocation of indirect costs. Yet optimizing decisions within the firm requires the use of pertinent cost and productivity information.

When cost accounting procedures are designed specifically to apply to various clearly identifiable centers within the store, it becomes possible to obtain cost data in terms of production units for each such center. When expense dollars are considered to be only indirectly related to sales, any resulting analysis is relegated largely to a role of comparison with the previous year(s)—and to a role of comparison with median averages of comparable firms and departments.

In effect, expense-center accounting becomes an extension of the functional classifications of expense. For example, where many functions are impersonal, such as general supervision, little or no relationship between the expenditure, its control, and over-all executive responsibility is present. The expense-center approach redefines, for example, general supervision into an allocable series of controllable costs related to the particular job of work or kind of service involved. The actual number of centers involved in this system approach varies directly with the volume of the store.

An illustration of expense-center accounting will be found in Appendix O. Among the many general operating standards for work and productivity centers are the following:

I. Sales
   A. Number of transactions
   B. Average sale
II. Wrapping and Packing Merchandise
   A. Number of packages per day or per week
III. Marking Merchandise
   A. Number of pieces machine marked
   B. Number of pieces hand marked
IV. Stenographic
   A. Number of letters per day by length average
   B. Form, dictated, or transcription
V. Delivery
   A. Number of packages by department and by methods of sale
   B. Distances traveled
   C. Number of pickups

VI. Other Store Operations
 A. Number of adjustments, by type,
  by department alterations
 B. Warehouse receiving—number of orders
 C. Warehouse workrooms—material processed

Also included are service shopping tests; standards could be set up for such items as wrapping, weight measurements and postage applied or costs, writing legibility, telephone service, employee honesty (Willmark, etc.), housekeeping, and customer correspondence.

Nonselling departments in larger stores are now generally referred to as either sales-supporting departments or work centers. Such areas, when they are set up on a work-center basis, are segmentized in activities on a production-unit standard basis. By obtaining information on a unit cost activity basis, areas which are high cost in relation to output values received can be easily pinpointed. Thus the principal utility of expense-center accounting is that of furnishing the data whereby the productivity units of work may be measured.[4] Each expense or work center includes a series of controllable costs allocated in terms of specific standards of work common throughout the entire department. For example, in the accounts-payable center, total costs within the center could be measured in relationship to the number of invoices handled; in selling departments costs could be related to transactions; in the credit department, the number of interviews and applications processed would be another unit. In effect, the more accurate the recording of actual unit cost of the functions performed, the greater the potential for improving their effectiveness.

ROLE OF MERCHANDISE-MANAGEMENT ACCOUNTING

Another recent concept in the field of retailing has been the development of merchandise-management accounting[5] which was discussed in the chapter on basic merchandising. This represents an extension of standard factory cost accounting techniques to the retail process. The purpose of MMA is to furnish buyers with specific guides as to actual profitability of the items handled in the store or departments. Applications to date have only been marginal, because buying decisions at the retail level are made on the basis of customer wants—not on the basis of "handling" costs.

Thus, customer demand, not accounting standards, is the proper criterion as to whether an item should be carried, dropped, or added. As a system of mer-

---

[4] With a fixed rate of sales, the fixed costs would be constant in total. But when divided by the number of units sold, an "average sale" would result; the average sale varies inversely with the number of units sold or transactions generated. Both fixed and variable expenses are directly related to output. The work centers make all costs traceable to specific activities. By this means, both direct, indirect, and common costs can be tied more perceptively to economic activities within the firm.

[5] Hereafter referred to as MMA, it was developed by Arthur Anderson and Co., Chicago, as a means of justifying the carrying of low-margin traffic appliances for stores in severely pressed competitive areas.

chandise control, MMA may have some applicability in areas where big-ticket hard goods are handled within the store; however, its utility within the framework of the total organization for decision making is severely limited. Bearing this out is one of the conclusions of a study by Professor Young:

> The results of the trial applications did not support the opinion of the retailers interviewed, that MMA would probably cost more than the results would be worth. MMA can be very flexible in the way the information is obtained and in the frequency and comprehensiveness of the analyses, according to the report.[6]

A decision to eliminate an item for sale may involve the use of an opportunity cost concept: if customer demand is present and the existing commodity shows a contribution to profit, it should probably be retained and reordered regardless of the MMA projection.

FUNCTIONS OF COST METHOD OF ACCOUNTING

Most retail firms today still use the cost method of accounting as their basic operating framework. Indirect expense allocation is another procedure where applications of cost accounting concepts are used. Regardless of which method of accounting is used, there are many store areas—such as workrooms for alterations, furniture, millinery, upholstery, candy making, and so on—which use the cost method of accounting.

Cost accounting methods have an important bearing on "proving" differences in costs in buying various quantities for discount purposes under the Robinson-Patman Act at the wholesale level or for purposes of justifying trade practices at the retail level.

THE PROBLEM OF COST

All marketing decisions require cost estimates. And sales maximization does not necessarily mean a lower overhead. Cost can also mean marginal analysis; this provides the appropriate economic framework for solving the problem of cost for retail and market control and their reappraisals.

A good accounting system is an integral part of any economic system and should furnish the basis for consistency in cost determination and decision making.

---

[6] Elmer R. Young, "Merchandise Management Accounting for Small Retailers," *Research Summary*, S.B.A., Washington, D.C., 1961. See also: Harold W. Jasper, "The Accountant-Director of Information Systems? Behavioral Scientist? Catalyst? *Miami Business Review*, Vol. XXXVI, No. 5, April 1965; Robert Beyer, "Management Services—Time for Decision," *The Journal of Accountancy*, March 1965, pp. 48–51; John A. Beckett, "Motivation and Systemation—New Realities for Industrial Management," *Essays* published by the University of New Hampshire, May 1963, especially p. 5; C. West Churchman, "Managerial Acceptance of Scientific Recommendations," *California Management Review*, Fall 1964, pp. 31–38. The above provide material for a good discussion of human motivations and decision making under uncertainty, where accounting reports are regarded as merely one aspect of the total information on costs.

The most important aspect of cost analysis is the criterion of relevancy—only those cost items that will affect or be affected by a decision being included. However, the problem of actual cost is always present in any retail-marketing situation. For example, it may be asked whether cost of merchandise includes a deduction for cash discounts from vendors or for the trade discount, or whether cost is the amount charged to the department with a "loading charge" added, whether an amount listed as a "true cost" is the amount with the proper indirect expenses added, or whether "depreciation" expenses should have been added to total "cost." Especially, outlay and opportunity costs should also be evaluated, and included when considering the nature of any expenditure.[7] In addition, future and historical costs should be considered when measurable degrees of anticipation are present.

In the total managerial-information network, direct-costing systems such as the contribution method of accounting have been adopted on the grounds that they provide the appropriate cost estimate for many departmental decisions. However, contribution costs do not represent total costs.

Long-run costs should be considered when adaptation to change may be a valid consideration. If "scale of output" is related to cost determination, then the actual cost may become too aggregative because sales can almost always be increased somewhat, although at higher proportionate costs.

Incremental costs are another consideration where the variation is based on the rate of sales. Marginal cost is not necessarily a discrete function, but more often a continuous one in retail firm costing. For example, a decision to increase sales-promotion expenditures would depend in part on what the incremental cost would be at a projected level of sales. The distinction is important, because marketing decisions always involve sales-volume estimates and estimates of the incremental additional costs involved in generating additional sales.[8]

CAPITAL BUDGETING IMPLICATIONS

Another method of costing is the capital budgeting or the discounted cash-flow method. This method represents an evaluation of the *net flow* of cash that is expected to result from any of a number of alternative applications of funds—such as an investment in one of several merchandise lines with varying turnover and attainable gross margins or investing in a new branch store.

Thus cost cannot be considered as a single variable. Quantitative, psychological, and social mechanisms are additional considerations of the cost-demand variables, as are price-sales relationships and existing competition. From among these there can be chosen the appropriate cost concepts for the pertinent framework

---

[7] See also George J. Stigler, *The Theory of Price* (rev. ed., New York: The Macmillan Co. 1952), chaps. vii and viii. Opportunity costs should be the central concept in all cost analysis. This would be either outlay cost or the imputed price that a factor's service would command in the most productive alternative use.

[8] See also Stephen Enke, "On Maximizing Profits: A Distinction between Chamberlin and Robinson," *American Economic Review*, XLI (1951), 578. For a more complete statement of the relevance of the profit-maximizing concept see P. J. Verdoorn, "Marketing for the Producer's Point of View," *Journal of Marketing*, XX (1955–1956), pp. 221–35.

for profit maximization. Also it is in the area of "variance," where actual results can be reconciled with those in the forecast budget. Once the reasons are determined for the operating variance, management can then proceed to correct the deficiencies with the proper guidelines.

In costing, the broad macro concept of the managerial-economic approach may be too general. For instance, specific cost information has to be developed for contract applications on "cost plus" or cost plus "fixed-fee" wholesale sales.[9] Thus the use of cost-accounting procedures may be a positive means of planning and projecting an improvement in the firm's net profit. However, market demand and customer wants must be deterministic—*not* cost analysis.

CASH DISCOUNTS AND "LOADING" CHARGES

In department stores, cash discounts from vendors are not considered as a reduction of the merchandise costs to the department; rather they are recorded as an offset to the expense involved in operating the accounts-payable department. Thus the cash-discount income appears as "other income," while nonoperating income in the form of discounts may be credited to the buying department at the end of the accounting period as in the net-profit plan of accounting. Such discounts are not considered in the determination of the department's IM or generated GM.

The rationale of handling cash discounts from vendors in this manner is that the buyer has no control over the payment of the merchandise invoices; thus, taking advantage of discounts from vendors is the financial responsibility of the control or "efficiency" index of the accounts-payable department. A further argument against giving the selling departments credit for such discounts is that cash discounts are not a part of the selling departments' income earned from operations. In addition, a policy of "no credit" for discounts in any of the larger firms automatically adds a "loading" charge to all merchandise invoices—an excess of from 2 to 3 per cent added to merchandise costs. In other words, a buyer would be required to earn a discount of 4 to 5 per cent above merchandise invoice costs, and this should be negotiated on all purchases. Management rationale here is that the larger amounts purchased should provide the economic base for a better-than-average purchase price in the market place—in some cases in spite of the Robinson-Patman Act.[10]

---

[9] Most larger retail stores have contract departments where large-volume single-order sales are negotiated, using cost-accounting standards.

[10] For example, a buyer may be required to buy only merchandise which has a 5-per-cent cash discount under such circumstances rather than negotiate for the greater cash discount that a seller might be willing to permit. The *gross amount* of the invoice is artificially increased so that the net (discounted) price will reflect the net price on which the vendor insists. For example:

Price of invoice $\qquad = \$1000$ less $2\%/10$ days
Net price of invoice $\qquad = \$980$
Price of invoice is increased to 1031.51 less $5\%/10$ days
$\qquad 980 = .95x$
$\qquad x = .95 \div 980 = 1031.58$
New set price of invoice $980.00

FUNCTIONS OF THE RETAIL METHOD OF INVENTORY AND PROFIT ACCOUNTING

Must department stores and other progressive retail firms operate by the retail method of inventory? For the use of this method, financial standards and ratio comparisons are available on both an area and a nationwide basis. The retail method permits the exchange of scientific data among retail firms because all data are framed in terms of their relationship to net sales. From a public-relations standpoint, a markup percentage based on retail is always less than markup percentage based on cost.[11]

Other applications of the retail method are discussed under the chapters on merchandising management. The analysis here will be basic and from a control standpoint.

The first step in the retail method is to divide all possible types of account-handling procedures and transactions into the following three sections:

Section I: This is illustrated in Table 40. It always results in "total merchandise handled" (TMH) at retail and at cost; the initial average markup percentage and its cost complement are also derived from this section.

TABLE 40
THE RETAIL METHOD OF INVENTORY: SECTION I
(For determining the TMH at cost and retail and getting IM percentage and reciprocal cost complement)

	COST	RETAIL	MU DOLLARS	MU PER CENT
Opening inventory (BOM)	$ 80,000	$130,000		
Gross purchases	(100,000)	(164,000)		
Return to vendors	(2,800)	(5,400)		
Net Purchases	97,200	158,600		
Transfers in (agreed cost)	800	(1,400)		
Transfers out (agreed cost)	—	—		
Net Transfers (in)		1,400		
Transportation and Freight	2,000			
Revision of retail upward		10,000		
Revision of retail downward				
TOTAL MERCHANDISE HANDLED	$180,000	$300,000	$120,000	40%—IM 60%—Cost Complement*

* This is the reciprocal percentage of IM and represents average cost of all merchandise handled until the end of accounting period.

The purpose of Section I is to arrive at the department or the store's initial cumulative average markup, which should be great enough to provide for total operating costs and leave a suitable margin for profit. This development of the markup is the merchandising division's responsibility. When price changes are made (such as "revisions of retail upward or downward") they are handled in Section I because they directly affect the initial average mark-on. As such, changes

---

[11] Case (A) $\dfrac{\$ \text{ markup} \quad \$4.00}{\$ \text{ cost} \qquad 6.00} = 66\frac{2}{3}\%$ initial markup (based on cost)

Case (B) $\dfrac{\$ \text{ markup} \quad \$4.00}{\$ \text{ retail} \quad 10.00} = 40\%$ initial markup (based on retail)

do not represent either appreciation or depreciation in the cost of the goods. Further, no items in Section I of the retail method of inventory must represent any depreciation or appreciation in the value of the merchandise received.

Section II: The aim here is to develop total retail deductions. Accounting for the changes in market value of the inventory is represented by markdowns, employees' discounts, and estimated shortages. Specific illustrations of this are found in Table 41, which is a listing of total retail deductions during the operating period. These items may be income-producing (such as sales) or recorded deductions (such as markdowns and discounts to employees).

TABLE 41

THE RETAIL METHOD OF INVENTORY: SECTION II

(For determining the total retail deductions and ending book inventory)

	COST	RETAIL	MU DOLLARS	MU PER CENT
Gross Sales		$216,000		
Customer refunds and allowances		16,000		
Net Sales		200,000	(Cash Deduction)	
Markdowns	(10.0%)	20,000		
Disc. Adjs. to Employees and customers	(1.0%)	2,000	(Non-Cash Deductions)	
Estimated stock shortages	(1.5%)	3,000		
TOTAL RETAIL DEDUCTIONS		$225,000		
TMH		$300,000		
Less TR deductions		225,000		
ENDING BOOK INVENTORY		75,000		
TMH (from Section I)		300,000		
Less: TR deductions (from Section II)		225,000		
Ending book inventory		75,000		
Ending physical inventory		76,000		
Stock shortage (overage in this case)*		+$ 1,000		

* (Estimated stock shortage was *overestimated* at 1.5% (or $3,000); thus shortage was actually 1% or $2,000.)

Both of these items make up the principal deductions in Section II, inasmuch as sales represent deductions from stock and markdowns represent depreciation in the retail selling price as well as deductions from stock. Markdowns are also used to clear stocks of bad buys, broken assortments, discontinued fashions, and damaged merchandise. When used as a sales stimulant, markdowns are generally of a "temporary" nature.

Section III: This evolves primarily from Sections I and II, and is illustrated in Table 42. Closing book inventory and shortages are included if physical inventory is taken. Gross and net costs of merchandise sold, maintained markup, net operating profit, gross margin and net profit are developed in this section.

Scope and Purpose

In effect, the retail method of inventory is a method of "inventory averaging" and a means whereby a book inventory determination is a simple procedure (as

TABLE 42
THE RETAIL METHOD OF INVENTORY: SECTION III

(a) Gross cost of merchandise sold $134,400 $(.60 \times \$225,000) - (.60 \times \$1,000)$
                                                      $(.60 = \text{reciprocal of IM})$

(b) Total cost of merchandise sold

$134,400	Discounts received	
[− 2,200*]	from vendors	$3,200
$132,200	Workroom costs (net)	1,000
	Nonoperating income	$2,200

(a) Net sales ($200,000) − G.C.M.S. ($134,400) = Maintenance markup ($65,600)
                                                   or 32.8%

(b) Net sales ($200,000) − T.C.M.S. ($132,200) = Gross margin   ($67,800)
                                                   or 33.9%

(c) Net profit = (Gross margin − Total operating expense) ($67,800 − $50,000) = $17,800
                                                   or 8.9% (before taxes)

* The difference between cash discounts from vendors and net alteration and workroom expenses is either added or subtracted from gross cost of merchandise sold. In this case, $2,200 was the excess of nonoperating income over nonoperating expenses.

would be the maintenance of a "perpetual" inventory record), as well as an important means of financial and merchandise control. By handling all data as inventory values, adjustments, sales, discounts, and markdowns at retail, the attained GM, operating profits and shortages can be ascertained at any time. The taking of a physical inventory is required only once a year and is a much simpler task than looking up a cost price on each item.

As pointed out, the maintained markup or gross margin represents the actual amount above the cost of goods received in the form of net sales. The key figure to be developed is "cost of merchandise sold" or "total merchandise costs." These data are developed as follows:

Cost Method:
  (Beginning inventory + purchases) + freight inward − (net sales + ending inventory) = Cost of goods sold.
Under the retail method total merchandise costs are developed by taking:
  TMH (Section I) − Total Retail Deductions (Section II) = Gross cost of merchandise sold (retail).
Then taking:
  (Gross cost of merchandise sold) × (Reciprocal or cost complement of initial cumulative markup) = Total merchandise costs.[12]

An understanding of the retail method of inventory can best be developed by dividing the accounting procedures into the three sections as shown above.

THE MARKET VALUE CONCEPT

It is important to understand the differences in procedure between the markdowns (which represent a depreciation in price) and a revision of retail downward or upward (which does not represent any change in the cost value of the

---

[12] Assuming complete offset of nonoperating income and expense.

goods). In the case of revision of a retail downward, appearing in Section I, its over-all effect is to: 1) reduce the dollar value of the total merchandise handled at retail; and 2) decrease the dollar markup and its equivalent initial percentage markup or mark-on.

When the percentage mark-on is reduced, it automatically increases the cost complement, increases the ending inventories at cost, decreases the cost of goods sold and increases the gross margin. For example:

$$
\begin{array}{ccc}
\text{TMH} = & \text{Cost} & \text{Retail} \\
\text{IM} = 40\% & \overline{60,000} & \overline{100,000}
\end{array}
$$

Revision of retail downward by $2,000 would reduce the retail value of Section I to $98,000 IM $= \dfrac{(90,000 - 60,000)}{98,000}$ (approximately 38.8%)

Ending book inventory at Retail = $30,000
    Case I —with MU of 40% = (100 − 40 = 60)
        EOM inventory at cost = $18,000 (60% of $30,000)
    Case II—with MU of 38% = (100 − 38 = 62) (cost complement)
        EOM inventory at cost = (approx.) $18,360 (61.2% of $30,000)

With a larger ending inventory, a smaller total merchandise cost and an overstated gross margin results.

Should a markdown be erroneously placed in Section I as a revision of retail downward, its placement there would result in understating the IM, overstating the ending inventory at cost, and overstating the GM, because all items in Section I must not reflect a depreciation in the value of the total inventory. The *automatic* valuation of the ending inventory at cost or market, whichever is lower, is an excellent advantage in using the retail method of inventory.

MARKDOWN AND SHRINKAGE CONTROL

The retail method is the only method of control which automatically pinpoints merchandise shortages by departments, thus indicating areas for managerial action. Shrinkage may be due to clerical errors, breakage, failure to record markdowns, or pilferage. Other discrepancies may occur when, in order to take advantage of anticipations and cash discounts, firms pay their invoices before actual receipt of goods or before full verification of quantities charged.

"Coverages" are always the result of accounting or clerical errors and are far more to be suspected and abnormal than shortages. For example, the ending book inventory will be overstated when sales are made at markdown prices without the markdown being recorded.

I TMH (retail)—	$100,000
II Total retail deductions—	70,000
III Ending book inventory—	30,000

Therefore, if $1,000 in markdowns are not recorded, then total retail deductions become understated by $1,000 to $69,000 and ending book inventory becomes overstated to $31,000; the maintained markup becomes overstated as well. Crediting sales to the wrong department or charging invoices to the wrong department also results in "overages" or shortages.

MARKDOWN ANALYSIS

Markdowns are retail deductions that result from merchandise depreciation or, stated alternatively, the failure of the market to maintain a retail price. Markdowns must be taken in the accounting period in which the reduction takes place, regardless of whether or not merchandise is sold. Otherwise, the net profit will be overstated. Additional markups and revisions of retail downward are part of the original invoice prices; markdowns are never part of original invoice data categories of Section I.

The reason that the cost complement of the initial cumulative markup is used is that this mark-on is the highest average in the course of the selling season. Its use reflects conservatism in action—with the result that the "cost complement" or "reciprocal" is smallest. Thus, when this figure is applied to the value of the ending inventory at retail, a more conservative figure results. For instance: [13]

When initial cumulative markup is	45%	(Case A)
Then the reciprocal or cost complement is	55%	
When initial cumulative markup is	40%	(Case B)
Then cost complement is	60%	

The beginning and closing inventories should always be valued on the same basis. Only by use of the initial cumulative markup can the ending inventory be correctly valued at cost.

MERCHANDISE TRANSFERS

The pricing of interdepartmental and interstore merchandise transfers should be handled in the same way as a merchandise purchase—provided that there has been no change in the market price and provided that "the transfer" is a "non-distress" type of movement. Problems arise only when there is some anxiety on the part of the disposing department to rid itself of particular merchandise. When this condition exists, the "sending" department should first take a markdown and send the merchandise at an "agreed" cost. In such cases, the difference between the actual cost of the merchandise and the "agreed" cost at which it is shipped

---

[13] Maintained markup and gross margin percents are based on actual sales (not inventories) and are always lower than initial, average, or cumulative markups (which are based on inventories, not sales). Therefore, when the physical ending inventory is taken and its retail value is $10,000, in Case A the ending inventory at cost would be $5,500 (.55 × 10,000); in Case B the ending inventory at retail would be $6,000 (.60 × 10,000), or overstated.

should be taken as an "additional" markdown in Section II, and recorded by the receiving department as a "purchase" in Section I at whatever cost has been agreed upon.

RELATIONSHIP OF RETAIL METHOD OF INVENTORY TO COST METHOD

The data resulting from use of the retail method of inventory is directly applicable to the firm's operating statement. For example, in the P & L statement of operations, the first item is net sales; this item would appear on the cost as well as on the retail methods of inventory:

Cost Method of Accounting

Operating Statement

Net sales		1,000,000
Purchases	700,000	
Begin. invent.	300,000	
Frt. in	20,000	
	1,020,000	
Less:		
Ending invent.	220,000	
Cost of goods sold		800,000
Gross profit		200,000
Rent		
Heat		
Light		
Taxes		
Insurance		
Depreciation		
Total operating exp.		150,000
Net operating profit		$50,000
Other income		
Other expense		(Equal)
Net profit before taxes (or 5% on sales)		$50,000 (5% of $1,000,000)
Net profit on net worth (before taxes)		$50,000 (16.6% of 300,000)
Net profit on total investment (before taxes)		$50,000 (10% of 500,000)

Retail Method of Inventory

(Section I) TMH (initial cumulative markup ⅓; cost complement ⅔)
            at cost   1,020,000
            at retail   1,530,000

(Section II) TR deductions   1,200,000
              EOM at retail   330,000   (1,530,000 −
              EOM at cost   220,000   1,200,000)
                                               (⅔ × 330,000)

∴ Cost of Merchandise Sold = 800,000
   (1,020,000 − 220,000)
                        And net sales   1,000,000
                        Cost of goods sold   800,000
                        Net operating expenses   150,000

Balance follows as in cost method—except that all relationships are based on retail;
∴ net operating profit = 50,000 [1,000,000 − (800,000 + 150,000)].

All operating expenses (such as rent, heat, light, taxes, insurance, and so on) are subtracted in detail form so as to arrive at the net operating profit. To this amount, the adjustments for nonoperating income and nonoperating expenses are computed so as to arrive at a final figure for net operating profit or gross margin before taxes. There are no basic differences between the normal cost accounting operating statement and that of the retail method of inventory statement. Without question, the retail method of inventory as a method of merchandising management has created the greatest possible impetus for scientific management.

Management Implication

In the use of the retail method of inventory, management has an effective tool for departmental analysis and budget planning for flow of funds. Actually, any business enterprise, to operate efficiently, must do so on a basis of forward planning and budgeting. In effect, the process of business can be said to consist of conversion of cash and credit into assets and the reconversion of these assets into greater amounts of cash and assets. The many ways in which this process is carried out depend on the philosophy of management. This concept of movement of people and merchandise can be said to represent an interacting flow of funds and assets and the means whereby critical evaluation of a firm's performance can be developed.[14]

MANAGEMENT OF FUNCTIONAL ACCOUNTING RECORDS

Business records furnish information for a superficial appraisal of the firm's financial condition. In this respect the balance sheet is a picture of the business at a particular point in time. Balance-sheet analysis for successive periods can pro-

[14] Bion B. Howard and Miller Upton, *Introduction to Business Finance* (New York: McGraw-Hill, 1953), p. 101.

vide management with the necessary historical perspective and trends for managerial planning and control. By means of the historical perspective approach, the "value added" by the conversion processes of the business operation can be readily traced.

A new type of statement analysis and functional procedure is the Yield Accounting Concept, which is shown in Figure XXXIX. This is a process cost system illustrative of the sorting, resorting, and double-sorting processes used by industry in a total systems approach to the conceptual changes in "value added" by marketing or retailing. To date, the total systems process has been only partially adopted. However, this system has much to commend it for the future as a managerial control system.

FIGURE XXXIX

YIELD ACCOUNTING SYSTEM

(Composed of functional units and models for simulation, optimization, and yield accounting)

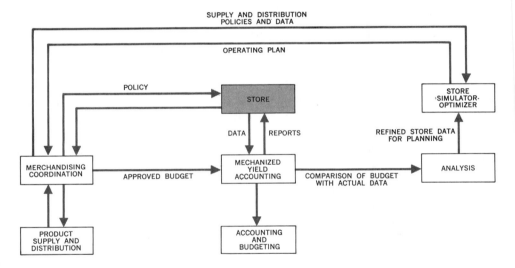

THE STORE HERE IS REGARDED AS A CATALYTIC SIMULATOR, ON WHICH ASSETS ARE CONVERTED TO MERCHANDISE WHICH IS REFINED BACK INTO CASH AS A BUSINESS PROCESS.
SOURCE: R. F. COOK *ET AL.*, "MECHANIZED YIELD ACCOUNTING PLAYS NEW ROLE IN REFINERY CONTROL," *PETROLEUM REFINER,* DECEMBER 1963, FROM WHICH THIS HAS BEEN DEVELOPED.

ANALYSES—FINANCIAL STATEMENTS

In the management of expense control and the attainment of gross margin goals, the most useful tool that management can utilize is a systematic pinpointing of areas of inefficient performance. The first approximations can be found in the balance sheet and P & L statements.

The two principal ways of analyzing financial statements are first, simple evaluation and analysis and second, ratio analysis. Using simple analysis, the total operation is examined from the standpoint of broad variations from typical performances found in other, similar businesses. Business record analysis not only provides a base for determining the presence of possible inefficiencies, but it also furnishes the basis for a situation analysis of the total operation of the firm.

The more important type of financial analysis is ratio analysis research. Data thus obtained lend themselves readily to industry ratios. Dun & Bradstreet develops its industry ratios on an annual basis. For example, in Table 43 the 1962 data ratios are shown by type of business.[15]

By far the easiest approach to financial analysis of the firm is through its flow of funds and net changes in working capital from one accounting period to another. These reviews are carried out by the evaluation of change of individual asset and current liability items, especially with respect to the manner in which such changes have influenced the net working capital of the firm. In judging the profit prospects of a firm, it is of great significance to the cash flows of the business. Cash flows in themselves summarize the changes in the cash position of the firm. For example, when current assets increase without an offsetting current liability, an increase in working capital results.

ELECTRONIC DATA PROCESSING (EDP)

Unquestionably, the integration of data processing and the resulting impact on accounting in a total information system cut across all organizational lines and the complex interrelationships of company and individual goals.[16]

Regardless of viewpoint, EDP systems are generally under the province of the controller. In effect, he is the "translator between engineering systems and long-run optimization goals of the business." [17] Thus the controller has charge of three broad categories of control which may be put into a system: controls over input, controls over the processing of data into the system, and controls related to the output of the system.

In management's never-ending search for an answer to the gross-margin squeeze, a tremendous amount of experimental research has been taking place. Computers have not changed management's need to obtain independent verification of financial results, and unbiased verification is still necessary in the substitution of machines for people.[18]

Fortunately, the advent of computers has made processing of research and experimental materials quite feasible in terms of time. Punched tapes, interlocking data equipment, IBM cards, and now optical scanning systems are replacing the hand- and machine-accounting systems and placing research and real time systems on a lower cost basis.

Most new EDP applications are in the area of pay roll and in the handling of item categories for automatic reordering. For example, in Table 44 are shown

[15] Ratios are for concerns in 12 retail lines, and with tangible net worths of over $75,000.
[16] See also L. G. Ifft, Jr., "Integration of Data Processing and its Impact on Accounting," *Technical Paper*, Volume 9, No. 49, 1962 (U. S. Steel Corp., N.Y.), pp. 17–22.
[17] See also results of research project by Professor Milton P. Brown and Miss Eleanor May in "The Functions of the Controller in Retail Store Organizations," reported in *Stores Magazine*, July–August 1962, Vol. 44, No. 7, pp. 16–18.
[18] Michael W. Maker, "The Controller's Role in EDP," *Retail Control*, December 1964, pp. 31–53.

Fourteen Important Ratios in Twelve Retail Lines
(1962 medians and quartiles)

Line of Business (and number of concerns reporting)	Current Assets to Current Debt (Times)	Net Profits on Net Sales (Per Cent)	Net Profits on Tangible Net Worth (Per Cent)	Net Profits on Net Working Capital (Per Cent)	Net Sales to Tangible Net Worth (Times)	Net Sales to Net Working Capital (Times)	Collection Period (Days)	Net Sales to Inventory (Times)	Fixed Assets to Tangible Net Worth (Per Cent)	Current Debt to Tangible Net Worth (Per Cent)	Total Debt to Tangible Net Worth (Per Cent)	Inventory to Net Working Capital (Per Cent)	Current Debt to Inventory (Per Cent)	Funded Debts to Net Working Capital (Per Cent)
Clothing, men's and boys' (151)	5.08	6.38	11.79	18.79	4.36	4.87	**	5.1	6.7	19.9	38.2	59.1	32.2	9.5
	2.74	2.78	5.74	8.91	2.37	2.99	**	3.7	15.0	41.9	73.1	85.9	66.8	30.9
	1.84	0.52	0.78	0.81	1.56	2.05	**	2.8	29.0	87.3	142.8	125.5	97.8	50.2
Clothing, men's and women's (76)	4.09	3.64	8.89	18.57	5.15	6.32	**	5.1	7.5	18.1	58.4	60.0	36.9	18.9
	3.02	1.28	3.66	4.21	2.70	3.67	**	4.1	21.8	36.7	90.6	79.2	66.7	33.5
	1.91	0.43	1.02	1.90	1.63	2.76	**	3.5	38.7	73.9	152.5	116.8	98.0	47.0
Department stores (278)	5.60	2.52	9.01	11.43	4.47	6.07	**	6.4	13.0	17.1	36.1	50.8	38.6	12.0
	3.53	1.30	4.65	6.34	3.08	4.30	**	5.2	25.9	29.4	62.0	69.7	59.6	27.8
	2.25	0.65	1.71	2.04	2.33	3.04	**	3.7	47.1	62.1	101.8	102.8	91.8	57.6
Discount stores (236)	2.10	2.20	20.04	29.60	12.98	19.93	**	7.9	15.5	68.9	109.6	128.5	64.5	23.1
	1.59	1.05	11.52	15.32	8.48	11.93	**	5.8	28.9	120.6	169.4	183.7	84.2	48.0
	1.34	0.54	3.97	5.47	5.93	8.07	**	4.4	53.9	206.2	262.5	278.1	109.0	85.8
Dry goods (82)	5.30	4.73	15.80	25.82	6.00	9.74	**	6.1	7.6	13.9	36.7	63.6	25.5	15.9
	3.14	2.87	9.64	12.32	3.15	3.90	**	4.5	16.9	34.5	82.7	96.5	51.3	32.0
	2.00	1.41	3.23	5.30	1.90	2.15	**	3.0	28.6	67.3	138.4	144.9	77.1	47.4
Furniture, 50 per cent or more instalment (168)	7.01	6.44	8.79	10.59	2.42	2.82	124	6.9	3.7	14.8	37.5	22.7	52.9	6.8
	3.99	3.10	4.91	5.75	1.59	1.70	164	4.5	9.4	35.5	61.9	39.2	93.2	16.6
	2.35	1.08	1.71	2.01	1.19	1.30	231	3.3	24.8	74.5	124.0	59.0	173.5	30.3
Groceries and meats, chain (66)	2.85	1.35	12.68	29.06	12.09	26.15	**	19.1	39.2	31.7	56.3	92.1	60.0	32.3
	1.94	1.02	10.32	18.99	8.73	17.71	**	14.7	54.0	44.0	82.2	117.7	71.9	49.0
	1.48	0.67	6.80	11.46	6.84	13.45	**	12.3	70.8	74.6	100.6	159.6	103.7	91.9
Groceries and meats, independent (66)	2.18	1.87	15.10	50.37	13.81	83.35	**	26.4	25.9	32.0	59.2	93.0	82.7	19.2
	1.52	1.09	8.62	22.60	9.17	31.02	**	20.9	59.7	49.0	90.3	144.6	118.5	68.3
	1.13	0.35	3.14	8.54	5.92	16.77	**	12.1	103.8	90.5	128.8	284.9	169.6	257.4
Hardware (67)	14.82	4.33	6.80	8.96	2.78	3.82	**	4.0	7.1	5.1	24.8	52.3	15.2	11.9
	5.97	1.87	2.89	4.82	1.57	2.29	**	3.4	14.9	16.5	46.1	74.3	38.7	22.5
	2.49	0.93	1.41	1.86	1.07	1.65	**	2.8	31.5	40.7	83.9	109.3	68.1	34.1
Lumber and building materials (185)	9.59	3.16	6.43	9.09	2.55	3.61	58	6.9	9.2	9.0	32.5	40.4	25.8	10.1
	4.76	1.70	3.17	4.51	1.88	2.68	79	4.9	17.3	20.1	51.6	56.9	50.5	24.7
	2.47	0.68	1.25	1.69	1.33	1.73	109	3.5	28.8	44.0	111.8	79.7	92.7	49.3
Shoes (75)	4.30	4.15	10.35	16.34	4.85	9.04	**	4.9	8.6	20.0	47.8	89.6	21.7	11.3
	2.70	1.97	4.60	8.57	3.05	4.38	**	3.6	20.9	40.9	90.3	125.0	49.4	24.2
	1.88	0.47	1.50	1.92	1.30	2.65	**	2.9	35.2	74.4	131.7	173.2	76.9	65.0
Women's specialty shops (196)	3.57	3.93	12.49	21.52	6.01	8.54	**	8.8	11.7	25.4	64.1	53.2	64.3	16.9
	2.13	1.83	5.05	6.90	3.61	4.93	**	6.2	20.9	60.9	102.6	92.6	97.8	35.2
	1.62	0.32	0.93	1.46	2.24	3.11	**	4.4	45.3	103.5	163.5	126.1	139.3	72.4

The figures from which the ratios are compiled are selected from a sampling of concerns whose tangible net worth, with few exceptions, exceeds $75,000. The financial statements are those appearing in credit reports on these businesses.

As reports containing year end statements are received on these concerns, copies are referred to statisticians who compute each of the "14 Ratios" on each of the concerns. The ratios are then punched on data processing cards, and arranged into industry groups.

After all computations have been completed, each group of ratios is graduated, industry by industry, into a series. The ratio one quarter down from the top becomes the UPPER QUARTILE. The ratio which falls halfway between top and bottom, that is, the one at the midpoint, is the MEDIAN. The ratio which is one quarter up from the bottom, or halfway between the MEDIAN and the bottom, becomes the LOWER QUARTILE. The purpose of these interquartile ranges is to show an upper and lower limit area, without reflecting the extreme top and bottom figures.

** Not computed; necessary information as to the division between cash sales and credit sales was available in too few cases to obtain an average collection period usable as a broad guide.

the use to which EDP equipment is being put in the Denver, Colorado, area. Computers are now handling accounting data and processing them into meaningful statistical forms more efficiently and at a lower cost than was previously thought possible. An RCA 501, for instance, can handle departmental sales inputs with a cash-register check. It then furnishes set data of sales audits of a standard item. These are processed in terms of stock number sequences sorted by departments and checked against cash register totals and cashiers' reports. The final output is information for a sales decision.

Instead of cards, punched tape used in conjunction with optical scanning systems (developed and now being used experimentally by some AMC stores) will probably turn out to be one of the more efficient EDP systems available.[19] These are only the beginning of broad movements in this direction by retailers.

From studies under the direction of the writer on the utilization of computer technology in department stores, it was found that stores apparently have no hesitation in automating accounts receivable, or other routine tasks. However, this "tends to drive out planning," for additional uses. Greater use of such hardware is needed for more effective operation.[20]

The Single Information System

The concept of the single information flow is that a piece of information is retained for use in only one place in the system so that it can be readily available when wanted at any organizational level. For example, sales information enters the system automatically from the point of sales and includes all necessary data for charges against customer accounts, sales commissions, unit control, evaluation of promotional effort, computation of operating statements, and sales analysis. This information is used by all divisions but is not duplicated in any divisional information file. Such an information system is technologically feasible with an on-line, real time-computer system with random entry, random access, and random information processing.[21]

The single information flow should be contrasted with the total systems approach, which ties together separate functional information systems. As an illustration of the total systems approach, the merchandising, control, finance, publicity, operations, and personnel divisions each maintains its own information system that is tied into a central processing unit. Duplication is necessary to some degree

---

[19] At the present time the Joseph Horne Company of Pittsburgh is pilot testing National Cash Register (NCR) scanning system and The Higbee Company of Cleveland, Ohio, is using an IBM system.

[20] C. F. Carpenter, "Effective Utilization of Computer Technology in Department Stores," unpublished research memorandum, Retail Research Center, Graduate School of Business, University of Pittsburgh, July 1964. In one of Mr. Carpenter's interviews with a department store personnel director, deep concern over the human factor in systems operations was expressed. Store employees were viewed as the store's most valuable asset, but it was agreed that more money is typically spent on the selection of a machine than in the selection of an employee.

[21] See Alfred L. Bauman, Jr., "Single Information Flow Philosophy," *Data Processing Yearbook 1963–64* (Detroit, Mich.: American Data Processing, Inc., 1963) p. 145.

TABLE 44

Status of Data of Sample Retail Firms in Denver Area*

Firm	Equipment — Mfr.	Model	Description	Unit Control	Payroll	Sales Audit	Accounts Payable	Purchase Distr.	Expense Distr.	Gen'l Books	Other
Department Store-A (including branches)	IBM " " " Kimball	1401G 047 083 523 026 195	Card-system computer Tape-to-card converter Sorter Gang punch Keypunch (3) Tag-to-card converter	X	X	X		(X)	(X)		Daily flash sales Monthly expense Sales clerks' productivity report Merchandise transfers
Specialty Store-A (including branches)	Univac " " " "	1004	Card system with paper-tape reader Tape-to-card converter (Kimball tags) Collator (1) Reproducer (1) Interpreter Sorter (2) Keypunch (2)	X	(X)	X	X	X	X	X	Addressing for direct mail
Moderate-price specialty chain	Univac " " " " "	1004	Card-system computer Tape-to-card converter Keypunch (3) Sorter (2) Collator (2) Interpreter Reproducer	X		X					Accounts receivable
Dry-goods chain	IBM " "	402 082 526	Accounting machine Sorter Reproducer	X	X		X	X			Open to buy Cash requirements Statement heading
Department Store-B (including branches)	IBM " " "	1401G 047 082–3 026	Card-system computer Tape-to-card converter Sorters Keypunches			X	X	X	X	X	Price revisions Classification
High-price specialty chain	NCR and UNIVAC Service Bureaus			X				X			
Supermarket chain	IBM	1440	Magnetic-disk drives (2)‡	(X)	(X)		(X)				

* From Colorado Controllers' Congress Association, May 1965.
† ( ) = In process.
‡ On order.

467

in order to preserve the autonomy of each divisional system. To the extent, however, that divisional goals conflict with company goals, biases will filter into the individual systems and will contaminate the information and mar its usefulness on a total system basis.

It is argued that the single information flow involving one file of information is less expensive and easier to manage than the total systems approach tying together multiple files of information. There exists, however, a strong natural tendency away from this approach, which stems from resistance to change and reluctance to surrender organizational prerogatives. Attempts to coordinate efforts of autonomous groups are frequently frustrated and yield to more expedient approaches which overlook differences. The information system of tomorrow may tend to become a patched-up version of the present system, incorporating all its limitations.

Adequate communications is a primary problem in systems development. If personnel could communicate perfectly with one another, most problems would vanish. The characteristics of perfect personal communication include:

> ... the subtle inferences and the implications perceived by individuals when interacting with others. They may be triggered by facial expressions, vocal inflections, or the circumstances surrounding the communication. The silent language thrives in an environment where conflicts of interest exist. To the extent that individuals are working towards the same ends, the communications problem between them is minimized. The problem of communications in a business thus becomes in part a problem of aligning individual goals with company goals.[22]

The understanding of human behavior is a basic determinant of the effectiveness of any business endeavor and its goals. A combination of skills such as in computer systems, in operations research, and in managing human relations is also needed before the development of fully integrated EDP systems can be effected in retailing.

THE INDUSTRIAL ENGINEERING APPROACH

The management of expense control operates in much the same way as does the management of process design or a systems procedure. In effect, the "total systems" concept in retailing would be best represented by a working methodology or framework which previously existed in the merchandising procedures of the store itself.

In utilizing this approach, a system for the entire operating division of the store is set up. For example, the best layout would be set up for internal traffic routing and movement of goods, from the point of receipt to the point of sale. By this means, the lowest possible cost consistent with customer services is determined and used.

The economic phasing of store operations to customer services is the important

---

[22] C. F. Carpenter, op. cit.

determinant of expense control. Another aspect of the industrial engineering approach is systems analysis, which insures continuing flexibility in the storage and shipment of merchandise for sale, for a branch store, or for expansions. In effect, the approach itself becomes a review of all existing systems under which the firm operates and achieves its over-all objectives.

RISK MANAGEMENT

All business assets are subject to loss, decay, or damage; some risks are transferable, others are not. For example, merchandise improperly bought, improperly sold, or incorrectly promoted represents damage of a noninsurable nature. Compensation for such losses is provided by an IM system and accompanying markdowns high enough to clear the merchandise from stock. (IM = Initial Markup.)

IM must also be large enough to provide for the normal, non-transferable risks in retailing, such as changes in styles, fluctuations in price levels, business cycles, population shifts, new competitive factors, etc. As pointed out above, these losses are absorbed as a cost of doing business and can be minimized through good management and buying controls.

Losses resulting from tangible property accidents or the hazards of daily contacts of the public, employees, and customers are insurable and thus transferable. Insurance management is part of the controller's responsibility; he carries out this function by developing an insurance program which effectively shifts the transferable risks associated with the operation of the firm.

In the purchase of insurance, protection from fire, theft, windstorm, and so on, is essential for the smaller retailer. So protected, he incurs a low permanent expense in return for freedom from the possibility of crippling losses. Insurance against liabilities incurred due to product sales, customer injuries while on the premises, and employee mishaps is also advisable.

For some businesses where values are high relative to bulk—such as diamonds and jewelry—substantial amounts of burglary and other protective insurance are needed. While each risk is a separate consideration, all risks can be covered by a single, comprehensive liability policy. Since 1960, Multi-Peril comprehensive policies have been available. These policies offer one complete policy for most insurance needs at the lowest possible cost.[23] This involves purchasing insurance from a merchandising standpoint. Insurance costs should run less than 3 per cent of total operating expenses.

Most insurance companies offer "all-coverage plans" (which, however, except

---

[23] See also James Stephenson, "Can Every Store Self-Insure Itself—If So, How?" *Retail Control*, September 1964, pp. 127–31. Mr. Stephenson (Superintendent, Multi-Line Department, Hartford Insurance Company, Atlanta, Ga.) pointed out that the Multi-Peril policy enables retailers to have coverage "on buildings, contents, business interruption, glass, public liability, personal injury (libel, slander, false arrest coverages), boiler and crime. In other words, the small to medium stores probably would have ended up with three property and casualty policies. One policy would cover their employees, workmen's compensation, and the third a Multi-Peril or package policy. Also, the larger insurance buyers with more complex operations and leaving fewer exposures uninsured would have greatly reduced their number of policies but probably could not have gotten by with as few as three."

workmen's compensation. Under the all-coverage plans, protection for libel, slander, and false arrest is also available at little additional cost.

In a study on insurance management of small retail firms in Oregon, it was found that:

1) fire insurance premiums accounted for about 40 per cent of total insurance premiums paid by the typical small retailer in the survey group. Many in the group were insured against relatively small fire losses but not against potential large losses;

2) the retailers generally thought insurance agents were more interested in making a sale than in performing a service. Lack of communication was a handicap to both agents and retailers;

3) many retailers bought insurance on the same property from different agents as a matter of business reciprocity. The agents and retailers surveyed knew this was not good business practice, but they were reluctant to change;

4) the adequacy of a retailer's liability insurance is extremely difficult to judge. Limits of potential loss cannot be predicted, because the extent of loss is often set by jury trial.[24]

The three principal types of insurable risks are those for loss of or damage to property owned or leased by the insured; liability risks imposed by law, either by explicit or implied contracts to which he is a party; and the risk of injury, illness, or death. The latter type of insurance is generally provided for in group insurance policies and is handled by the firm for all its employees. (In Appendix M will be found the classification of transferable risks as part of managerial insurance considerations.)

SUMMARY AND CONCLUSIONS

Many of the aspects of retail accounting, especially those of the retail method of inventory, were analyzed in this chapter. The relationship of the accounting system and resulting decision processes were analyzed as a functional staff tool for historical analysis, planning, and decision making.

In evaluating organization controls through accounting procedures, management is dealing with a dynamic operating system. Thus the use of static figures (such as those found on balance-sheet statements) has severe limitations, unless the data are developed over periods of several years so as to pinpoint changes.

Certain inadequacies of the natural classifications of expenses for managerial decision making were also reviewed. The importance of store systems and their flexibility were traced as a "path" of critical evaluations for pinpointing areas where efficiency could be improved. The functions of EDP systems in the organization and "risk" management as part of the control function were reviewed from the standpoint of the reappraisal functions.

---

[24] Donald A. Watson and A. Gerlof Homan, "Insurance Management in Small Retail Firms," *Management Research Summary*, SBA, Washington, D.C., August 1962.

Part Eight

Executive Management and Business Statesmanship

Chapter 28: *The Interrelationship of Government and Business*

The interaction of government and business generates a social process that creates public values. This creation of public values in a marketing economy involves the utilization of mass distribution facilities to move commodities to points of consumption. The system of distribution in any economy is affected directly by the political system under which it operates and by the economic variables of all its interacting forces.[1]

Within this framework, competitive markets force firms to operate at the highest possible level of efficiency and flexibility. Thus, the economy tends to be flexible, independent, and at least outwardly competitive. In this setting, elements of oligopolistic, imperfect, and monopolistic competitive tendencies appear.

Everyone is a consumer. It follows, then, that any economic activity which can reduce either production or selling costs, or both, with resulting savings passed on to the consumer, would be desirable. This is basic to the creation

---

[1] See also Otto Kleppner, *Advertising Procedure* (4th ed., Englewood, N.J.: Prentice-Hall), p. 669; Clair Wilcox, *Public Policies Toward Business* (rev. ed., Homewood, Ill.: Richard D. Irwin, Inc., 1960); Sam Rosen, *National Income* (New York: Holt, Rinehart and Winston, Inc., 1963); Harold G. Moulton, *Controlling Factors in Economic Development* (Washington, D.C.: The Brookings Institution, 1949); and P. W. S. Andrews, *On Competition in Economic Theory* (London: Macmillan & Co. Ltd., 1964).

of an affluent society and a more efficient government—the twin principles of a better social framework in which citizens participate.

At the retail market levels, new techniques in advertising, promotion, and merchandising are fast becoming the self-regulators of competition. Where protection of the consumer interest is deemed warranted, the government's role in the field of distribution has become more important. In addition to taxation, the local, state, and federal governments are interacting increasingly at regulatory and participating levels.

Social Security, Medicare, "Fair Trade" legislation, unfair practices Acts (minimum pricing legislation), deceptive pricing, advertising regulation, Sunday Blue Laws, Pure Food and Drug Acts, Equal Opportunity Laws, and adherence to fair labor standards Acts are among many of the various aspects of controls and regulations under which business is conducted.

It is especially important to note that at the retail level neither Congress nor the courts have recognized any official impairment in our market and retailing system, because, for enforcement purposes, they have subdivided the antitrust law into a series of industry markets. Where resale price maintenance contracts are legal, the only price competition that is not in force is that on pertinent brands.[2] Of course, monopolistic price controls on milk products in some states also work against the consumer. Sellers can never free themselves from price competition—whether they attempt to apply "Fair Trade" legislation or price controls against their competitors—because, in any competitive market, artificial price levels cannot be maintained.

The struggle to maintain competition has three aspects: that in which manufacturers of nationally advertised branded items are concerned; that involving distributors, wholesalers, and retailers; and that in which both the aforementioned as well as the federal, state, and local governments participate.

IMPORTANCE OF COMPETITION AT THE RETAIL LEVEL

Competition at the retail level directly involves the psychological propensity to consume. As aggregate income increases, consumers spend more on goods and services but not in proportion to the increases in income. That means that as long as income in the aggregate continues to increase, there will be a continued strong allocation for consumption expenditures, but not proportionately so. Competition at the retail level enables the consumer to maximize his satisfactions in the framework of opportunity cost, subjective utilities, and general equilibrium operations.[3]

The total propensity to consume is as highly stable as Keynes stipulates, and

---

[2] The McGuire Act and now the Quality Stabilization Approach, which is currently favored for passage. See also P. W. S. Andrews and Frank A. Friday, *Fair Trade* (London: Macmillan & Co., Ltd., 1960).

[3] Helen G. Canoyer, "Some Observations Concerning Economics of Consumption" (Bloomington: Indiana Marketing Symposium, 1952), Schuyler F. Otteson (ed.).

consumption is also a fairly stable element in the economy. However, consumers can and do change their patterns of consumption, and without previous notice.[4]

To illustrate: Strong consumer demand leads to sales increases, which are projected into further cyclical growth and production of both industrial and consumer goods. As long as such self-generating cycles continue, competition is fostered and smaller and even marginal firms prosper. However, when consumer spending levels off, smaller competitors are driven out of business and the fewer remaining sellers can lessen their competitive efforts with the result that the market stabilizes and general stagnation takes place.

When such situations occur, Keynes felt that government action has to provide the necessary stimulation for regenerating an upward economic cycle. This is, apparently, the kind of economic ambiance in which business is being conducted today. In furthering such economic controls and maintaining the economic health of our business economy, the Federal Reserve Board adjusts the discount rate and also controls the market for securities by either upward or downward "pushes" through their "open market operations." Both of these operations directly and indirectly affect national income, as does tax policy.[5] National income also is affected by the rate of investment and capital spending and by both short- and long-term interest rates. Keynes relates his consumption function to full employment and to national income generated to a maximand under competitive conditions. Competition, full employment, and national income are then all "keyed" in a single mass unit to the consumption function which in the long view never exceeds long-run income levels.[6]

PUBLIC POLICY OBJECTIVES

It has been a policy publicly advocated that competition and private enterprise, though not in the utilities, are desirable. However, government policy aims at emphasizing workable competition and ignoring impracticable notions of pure competition.

Today, applied variations of Keynes's economic theories are being used to suggest that the government should be committed to a maintenance of a high level national income with projected small percentage increases over time. And, because of built-in government controls, it is very doubtful that our economy will ever again experience a protracted depression similar to that of the thirties. Slightly rolling readjustments and short-term recessions of perhaps two to three years' length, varying with the marginal productivity of capital, is the present general trend of the economy.

---

[4] J. M. Keynes, *The General Theory of Employment, Interest and Money* (New York: Harcourt, Brace & Co., 1936). See also Wright's interpretation of Engels' Laws of Consumption. E. L. Feige, "The Demand for Liquid Assets: A Temporal Cross-Section Analysis," The Ford Foundation, Doctoral Dissertation Series, 1963 Award Winner.

[5] See also E. Sussna, "A Proposed Computer Simulation of Federal Reserve Open Market Operations," unpublished research memorandum, Graduate School of Business, University of Pittsburgh (September 1962).

[6] J. M. Keynes, op. cit.

The theoretical assumptions of the classical and neoclassical economists—that an economy operating at too high a level eventually eats up all its capital investment potential—has never been disproved. It is therefore assumed that there may be upward limits to full utilization of resources. For this reason, the federal government seeks to confine business and labor within "noninflationary wage-price guideposts," to offer equal employment opportunities for all, to impose voluntary controls, to seek equilibrium in the balance of payments gap, and to promote the advancement of national interest in economic development on Earth and the exploration of outer space. Of greater importance, perhaps, is the fact that government and business are working together to formulate and adapt fiscal policy so as to achieve full employment and more rapid economic development.[7]

In Figure XL is shown an illustration of the interrelationship of government, business, and society. Within this framework, the maintenance of competition involves a never-ending vigil of regulation, court cases, consent decrees, and promulgations of trade practice rules.

THE STAKE IN EFFICIENT DISTRIBUTION

The cost of distribution and the process of moving goods from the points of production to the points of consumption have been estimated to range from 55 to 60 per cent of the total purchase price of all consumer commodities. These marketing-distribution costs include all the marketing functional applications of time, place, and possession utilities.

Change of form utilities should not be included with distribution costs; for instance, the cost of freezing foods is a production change of form cost, not a marketing cost. Improved productivity can lower the over-all cost of what consumers buy, and, at the same time, increase the amount of discretionary income available for consumers' purchases. In effect, any reduction in the cost of living automatically increases the consumer's spending base. Most individuals in the middle- and lower-income groups are generally predisposed to spend more and to save less.

The three states of the market already mentioned (monopoly, oligopoly, and competition) coexist. For example, Army or Navy Post Exchanges (PX's) operate internally as beneficent monopolies and externally as competitive market units. The existence of any institution, so long as it continues to perform essential functions in a reasonably efficient manner, is justified and achieves business continuity. Consumer cooperatives are also classified in this way.

Only in a voluntary competitive enterprise where there is adequate reward for efficiency can competition exist. In this setting, the consumer receives the widest possible variety of products and services from which to choose. The market

[7] "Business and Government: A Changing Balance of Power," Business Week, July 17, 1965, p. 85. See also R. Joseph Monsen, Jr., and Mark W. Cannon, The Makers of Public Policy (New York: McGraw-Hill Co., 1965).

reward for ineffective participation is failure—disappearance from the market place.

Because the marketing-retailing processes do not directly involve a change in the form of the commodities handled, the social and economic "values added" that are created may be rather obscure to the unthinking consumer. The values received by the consumer (of having wanted merchandise at the right time, place, price and in the right quantity) are, in effect, the value that the consumer himself places on the offer. Thus the creation of public values, especially in terms of satisfaction, is not solely a function of land use and entrepreneurial risk in market institutions. Rather, public values are a result of market and retail distribution—satisfying the consumer's desire for a wide variety of goods or services from which to choose.

In efforts both to protect the consumer and to make him more efficient, the government inspects weights and measures, and has agencies that seek out product flaws and possible harmful products and attempt to eliminate misleading and deceptive advertising. The government also fosters product testing services and encourages consumer education in both government and civic groups.[8]

In addition, government agencies at all levels—local, state, and federal, as well as university bureaus of business research—gather data about all the economic variables that affect the efficiency of the distribution functions in the economy. For example, at the present time, to implement the government's war on poverty, great emphasis is placed on statistics concerning consumer income and the consumer price index.[9]

FUNCTION OF REGULATORY AGENCIES

In 1914, the Federal Trade Commission Act was passed to set up guides, to regulate fair competition, and to prevent monopolies in restraint of trade; its intention was to preserve competition, not to restrict it. The Robinson-Patman Act (an amendment to the Sherman and Clayton Acts) was passed to prohibit price discrimination in interstate commerce. The principal provisions of the Clayton Act concern the prevention of "tying in" clauses in purchase contracts, interlocking directorates, and exclusive dealer arrangements where such actions tend to restrict competition and discriminate. "Fair Trade" legislation does not work either in the consumer interest or in the interest of the company taking advantage

[8] For example, the federal government maintains testing bureaus such as the National Bureau of Standards in Washington for the protection of consumers, a geological service for use in public land explorations, and National Bureaus of the Departments of Commerce and Labor, among others.

[9] *Current Population Reports,* Series P–60, No. 43, as found in *Consumer Income* (Series P–60, No. 45), June 18, 1965, U. S. Department of Commerce, Bureau of the Census, Washington, D.C.; and such publications as the University of Denver's *Denver Metropolitan Area Consumer Price Index,* which is based on data supplied by the U. S. Department of Labor, Bureau of Labor Statistics. In the former publication, it was found that "the median income for all families in 1963 was $6,200. Forty-four per cent of the 11-million unrelated individuals had total money incomes of less than $1,500 in 1963, whereas 28 per cent had an income of less than $1,000." The median income for all unrelated individuals was $1,800.

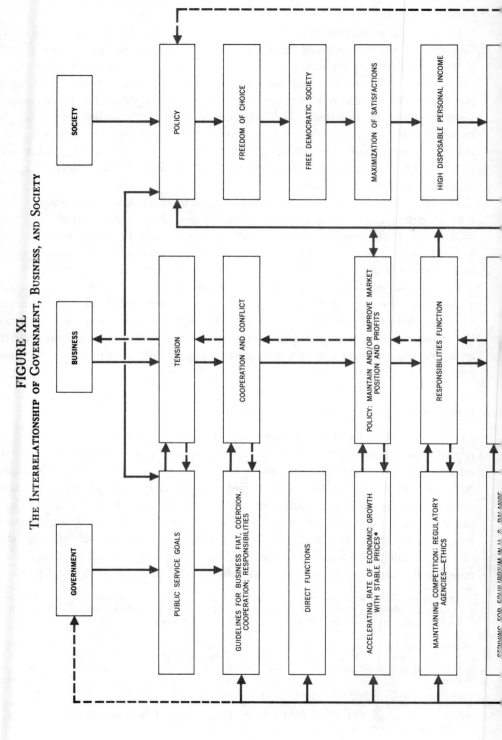

FIGURE XL
The Interrelationship of Government, Business, and Society

GOVERNMENT

BUSINESS

SOCIETY

PUBLIC SERVICE GOALS

TENSION

POLICY

GUIDELINES FOR BUSINESS FIAT, COERCION, COOPERATION; RESPONSIBILITIES

COOPERATION AND CONFLICT

FREEDOM OF CHOICE

DIRECT FUNCTIONS

FREE DEMOCRATIC SOCIETY

ACCELERATING RATE OF ECONOMIC GROWTH WITH STABLE PRICES*

POLICY: MAINTAIN AND/OR IMPROVE MARKET POSITION AND PROFITS

MAXIMIZATION OF SATISFACTIONS

MAINTAINING COMPETITION: REGULATORY AGENCIES—ETHICS

RESPONSIBILITIES FUNCTION

HIGH DISPOSABLE PERSONAL INCOME

478

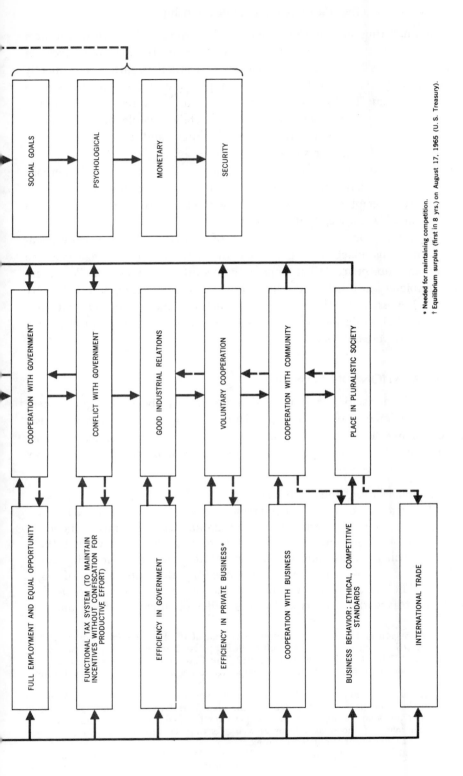

SOCIAL GOALS

PSYCHOLOGICAL

MONETARY

SECURITY

COOPERATION WITH GOVERNMENT

CONFLICT WITH GOVERNMENT

GOOD INDUSTRIAL RELATIONS

VOLUNTARY COOPERATION

COOPERATION WITH COMMUNITY

PLACE IN PLURALISTIC SOCIETY

FULL EMPLOYMENT AND EQUAL OPPORTUNITY

FUNCTIONAL TAX SYSTEM (TO MAINTAIN INCENTIVES WITHOUT CONFISCATION FOR PRODUCTIVE EFFORT)

EFFICIENCY IN GOVERNMENT

EFFICIENCY IN PRIVATE BUSINESS*

COOPERATION WITH BUSINESS

BUSINESS BEHAVIOR: ETHICAL, COMPETITIVE STANDARDS

INTERNATIONAL TRADE

* Needed for maintaining competition.

† Equilibrium surplus (first in 8 yrs.) on August 17, 1965 (U. S. Treasury).

of this legislation,[10] thus negating or offsetting the primary objective of business legislation, which is the fostering of competition. At times, the regulatory agencies attempt to "make laws" by their interpretations of legislation, rather than merely to carry out the enforcement of laws.[11] For example, one of the principal *raisons d'être* of the Federal Trade Commission Act is to interpret the Robinson-Patman Act and to see that no one buyer—be he retailer, wholesaler, distributor, or manufacturer—should be permitted to acquire merchandise or commodities, regardless of quantity, at an excessive discount.

This rule was based on the fact that too large a discount, though perhaps justified on a "savings" basis, would be discriminatory in character. It is obvious, of course, that the receipt of large discounts by a seller permits the recipient to sell the product at a lower price, should he so desire.

In research studies concerning enforcement of legislation by regulatory agencies, retailers and manufacturers agree that the activities of the agencies are generally fair and objective. What apparently disturbs retail and market managers is the ambiguity in much of the legislation, its interpretation, and its "spotty enforcement." For example, those cited for violations resent the fact that they were thus designated while individuals whom they considered guilty of the same or worse infractions were not touched.[12]

EFFECT OF TAXATION ON SPENDING

In addition to the legislation and regulation mentioned above, the government acts as a directing force through social legislation and by spending taxation. Also, by selectively taxing "undesirable" commodities and services and selective spending, the government influences the social habits and shopping patterns of consumers.

In these policy areas, there are many popular mythologies of American politics. "The realities of government taxing and spending are obscured in a fog of rhetoric." The voters are told by one group that unbalanced budgets are always bad; that government spending is ruining the country; that the national debt will be a crushing burden on future generations; and that the strength of the federal system is being sapped by the bureaucracy of big government. Another group always trumpets the virtues of government spending over private spending; scoffs at the possibility of inflation arising out of

[10] See also Harvey Averch and Leland L. Johnson, "Behavior of the Firm Under Regulatory Constraint," *American Economic Review*, December 1962, pp. 1052–69; and George J. Stigler and Claire Friedland, "What Can Regulators Regulate? The Case of Electricity," *Journal of Law and Economics*, October 1962, pp. 1–16. In a competitive economy, artificial price levels cannot be maintained.

[11] This was applied in a cease and desist order on list pricing Norelco shavers by the North American Phillips Co. in their newspaper advertisement for the New York City and Philadelphia areas in 1963. The writer prepared the reply for the company for the Federal Trade Commission, and pointed out that many of the smaller firms as well as stamp redemption firms in these areas were selling Norelco shavers at stipulated list price.

[12] See "Retailers Find Flaws in Fur Labeling Act," *Women's Wear Daily*, July 19, 1957, based on Retail Research Center Studies, Graduate School of Business, University of Pittsburgh, 1963–1965.

deficits; and deprecates the need for economy and efficiency in government.

The myths are recited with varying degrees of sophistication. On the one hand they range from expressions of concern over growing governmental centralization to warnings of impending national bankruptcy; on the other they range from suggestions of an economic slowdown to predictions that America will lose its preeminence in the world economy.[13]

In the realm of taxation, the high taxes placed on liquor, cigarettes, and gambling, and the health warnings on cigarette packages are illustrations of the discouragement of selected spending. Where the sales tax also applies to food purchases may be considered a similar category. Governing bodies, which are constantly seeking new ways of securing tax money, overlook or are lax in permitting many inequities to develop over time. In some cases where necessities are considered luxuries by the lawmakers, they are also selectively taxed as an excise. An example is gasoline, which today is really a necessity, not a luxury; another is the lumping of baby powder with exotic perfumes as a cosmetic.

Nevertheless, it is the *ultimate consumer* who must always foot the bill and pay taxes in the total purchase price of what he wants. This applies, whether or not taxes are included separately as an addition to the final price. Only in the case of excise and sales tax is there a clear-cut statement as to the nature of the actual additive tax.

The firm that either collects or pays taxes incurs handling costs. This process has a bearing on the firm's legal structure, on its location, and its business policies.

The farther back in the channel that a tax is imposed, the greater the resulting burden at the consumer level, because each functionary in the channel must base his selling price on the total input cost of his purchase.

Most excise taxes were repealed in June 1965. This repeal tends to increase sales volume. When and if excise taxes are re-enacted, sales volume decreases.

In January 1966, there was a 1-per-cent increase in the Social Security tax schedule of individuals to pay for Medicare. It is estimated that this tax will decrease the total disposable personal income some $5.5 billion.[14]

Tax legislation influences the legal form of organization, especially where taxable versus nontaxable exchanges are involved—for example, when depreciable property is transferred. Real property is not affected.[15]

[13] *The Brookings Bulletin*, Vol. 4, No. 2, Summer 1965, Washington, D.C. See also David J. Ott and Attiat F. Ott, "Federal Budget Policy," and James A. Maxwell, "Financing State and Local Governments," The Brookings Institution, Washington, D.C. In these recent publications federal policies and programs which affect employment opportunities and disposable income are discussed. In the Maxwell book, the expenditures and taxing policies of state and local governments which spend more than twice as much as the federal government in nondefense services are reviewed from the standpoint of cost emanating primarily from local sources. Other Brookings publications on public policies and investments are by Robert Dorfman, "Measuring Benefits of Government Investment," and Herbert C. Morton (ed.) "Brookings Papers on Public Policy," Washington, D.C., May 1965.

[14] "Taxes, 1965," *Forbes*, December 15, 1964, pp. 15–17.

[15] See Internal Revenue Code Sec. 1245, enacted as part of the 1962 Revenue Act. See also Robert H. Raymond and Clifford M. Hicks, "Federal Taxes and the Legal Form of Small Firms," *Management Research Summary*, Washington, D.C., 1963.

MAINTENANCE OF COMPETITION

Full dependence upon the effectiveness of the antitrust laws in implementing antitrust policy is not enough for the preservation of competition. Adequate supplies of goods to insure buyer's markets are also necessary. The maintenance of competition as a public economic policy is an evolution of the theoretical concepts of Adam Smith, David Ricardo, and other classical economists; their dicta are still used in the social control of industry.

In recent years it has become quite fashionable in many academic and business circles to assume that the competitive system of enterprise is on its way out. Close-range analysis of the economic positions of many private sectors in the economy has led many economists to assume the eventual development of a collective society. Indeed, it might be argued that there is no longer any high degree of interfirm competition at a retail level—the last remaining semblance of open competition. Such arguments are generally based on the fact that there exists a surprising degree of similarity in price and offerings in practically all market areas—discount-house and new market entries notwithstanding.

Yet the economic effectiveness of the independent merchant has not diminished significantly. Most of these firms are small and are maintaining their share of the market, as shown by Figure XLI. During the last three decades, the number of retail establishments has varied around 1.75 million with only minor proportionate changes in volume accruing to chains and multiunit firms.[16]

Today, there are approximately 4.7 million out of a total of some 4.9 million firms classified as "small" by the SBA. These are described as "self-initiated, largely self-financed, and self-managed." In order to help small businesses, the SBA has a loan program, technical advisory services, and educational programs to help them compete more effectively. In the fall of 1965, the National Bureau of Standards provided the SBA with further data on existing business structures so that more assistance would be available to help creative managers of small business.[17]

In maintaining competition, there are still exploitation policies of competitive firms to be supervised by the Federal Trade Commission (FTC). Confiscatory inheritance and tax policies have led to the growth of foundations. Constant supervision of corporate finances by regulatory agencies such as the Securities and Exchange Commission and permissive applications of investment banking procedures by individual states are not fully in the public domain. Thus these must be regulated outside the pale of competitive enterprise as we know it today.

The government is committed through various interpretations of antitrust legislation—starting with the Sherman Antitrust Act of 1890—to the preservation of competition and competitive enterprises. This policy has been only moderately successful, because the criteria for evaluating monopoly keep changing, along with

---

[16] See Table 6, Chapter 3. Note this number of establishments, despite the elimination of establishments generating less than $20,000 annual volume in the 1954 Census of Business.
[17] "A Future for Small Business," *Business Week*, July 31, 1965, pp. 35–38.

FIGURE XLI
SMALL BUSINESS PROJECTIONS*

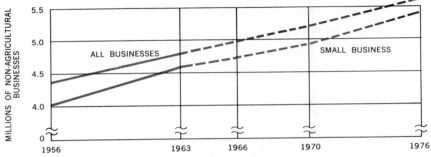

Data: Commerce Dept.; National Planning Assn., BW ests.

LESS OPPORTUNITY FOR THE SMALLER FIRM IN MANUFACTURING

TOTAL VALUE ADDED BY LARGEST COMPANIES IN MANUFACTURING

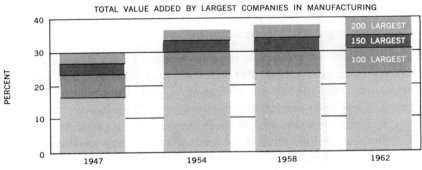

Data: Commerce Dept.

PROPORTIONATE BUSINESS—CHAIN STORES

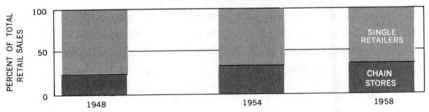

Data: Commerce Dept.; U.S. Congress—House Select Committee on Small Business

SERVICE EXPENDITURES

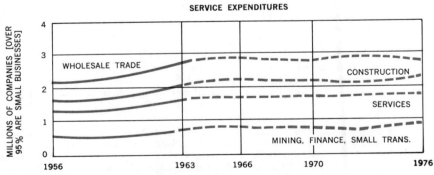

Data: Commerce Dept.; National Planning Assn. ests.

* Developed from Business Week, "A Future for Small Business," July 31, 1965, p. 35.

483

court interpretations and philosophies of government. For example, when a firm has grown very large it may possess concentrated strength and contain a potential for monopolistic characteristics; however, size, per se, is no longer the principal criterion for antitrust action. The size of the market share of the firm is more deterministic of market concentration than market power or "follow-the-leader" pricing policies.

Direct social control of industrial systems presents many difficulties and dangers. The sheer unfairness of many policies of the large firms in their explanation of price competition also indicates much to be desired.[18]

For example, many individuals in top managerial echelons feel that there is an excessive preoccupation and concern with measuring concentration in relatively narrowly defined markets when the world is undergoing a change in the scope of markets comparable to the great change of the turn of the twentieth century.[19]

Dependence on Regulatory Agencies

Within the domain of regulation are interpretations of various kinds of what constitutes price discrimination. For example, in June 1963, the United States Supreme Court ruled that the use of trading stamps is not a price reduction but constitutes a cash discount. This directly affects "Fair-traded" items and still permits stores to discriminate on the price of such items. The Supreme Court has also ruled that a seller's charging of different prices to customers in different parts of the country also constitutes price discrimination.[20]

The issues at stake are still highly controversial. Sections 2 (d) and (e) of the Clayton Act deal directly with discriminations in the field of "promotional services" through cooperative advertising allowances—in other words, varying "discounts" for the purchasers of products who resell the articles they buy. There has been violation of the law if a buyer induces a discriminatory "promotional allowance" as distinguished from a "price concession." [21]

---

[18] See A. R. Burns, "The Anti-Trust Laws and the Regulation of Price Competition, New and Contemporary Principles," Duke University, School of Law, Vol. IV, No. 3, June 1937, pp. 301–20; and F. M. Westfield, "Regulation and Conspiracy," *The American Economic Review*, Vol. LV, No. 3, June 1965, pp. 424–44.

[19] From a monograph by John J. Scott, entitled "Antitrust and Bigness," General Counsel, Socony Mobil Oil Co., Inc., June 1965.

[20] The selling prices of Anheuser-Busch, Inc. to St. Louis customers in 1954 and 1955, in contrast to Busch's other customers elsewhere, constituted discrimination, it was ruled. The Court was quick to add, however, that as long as price discrimination is not in bad faith, it is legal.

[21] See also James J. Bliss, "The Real Issue in the Co-op Ad. Controversy," *Stores*, July–August 1962, NRMA, New York City. Mr. Bliss comments specifically,

In situations where the seller pays the buyer for performing the service, Section 2 (d) applies; where the seller furnishes the service itself to the buyer, 2 (e) applies. In either case, the requirement is that the seller treat all competing customers on proportionally equal terms.

In recent decisions,

the Second Circuit Court of Appeals ruled, in the Grand Union Co. and American News Co. cases that despite the omission of buyers in Sections 2 (d) and (e), the inducement by purchasers of favored advertising allowances is "unlawful" under Section 5 of the Federal Trade Commission Act as an "unfair trade practice." In these decisions, the court acknowledged that Robinson-Patman applied only to sellers but concluded that this omission was more "inadvertent" than "studious." A similar conclusion was reached recently

Many of the legal requirements of cooperative advertising extensions are vague and uncertain; however, in no sense should it be construed that advertising allowances have become illegal.

Another area where price discrimination often occurs is in the manufacturer's offering of co-op advertising to selected customers.

In a study of the effect of the Robinson-Patman Act on competition, it was found that the Federal Trade Commission's supervision and regulation of the Robinson-Patman Act was generally in the public welfare and was constructively enforced.[22]

Finally, the effect of surveillance and enforcement policies of the Commission has been to encourage voluntary compliance. At the same time, the Commission has indicated that it would seek voluntary compliance from intrastate firms as well as those interstate in character.[23]

EFFECT OF MERGERS AND ACQUISITIONS

Today, independent firms combine for the purpose of strengthening their total effectiveness. By scientific market management and the pooling of their knowledge and resources, independents feel that they can compete more effectively. This is essentially the type of approach used by larger chains through their buying offices; in these offices, systems of vertical and horizontal integration are developed, and specialized management is used throughout the resulting organization.

Independents combine also to secure wider markets, a firmer base, and additional economic retail locations which follow population concentrations that are highly mobile in character. If a suburban movement becomes sizable, new stores must move in. Existing stores and plants must follow, and provide the convenience factor in shopping that customers demand. Failure to expand merely invites other entries into the market. Often the capital needed to expand into new market areas may force a merger. The need to provide a market for the owner-

---

by another Court of Appeals decision involving Giant Foods, Inc. These cases, as yet, have not been reviewed by the U. S. Supreme Court.

    In effect, therefore, the FTC and the courts have invoked "catch-all" Section 5 of the FTC Act to apply the provisions of Sections 2 (d) and (e) of the Robinson-Patman Act to buyers as well as sellers.

[22] John R. Davidson, "A Study of the Effect of the Robinson-Patman Act upon Cooperative Advertising Policies and Practices," unpublished doctoral dissertation, Graduate School, Ohio State University, Columbus, Ohio, 1959. Professor Davidson reviewed and analyzed the Robinson-Patman Act's effect on maintaining competition from the standpoint of price discrimination generally, and with pseudo brokerage charges and disproportionate cooperative advertising services and allowances specifically. He concluded, further, that the Act has had a salutary effect in reducing the dangers of competitive abuses in our economy. Its language has permitted interpretation and application to changing competitive conditions.

    The Commission's enforcement policy and the promulgation of trade practice rules exert a wholesome influence upon present-day users, thereby enhancing the favor and trust with which vertical cooperative advertising practices are viewed. The solution of problems of present-day abuses lies in the use of effective administrative procedures.

[23] For instance, in a drive to organize employees in the Famous-Barr Company (a subsidiary of the May Department Stores) in St. Louis, the NLRB ruled that the mere commuting travel of an elevator operator who resided just across the Mississippi River (less than two miles from the store) automatically made the company an interstate one.

ship shares in independent firms also induces firms to merge or to be bought.[24] Other alternatives inducing mergers are gifts before death, survivor purchase agreements, and stock retirement plans.[25]

Today, merger and combination movements are taking place in all industries as well as in retail firms. As combinations increase, the preservation of economic freedom and competition becomes a very important part of total economic progress, especially for the consumer. In many areas throughout the country competition is no longer a vital factor.

Unfortunately, workable competition does not continue in accordance with Adam Smith's stipulations of the "invisible hand." As pointed out, government legislation has been initiated in order to preserve competition, not to hamper it. Often, lack of business regulation and a laissez-faire attitude leads to a stifling of competition, not its promotion. In the complete competitive system of enterprise when marginal firms are eliminated from the market, those remaining tend to combine and restrict their competitive scope.

For example, in August 1965, Federated Department Stores, Inc., of Cincinnati, Ohio, signed a consent order with the Federal Trade Commission that forbids it to make certain acquisitions for five years from the date of signing without specific FTC advance approval. Other department stores reputed to be on the FTC list for limitation and scope of further acquisitions are Allied Stores, Inc., New York, after its acquisition of Wolff & Marx Company, San Antonio, Texas.[26]

The Evaluative Aspect

A good criterion in the evaluation of mergers and combinations as well as competition is, "Will it benefit the consumer's long-run interests?"

For example, the consumer today is faced with all manner of oligopolistic and monopolistic practices. In addition, there is a "beneficial" monopoly of size in a merger, which may be economic and result in improved effectiveness, not restraint in the market place. For example, the larger firm in striving for efficiency stresses rapid turnover at a lower gross margin as a more effective means of competing. Such procedures, of course, benefit both the market functionary as well as the consumer. This is not so when a firm engages in "umbrella" pricing practices.

PRICE AND TIME MONOPOLY

Firms survive and prosper at the retail level on both a competitive and a monopolistic basis. No two trading areas are exactly alike. In analyses of consumption patterns, it has been found that the degree of competition at the retail level varies

---

[24] The Rike-Kumler Company of Dayton, Ohio, an eminently successful and dominant firm in south central Ohio, merged with Federated Department Stores, Inc., and primarily for this purpose.
[25] For the alleviation of hardship when businesses dissolve or merge, much pressure has been applied to reduce estate tax rates and mitigate rulings which impede small businesses.
[26] Women's Wear Daily, August 11, 1965, pp. 1, 59.

greatly from one type of store to another and from one trading area to another.

In any economy where supply exceeds demand and where there is a multiplicity of substitutable brands and items on the market, price monopoly is not possible, except for selected new products or innovations—and these not for long periods of time.

However, temporary monopolies can be fostered wherein discriminatory terms, conditions, prices, and advertising allowances are given in violation of the Robinson-Patman Act.[27]

The legal form of price monopoly has been that set up under "Fair-Trade" agreements. This type of legislation has been attempted at both the state and federal levels for more than thirty years. Almost half the forty-five states (except Missouri, Texas, and Vermont) which originally enacted "Fair-Trade" laws have either repealed or altered them significantly. A new "Fair-Trade" law, under the name of the "Quality Stabilization Approach," is presently under consideration in both Houses of the federal government. As before, the justification for such legislation is the protection of the small retailer. This reasoning contradicts the Department of Justice's statistics which show more small business bankruptcies in states with "Fair-Trade" laws than without them.[28]

As to time monopolies, state and local governments have been involved in the enforcement of Sunday Blue Laws, where business and service establishments are forced to remain closed. While such legislation may be based on religious grounds, it serves to eliminate time competition.

Another form of time monopoly that is growing in competitive importance is the choice of opening and closing hours on bases other than those set by large stores or chains. The rescheduling of open hours is most often encountered in the food field.

Competitive effectiveness and real profitability are generated only when the price offerings of a firm fluctuate within relatively narrow ranges, time monopolies notwithstanding.

Where time monopolies really pay off is in the new highway locations with parking facilities that do not depend on retail affinities but on growing access and egress to highways. Many of these new outlets which are permitted to stay open on Sunday and late in the evening carry increasingly wider inventory diversifications. Such outlets are expanding faster than new shopping centers.

---

[27] Further practices which affect price competition occur whenever only one competitor receives exclusives, preferences, and discriminations in both price and other treatment, refusals to sell and granting of return policy, retail price maintenance, no charge for unsold merchandise and consignment, limiting colors and numbers, advance sales, high minimum requirements, late shipments and losses.

[28] "Price Fixing by Stealth and Guile," Consumer Reports, October 1963, pp. 462–63. Much evaluative analysis in the area of price maintenance under the former Miller-Tydings Act (1937) and the McGuire Act (1951) and now the present series of attempts at re-enactment is being made by Dr. Joseph M. Klamon, Professor of Marketing, Washington University. See also Phillip Almarin, Market Structure, Organization, and Performance (Cambridge: Harvard University Press, 1962); P. W. S. Andrews and Frank A. Friday, Fair Trade: Resale Price Maintenance Reexamined (London: Macmillan & Co. Ltd., 1960); James J. Bliss and Ira M. Millstein (eds.), Manual of Federal Trade Regulations Affecting Retailers (NRMA, New York: 1963).

LOCATIONAL AND FRANCHISE MONOPOLIES

With the advent of paved road networks, very few locational monopolies remain. Customer mobility is such that comparative prices must be "in line." When significant price differentiations occur in comparable commodities, consumers merely drive elsewhere to shop.

Of greater significance is the merchandising monopoly, where certain lines or certain brands are handled on an exclusive basis by franchised firms. The franchise system itself is also being attacked today as restrictive. This is within the purview of Sections 1 and 2 of the Sherman Act and Clayton Act, not the Robinson-Patman Act. Most proscriptions regarding exclusive franchises or refusal to deal are representative of "any conspiracy, combination, contract in restraint of trade," and of Section 2 of the Sherman Act which states: "attempts to monopolize, conspiracies to monopolize, and monopolizing any part of trade and commerce is illegal."

Exclusive brands, high-fashion items, and private branding help to avoid direct price competition, because no two items are exactly comparable. Only when products can easily be substituted for one another are merchandising monopolies along these lines justified.

In many cases, merchandise line or brand exclusives may represent the principal means of building up store prestige image—a vital necessity for many retail stores. As pointed out above, this is not legal under the Sherman Act. Yet sub rosa exclusives are constantly being given. In pending litigation, the legality of the entire franchise system is being tested in the Supreme Court.[29]

LEGISLATION AFFECTING DISTRIBUTION

Congress is continually being besieged for legislative help, especially in the field of distribution and particularly on the question of exclusive territories. A bill now pending would give "non-dominant" companies the right to segregate their markets among their own distributors. Legislation along these lines was spearheaded by the antitrust attack against General Motors Corporation, who allegedly violated the Sherman Act by discouraging its dealers from selling to and through auto discounters. The action was initiated as a result of General Motors' attempt to force dealers to live up to franchise agreements.[30]

---

[29] The entire issue is somewhat clouded, as the Supreme Court in the White Motor Company case refused to declare illegal per se geographical restrictions which White assigned to its dealers. Justice William J. Brennan, Jr., added that this would make it necessary "for a manufacturer to subdivide his sales territory in order to ensure that his product will be adequately advertised, promoted, and serviced." And he agreed with Douglas that "we do not know enough of the business stuff out of which these arrangements emerge to be certain how they fit into the antitrust picture." "Is the Franchise System Legal?" *Business Week*, April 3, 1965, pp. 66–68.

[30] *Ibid.* See also Stanley C. Hollander, *Restraints Upon Retail Competition* (East Lansing, Mich.: Bureau of Business Research, Graduate School of Business, Michigan State University 1965). Professor Hollander concludes that in essence what is being sought by legislation affecting distribution is "a policy which can best serve the American consumer" (p. 90).

In other, similar litigation, various apparel trade associations have always frowned on the practice of quantity discounts, advertising allowances, and subsidies for retailers and resident buying offices. Much of the pressure for the enactment of the Robinson-Patman Act came from sources such as these, because it was felt that discriminatory procedures were contrary to the spirit of their trade regulations. It is a fact that more often than not that "the greater strength of legal suasion over voluntary agreement is notable." [31]

In effect, there are four general types of legislation which affect distribution: these may be classified into major, minor, federal, and state and local. This legislation is largely designed for the consumer interest. Typical examples are:

1. *Major:* antitrust legislation, tariffs, maintenance of competition, the Pure Food and Drug Act.
2. *Minor:* factory, warehouse, and store inspection, safety and sanitary conditions.
3. *Control Without Ownership:* Federal Trade Commission Act, Federal Communications Commission, Antitrust Division of the Department of Justice.
4. *Government Ownership:* Tennessee Valley Authority, Post Exchanges.

In the administration and regulation of legislation, the following procedural and miscellaneous considerations are involved: [32]

1. *Regulation of Monopolistic Methods*
   a. Market Control and Collusive Practices
   b. Market Exclusion Tactics
2. *Regulation of Products*
   a. Product Standards and Quality
   b. Packaging and Conditions of Offer
3. *Regulation of Price Competition*
   a. Price Discrimination and Control
   b. Resale Price Maintenance (where applicable)
4. *Regulation of Channels of Distribution*
   a. Exclusive Dealing Arrangements, Franchises
5. *Regulation of Unfair Competition*
   a. Truth in Advertising
   b. Promotional Discounts

Other government regulations of business are:

I. *Methods of Government Regulation*
   A. Enforcement of competition
   B. Regulation of competition
   C. Managerial functions
   D. Investigations of practices
   E. By taxation
   F. Prices and production
   G. By standards of quality
   H. By yardstick of government competition
II. *Market Management*
   A. Commerce clause, Constitution
      1. Interstate and intrastate commerce

[31] In an early column of Samuel Feinberg, *Women's Wear Daily,* New York.
[32] Classification developed from "Legal Developments in Marketing" section of *The Journal of Marketing.* Steuart H. Britt (ed.). See especially July 1965 issue, Vol. 29, No. 3, pp. 67, 71.

III. *Principles of Federal Legislation*
  A. Sherman Act, 1890
    1. Original antitrust act
    2. Interpreted too narrowly
  B. Clayton Act, 1914
    1. Amended Sherman Act
    2. Declared certain acts in restraint of trade
  C. Federal Trade Commission Act, 1914
    1. Declared unfair method of competition unlawful
    2. Set up enforcing commission
  D. Robinson-Patman Act, 1936
  E. Fair-Trade Laws: Miller-Tydings Act, 1937; McGuire Act, 1951
    1. Amends Clayton Act
    2. Legalizes certain resale price maintenance contracts
  F. Lea-Wheeler Act, 1938
    1. Amends Fed. Trade Com. Act
    2. Broadened powers of commission to cover unfair or deceptive acts. Covers truth in advertising
  G. Wagner Labor Act, 1935
     Taft-Hartley Act, 1947
    1. Right to organize, bargain
    2. Defined unfair labor practices
    3. Set up NLRB
  H. Fair Labor Standards Act, 1938
     Full Employment Act, 1946
     Equal Opportunity Act, 1965
    1. Minimum wage and maximum hours
  I. Fed. Food, Drug, and Cosmetics Act
    1. Adulteration, labeling, packaging
    2. Misleading advertising
  J. Wool Products Labeling Act, 1939

IV. *State Legislation*
  A. Business and Occupational Restrictions: Optical goods, drug products, convict-made goods, firearms
  B. Resale Price Agreement Laws (California—1931): Fair-Trade Acts to 1951 (45 states)
  C. Unfair Practices Acts: Prohibits sales below cost
  D. Antidiscrimination Acts: state version of Robinson-Patman Act
  E. Wages and Hours legislation
  F. Unemployment and Workmen's Compensation Laws
  G. Black and White Laws, "Blue Sky" Ordinances
  H. Food, Drug, and Cosmetic Laws
  I. Free Goods and Premium Laws
  J. Sample Laws
  K. Advertising
  L. "Anticonsumer discount" Acts

V. *Municipal Laws*
  A. Fire Regulations
  B. Zoning Regulations
  C. Traffic Regulations
  D. Public Health Laws
  E. Building regulations

GOVERNMENT AS A FACTOR IN PRODUCTION AND BUSINESS

Government in any modern economy is a factor in production by claiming a distributive share of the fruits of production, as do land, labor, capital, and management. From the standpoint of economic bargaining and control, government regulates the forces of action over competition. The government is a monopolist, in the sense that it does not have to bid for trade or to force price levels in either direction. Essentially, government is a neutral factor in business and in favor of the consumer because, in any society, everyone is a consumer.

However, the government might step into an adverse situation and encourage cooperatives, where a so-called competitive framework is not working in the consumer interest. For instance, in Europe and in some areas of the United States, consumers have organized in order to eliminate the middleman's profit, thus hoping to lower costs. However, as a proven marketing principle, although it is always possible to eliminate the middleman, it is never possible to eliminate his function. Only when the middleman's functions are inefficient will consumer movements seeking more efficient distribution succeed. As a result, only limited success has been achieved in the United States, because price fixing and restrictive markets are not commonplace at the retail level.[33]

Individuals are responsible to the law, and must take the responsibility of participants in a free, democratic society. In a similar manner, corporations as separate legal entities are responsible, and have "personal responsibility" in a form of extension of the individual rights of their owner-stockholders. The corporation today clearly recognizes the government as a factor in production and a business determinant. As a result, our system of enterprise is a proven success of "our mutual-consent cooperative free enterprise system." [34] In turn, government and society recognizes the corporation's rights to private property as a means of efficient production of socially desirable and economically wanted goods.

Businessmen are interested in government insofar as changes of policy may result in new legislation. For example, the creation of small loan companies legislation under the sponsorship of the Russell Sage Foundation in 1914 has enabled hundreds of thousands of consumers to make ends meet in times of stress.

Also in the development of business enterprise the government protects inventors with patents and artists with copyrights, furnishes marketing aids for all businesses and statistical criteria for better development and growth.

In effect, business activity under constitutional law is subject to the dicta of legislative bodies who have the power to make "reasonable" laws under the "police powers" of the state. As pointed out, most legislation affecting business is essentially designed to protect competition and the public health and welfare. For example, minimum wage legislation now also applies to almost all employers.

Interrelationship with Trade Associations

Trade associations may be defined as a group of competing, independent members who operate in similar levels of enterprise; the association becomes the spark plug or clearing house for increasing over-all productivity, making store planning more effective, and furnishing store management with more scientific guides in

---

[33] To be successful, consumer movements should be based on homogenous groups of individuals living in contiguous areas; community organizations along these lines would necessitate democratic control and cash sales at prevailing market prices. In the United States today there are approximately 44,000 consumer cooperatives, two-thirds of them in the field- and farm-store categories, and one-third food stores. More than half of the cooperatives in existence are located in the Middle West and in smaller towns and cities, although there has been some growth in this direction in suburban areas. As long as retail and wholesale enterprise remain competitive, there is little likelihood of any significant expansions in this direction, despite government sponsorship.

[34] Rodman C. Rockefeller, "The New Nature of Corporations" (Business Week, July 17, 1965), p. 100.

the solving of individual business problems. Trade associations vary from chambers of commerce, with a part-time secretary, to those of a particular industry and of great size.

Some larger associations combine retailers, wholesalers, and manufacturers whose operating methodology creates a continuing interaction in a restricted area.[35] Especially in the field of retail distribution, trade associations have developed standard accounting practices, means for cooperative advertising, and methodologies for the standardization of activities. They also act as a watchdog on legislation likely to be detrimental to their interests.

More than ever, businessmen are combining through trade associations and trade practice rules (the latter under government sponsorship). As business competitors entrepreneurs are forbidden to organize or "conspire" in restraint of trade. However, they can exchange ideas and facts on a common interchange basis—even regarding the handling of new merchandise lines or on the general "opening up" of new locations. The government encourages such interchanges in order to improve competitive effectiveness without market chaos.

The development of the Harvard Reports, the MOR Statistics of the NRMA, the Federal Reserve Bank publications and trade association statistics have all been instrumental in fostering increasing cooperation tending toward greater efficiency and at the same time greater operating similarities. The area of teamwork in business not only pertains to improvement in business operations but also to those involved in lobbying for protective purposes. Today, the interchange of ideas and information does help to improve organizational efficiency—especially in production costs, labor relations, market management, and public relations.

Regardless of the trade association, the total over-all objectives are purported to improve ethical standards of business and of competition in the markets wherein member firms operate. Unfortunately, more often than not trade associations attempt to act in building up "private preserves" through lobbying in legislatures.

The legislative activities of trade associations range all the way from merely presenting a point of view to state legislatures to lobbying for major bills. Their activities are often suspect: especially when suggestions in the area of pricing and market segmentation are presented. Service groups such as Rotary Clubs and Better Business Bureaus seek to improve ethical practices in business operations, especially creditability and honesty in local media advertising.[36]

SUMMARY AND CONCLUSIONS

In this chapter the interaction of government and business and their underlying economic philosophies were examined from the standpoint of the government's

---

[35] Classifications may be by region (national, state, or local); by membership alone; or by the marketing of a single line of products. As far back as 1911, trade associations began to control business under the Eddy Formula. (This consisted of the interchange of information, exact knowledge of market conditions, and intelligent use of information acquired. Thus, the effects of competition were tempered.)

[36] H. H. Maynard and W. Weidler, *Introduction to Business Management* (4th ed., New York: Ronald Press, 1951), p. 522.

stake in efficient distribution. The manner in which governmental policy objectives operate to further competition was also analyzed.

It was pointed out that size, per se, is no longer undesirable. There are many instances where large-scale enterprise is not only desirable but would act to maintain high levels of productivity and pass such savings on to the public in the form of lower prices. A high social premium is created by lower prices, regardless of whether the underlying motivations of such pricing policies are to maintain or increase market share. The performance, behavior, or ethical rationality of a firm in meeting the consumer interest are far more crucial aspects for examination than those of size alone.

As an aspect of competition, the regulatory aspects of the Robinson-Patman Act were reviewed. It was brought out also that so-called "Fair-Trade" legislation creates artificial price levels which cannot be maintained in any competitive system in the long run.

Government and business now interact in almost every sphere: equal employment opportunities, "voluntary" programs by businessmen and banking interests, the war against poverty, science and technology in economic development. In taxation and certain public policy areas, friction continues. Nevertheless the traditional free-enterprise economy and economic freedom is now for all intents and purposes a "voluntary" partnership.

Thus there are no longer any simple divisions between government and business. The wide diffusion of ownership and control of business in our pluralistic society means that there has begun a merging of goals between business, government, and society.

In conclusion, as the interrelationships of government and business increase, the complex interacting variables of government must also be weighed and evaluated as precursors to top management decision making and problem solving. Such variables are parts of the function of executive leadership everywhere.

Chapter 29: *Executive Leadership and Adaptation to Change*

Management is everywhere the function of executive leadership, which is vital to the success of any enterprise or organization. To be effective, executive leadership must adapt to change in much the same manner as it adapts to changing business conditions and solves its problems.

Executive management must not only be concerned with the enterprise itself but also, and to an even greater extent, with its external setting as a socioeconomic institution in the business community. In other words, executive management today must be a pervasive force not only in the firm which it leads but throughout the community in which it operates. This involves creative planning, which is a logical staff development in administrative management as a firm continues to grow.[1]

---

[1] See also R. C. Davis, *The Fundamentals of Top Management* (New York: Harper and Row, 1963). See also Malcolm P. McNair (A. B. Smith, ed.), *Competitive Distribution in a Free High-Level Economy and Its Implications for the University* (Pittsburgh, Pa.: University of Pittsburgh Press, 1958). In this discussion, the changing role of distribution in the economy is reviewed.

PROFESSIONALISM IN EXECUTIVE LEADERSHIP

Creative planning involves potential alternative moves to meet change and market uncertainties. Since the turn of the century, increasing numbers of business firms have been managed by professional managers with their own sets of rules for business success. Professional management is a self-perpetuating society or class—much more so than any ownership groups of the past.

Professional executive leadership involves skill in meeting problems and ability to contribute knowledge. Within the province of market and retail management, satisfying consumer wants is a productive process. Professional management best meets the dynamic needs of the market place when the totality of its efforts is greater than the sum of all its parts.

Professional management develops an effective attitude on the part of the total organization in adjusting to consumer wants. The marketing management part of the productive process involves the total process in satisfying consumer wants.

Effectiveness, in a managerial economic sense, advances the art and science of marketing through the development of new concepts in market orientation and makes available new and useful products to the public. This is carried out without loss of the managerial viewpoint (the creative attitude necessary to inject innovations into marketing). An integrated management approach also means that this is carried out without loss of effectiveness in profitable operations.

No two firms operate similarly. Market managers must be aware of how best to meet market segmentations, channelized competition, and know the cost-profit potentials of meeting any and all market challenges.

This involves the realization that companies and products are not alike though they may have the same "designations." Basic to effective distribution is an understanding of the real nature of products (an understanding and a visualization of the product offer in terms of satisfaction to users)—not just their physical attributes. By this means their correct management in the market is assured.

Management philosophy determines policy and action. For example, in Pittsburgh there are three major department stores, each with completely different policies and operating philosophies. Yet each is successful.[2] In the field of market and retail management, there are no clear-cut policy areas for any community—the variables are primarily qualitative and not quantitative.

In the entire framework of executive leadership, manufacturers, wholesalers, and retailers must thoroughly understand that marketing is productive, not parasitic, and contains important sociological, governmental, and psychological contributions to organized society.

The larger the organization, the more likely it is that its direction and control will be in the hands of professional administrative management. The gap between professional management and knowledgeable management consultants who work

[2] The Joseph Horne Co. (formerly an AMC, and now an Associated Dry Goods, affiliate), Kaufmann's (a May department store), and Gimbel Brothers Co. (research and observations by the author).

on an independent basis for many firms is narrowing. Both groups are generally capable of sizing up a problem, planning a program of action, and developing control and reappraisal plans. Executive leaders must not only be good "generalists," but they also boast particular specializations to be used as the basis for a particular philosophy of management and a springboard for action.

EFFECT OF SIZE OF FIRM AND SCALE OF PLANT

Effectiveness is no longer the natural concomitant of a large scale in plants or firms. As pointed out previously (in Chapters Two and Eleven), marginal analysis shows the applicability of the U-shaped cost curve as a basis for deciding on the firm's level of operation. The larger firms and those in growth cycles no longer have the wide flexibility of operating at the low end of the cost curve, as commonly supposed. That is one of the primary reasons for the cyclically recurring cost-profit squeezes in large-scale industries and retail firms. Because of organizational rigidities and inability to adapt to change, many large-scale enterprises create dis-economies rather than economies of scale.

In the smaller firm, decisions are made much more quickly and easily, fewer specialists are required, and there are better communications. The need for maximum coordination in the smaller firm is less, because most management people here are "generalists" and manage a number of functions rather than single specialized functions. As a result, continuing over-views of the operation are much more possible.

Coordination and communications are the two vital aspects of the present state of the science of the managerial arts for organizations of all sizes. Also, the greater the specialization of the executive manager, the more complex the views that have to be reconciled to create effective operations. Recognition of such decision variables required of management means recognition of the importance of scientific approach to decision making and problem solving.[3]

THE CHANGING ROLE OF EXECUTIVE LEADERSHIP

Executive leadership is much more than planning, activating, reappraising, organizing, and controlling business operations. To achieve these ends there are no simple sets of rules or policies that can be universally applied. For instance, there

---

[3] See also Mary S. C. Henderson, "Managerial Innovations of John Diebold," Washington, D.C.: LeBaron Foundation, 1965. In these texts, the science of information dissemination for use in systems technology of "bundles of functions" is reviewed as "adaptations to change." While this terminology is not used specifically, the implications are readily apparent. Decision behavior and problem solving under various conditions of risk and uncertainty are qualitatively and quantitatively reviewed. See also: William Fellner, *Probability and Profit* (Homewood, Ill.: Richard D. Irwin, 1965); Howard Raiffa and R. O. Schlaifer, *Applied Statistical Decision Theory* (Cambridge: Graduate School of Business Administration, Harvard University, 1961); John Von Neumann and O. Morgenstern, *Theory of Games and Economic Behavior* (2nd ed., Princeton, N. J.: Princeton University Press, 1947); Michael A. Wallach, Nathan Kogan, and Daryl J. Bem, "Group Influence on Individual Risk Taking," *Journal of Abnormal and Social Psychology*, Vol. 65, No. 2, pp. 75–86, for further elaboration on managerial uses of simulation techniques, probability theory, and underlying considerations for decision making.

is no one store policy for choice of location and type of store most economic for that location.

Today, with approximately 1,710,000 retail establishments, there are thousands of differing policies applied for solving essentially similar operating problems. Policies vary widely in handling of transportation, parking, delivery, and the avoidance of congestion—even for similar stores in similar locales. Policies must be flexible in order to adapt to change.

THE ORGANIC FUNCTIONS OF CHANGE

An organic function of management is one that is indispensable to the success of a business organization. Adjustment to change requires flexible policy formulation and administration. For example, the Western Electric distribution system in recent years has been put under tremendous pressure induced by changes in product-line characteristics and a revision of the Telephone Company's concept of the service they should expect.

Until recent years, also, communications equipment and products were largely utilitarian with differences in product characteristics closely related to function. Style and individuality (tailored service) have become important devices by which the Telephone Company has increased sales and, indeed, are the two areas where Western Electric is facing competition in its sales to its parent firms.

> The most basic job, then is to get customers for the Telephone Company, to help them turn public interest and orders into sales and revenue. As the public becomes harder to please, the company must focus increasing attention on the quality of the total distribution operation.[4]

Society is dynamic. Hence, all functionaries catering to or serving within a society must also be dynamic and must adapt to necessary social and industrial changes. An organic function defined as above means that successful adaptation to change then becomes an indispensable trait of executive leadership.

Policy is the governing principle and indicates not only the general manner of the business operation but also whether the business leader tends to make his decisions for the firm chiefly by intuitive methods of trial and error or by more "scientific" means. Any nonsystematic, inflexible basis of management—especially in retail markets—is not economic because the day-to-day market forces are dynamic and almost completely unpredictable.

Influence of Change on Objectives

A tremendous amount of catalogue business has been generated from urban and suburban areas, despite numbers of stores within easy reach. As a result, branch-store policies are today being completely re-evaluated, especially from the standpoint of merchandise lines handled and assortments and services offered.

---

4 W. F. Miller, "Decentralization and Intracompany Marketing Concepts," unpublished memorandum under the direction of the writer, Graduate School of Business, University of Pittsburgh, 1963.

The Pervasiveness of Change

Executive management in the retail firm can be said to use a social-physics approach to management. Problems are stated in terms of movement of resources, personnel, and materials and in creating satisfactions and utilities of higher values. In any concepts of social utility, standards are set up to develop measures of input-output relationships for representative firms. In the case of retail firms, measures are in terms of "Value Added."

The marginal rate of substitution and input-output ratio standards are based on the fact that comparisons between inter- and intra-firm performances are also valid and useful comparisons. In practice, efficiency in itself has little significance as a goal. However, profit maximization as the goal of a firm has real significance as a social utility concept. This is another evaluative criterion for effective executive leadership.

Pervasive change in a firm means much more than the legal, formal organizational relationships involved. For example, there are generally four types of change which are pervasive: obsolescence of cost, function, reliability, and style. Such changes require continuing managerial attention and adjustments.

Style obsolescence, for instance, except for fashion merchandise, is less critical in durables because their fashion and prestige status effect continues for much longer periods. What styles are in fashion have a much greater impact on soft lines where six to nine months lead time planning for change is basic to the success of the firm.

Another facet of executive planning is forecasting change in a firm's share of the market. Any upward movement in its share of the market is an indicator of the store's strength, competitive position, and potential for growth.

Pervasive changes in the market can be forecast well in advance. For example, in the income revolution there are "broad-middle" and upper-middle income group families who possess relatively high proportions of discretionary income.

With larger amounts of money in reserve than ever before, the first effect has been the "easing of normal extensions" of installment credit. Other changes in the "present-future" are growing psychological-sociological status changes in owning at least two cars, exceptionally good carpeting, good housing and furnishings, as well as "more-than-economic" durable goods in general. With the rise in the consumer's economic intelligence, newspapers, radio, television—in fact all communications media—are becoming more effective.

Economic intelligence as well as knowledge in the social and physical sciences has been increasing at a geometric rate especially during the last two decades. Because of higher real incomes, more leisure, and a greater availability of credit, consumers have almost completely changed their patterns of consumption. Executive leaders must evaluate and assess all such changes if they are to compete effectively.[5]

---

[5] Pervasive changes in trading areas are clearly illustrated by classification in the "life cycles" of consumers. In terms of stages, they could resemble the following:
　　1) The Bachelor Stage　　—young single people;

Change and Innovation

Changes in shopping habits, living patterns, social desires, and leisure time are continuing to force changes in store operating and merchandising policies. With changing demands in retail markets, great pressures have been generating to reduce costs, offer fewer services, and promote more cut prices. Firms that change their promotional policies in response to changing shifts in their demand schedules do so with the hope that they can thereby generate increases in economic sales.

Discount house innovations, scrambled merchandising techniques, innovations in selling, and strong promotions mail order selling have all been initiated in attempts to meet change. Where inflexibility, inability and unwillingness to meet change is overcome, executive management is able to maintain or improve the market position of its firm.

Goals of Consumer and Economic Units: Reactions, and Conflict

Consumers, too, seek to maximize. Consumers differ from firms in that they attempt to optimize satisfactions from relatively scarce amounts of disposable personal income. Each consumer buys on the basis of personal utility scales (utiles) as he seeks the most effective allocation of funds among various goods and services. Firms seek to maximize also, but their goals are primarily long-run profit maximization, a harshly rational goal.

Firms achieve their objectives by offering optimum packages of utilities to potential purchasers. Neither consumers nor business firms ever fully succeed in allocating resources in such a fashion so as to be completely efficient. Rather, both suppliers and buyers compromise in their attempts at maximands. The firm attempts to operate at points where marginal costs will equal marginal revenues and the consumer will purchase what is available at the "points of exhaustion."

The factor-owner suppliers of capital also seek to maximize returns for the money units which they supply to the business. While their objectives may seem to conflict directly with that of consumers and functional management, differences of taste and opinion happily permit feasible equilibrium solutions. Thus, economic factor units that are directly opposed—each feeling that their points of individual maximand have been reached—consummate transactions.

Employees of retail firms also strive to maximize their satisfactions. They demand the highest possible return in exchange for their labor units. Psychic and other nonmonetary returns must also be furnished by management if over-all satisfactions are to result. Thus all the "sellers" of factors of production, although

---

2) Newly Married Couples—young, no children;
3) The Full Nest I   —young married couples with dependent children;
4) The Full Nest II   —older married couples with dependent children;
5) The Empty Nest   —older married couples with no children living with them;
6) The Solitary Survivor —older single people.

Each of the groups has a different pattern of consumption, a differing goal, and must be catered to differently. (*Life Study of Consumer Expenditures*, Vols. 1 and 2, Alfred Politz Research, Inc., N.Y., 1957.)

seeking maximization of satisfactions, continually run the gauntlet of economic conflict. To exist, each must settle for compromise goals of satisfactions at points of equilibrium.

With respect to labor factor units equilibrium depends on the particular units of substitutable labor available in particular areas. In the case of investment units, the adequacy of competing investment opportunities determines the amount of funds available for loan to retail firms. With consumers, the conveniences involved in driving-time distances to stores determine the strength of a store's patronage motives. This means that the greater number of investment or purchase choices available to each investor or consumer serves to improve the satisfactions available for the entire system as a whole.

For example, individual workers have little control over working hours but relatively great control over the allocation of their disposable personal income. At the same time, workers as a group through unions do influence the length of the work day, work week, leisure time, and break periods. Likewise, satisfied consumers develop patronage preferences, although their attempts to maximize may be said to be in conflict with a firm's attempt to maximize. Yet stores which succeed in creating public values and customer satisfactions are assured of public support and business continuity, although creating better public values may be costlier.

BUSINESS AND COMMUNITY LEADERSHIP

The economic setting in which business operates provides mutually supporting productive action. Again this involves adaptation to change. This means that social responsibilities of business leaders everywhere cannot be relegated solely to those of just the firm itself and its customers. Social responsibilities involve much more than merely offering competitive salaries and fringe benefits for generating a favorable public image. The business leader must also be a business statesman in the community and a leader in the area of economic legislation.

Almost all the time, legislation is passed without many of those most directly affected being aware of its implications. Executives who head businesses tinged with strong public relations implications generally fear that too much political activity would seriously alienate many of their customers. This is probably one of the more important reasons for passivity in this field. However, political activity is fully justified and ties in directly with executive management's role in business and in the community.

In addition, executive managers should participate in community and welfare activities. This may involve, for example, acceptance of the chairmanship of the community-chest drive or the development of the local Red Cross. Participation is important in that it concerns the sense of legitimacy that any populace feels toward its own institutions and their leadership.[6] The sense of legitimacy, of course, is tied up with the feelings that individuals have and that are shared by

---

[6] Chadwick J. Haberstroh, "The Legitimacy of Managerial Authority," unpublished paper, College of Business Administration, University of Denver, February 1964.

large groups of people. A uniformity of opinion of people on very basic moral questions is the central concept of the ideologies of American society. Such concepts support the position of business managers everywhere. More specifically, in the community, the "organization man" could also be mentioned. The ethical codes of individual corporations are often too restrictive of the human rights of their employees. These are often violated both in the structured role of the organization man and his function as a community leader.

RESEARCH AS A MANAGERIAL STAFF FUNCTION

New techniques in OR, cybernetics, lead-time analysis, and administrative procedures in both executive and operative management are some of the research tools now being used. The value of research for practical applications can only be fully enhanced or exploited if the research directors are either part of the top management team or report directly to executive management. The research activities of a firm should not only cover immediate, short-range marketing problems, but should furnish the basis for all types of decisions.

Management also seeks recommendations for action from the results of past decisions based on similar problems. In essence, the effectiveness of the decision-making function of management depends on the quality of the information on which it is based. For example, staff investigations and analysis include a great many criteria. Some of those used to measure the effectiveness of individual divisions, departments or activities follow:

I. Methods of determining the objectives
   A. Primary objectives
      1. Various marketing research techniques
   B. Collateral and secondary objectives
      1. The questionnaire method of difficulty analysis
      2. Interview and observational methods based on:
         a. Comparative records by projects and organizational groups of:
            (1) Recurring interferences with performance
            (2) Actual results accomplished
         b. Executive statements concerning results that are being accomplished and their causes
      3. Morale surveys
II. Methods of investigating causes
   A. Formal methods
      1. The laboratory research techniques of the physical sciences
      2. The statistical research techniques of the social sciences
   B. Methods of functional analysis
      1. Organizational techniques of:
         a. Job analysis
         b. Time and duty study
      2. Procedural techniques of:
         a. Process or methods analysis
         b. Motion and time study

It is not enough for management to view such analyses on a "when-and-if" basis; there must be continuing evaluative research throughout the organization and its interacting markets.

Most executive leaders of business organizations are not scientists. Yet only through scientific and analytical investigations can their philosophies of management be correctly channeled. A philosophy of management is based on ideas. Most ideas are formulated haphazardly rather than logically. Often, decisions and policies are postponed, as the decision maker feels that the application of a solution to a problem would be only marginally useful. Thus, many decisions are made on an "as-needed" basis.

Planned research can provide executive management with the ability to protect or expand its share of the market. It can also provide management with a "running detail" on what time, what kinds, what areas, and at what prices sales and profits can be optimized. While it may be axiomatic to predict that discretionary consumer spending is bound to increase, exactly how and in what areas such expenditures will develop become the important criteria. Some pertinent areas for applications of research for management are:[7]

1) How to measure and compete effectively with new forms of competition as these appear.
2) How to develop productive innovations in the market place.
3) How and to what extent to utilize new approaches to market and marketing management.
4) How best to develop "marketing mix" for stores in differing markets.
5) How to make optimum use of operations research and other new techniques in policy formulations.
6) How most effectively to analyze branch-store profitability.
7) How best to handle contributions of particular merchandise lines and classifications.
8) To assess whether computer applications of distribution cost analysis are really helpful to the store's competitive position.
9) To find whether there are any real advantages to computer forecasting through the use of quantitative economic indicators, or of a single indicator.
10) To assess whether the firm is really adapting to change.

Unfortunately, many market organizations do not have formal market research departments and cannot carry out research. For example, in a market survey in 1963, more than one-half of the companies surveyed did not have formal research departments; in the others, research was integrated informally in various departments primarily in the central divisions. Further, a great many so-called research personnel were found to be low-level fact gatherers, lacking in either proper statistical or research backgrounds, or both.

---

[7] R. D. Entenberg, unpublished paper, College of Business Administration, University of Denver, 1963–1965.

SCIENTIFIC MANAGEMENT PROCESSES

Executive management also controls the organization by flexibly time-planning the attainment of organizational objectives.

Scientific planning involves the use of both theory and practice. A staff planner generally submits for evaluation as a prelude to action a program which includes strategy alternatives, program design, and the methodologies to be used as stimuli for action. Means and goals must be matched in terms of time.

In the design of any management system, the relationships between the systems concept and management should be set up in a flow design, showing accompanying constraints. For instance, a system set up as an organized, complex assemblage of parts must still form a unitary whole covering a totality of concepts. A firm is a complex system in an environment not unlike our mountain and river systems, or the solar system. The firm itself (like a body) is a complex organism including the skeletal system, the circulatory system, and the nervous system. The executive leader of the firm comes into daily contact with such phenomena as transportation systems, communication systems, and economic systems.[8]

Subsystems and Planning

Where there is a full-time corporate planner, he is generally responsible for presenting top management with the objectives, format, and other elements which constitute the guiding framework in any planning process. The detailed planning, of course, is generally carried out by major line managers. Once submitted, they should be reviewed and coordinated by the corporate planner and evaluated by top executive management.

Planning also involves an OR outlook by the firm's executive management. Feedback analysis and strategy reappraisals are all part of the planning process. Many firms use "sensitivity charts," like those used by quality-control engineers; these indicate when a deviation from previously set plans or criteria has occurred. With charts of sensitivity analysis, goal achievement becomes possible.

Thus planning in any scientific management process involves administrative control. In turn, control may be open- or closed-ended. Open-end control pinpoints strategy procedures for achieving stipulated functions. Closed-end controls involve the reappraisal processes of reintroducing into a system the differences between actual results and those planned. Administrative measures of control interact, supplement, and change from open to closed ends of control as organizational needs change.

---

[8] See also Richard A. Johnson, Fremont E. Kast, and James E. Rosenzweig, "Designing Management Systems," *The Business Quarterly*, Vol. 29, No. 2, Summer 1964, pp. 59–67. The authors also emphasize that the systems concept is a frame of mind—a willingness on the part of executives to accept a theory of subsystems integrated into a processing composite whole. Within such a framework a "resource-allocation" planning group and an operations planning group can carry out the work of the organization in an atmosphere of creativity and innovation (p. 65).

See also E. T. Grether, "An Emerging Apologetic of Managerialism?: Theory in Marketing 1964," *Journal of Marketing Research*, Vol. II, May 1965, pp. 190–95.

In experimental studies, relating planning activities to performance and attitude in the achievement of organizational goals, findings indicate that "participation and planning on one hand and morale and productivity on the other" show a strong positive relationship.[9] Thus executive management should permit organizational planning down to the lowest reasonable echelon.

More specifically, there is a sort of "law of averages truth" [10] that accompanies the use of the scientific method in management. The "truth" is based on the observation and classification of facts, which are then applied to the general laws resulting from accumulated specialized knowledge existing in pertinent decision areas. The development of laws and principles at all levels of an operation means that almost all management decision centers can be programed. In effect, applications of automation and cybernetic techniques represent the ultimate in scientific management.

In other studies of a more quantitative nature on managerial planning and its effect on decision optimization, combinations of mathematical equations and the computer are being used. The process is essentially one of simulating business policy in a framework of uncertainty. This kind of simulation technique is called a "venture simulator." The venture simulator permits the investigations of many combinations and permutations for possible managerial decisions, regardless of planning methods. Once carried out, such concepts of venture analysis can be applied to the firm's market strategy.[11]

In any scientific processes, the management report summaries are key guides. While the subjects covered may be multitudinous, the same general formats are used that are shown in Table 45. In each case, the more concise and brief is the report the better. At the same time, no important information should be omitted. The length of a management summary report should not exceed one page.

COORDINATION, DELEGATION, AND THE "ONE-MAN" ORGANIZATION

A good manager delegates authority and responsibility within the framework of organization goals. Responsibility means "a charge" for which an individual is accountable. Authority without responsibility results in weak management. Executive management can delegate the authority but remains ultimately responsible for the action of the subordinate to whom it has delegated. The fact that the subordinate accepts the task obliges him to do it, but does not relieve his superior of responsibility. All decision makers in an organization should have access to a body of information available to all executives. Further, the exact meanings of words should be defined so that the correct applications are conveyed at all times.

[9] Bernard M. Bass and Harold J. Leavitt, "Some Experiments in Planning and Operating," *Management Science*, Vol. 9, No. 4, July 1963. See also R. Likert, *New Patterns of Management* (New York: McGraw-Hill, 1961).

[10] Defined here as an empirical reality at a particular point in time.

[11] J. J. Tozzi and Paul E. Leitzinger, "A Theoretical Model for Managerial Decision Making," unpublished research memorandum, Retail Research Center, University of Pittsburgh, 1963. The authors point out that the output data from the "venture simulator" is no more accurate than the statistical parameter from which the mathematical equations are derived.

TABLE 45

ILLUSTRATION OF SUMMARY STAFF REPORT*

Subject:	Title of (research) report
Purpose:	Reason for writing the report—conditions initiating the investigation
Factual Data:	Subject involved, conditions of the problem, difficulties, brief statement of alternatives, and corresponding page references to body of the report that will permit quick verification of essential facts presented. No opinions. Single spaced, with line between subjects.
Conclusions:	Principal judgments concerning limiting factors and controlling principles. These judgments should flow logically from and be supported by essential facts presented above; of greater importance, the essentials must be worded so as to facilitate an actionable conclusion by management.
Recommendations:	This contains the researcher's opinion and suggestion of solutions that appear to hold the greatest promise of success. (Note: data developed from hypotheses presented and investigated should flow logically from and be supported by the facts.)

Submitted by:

_____

Director, Research

* Based on suggestions from Professor R. C. Davis, Ohio State University, Columbus, Ohio, 1954.

Executive coordination is the development and maintenance of a proper series of relationships among subordinate staff so that effective plans of action result. The larger the organization, the greater the need for coordination among the various specialized managerial groups in a store.

The coordination of staff functions is both a tool and an informational source of executive management; thus good management is directly dependent on effective staff coordination. The technical staff assists top management in creative planning in areas requiring their skill.

Executive coordination can represent either mental or physical control and the processing of directives in the order of their importance. In the smaller organization, control is exercised, more often than not, through a "one-man" organization. The one-man organization pays off only when planning and the proper delegation of authority takes place and the "principle of exception" (the bringing of only the most urgent problems directly to the attention of top management), is used, as it is in most retail firms. The method is desirable, and counteracts frequent— and often ill-advised—decisions made on the selling floor. It is used quite frequently as a typical *modus operandi* by most executives in retail firms. This occurs because of the frequency of decisions made on the "selling floor"—often without reference to policy.

From a psychological standpoint, the one-man organization is highly tinged with emotion. When emotions are involved in managerial decision processes, formal organizational procedures are rarely set up; in many such cases, authority and responsibility grow like Topsy—without planning. Such lack of planning creates limiting factors in the operation of the enterprise itself. For example, management training in the smaller organization comes into the picture often on the expediency basis of "seniority or trustworthiness," rather than on that of an individual's capabilities and potential.

THE INFORMAL ORGANIZATIONAL STRUCTURE

In the retail organization, both line and staff interact almost constantly on an informal basis, regardless of officially assigned responsibilities. Often, the interaction is so great that classifications into line or staff themselves become academic. There is also a constant intermingling of functions, organizational charts notwithstanding. With a very great deal of informal interaction at all organizational levels, the informal organization in the retail firm becomes a potent factor.

Whenever normal chains of command are blocked and stipulated spans of control are either bypassed or ignored, the formal organizational structure becomes an informal one. This can occur at any echelon in the firm.

The growth of the informal organization does not entail loss in organizational flexibility—flexibility in the ability to meet changing competition, varying work loads, and in the management of resources. Organizational flexibility is a prerequisite for developing optimum solutions for changing problems that arise; effective adjustments to change, as pointed out, call for the highest type of executive leadership. For example, temporary changes in business conditions should be matters of calm and rapid adjustment. In many firms, when a cost-profit squeeze occurs, its management insists on strict adherence to operating policy. This in turn increases organizational rigidity, and as a consequence, operating effectiveness is lost.

The understanding of the use of standards—such as financial and operating ratios—assists executive management in finding the best and most rapid way of adapting to change.

ECONOMIC MANAGEMENT OF RESOURCE ALLOCATION

When new competitors and innovations enter retail markets, existing firms should re-evaluate all market policies for needed changes. When new competitors enter a market, overinvestment (in terms of "overstored" conditions) may be the initial impact.[12] During the initial period of growth, being in the right location, at the right time, with the right price, and with the right merchandise suffices. As a

---

[12] The Colorado Springs, Colo., area was such an "overstored" complex in 1965 because of the many new entrants into the market. It was estimated by the writer that it would take a minimum of two years, even under an accelerated growth pattern, for market demand to warrant the economics of the investment in the new and existing retail facilities. (Based on research studies of the area, supervised by the writer as Director of the Division of Research, University of Denver, April 1965.)

business grows, so should its profits, providing that overinvestment and over-expansion have not taken place.[13]

Incremental costs are a "sensitive" indicator of whether or not the rate of growth which a firm maintains is economic. The older the firm, the greater the managerial skills needed to maintain growth and profitability because of natural organizational rigidities that accompany age. When growth finally levels off, built-in costs of prior periods may become highly uneconomic. To isolate any additional, overoptimistic inputs costs, executive management should reassess the profitability of all incremental resource inputs.

The productivity of capital in any specific projection measures the cost of expansion. Such appraisals may involve as much as a twenty-year forecast. However, ten- to twelve-year forecasts are much more realistic.

One of the more acceptable methods by which such projections can be carried out is the discounted cash-flow method. In essence, this method measures the present impact of any capital outlay upon future earnings. Unless this is carried out, executive management may find that its capital outlays, costing 12 to 15 per cent, will go into projects producing only a 4- to 5-per-cent return.

Any investment which cannot project the existing rate of return for the firm should not be made unless market competition warrants the investment. This is often difficult to ascertain, because privately owned, rapidly growing companies often have fixed incumbrances in the form of long-term leases and repayments of so-called equity capital. Regardless of this, only the combined "cost of capital" should be the standard of comparison. On this basis, market data often show that the total cost of capital for new equity investments ranges from 12 to 15 per cent.

Thus management, through an "ordered weighing" of various alternatives allocates resource inputs and ties in forecasts of volume-profit outputs for the various alternatives. The process of ordered weighing of variables is set up in order to maximize the effectiveness of the firm's assets.

Resource allocation deals with the future. It is a form of preplanning set up in terms of likely consequences. Executive management makes such decisions in terms of maximizing the total effectiveness of the firm, not just a department or a branch. For example, resource allocations are made in plant or store space; in funds for particular decor, color and fixturing; and in personnel suitable to insure effective utilization of the space with an operations research approach—an awareness of the interrelationship of the part and the whole.

Executive management actually uses economic theory to arrive at decisions in the areas of resource allocations. Below are some of the principles (set up in aggregative form) used by executive management and controllers of many of the leading department stores, chains, and multi-unit stores throughout the United

---

[13] Joel Dean, "How to Meet the Rising Costs of Doing Business," Paper, Supermarket Institute, Chicago, 1959, p. 8.

States.[14] A descriptive model of the managerial decision process is shown in Figure XLII.

FIGURE XLII
DESCRIPTIVE MODEL:
USE OF ECONOMIC THEORY BY EXECUTIVE MANAGEMENT IN ALLOCATION OF RESOURCES

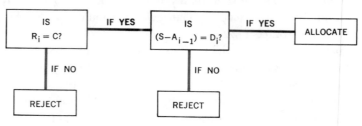

R_i = RATE OF RETURN ON THE PARTICULAR ALLOCATION
C = COST OF FUNDS TO THE FIRM
S = TOTAL SUPPLY OF AVAILABLE FUNDS
A = CUMULATIVE TOTAL OF FUNDS ALLOCATED FOR ALL PROPOSALS (i) TO DATE
D_i = DEMAND FOR FUNDS BY PROPOSAL (i)

CAPITAL BUDGETING DECISIONS

An important aspect of the allocation of resources is the bearing it has on investment decision. Every organization maintains lists of opportunities for investment of funds outside the organization. On the other hand, capital investment programs within the firm have differing criteria—for example, the payback period (the time required to cover the original investment). There are various types of projections for each kind of investment both outside and within the firm. (Projections are always experimental, because working conditions in the future may differ markedly from those in which the experiment was carried out.)

Nevertheless, executive management must plan and make decisions on the basis of planning projections. For example, in the area of capital budgeting, the allocation of funds can be reduced significantly if the performance of the firm as a whole as well as its components are first selectively analyzed. In research studies on optimizing the returns on investment, the allocation of gross assets to minimize risk and maximize return is generally chosen.

Although no attempt is made here to draw comparisons between the quality of executive leadership and growth rates, the organization's design for growth should nevertheless be a factor in all major decisions. For example, in many cases the Markowitz model of "expected return–variance of return" theory is used as a basis for problem solving. In this model, the investment holdings are

---

[14] R. D. Entenberg, "Resource Allocation: Theory, Principles, and Models," research paper presented to NRMA Annual Convention, January 1965, New York City.

compared to the total capital assets of the firm on a fixed "normal" return basis. The projections, similar to capital budgeting decisions, assume that any variance from the norm or risk is undesirable, while a definite normal rate of return is to be desired.[15]

DESIGN FOR GROWTH

One of the principal advantages of a large firm or plant is the possibility of a sale-leaseback method of expansion. This operates in much the same fashion as consumer credit. The individual supplying the financing for purchase of a building or equipment bases his investment on a prospective rate of return consistent with the risk involved. This is an excellent device for using the discounting cash-flow technique. Executive management, before making a capital investment, evaluates the investment on this basis—taking into account the flows of return of cash over time at the proper discount rate. This method also takes into account the residual value accruing to the owner of the property as part of the return.

There is much to be said for ownership of facilities, which entails the freedom to remodel or move as determined by changes in the market structure or population movement—and represents a more unrestrictive and permissive managerial adaptation to change. When a sale-leaseback arrangement is made, it should be considered as a long-term debt instrument and so treated on the balance sheet. When a sale-leaseback arrangement is viewed in this manner, there is less likelihood of restriction of movement occurring should interest costs become high.[16]

In a study by the Brookings Institution, it was pointed out that any design for growth would have to include gains in equipment efficiency for any fast expansion. Industry is getting more output per dollar investment while spending proportionately less for new plant and equipment. With comparatively stable prices and with capacity exceeding demand, output and growth increase. In other words, any design for growth must take place in a framework of either more government spending or more tax cuts. Only by such means can investment in capital equipment continue to produce increasing amounts of output per dollar investment.[17]

---

[15] H. M. Markowitz, *Portfolio Selection* (New York: Wiley & Sons, 1958). See also W. J. Baumol, *Economic Theory and Operations Analysis* (New York: Macmillan, 1962); H. Bierman and S. Smidt, *The Capital Budgeting Decision* (New York: Macmillan, 1960); G. Tintner, *Mathematics and Statistics for Economists* (New York: Holt, Rinehart & Winston, 1960).

[16] Joel Dean, *op. cit.* Any test of the marginal productivity of capital matched to the marginal profitability of investment—in the long run—is no longer academic. Only by this means can the proper rate in channeling take place..

[17] "Changing the Rules on Growth," *Business Week*, March 6, 1965, pp. 142–44. This *Business Week* report is based on a Brookings Institution Study on "Investment Demand" by Bert Hickman. The Hickman study shows that "in 1948, a dollar's worth of capital invested in plant and equipment produced, on the average, 72¢ worth of output a year. By 1957, a dollar's worth of capital stock was yielding an annual output of 85¢. And in 1962—the last year for which Hickman provides an estimate—$1 in capital stock was yielding 92¢ output. All these figures are stated in terms of constant dollars. Thus, from 1948 to 1962, the real increase in the productivity of capital equipment was 28%.... This figure represents the average gain for the

Some thirty years ago, there was widespread general acceptance of the explanations and results of the work of Simon S. Kuznetz and Arthur F. Burns. As a result, little additional work was carried out in growth patterns and long-term forecasts. Nevertheless, firms such as the Prudential Insurance Company, Sears, Roebuck, the Federated Department Stores Company, the Allied Stores Corporation as well as many other retail firms operate from short- as well as long-range forecasts. Their design for growth is based essentially on approaches developed from behavior analysis in the formation of the disaggregated sectors of the economy.[18]

DECISION VARIABLES AND SPANS OF CONTROL

Decision making is no longer an individual process. The personal experiences of any single individual are generally an inadequate basis for major policy determinations. The smaller, one-man organization might prove self-limiting in the long run, although it may be a successful operation.

The minute a firm translates itself from a single to a multiunit institution, the decision-making and coordinating processes immediately become too complex for the one-man organization; as a result, executive management must then rely on an increasing number of individuals in order to optimize decisions within the firm. This means an orderly increase in the span of executive control. With scalar growth comes a division of labor. As this occurs, executive responsibility is delegated among more individuals and specialists. Again, coordination and communications become the key factor in organizational growth, otherwise the overall policy objectives of the firm are easily lost. Built-in uneconomic cost centers and empire building become relatively easy to induce.

Another aspect of organizational growth is vertical and horizontal integration within the firm. For example, many stores operate their own alteration shops and workrooms, manufacture their own candy and baked goods, and handle the complete servicing of all goods that they sell in order to maximize effective growth. Growth alone does not insure profit, because very often functional duplications accompany it. Effective growth should involve integration of specialized functions.

As an organizational principle, the span of executive control is pretty generally recognized as a definite managerial consideration. When executive leaders use the span of control to establish a sounder operation, both productivity and morale increase throughout the organization. In an article on this point which discussed

---

entire economy. The gains in the productivity of capital differ widely from industry to industry."

[18] Bela Gold, "Industry Growth Patterns: Theory and Empirical Results," Pittsburgh: Graduate School of Business, 1964. See also H. H. Landsberg, L. L. Fischman, and J. L. Fisher, *Resources in America's Future* (Baltimore: Johns Hopkins Press, 1963); George J. Stigler, *Trends in Output and Employment* (New York: National Bureau of Economics Research, 1947), p. 26.

the development of a scientific system, seven factors were selected as having a direct bearing on the span of executive control:

Similarity of functions supervised,
Geographic contiguity of functions supervised,
Complexity of functions supervised,
Direction and control required by the personnel supervised,
Coordination required of the supervisor,
Planning required of the supervisor,
Organizational assistance received by the supervisor.[19]

Professor R. C. Davis of Ohio State University states that the span of executive control should rarely exceed seven functions, with five being the most productive; the span of operative control would revolve around fifteen, depending on the above list of criteria.

Within this framework, an additional concept of a span of control by executive management was developed at the Hughes Aircraft Company in Fullerton, California. This was developed by Phil N. Scheid, Manager, Management Operations, Ground Systems Group. The title of his system, which is based on management studies, analysis, and experimentation, is COACH, an acronym from "Charter of Accountability Concept—Hughes." This span system is based on the establishment of written "charters" for each major division and group office of the organization.

The system is equally applicable to both line and staff organizations which strive for goal achievement as well as improved performance. The system is based on the integration of scientific management, revisionist management, and behavioral management. Mr. Scheid concludes that the COACH concept can provide "the appropriate blend of executive leadership required to maintain and improve the American business system and the largely untapped reservoir of latent creative energy within each staff or line supervisor and manager, eager for the opportunity to demonstrate his total capability." [20]

FUNCTIONAL EVALUATION—EXECUTIVE LEADERSHIP

Executive managers are measured by their decisions in critical areas: credit policies, merchandising policies, operating policies, branch store policies (accounting methods, central versus decentralized controls, common versus individual inventories, etc.), and in the effective use of calculated risks in the operation of the firm.

The general evaluation of the executive leaders in the organization also rests on the manner in which the staff evolution and control takes place. The evolution

---

[19] C. W. Barkdull, "Span of Control—A Method of Evaluation," *Michigan Business Review*, May 1963, pp. 25–32.

[20] Phil N. Scheid, "The Concept and Charter of Accountability," Fullerton, Calif.: Hughes Aircraft, No. 1964. See also Warren G. Bennis, "Revisionist Theory of Leadership," *Harvard Business Review*, January–February 1961; Harold J. Leavitt and Thomas L. Whisler, "Managements in the 1980's," *Harvard Business Review*, November–December 1958.

in the chain of command should first include organized society. From organized society evolves the framework for standards of business conduct. These first two considerations then evolve as follows:

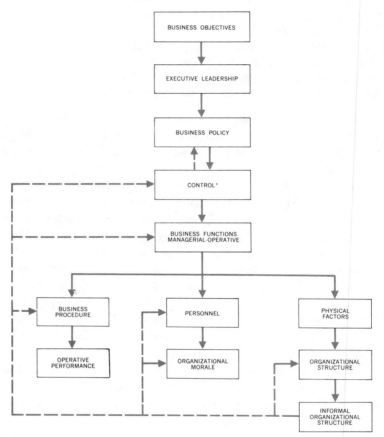

* THE ORGANIC FUNCTIONS OF CONTROL AND THEIR SUBFUNCTIONS ARE PRELIMINARY STAFF CONSIDERATIONS; THESE CONSIST OF:
1. ROUTINE PLANNING, 2. SCHEDULING, 3. PREPARATION, 4. DISPATCHING — (1) THROUGH (4) WOULD INCLUDE CONCURRENT LINE CONTROL FUNCTIONS — 5. DIRECTING, 6. STAFF SUPERVISION, 7. COMPARING, 8. RE-APPRAISING, 9. CORRECTIVE ACTION (LINE).

General criteria used in evaluating the competency of executive leadership include the executive's ability to anticipate goals for the business future, the use of positive rather than negative methods of leadership, the quality of the executive's subordinates, the degree of voluntary, enthusiastic cooperation in the operative ranks of the organization, the nature and degree of the organization's discipline, and the existence of genuine confidence between executive and operative employees.

In fact, managerial acumen is judged by the firm's net profit per dollar of sales volume, its net profit return on total capitalization, the net return on total equity or net worth investment, total revenues in terms of share of market, and by concepts and plans for growth.

Within this framework, stability, flexibility, and organizational balance indicate executive management's capacity for growth, as well as that of the organization. The measurement for the capacity for growth is essentially a qualitative one, and involves staff investigation and analysis.

Decision Processes

Decision making and resulting courses of action underlie the entire field of human behavior. Each of us has a built-in, culturally adjusted, biological decision maker, through which alternatives are automatically weighed, accepted, or rejected. One's memory bank is a continuing source of information; a course of action cannot be assumed to have been made solely on the basis of information given to an individual. Conclusions indicate those segments of the decision process which are based upon accepted "facts" derived from experience. For example, when an executive makes a decision or solves a problem in a new area for the first time, a learning pattern is initiated by the executive and the firm.[21] This learning pattern is either reinforced or negated through further trial and error. In a paper presented to the NRMA, the writer pointed out that:

> Within the firm, the effectiveness of the decision makers at all executive echelons depends on the learning experiences resulting from the various types of information flows to which they have been exposed. Regardless of whether or not decision makers act rationally or irrationally, they must forecast results on the basis of the empirical "whys" of decision choices. The manner in which the "whys" are measured and evaluated by executive management determines the long-run success of the organization and the firm's evolving pattern of market competition.[22]

One of the more serious problems facing business managers today is an understanding of the true nature of the information function.

> In some cases, sufficient or timely information for solving business problems is lacking. In many other cases, it is quite obvious that businesses have more information than they actually know how to use. The main problem for executive management is to encompass the utilization of what is already available and using it.[23]

Generalization and Executive Leadership

Many executives will not make a decision until organizational needs reach certain pressure levels that are indices of sensitivity varying with organizations and individuals. The greater the sensitivity of the executive leader to change, the less the threshold of pressure needed for adaptation of the firm to new market con-

---

[21] See Herbert A. Simon, *The New Science of Management Decision*, The Ford Foundation Distinguished Lectures, Vol. III (New York: Harper & Bros., 1960). Professor Simon states that decision making should be considered synonymous with management.

[22] R. D. Entenberg, "Decision Making Processes, Communications, and the Flow of Information Within the Retail Organization," paper presented to management session of the NRMA, January 1963, New York City.

[23] *Ibid.*

ditions. Also, before decisions can be made, an executive must have a perceptive instinct to recognize that a problem exists. Once recognized, the ability to articulate the problem, and state the issue with clarity is a must. Too often, organizational crises continue because no one senses the real problem until it is too late to take appropriate and economic action.

In this respect, the specialist, whether it be in education or business is at a distinct disadvantage at higher levels of authority and responsibility. The nature of the problems encountered at such levels calls for a generalized approach. The man who thinks only as an accountant, a lawyer, or a treasurer might miss the fact that higher echelon decisions must be made with consideration for the firm as a whole.

The generalist in the broad sense is the individual who has opened his mind to the widest possible range of intellectual experiences so that unfamiliar problems are quickly recognized or anticipated. He is then in a position to gather as much information as quickly as possible about an unfamiliar problem in order to focus on all possible alternatives and permit sequential decisions on a narrowing scale basis to take place quickly. This is the mark of a good executive leader.[24]

GENERAL SUMMARY AND CONCLUSIONS

In this concluding chapter, an analysis of management as the function of executive leadership was presented. The importance of continuing research, both as a line and staff function, was analyzed from the standpoint of the objective of enterprise. It was pointed out that effective administrative management cannot be generated without planned methodology based on information that will facilitate adaptation to change.

The major decisions that must be taken within any business organization concern: 1) setting corporate policy, 2) selection of key executives, 3) determination of organizational structure, 4) diversification and expansion policies, and 5) capital budgeting decisions. Corporate policy decisions which affect people within the organization are probably the most important and, often, the most trying. With an infinite multiplicity of decisions to be made at all organizational echelons, mistakes are to be expected.

The more facts that are required from different sources, the more complex the organization and the greater the effectiveness of the informal organizational structure. Not only is there a narrow dividing line between the formal and informal operating structures in the retail marketing firm, but at times the various echelons are difficult to distinguish. In addition, the line between the executive manager who intelligently applies the experience of others in a systematic manner for decision making and the executive who thinks logically and learns well from his own experience is also difficult to distinguish.

Growth at all levels of the firm is more than one dimension. Growth involves

---

[24] *Ibid.*

processing, planning, and staff evolution—not just the addition of new work centers on a vertical and a horizontal basis. These facets are critical aspects of any evaluation of executive leadership.

It was also pointed out that an executive's ability to maintain confidence and freedom of action is crucial. In this respect, restrictions of managerial actions can make the difference between a really successful operation and a marginal one.

Finally, businesses succeed or fail on the basis of the managerial inputs. In turn, quality and effectiveness depend on timing. And correct timing depends on the degree to which the managerial inputs have been adjusted to current conditions.

Executive leadership, as the art-science of management, involves decision making of the highest order. All business and academic experiences, qualitative and quantitative, involve executive decision making. Such decisions are made in a challenging framework of continuing uncertainty and change. The ability of an executive leader to solve business problems in such a framework measures his ability to adapt and grow.

In effect, the managerial-economic approach to effective retail and market distribution can furnish the perspectives necessary to cope with any and all changes and, in the process, enable the organization to grow.

APPENDIXES

Appendix A

Definition of Terms

Retail trade, as defined in major groups 52 through 59 (521–5999) of the 1957 edition of the Standard Industrial Classification (SIC) Manual, is covered in the 1963 Census. The manual includes establishments primarily engaged in selling merchandise to personal, household, and farm users. Liquor stores operated by state and local governments, classified in SIC major groups 92 and 93, are also included. Excluded from retail trade are places of business operated by institutions and open only to their own members or personnel; this includes restaurants and bars operated by clubs, school cafeterias, eating places operated by industrial and commercial enterprises for their own employees, and establishments operated by agencies of the Federal Government on military posts, hospitals, etc.[1]

Establishments covered by the Census in 1963 were assigned a "kind-of-business" classification in accordance with the provisions of the 1957 edition of the SIC Manual. Because in some instances a more detailed classification is required for Census purposes than is available in the SIC Manual, additional kinds of business have been identified with the SIC categories.

Kind of Business. It should be noted that kind-of-business classifications are not interchangeable with commodity classifications. Most businesses sell a number of kinds of commodities. The kind of business code assigned reflects generally either the individual commodity or commodity group which is the primary source of the establishment's receipts, or some mixture of different commodities which characterize the establishment's business. Thus, the classification of establishments by kind of business usually does not make it possible to determine either the number of establishments handling a particular commodity or the sales of that commodity. For example, the "food group" classification excludes stores selling some food if the sale of food is not the primary source of receipts; moreover, even though stores are classified as "food stores," some of their receipts may be derived from the sale of nonfood products.

Standard Metropolitan Statistical Areas. Area titles and definitions of the 2 Standard Consolidated Areas and the 217 Standard Metropolitan Statistical Areas in the United States established by the Bureau of the Budget as of August 4, 1964.

---

[1] Retail Trade, United States 1963 Census of Business (BC63–RA1) United States Department of Commerce, Bureau of the Census, pp. 223–29.

Appendix B

Definitions and Key Characteristics of Selected Store Organizations

CHAIN STORES. Consist of two or more centrally owned units, handling on the same plane of distribution substantially similar lines of merchandise. Emphasis is placed on central ownership rather than local management control. The central organization has regular control over its retail units and assumes full financial responsibility.

Advantages. Most of the advantages of chain stores are basically the same as those inherent in other forms of large-scale enterprise.

a. Buying power—This type of organization is able to buy on more favorable terms than the single-unit store in the same line.
b. Buying skill—Most purchases are made through central buying by merchandising experts who spend all of their time initiating and maintaining market contracts, collecting information, and conducting negotiations.
c. Low operating costs—By integration of the wholesaling and manufacturing operations in store-owned warehouses, chain stores in many cases demand and receive functional discounts. Their warehouse operation involves low handling and shipping costs, because credit and sales problems are eliminated and deliveries can be scheduled more efficiently.
d. Curtailment of services to the consumer—Most chains generally offer more limited service and usually sell only for cash.
e. Limited composition of stock—Chains tend to concentrate on items with widespread demand so that a higher turnover, smaller risk, and lower investment and insurance costs result.
f. Advertising advantages—When stores are concentrated in a single market, newspaper, radio, and television advertising is economic.
g. Experimentation in merchandise—Because of wide geographical dispersion, they can test merchandise selectively without great risk.
h. Risk distribution and competitive superiority—The wide territorial distribution of the retail units of many chains reduces their risks, as a decline in sales in one store may be offset by corresponding sales increases elsewhere.

Disadvantages.

a. General limitation of service and standardization of operating procedures—

Because of the many different sizes of stores in heterogeneous markets, standardization of operating procedures often proves too inflexible for maximizing efficiency throughout the organization.

b. *Personnel limitations*—There is less personal contact between store management and the local public.

c. *Public opinion and legal limitations*—Charges of monopoly and "driving out" the small businessman are commonplace.

The chain's ability to receive discriminatory advantages in purchasing is limited by the Robinson-Patman Act. Its freedom to engage in loss-leader pricing was curtailed to some extent by the state Unfair Sales Act. Many states have taxed chains, thus decreasing their competitive effectiveness.

d. *Increasing efficiency of independents*—Independents are, as a whole, carrying on their business much more efficiently than in the past, and in many instances perform more effectively than chains.

Future. Their future expansion is limited to the fact that a certain portion of the public still demands services which most large centrally managed chains cannot or will not give. They have earned the right to exist, and are moving towards complete self-service and "check-out." This will modify the type of merchandise they carry. Legal limitations and union activities will limit their competitive effectiveness. Independent stores will continue to give them more competition. In some fields, such as auto accessory and appliance stores, it will be difficult for them to maintain their present relative position.

Trend. The chain store had a phenomenal development in the 1920's. By 1929 the number of both organizations and stores reached a peak. Before that, the profits from chain-store operations had been relatively high. Since this time fewer chains formed by mergers and acquisitions are in existence. Chains have reached the point of saturation in many cities and towns. They are not well suited for certain lines of goods. Although chains have not been able to acquire more than about 30 per cent of all retail-store sales, their market share, especially in the case of supermarkets, reaches saturation points in many local markets with absorption well over double the national average.

VOLUNTARY CHAINS. Cooperative chains in which the retailer members preserve individual ownership of their stores. They operate with voluntary and contractual central organization. The individual store assumes full financial responsibility for its acts. They are generally wholesale-sponsored.

Advantages. The voluntary chain has inherent strength and stability because of centralized planning, which an individual store cannot afford. There has been establishment of physical standards for store operations, and some co-ops permit the sponsor to cancel the membership of any retailer who fails to keep his store up to set standards. They secure better prices through more advantageous discounts, advertising allowances, and improved displays. Their advertising costs are lower because of the centralized cooperative effort.

Disadvantages. There is a lack of strong central control, and sponsors are limited in the encouragement of better merchandising methods. Sometimes the retailer is forced to concentrate on the wholesaler's private brands. When both national and wholesaler's brands are carried, inventories may become uneconomic.

Future. Despite these weaknesses, the voluntary chains will continue to expand. It appears that the concept of voluntary chains has wide association and application and has unquestionably strengthened the position of the independent merchant. Future expansion is limited almost solely by the number of qualified stores developed as a result of voluntary group activities.

Trend. A great increase in sales volume was experienced over the period 1948–1954. In 1955 it was estimated that nearly two-thirds of the total sales volume of independent grocery stores was accounted for by members of cooperatives and voluntary chains. Voluntary chains have developed primarily in lines of merchandise where it is feasible for merchants to utilize a primary source of supply, such as food groups, on the wholesale level. Up to this time little voluntary chain activity other than group buying has been observed. In the case of fashion merchandising, which involves assembling from numerous sources, inability to adapt to local preferences is a major handicap to growth.

DEPARTMENT STORES. Retail stores carrying general lines of apparel (such as suits, coats, dresses, furnishings), home furnishings, jewelry, floor coverings, linens, major household appliances—the lines arranged in separate departments which function under a single department manager or buyer. Establishments in this classification employ twenty-five or more people.

Advantages. The larger department stores offer wide varieties of merchandise in depth. There is also a wide range of customer services available, such as delivery, liberal adjustments, several forms of credit, fashion shows, lounges, and telephones. Because of increasing costs, there has been a trend toward reducing services or making separate service charges where possible. Because of generally alert management, adapting to change and new scientific techniques, they will continue as an important part of the retail structure.

Peculiar advantage of size. Division of labor differs from the chain-store organization, with buyers generally at the head of each department. Because of wide range of merchandise, salespeople must develop a high degree of product knowledge and selling skill. Almost any type of skill can be found in department stores, such as merchandise experts, advertising and display specialists, credit personnel, accountants, training specialists, warehouse employees, etc. Generally, management of those stores assume active roles in community affairs.

Disadvantages. They suffer from a lack of personal contact between top management and consumers. Complex supervisory procedures within the organization cause difficulties.

There are generally high-fixed costs caused by the dwindling volume of downtown locations. There are often congestion and parking difficulties. It is almost impossible for the customers to get acquainted with the salespeople.

They are not generally willing to research for adequate feedback on consumer wants.

Future. They are a mature type of institution striving to serve all segments of the consuming public. It is apparent that they are struggling to maintain their position in the face of newer forms of competition, such as discount houses. An important reason for optimism is that their top management is generally alert to dynamic changes. Most have great financial strength.

Trend. The trend is toward basement stores, leased departments, and branch stores. The basement-store trends are to self-service and check-out-type sections of budget merchandise. The leased departments operate as a concession for individuals or chains for departments such as millinery, jewelry, shoes, auto accessories, or beauty salons.

VARIETY STORES. Retail establishments primarily engaged in selling a variety of merchandise in the lower and popular price ranges—such as stationery, gift items, ladies' accessories, toilet articles, light housewares, toys, etc. These stores are frequently known as 5¢ to $1 stores, although barriers on handling higher-priced lines are no longer present. Sales usually are made on a cash-and-carry basis, with the open simplified selling method of display encouraging customer selection of merchandise. Credit, stamps, and increased use of advertising have been new competitive trends.

Advantages. Merchandise is openly displayed, consisting for the most part of low-priced consumer goods in a wide assortment.

Disadvantages. There is not enough personal contact between clerks and customers. Most sales personnel are inadequately trained and young; there is a high personnel turnover. Very slow to adapt to new forms of competition because of conservative policy formulation.

Future. They will continue to expand in shopping centers and suburban areas.

Trend. Variety stores will move faster into self-service, check-out discount store types of operations and trade up into most merchandise classifications. They are found in both downtown and outlying shopping districts, and at points of heavy consumer traffic. Chain organizations dominate this type of organization, and geographical expansion will be primarily in shopping centers. Stores in this general merchandising group have declined in sales volume and are still losing competitive position.

SUPERMARKETS. Large retail food stores selling a wide variety of consumer products, supplemented by a variety of non-food commodities and other convenience and specialty goods. Their principal promotional appeal is self-service, mass displays, wide assortments, generally convenient parking, heavy weekend advertising and promotional gimmicks of all kinds.

Advantages. Their price appeal results from selling "own-brand" merchandise. They can also sell national brands more cheaply because of quantity purchases. They carry wide ranges of merchandise because of their increasingly large physical layouts. Many impulse purchases result from the physical layout, mass displays, and self-service check-out.

Disadvantages. They compete with other supermarkets. They need some types of personal selling. Congestion is found at the check-out counter. Not enough services such as delivery are provided. The large store may confuse a customer, and pilferage is quite common. The increasing use of stamps as an "extra" has served to add expense rather than result in sustained additional volume.

Future. Supermarkets are competing with other supermarkets increasingly, and as "frills" are added they will become less competitive in relation to the independents who often have lower cost structures. They will continue to grow with the population but at a smaller rate.

Trend. The trend is toward extension of self-service to all sections, such as delicatessen, meats, and coffee. More store refinements will be added, with more nonfood items handled. Use of scientific work-simplification methods are being used, along with trading stamps.

AUTOMOBILE SUPPLY STORES. Retail establishments primarily engaged in selling auto tires, batteries, seat covers, parts, and accessories. Such establishments frequently have facilities for tire recapping and selected installation.

Advantages. There are few seasonal ups and downs, and commodities sold are not perishable. They cater to a do-it-yourself individual who wants to save costly garage and service charges. Mainly they do business on a cash basis. They have a large assortment of merchandise of a related variety and enjoy much advertising support from the manufacturer.

Disadvantages. There is often chaotic price competition; stores must be open long hours. A high capital investment is needed to enter into the business. Unless it is of the "wholesale" sponsored variety, many merchandise items are low in price, and there are many items which must be assembled before they can be displayed for sale.

Future. They will be selling more and more unrelated items and build new locations in suburban areas. Merchandise will be made more attractive, with more emphasis on do-it-yourself techniques. However, many of these stores will be forced to go "discount" because of intense competition from this direction.

Trend. The trend is to sell merchandise at unprofitable mark-ons and to sell more and more unrelated goods.

MAIL-ORDER HOUSES. Classified as "non-store" retailers. They may furnish potential customers with a catalogue describing the merchandise and prices, or sales are often made on a house-to-house basis. They also advertise in magazines, newspapers, and other media. The establishments are subdivided into various classifications, generally on the basis of the merchandise that they handle. Many are an integral part of well-known retail institutions.

Advantages. Mail-order houses are not greatly affected by local congestion, depression, or strikes. Prices are somewhat lower than average retail prices, but postal and delivery charges tend to negate this advantage. Buying from catalogues is relatively easy, and shopping can be done at any convenient time of the day or night. There is none of the sales pressure and confusion of crowded stores. The warehouse is generally located in a low-rent area. A great proportion of their business is on a cash basis.

Disadvantages. It is not possible to examine merchandise beforehand. Many people hesitate to order by mail because of sizing problems. Mail purchases take time for delivery. Catalogues and merchandise prices must be planned well in advance of the season, regardless of possible fluctuations.

Future. Such selling is becoming more important in metropolitan as well as rural areas. It is also relatively easy for unscrupulous operators to mislead purchasers in these areas. Credit selling and new methods of sizing and selection methods will increase their importance.

Trend. They now compete with specialty and department stores. Sales promotion activities have been thoroughly and efficiently organized, and shipping warehouses are well located. "Money-back" guarantees are becoming increasingly important. They promote mainly "own-brand" merchandise. They will continue to sell items that are novel or not generally available in retail stores.

SPECIALTY STORES. Retail establishments primarily engaged in selling single-line merchandise classifications such as ladies' or men's wear, shoes, lingerie, etc.

Advantages. They handle one or more individual lines of merchandise in depth, and cater to customers who demand selection in depth before purchasing. Management knows its customers well, can purchase for their taste, and customer-salesperson contact is common. Their cost of doing business is generally low. The proprietor emphasizes service and quality rather than price. The stores are less concerned with price competition because of lines which they handle. They are located in easily accessible string-street locations downtown and in shopping centers.

Disadvantages. There is heavy dependence on buying offices for advice and proper operation. They are not able to advertise economically. The risk is great because inventories are on a "restricted line." Often these stores are one-man organizations and are subject to liquidation should the owner retire. There is little impulse buying, and stores are often too small to expand properly into related lines.

Future. Specialty stores will continue to be important in distribution in the urban and rural shopping communities.

Trend. Because they specialize, they have a very strong core of loyal customers. They carry stock that is often not carried by other stores. There has been a tendency for people to open shops without experience or without sufficient capital. Failure rates will continue to be high. Nevertheless, new entries will constantly venture into the field.

Appendix C

Concept of the Standard Metropolitan Statistical Areas[1]

The concept of "Standard Metropolitan Statistical Areas" has been developed to meet the need for the presentation of general-purpose statistics by agencies of the Federal Government, in accordance with specific criteria for defining such areas. On the basis of these criteria, definitions of the areas in terms of geographic boundaries are established by the Bureau of the Budget with the advice of the Federal Committee on Standard Metropolitan Statistical Areas, which is composed of representatives of the major federal statistical agencies.

Standard definitions of metropolitan statistical areas were first issued in 1949, as "Standard Metropolitan Areas." They were developed to replace four different sets of definitions then in use for various statistical series—"metropolitan districts," "metropolitan counties," "industrial areas," and "labor market areas." Because of the use of these different definitions, it was not possible to relate the statistics on population, industrial production, labor force, and other series for the area in question, since each series included a slightly different territory.

The primary objective in establishing standard definitions of metropolitan areas was thus to make it possible for all federal statistical agencies to utilize the same boundaries in publishing statistical data useful for analyzing metropolitan problems. The term "standard metropolitan area" has been changed to "standard metropolitan statistical area" in order to describe more accurately the objective of the definitions.

In order to achieve this purpose, objective criteria of a quantitative character have been established to define the areas. The criteria were revised and reissued in March 1958, following review and minor revisions by the Federal Committee on Standard Metropolitan Statistical Areas.

The general concept of a metropolitan area is one of an integrated economic and social unit with a recognized large population nucleus. To serve the statistical purposes for which metropolitan areas are defined, its parts must themselves be areas for which statistics are usually or often collected. Thus, each standard metropolitan statistical area must contain at least one city of at least 50,000 inhabitants

---

[1] See *Standard Metropolitan Statistical Areas* (Washington, D.C., Office of Statistical Standards, Bureau of the Budget, Executive Office of the President) 1961.

(see also criterion 1[b]). The standard metropolitan statistical area will then include the county of such a central city and adjacent counties that are found to be metropolitan in character and economically and socially integrated with the county of the central city. In New England the requirement with regard to a central city as a nucleus still holds, but the units making up the area are the towns rather than counties. The county (or town in New England) is the basic statistical unit. A standard metropolitan statistical area may contain more than one city of 50,000 population. The largest city is considered the nucleus and usually gives the name to the area. The name may include other cities in the area if such cities have populations of 250,000 or have at least one-third the population of the largest city and a minimum population of 25,000. Standard metropolitan statistical areas may cross state lines....

The definitions presented here are designed to serve a wide variety of statistical and analytical purposes. Adoption of these areas for any specific purpose should be judged, however, in the light of the appropriateness of the criteria by which they are defined. Area definitions are used in presenting data from the Censuses of Business, Manufactures, and Mineral Industries; the Censuses of Population and Housing; and the Census of Governments; in presenting current economic and social data; and in analyses of local area problems.

Present Retail-Store Classifications: Present retail census data are compiled on an "establishment" basis and grouped into categories classified according to predetermined structure characteristics.

Kind of Business: The "kind-of-business" grouping of stores is based on general-commodity group sales by merchandise lines. The extent and relative importance of the specific lines carried and sold cannot be evaluated very accurately because of the wide overlapping of similar merchandise classifications handled by separate intra-store departments and groupings. However, the "kind-of-business" classification does point out in broad general terms the type of information available in census data, and this information is basic to any projected conceptual changes in the collection of the data.

Ownership Clauses: This grouping should be expanded to include subclassifications of "affiliated" as well as "non-affiliated" independent stores. Such an expansion would refer to whether the independent store worked co-operatively in promotion, merchandising, and operation through the sponsorship of manufacturers, wholesalers, or through "joint" efforts with other retailers. This change would be of particular significance to many consumer-goods manufacturers and distributors—especially those in grocery, automotive, accessory, variety, and drug businesses.

Sales-Volume Size: Retail establishments are grouped according to comparative sales size and by geographical areas. Basic trends concerning market concentrations, competitive conditions, and general types of consumption expenditures made can be determined from this grouping.

Classifications by Functions Performed: The value of the grouping by functions performed becomes a useful analytical tool when the relative operating costs of stores handling similar merchandise and offering similar services can be compared.

If this grouping could be further subdivided according to type of shopping locale, its usefulness would be considerably enhanced.

Extent and Nature of Merchandise Lines Handled: The extent and nature of the product lines handled are greatly influenced by the size of trading areas, degree of population concentration, and the location of stores within the trading area. Selected "kind-of-business" groupings—such as food stores, general merchandise stores, and drugstores—are combined according to the nature and extent of the lines handled—into general stores, single-line stores, specialty stores, departmentalized specialty stores, department stores, variety stores, etc.

The shortcoming of these groupings is that the same or similar lines, as well as the varieties and assortments offered, are not carried by all stores within each group. No clear lines of demarcation exist; and broad-line classifications of merchandise offerings invariably involve extensive degrees of "value-judgment" interpretations.

Because the number of retail establishments carrying complementary or supplementary commodity lines is likely to increase rather than to decrease, the analytical usefulness of such classifications tends to be limited.

Classification by Location: Present criteria are set up for classifications according to size of geographical and political subdivisions without regard to "natural" or "planned" shopping areas. This imposes severe limitations on the usefulness of this grouping.

The encompassing trading area of large concentrations of population represents only a "first approximation" for scientific market analysis. There are so many different types of "shopping" and "buying" areas within "Standard Metropolitan Areas" that determination of markets is too often the result of educated guesswork. Purchase motivations, services, functions performed, types of goods offered, prices charged, and the extent of lines carried are almost completely interrelated with specific shopping-area location. Census data compiled according to geographical and political subdivisions leave much to be desired.

Further Problems: Lack of any specific trading-area identity is much more acute when marketing analysis is needed with reference to "shopping" goods and "specialty" goods. On the other hand, marketing analysis of widely distributed "convenience" goods is less dependent on correlations to particular types of shopping locales.

Again, the field of retailing is so dynamic and complex that data which would furnish optimum market measures will probably always represent broad generalizations and compromises.

Another widely used generalization that tends to be applied too broadly is the term "credit." "Credit" in itself is incomplete for purposes of setting up standards of comparison for this type of sales transaction. A credit sale may involve a 30-day charge account; a "revolving," "delayed," a "straight" installment sale; a combination of any of these; or still other types of deferred payment plans. Every type of credit offered has a direct bearing on size of store, frequency of purchase, amount of sale, price lines, clientele, functions performed, capital needed, and nature and extent of the lines handled. The economic groups residing in an establishment's trading area represent another important determinant of the type and the extent of credit offered.

Changes Indicated: A valid workable basis for a practical classification of retail establishments can be developed with the present "kind-of-business" groupings as a base. To be entirely comprehensive, the suggested changes and expansions should also include present groupings in terms of significant and contiguous population segments. Such segments could then be further subdivided into various trading-area classifications as detailed below. Each trading area, district, or center, in turn, would have a "kind-of-business" classification by size (as pointed out above), with further subdivisions by ownership status and by the kind of services offered.

In this manner, Census data enumerating similar types of stores with like volumes in similar trading areas, in similar types of shopping centers, handling similar lines, and offering similar groups of services would provide much more scientific bases for meaningful comparisons and analyses.

SUGGESTED REVISIONS

Accordingly, the following expansions and additions to present Census classifications are suggested:

Group I—Consisting of four broad divisions:

This group would include, as a first step, the listing of establishments by sales, according to kind-of-business classification *and* according to specific shopping-district locations by area segments as shown below. Suggested shopping-district classifications and subdivisions are listed and defined under Group II.

(a) The 217 largest cities.
(b) Cities of 25,000 inhabitants or more, exclusive of those included with "a."
(c) Cities of 10,000 to 24,999.
(d) Rural areas under 2,500 to cities with populations up to 9,999.

Regarding Group I(a), a total of 217 cities were listed as the 178 "Standard Metropolitan Areas" in 1954. These metropolitan centers included 56.5 per cent of the country's total population, and accounted for almost $110 billion (approximately 64.7 per cent) of all retail-store sales. A "standard metropolitan area" has been defined by the Bureau of the Census as consisting of counties containing a city of 50,000 or more population as a basic framework.

Group II—Consisting of five locational subdivisions:

This group would represent the first subdivision for each category of Group I. The initial grouping would be by geographical area. A second regrouping could then be carried out according to comparable shopping district locations, irrespective of geographical areas. This would form a cohesive central core of *like* retail units in *similar* external settings as follows:

(a) *Central business districts*—This would include the sections within a town or city where all or mostly all communications, streets, and transportation converge, and where the principal shopping and specialty goods stores are concentrated. Their radii would be determined by population concentrations. Extremely large cities are quite likely to have more than one such district, while smaller cities, especially those adjacent to or contiguous with larger cities, may not have such a "district."

(b) *Regional shopping centers*—These would consist of "planned" centers that may have as many as 100 retail units, consisting of shopping, specialty, and convenience stores of all kinds. Such regional centers usually have a minimum total area of approximately forty acres and parking provisions for more than 4,000 cars.

(c) *Sectional, suburban, and intra-city secondary shopping locations*—These would include any sections where important segments of a town's or city's communications and transportation facilities emanate in conjunction with close proximity to extensive residential areas. Both "controlled" and "sporadic" secondary shopping districts would be in this category; this would include planned centers of approximately thirty-five to fifty stores on the order of the regional centers in II(b), but on smaller scales.

(d) *Neighborhood "string streets" and "convenience" centers*—These areas generally consist of contiguous "convenience" goods stores with only minimum differences between them (food, drug, bakery, etc.). Such store groups are generally developed along main traffic arteries. "Planned" shopping plazas of six to twelve convenience stores would be included in this subdivision.

(e) *Small clusters and scattered stores*—These would include all types, sizes, and varieties of establishments not classified elsewhere.

In the case of Group II(c), a "controlled" shopping-center classification would indicate those centers sponsored by private or collective efforts, and so planned that all developments benefit both the surrounding community and itself. A "sporadic" classification would be one where stores have evolved naturally into a full-blown secondary shopping district or section in response to locational needs.

"House-to-house" sales could be enumerated properly only if an established sales office is maintained. Where "selling effort" areas are undefined, location of main offices would be the determining factor of locational area. Mail-order sales which are solicited and processed through identifiable local offices would be considered as having originated in that "establishment." Mail-order and vending machines are also grouped in a "non-store" category in the present Census. All such sales would be more realistically grouped if included with total sales of the originating retail establishments.

Group III—By kind-of-business, ownership classes, co-operative affiliations, and service function type:

(A) *Independents*
  (1) *Non-affiliated*—(By kind-of-business)
    (1a) *Full service* (where 50 per cent or more of total sales are made on a full-service basis—includes credit and delivery).
    (1b) *Limited service* (where 50 per cent or more of total sales are made on a simplified, self-selection, self-service, and/or cash-and-carry basis).
  (2) *Affiliated* (By kind-of-business as 1-a or 1-b) for co-operative efforts through:

    (2a) Manufacturer-sponsored voluntary chains
    (2b) Wholesale-sponsored voluntary chains
    (2c) Ownership-group activities
    (2d) Joint buying, merchandising, etc., with other retailers

(B) *Multi-units*—(By kind-of-business as 1-a or 1-b above)
    (1) Chains
    (2) Ownership groups
    (3) Independents with three or more satellite branches

(C) *Utility, government, and consumer-operated stores* (including permanently leased stalls in public or farmers' markets)[2]

A further note on *Kind-of-Business Classifications*:[3]

Retail trade, as defined in major groups 52 through 59 of the 1957 edition of the SIC *Manual*, and as covered in the 1958 Census, includes establishments primarily engaged in selling merchandise to personal, household, and farm users. In this report, liquor stores operated by State and local governments, classified in SIC major groups 92 and 93, also are included. Excluded from retail trade are places of business operated by institutions and open only to their own members or personnel, such as restaurants and bars operated by clubs, school cafeterias, eating places operated by industrial and commercial enterprises for their own employees, establishments operated by agencies of the Federal Government on military posts, hospitals, etc.

Establishments covered by the census were assigned a kind-of-business classification in accordance with the provisions of the 1957 edition of the SIC *Manual*. However, because in some instances a more detailed classification is required for Census purposes than is available in the SIC *Manual*, additional kinds of business have been identified within the SIC categories.

It should be noted that kind-of-business classifications are not interchangeable with commodity classifications. Most businesses sell a number of kinds of commodities. The kind of business code assigned generally reflects either the individual commodity or commodity group which is the primary source of the establishment's receipts or some mixture of different commodities which characterize the establishment's business. Thus, the classification of establishments by kind of business generally does not make it possible to determine either the number of establishments handling a particular commodity or the sales of that commodity. For example, the "food group" classification excludes stores selling some food if the sale of food is not the primary source of receipts moreover, even though stores are classified as "food stores" some of their receipts may be derived from the sale of non-food products.

---

[2] Robert D. Entenberg. "Suggested Changes in Census Classifications of Retail Trade," *Journal of Marketing*, Spring 1960, 39–43.

[3] 1958 Census of Business, Retail Trade Pennsylvania, U. S. Department of Congress, pp. 38–114.

Appendix D

Criteria Followed in Establishing Standard Metropolitan Statistical Areas

The definition of an individual standard metropolitan statistical area involves two considerations: first, a city or cities of specified population to constitute the central city and to identify the county in which it is located as the central county; and, second, economic and social relationships with contiguous counties[1] which are metropolitan in character, so that the periphery of the specific metropolitan area may be determined. Standard metropolitan statistical areas may cross state lines.

POPULATION CRITERIA

1. Each standard metropolitan statistical area must include at least:
(a) One city with 50,000 or more inhabitants, or
(b) Two cities having contiguous boundaries and constituting, for general economic and social purposes, a single community with a combined population of at least 50,000, the smaller of which must have a population of at least 15,000.

2. If two or more adjacent counties each have a city of 50,000 inhabitants or more (or twin cities under 1[b]) and the cities are within 20 miles of each other (city limits to city limits), they will be included in the same area unless there is definite evidence that the two cities are not economically and socially integrated.

CRITERIA OF METROPOLITAN CHARACTER

The criteria of metropolitan character relate primarily to the attributes of the county as a place of work or as a home for a concentration of nonagricultural workers. Specifically, these criteria are:

3. At least 75% of the labor force of the county must be in the nonagricultural labor force.[2]

---

[1] A "contiguous" county either adjoins the county or counties containing the largest city in the area, or adjoins an intermediate county integrated with the central county. There is no limit to the number of tiers of outlying metropolitan counties so long as all other criteria are met.

4. In addition to criterion 3, the county must meet at least one of the following conditions:

(a) It must have 50% or more of its population living in contiguous minor civil divisions [3] with a density of at least 150 persons per square mile, in an unbroken chain of minor civil divisions with such density radiating from a central city [4] in the area.

(b) The number of nonagricultural workers employed in the county must equal at least 10% of the number of nonagricultural workers employed in the county containing the largest city in the area, or be the place of employment of 10,000 nonagricultural workers.

(c) The nonagricultural labor force living in the county must equal at least 10% of the number of the nonagricultural labor force living in the county containing the largest city in the area, or be the place of residence of a nonagricultural labor force of 10,000.

5. In New England, the city and town are administratively more important than the county, and data are compiled locally for such minor civil divisions. Here, towns and cities are the units used in defining standard metropolitan statistical areas. In New England, because smaller units are used and more restricted areas result, a population density criterion of at least 100 persons per square mile is used as the measure of metropolitan character.

CRITERIA OF INTEGRATION

The criteria of integration relate primarily to the extent of economic and social communication between the outlying counties and central county.

6. A county is regarded as integrated with the county or counties containing the central cities of the area if either of the following criteria is met:

(a) If 15% of the workers living in the county work in the county or counties containing central cities of the area, or

(b) If 25% of those working in the county live in the county or counties containing central cities of the area.

Only where data for criteria 6(a) and 6(b) are not conclusive are other related types of information used as necessary. This information includes such items as average telephone calls per subscriber per month from the county to the county containing central cities of the area; percent of the population in the county located in the central city telephone exchange area; newspaper circulation reports prepared by the Audit Bureau of Circulation; analysis of charge accounts in retail stores of central cities to determine the extent of their use by residents of the contiguous county; delivery service practices of retail stores in central cities; official traffic counts; the extent of public transportation facilities in opera-

---

[2] Nonagricultural labor force is defined as those employed in nonagricultural occupations, those experienced unemployed whose last occupation was a nonagricultural occupation, members of the Armed Forces, and new workers.

[3] A contiguous minor civil division either adjoins a central city in a standard metropolitan statistical area or adjoins an intermediate minor civil division of qualifying population density. There is no limit to the number of tiers of contiguous minor civil divisions so long as the minimum density requirement is met in each tier.

[4] Central cities are those appearing in the standard metropolitan statistical area title.

tion between central cities and communities in the contiguous county; and the extent to which local planning groups and other civic organizations operate jointly.

CRITERIA FOR TITLES

7. The following criteria are used for determining titles for standard metropolitan statistical areas:

(a) The name of the standard metropolitan statistical area is that of the largest city.

(b) The addition of up to two city names may be made in the area title, on the basis and in the order of the following criteria:

(1) The additional city or cities have at least 250,000 inhabitants.

(2) The additional city or cities have a population of one-third or more of that of the largest city and a minimum population of 25,000, except that both city names are used in those instances where cities qualify under criterion 1(b).

(c) In addition to city names, the area titles will contain the name of the state or states included in the area.

The definitions and titles of standard metropolitan statistical areas are established by the Bureau of the Budget with the advice of the Federal Committee on Standard Metropolitan Statistical Areas. This Committee is composed of representatives of the major statistical agencies of the Federal Government. In applying the foregoing criteria, data from the following sources are used by the Committee:

Population, labor force, density, and occupational data: Bureau of the Census, Department of Agriculture, and Bureau of Employment Security.

Employment by place of work: Bureau of Old-Age and Survivors Insurance, Department of Labor, and Department of Defense.

Volume of commuting: Bureau of Employment Security in cooperation with the affiliated state employment security agencies, and the Bureau of the Census.

Volume of telephone communications: American Telephone & Telegraph Co. and other telephone companies.

Newspaper circulation: Audit Bureau of Circulation reports.

Data on charge accounts, delivery service practices, traffic volume, and public transportation, and related information: informed local groups.

Appendix E

Current Business Reports Available[1]

Listed below are selected Bureau of the Census publications which are based on data collected in various recurring current surveys of the Bureau. Although most of them are limited to businesses within the scope of the Business Census, there are some exceptions, particularly County Business Patterns:

I. *County Business Patterns (CBP).* Data on mid-March employment and January–March pay rolls taxable under the Federal Insurance Contributions Act are published in these reports for the United States, states, counties, and standard metropolitan statistical areas. These statistics are shown for many kinds of business under the following broad industry groups: agricultural services, forestry, fisheries; mining; contract construction; manufacturing; public utilities; wholesale trade; retail trade; finance; insurance and real estate; and services. Beginning with 1964 data, CBP data will be issued annually with the report for the first quarter 1964 scheduled for release about mid-1965.

II. *Retail Trade Reports.*

A. *Weekly Retail Sales:* Issued each Thursday, this report presents estimated weekly sales of retail stores in the United States, by kind-of-business groups and for all kinds of business combined, for weeks of the current month to date and all weeks of the previous month. Percentage changes in sales in the most recent week, the most recent 4-week period, and comparable periods a year ago are also shown.

B. *Advance Monthly Retail Sales:* Issued about 10 days after the close of the data month, this report presents monthly estimates of sales of retail stores by kind-of-business groups and for all kinds of business combined. Data are shown for current month, preceding month, and same month a year ago, both unadjusted and adjusted for seasonal variations and trading-day differences.

C. *Monthly Retail Trade:* This report includes estimated dollar sales and end-of-month accounts receivable, by kind of business, for all retail stores and for stores of organizations operating 11 or more retail stores for

[1] U.S. Bureau of the Census, Census of Business, 1963, *Retail Trade: United States Summary*, BC63–RA1, Washington, D.C., 1965.

535

the United States for the current month, with comparisons for previous months. Data are shown both unadjusted and adjusted for seasonal variation and trading-day differences.

D. *Monthly Retail Trade—Area Sales Supplement:* This supplement to the Monthly Retail Trade Report provides estimates of sales of retail stores by geographic regions, divisions, selected states, and standard metropolitan statistical areas for the current month, with comparisons for previous months.

E. *Retail Trade—Annual Report:* This report provides annual retail sales by kind of business and per capita sales of selected kinds of business, for the United States, geographic regions, divisions, and selected states. United States figures by kind of business are given on the cost value of year-end merchandise inventories, sales-inventory ratios, and year-end accounts receivable balances, by charge and installment accounts. Separate figures also are provided for retail stores and organizations operating 11 or more retail stores and, for the food and general merchandise groups, for organizations operating 4 or more retail stores.

III. *Monthly Wholesale Trade Report.* This report includes estimated dollar sales, end-of-month inventories, and stock-sales ratios of merchant wholesalers, by kind of business for the current month, with comparisons for previous months. Dollar volume sales estimates are shown by geographic division in total and for durable and nondurable kind-of-business subtotals. Sales and inventory trends (per cent changes) are shown by detailed kinds of business at the national level and for selected categories by geographic division. Measures of sampling variability are given. United States data are shown adjusted for seasonal variations and, in the case of sales, also for trading-day differences.

IV. *Other Current Business Reports.*

Canned Food Report: This report is issued on 4 dates—January 1, April 1, June 1, and November 1—to show total stocks of wholesale distributors and canners, including warehouses of retail multiunit organizations, of selected canned food items (vegetables, fruits, juices, fish). In all reports data are shown in actual cases for total stocks and for canners' carry-over, pack, and total supply. In the January 1 report separate data are shown for the No. 10 can size, as well as for warehouse stocks of retail multiunit organizations. Data on canners are furnished by the Canners' Association.

Green Coffee Inventories and Roastings: This quarterly report provides estimates of green coffee inventories held by roasters, importers, and dealers, the quantity of green coffee roasted, and the amount roasted for soluble use, by quarters, for the current and previous 3 years. Also included are quarterly imports of green coffee during the same period.

Appendix F

Economics of Forecasting Business Fluctuations

I. Nonrecurring or nonperiodical change
  A. Trends
    1. Definition
    2. Direction
  B. Irregular or accidental fluctuations
    1. Examples
    2. Difference from other forms
    3. Theory of cancellation of factors
  C. Structural changes
    1. Definition
    2. Examples

II. Recurring or periodical fluctuations
  A. Seasonal
    1. Natural
    2. Artificial
  B. Cyclical
    1. Difference from trends
    2. Difference from seasonal
    3. Characteristics
    4. Definition
    5. Types
    6. Normal process

III. The time series
  A. The index number
    1. Use
    2. Types
  B. Correction of figures
    1. For price changes
    2. For trend
    3. For seasonal variation
    4. For trend and seasonal variation

Appendix G

Some of the So-Called Business Barometers

I. *Financial:*
  A. Interest Rates
    1. Call
    2. Time (4–6 mos.)
    3. Commercial Paper
    4. Acceptances
    5. Short Term (60–90 days)
    6. Rediscount Rate
  B. Bank Debits
  C. Brokers Loans
  D. Balance of Payments Status
  E. Credit Conditions (Federal Reserve System) (Amount in Use)
     Purchase of Bills
     Purchase of Government Securities
  F. Volume of Loanable Funds
  G. Borrowing by Member Banks
  H. Money in Circulation
  I. Bank Deposits
  J. Gold Stocks
II. *Distribution:*
  A. Car loadings
  B. Mail Order Sales
  C. Retail and Wholesale Sales
  D. Truck Movement
  E. Installment Sales
III. *Industrial:*
  A. Production in Basic Industries
  B. Building and Construction
  C. Steel Ingot Production
  D. Automobile Production
  E. Electric Power Production
  F. Bituminous Coal Production
  G. Airplane Production

IV. *Prices:*
   A. Wholesale
   B. Farm Products
   C. Manufactured Products
   D. Ratio of Farm Products to Manufactured Products
   E. Sensitive Commodities
   F. Cost of Living
V. *Profits:*
   A. Corporation Earnings
   B. Failures
   C. New Corporations (Number)
   D. National Income
VI. *Inventories:*
   A. Raw Commodities: Wheat, Coal, Meats, Copper
   B. Finished Goods
   C. Freight Cars and Engines
   D. Retail
   E. Wholesale
VII. *Stock Market:*
   A. Stock Prices
   B. Bond Prices
   C. New Security Flotations
VIII. *Employment:*
   A. Number Employed
   B. Amount of Pay Rolls
   C. Man-Hours
   D. Number Unemployed
IX. *Unfilled and New Orders:*
   A. Machine and Tool
   B. Freight Cars and Engines
   C. Textiles
   D. Total Industry
X. *Business Ratios:*
   A. Corn-Hog Ratio
   B. Cotton-Cotton-Cloth Ratio
   C. Financial Ratios
   D. Inventories-Sales Ratios
XI. *Foreign Trade:*
   A. Exports
   B. Imports
XII. *Handbooks:*
   A. Industrial Market Data
   B. Consumer Market Data (U.S. Department of Commerce)

Appendix H

Other Statistics
by Selected Institutional Sources

I. Governmental Agencies:
 A. Foreign governments, United Nations, World Bank
 B. U. S. Government; all departments, especially:
    Department of Commerce
    Department of Agriculture
    Interior Department
    Bureau of the Budget, Office of the President
 C. Statistical Department, most states
 D. Some counties and larger cities.

II. Semipublic Agencies:

Federal Reserve Board, Washington	Federal Communications Commission
Federal Reserve Banks (12 Districts)	Various Port Authorities
Home Loan banks	Army Engineers
Reconstruction Finance Corporation	Securities & Exchange Commission
Interstate Commerce Commission	University bureaus of research,
Federal Trade Commission	social and economic research

III. Private Financial Institutions and Insurance Companies:

American Stock Exchange	Chase Manhattan National Bank
New York Stock Exchange	New York Trust Company
Most large commercial banks:	1st National Bank of Chicago
National City Bank (New York)	Dun & Bradstreet

IV. Research Agencies:
 A. Financed by private funds: Rockefeller Foundation, Falk Foundation, Buhl Foundation National Bureau of Economic Research, Mellon Institute, National Industrial Conference Board, Committee for Economic Development;
 B. Financed partly by private funds and partly by institutions.

540

V. *Trade Associations:*

American Iron and Steel Institute
Machine Tool Association
Foundry Equipment Association
National Retail Merchants
  Association
Rubber Association of America

American Petroleum Institute
American Institute of Meat
  Packers
American Management Association
Supermarket Institute

VI. *Private Trade Papers and Services:*

Barron's
Babson Globe News
Moody Monthly
Commercial &
  Financial Chronicle

Sales Management Magazine
Dun & Bradstreet
Wall Street Journal
Women's Wear Daily

Iron Age
Standard & Poor
Daily News Record

VII. *Individual Company Public Statements and Reports.*

Appendix I

Reference Sources

Each time series discussed in this booklet is included in the following monthly publications:

Survey of Current Business, U. S. Department of Commerce, Office of Business Economics

Business Cycle Developments, U. S. Department of Commerce, Bureau of the Census

Federal Reserve Bulletin, Board of Governors of the Federal Reserve System

Economic Indicators, Joint Economic Committee, U. S. Congress.

These publications carry a broad collection of economic data but do not always include detailed components of each series. For each series in the Survey of Current Business, the biennial supplement entitled Business Statistics gives historical data and a brief description of series and sources.

The bibliographical note which follows lists, for each heading discussed in this booklet, the agencies compiling the original data, the primary sources of detailed current and historical data, and official publications which give technical explanations of the concepts and estimating procedures. Publications containing current data are indicated by an asterisk (*) and are listed in the order of dates released. Unless otherwise specified, these sources are published monthly. The listing is not intended to be a comprehensive bibliography.

GROSS NATIONAL PRODUCT AND NATIONAL INCOME

U. S. Department of Commerce, Office of Business Economics:

*Survey of Current Business. Quarterly estimates in the issue for the second month following the end of each quarter; preliminary annual estimates in the February issue and revised estimates in the July issue; monthly personal income estimates for the United States in each issue and annual estimates by states in the August issue.

U. S. Income and Output, 1958; 1954 National Income; Personal Income by States Since 1929. Supplements to the Survey, with historical data and explanation of concepts and estimating procedures.

THE LABOR FORCE AND UNEMPLOYMENT

U. S. Department of Labor, Bureau of Labor Statistics, and Bureau of Employment Security:

*Monthly Report on the Labor Force, BLS. Selected components of the
household labor force, nonfarm pay-roll employment, and insured unemployment series.

*Employment and Earnings, BLS. Additional detail on the labor force and
pay-roll employment (including data by states), and a brief explanation of
estimating procedures for each series. Additional information on concepts and
estimating procedures available from the Bureau in various "Technical Notes"
listed in this source.

*Unemployment Insurance Claims (weekly); *The Unemployment Insurance
Review (includes a separate monthly report on unemployment insurance statistics); *Area Labor Market Trends, BES. Detail on the insured unemployment series. Technical notes given in the March 1960 issue of The Labor
Market and Employment Security (reprints available).

*Monthly Labor Review, BLS. Detailed components (no area data) for each
series for a 13-month period.

Employment and Earnings Statistics for the U. S., 1909–62 (BLS Bulletin 1312–
1); Employment and Earnings Statistics for States and Areas, 1939–62 (BLS
Bulletin 1370). Historical data.

INDUSTRIAL PRODUCTION

Board of Governors of the Federal Reserve System:

*Business Indexes, Release G.12.3. All components.

*Federal Reserve Bulletin. All groupings but not individual series.

Industrial Production, 1957–59 Base. Historical data from 1919 for total and
major industry groupings and from 1947 for other series. Listing of source
and description of basic data, with 1957–59 proportions for industries and
markets.

Industrial Production, 1959 Revision. Description of computational methods and
uses with emphasis on market groupings introduced in this revision.

WHOLESALE AND CONSUMER PRICES

U. S. Department of Labor, Bureau of Labor Statistics:

*Wholesale Price Index, weekly index, news release, and *Wholesale (Primary
Market) Price Index, news release. Major commodity groups and subgroups.

*Wholesale Prices and Price Indexes. All components. The February 1962
(Preliminary) issue contains historical data for major series and the rebasing
factors to 1957–59 = 100 for all series. The March 1958 (Preliminary) and
the June 1961 (Preliminary) issues contain detailed descriptions of the
revisions of the weighting structures based on 1954 and 1958 sales data,
respectively.

*Consumer Price Index, news release. Major group, subgroup, and special
group indexes for U. S.; major groups for cities.

*Consumer Price Index. Additional detail. All items and food indexes for cities; average retail prices of selected foods.

*Monthly Labor Review. All components except individual items for a 13-month period for both price series; CPI by cities for all items and food. Explanatory articles in the February 1953 issue (1953 revision of CPI), the December 1955 issue (WPI indexes by stage-of-processing), and the February 1962 issue (WPI weight revisions, 1890–1960).

*Consumer Price Index: Quarterly Price Indexes for Selected Items and Groups. Individual commodities and services based on a subsample of cities. Historical data in a special September 1962 release with the same title.

*Wholesale Prices and Price Indexes (annual). All components by months and annual averages. Also contains brief descriptions of the indexes and specifications for items priced. The 1957 report (Bulletin 1235) contains description of indexes by durability of product.

Consumer Prices in the United States, 1953–58 (Bulletin 1256); 1949–52 (Bulletin 1165); 1942–48 (Bulletin 966). Historical data.

Techniques of Preparing Major BLS Statistical Series (Bulletin 1168). Detailed description of the indexes and their uses and limitations. (Chapter 9, CPI based on 1953 revision; Chapter 10, WPI.)

"An Abbreviated Description of the Revised Consumer Price Index" and "Major Changes in the Consumer Price Index." Unpublished, March 1964.

SEASONAL ADJUSTMENT

"Adjustment for Seasonal Variation," Federal Reserve Bulletin, June 1941 (reprints available), Board of Governors of the Federal Reserve System, Washington, D.C. Description of basic ratio-to-moving-average method.

Shiskin, Julius. Electronic Computers and Business Indicators, Occasional Paper No. 57, National Bureau of Economic Research, New York, 1957. Census Method II.

Seasonal Adjustment on Electronic Computers, Organization for Economic Cooperation and Development, Paris, France, 1961. Copies available from OECD, Washington, D.C. Census Method II.

"Specifications for the X-9 Version of the Census Method II Seasonal Adjustment Program," and "Specifications for the X-10 Version of the Census Method II Seasonal Adjustment Program," Bureau of the Census, Office of Chief Economic Statistician, Washington, D.C., March 6, 1962.

1960 Proceedings of the Business and Economic Statistics Section, American Statistical Association, Washington, D.C., 1960. Six papers, including one on the BLS method, presented in a session on seasonal adjustments.

The BLS Seasonal Factor Method: Its Application by Electronic Computer, U. S. Department of Labor, Bureau of Labor Statistics, June 1963.

BUSINESS CYCLE INDICATORS

National Bureau of Economic Research, Inc., New York:
Burns, Arthur F. and Mitchell, Wesley C., Measuring Business Cycles (New York, 1946).

Mitchell, Wesley C., *What Happens During Business Cycles* (New York, 1951).

Moore, Geoffrey H., Editor, *Business Cycle Indicators* (Vols. I and II, Princeton University Press, 1961). Articles on selection, interpretation, and application of business indicators; detailed description of the 1960 list of 26 major indicators; historical data through 1958 for 50 indicators.

Shiskin, Julius. *Signals of Recession and Recovery—An Experiment With Monthly Reporting*, Occasional Paper No. 77, New York, 1961. Description of the background and rationale for the monthly report, *Business Cycle Developments* (see below); timing classification and summary measures of leads and lags for 72 business cycle indicators; 1958–61 data for 65 business indicators; selected cyclical measures for 1948–61.

*Business Cycle Developments, U. S. Department of Commerce, Bureau of the Census. Includes basic data for NBER's 30 leading, 15 roughly coincident, and 7 lagging indicators, plus 18 other U. S. series with business cycle significance; analytical and cyclical measures for selected series.

Appendix J

The Manpower Act of 1965[1]

The Manpower Act of 1965[2] amends the MDTA by providing for expanded research and experimental programs; stimulation of job development programs; liberalized training allowances with respect to amount, duration, and eligibility, designed to encourage and facilitate training for those in greatest need of it; consolidation of manpower training programs provided under the Area Redevelopment Act and the Manpower Development and Training Act; expanded use of private training facilities; refresher training for unemployed professional workers; and amendments of a technical nature which improve the administration of the act. At the same time training under title II of the MDTA is extended for another 3 years, and its financing is radically altered with respect to the State-matching provision.

Specifically, the amendments may be summarized as follows:

TERMINATION DATE AND FINANCING PROVISIONS

The former June 30, 1966, termination date of the training program authorized under title II has been extended to June 30, 1969.

Funds originally required from the States on a matching requirement basis was postponed for another year and thereafter reduced to sharing of only 10 percent of the training costs. Thus, under this amendment, the States will no longer be required to share training allowance costs. Moreover, since training costs may be matched "in kind" instead of cash, no real hardship should be imposed on the ability of the States to continue to participate in the program beginning with fiscal year 1967.

With these two basic amendments, the States can now plan more effectively because of the certainty of continuing Federal assistance.

EXPANSION OF RESEARCH AND EXPERIMENTAL PROGRAMS—AMENDMENTS TO TITLE I

A greatly expanded and coordinated research program results from the newly enacted amendments. In essence, they not only permit a more comprehensive

---

[1] By Rose Rosofsky, Office of Manpower, Automation and Training. Reprinted from *Manpower Training Facts*, May 1965.
[2] Public Law 89–15, April 26, 1965.

program of basic research, but also bring together under title I all experimental, developmental, demonstration, and pilot projects. Thus, a clear distinction is made between these and regular, conventional training projects carried on under title II, and these projects can be conducted without regard to limitations imposed by matching requirements or apportionment of funds among the States.

The amendments provide that:

—Basic research funding is increased, and the Secretary of Labor is authorized to make grants as well as enter into contracts for research and experimental programs. The expanded funding and new provision for grants will give greater scope and flexibility to the total research and experimental effort.

—The program of experimental and demonstration projects to test new methods for rehabilitation of disadvantaged groups in the labor force is placed in title I and a clear mandate given for its expanison—an endorsement of the success, effectiveness, and potential of this program which started as a limited pioneering measure.

—The Secretary of Labor is directed to stimulate and assist job development programs to expand unmet employment needs in service and related occupations, giving emphasis and direction to active job development as part of a comprehensive manpower program.

—Labor mobility demonstration projects originally authorized under the 1963 amendments are now incorporated as part of title I. These projects are extended for 2 years, appropriations are increased from $4 million to $5 million per year, limitations on the type of relocation expenses to be reimbursed have been removed, and provisions have been added for deferred repayment of loans.

—Finally, a pilot program is authorized to experiment with the placement of persons having difficulty in securing employment for reasons other than ability to perform. This new authority is intended particularly to assist in placement of trainees who have difficulty in securing indemnity bonding required for employment, usually due to former police records.

THE TRAINING PROGRAM—AMENDMENTS TO TITLE II

Extensive changes were made in the provisions relating to income maintenance for trainees. These amendments will remove or relieve financial pressures which tend to discourage or curtail training. They will have the effect of extending training opportunities, particularly for those most in need of them. The principal amendments are as follows:

—The period during which training allowances may be paid is extended to 104 weeks. This will provide the flexibility for lengthening training courses, particularly those combining basic education and occupational training, which of necessity often have been too accelerated to achieve desired results even to the extent of causing dropouts from training. It will also open the doors to training in more of the technical and advanced skills in growing demand which require more extensive preparation.

—Eligibility for training allowances is extended for single persons not living as members of a family or household group—filling a gap which heretofore precluded training for many needy unemployed persons.

—Eligibility for training allowances is also broadened to permit more than one unemployed member of a family or household to receive a regular training allowance, provided that the head of the household is unemployed. This will relieve economic pressures, particularly for unemployed workers in the larger families—opening further training opportunities.

—Allowance payments are increased to relieve the financial strain of training for those with heavy family responsibilities. The amendments provide for an additional $5 per week for each dependent over two, up to a maximum of four additional dependents.

—To further relieve financial hardships imposed on trainees, the act is amended to permit the payment of expenses for daily commuting between the residence and place of training.

—Discretionary increases in subsistence and transportation allowances are permitted for training referrals in noncontiguous States and in areas outside the continental United States, where higher transportation and living costs make the present limitations inadequate.

—To stabilize and avoid fluctuation in the rate of training allowances, the method of computation of State unemployment compensation payments upon which the allowances are based is amended. The base period for such computation is changed from the average for the single most recent quarter to the average gross unemployment payments made over the most recent four calendar quarters period.

—The provision for payment of youth training allowances is also amended to permit these trainees to continue to draw allowances even if they reach age 22 during the training program. As a corollary to this amendment, the Secretary is given administrative flexibility in conforming with the 25-percent limitation on youths receiving training allowances. These amendments remove undue technical rigidities and provide flexibility for effective administration of the important youth training provisions of the act.

Other amendments to title II of the act provide that:

—Trainees enrolled in on-the-job training programs are authorized to engage in part-time work outside of their training program for up to 20 hours of paid employment per week without reduction in the training allowance—an elimination of the distinction created by the 1963 amendments when this provision was enacted for institutional trainees only.

—The provision for the use of private training institutions, with stress on their usefulness for individual referrals, is emphasized and encouraged when their cost and the effectiveness of training are comparable to public institutions. Under the new amendment the 10-percent State-matching provision, effective July 1, 1966, may be waived for private institutions by the Secretary of Health, Education, and Welfare if he determines that 100-percent Federal payment is necessary to meet the act's objectives.

—The training provisions of sections 16 and 17 of the ARA are repealed and merged with those of the MDTA under a separate new provision. This amendment is essentially a legal consolidation of these two training programs of very similar purpose. It rationalizes them by equalizing and conforming such important provisions as duration of training, eligibility for increased training allowances, and for daily transportation expenses. Training for redevelopment areas under the new provision of the MDTA will continue as in the past, except that (1) the Secretaries of Labor and of Commerce will determine training and retraining needs, and (2) all unemployed and underemployed persons residing in redevelopment areas will be eligible for training and training allowances. This new provision also authorizes full Federal financing, without apportionment among the States; and separate funds are authorized to be appropriated for its implementation.

MISCELLANEOUS—AMENDMENT OF TITLE III

To facilitate fiscal management of the training program and to overcome funding difficulties and complications experienced in the past, title III is amended to provide that the cost of all training programs, including training allowances, approved during a fiscal year are to be paid from funds appropriated for that year.

A new rule is also established for reapportionment of funds among the States to give more stability to State planning for training programs. It provides that no funds shall be reapportioned among the States prior to expiration of the first half of the fiscal year and only upon 30 days' prior notice, except that such prior notice shall not apply during the last quarter of the fiscal year.

Finally, the Secretaries of Labor and of Health, Education, and Welfare may, under such rules and regulations as they prescribe, make contracts or agreements permitting the States to approve programs whose cost does not exceed $75,000.

Appendix K

The Functions of a Diversified Sales Finance Company[1]

The following outline of the nationwide services of a "Credit Company" and its subsidiaries (finance companies, insurance companies, and manufacturing companies) illustrates the functions of a diversified sales finance company.

FINANCE COMPANIES

Five main types of financing services are provided.

Wholesale Financing is furnished to finance the current wholesale purchases from manufacturers, by distributors and dealers—especially of automobiles, refrigerators, radios, television sets, heating equipment, time- and labor-saving machinery and other articles usually sold on the installment plan—while carried in stock awaiting resale to customers.

Installment Financing is supplied to finance the retail sale of products sold on the installment plan by manufacturers, distributors and dealers—especially of automobiles, home appliances, radios and television sets, heating equipment, time- and labor-saving machinery.

Commercial Financing embraces the purchase of current open accounts receivable from manufacturers, wholesalers, mills, and converters, on the "Non-Notification" plan of not giving notice to customers of the assignment of the invoices: (1) entirely without recourse as to credit losses on approved accounts; (2) with limited liability on credit losses; or (3) with full guarantee of the sellers. Concerns selling their receivables continue to pass their credit cards and make collections direct from their customers and receive 80% to 95% cash upon delivery of shipping evidence, balance when collected. Advances are also made on inventories, fixed assets, other security, and on open credit.

Factoring involves the purchase of current open accounts receivable from mills, manufacturers, converters, and wholesalers and the assumption of all credit risk thereon. Such concerns can "Factor" their entire annual sales volume through

---

[1] Clyde William Phelps, *Accounts Receivable Financing as a Method of Securing Business Loans* (Studies in Commercial Financing, 2nd ed., Commercial Credit Company, Baltimore, 1963).

550

Textile Banking Company, Inc., of New York. This company passes upon credits, purchases the accounts receivable, makes all collections direct from the customers and assumes all credit losses on approved accounts. Advances are also made on inventories, fixed assets, other security, and on open credit.

Direct Loans are made generally through subsidiary industrial banks or personal loan companies to individual owners of automobiles, secured by liens upon such automobiles, and usually with insurance against fire, theft, collision and accidental physical damage. Some of these subsidiaries also make loans with liens upon other articles usually sold on the installment plan, as well as so-called unsecured "character" and "comaker" loans.

INSURANCE COMPANIES

The insurance subsidiary provides three main kinds of insurance service.

Credit Insurance protects manufacturers, wholesalers, mills and converters against excessive losses on their accounts receivable, who pass their own credits, carry and collect their receivables and are reimbursed by American Credit Indemnity Company of New York, for losses in excess of an agreed percentage of annual sales. This company also guarantees payment of accounts by individual customers. Collection service facilities are maintained for its customers.

Health Insurance is provided by a subsidiary which writes individual or group health and accident insurance, including hospitalization and surgical benefits.

Automobile Insurance protects new and used automobiles and trucks against loss by fire, theft, collision and accidental physical damage. This subsidiary confines its insurance usually to articles sold on the installment plan and financed by the Finance Companies.

MANUFACTURING COMPANIES

The manufacturing subsidiaries of Commercial Credit Company operate and finance in eight different fields: pork products; name plates, instrument dials and products made from metal, glass and plastics; special heavy machinery and iron castings, heat interchangers, filters, evaporators, etc.; pipe fittings cast in malleable, gray iron, brass or bronze; roller and ball-bearing equipment; signal lights, cap pistols and caps, fuses, plastics, etc.; oil burner equipment, cap pistols and caps, hardware and plastics; and printing machinery and presses.

Appendix L

Effective Methods and Ideas for Improving Off-Season Sales[1]

(1) Advance the selling season of new merchandise to the time that close-outs of season-end merchandise are started.

(2) Offer close-outs at "sacrifice" prices as early as possible—either during the initial part of your slack season or even during the closing phases of a busy season. But remember that close-out sales should not be put on for more than 2 weeks at any one time. Anything longer loses its sales impact.

(3) About midway through a slack period, start building up your new merchandise displays for the coming season.

(4) Adopt a "model stock plan" as a permanent operating technique used to make sure that fresh merchandise of appropriate assortment and price is always on hand.

(5) Cultivate "personal touch" as much as possible in all customer contacts. This can pay dividends in sales during your slack season. Customers should be treated in a courteous and friendly manner regardless of how little they buy.

(6) Use more "in-home" selling where feasible: floor coverings, appliances, television, and the like, are especially suited to this approach. Trading-up opportunities are greater and sales more easily closed when "in-home" selling is carried out intelligently.

(7) In the convenience-goods field, small stores need not be squeezed out by supermarkets. There are hosts of items, especially in meats and produce, on which the small firm manager has little price competition. Among other things, for instance, "ready-to-eat" meals can be featured.

(8) A clearing house for babysitters is an excellent service device for gaining year-round store interest.

(9) A playroom operated jointly by stores in the same sections or shopping center is a worthwhile promotional device which attracts busy young mothers. In the same vein, special open-house nights with other local stores participating have proved helpful.

---

[1] By Robert D. Entenberg, *Methods for Improving Off-Season Sales*, *Small Marketers Aids*, *Small Business Administration*, No. 32, Washington, D.C., April 1958.

(10) Use circulars and direct mail in conjunction with advertising in neighborhood newspapers. Such material can be set up at small cost. A comparatively inexpensive dual-cylinder stencil duplicator can be used for quantity reproductions of fashion sketches and other illustrations. Basic appeals during off-seasons should generally be "value" and "price." Slack season promotions can be productive when the "value" aspect of merchandise—at a particular time—is suitably stressed. "Best price" items should be attractively and prominently displayed so that they may be easily recognized.

(11) Develop programs of "related merchandising" and use them extensively. For example: men's jewelry with shirts and ties; gloves with mufflers and belts; and handkerchiefs with sportswear.

(12) Prize contests can also be sales builders. For example, a free prize may be given to each hundredth customer (100th, 200th, 300th, and so on), with names of winners posted weekly in your show windows or inside the store and prizes selected from the merchandise being featured.

(13) Dawn-to-midnight promotions often work well in shopping goods stores.

(14) Gifts for newly-weds and new parents who live in a store's trading area are sales boosters. Along this line, smaller stores should not hesitate to sponsor a "welcome wagon" for newcomers to the community.

(15) If you carry merchandise eligible for home improvement loans, you should insist that all salespeople know the details. Loan terms and repayment schedules are important parts of the sales picture.

(16) Ask your customers what they would suggest to improve off-season service, assortments, and attractions.

(17) Put new emphasis on personalized tags, labels, boxes, and wrappings.

(18) Use "bargain tables" regularly in all slow periods to offer unadvertised specials. When consistently presented, this merchandising technique can be an effective builder of store traffic.

(19) Offer merchandise guarantees regardless of price.

(20) Encourage customers making purchases of shopping and specialty goods to register their names on a purchase-record card. Having such a card is a great asset in developing an up-to-date, personalized mailing list for promotional material. For example, you can send birthday and other personal greetings in addition to announcements of sale.

Appendix M

Transferable Risks: Insurance Considerations

Costs must be carefully weighed against the requirements of the firm. Effective management in this direction means the purchase of the greatest possible amount of coverage for the lowest possible premium payments. More specifically, protection for cash involves possible loss by fire, interior robbery, outside robbery (on way to bank or from a collection), messenger robbery, burglary of safe, embezzlement, check alterations, forgery, and burglary of safety deposit box. Other types of asset losses are:

Notes receivable, government and other marketable securities: Fire, interior robbery, messenger robbery, embezzlement, burglary of safe, (or) burglary of safety deposit box.

Accounts receivable: Burglary of records, destruction of records by fire, (or) "simple" nonpayment.

Merchandise: Fire, burglary, robbery, (or) theft; damage by smoke, smudge, water, accidental operation of automatic sprinkler, steam, flood, explosion, (or) electric-current interruption. Liability on account of injury arising from the sale of merchandise.

Delivery equipment: Fire, theft, collision, (or) explosion; damage by fire, theft, collision, (or) explosion; liability on account of injury to employees and others (or) damage to automobiles and property of others.

Furniture and fixtures: Fire, theft, (or) burglary; damage by fire, theft, burglary, explosion, water, flood, smoke, (or) smudge; accidental operation of automatic sprinkler, heat, or water systems; liability on account of accidents to employees and customers.

Building and equipment: Fire, tornado, explosion, windstorm, lightning, (or) cancellation of lease; operation of automobiles by others; flood, accidental operation of sprinkler, plumbing, and heating systems and electrical equipment; breaking of display windows; liability on account of acts of contractors and their employees; injury to customers caused by falling plaster, bricks, slate, glass signs, snow, fire-escape ladders, and by defective railings; failure of elevators; explosion of boiler, etc.; and finally with respect to land—loss of title.

Because cash securities and receivables assets are highly liquid assets, they are not generally covered in the standard fire insurance policy. In such cases, the moral risk is too great a hazard when weighed in relationship to the costs of the premiums. However, "special agreements" may be obtained on insuring accounts receivables records. For insurance purposes, inventory valuations are determined at invoice cost or from the retail method cost complement approach. When direct and indirect expenses incurred in the merchandising and sales supporting operations are added, the valuation may be higher. Generally, the invoice cost of the merchandise is increased by the amount of expense incurred in getting it ready for sale.

In the standard fire-insurance policy contract, the actual cash value of the items plus replacement costs form the general basis for evaluation. Where furniture and fixtures are a permanent part of the building, such items must be covered in a subsequent paragraph or clause. Coverage for fire is generally very broad and includes cash registers, display fixtures, scales, safes, typewriters, paintings, and miscellaneous items needed for conduct of the business. It should be pointed out that most fire loss rarely exceeds 75 per cent of the total value involved. By taking advantage of a coinsurance clause to any standard fire insurance policy, a considerable amount of the premiums can be saved.

In taking advantage of a coinsurance clause, the insurer takes out protection up to a certain percentage of the value of a building, for instance, then the firm becomes a coinsurer with the insurance company in the case of any possible loss. For example, a building valued at $500,000 having an 80 per cent coinsurance clause requires that $400,000 of insurance be bought to meet the policy's requirement. By this means all losses up to $400,000 are covered by the insurance company. Any loss above this amount is sustained by the insured firm.

Should the insured not meet the 80 per cent coinsurance requirement, he would become a coinsurer for the percentage of insurance not carried to meet the clause requirement. For example, if the insured only takes out $300,000 worth of insurance where $400,000 is required, the insured would be responsible for ¼ of all losses up to the total amount of the policy.[1] This can be expressed as a formula:

$$\frac{\text{Amount of insurance carried}}{\text{Coinsurance percentage} \times \text{Value of property}} = \% \text{ Insurance Co. pays}$$

For example, on a $100,000 loss, under conditions as described above:

$$\frac{\$300,000}{80\% \times \$500,000} = \frac{\$300,000}{\$400,000} = 75\%$$

∴ Insurance company payment = $75,000 (.75 × $100,000)

Firm's payment = $25,000

---

[1] See also D. J. Duncan and C. F. Phillips, *Retailing, Principles and Methods*, 6th ed. (Homewood, Ill.: Richard D. Irwin, Inc., 1963), pp. 715–738.

BUSINESS INTERRUPTION INSURANCE

An important form of insurance is business interruption insurance, known officially as "use and occupancy." Any reduction in gross earnings which results directly from fire or windstorm is, in effect, compensated after "normal" charges and expenses (including pay-roll) are deducted. This insurance indemnifies the purchaser only for the actual loss sustained. In other words, any out-of-pocket expense such as rent, pay roll, etc. (when paid by the insurance company) is deducted from the estimated gross earnings in determining the amount of the loss. Commissions and rents from leased departments, of course, are considered parts of the loss of gross earnings. Should only partial operation be permissible, this would count as an offset against the total amount of the loss.

In the case of Burglary, Robbery, and Theft Insurance, robbery is distinguished from burglary in that it involves violence or threat of violence to the person in charge of a company's assets either internally or externally (such as the use of outside messenger services). Bonding is used to insure against theft or larceny from internal sources.

INSURANCE CONTROL

Insurance policies and premium schedules differ from one state to another, as do plans and premiums of the insurance companies themselves, although most policies are standardized by the Control Fire Insurance Board. The purchase of insurance involves a weighing of variables, such as cash costs versus needs on a calculated risk basis. Calculated risks would rarely be taken in the case of Workman's Compensation, fire, or automobile liability coverages.

Appendix N

Illustration of Pre-Interview Evaluation Form for Executive Training and Placement

[NOTE: Appendix N is a double-page illustration, presented on the two pages that follow.]

APPENDIX N

PRE-INTERVIEW EVALUATION FORM FOR EXECUTIVE TRAINING AND PLACEMENT

UNIVERSITY OF PITTSBURGH : PLACEMENT SERVICE

Standard Rating Form

Name of Applicant

I. PERSONAL DATA

(a.) Knew applicant approximately _____ years _____ months; Personally _____, as a student _____, through connection with extracurricular activities _____, other _____

(b.) Graduating from: (encircle) COLLEGE, BUSINESS ADMINISTRATION, ENGINEERING AND MINES, EDUCATION, RETAILING, LAW, GRADUATE SCHOOL, GRADUATE SCHOOL OF SOCIAL WORK.

(c.) Major field of concentration _____

II. INVENTORY OF APPLICANT'S PERSONAL TRAITS

Directions: Place an "x" on the line at the point which describes the student you are rating. Consider the whole line as a continuum. Ignore any trait which you do not feel competent to rate.

1. APPEARANCE

Invariably clothed and groomed in the best of taste.	Is always suitably dressed. Stays neat all day. Makes a good impression.	Generally avoids offending against good taste in grooming or attire.	Occasionally offends by poor taste in clothes or grooming. Does not maintain neat appearance throughout the day.	Comes to school sloppily dressed. Frequently offends against good taste in either grooming or dress.

2. DEPENDABILITY

Unvaryingly punctual in completing assignments and in keeping appointments.	Seldom late with assignments or appointments.	Normally is reasonably prompt in completing assignments and keeping appointments.	Makes excuses and alibis for nonfulfillment of promises and obligations.	Frequently absent or late. Cannot be counted on.

3. PERSISTENCE

Exceedingly persistent without being offensive. Voluntarily bends every energy to finish task.	Unusually persistent. Seldom deterred by difficulties.	Fairly persistent. Ordinarily finishes a task before leaving it.	Tends to leave difficult tasks unfinished unless encouraged to continue.	Easily deterred by obstacles. Often gives up even if urged to continue.

4. SELF-CONTROL. Stability under stress

Excellent composure even under difficult conditions.	Even temperament. In good spirits most of the time. Not irritated by minor mishaps.	Satisfactory self-control in ordinary situations.	Rather prone to anger and moodiness.	Easily upset by minor incidents. Moody. Irritable.

5. ADJUSTABILITY

Appears to feel secure in his social relationships and is accepted by the groups of which he is a part.	Appears to have some anxiety about his social relationships, although he is accepted by the group of which he is a part.	Shows the desire to have an established place in the group, but is, in general, treated with indifference.	Withdrawn from others to an extent that prevents his being a fully accepted member of his group.	Has characteristics of person or behavior that prevent his being an accepted member of his group.

His influence habitually shapes the opinions, activities, or ideas of his associates. | Approaches tasks with energy, imagination, and originality; contributes something that is his own. | Acitvely searches for better ways of doing things. Makes many good suggestions. | Can see only one method of attack, usually suggested by someone else. | Is a nonentity, always carried along by nearest and strongest influence.

III. INVENTORY OF APPLICANT'S PROFESSIONAL QUALITIES

7. INTELLECTUAL CAPACITY

Outstanding ability to understand directions and to grasp new ideas. Exceptionally wide awake and alert.	Quick to grasp new ideas. Usually understands directions at once.	Ability to understand new ideas and instructions about average.	Instructions must be repeated several times before fully understood. Does not understand new ideas quickly.	Grasps new ideas and understands instructions very slowly. Very slow to learn.

8. ANALYTICAL ABILITY

Has ability to size up a problem, get and evaluate the facts, reach sound conclusions, and present them in clear and concise manner.	Can size up a problem and reach sound conclusions but needs help in presenting them.	Is resourceful when faced with problems.	Desires to analyze and tackle problems but approach is fumbling and vague.	Baffled by even the simplest dilemma.

9. ATTITUDE TOWARD HIS PROFESSION

Extraordinarily enthusiastic about his work.	Shows eager interest in work. Proud to be a member of his profession.	Shows normal interest, all that is ordinarily expected.	Sometimes appears indifferent. Does not express pride in profession.	Lacks interest. Should be in another line of work.

IV. COMMUNICATION SKILLS

Proficiency in oral expression: High____   Medium____   Low____

Ability to express his ideas in writing: High____   Medium____   Low____

V. SPECIAL WORK INTERESTS:

VI. RECOMMENDED FIELD. I believe the applicant is suited for:

Sales ____	Clerical ____	Accounting ____	Administration ____
Research ____	Design ____	Production ____	Teaching ____
Development ____	Test ____	Routine ____	Other (Specify) ____

VII. COMMENTS: (1) Include any knowledge of work experience; (2) Mention any strong or weak points not covered above.

Signature _____   Title _____

Appendix O

Relationship of Expenses and Work Centers[1]

EXHIBIT "A–1"

Sales Factors

Cost of Sales
(a) Gross Margin
(b) Controllable Expenses
(c) Contribution
(d) Management Expenses

Net Profit
(a) Gross Margin is the essence of the Retail Method of Inventory. The basic elements are: mark-on, markdowns, workroom cost, and cash discounts.
(b) Controllable Expenses and Management Expenses classified by Expense Centers are the essence of Expense Center Accounting. Exhibit "C" shows the chart of Expense Centers.
(c) Contribution profit by item is the essence of Merchandise Management Accounting. This is in effect a breakdown of contribution profit by department. It is designed to provide expense facts and profitability facts by item as a guide to more profitable item merchandising.

EXHIBIT "A"

Expense Classifications by Functions and Subfunctions
    21—Executive Office
    22—Accounting Office
    23—Accts. Receivable and Credit
    24—Superintendency
    25—General Store
TOTAL ADMINISTRATIVE
    31—Operating and Housekeeping
    32—Fixed Plan & Equipment Costs
    33—Light, Heat and Power
TOTAL OCCUPANCY
    42—Sales Promotion Office
    43—Newspaper and Gen. Advtg.
    44—Direct Mail and Circulars
    45—Display
TOTAL PUBLICITY
    52—Merchandise Mgmt. & Buying
    53—Central Buying Office
    54—Receiving and Marking
TOTAL BUYING
    61—Compensation and Salespersons
    62— General Selling
    63—Delivery
TOTAL SELLING
TOTAL SALARIES
TOTAL OTHER EXPENSES
TOTAL EXPENSES

---

[1] This appendix is based on Exhibits developed by H. L. Margules, Controller, Gimbel Bros., Pittsburgh, Pa. (May 22, 1957).

560

EXHIBIT "B"

PAY ROLL
22–01–10 Controller's Office
22–01–20 Auditing
22–01–30 Accounts Payable
22–01–40 Statistical
22–01–50 Payroll Office
22–01–60 Cash Office
22–01–70 Incoming, Outgoing Mail
22–01–75 Central File
TOTAL

SUPPLIES
22–06–10 Printed Forms & Other
        Supplies
22–06–30 Tabulating Supplies
TOTAL

UNCLASSIFIED
22–08–10 Net Cash Shortages
22–08–20 Equipment Hire
22–08–30 Miscellaneous
22–08–35 Supper Expense
TOTAL

22–09–10 TRAVELING

22–10–10 POSTAGE

22–15–10 CONTRA CREDIT

TOTAL ACCOUNTING OFFICE

EXHIBIT "E"

1. Old Manual

Census	Dollars	% to Sales
100	$4,400	4.4

2. New Manual

Sales	Work Load	R.W.L.	Productivity	Hours	R.H.	Pay Rate	Dollars	% to Sales
100,000	10,000	10.0	2.5	4,000	4.0	$1.10	$4,400	4.4

Work Load		Productivity	=	Hours Worked	×	Pay Rate	=	Dollars
10,000	÷	2.5		4,000		$1.10	=	$4,400

R.W.L.		Productivity	=	R.H.	×	Pay Rate	=	% to Sales
10.0	÷	2.5		4.0		$1.10	=	4.4

EXHIBIT "C"—NEW MANUAL
Chart of Expense Centers and Measuring Units

Expense Center	Recommended Measuring Unit
110—General Management	None
121—Real Estate Costs—excluding Service and Warehouse Buildings	None
128—Real Estate Costs—Service and Warehouse Buildings	None
131—Furniture and Fixture Costs—excluding Service and Warehouse Buildings	None
138—Furniture and Fixture Costs—Service and Warehouse Buildings	None
140—Other fixed and Policy Expenses	None
211—Control and Office Management	None

215—Mail and Messenger Service	None
221—General Accounting and Statistical	None
225—Timekeeping and Pay Roll	Payments made
230—Accounts Payable	Merchandise and Expense Invoices handled
240—Cash Office	Cash Received
250—Sales Audit	Gross Sales Transactions
310—Credit	Gross Credit Sales Transactions
321—Pre-Billing	Gross Credit Sales Transactions
325—Billing	Gross Credit Sales Transactions
330—Bill Adjustments	Bill Adjustments Completed
340—Lay-Away	Gross Lay-Away Sales Transactions
410—Publicity and Display Management	None
421—Art Work and Photography	Column Inches of Newspaper and Shopping News Advertising
422—Copy Production	Column Inches of Newspaper and Shopping News Advertising
423—Newspaper and Shopping News	None
425—Direct Mail	None
427—Radio and Television	None
429—Other Advertising and Publicity	None
430—Shows and Exhibits	None
441—Display Production	None
445—Sign Shop	Square inches of signs made
511—Service and Operations Management	None
515—Supply Purchasing	None
520—General Telephone Service	None (See alternate measuring units)
530—Protection	Selling Area Times Selling Days
540—Miscellaneous Customer Service	None
560—Elevators and Escalators	Elevator Hours
570—Cleaning	Selling Area Times Selling Days
581—Maintenance of Properties	None
585—Utilities	None
611—Personnel	None
613—Employment	Hours worked by all Store Employees
615—Training	Hours worked by all Store Employees
617—Training Squad	None
621—Hospital and Medical Service	Hours worked by all Store Employees
625—Other Employee Welfare Activity	Hours worked by all Store Employees
630—Supplementary Benefits	None
721—Receiving	Cost value of Merchandise Received
725—Returns to Vendors	Returns to Vendors
730—Checking and Marking	Pieces marked and remarked
750—Transfer Hauling	None (See alternate measuring units)
761—Delivery—General	None

763—Freight, Express and Parcel Post	Packages Handled
765—Package Delivery	Packages Delivered
767—Furniture Delivery	Furniture and Bulk Pieces Delivered
769—Garage	Delivery Mileage (Truck)
821—Direct Selling—Owned Retail Departments	Gross Sales Transactions
825—Direct Selling—Owned Cost Departments	Gross Sales Transactions
831—Other Direct and General Selling	None
834—Mail and Telephone Order	Mail and Telephone Orders written
837—Personal Shopping Service	Personal shopping transactions
840—Maintenance of Stock	None (See alternate measuring units)
851—Retail Selling Supervision	Retail selling man hours
855—Cost Selling Supervision	Cost selling man hours
861—Merchandise Adjustment	Merchandise complaints completed
863—Service Desks	Exchange and return transactions handled
865—Customers' Returned Goods Room	Return transactions handled
867—Cashiering, Inspection, Wrapping and Light Packing	None (See alternate measuring units)
869—Crating and Heavy Packing	None (See alternate measuring units)
910—Merchandise Management	None
921—Buying	None
924—Comparison Shopping	None (See alternate measuring units)
927—Testing	None (See alternate measuring units)
930—Domestic and Foreign Buying Offices	None

EXHIBIT "D"—NEW MANUAL
Expense Accounts in Expense Center 230
Accounts Payable

230–01–1	Invoice and Order
230–01–2	Accounts Payable
230–06	Supplies
230–07	Services Purchased
230–08	Unclassified

Appendix P

Developing Purchase Motivations Through Prestige and a Fashion Image

In no other aspect of merchandising is the prestige of the retailer more at stake than in the realm of fashion.

Department and specialty stores such as the Joseph Horne Company of Pittsburgh and Neiman-Marcus of Dallas, Texas, are representative of retail firms which base their total store concept on prestige acceptance. Prestige and status are not, of course, desirable unless these organizational attributes can be transferred into dynamic patronage motives and subsequently into an effective merchandising profit and an adequate return on net investment in the business.

It is usually the fashion coordinator who is responsible for the prestige position of the store as a fashion authority. By working with merchandising and promotion executives the fashion coordinator recommends purchases based on 1) forecast fashions, 2) current fashions, and 3) current volume fashions in the desired store image in terms of customer wants.

THE COORDINATION PROCESS

Three steps in the process of fashion coordination were presented by Elizabeth M. Patrick, fashion director of L. S. Ayres & Company, Indianapolis, as follows:

(1) Preseason prediction: gathering information from all the authorities—magazines, leather people, manufacturers, designers, etc.—and then editing the data in terms of the store personality, its spirit, and competitive situation.
(2) In-market coordination: selection of items on the basis of the preseason predictions.
(3) Interpretation at the store: working with merchandise managers, window and display men, publicity and display men, publicity and salespeople.

CASE HISTORY

At J. Gardenia & Company in Washington, D.C., a high-prestige multifloor specialty firm, public relations, publicity, and fashion coordination are handled in the same office. Miss Ruby S. Messenger, manager of this office, described the store's procedures and techniques of fashion coordination:

It begins with getting all possible information from all possible sources that can contribute news on what's happening or going to happen—not only in trade circles but also in people's lives and in the national economy.

The information comes to the fashion coordinator's office. From there it is directed to buyers, controllers, publicity people, and key sales personnel, marked "for information only." Thus buyers are given advance informational preparation for their market trips. The management staff, which cooperates on storewide fashion promotions, is thus kept up to date.

After market trips, there is a meeting of buyers, department heads of merchandise, display and publicity and all store executives including the chairman of the board. Each buyer summarizes his impression of the events at his market. Out of these reports a dominant theme results. When a single color theme is selected, it is never one specified shade; it must be a series or set of colors which can be harmonized into different versions of any color available in different markets.

The fashion coordinator also prepares a three-month promotion plan. It covers all tie-ins, all fashion shows—both in and out of the store—advertising, and pertinent public relations. Copies are sent to every department head and to all executives, including each branch store manager. The plan is up-dated every month, so that the store is always operating on the basis of a current three-month projection.

To assure the sales staff that it is well informed about fashion news and store plans, fashion shows for all employees are put on at the beginning of the two major seasons. Merchandise shown includes every garment for the woman, "top to bottom—inside out." Printed and illustrated literature is also distributed through the personnel department to everyone in the store, including all individuals in non-selling, sales-supporting activities.

For in-store fashion shows, Miss Messenger works closely with designers on all price levels; she frequently has them visit the store.

Author and Source Index

NOTE: Throughout this Index, the appearance of (F) or (T) after a page number indicates that the entry cited is contained in a Figure or Table, respectively, on that page.

Subject Index

NOTE: Throughout this Index, the appearance of (F) or (T) after a page number indicates that the entry cited is contained in a Figure or Table, respectively, on that page.